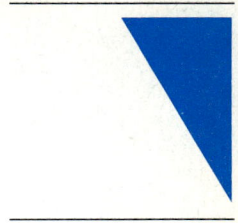

MACROECONOMICS

MACROECONOMICS
SECOND EDITION

David R. Kamerschen
Professor of Economics
University of Georgia

Richard B. McKenzie
Professor of Economics
University of Mississippi

Clark Nardinelli
Associate Professor of Economics
Clemson University

HOUGHTON MIFFLIN COMPANY   Boston
Dallas   Geneva, Illinois
Palo Alto   Princeton, New Jersey

Chapter Epigraphs

CHAPTER 1. Frank H. Knight, "Economics, Political Science, and Education," in *Freedom and Reform: Essays in Economics and Social Philosophy* (Indianapolis, Ind.: Liberty Press, 1982), p. 386.

CHAPTER 2. Lionel Robbins, *The Nature and Significance of Economic Science*, 2nd ed. (New York: Macmillan, 1973), p. 16.

CHAPTER 3. Friedrich A. Hayek, *Law, Legislation, and Liberty* (Chicago: University of Chicago Press, 1979) III, p. 74.

CHAPTER 4. John Locke, *The Second Treatise of Government*, ed. Thomas P. Peardon (New York: The Liberal Arts Press, 1954), pp. 32–33.

CHAPTER 5. Lewis Carroll, *Through the Looking Glass and What Alice Found There* (A number of modern sources are available.)

CHAPTER 6. Henry C. Wallich, "Honest Money," *Macroeconomics 1979: Readings on Contemporary Issues* (Ithaca, N.Y.: Cornell University Press, 1979), p. 43.

CHAPTER 7. David T. Bazelon, *The Paper Economy* (New York: Vintage Books, 1965), p. 73.

CHAPTER 8. Milton Friedman, *Dollars and Deficits: Inflation, Monetary Policy, and the Balance of Payments* (Englewood Cliffs, N.J.: Prentice-Hall, 1968), p. 165.

CHAPTER 9. Roger Leroy Miller, Raburn M. Williams, *The Economics of Natural Issues* (San Francisco: Canfield Press, 1972), p. 114.

CHAPTER 10. E. Ray Canterbery, *Economics on a New Frontier* (Belmont, Calif.: Wadsworth Publishing, 1968), p. i.

CHAPTER 11. Alvin H. Hansen, "The General Theory," in M. G. Mueller, ed., *Readings in Macroeconomics,* 2nd ed. (New York: Holt, Rinehart and Winston, 1971), p. 23.

Part Opener Photographs

PART I   Erich Hartmann/Magnum
PART II   Eric Neurath/Stock, Boston
PART III Sylvia Plachy/Archive
PART IV   Ellis Herwig/Stock, Boston
PART V   Roger Malloch/Magnum
PART VI   Ira Kirschenbaum/Stock, Boston
PART VII Peter Menzel/Stock, Boston

Cover photograph by Thomas Leighton

Printed in the U.S.A.

Library of Congress Catalog Card Number: 88-81339

ISBN: 0-395-38108-8

BCDEFGHIJ-VH-9543210-89

CHAPTER 12. Walter W. Heller, "Ford's Budget and the Economy," *Wall Street Journal* (February 5, 1976), p. 18.

CHAPTER 13. Arthur Okun, *The Political Economy of Prosperity* (New York: W. W. Norton, 1970), p. 100.

CHAPTER 14. Robert E. Lucas, Jr. "Tobin and Monetarism: A Review Article," *Journal of Economic Literature* 19 (June 1981), p. 566.

CHAPTER 15. John A. Tatom, "We Are All Supply-Siders Now!," *Federal Reserve Bank of St. Louis Review* (May, 1981), pp. 18–30.

CHAPTER 16. Abraham Lincoln, speech in Clinton, Illinois, September 8, 1858.

CHAPTER 17. David Ricardo, *Notes on Malthus' Principles of Political Economy*, quoted in Jacob Viner, *Studies in the Theory of International Trade* (New York: Augustus M. Kelly, 1965), p. 441.

CHAPTER 18. Robert Z. Aliber, *The International Money Game* (New York: Basic Books, 1973), p. 12.

CHAPTER 19. Herbert Stein, "Leave the Trade Deficit Alone," *Wall Street Journal* (March 11, 1987), p. 36.

CHAPTER 20. Barry Commoner, *The Poverty of Power: Energy and the Economic Crisis* (New York: Alfred A. Knopf, 1976), p. 257.

CHAPTER 21. Karl Marx, *The Communist Manifesto* (Chicago: Henry Regnery, 1954), p. 23.

CHAPTER 22. Saul K. Padover, ed., *Thomas Jefferson on Democracy* (New York Appleton-Century, 1939), p. 19.

Acknowledgments

William R. Allen. "Mouse Wisdom: Foreign Trade and Economic Health," from *The Midnight Economist,* February 1988, pp. 3–4. Copyright © 1988 by the Institute for Contemporary Studies. Reprinted by permission.

Robert J. Barro. "A Deficit Nearly on Target," from *The Wall Street Journal,* January 30, 1985. Reprinted by permission of *The Wall Street Journal.* © Dow Jones & Company, Inc. 1985. All rights reserved.

Gary Becker. "The NCAA: A Cartel in Sheepskin Clothing," reprinted from the September 14, 1987 issue of *Business Week* by special permission. Copyright © 1987 by McGraw-Hill, Inc.

A. S. Binder. *Hard Heads, Soft Hearts,* © 1987, Addison-Wesley Publishing Co., Inc., Reading, Massachusetts. Table 6.3 adapted from Table 2 (data from the Economic Report of the President and Economic Indicators), p. 40; excerpt in Chapter 15 from p. 106; excerpt in Chapter 16 from pp. 105–106; excerpt in Chapter 17 from pp. 118–119. Reprinted by permission.

Milton Friedman. "The Fed Has No Clothes," from *The Wall Street Journal,* April 15, 1988. Reprinted by permission of *The Wall Street Journal.* © Dow Jones & Company, Inc., 1988. All rights reserved.

James Gleick. "Prisoner's Dilemma: Why People Cooperate," from *The New York Times,* June 17, 1986. Copyright © 1986 by The New York Times Company. Reprinted by permission.

Carl Haub and Mary Mederios Kent. *1988 World Population Data Sheet* (Washington, D.C.: Population Reference Bureau, Inc., 1988.) Reprinted by permission.

Thomas Humphrey. "What Economists Do At the Richmond Fed" reprinted by permission of the author.

Peter T. Kilborn. "International Economics Talks: A Who's Who," from *The New York Times,* October 7, 1985. Copyright © 1985 by The New York Times Company. Reprinted by permission.

Richard B. McKenzie. "Textile Gripes are Made of Whole Cloth," from *The Wall Street Journal,* April 8, 1988. © Dow Jones & Company, Inc., 1988. All rights reserved.

"The Rush to 'Privatize,'" *New York Times* editorial, January 13, 1986. Copyright © 1986 by The New York Times Company. Reprinted by permission.

Table 15.1, "Rates and Revenues (1975–1982; Percentage Change in 1972 Dollars)," from *Organization for Economic Cooperation and Development Revenue Statistics,* Polyconomics, Inc. Reprinted by permission.

Alan Reynolds. "Less Will Get You More," from *The Wall Street Journal,* January 23, 1985. Reprinted by permission of *The Wall Street Journal.* © Dow Jones & Company, Inc., 1985. All rights reserved.

James C. Self, Sr. "Textile Protectionism: The Case for Protection," from *The Greenville (S.C.) News/Piedmont,* April 3, 1988, p. 3E. Copyright © 1988. Reprinted with permission.

Leonard Silk. "Underground's Hidden Income," from *The New York Times,* September 19, 1986. Copyright © 1986 by The New York Times Company. Reprinted by permission.

Gordon Tullock, *Toward a Mathematics of Politics.* Excerpt in Chapter 22 adapted by permission of the University of Michigan Press.

Richard Vedder and Lowell Galloway. "Soaking the Rich Through Tax Cuts," from *The Wall Street Journal,* March 21, 1985. Reprinted by permission of *The Wall Street Journal.* © Dow Jones and Company, 1985. All rights reserved.

Table 18.1 reprinted by permission of *The Wall Street Journal,* February 1, 1988, © Dow Jones & Company, Inc., 1988. All rights reserved.

World Bank. Six tables from *World Development Report 1987,* published by Oxford University Press. Reprinted by permission of the World Bank.

DEDICATIONS

To Gena, my wife and best friend, for her love, understanding, and companionship   DRK

To my wife Karen with love   RBM

To Laurie, who makes everything else possible   CN

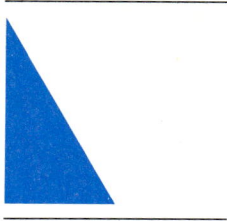

Preface

Whether or not we realize it, we all make countless economic decisions every day. Is it better to live in the Northeast or the Southwest? Better to buy clothes or books? Better to eat at home or go to a restaurant? Economics plays a prominent role in all our lives, but we often don't understand how or why.

On the surface, economics seems to be a complex—even arcane—welter of facts and figures. In reality, however, economics is based on a few central theories. Our aim in this text is to explore these economic principles in order to clarify the science of economics for the student. Using theory as the "engine of analysis" to provide the necessary structure and methodology, this text applies it to the economic policies that affect us and the economic problems we all face. The intent is that students completing this text will have a better understanding of why inflation and unemployment occur, how the market power of a monopoly affects the way a market works, the power and limits of governments to remedy economic problems, and other issues.

Consensus among economists has been hard to achieve in the 1980s. Old solutions have failed to work, new solutions have been proposed, and we are typically confronted by several quite different answers to any given question. But another central purpose of this text is to show students that a surprisingly small number of concepts, principles, and models are common to any proposed solution, and that the different views of different economists are more a matter of interpretation than of methodology.

The Text

With these central purposes in mind, ECONOMICS, Second Edition, has been designed to be comprehensible and adaptable to most curricula, to be rich in applications, and to make economics easier to learn.

A Text That is Comprehensive and Adaptable to Most Curricula

Part I forms an introduction to macroeconomics (Parts II through V) or microeconomics (Parts VI through IX), so ECONOMICS, Second Edition, is equally suited for a macro/micro sequence or a micro/macro sequence.

Macro

Parts II through V form the core of the macro section, and treat money and monetary policy before covering national income and fiscal policy. Part IV ends with a thorough development of aggregate supply and demand, which was introduced in Chapter 6. In Part V, "Alternative Views of the Macroeconomy," monetarism, supply-side economics, and rational expectations theory are covered in three self-contained chapters. They are unified by reference to the aggregate supply/demand model, but each is complete in itself, allowing instructors to choose whether or not to assign any or all of these chapters.

Micro

Parts VI through VIII form the core of the micro section. Appendices treating indifference curves, isoquants, isocosts, and several other optional topics allow instructors to choose whether or not to cover them in their principles course. In Part IX, optional chapters covering market failures, government controls, agriculture, and public choice provide further flexibility in choosing specific areas of microeconomics applications.

Key Features of the Second Edition

In revising ECONOMICS, Second Edition, we sought the advice of many users of the first edition. We were heartened by their encouragements and attentive to their criticisms. In general, we feel the second edition reflects the improved coverage that three authors, each writing extensively within his own specialty areas, can bring to an introductory text. More specifically, the second edition features:

○ New chapter pedagogy
○ Fully integrated ancillary package
○ Extensively revised Macroeconomics, especially in the coverage of monetarism and money and banking

○ Increased coverage of production and cost in Microeconomics, plus a continued focus on applications

○ Revised coverage of industrial market theory

○ Improved coverage of international economics

○ New coverage of the national debt and the balance of payments

○ Many new "Perspectives" boxes

○ Nine special "Dialogues," in which economists argue two sides of an important issue

○ An all new Appendix, "The Nobel Laureates in Economics," which includes biographical information and drawings of these premier economists.

○ A new computerized Test Bank, which can draw all the figures that accompany graphing-type questions

○ A new computerized version of the Study Guide with graph manipulation capabilities and exercises designed to make graphs and graphing useful tools (rather than painful obstacles) for introductory-level Economics students.

A Text That is Rich in Issues and Applications

"Perspectives"—most written specifically for this text—draw on the experiences and insights of a wide range of economists to illuminate current issues, applications, and historical background. Flat tax proposals, the federal deficit, the "underground" economy, Perestroika, and many other topics are covered. Informative, authoritative, and thought-provoking, these short essays show the many perspectives of economic analysis, and acquaint students with the kinds of questions economists ask and some of the answers they propose. Short biographical "Perspectives" on well-known and influential economists offer insights into the thoughts and teachings of these men and women. "Dialogues" present opposing views on a variety of topics that frequently provoke debate—sex discrimination, the minimum wage, and the like. These "Dialogues" acquaint students with the tools of discourse economists use.

A Text That Makes Economics Easier to Learn

Right from Chapter 1, in which the concepts of scarcity and choice are clarified through an eyewitness account of life in a prisoner-of-war camp, abstract terms are presented in the context of realistic, integrated examples. All new terms are highlighted, defined immediately in the margins, reviewed at the end of the chapter, and defined again in the end-of-text glossary. In addition, the index indicates the page on which each new term was initially defined in context.

Kamerschen/McKenzie/Nardinelli ECONOMICS, Second Edition, is the first economics text to use a fully integrated pedagogical system. Each chapter begins with a list of Key Questions that focus on the central concepts to be introduced in the chapter. The Key Questions are then repeated in the margin next to the text area where the questions are "answered"— where the concepts are discussed. The chapter review includes a Review of Key Questions, and all Review Questions are cross-referenced to the Key Questions.

The ancillary package makes full use of the text Key Questions as well. In the Study Guide, the Chapter Summary is organized around the Key Questions; all Discussion Questions and Multiple Choice Questions are also cross-referenced to the text Key Questions. In the Test Bank, all questions are cross-referenced to the text Key Questions, and are also designated by level of difficulty. The instructor can select questions to test the student's ability to recall (R), apply (A), or analyze (N) the economic concepts they have learned. The Instructor's Handbook includes the Review of Key Questions section from the text, and cross-references all Teaching Tips to the Key Questions.

The Complete Teaching/Learning System

For the Instructor

Instructor's Manual, prepared by the authors. For each chapter, provides:

Chapter Objectives
New Terms
Review of Key Questions
Teaching Tips, cross-referenced to Key Questions
Suggested answers to all Review Questions in the text

Transparency Masters for every figure in the book are also provided in the Instructor's Manual.

Test Bank, by Douglas Copeland, Avila College, contains over 2,000 test items with level of difficulty designations (R for Recall, A for Application, and N for Analysis) and Key Question references.

Computerized Test Bank with Graphing Capabilities, available for IBM PCs or compatibles with at least 256K of memory, two disk drives, and a graphics-quality printer (Epson or compatible) will print out any test the instructor selects and draw all the graphs in the selected questions, eliminating the need to paste the graphs in later.

Two-Color Overhead Transparencies, with 104 key figures from the text, reproduced on Mylar for clear, legible projection.

For the Student

Economics, Second Edition, hardcover text
Macroeconomics, Second Edition and
Microeconomics, Second Edition, paperbacks.
Both volumes include chapters on introduction to economics, public choice, international trade and finance, comparative economic systems, and economic development.

Study Guide, by Douglas Copeland, Avila College. For every chapter, the Study Guide provides:

Chapter Summary organized around text Key Questions
Review Terms and Concepts
Completion Exercises
Problems and Applications
True/False Questions
Multiple Choice Questions, cross-referenced to text Key Questions
Discussion Questions, cross-referenced to text Key Questions

Acknowledgments

Several of our colleagues helped bring economics issues to life by contributing articles for the "Perspectives" and "Dialogues" in the text. For their assistance, we would like to thank (in order of appearance): Rudolph White, University of Georgia; William F. Shughart II, University of Mississippi; Dennis Placone, International Trade Commission; Thomas Humphrey, Federal Reserve Bank of Richmond; Dwight Lee, University of Georgia; N. Keith Womer, University of Mississippi; Courtenay C. Stone and Daniel Thornton, Federal Reserve Bank of St. Louis; Thomas M. Humbert, Office of Congressman Jack Kemp; Edward L. Hudgins, Heritage Foundation; Russell Shannon, Clemson University; Katsuro Sakoh, Johns Hopkins University; Lawrence S. Moss, Babson College; and Martin Snitzer, Virginia Tech. We also thank Kate Salley Palmer for her drawings of the Nobel Laureates.

Reviewers

Many reviewers offered invaluable suggestions for the revision of ECONOMICS, Second Edition. We deeply appreciate their help.

Henry Adu,
Johnston Technical College, Smithfield, NC

Carl Brehm,
Kenyon College, Gambier, OH

Richard V. Burkhauser,
Vanderbilt University, Nashville, TN

Jen-Chi Cheng,
Vanderbilt University, Nashville, TN

Marshall R. Colberg,
Florida State University, Tallahassee, FL

Elynor Daris,
Georgia Southern College, Statesboro, GA

Charles P. DeLorme, Jr.
University of Georgia, Athens, GA

Claude Farrell,
University of North Carolina, Wilmington, NC

Hamid Fathi,
Erie Community College, Buffalo, NY

Ralph T. Frasco,
University of Dayton, Dayton, OH

Mark Gardner,
Piedmont College, Demorest, GA

Amyra Grossbard-Shechtman,
San Diego State University, San Diego, CA

Gena F. Hampton
Gainesville College, Gainesville, GA

Randall B. Hayden,
Wichita State University, Wichita, KS

Thomas Humphrey,
Federal Reserve Bank of Richmond

Christopher N. Inya,
Monroe Community College, Rochester, NY

Arthur Kartman,
San Diego State University, San Diego, CA

Darrell E. Parker,
Winthrop College, Rock Hill, SC

Dennis Peters,
Normandale Community College, Bloomington, MN

Ali Saad,
Bernard Baruch College of CUNY, New York, NY

Russell Shannon
Clemson University, Clemson, SC

Scott Sumner,
Bentley College, Waltham, MA

D. F. Swanson,
Indiana University Southeast, New Albany, IN

Thomas G. Talty,
Erie Community College, Buffalo, NY

George R. Thomas,
Johnston Technical College, Smithfield, NC

Linda Vansickle
University of Georgia, Athens, GA

Chiou-Nan Yeh,
Alabama State University, Montgomery, AL

Contents in Brief

Contents

PART II
THE MACROECONOMY

5 Measurements of the Macroeconomy 105

6 Macroeconomic Problems and Policies 135

15 Supply-Side Economics

21 Economic Growth and Development 551

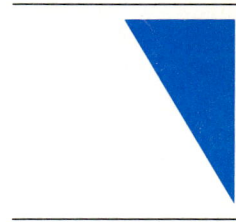

MACROECONOMICS

PART I

Introduction

The Economic Way of Thinking

In economics in particular, education seems to be largely a matter of unlearning and "disteaching" rather than constructive action. A once famous American humorist observed that "it's not ignorance does so much damage; it's knowin' so dernd much that ain't so." . . . It seems that the hardest things to learn and to teach are things that everyone already knows.
  Frank H. Knight

KEY QUESTIONS

▲ 1. What is the central concern underlying economic analysis?

▲ 2. What topics does economics cover?

▲ 3. What role does theory play in economics?

▲ 4. What are the major approaches to economic inquiry?

▲ 5. What are the two major branches of economics as a course of study?

NEW TERMS

Capital (investment goods)
Economics
Entrepreneur
Labor
Land
Macroeconomics
Market

Microeconomics
Normative economics
Positive economics
Resources
Scarcity
Technology
Theory

Frank Knight was a wise professor. Through long years of teaching he realized that students in beginning economics face a difficult task. They must learn many things in a rigorous manner that, on reflection and with experience, amount to common sense. To do that, however, they must set aside—or "unlearn"—many preconceived notions of the economy and of the course itself.

As all good teachers must do, we intend to challenge you in this course to rethink your views on the economy. We will ask you to develop new methods of analysis, maintaining all the while that there is, indeed, an "economic way of thinking" that deserves mastering. We will also ask you to reconsider, in light of the new methods of thinking, old policy issues about which you may have fixed views. These tasks will not always be easy for you, but we are convinced that the rewards from the study ahead are substantial. The greatest reward may be that this first economics course will help you to better understand the way the world works. Much of what this course is about is, oddly enough, crystallized in a story of what happened in a prisoner-of-war camp.

The Emergence of a Market

1. What is the central concern underlying economic analysis?

Market: the process by which buyers and sellers determine what they are willing to buy and sell and on what terms.

Economic systems spring from people's drive to improve their welfare. R. A. Radford, an American soldier who was captured and imprisoned during the Second World War, left a vivid account of the primitive market for goods and services that grew up in his prisoner-of-war camp.[1] A **market** is the process by which buyers and sellers determine what they are willing to buy and sell and on what terms. That is, it is the process by which buyers and sellers decide the prices and quantities of goods that are to be bought and sold. Because the inmates had few opportunities to produce the things they wanted, they turned to a system of exchanges based on the cigarettes,

1. R. A. Radford, "The Economic Organization of a P.O.W. Camp," *Economica* (November 1945), pp. 180–201.

toiletries, chocolate, and other rations distributed to them periodically by the Red Cross.

The Red Cross distributed the supplies equally among the prisoners, but "very soon after capture . . . [the prisoners] realized that it was both undesirable and unnecessary, in view of the limited size and the equality of supplies, to give away or to accept gifts of cigarettes or food. Goodwill developed into trading as a more equitable means of maximizing individual satisfaction."[2] As the weeks went by, trade expanded and the prices of goods stabilized. A soldier who hoped to receive a high price for his soap found he had to compete with others who also wanted to trade soap. Soon shops emerged, and middlemen began to take advantage of discrepancies in the prices offered in different bungalows.

A priest, for example, found that he could exchange a pack of cigarettes for a pound of cheese in one bungalow, trade the cheese for a pack and a half of cigarettes in a second bungalow, and return home with more cigarettes than he had begun with. Although he was acting in his own self-interest, he had provided the people in the second bungalow with something they wanted—more cheese than they would otherwise have had. In fact, prices for cheese and cigarettes differed partly because prisoners had different desires, and partly because they could not all interact freely. In exploiting the discrepancy in prices, the priest moved the camp's store of cheese from the first bungalow, where it was worth less, to the second bungalow, where it was worth more. Everyone involved in the trade benefited from the priest's enterprise.

Entrepreneur: an enterprising person who discovers potentially profitable opportunities and organizes, directs, and manages productive ventures.

A few entrepreneurs in the camp hoarded cigarettes and used them to buy up the troops' rations shortly after issue—and then sold the rations just before the next issue, at higher prices. An **entrepreneur** is an enterprising person who discovers potentially profitable opportunities and organizes, directs, and manages productive ventures. Although these entrepreneurs were pursuing their own private interest, like the priest, they were providing a service to the other prisoners. They bought the rations when people wanted to get rid of them and sold them when people were running short. The difference between the low price at which they bought and the high price at which they sold gave them the incentive they needed to make the trades, hold on to the rations, and assume the risk that the price of rations might not rise.

Soon the troops began to use cigarettes as money, quoting prices in packs or fractions of packs. (Only the less desirable brands of cigarette were used this way; the better brands were smoked.) Because cigarettes were generally acceptable, the soldier who wanted soap no longer had to search out those who might want his jam; he could buy the soap with cigarettes. Even nonsmokers began to accept cigarettes in trade.

This makeshift monetary system adjusted itself to allow for changes in the money supply. On the day the Red Cross distributed new supplies of cigarettes, prices rose, reflecting the influx of new money. After nights

_____

2. Ibid., p. 190.

spent listening to nearby bombing, when the nervous prisoners had smoked up their holdings of cigarettes, prices fell. Radford saw a form of social order emerging in these spontaneous, voluntary, and completely undirected efforts. Even in this unlikely environment, the human tendency toward mutually advantageous interaction had asserted itself.

Today markets for numerous new and used products spring up spontaneously in much the same way. At the end of each semester college students can be found trading books among themselves, or standing in line at the bookstore to resell books they bought at the beginning of the semester. Garage sales are now common in practically all communities. Indeed, like the priest in the POW camp, many people go to garage sales to buy what they believe they can resell—at a higher price, of course.

More than two hundred years ago, Adam Smith outlined a society that resembled these POW camp markets in his classic *Wealth of Nations*. Smith, considered the first economist, asked why markets arise and how they contribute to the social welfare. In answering that question, he defined the economic problem.

The Economic Problem

Our world is not nearly as restrictive as Radford's prison, but it is no Garden of Eden either. Most of us are constantly occupied in securing the food, clothing, and shelter we need to exist, to say nothing of those things we would only like to have—a tape deck, a night on the town. Indeed, if we think seriously about the world around us, we can make two general observations.

First, the world is more or less fixed in size and limited in its resources. **Resources** are things used in the production of goods and services. There are only so many acres of land, gallons of water, trees, rivers, wind currents, oil and mineral deposits, trained workers, and machines that can be used in any one period to produce the things we need and want. We can plant more trees, find more oil, and increase our stock of human talent, but there are limits on what we can accomplish with the resources at our disposal.

Economists group resources into four broad categories: land, labor, capital (also called investment goods), and technology. **Land** includes the surface area of the world and everything in nature—minerals, chemicals, plants—that is useful in the production process. **Labor** includes any way in which human energy, physical or mental, can be usefully expended. **Capital** (investment goods) includes any output of a production process that is designed to be used later in other production processes. Plant and equipment—things produced to produce other things—are examples of these manufactured means of production. **Technology** is the knowledge of how resources can be combined in productive ways.

To this list some economists would add a fifth category, entrepreneurial talent. The entrepreneur is critical to the success of any economy, especially if it relies heavily on markets. Because entrepreneurs discover

Resources: things used in the production of goods and services.

Land: the surface area of the world and everything in nature—minerals, chemicals, plants—that is useful in the production process.

Labor: any way in which human energy, physical or mental, can be usefully expended.

Capital (investment goods): any output of a production process that is designed to be used later in other production processes. Includes plant and equipment.

Technology: the knowledge of how resources can be combined in productive ways.

more effective and profitable ways of organizing resources to produce the goods and services people want, they are often considered a resource in themselves.

Our second general observation is that in contrast to the world's physical limitations, human wants abound. You yourself would probably like to have books, notebooks, pens, and a calculator, perhaps even a computer with 640K worth of memory and a 20 megabyte hard-disk drive. A stereo system, a car, more clothes, a plane ticket home, a seat at a big concert or ballgame—you could probably go on for a long time, especially when you realize how many basics, like three good meals a day, you normally take for granted.

Scarcity: the fact that we cannot all have everything we want all the time.

In fact, most people want far more than they can ever have. One of the unavoidable conditions of life is the fundamental fact of scarcity. **Scarcity** is the fact that we cannot all have everything we want all the time. Put simply, there isn't enough of everything to go around. Consequently society must face several unavoidable questions:

1. What will be produced? More guns or more butter? More schools or more prisons? More cars or more art, more textbooks or more "Saturday night specials"?

2. How will those things be produced, considering the resources at our disposal? Shall we use a great deal of labor and little mechanical power, or vice versa?

3. Who will receive the goods and services produced? Shall we distribute them equally? If not, then on what other basis shall we distribute them?

4. Perhaps most important, how shall we answer all these questions? Shall we allow for individual freedom of choice, or shall we make all these decisions collectively?

These questions have no easy answers. Most of us spend our lives attempting to come to grips with them on an individual level. What should I do with my time today—study or walk through the woods? How should I study—in the library or at home with the stereo on? Who is going to benefit from my efforts—me or my mother, who wants me to succeed? Am I going to live by principle or by habit? Take each day as it comes or plan ahead? In a broader sense, these questions are fundamental not just to the individual but to all the social sciences, economics in particular. Scarcity is the root of economics. **Economics** is the study of how people cope with scarcity—with the pressing problem of how to allocate their limited resources among their competing wants to satisfy as many of those wants as possible.

Economics: the study of how people cope with scarcity—with the pressing problem of how to allocate their limited resources among their competing wants to satisfy as many of those wants as possible.

The problem of allocating resources among competing wants is not as simple as it may first appear. You may think that economics is an examination of how one person or a small group of people makes fundamental social choices on resource use. That is not the case. The problem is that we have information about our wants and the resources at our disposal that may be known to no one else. For example, you may know you want a new

PERSPECTIVES
Adam Smith (1723–1790)

"It is not from the benevolence of the butcher, the brewer, or the baker, that we expect our dinner, but from their regard to their own interest. We address ourselves, not to their humanity but to their self-love, and never talk to them of our own necessities but of their advantages."

When this passage from Adam Smith's *An Inquiry into the Nature and Causes of the Wealth of Nations* (1776) is taken out of context, as it so often is, it may convey a narrow and cynical view of human behavior. Understood in context, however, Smith's statement is merely a logical one. In a complex society, one simply cannot rely on the kindness of others for all one's wants and needs. People are charitable—at least most people are—but they have their limits. As Smith wrote, the individual "at all times stands in need of the cooperation and assistance of great multitudes [of people], while his whole life is scarcely sufficient to gain the friendship of a few persons . . . He will more likely prevail if he can interest their self-love in his favor, and show them that it is for their own advantage to do what he requires of them."

Smith saw the market as a means of enlisting cooperation among strangers. "Give me what I want and I will give you what you want" is the proposition that lies at the base of every market transaction. The butcher, the brewer, and the baker may not know their customers, but by pursuing their own interest, they provide the meat, beer, and bread that others need in order to put dinner on the table.

Prevailing opinion in Smith's time held that in a market exchange, one party profits at the expense of the other. Smith, however, reasoned that if both parties enter into an exchange *voluntarily*, and each gives up something of value for something else of value, both parties perceive they will benefit. They may not be as well off as they would like to be, but their welfare has been improved by the transaction. Through trade, they have each obtained something they want but cannot produce themselves.

Smith's ideas also conflicted with the mercantilist philosophy of trade, which held that the unregulated pursuit of private interest would inevitably lead to disorder. In Europe in the seventeenth and eighteenth centuries, wages, prices, interest rates, employment, foreign trade, and the quality of goods and services were all strictly controlled by government. The object of this control was to ensure the ruling class's vision of social justice through the administration of what was produced and how it was produced and distributed. Yet to Smith, self-interest was obviously a constructive, coordinating force. In the drive to fulfill their own needs, self-interested people had to appeal to the interests of others. Self-interest is an incentive—a reason to cooperate and coordinate one's activities with others'.

calculator because your statistics class requires you to have one, and even your friends (much less the people at Hewlett-Packard or Casio) do not yet know your purchase plans. You may also be the only person who knows how much labor you have, which is determined by exactly how long and intensely you are willing to work at various tasks. At the same time, you may know little about the wants and resources that other people around the country and world may have. Before resources can be effectively allocated, the information we hold about our individual wants and resources must somehow be communicated to others. This means economics must be con-

Critics of the market system saw profit as an unfair drain on workers' earnings, but Smith viewed it as an incentive—the reward that encourages the producer to meet the interests of others. He felt that competition among producers would keep profits and prices low, so consumers would not be overcharged. In Smith's words, self-interest acts like an "invisible hand" that guides individuals to work for the common interest in the pursuit of their own gain.

Smith saw government as necessary, but only to provide for national defense, for the administration of law and justice, and for certain essential public works that cannot be provided efficiently by the market, such as roads and education. He objected to further government involvement in the market for three reasons. First, government means collective decision making, which runs counter to the individual self-interest that is the foundation of the market system. To Smith, individual choices were important. Leaving decisions to the individual seemed the best way to ensure that good choices would be made.

Second, Smith argued that government restrictions on the market can prevent mutually beneficial trades and reduce the welfare of potential traders. Government-imposed tariffs on imports are a good example of this negative effect. Tariffs increase the price of imports and encourage consumers to buy more domestic substitutes than they would otherwise, at a higher price. As a result, consumers get less for their dollar.

Third, Smith felt that businesspeople would exploit any government power over the economy to further their own interests. He once wrote, "The proposal of any new law or regulations of commerce which comes from this order [of entrepreneurs], ought always to be listened to with great precaution, and ought never to be adopted till after having been long and carefully examined . . . with the most suspicious attention. It comes from an order of men . . . who have generally an interest to deceive and even to oppress the public . . ." Businesspeople, said Smith, seldom come together except to conspire against the public—that is, to restrict trade in their favor. He felt that the competition inherent in the market system would help to minimize such collusion.

Although he may never have used the word, Smith was well aware of the imperfections of the market system. He recognized the risk of monopoly, which he saw as an evil fostered primarily by government. He also acknowledged that the market often adjusts slowly to change and may fail to produce adequate quantities of certain goods without government intervention. *Wealth of Nations* did not attempt to prove that the free market system is perfect. Rather, it was a classic statement on the relative merits of the market system, compared with the alternatives.

cerned with *systems* of communication. Indeed, the field is extensively concerned with how information about wants and resources is transmitted or shared through, for example, prices in the market process and votes in the political process.

Markets like the one in the POW camp emerge in direct response to scarcity. Because people want more than is immediately available, they produce some goods and services for trade. By exchanging things they like less for things they like more, they reallocate their resources and enhance their welfare as individuals.

The Scope of Economics

◢ 2. What topics does
economics cover?

Beginning students often associate economics with a rather narrow portion of the human experience: the pursuit of wealth; money and taxes; commercial and industrial life. Critics often suggest that economists are oblivious to the aesthetic and ethical dimensions of human experience. Such criticism is not altogether unjustified. Increasingly, however, economists are expanding their horizons and applying the laws of economics to the full spectrum of human activities.

The struggle to improve one's lot is not limited to the attainment of material goals. Although most economic principles have to do with the pursuit of material gain, they can be relevant to aesthetic and humanistic goals as well. The appreciation of a poem or play can be the subject of economic inquiry. Poems and plays, and the time in which to appreciate them, are also scarce.

Jacob Viner, an economist active in the first half of this century, once defined economics as what economists do. Today economists study an increasingly diverse array of topics. As always, they are involved in describing market processes, methods of trade, and commercial and industrial patterns. They also pay considerable attention to poverty and wealth; to racial, sexual, and religious discrimination; to politics and bureaucracy; to crime and criminal law; and to revolution. There is even an economics of group interaction, in which economic principles are applied to marital and family problems. Thus, although economists are still working on the conventional problems of inflation, unemployment, and international monetary problems, they are also studying the delivery of housing to the disadvantaged or of health care to the very young and the elderly. In one way or another, today's economists are tackling a wide variety of subjects—from committee structure to the criminal justice system, ethics, voting rules, and the legislative process.

What is the unifying factor in these diverse inquiries? What ties them all together and distinguishes the economist's work from that of other social scientists? Economists take a distinctive approach to the study of human behavior. They employ a mode of analysis based on certain presuppositions about human behavior. For example, much economic analysis starts with the general proposition that people prefer more to less of those things they want and that they seek to maximize their welfare by making reasonably consistent choices in the things they buy and sell. These propositions enable economists to derive the "law of demand" (people will buy more of any good at a lower price than at a higher price, and vice versa) and many other principles of human behavior.

One purpose of this book is to describe this special approach in considerable detail—to develop in precise terms the commonly accepted principles of economic analysis and to demonstrate how they can be used to understand a variety of problems, including pollution, unemployment, crime, and ticket scalping. In every case, economic analysis is useful only if it is based on a sound theory that can be evaluated in terms of real-world experience.

Developing and Using Economic Theories

▲ 3. **What role does theory play in economics?**

The real world of economics is staggeringly complex. Each day millions of people engage in innumerable transactions, only some of them involving money, and many of them undertaken for contradictory reasons. To make sense of all these activities, economists turn to theory.

A theory is a model of how the world is put together; it is an attempt to uncover some order in the seemingly random events of daily life. Economic theory is abstract, but not in the sense that its models lack concreteness. On the contrary, good models are laid out with great precision. Economic theories are simplified models *abstracted from* the complexity of the real world. The economist deliberately concentrates on just a few outstanding features of a problem in an effort to discover the laws that govern their relationship. A **theory** is a set of abstractions about the real world. An economic theory is a simplified explanation of how the economy or part of the economy functions or would function under specific conditions.

Theory: a set of abstractions about the real world. An economic theory is a simplified explanation of how the economy or part of the economy functions or would function under specific conditions.

Quite often the economist must also make unproved assumptions, called simplifying assumptions, about the parts of the economy under study. For example, in examining the effects of price and availability on the amount of food sold, the economist might assume that people eat only oranges and bananas in the model society in question. Such a simplifying assumption is permissible in constructing a model, for two reasons. First, it makes the discussion more manageable. Second, it does not alter the problem under study or destroy its relevance to the real world.

As following chapters will reveal, economic theorizing is largely deductive—that is, the analysis proceeds from very general propositions (such as "more is preferred to less") to much more precise statements or predictions (for example, "the quantity purchased will rise when the price falls").[3] Economic theories sometimes vary in their premises and conclusions, but all develop through the following three steps.

First, a few very general premises or propositions are stated. "More is preferred to less" or "People will seek to maximize their welfare" are examples of such propositions. The premises tend to be so general that they are beyond dispute, at least to the economists developing the theory.

Second, logical deductions, which are tentative predictions about behavior, are drawn from the premises. From the premise "People will seek to maximize their welfare" we can deduce how people will tend to allocate their incomes at certain prices. We can then conclude that they will purchase more of a good when its price falls. Mathematics and graphic analysis are often very useful in deducing the consequences of premises.

Third, the predictions are tested against observable experience. Theory may tell us that people buy more at lower prices than at higher prices, but the critical question is whether that prediction is borne out in the real

---

3. In contrast, inductive theorizing proceeds from very precise statements about observable relationships (such as "people are laid off when plants close") to much more general propositions (for example, "plant closings increase unemployment").

PERSPECTIVES

What Do Economists Do?

Rudolph White, University of Georgia

According to the U.S. Department of Labor, there were approximately 96,000 professional workers classified as economists in 1986. These economists worked in private industry, in colleges and universities, and at all levels of government. Over 300,000 students have earned bachelor degrees in economics since 1960, which indicates that less than one-third of students with bachelor degrees in economics become practicing economists.

Many economics graduates go to work as financial analysts, bank officers, credit analysts, policy analysts, and stockbrokers. Many others go on to graduate school in economics or into other professional schools, most notably graduate schools of business, law, and public administration. After completing training programs specific to their employing firms, many "econ" graduates assume management posts. The following major corporations often hire economists for accounting, finance, and various management positions: AT&T, International Paper, Chrysler, CIGNA, Price Waterhouse, Standard Oil of Ohio, Libby-Owens-Ford, Duke Power, and Michigan Bell Telephone. Such a list does not capture the numerous smaller fast-growing firms in your area of the country.

Clearly, economists do many things. As practicing professionals in business, they are often called on to evaluate various investment opportunities. For example, economists might be asked to assess the profitability of the development of a new product, the construction of a new plant, or the purchase of an existing firm. This may mean that they must use statistical analysis to forecast the future movement in overall economic activity (measured by production, interest rates, unemployment, and price level, for example) in the country and to estimate future production costs and sales.

Business economists may also be asked to assess the likely impact of pending congressional legislation on the financial health of a company. For example, economists at General Motors have been called on to determine how mandatory pollution control equipment and air bags would likely affect the size of the U.S. automobile market and, more specifically, GM sales, employment, and profits. Economists with the American Textile Manufacturers Association have been asked to estimate how additional import restrictions will affect jobs, wages, and profits in the industry.

Economists who work on congressional staffs often advise their senators and representatives on how various pieces of pending legislation will affect their states and districts and what position they should take. Special interest groups in Washington often employ economists to formulate the strongest possible arguments for or against pending legislation. For instance, soft drink bottlers might employ economists to develop arguments that can be used to defeat a proposed tax levied on each soft drink sold in the country.

Academic economists are probably the most publicly visible economists because they do a great deal of teaching at the undergraduate and graduate levels. They also undertake consulting projects for governments and businesses and do basic research. Their research topics are varied. Some may be concerned with questions of why prices are rising, unemployment is falling, or homelessness is rising. They may also investigate the impact of, say, a change in highway speeds on highway accidents, deaths, and financial losses from automotive accidents. Others may seek to answer more fundamental questions, such as "Why do 'firms' exist?" or "How can 'government' be justified?"

In many of their endeavors, economists use simplified models of human behavior and interaction. They try to make predictions, based on the rules of logic, and seek to test their predictions against real world observations. Economists might reason that because the deregulation of airlines (which occurred in 1978) has reduced air fares, more people have been flying and (possibly) fewer people have been driving their cars on the nation's highways. They might then reason that the number of highway deaths is directly linked to the

continued

TABLE 1.1 Earnings and Employment 1986, Occupations Employing 50,000 or More People

Occupation (Not Self-Employed)	Rank	Median Weekly Earnings	Number Employed (000)	Percentage of Women Employed in Occupation
All occupations		$358	78,727	41.3
Judges	1	767	28	20.0
Lawyers	1	767	314	25.2
Airline pilots	3	754	54	1.9
Chemical engineers	4	721	55	10.9
Aerospace engineers	5	708	95	4.2
Electrical engineers	6	704	571	7.8
Economists	**6**	**704**	**96**	**38.5**
Mechanical engineers	8	687	283	3.9
Marketing managers	9	680	421	24.0
Physicians	10	653	219	26.9
Purchasing managers	11	633	101	32.7
Computer systems analyst	12	631	337	35.0
Industrial engineers	13	628	191	9.9
Locomotive operators	14	625	57	1.8
Personnel managers	15	621	109	47.7
Civil engineers	16	618	209	3.3
Operations Res.	17	617	203	37.9
Educational administrator	18	610	440	43.0
Security sales	19	608	215	24.2
Pharmacists	20	607	109	34.9
Chemists (excluding biologists)	21	601	116	20.7
College teacher	22	600	443	27.5
Financial managers	23	584	396	37.9
Architects	24	577	87	11.1
Social scientists	25	569	229	42.8
Telephone installers	26	568	64	6.3
Management analysts	27	567	102	39.2
Police supervisors	28	558	89	5.6
Water transport operators	29	547	51	2.0
Production supervisors	30	524	219	9.1
Extractive operator	31	520	155	1.3
Computer programmers	32	519	503	34.2
Public relations	33	518	130	48.5
Repair data processors	34	514	127	8.7
Electrical installers	34	514	106	1.9
Public administrators	36	513	434	40.6
Tool and die makers	37	506	151	1.3
Aircraft mechanics	38	505	96	3.1
Health managers	39	503	113	59.3
Biological scientists	39	503	59	37.3
Millwrights	41	501	93	6.3
Underwriters	42	500	600	46.5
Construction supervisors	42	500	420	1.4
Educational counselors	43	494	146	50.7
Statistical engineers	44	493	103	1.0
Sales representatives	45	492	1,226	17.0
Psychologists	46	491	100	49.0

Source: Adapted from *Monthly Labor Review* (June 1987).

What Do Economists Do?

continued

volume of highway traffic—that is, the lower the amount of driving, the lower the number of automobile accidents and deaths. Hence, economists might predict that airline deregulation has reduced the number of highway deaths. Of course, such a conclusion would have to be checked by statistical analysis with what has actually happened to highway deaths since airline deregulation.

For their work, economists are paid relatively well. As Table 1.1 reveals, the median weekly salary of economists was $704 in 1986 and ranked sixth among occupations employing 50,000 or more people that year. Judges, lawyers, airline pilots, and chemical, aerospace, and electrical engineers outranked economists, but not by more than 9 percent in terms of median weekly salary.

Nearly 40 percent of all practicing economists are women.

Your reason for taking this first course in economics may not be, at this point, directly related to expected financial returns. You may be taking the course as an elective or as a graduation or major requirement. The course may be a requirement because faculty members in other disciplines believe that you need a firm grounding in economic principles to pursue your chosen career. The course is designed to do much more than that. It can enable you to better understand the events that you see around you on campus and read about in newspapers. More than anything else, economics seeks to provide you with a means of thinking about the world and your place in it.

world. Do people actually buy more apples when the price falls? Empirical tests require data to be carefully selected and statistically analyzed.

Empirical tests can never prove a theory's validity. The behavior that is observed—more apples purchased, for instance—may be caused by factors not considered in the theory. That is, the quantity of apples purchased may increase for some reason other than a drop in price. Empirical tests can only fail to disprove a theory. If a theory is repeatedly evaluated in different circumstances and is not disproven, however, its usefulness and general applicability increase. Economists have considerable confidence in the proposition that price and quantity purchased are inversely related because it has been repeatedly tested and found to be accurate.

Although a theory is not a complete and realistic description of the real world, a good theory should incorporate enough data to simulate real life. That is, it should provide some explanation for past experiences and permit reasonably accurate predictions of the future. When you evaluate a new theory, ask yourself: Does this theory explain what has been observed? Does it provide a better basis for prediction than other theories?

Positive and Normative Economics

◢ 4. What are the major approaches to economic theory?

Economic thinking is often divided into two categories—positive and normative. **Positive economics** is that branch of economic inquiry that is concerned with the world as it is rather than as it should be. It deals only with the consequences of changes in economic conditions or policies. A positive

Positive economics: that branch of economic inquiry that is concerned with the world as it is rather than as it should be.

Normative economics: that branch of economic inquiry that deals with value judgments—with what prices, production levels, incomes, and government policies *ought* to be.

economist suspends questions of values when dealing with issues like crime or minimum wage laws. The object is to predict the effect of changes in the criminal code or the minimum wage rate—not to evaluate the fairness of such changes. **Normative economics** is that branch of economic inquiry that deals with value judgments—with what prices, production levels, incomes, and government policies *ought* to be. A normative economist does not shrink from the question of what the minimum wage rate ought to be. To arrive at an answer, the economist weighs the results of various minimum wage rates on the groups affected by them—the unemployed, employers, taxpayers, and so on. Then, on the basis of value judgments of the relative need or merit of each group, the normative economist recommends a specific minimum wage rate. Of course, values differ from one person to the next. In the analytical jump from recognizing the alternatives to prescribing a solution, scientific thinking gives way to ethical judgment.

Microeconomics and Macroeconomics

5. What are the two major branches of economics as a course of study?

Microeconomics: the study of the individual markets—for corn, records, books, and so forth—that operate within the broad national economy.

The discipline of economics is divided into two main parts—microeconomics and macroeconomics. As the term *micro* (as in microscope) suggests, **microeconomics** is the study of the individual markets—for corn, records, books, and so forth—that operate within the broad national economy. When economists measure, explain, and predict the demand for specific products like bicycles and hand calculators, they are dealing with microeconomics. Much of the work of economists is concerned with microeconomic analysis—that is, with the interpretation of events in the marketplace and of personal choices among products.

Questions of interest to microeconomists include:

What determines the price of particular goods and services?

What determines the output of individual firms and industries?

What determines the wages workers receive? The interest rates lenders receive? The profits businesses receive?

How do government policies—like minimum wage laws, price controls, tariffs, and excise taxes—affect the price and output levels of individual markets?

Macroeconomics: the study of the national economy as a whole or of its major components. Deals with the "big picture," not the details, of the nation's economic activity.

Economists are also interested in measuring, explaining, and predicting the performance of the economic system itself. To do so they study broad subdivisions of the economy, such as the total output of all firms that produce goods and services. **Macroeconomics** is the study of the national economy as a whole or of its major components. It deals with the "big picture," not the details, of the nation's economic activity.

Instead of concentrating on how many bicycles or hand calculators are sold, macroeconomists watch how many goods and services consumers purchase in total or how much money all producers spend on new plant and equipment. Instead of tracking the price of a particular good in a particular market, macroeconomics monitors the general price level or average of all prices. Instead of focusing on the wage rate and the number of people employed as plumbers or engineers, macroeconomists study incomes of all employees and the total number of people employed throughout the economy. In short, macroeconomics involves the study of national production, unemployment, and inflation. For that reason it is often referred to as aggregate economics.

Typical macroeconomic questions include:

What determines the general price level? The rate of inflation?

What determines national income and production levels?

What determines national employment and unemployment levels?

What effects do government monetary and budgetary policies have on the general price, income, production, employment, and unemployment levels?

What, if anything, can government do to combat inflation, unemployment, and recession?

These questions are of more than academic interest. The theories that have been developed to answer them can be applied to problems and issues of the real world. Throughout this book, as well as in specific chapters on topics like inflation, regulation and deregulation, and price controls and consumer protection, we will examine the practical applications of economic theory. In some basic way, scarcity—and the economic question of how to deal with it—touches all of us.

Chapter Review

Review of Key Questions

◢   *1. What is the central concern underlying economic analysis?*

Economics deals primarily with problems that arise from scarcity—that is, our inability to satisfy all wants with the limited resources available. Because of scarcity, we must make difficult choices about how best to allocate resources on individual, community, and national levels.

◢   *2. What topics does economics cover?*

Economics is concerned, generally, with how people seek to improve their welfare. Accordingly, economics is a study of the level of production of individual goods and within the entire economy, the level of employment (and unemployment), the quantity of money, and the rate of inflation. However, economics is not restricted to the "material" dimensions of life. The techniques of economic analysis could also be applied to people's decisions to read a poem or watch a sunset.

◢   *3. What role does theory play in economics?*

The real world is too complex to be studied in its entirety. In order to improve our understanding of the world, we must simplify the analysis by abstracting key relationships from the complex world and form a "model" or "theory" of how the world works. The usefulness of theory cannot be judged by how completely it is intended to describe the world because it leaves out many details that clutter thinking. Rather, the usefulness of theory must be judged by what it is intended to accomplish. An important purpose of economic theory is to generate predictions about real-world events that can be subjected to empirical tests.

◢ *4. What are the major approaches to economic inquiry?*

Economic analysis has two approaches—*positive* and *normative*. Positive economics deals primarily with predictions of how the economy actually operates. Normative economics concerns value judgments about how the economy should operate.

◢ *5. What are the two major branches of economics as a course of study?*

As a course of study, economics is divided into *microeconomics* and *macroeconomics*. Microeconomic analysis deals with individual markets, such as the market for corn. Macroeconomic analysis studies the operation of the entire national economy and its major subdivisions, such as the level of business investment.

Further Topics

Economics is a discipline best described as the study of human interaction in the context of scarcity. It is the study of how, individually and collectively, people use their scarce resources to satisfy as many of their wants as possible. The economic method is founded in a set of presuppositions about human behavior on which economists construct theoretical models. A major purpose of this book is to describe the analytical tools economists use and in that way show how they study human behavior.

Review of New Terms

Capital (investment goods) Any output of a production process that is designed to be used later in other production processes. Includes plant and equipment.

Economics The study of how people cope with scarcity—with the pressing problem of how to allocate their limited resources among their competing wants to satisfy as many of those wants as possible.

Entrepreneur An enterprising person who discovers potentially profitable opportunities and organizes, directs, and manages productive ventures.

Labor Any way in which human energy, physical or mental, can be usefully expended.

Land The surface area of the world and everything in nature—minerals, chemicals, plants—that is useful in the production process.

Macroeconomics The study of the national economy as a whole or of its major components. Deals with the "big picture," not the details, of the nation's economic activity.

Market The process by which buyers and sellers determine what they are willing to buy and sell and on what terms. That is, the process by which buyers and sellers decide the prices and quantities of goods to be bought and sold.

Microeconomics The study of the individual markets—for corn, records, books, and so forth—that operate within the broad national economy.

Normative economics That branch of economic inquiry that deals with value judgments—with what prices, production levels, incomes, and government policies ought to be.

Positive economics That branch of economic inquiry that is concerned with the world as it is rather than as it should be. Deals only with the consequences of changes in economic conditions or policies.

Resources Things used in the production of goods and services.

Scarcity The fact that we cannot all have everything we want all the time.

Technology The knowledge of how resources can be combined in productive ways.

Theory A set of abstractions about the real world. An economic theory is a simplified explanation of how the economy or part of the economy functions or would function under specific conditions.

Review Questions

1. In the prison camp described on pages 4–6, rations were distributed equally. Why did trade within and among bungalows result? (◢ 1)
2. Recall the priest who traded cigarettes for cheese, and cheese for cigarettes, so that he ended up with more cigarettes than he had initially. Did someone else in the camp lose by the priest's activities? How was the priest able to end up better off than when he began? What did his activities do to the price of cheese in the different bungalows? (◢ 1)
3. Theories may be defective, but economists continue to use them. Why? (◢ 3)
4. An introductory economics book could include theories more complex than those in this book. What might be the tradeoffs in dealing with more complex theories? (◢ 2, ◢ 3)
5. How can values influence scientific inquiry? How can value-free (positive) economic analysis affect policy assessments? (◢ 4)
6. What is the difference between micro- and macroeconomics? (◢ 5)

Scarcity and Production Possibilities

Economics is the science which studies human behavior as a relationship between ends and means which have alternative uses.
  Lionel Robbins

KEY QUESTIONS

▲ 1. How are the concepts of scarcity and cost related?

▲ 2. What are production possibilities curves and what does their downward slope imply?

▲ 3. What does investment do to future production opportunities?

▲ 4. How do current choices between private and public goods affect future production opportunities?

▲ 5. How do people, acting individually and collectively, change their production opportunities?

▲ 6. Why do people benefit from trade?

▲ 7. How are major sectors of the economy tied together?

NEW TERMS

Circular flow of income
Comparative advantage
Consumption goods
Cost (opportunity cost)
Diseconomies of scale
Economies of scale
Money

Private goods
Production possibilities curve
  (production possibilities
  frontier)
Public goods
Specialization of labor

The last chapter introduced the basic economic problem: the conflict between unlimited human wants and limited resources. Using graphic analysis, this chapter examines the decisions that must be made individually and collectively as a result of the conflict. Two concepts—the production possibilities curve and the circular flow of income—are particularly important to the discussion.

The appendix at the end of this chapter outlines the basic features and uses of graphs. If you are unsure how to use or read graphs, turn to page 39 before reading further.

The Implications of Scarcity

◢ 1. How are the concepts of scarcity and cost related?

Scarcity is a fact of life. Individually and collectively we cannot have all that we want; we are forced to live within our means. The essential economic problem is this: Our ability to imagine the goods and services we would like to have far exceeds our ability to produce them—that is, to transform the resources at our disposal into the goods and services we want.

From the basic observation of scarcity, three conclusions flow. First, there is always more than one use for a resource. Time not spent studying can be used to farm, to run computers, or to raise a family. There is always something constructive for people (or machinery, or land) to do. Economically speaking, a person is unemployed because some barrier—distance or lack of skill—separates him or her from productive work, not because none exists. Technological change may eliminate the need for labor in a given industry, but it also frees labor to do other things and satisfy other wants.

Second, we must choose among alternative uses for resources. Choice is an inescapable, sometimes agonizing, part of the economic process. Whenever we do anything, we forgo the opportunity to do other things. If we go to a movie, we choose not to study. If we produce textiles, we forgo the chance to make machines or a variety of other products and services. If we expand public education, we must do without extra police protection—or raise taxes and do without private goods. "You can't have your cake and eat it too" is a well-worn adage but an economically apt one.

Third, every choice has a cost. Although often stated in dollars and cents, an item's cost is more accurately defined as the value of what could have been purchased instead. Dollars and cents are only a means of measuring this opportunity cost. **Cost** (or, more precisely, opportunity cost) is the value of the most highly preferred alternative not taken.

Cost (opportunity cost): the value of the most highly preferred alternative not taken.

As long as resources are scarce and we can choose among them, everything we do will have a cost. There is a cost to studying, to producing textiles, and to providing public education. Although we talk about cost in terms of dollars and cents, cost itself will never be seen—can never be seen—for it is the option not taken or the value of what we could have done but didn't.

The Production Possibilities Curve

▲ **2. What are production possibilities curves and what does their downward slope imply?**

The limitations and choices inherent in the economy can be represented graphically. Assume that a nation can produce only two goods—guns (measured in numbers of guns) and butter (measured in pounds). Although this economy can produce only so much, choices among alternatives do exist. Resources can be shifted from one line of production to another, changing the combination of guns and butter produced. At one extreme, the nation can devote all its resources to making guns, producing no butter at all. Alternatively, it can make only butter. Resources also can be divided between the two production processes, yielding some combination of guns and butter. If all possible production combinations are plotted on a graph (with guns on the horizontal axis and butter on the vertical), the result is a production possibilities curve. A **production possibilities curve** (sometimes called a production possibilities frontier or a product transformation curve) is a graphical representation of the various combinations of goods that can be produced when all resources are fully and efficiently employed. It shows all the production combinations possible when all resources available are used in the most productive way possible, given the best known technology (see Figure 2.1).

Production possibilities curve (production possibilities frontier): a graphical representation of the various combinations of goods that can be produced when all resources are fully and efficiently employed.

Linear Production Possibilities Curves

The production possibilities curve can take several shapes, two of which are shown in Figure 2.1. All are downward sloping from left to right. (Such curves are said to have a *negative slope*—see the Appendix, page 39, for an explanation of the term *slope*.) Why? Suppose we are using all our resources to produce guns; that is, we are at point *a* in Figure 2.1, panel (a). Then the only way we can produce butter is to move some resources away from the production of guns. Such a shift necessarily means a cut in the number of guns produced. We move from point *a* to point *b*—upward and to the left.

The movement from *a* to *b* on the curve in Figure 2.1(a) can be seen as the cost of producing the butter. That is, the cost of the 80 pounds of butter gained is the *value* of the 50 guns given up. It is important to remember that cost is the value, not the number, of what is given up. In Figure 2.1(a), the slope of the curve, $-80/50$ or $-8/5$, is constant (because the curve is straight). Therefore the *number* of guns forgone for each additional unit of butter remains constant. The value of additional units of butter, in economic terms, does not necessarily remain constant, however.

(a) Linear Curve

(b) Bowed Curve

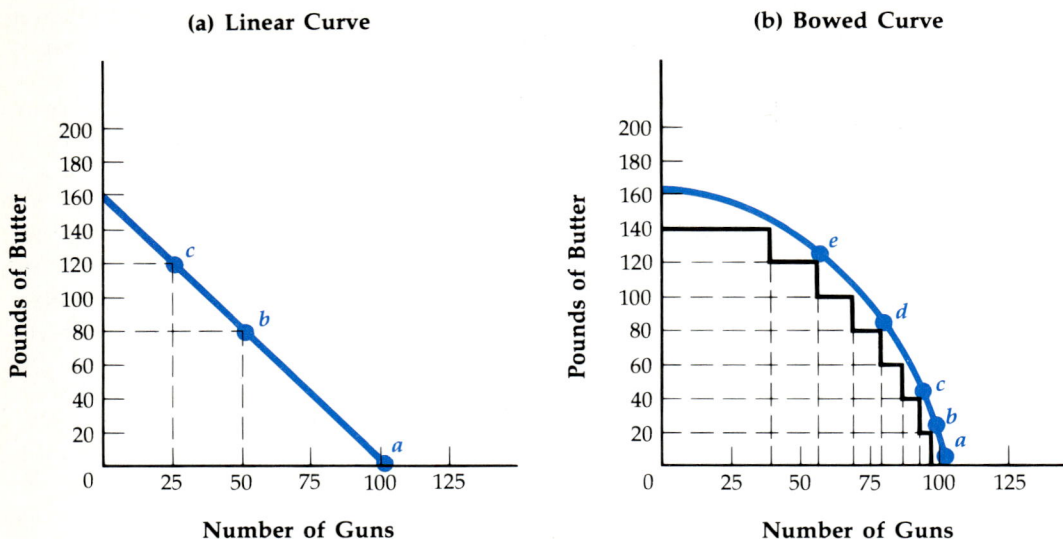

FIGURE 2.1 Production Possibilities Curves

All production possibilities curves slope downward from the left to the right. When resources are fully and efficiently employed, more of one good, like guns, can be produced
only by giving up some of another good, like butter.

A production possibilities curve that takes the form of a straight line—as in panel (a)—
indicates that the number of goods that must be given up for a specific amount of a second
good remains constant as production increases. A production possibilities curve that is
bowed out—as in panel (b)—indicates that as production increases, more and more goods
must be given up to gain the same amount of the second good.

In fact, as we move up along the curve, acquiring more butter and
giving up more guns, the relative value of guns and butter is almost certain
to change. As more guns are given up, they will be taken away from uses
that are increasingly valuable, and the cost of additional units of butter will
tend to rise as more are produced. At the same time, the relative value of
the additional units of butter will tend to fall because they will be used for
less and less valuable purposes. Just how far up the curve we will go depends entirely on the relative values of the two commodities. If we stop
at c, that is the point where additional units of butter are not worth their
cost to us.

Bowed Production Possibilities Curves

The curve in Figure 2.1(b) is bowed out from (or, to use mathematical
jargon, "concave to") the origin. What does such a shape imply? As the
curve approaches the intersection on the vertical axis, it becomes flatter or
lower in slope. The number of guns that must be forgone for each additional unit of butter goes up progressively. When we moved from a to b,
expanding our production of butter by 20 pounds, we gave up only 5 guns.

If we move further up the curve from *b* to *c*, however, we must forgo significantly more guns than before—7 instead of 5—to get 20 more pounds of butter. Similarly, as we move up the curve from *c* to *d* and from *d* to *e*, we give up proportionally more guns for each 20 pounds of butter.

These increases in the number of units forgone stem from the tendency to use resources as efficiently as possible. As we divide up our resources between butter and guns, we put those resources that are better suited to butter production into the butter industry and those better suited to guns into the gun industry. If we then want to increase butter production, we must move some resources from guns to butter. We have already put the most suitable resources into butter; now we must add resources that are less suitable. Thus for each additional pound of butter, we must give up progressively more of our gun resources.

In Figure 2.1(b), the *cost* of producing each additional unit of butter increases for two reasons. First, as in Figure 2.1(a), the value of the guns forgone rises. Second, each time butter production is expanded, the resources transferred from guns will be less efficient for butter production; thus more and more guns must be given up.

Points Inside and Outside the Curve

The production possibilities curve assumes that resources are fully and efficiently employed. (That is, they are used where they will do the most good, in terms of what people want most.) If those two conditions are not met, then the economy will not be operating on the production possibilities curve but at some point within it, like point *u* in Figure 2.2. At point *u*,

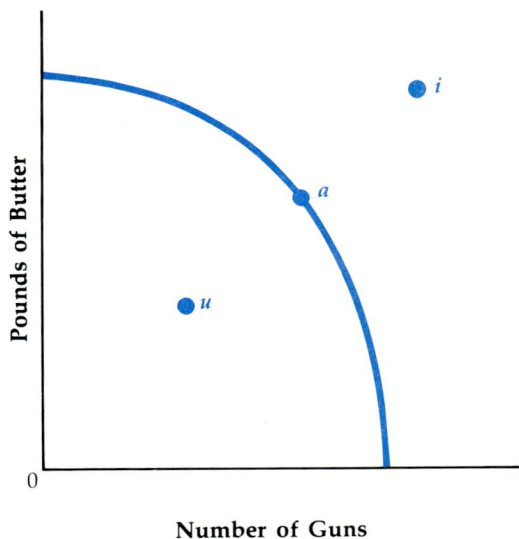

FIGURE 2.2 Maximizing Production
Any point on a production possibilities curve (such as *a*) represents full and efficient use of resources. Points inside the production possibilities curve (such as *u*) represent incomplete or inefficient use of at least one resource. Points outside the curve (*i*, for instance) are beyond an economy's resources.

fewer goods than possible are being produced. From such a point, we should be able to move to a point on the curve, like *a*, expanding the production of both guns and butter at the same time. In that respect, a movement from *u* to *a* is costless—nothing is forgone to increase production. Making sure that our economy is not functioning somewhere in the interior of the production possibilities curve, where resources are underutilized, is one of the major tasks for economic policymakers.

Points outside, or to the right of, the production possibilities curve are by definition impossible to achieve. To suggest, for instance, that we should choose to produce at a point like *i* is equivalent to saying that we should produce more than we are capable of producing (*i* stands for "impossible"). In the heat of debate, our political leaders sometimes seem to suggest just such impossible goals. Our production limitations (and the problems of choice) cannot be escaped. We cannot move to a point like *i* by printing more money. The additional dollars add nothing to our stock of real resources.

Partly because economists are constantly insisting that we recognize the obvious, economics is often referred to as the "dismal science." In fact we are generally either on or close to our production possibilities frontier. Getting more of one thing thus means giving up something else. We do have options, but they are options constrained by reality. To borrow the words of Ben Franklin, choices are as certain as death and taxes.

The Choice Between Investment and Consumption

▲ **3. What does investment do to future production opportunities?**

Choices span the spectrum of goods and services. We must choose not only between the goods and services we can have today, but between current goods and services and those we can have in the future. When we choose an apple from our barrel, we also choose to have one less apple for the future. In the same way, our choices between capital or investment goods and consumption goods influence both our present and future incomes and our consumption patterns over time. Recall from Chapter 1 that an investment or capital good is any output of a production process that is designed to be used in other production processes—for example, plant and equipment. Investment goods (capital) are manufactured means of production. A **consumption good** is any good that is produced to be used and enjoyed more or less immediately by its purchaser, like ice cream.

Consumption goods: goods that are produced to be used and enjoyed more or less immediately by their purchasers.

Figure 2.3 shows the economic consequences of various levels of investment. Assume that a nation's production possibilities curve is C_2I_3. Assume also that the nation chooses to produce at point *a*, representing C_1 consumption goods and I_1 investment goods. Several consequences follow from such a decision.

First, like consumption goods, investment goods come at a cost. That cost is the value of the consumption goods forgone, in this case, $C_2 - C_1$.

Second, investment goods are means of production; they add to a nation's stock of plant and equipment. As long as the level of investment—in this case, I_1—does more than replace old, worn-out plant and equip-

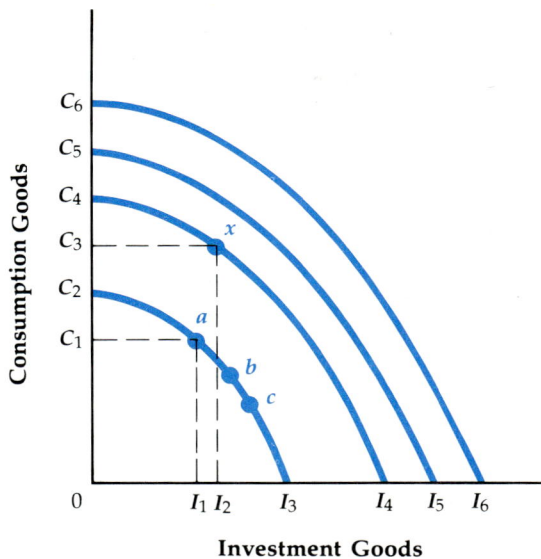

FIGURE 2.3   Investment Versus Consumption
A nation's future production capability depends on the choices it makes between consumption and investment goods. The more investment goods it produces, the further to the right its production possibilities curve will shift. If a nation produces at point a on curve C_2I_3, its production possibilities curve will shift to C_4I_4. If it chooses point b, its curve will shift to C_5I_5; from point c, it will shift to C_6I_6.

ment, it increases future production capabilities. That is, because of the new plant and equipment, the nation's production possibilities curve will gradually shift to the right, perhaps to C_4I_4. This rightward shift of the production possibilities curve indicates economic growth.

Third, when the production possibilities curve shifts to the right, a nation's ability to afford consumption goods increases. When a nation that was producing initially at point a moves to point x, consumption increases from C_1 to C_3. Thus by forgoing a small amount of consumption goods $(C_2 - C_1)$ in the beginning, a nation gains a larger amount of consumption goods $(C_3 - C_2)$ in the future. This increased future consumption does not require a decrease in future investment. Investment increases too, from I_1 to I_2.

Fourth, this greater investment capability increases the potential for future growth. Every time investment increases, the production possibilities curve shifts further to the right—to C_5I_5, C_6I_6, and so on.

Fifth, the more a nation invests initially, the greater the shift in its future production possibilities. If a nation chooses to invest more than I_1— for example, choosing point b instead of point a on curve C_2I_3—its production possibilities curve will shift further to the right, perhaps to C_5I_5, than it would with I_1 investment. Choosing point c can cause the curve to shift still further, perhaps to C_6I_6. The more a nation invests initially, however, the more it must forgo in the way of consumption goods.

Thus a nation's long-term economic growth depends heavily on its ability to forgo current consumption in order to invest. Suppose three nations—A, B, and C—start out on the same production possibilities curve,

C_2I_3. Simply by choosing different points on that curve—*a*, *b*, or *c*—they can end up with vastly different future production possibilities curves and future consumption patterns. What happens tomorrow depends critically on the choices made today.

Ideally, at what point should a nation produce initially: *a*, *b*, or *c*? At first it may seem that the answer is obviously *c* (and if not *c*, then *b*). Does the value of the future consumption gained exceed the value of the current consumption forgone? Not necessarily. If a nation chooses to produce at point *a* when it could have produced at point *c*, we must presume that its citizens do not value the benefits of future consumption as much as current consumption.

The position of the production possibilities curve also depends on the types of investment projects that are undertaken. A nation that merely duplicates existing plant and equipment, rather than improving them, will not do as well in the future as a nation that invests heavily in research and innovative technology. Of course innovation can be risky; not all new ideas are better ideas. Again the benefits of increased investment must be weighed against the cost to those who will pay for it.

In the United States, investment goods accounted for 14 to 16 percent of the total market value of all goods and services produced over the past two decades. That was higher than the percentage for economically stagnant Great Britain, but significantly lower than the percentage for dynamic Japan. During the early 1980s, the United States invested slightly less of its output (13 percent) in investment goods. The reasons cited most frequently for the drop in investment were the uncertainties produced by inflation; the reduced willingness of Americans to save (there can be no investment without saving); higher taxes; greater government regulation of industry; high interest rates; and reduced industry profits. In the mid-1980s, the decline in investment as a percentage of national output was reversed. The rise in investment spending was still on the rise in 1988. With unemployment falling, producers needed an expanded capital base to meet the rising domestic and international demand for U.S. goods and services.

The Choice Between Private and Public Goods

▲ 4. How do current choices between private and public goods affect future production opportunities?

Private goods: goods that are bought or produced and used by people as individuals or as members of small voluntary groups.

Just as a society must decide between consumption and investment, it must choose between individual and collective consumption or investment. Politicians may be fond of so-called free lunch programs, and local officials may vie with each other for "federal handouts" with which to finance municipal projects. However, these publicly funded goods are "free" only in a very limited sense. When a particular city receives federal funds, local taxpayers' federal income tax bills may not change very much. Nevertheless federal programs always involve a cost. One task of the economist is to spot that cost and bring it to the attention of decision makers.

Figure 2.4 shows the production possibilities curve for private goods and public goods. **Private goods** are goods that are bought or produced and used by people as individuals or as members of small voluntary groups,

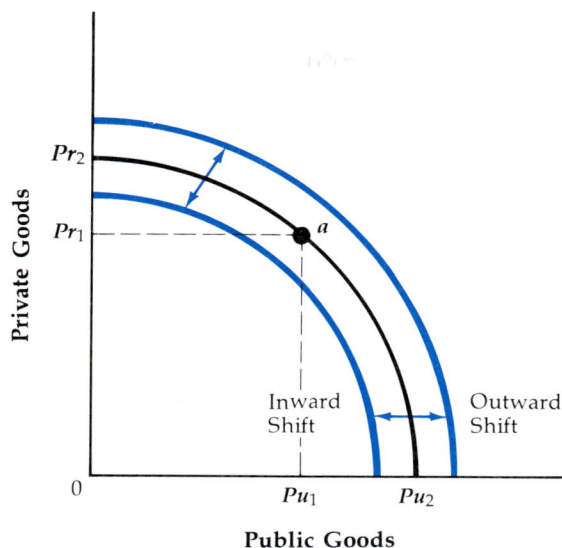

FIGURE 2.4 Public Versus Private Goods
A nation's future production possibilities curve depends on the choices it makes between public and private goods. Production of some public goods—for example, pollution control devices or police protection—can shift the production possibilities curve outward. Production of other public goods—welfare assistance that discourages people from working or acquiring education, for example—can shift the production possibilities curve inward.

Public goods: goods that are bought or produced and used by large groups of people or by governments.

like baseballs and food. **Public goods** are goods that are bought or produced and used by large groups of people or by governments, like police protection or national defense. Public goods can benefit many people at once. As with other production possibilities curves, a society can operate at any point along the curve. Operating at point a will produce a combination of Pr_1 private goods and Pu_1 public goods. In this case, the cost of the public goods is the difference between Pr_2 and Pr_1 on the vertical axis. That is, to obtain Pu_1 public goods, we must give up $Pr_2 - Pr_1$ private goods. As individuals, we forgo so many cars, stereos, or computers to get missiles and water treatment plants instead.

Our choices between public and private goods can also (but do not necessarily) affect our nation's future production possibilities curve. The purchase of public goods can shift the curve in either direction. The curve may shift to the right, for instance, if government-provided goods allow the private sector to operate more efficiently by reducing the costs businesses have to bear. Up to a point, police protection enables producers to devote more of their resources to production and investment and fewer to protecting their property from thieves and vandals. If government-provided goods increase the nation's stock of plant and equipment (for example, dams, hospitals, and sewer systems) or enhance people's ability to produce (through student loans, for example), the curve may shift to the right. Government-enforced environmental controls may also have a positive effect, if they make producers and consumers more aware of the environmental costs of products and thus less wasteful of resources.

Government-provided goods may shift the nation's production possibilities curve to the left, however, if they discourage people from working or reduce the resources available for production. If welfare allows people to remain out of work longer than they need to, for instance, it reduces the nation's production possibilities. Government-provided goods may also have a negative effect if, like taxes on the interest earned on savings accounts, they reduce people's incentive to save, increasing consumption at the expense of investment. Finally, government production of goods may be wasteful. If resources are idle or underutilized because of political maneuvering, fewer goods, public and private, will be produced than is possible.

The exact extent to which government affects the movement of the production possibilities curve has been the subject of considerable study by economists, but no consensus has been reached. This question can have no simple answer.

Shifting the Production Possibilities Curve

▲ 5. How do people, acting individually and collectively, change their production opportunities?

Given limited resources and unlimited wants, people have become quite creative in devising ways to get the most out of scarce resources and expand their production possibilities. Among the wide variety of techniques they have developed, several deserve to be mentioned.

Substitution of Resources

People have discovered new resources and substituted them where possible for scarce ones. Chemists developed fertilizers to increase the yield of farmland and free scarce land for other uses. Prospectors developed hydrocarbon fuels as a substitute for scarce human and animal energy. More recently scientists invented solar energy collectors to replace dwindling hydrocarbon fuels. The progressive substitution of nonhuman for human energy sources has increased society's production possibilities.

Cost Sharing

To share the cost of capital equipment ("spread the overhead") and the risk that must be assumed by investors, people have developed a variety of social structures, from families and cooperatives to corporations and insurance companies.

Specialization of Labor

Specialization of labor: the process of dividing and assigning different production tasks to individuals with differing skills and talents.

To increase the productivity of labor, people have learned to divide up the tasks of production, a process called specialization of labor. **Specialization of labor** is the process of dividing and assigning different production tasks to individuals with differing skills and talents. Specialization usually (but not always) increases production because when people concentrate on a limited number of tasks, they tend to become more proficient at them.

They spend more time in actual production and less in shifting from one task to another. Specialization also reduces the duplication of tools that is necessary when people attempt to be self-sufficient.

Economies of Scale

Economies of scale:
decreases in per unit cost due to an increase in the rate of production when the use of all resources is expanded.

Partly because it promotes specialization, production on a large, even massive, scale can reduce the cost per unit of production. **Economies of scale** are decreases in per unit cost due to an increase in the rate of production when the use of all resources is expanded. Economies of scale occur when an increase in resource inputs brings a proportionally greater increase in output during a given period of time. Large-scale production also allows the use of larger, faster, more efficient equipment. For example, if large computers can be fully used twenty-four hours a day, their speed—hundreds of thousands of calculations per second—makes up for their expense. When they are fully used, their cost per unit of calculation is less than the cost per unit of a desk-top calculator.

Diseconomies of scale:
increases in per unit cost due to an increase in the rate of production when the use of all resources is expanded.

There are limits, of course, to a firm's ability to reduce costs by expanding its scale of operation. Beyond some point, expansion brings an increase in the cost of producing each unit, called a diseconomy of scale. **Diseconomies of scale** are increases in per unit cost due to an increase in the rate of production when the use of all resources is expanded. Diseconomies of scale occur when an increase in resource inputs is not matched by a proportionate increase in output. Diseconomies of scale are generally attributed to the communication problems that plague large, bureaucratic organizations. When those at the top of the organizational hierarchy lose touch with those at the bottom, the firm functions less efficiently.

Trade

As the priest in the POW camp found (see pages 4–6), the inconveniences associated with scarcity can be reduced by trade. Commerce allows people to exchange goods and services they value less for those they value more. It also increases people's opportunity to specialize, expand the scale of their operations, and take advantage of resulting economies of scale. Perhaps most important, trade allows people to capitalize on any advantage they may have in production cost.

Money as a Resource

In a very simple economy, barter (the exchange of goods for goods) is an acceptable means of trade, but it requires a coincidence of wants. A person who has a good to sell—say, pigs—must find someone who not only wants that particular good but wants to give up something the pig owner desires—chickens, perhaps. The time the pig farmer spends searching for a compatible trader is time that cannot be spent farming and producing.

PERSPECTIVES
David Ricardo (1772–1823)

From the time of its initial publication in 1776, Adam Smith's *An Inquiry into the Nature and Causes of the Wealth of Nations* dominated economic thinking in the English-speaking world. One of Smith's most brilliant and enthusiastic admirers was a young businessman, David Ricardo. Ricardo was the third of seventeen children of a Sephardic Jewish stock broker. He began work for his father on the London stock exchange when he was fourteen. At age twenty-one he renounced his faith and broke with his father in order to marry a young Quaker. Ricardo then went into business for himself as an independent broker. He gradually accumulated a large fortune and a large family. By the time he was in his mid-forties he was able to retire from business and live the life of a country gentleman. In 1817 he entered Parliament, serving until his death in 1823.

Although he died one of the richest men in England and a member of Parliament, Ricardo is not remembered for his accomplishments in the practical worlds of business and politics. Rather he is remembered for his contributions to the world of economic thought. From the time of his first reading of Smith (in 1799) he began to think and then write on the economic problems of the day. He attempted to fill in what he regarded as the theoretical gaps in the work of Smith and in so doing created his own distinctive school of thought. His *Principles of Political Economy and Taxation* (1817) incorporated many important theoretical advances, including the theory of comparative advantage.

Smith had justified free international trade on the grounds of absolute advantage—that each good should be produced by the nation that can produce it at lowest cost. Ricardo demonstrated that free trade would produce universal benefits even when one nation had an absolute advantage in the production of all goods. All that was necessary was for trading to take place according to comparative advantage. With a simple numerical example involving two countries (England and Portugal) and two goods (wine and cloth), Ricardo proved that free trade would benefit both even if Portugal could produce both wine and cloth at a lower absolute cost than England. Portugal would export wine and import cloth because its cost of producing wine fell below that of England by proportionally more than did its cost of producing cloth. In other words, the relative price of wine was lower in Portugal, while the relative price of cloth was lower in England.

Ricardo made many other contributions to economic theory, including his theory of value, his theory of money and prices, and his theory of rent. His greatest influence on modern economics, however, may be his method. The work of Adam Smith blended history, theory, and simple examples in an eclectic mixture. In contrast to Smith, Ricardo proceeded from assumption to conclusion in a tightly woven, rigorous theoretical model. The abstract models that characterize modern economics began with the formal models developed by Ricardo.

Money: any generally accepted medium of exchange or trade that also serves as a store of purchasing power.

Money was developed to make trading more efficient and to reduce the time spent looking for traders. Instead of searching for someone who wants pork and has chickens to sell, a pig farmer can sell his pigs for cash and use the cash to buy chickens. With the time he saves, he can produce more food. Money can serve as a medium of exchange because it is an accepted store of purchasing power. That is, people who want to postpone consumption can leave their money in a safe place, knowing that when they do want to spend it, it will still be valuable. **Money** is any generally accepted medium of exchange or trade that also serves as a store of purchasing power.

Without money, people would have to save for future purchases by holding on to a variety of goods that could be used in trade. Their resources would be tied up in storage and would be unavailable for the production of other goods and services. Money, however, can be used productively while it is being stored for future use. A banker can lend it to someone who needs to buy a new machine, for instance. Thus money frees resources to be used in productive activity. It expands society's production possibilities frontier.

Taking Advantage of Comparative Advantage

▲ **6. Why do people benefit from trade?**

One of the benefits of trade is that it allows people to capitalize on any advantages they may have in cost of production. Consider a world in which there are only two people, Fred and Harry. Let's imagine that they live on an island and that they can produce only two goods, coconuts and papayas. The table below shows how much each man can produce. In one hour Fred can produce four coconuts or eight papayas; Harry can produce six coconuts or twenty-four papayas. Harry is more productive than Fred in either case, yet both can gain by specializing and trading with each other.

	Number of Coconuts Produced per Hour	Number of Papayas Produced per Hour
Fred	4	8
Harry	6	24

To see why, we must look at the relative cost of producing coconuts and papayas. If Fred produces four coconuts, he loses the opportunity to produce eight papayas. In other words, the cost of the four coconuts is eight papayas—or to put it another way, the cost of one coconut is two papayas. Fred would be better off if he could trade one coconut for more than two papayas because two papayas is what he has to give up to produce the coconut.

From Harry's point of view, the cost of one coconut is four papayas. (To produce six coconuts, Harry has to give up twenty-four papayas.) If Harry could get a coconut for less than four papayas, he would be better off. He could produce four papayas, trade some for a coconut, and have some left over to eat.

The cost of producing coconuts may be summarized as follows:

Fred: 1 coconut = 2 papayas

Harry: 1 coconut = 4 papayas

Comparative advantage: a relatively lower cost of production, or the capacity to produce a product at a lower cost than a competitor, in terms of the goods that must be given up.

Fred can produce one coconut at less cost (in terms of the papayas that must be given up) than Harry can. Similarly, one papaya is less costly to produce (in terms of the coconuts that must be given up) for Harry than for Fred. In terms of the relative cost of production, Fred has a comparative advantage in the production of coconuts, and Harry has a comparative advantage in papaya production. A **comparative advantage** is a relatively lower cost of production, or the capacity to produce a product at a lower cost than a competitor, in terms of the goods that must be given up.

If Fred and Harry specialize in the fruits for which they have a comparative advantage and then trade with each other, each will benefit. Remember that Fred would be better off it he could trade one coconut for more than two papayas. Thus if he and Harry agree to an exchange at the rate of one coconut for three papayas, he will obviously benefit. He will produce one coconut, giving up two papayas in the process, but will get three papayas in return from Harry. Harry will also benefit. He can produce four papayas, giving up one coconut in the process, and trade three of those papayas to Fred for one coconut. Harry will end up with the same number of coconuts he would have had if he had produced coconuts instead of papayas, but he will have one papaya as well.

If both Fred and Harry are better off, their total production must have increased. Through specialization and trade Fred and Harry have cut their cost of production and moved closer to their joint production possibilities frontier. They have used scarce resources more efficiently than they would have otherwise.

The Circular Flow of Income

▲ **7. How are major sectors of the economy tied together?**

Circular flow of income: the integrated flow of resources, goods, and services between or among broad sectors of the economy, like producers, consumers, and government.

Trade not only enhances people's welfare but increases their dependence on one another. This interdependence can be illustrated by what is called a circular flow diagram (see Figure 2.5). The **circular flow of income** is the integrated flow of resources, goods, and services between or among broad sectors of the economy, like producers, consumers, and government. In simplified form, this diagram shows the flow of resources, goods, and services between two sectors of the private economy—producers (bottom) and consumers (top). The consumers have two basic functions: to provide the resources (land, labor, and capital) needed by the producers and to consume the goods and services produced. The producers also have two basic functions: to assemble the necessary resources provided by consumers and to produce the goods and services consumers want. The integrated nature of the economy is symbolized by the arrows that represent the flows of resources, final products, and money payments to and from consumers and producers.

For a barter economy, the diagram would be even simpler. There would be only two arrows—one representing the flow of resources from the consumer to the producer, the other representing the flow of goods and services from the producer back to the consumer. In this primitive economy, the goods on the right side of the diagram would trade for the resources on the left side. The price of labor, for example, would be stated in so many gadgets produced, and the price of gadgets would be stated in so many hours of labor. Such a system would be extremely inefficient, for people would waste a great deal of time searching for beneficial trades.

Though money eases the difficulties of trading, it tends to obscure the interdependence of producers and consumers. When money is used for trade, producers secure their income from particular consumers, not caring whether those consumers work for them or provide them with resources. Laborers secure a money payment for their services from producers, which

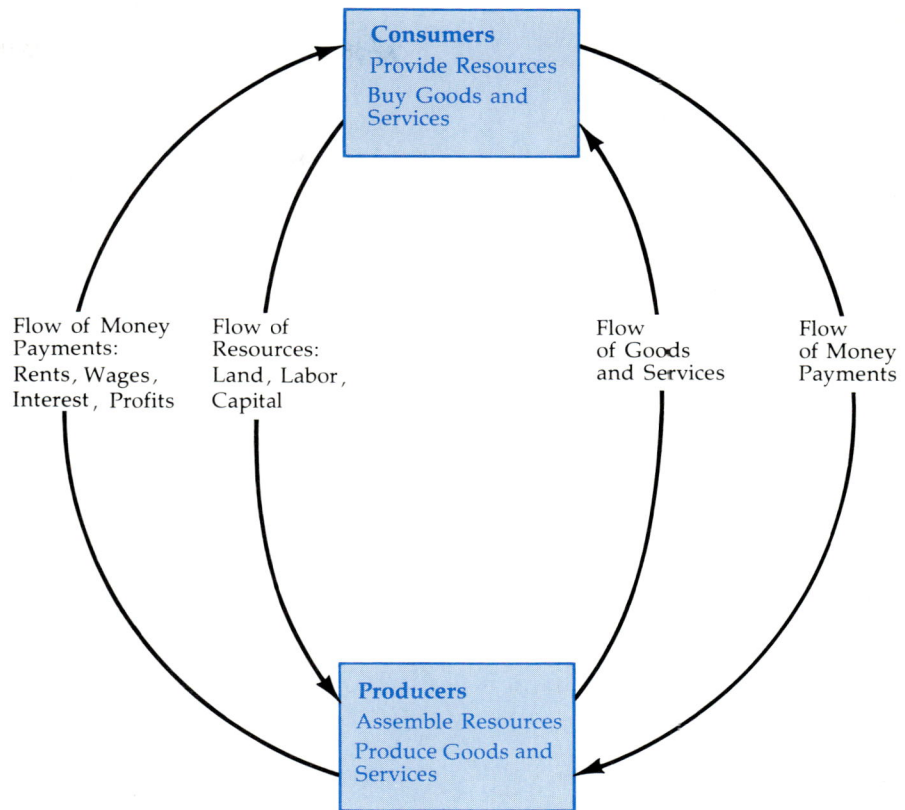

FIGURE 2.5 The Circular Flow of Income

Consumers and producers generate opposing flows of resources and money payments for those resources, in the form of wages, rents, interest, and profits (left side). In the same way, they generate opposing flows of goods and services and money payments for those goods and services (right side).

they use to buy goods from a variety of producers, not necessarily those they work for. Prices are stated in terms of dollars (or pounds sterling, or lira), and people may get the mistaken impression that their incomes are unrelated to production, except in a remote and tenuous way. After all, they don't get paid with the goods they produce.

Yet the two sectors are closely interrelated. The health of the business sector (producers) clearly depends on the expenditures made by the consuming sector. Without that flow of money payments from consumers, producers would be unable to pay for the resources they buy from consumers. Likewise, conditions in the consuming sector depend on the success of firms in the business sector. If the business sector cannot sell its goods and services, producers will not be able to pay workers' salaries. Thus an integrated, money-based trade can multiply the effects of disruptions in trade. If the circular flow of money is interrupted, production may slow, consumption may fall off, and laborers may be thrown out of work. Such interruptions in the circular flow, called recessions, are a subject of considerable concern to macroeconomists.

Figure 2.5 does not reflect the full complexity of the exchange relationships that exist among people. In the real world, the business sector has internal flows of its own. Producers funnel resources to other producers in the form of raw materials and investment goods like machinery. They make payments to each other in the form of money. A more realistic, although still incomplete, description of the circular flow is contained in Figure 2.6.

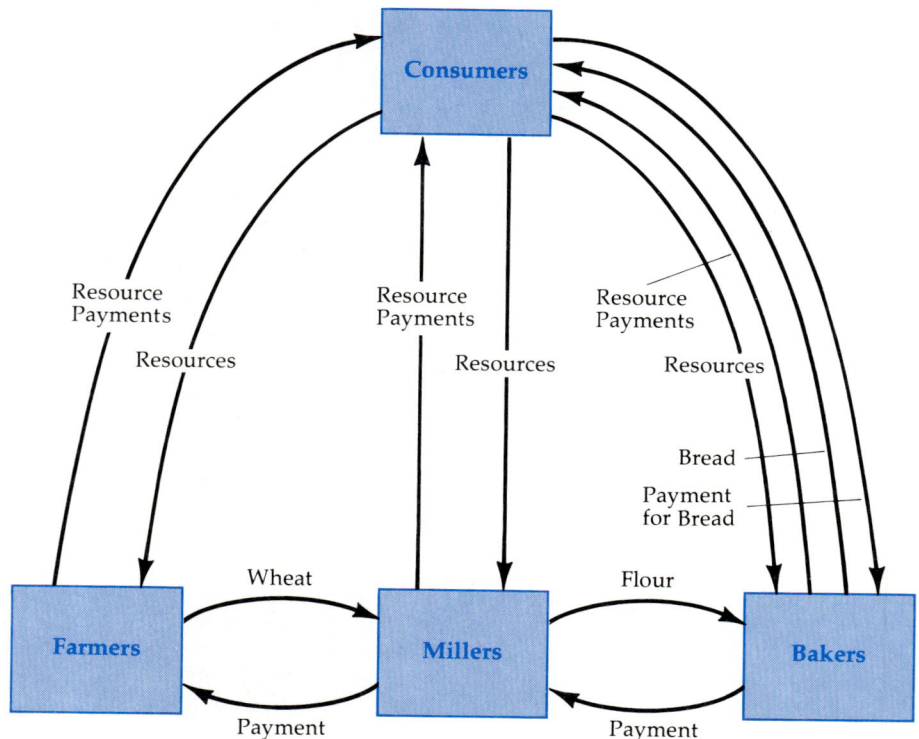

FIGURE 2.6   The Circular Flow of Income: A More Complicated Model
Resources (goods and services) and money payments for them flow not just between consumers and producers but among producers as well. All producers buy resources from households with money payments. Farmers, for instance, receive resources from consumer households, for which they make money payments. They also sell their wheat to millers, who make flour and sell it to bakers—who then make bread and sell it to consumers.

Producers have been divided into three representative groups: farmers, millers, and bakers. All three buy certain resources, like labor, from consumers. In addition, the millers buy their basic resource, wheat, from the farmers, and the bakers buy their basic resource, flour, from the millers.

Actual trading arrangements are extraordinarily complex. Farmers, for example, must buy machinery to produce wheat. Farm equipment producers must buy metal, plastics, and hundreds of other resources to manufacture the machinery they sell to the farmers. Metal producers must buy equipment to process and finish their product. Both metal producers and equipment manufacturers must have food to eat. Furthermore, all these trades must be handled by a communications and transportation network that can deliver all the resources and products needed to the appropriate destinations at the appropriate time. Traders also must be able to adjust their relationships to changes in consumer demand.

Government further complicates the circular flow by drawing off money in the form of taxes and then injecting it back into the circular flow in the form of government purchases, for everything from planes to welfare checks. There is also private saving, which channels purchasing power through banks to consumers of cars, houses, and furniture and through stock and bond markets to investors in inventory, plant, and equipment. It is a wonder that the system works at all. The economy is an extraordinarily complex web of fragile but productive interrelationships, all formed for one overriding purpose: to make the most of society's production possibilities, given the inescapable fact of scarcity.

Chapter Review

Review of Key Questions

1. *How are the concepts of scarcity and cost related?*

   Scarcity means that we cannot accomplish all that we want. We must make choices, which means that when we do anything, we must forgo doing something else. Cost is the value of the alternative not taken.

2. *What are production possibilities curves and what does their downward slope imply?*

   Production possibilities curves are a graphical means of illustrating the various combinations of goods and services that can be produced by a person, community, or country. Their downward slope illustrates a basic principle of production: greater production of one good can be obtained only at increasing additional cost.

3. *What does investment do to future production opportunities?*

   A decision to consume goods and services implies a decision to forgo investment goods. Because investment goods are used to produce other goods and services, the level of investment we choose will affect the position of our production possibilities curve in the future. In this way, current and future choices are inextricably related.

▲   *4. How do current choices between private and public goods affect future production opportunities?*

A decision to produce public goods is a decision to forgo private goods. The production of public goods can shift the future production possibilities curve to the left or right, depending on how these public goods affect people's tendency to produce, work, save, and invest.

▲   *5. How do people, acting individually and collectively, change their production opportunities?*

People have devised a number of ways to improve the productivity of resources in the face of scarcity. They have developed substitute resources, organized to share costs, specialized their labor, and expanded production in order to realize economies of scale. They have developed trading relationships based on comparative advantages in cost of production and used money to put otherwise idle resources to work. Trade increases production by encouraging the most efficient use of resources.

▲   *6. Why do people benefit from trade?*

People trade in order to gain in some way. As long as they specialize in the production of these goods and services in which they have a comparative cost advantage, trade can be mutually beneficial. By specializing and reducing the cost of production, trading partners raise total production.

▲   *7. How are major sectors of the economy tied together?*

Circular flow diagrams show the economic interdependence of consumers and producers. Producers depend on consumer expenditures, and consumers depend on payments from producers for their land, labor, and capital. Disruptions in the flow of income between these two sectors can lead to reductions in national production, income, and employment.

Further Topics

Like scarcity, choice is pervasive. We must choose between a variety of goods and services, between public and private goods, between consumption and investment, and between old and new technology. The choices we make have huge consequences for both the present and the future. Our ability to grow and become more productive tomorrow depends on our willingness to save today. Greater future output does not necessarily imply greater welfare over time, however. Tomorrow's growth may not be worth today's sacrifice, in terms of consumption forgone.

Production possibilities curves can be useful in illustrating these and other choices we must make. They also can be easily misunderstood. The production possibilities curve may suggest that society's choices are more or less apparent: we simply have to plot the curve, observe the options, and choose. For several reasons, our economic difficulties cannot be solved as easily as that.

First, we lack a great deal of information about what our society can produce at the limit. If we produced only two goods, finding the production possibilities frontier might be relatively simple, but we produce millions of products, requiring many kinds of resources. The tradeoffs among those resources and the goods made from them are extraordinarily complex. Furthermore, we do not know very much about the quantity of existing resources. For instance, we do not know how much labor really exists in total because we do not know how hard and long people are actually willing to work. The people who interact with one another in the labor market are the ones who know the answer to that question. Social scientists and policymakers may know something about the operation of the economy, but there is a great deal they do not and cannot know.

In short, although production possibilities curves help us to envision the types of choices we must make, the actual options open to us do not result from the curves but from the economic process. They are the product of the millions of interrelated choices made daily by individuals, groups, and government. Our resources and our choices as to how those resources will be employed determine our production possibilities and our position on the production possibilities curve. In the next chapter we will see how people make choices through the market process and how, through the pricing system, they determine their society's production possibilities.

Review of New Terms

Circular flow of income The integrated flow of resources, goods, and services between or among broad sectors of the economy, like producers, consumers, and government.

Comparative advantage A relatively lower cost of production, or the capacity to produce a product at a lower cost than a competitor, in terms of the goods that must be given up.

Consumption goods Goods that are produced to be used and enjoyed more or less immediately by their purchasers.

Cost (opportunity cost) The value of the most highly preferred alternative not taken.

Diseconomies of scale Increases in per unit cost due to an increase in the rate of production when the use of all resources is expanded.

Economies of scale Decreases in per unit cost due to an increase in the rate of production when the use of all resources is expanded.

Money Any generally accepted medium of exchange or trade that also serves as a store of purchasing power.

Private goods Goods that are bought or produced and used by people as individuals or as members of small voluntary groups.

Production possibilities curve (production possibilities frontier) A graphical representation of the various combinations of goods that can be produced when all resources are fully and efficiently employed.

Public goods Goods that are bought or produced and used by large groups of people or by governments.

Specialization of labor The process of dividing and assigning different production tasks to individuals with differing skills and talents.

Review Questions

1. What is cost? (▲ 1)

2. What determines the shape and position of a nation's production possibilities curve? (▲ 2)

3. Suppose a nation is producing at some point inside the production possibilities curve. If the government implements a policy that moves the nation onto the production frontier, is there a cost to the additional goods produced? (▲ 1, ▲ 2)

4. Suppose a nation's yearly purchase of investment goods is less than its yearly loss of investment goods through wear and tear. What will happen to the nation's production possibilities curve? (▲ 3)

5. Evaluate the following statement: "Greater investment today will enable this nation to produce more in the future. It will reduce the cost of future investment and enable us to grow even faster in the future. Our government should therefore devise a policy that will stimulate business investment." (▲ 3, ▲ 4)

6. Does a nation's production possibilities curve depend on its distribution of wealth and income? On the existence and distribution of property rights? On the level of taxation and type of tax levied? levied? (▲ 2, ▲ 5)

7. Suppose that Joan's and Terry's hourly production rates for squashes and turnips are as follows:

Case I	Squashes	Turnips
Joan	10	50
Terry	40	800

Case II	Squashes	Turnips
Joan	20	30
Terry	100	50

For each case, determine who should specialize in producing squashes and then suggest an exchange rate for squashes and turnips that will benefit both Joan and Terry. (▲ 6)

8. On what does the income of households depend? (▲ 7)

Graphic Analysis

Economists often use graphs to illustrate the relationships between and among economic variables. Graphs are pictorial representations of the presumed relationships between or among variables. Graphs can display a great deal of information in a small area; they show at a glance how two or more variables are related.

The Features of Graphs

The major features of a graph are shown in Figure 2.A1. In the lower left corner is the *origin*, the point at which the value of both variables represented in the graph is zero. Extending out from the origin are the horizontal, or X, axis (also called the abscissa) and the vertical, or Y, axis (also called the ordinate). The relationship among variables is shown graphically by a series of points in the interior of the graph (between the vertical and horizontal axes). The points combine various values scaled along the two axes.

For example, suppose we scale the number of bushels of apples consumers will buy at different prices along the horizontal axis, and the various prices per bushel along the vertical axis. If consumers buy 50 bushels of apples a day when the price of apples is $5 a bushel, that price-quantity combination can be represented by point *a* on the graph. Other price-quantity combinations like *b* and *c* can be plotted and connected to form a line, or curve, like the one in color in the figure.

The Slope of Curves

The curves plotted on a graph can have almost any shape. One important characteristic of their shape is the slope. The *slope* is the ratio of the vertical movement up a curve (sometimes called the "rise") to the corresponding horizontal movement along the curve (also called the "run"). Mathematically, the slope can be expressed as follows:

$$\text{slope} = \frac{\text{rise}}{\text{run}} = \frac{\Delta y}{\Delta x}$$

where Δ = change in

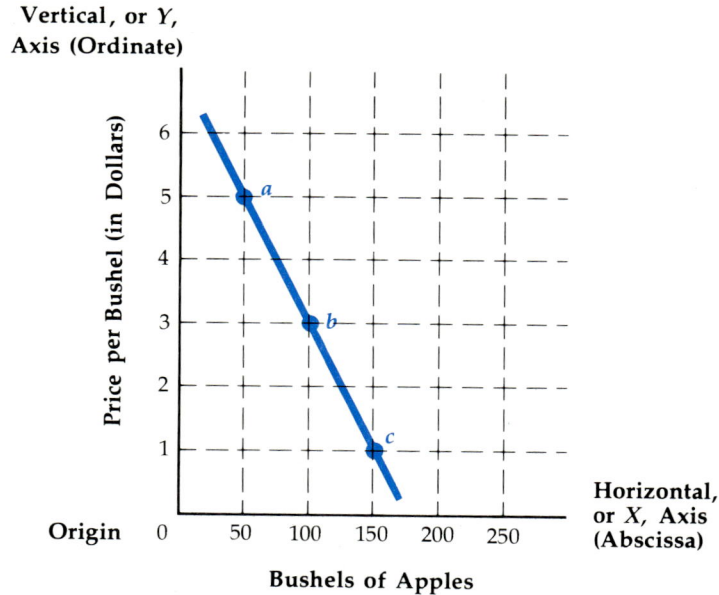

FIGURE 2.A1   Features of a Graph
The vertical axis of a graph is sometimes called the *Y* axis, or the ordinate. The horizontal axis is called the *X* axis, or the abscissa. The point of intersection of the two axes is called the origin. A series of points inside the graph portray assumed or deduced relationships between the variables on the *X* and *Y* axes, like the price and quantity of apples sold. The line that connects those points is called a curve. The curve shown here has a negative slope (moves downward from left to right).

That is, the slope is equal to the ratio of the change in the value on the vertical axis to the change in the value on the horizontal axis.

The slope can be either positive or negative, depending on which way the curve slants. It is said to be positive when the curve moves up toward the right and negative when it moves down toward the right. Figure 2.A1 shows a curve with a negative slope. As the price per bushel goes down (vertical axis), the number of bushels sold goes up (horizontal axis). This kind of relationship, called an inverse relationship, produces a negative slope. If the price of a bushel of apples falls from \$5 to \$3 while the quantity consumers purchase rises from 50 to 100 bushels, the slope of the curve will be $\frac{-2}{50}$, or -0.04:

$$\text{slope} = \frac{\Delta y}{\Delta x} = \frac{P_1 - P_2}{Q_1 - Q_2} = \frac{(\$3 - \$5)}{(100 - 50)} = \frac{-2}{50} = -0.04$$

When the change in both x and y is positive, the ratio, or slope, is positive, and the relationship between x and y is said to be direct. The curve slants up toward the right, as in Figure 2.A2(a).

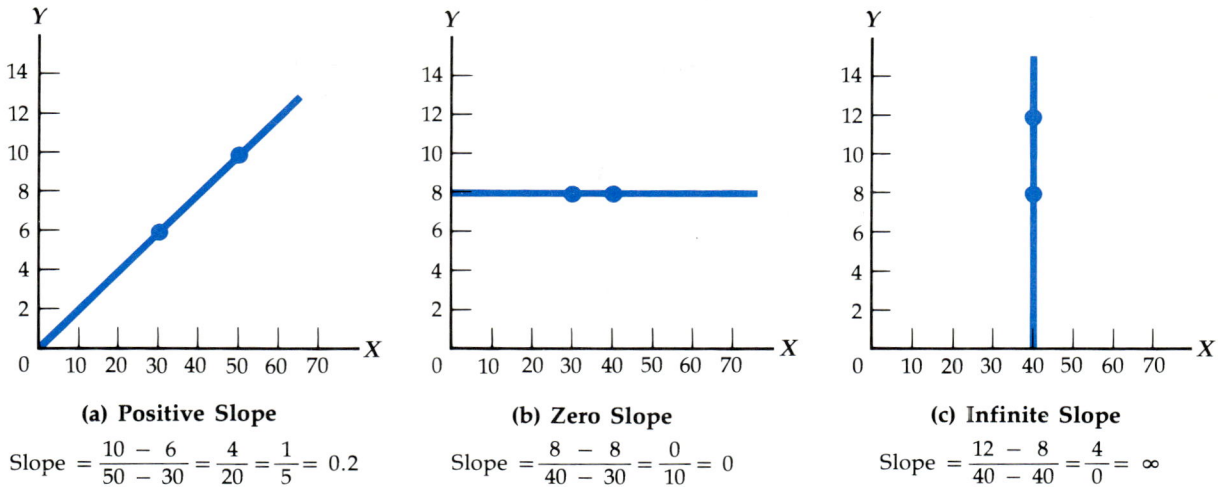

(a) Positive Slope

$$\text{Slope} = \frac{10 - 6}{50 - 30} = \frac{4}{20} = \frac{1}{5} = 0.2$$

(b) Zero Slope

$$\text{Slope} = \frac{8 - 8}{40 - 30} = \frac{0}{10} = 0$$

(c) Infinite Slope

$$\text{Slope} = \frac{12 - 8}{40 - 40} = \frac{4}{0} = \infty$$

FIGURE 2.A2 Curves with Various Slopes

Curves that move upward from the left to the right—panel (a)—are said to have a positive slope. Curves that are horizontal to the X axis—panel (b)—have a zero slope; curves that are vertical to the X axis—panel (c)—have an infinite slope.

A curve that runs parallel to the horizontal axis has a slope of zero—it has no vertical rise or fall (see Figure 2.A2(b)). When its zero numerator (the rise) is divided by a positive denominator, the result is zero. A curve that runs perpendicular to the horizontal axis has a slope of infinity—even with no horizontal movement, it continues upward indefinitely (see Figure 2.A2(c)). When its positive numerator is divided by a zero denominator, the result is infinity.

Curves with Changing Slopes

Straight curves (sometimes called linear curves) like the ones in Figures 2.A1 and 2.A2 have the same slope at all points. The rise is always the same for any given run, no matter where on the curve it is measured. Thus the ratio of the rise to the run is said to be constant. Not all curves are straight lines, however. The slope of the curve in Figure 2.A3, for example, is steeper near the origin than at the other end. Because the slope of a curve like this is constantly changing, it must be measured at specific points on the curve.

To obtain the slope at any given point on such a curve, draw a straight line tangent to the curve, as in Figure 2.A3. Measure the rise and the run between any two points on that tangent straight line, and divide the rise by

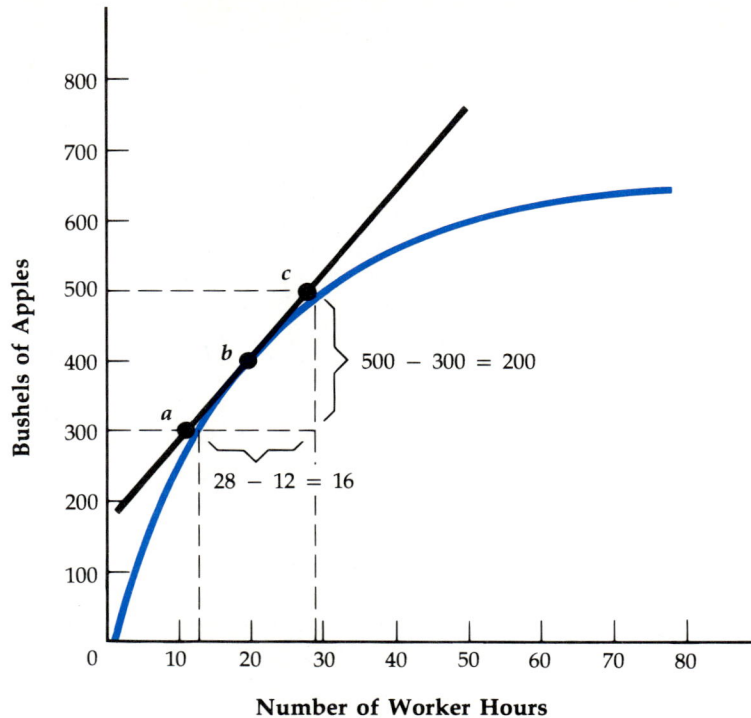

FIGURE 2.A3 Curves with a Changing Slope
Because this curve bends downward as it moves from the left up to the right, it is said to have a decreasing positive slope

$$\left(\text{slope at } b = \frac{200}{16} = \frac{25}{2} = 12.5\right).$$

the run. In Figure 2.A3, the rise of the line tangent to point b, measured between points a and c, is 200; the run is 16 (28 − 12). Hence the slope is

$$\frac{200}{16} \text{ or } \frac{25}{2}$$

The changing slope of a curve has practical implications. In Figure 2.A3, the rising curve shows the contribution made by additional worker hours to the total output of apples. As the curve rises past point b, its slope becomes progressively flatter. In other words, beyond a certain point, as the number of hours worked grows, each new hour adds less to total output.

The Uses and Misuses of Graphs

A comparison of Figure 2.A4 and Table 2.A1 demonstrates the efficiency of graphs in displaying economic variables. The table and the graph both show a measure of the nation's overall price level—the consumer price

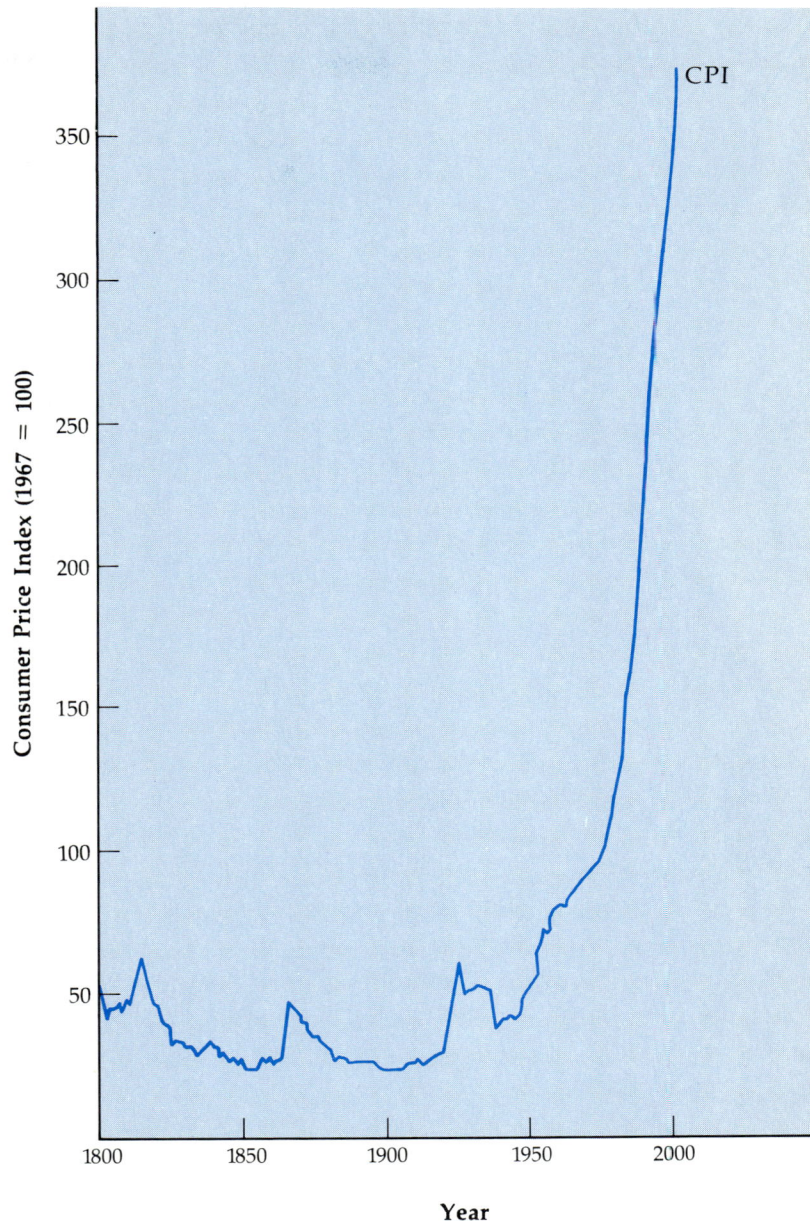

FIGURE 2.A4 U.S. Price Level, 1880–1987

The general movement of prices over a long period of time can be shown graphically by plotting the consumer price index (vertical axis) for each year (horizontal axis). At a glance one can see that the price level moved up and down at relatively low levels between 1800 and 1940. Over recent decades, however, it has risen sharply.

Sources: U.S. Bureau of the Census, *Historical Statistics of the United States* (Washington, D.C.: U.S. Government Printing Office, 1975), pp. 210–211; *Economic Report of the President* (Washington, D.C.: U.S. Government Printing Office, 1988), p. 313.

TABLE 2.A1	U.S. Price Level, 1800–1987				
Year	CPI[a]	Year	CPI	Year	CPI
1800	51	1865	46	1930	50
1805	45	1870	38	1935	41
1810	47	1875	33	1940	42
1815	55	1880	29	1945	54
1820	42	1885	27	1950	72
1825	34	1890	27	1955	80
1830	32	1895	25	1960	89
1835	31	1900	25	1965	95
1840	30	1905	27	1970	116
1845	28	1910	28	1975	161
1850	25	1915	30	1980	247
1855	28	1920	60	1985	322
1860	27	1925	53	Jan. 1988	347

a. CPI stands for consumer price index; 1967 = 100.

Sources: U.S. Bureau of the Census, *Historical Statistics of the United States: Colonial Times to 1970* (Washington, D.C.: U.S. Government Printing Office, 1975), pp. 210–211; *Economic Report of the President* (Washington, D.C.: U.S. Government Printing Office, 1988), p. 313.

index—over time. By scrutinizing the figures in the table, you can determine that the price level rose and fell several times during the nineteenth century, before skyrocketing in the second half of this century. Figure 2.A4 shows the same trend at a glance, however. The dramatic upward surge in prices from 1940 on shows that significant inflation is a modern phenomenon.

Graphs, like statistics, can be misused. The mere plotting of two variables on a graph does not establish a cause-and-effect relationship between them. For instance, the number of major-league home runs hit each season can be plotted against the annual snowfalls in Rochester, New York—but the resulting curve will make no sense, regardless of its shape and slope. A graph proves nothing about the way in which two variables are influenced by one another. Relationships are established by theory.

The Elements of Supply and Demand

Competition, if not prevented, tends to bring about a state of affairs in which: first, everything will be produced which somebody knows how to produce and which he can sell profitably at a price at which buyers will prefer it to the available alternatives; second, everything that is produced is produced by persons who can do so at least as cheaply as anybody else who in fact is not producing it; and third, that everything will be sold at prices lower than, or at least as low as, those at which it could be sold by anybody who in fact does not do so.
    Friedrich Hayek

KEY QUESTIONS

▲ 1. What is the competitive market process?

▲ 2. What are the supply and demand curves and how can they be used to understand the market process?

▲ 3. When does the market operate "efficiently"?

▲ 4. What are the many ways firms compete?

▲ 5. How do competitive markets adjust to changes in conditions in the "short run" and "long run"?

▲ 6. What are the shortcomings of competitive markets?

NEW TERMS

Competition
Decrease in demand
Decrease in supply
Demand
Efficiency
Equilibrium price
Equilibrium quantity
Increase in demand
Increase in supply

Long-run equilibrium
Market shortage
Market surplus
Perfect competition
Price ceiling
Price floor
Short-run equilibrium
Supply

In the heart of New York City, Fred Lieberman's small grocery is dwarfed by the tall buildings that surround it. Yet it is remarkable for what it accomplishes. Lieberman's carries thousands of items, most of which are not produced locally, and some of which come thousands of miles from other parts of this country or abroad. A man of modest means, with little knowledge of production processes, Fred Lieberman has nevertheless been able to stock his store with many if not most of the foods and toiletries his customers need and want. Occasionally Lieberman's runs out of certain items, but most of the time the stock is ample. Its supply is so dependable that customers tend to take it for granted, forgetting that Lieberman's is one small strand in an extremely complex economic network.

How does Fred Lieberman get the goods he sells, and how does he know which ones to sell and at what price? The simplest answer is that the goods he offers and the prices at which they sell are determined through the market process—the interaction of many buyers and sellers trading what they have (their labor or other resources) for what they want. Lieberman stocks his store by appealing to the private interests of suppliers—by paying them competitive prices. His customers pay him extra for the convenience of purchasing goods in their neighborhood grocery—in the process appealing to his private interests. To determine what he should buy, Fred Lieberman considers his suppliers' prices. To determine what and how much they should buy, his customers consider the prices he charges. The Nobel Prize–winning economist Friedrich Hayek has suggested that the market process is manageable for people like Fred Lieberman precisely because prices condense into usable form a great deal of information, signaling quickly what people want, what goods cost, and what resources are readily available. Prices guide and coordinate the sellers' production decisions and consumers' purchases.

How are prices determined? In competitive markets, as this chapter describes, prices are established by the forces of supply and demand.

The Competitive Market Process

◢ **1. What is the competitive market process?**

So far, our discussion of markets and their consequences has been rather casual. In this section we will define precisely such terms as *market* and *competition*. In later sections we will examine the way markets work and learn why, in a limited sense, markets can be considered efficient systems for determining what and how much to produce.

The Market Setting

Most people tend to think of a market as a geographical location—a shopping center, an auction barn, a business district. From an economic perspective, however, it is more useful to think of a market as a process. You may recall from Chapter 1 that a market is defined as the process by which buyers and sellers determine what they are willing to buy and sell and on what terms. That is, it is the process by which buyers and sellers decide the prices and quantities of goods to be bought and sold.

In this process, individual market participants search for information relevant to their own interests. Buyers ask about the models, sizes, colors, and quantities available and the prices they must pay for them. Sellers inquire about the types of goods and services buyers want and the prices they are willing to pay.

This market process is self-correcting. Buyers and sellers routinely revise their plans on the basis of experience. As Israel Kirzner has written,

> The overambitious plans of one period will be replaced by more realistic ones; market opportunities overlooked in one period will be exploited in the next. In other words, even without changes in the basic data of the market (i.e., in consumer tastes, technological possibilities, and resource availabilities), the decisions made in one period of time generate systematic alterations in corresponding decisions for the succeeding period.[1]

The market is made up of people, consumers and entrepreneurs, attempting to buy and sell on the best terms possible. Through the groping process of give and take, they move from relative ignorance about others' wants and needs to a reasonably accurate understanding of how much can be bought and sold and at what price. The market functions as an ongoing information and exchange system.

Competition Among Buyers and Among Sellers

Competition: the process by which market participants, in pursuing their own interests, attempt to outdo, outprice, outproduce, and outmaneuver each other.

Part and parcel of the market process is the concept of competition. **Competition** is the process by which market participants, in pursuing their own interests, attempt to outdo, outprice, outproduce, and outmaneuver each

---

1. Israel Kirzner, *Competition and Entrepreneurship* (Chicago: University of Chicago Press, 1973), p. 10.

other. By extension, competition is also the process by which market participants attempt to avoid being outdone, outpriced, outproduced, or outmaneuvered by others.

Competition does not occur between buyer and seller, but among buyers or among sellers. Buyers compete with other buyers for the limited number of goods on the market. To compete, they must discover what other buyers are bidding and offer the seller better terms—a higher price or the same price for a lower-quality product. Sellers compete with other sellers for the consumer's dollar. They must learn what their rivals are doing and attempt to do it better or differently—to lower the price or enhance the product's appeal.

This kind of competition stimulates the exchange of information, forcing competitors to reveal their plans to prospective buyers or sellers. The exchange of information can be seen clearly at auctions. Before the bidding begins, buyers look over the merchandise and the other buyers, attempting to determine how high others might be willing to bid for a particular piece. During the auction, this specific information is revealed as buyers call out their bids and others try to top them. Information exchange is less apparent in department stores, where competition is often restricted. Even there, however, comparison shopping will often reveal some sellers who are offering lower prices in an attempt to attract consumers.

In competing with each other, sellers reveal information that is ultimately of use to buyers. Buyers likewise inform sellers. From the consumer's point of view,

> The function of competition is here precisely to teach us *who* will serve us well: which grocer or travel agent, which department store or hotel, which doctor or solicitor, we can expect to provide the most satisfactory solution for whatever particular personal problem we may have to face.[2]

From the seller's point of view—say, the auctioneer's—competition among buyers brings the highest prices possible.

Competition among sellers takes many forms, including the price, quality, weight, volume, color, texture, power, durability, and smell of products, as well as the credit terms offered to buyers. Sellers also compete for consumers' attention by appealing to their hunger and sex drives or their fear of death, pain, and loud noises. All these forms of competition can be divided into two basic categories—price and nonprice competition. Price competition is of particular interest to economists, who see it as an important source of information for market participants and a coordinating force that brings the quantity produced into line with the quantity consumers are willing and able to buy. In the following sections, we will construct a model of the competitive market and use it to explore the process of price competition. Nonprice competition will be covered in a later section.

---

2. Friedrich H. Hayek, "The Meaning of Competition," *Individualism and Economic Order* (Chicago: University of Chicago Press, 1948), p. 97.

Supply and Demand: A Market Model

▲ 2. What are the supply and demand curves and how can they be used to understand the market process?

A fully competitive market is made up of many buyers and sellers searching for opportunities or ready to enter the market when opportunities arise. To be described as competitive, therefore, a market must include a significant number of actual or potential competitors. A fully competitive market offers freedom of entry: there are no legal or economic barriers to producing and selling goods in the market.

Our market model assumes perfect competition—an ideal situation that is seldom, if ever, achieved in real life but that will simplify our calculations. **Perfect competition** is a market composed of numerous independent sellers and buyers of an identical product, such that no one individual seller or buyer has the ability to affect the market price by changing the production level. Entry into and exit from a perfectly competitive market is unrestricted. Producers can start up or shut down production at will. Anyone can enter the market, duplicate the good, and compete for consumers' dollars. Since each competitor produces only a small share of the total output, the individual competitor cannot significantly influence the degree of competition or the market price by entering or leaving the market.

Perfect competition: a market composed of numerous independent sellers and buyers of an identical product, such that no one individual or buyer has the ability to affect the market price by changing the production level. Entry into and exit from a perfectly competitive market is unrestricted.

This kind of market is well suited to graphic analysis. Our discussion will concentrate on how buyers and sellers interact to determine the price of tomatoes, a product Mr. Lieberman almost always carries. It will employ two curves. The first represents buyers' behavior, which is called their demand for the product.

The Elements of Demand

Demand: the assumed inverse relationship between the price of a good or service and the quantity consumers are willing and able to buy during a given period, all other things held constant.

To the general public, demand is simply what people want, but to economists, demand has a much more technical meaning. **Demand** is the assumed inverse relationship between the price of a good or service and the quantity consumers are willing and able to buy during a given period, all other things held constant.

Demand as a Relationship

The relationship between price and quantity is normally assumed to be inverse. That is, when the price of a good rises, the quantity sold *ceteris paribus* (Latin for "everything else held constant"), will go down. Conversely, when the price of a good falls, the quantity sold goes up. Demand is not a quantity but a relationship. A given quantity sold at a particular price is properly called *quantity demanded*.

Both tables and graphs can be used to describe the assumed inverse relationship between price and quantity.

Demand as a Table or a Graph

Demand may be thought of as a schedule of the various quantities of a particular good consumers will buy at various prices. As the price goes down, the quantity purchased goes up and vice versa. Table 3.1 contains a

Price-Quantity Combinations	Price per Bushel	Number of Bushels
A	$0	110,000
B	1	100,000
C	2	90,000
D	3	80,000
E	4	70,000
F	5	60,000
G	6	50,000
H	7	40,000
I	8	30,000
J	9	20,000
K	10	10,000
L	11	0

hypothetical schedule of the demand for tomatoes in the New York area during a typical week. The middle column shows prices that might be charged. The column on the right shows the number of bushels consumers will buy at those prices. Note that as the price rises from zero to $11 a bushel, the number of bushels purchased drops from 110,000 to zero.

Demand may also be thought of as a curve. If price is scaled on a graph's vertical axis and quantity on the horizontal axis, the demand curve has a negative slope (downward and to the right), reflecting the assumed inverse relationship between price and quantity. The shape of the market demand curve is shown in Figure 3.1, which is based on the data from Table 3.1. Points a through l on the graph correspond to the price-quantity combinations A through L in the table. Note that as the price falls from P_2 ($8) to P_1 ($5), consumers move down their demand curve from a quantity of Q_1 (30) to the larger quantity Q_2 (60).[3]

The Slope and Determinants of Demand

Price and quantity are assumed to be inversely related for two reasons.

First, as the price of a good decreases (and the prices of all other goods stay the same—remember *ceteris paribus*), the purchasing power of consumer incomes rises. More consumers are able to buy the good, and many will buy more of most goods. (This response is called the income effect.)

In addition, as the price of a good decreases (and the prices of all other goods remain the same), the good becomes relatively cheaper, and consumers will substitute that good for others. (This response is called the substitution effect.)

---

3. Mathematically, the demand relationship may be stated as $Q_d = a - bP$, where Q_d is the quantity demanded at every price; a is the quantity consumers will buy when the price is zero; b is the slope of the demand curve; and P is the price of the good. Thus the demand function for tomatoes described in Table 3.1 and Figure 3.1 may be written as $Q_d = 110,000 - 10,000 P$.

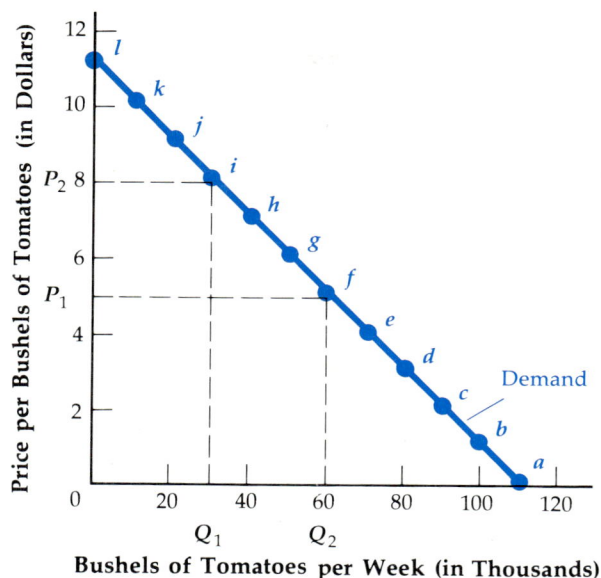

FIGURE 3.1 Market Demand for Tomatoes
Demand, the assumed inverse relationship between price and quantity purchased, can be represented by a curve that slopes down toward the right. Here, as the price falls from $11 to zero, the number of bushels of tomatoes purchased per week rises from zero to 110,000.

In sum, when the price of tomatoes (or razorblades or any other good) falls, more tomatoes will be purchased because more people will be buying them for more purposes.

Although price is an important part of the definition of demand, it is not the only determinant of how much of a good people will want. It may not even be the most important. The major factors that affect market demand are called determinants of demand. They are

○ consumer tastes or preferences

○ the prices of other goods

○ consumer incomes

○ number of consumers

○ expectations concerning future prices and incomes

A host of other factors, like weather, may also influence the demand for particular goods—ice cream, for instance.

A change in any of these determinants of demand will cause either an increase or a decrease in demand. An **increase in demand** is an increase in the quantity demanded at each and every price. It is represented graphically by a rightward, or outward, shift in the demand curve. A **decrease in demand** is a decrease in the quantity demanded at each and every price. It is represented graphically by a leftward, or inward, shift of the demand curve. Figure 3.2 illustrates the shifts in the demand curve that result from a change in one of the determinants of demand. The outward shift from D_1 to D_2 indicates an increase in demand: consumers now want more of a good

Increase in demand: an increase in the quantity demanded at each and every price, represented graphically by a rightward, or outward, shift in the demand curve.

Decrease in demand: a decrease in the quantity demanded at each and every price, represented graphically by a leftward, or inward, shift of the demand curve.

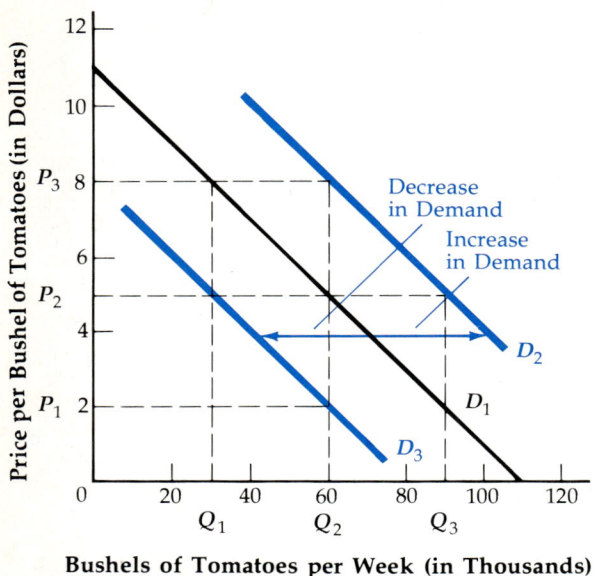

FIGURE 3.2 Shifts in the Demand Curve
An increase in demand is represented by a rightward, or outward, shift in the demand curve, from D_1 to D_2. A decrease in demand is represented by a leftward, or inward, shift in the demand curve, from D_1 to D_3.

at each and every price. For example, they want Q_3 instead of Q_2 tomatoes at price P_2. Consumers are also willing to pay a higher price now for any quantity. For example, they will pay P_3 instead of P_2 for Q_2 tomatoes. The inward shift from D_1 to D_3 indicates a decrease in demand: consumers want less of a good at each and every price—Q_1 instead of Q_2 tomatoes at price P_2. And they are willing to pay less than before for any quantity—P_1 instead of P_2 for Q_2 tomatoes.

A change in a determinant of demand may be translated into an increase or decrease in market demand in numerous ways. An increase in market demand can be caused by

An increase in consumers' desire for the good. If people truly want the good more, they will buy more of the good at any given price or pay a higher price for any given quantity.

An increase in the number of buyers. If more people will buy the good at any given price, they will also pay a higher price for any given quantity.

An increase in the price of substitute goods (which can be used in place of the good in question). If the price of oranges increases, the demand for grapefruit will increase.

A decrease in the price of complement goods (which are used in conjunction with the good in question). If the price of stereo systems falls, the demand for records, tapes, and CDs will rise.

Generally speaking (but not always), an increase in consumer incomes. An increase in people's incomes may increase the demand for luxury goods, such as new cars. It may also decrease demand for low-quality goods (like hamburger) because people can now afford better-quality products (like steak).

An expected increase in the future price of the good in question. If people expect the price of cars to rise faster than the prices of other goods, then (depending on exactly when they expect the increase) they may buy more cars now, thus avoiding the expected additional cost in the future.

An expected increase in the future price of a substitute good. If people expect the price of oranges to fall in the future, then (depending on exactly when they expect the price decrease) they may reduce their current demand for grapefruit, so they can buy more oranges in the future.

An expected increase in future incomes of buyers. College seniors' demand for cars tends to increase as graduation approaches and they anticipate a rise in income.

The determinants of a decrease in market demand are just the opposite:

A decrease in consumers' desire or taste for the good.

A decrease in the number of buyers.

A decrease in the price of substitute goods.

An increase in the price of complement goods.

Usually (but not always), a decrease in consumer incomes.

An expected decrease in the future price of the good in question.

An expected decrease in the future price of a substitute good.

An expected decrease in future incomes of buyers.

The Elements of Supply

On the other side of the market are producers of goods. The average person thinks of supply as the quantity of a good producers are willing to sell. To economists, however, supply means something quite different. **Supply** is the assumed relationship between the quantity of a good producers are willing to offer during a given period and the price, everything else held constant. Generally, because additional costs tend to rise with expanded production, this relationship is presumed to be positive. Like demand, supply is not a given quantity—that is called quantity supplied. Rather it is a relationship between price and quantity. As the price of a good rises, producers are generally willing to offer a larger quantity. The reverse is equally true: as price decreases, so does quantity supplied. Like demand, supply can also be described in a table or a graph.

Supply: the assumed relationship between the quantity of a good producers are willing to offer during a given period and the price, everything else held constant.

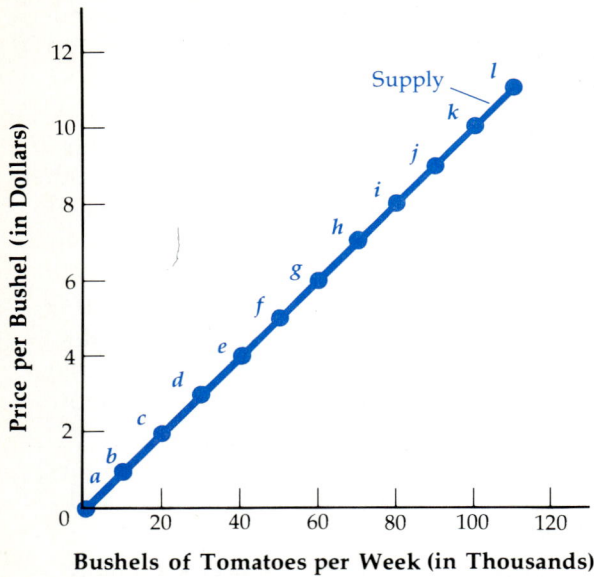

FIGURE 3.3 Supply of Tomatoes
Supply, the assumed relationship between price and quantity produced, can be represented by a curve that slopes up toward the right. Here, as the price rises from zero to $11, the number of bushels of tomatoes offered for sale during the course of a week rises from zero to 110,000.

Supply as a Table or a Graph

Supply may be described as a schedule of the quantities producers will offer at various prices during a given period of time. Table 3.2 shows such a supply schedule. As the price of tomatoes goes up from zero to $11 a bushel, the quantity offered rises from zero to 110,000, reflecting the assumed positive relationship between price and quantity.

Supply may also be thought of as a curve. If the quantity producers will offer is scaled on the horizontal axis of a graph and the price of the good is scaled on the vertical axis, the supply curve will slope upward to the right, reflecting the assumed positive relationship between price and quantity. In Figure 3.3, which was plotted from the data in Table 3.2, points *a* through *l* represent the price-quantity combinations *A* through *L*. Note how a change in the price causes a movement along the supply curve.[4]

The Slope and Determinants of Supply

The quantity producers will offer on the market depends on their production costs. Obviously the total cost of production will rise when more is produced because more resources will be required to expand output. The additional or marginal cost of each additional bushel produced also tends to rise as total output expands. In other words, it costs more to produce the

---

4. Mathematically, the supply relationship may be stated as $Q_s = a + bP$, where Q_s is the quantity supplied; a is the quantity producers will supply when the price is zero; b is the slope; and P is the price. Thus the supply function of tomatoes represented in Table 3.2 and Figure 3.3 may be written $Q_s = 0 + 10,000\,P$.

TABLE 3.2 Supply of Tomatoes

Price-Quantity Combination	Price per Bushel	Number of Bushels
A	0	0
B	1	10
C	2	20
D	3	30
E	4	40
F	5	50
G	6	60
H	7	70
I	8	80
J	9	90
K	10	100
L	11	110

second bushel of tomatoes than the first, and more to produce the third than the second. Firms will not expand their output unless they can cover their higher unit costs with a higher price. This is the reason the supply curve is thought to slope upward.

Anything that affects production costs will influence supply and the position of the supply curve. Such factors, which are called determinants of supply, include

- change in productivity due to a change in technology
- change in the profitability of producing other goods
- change in the scarcity (and prices) of various productive resources

Increase in supply: an increase in the quantity producers are willing and able to offer at each and every price, represented graphically by a rightward, or outward, shift in the supply curve.

Decrease in supply: a decrease in the quantity producers are willing and able to offer at each and every price, represented graphically by a leftward, or inward, shift of the supply curve.

Many other factors, such as weather, can also affect production costs. A change in any of these determinants of supply can either increase or decrease supply. An **increase in supply** is an increase in the quantity producers are willing and able to offer at each and every price. It is represented graphically by a rightward, or outward, shift in the supply curve. A **decrease in supply** is a decrease in the quantity producers are willing and able to offer at each and every price. It is represented graphically by a leftward, or inward, shift of the supply curve.

In Figure 3.4, an increase in supply is represented by the shift from S_1 to S_2. Producers are willing to produce a larger quantity at each price—Q_3 instead of Q_2 at price P_2, for example. They will also accept a lower price for each quantity—P_1 instead of P_2 for quantity Q_2. Conversely, the decrease in supply represented by the shift from S_1 to S_3 means that producers will offer less at each price—Q_1 instead of Q_2 at price P_2. They must also have a higher price for each quantity—P_3 instead of P_2 for quantity Q_2.

A few examples will illustrate the impact of changes in the determinants of supply. If firms learn how to produce more goods with the same or fewer resources, the cost of producing any given quantity will fall. Because of the technological improvement, firms will be able to offer a larger quan-

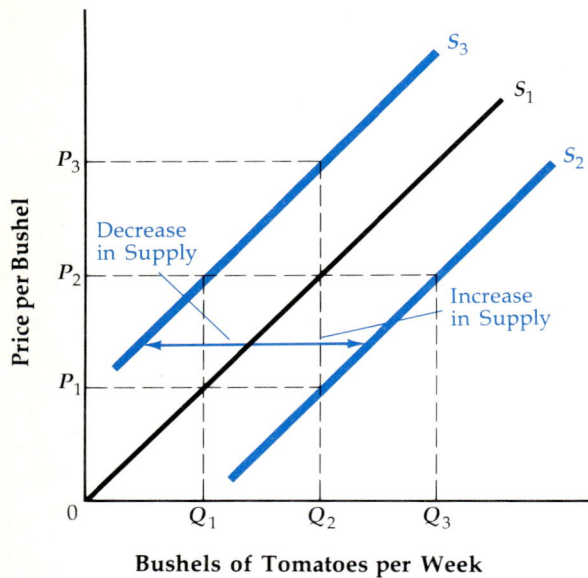

FIGURE 3.4 Shifts in the Supply Curve
A rightward, or outward, shift in the supply curve, from S_1 to S_2, represents an increase in supply. A leftward, or inward, shift in the supply curve, from S_1 to S_3, represents a decrease in supply.

tity at any given price or the same quantity at a lower price. The supply will increase, shifting the supply curve outward to the right.

Similarly, if the profitability of producing oranges increases relative to grapefruit, grapefruit producers will shift their resources to oranges. The supply of oranges will increase, shifting the supply curve to the right. Finally, if lumber (or labor or equipment) becomes scarcer, its price will rise, increasing the cost of new housing and reducing the supply. The supply curve will shift inward to the left.

Market Equilibrium

Supply and demand represent the two sides of the market—sellers and buyers. By plotting the supply and demand curves together, as in Figure 3.5 we can predict how buyers and sellers will interact with one another. At any price other than the one at the intersection of the two curves, the desires of buyers and sellers will be inconsistent, and a market surplus or shortage of tomatoes will result.

Market Surpluses

Market surplus: the amount by which the quantity supplied exceeds the quantity demanded at any given price. Graphically, the excess supply that occurs at any price above the intersection of the supply and demand curves.

Suppose that the price of a bushel of tomatoes is $9, or P_2 in Figure 3.5. At this price the quantity demanded by consumers is 20,000 bushels, much less than the quantity offered by producers, 90,000. There is a market surplus, or excess supply, of 70,000 bushels. A **market surplus** is the amount by

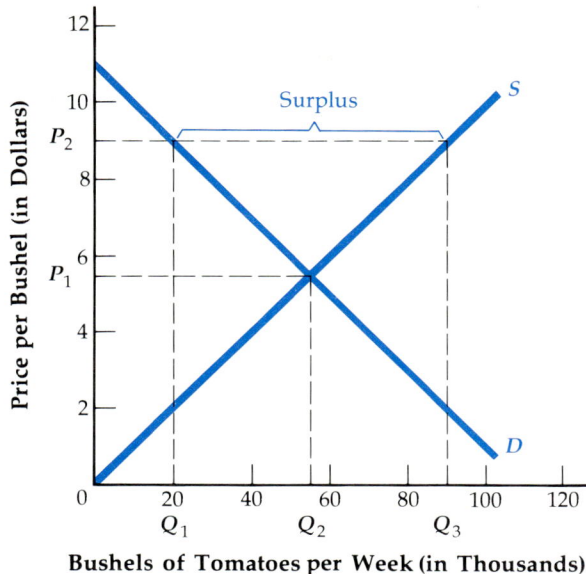

FIGURE 3.5   Market Surplus
If a price is higher than the intersection of the supply
and demand curves, a market surplus—a greater quantity supplied, Q_3, than demanded, Q_1—results. Competitive pressure will push the price down to the equilibrium
price P_1, the price at which the quantity supplied equals
the quantity demanded (Q_2).

Equilibrium price: the
price toward which a
competitive market will
move, and at which it will
remain once there, every-
thing else held constant.
The price at which the
market "clears"—that is,
at which the quantity
demanded by consumers
is matched exactly by the
quantity offered by pro-
ducers.

Equilibrium quantity:
the output (or sales) level
toward which the market
will move, and at which it
will remain once there,
everything else held con-
stant. Reached when the
quantity demanded
equals the quantity sup-
plied (at the equilibrium
price).

which the quantity supplied exceeds the quantity demanded at any given
price. Graphically, it is the excess supply that occurs at any price above the
intersection of the supply and demand curves.

What will happen in this situation? Producers who cannot sell their
tomatoes will have to compete by offering to sell at a lower price, forcing
other producers to follow suit. As the competitive process forces the price
down, the quantity consumers are willing to buy will expand, while the
quantity producers are willing to sell will decrease. The result will be a
contraction of the surplus, until it is finally eliminated at a price of $5.50 or
P_1 (at the intersection of the two curves). At that price, producers will be
selling all they want to; they will see no reason to lower prices further.
Similarly, consumers will see no reason to pay more; they will be buying all
they want. This point, where the wants of buyers and sellers intersect, is
called the equilibrium price. The **equilibrium price** is the price toward
which a competitive market will move, and at which it will remain once
there, everything else held constant. It is the price at which the market
"clears"—that is, at which the quantity demanded by consumers is matched
exactly by the quantity offered by producers. At the equilibrium price, the
quantities desired by buyers and sellers are also equal. This is the equilibrium quantity. The **equilibrium quantity** is the output (or sales) level toward which the market will move, and at which it will remain once there,
everything else held constant.

In sum, a surplus emerges when the price asked is above the equilibrium price. It will be eliminated, through competition among sellers, when
the price drops to the equilibrium price.

Market Shortages

Suppose the price asked is below the equilibrium price, as in Figure 3.6. At the relatively low price of $1, or P_1, buyers want to purchase 100,000 bushels—substantially more than the 10,000 bushels producers are willing to offer. The result is a market shortage. A **market shortage** is the amount by which the quantity demanded exceeds the quantity supplied at any given price. Graphically, it is the shortfall that occurs at any price below the intersection of the supply and demand curves.

As with a market surplus, competition will correct the discrepancy between buyers' and sellers' plans. Buyers who want tomatoes but are unable to get them at a price of $1 will bid higher prices, as at an auction. As the price rises, a larger quantity will be supplied because suppliers will be better able to cover their increasing production costs. At the same time the quantity demanded will contract as buyers seek substitutes that are now relatively less expensive compared with tomatoes. At the equilibrium price of $5.50, or P_2, the market shortage will be eliminated. Buyers will have no reason to bid prices up further, for they will be getting all the tomatoes they want at that price. Sellers will have no reason to expand production further; they will be selling all they want to at that price. The equilibrium price will remain the same until some force shifts the position of either the supply or the demand curve. If such a shift occurs, the price will move toward a new equilibrium at the new intersection of the supply and demand curves.

The Effect of Changes in Demand and Supply

Figure 3.7 shows the effects of shifts in demand and supply on the equilibrium price and quantity. In panel (a), an increase in demand from D_1 to D_2

Market shortage: the amount by which the quantity demanded exceeds the quantity supplied at any given price. Graphically, the shortfall that occurs at any price below the intersection of the supply and demand curves.

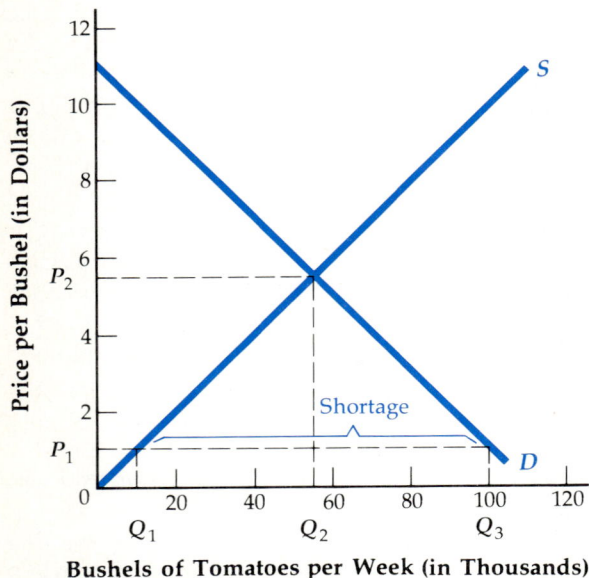

FIGURE 3.6 Market Shortage
A price that is below the intersection of the supply and demand curves will create a shortage—a greater quantity demanded, Q_3, than supplied, Q_1. Competitive pressure will push the price up to the equilibrium price P_2, the price at which the quantity supplied equals the quantity demanded.

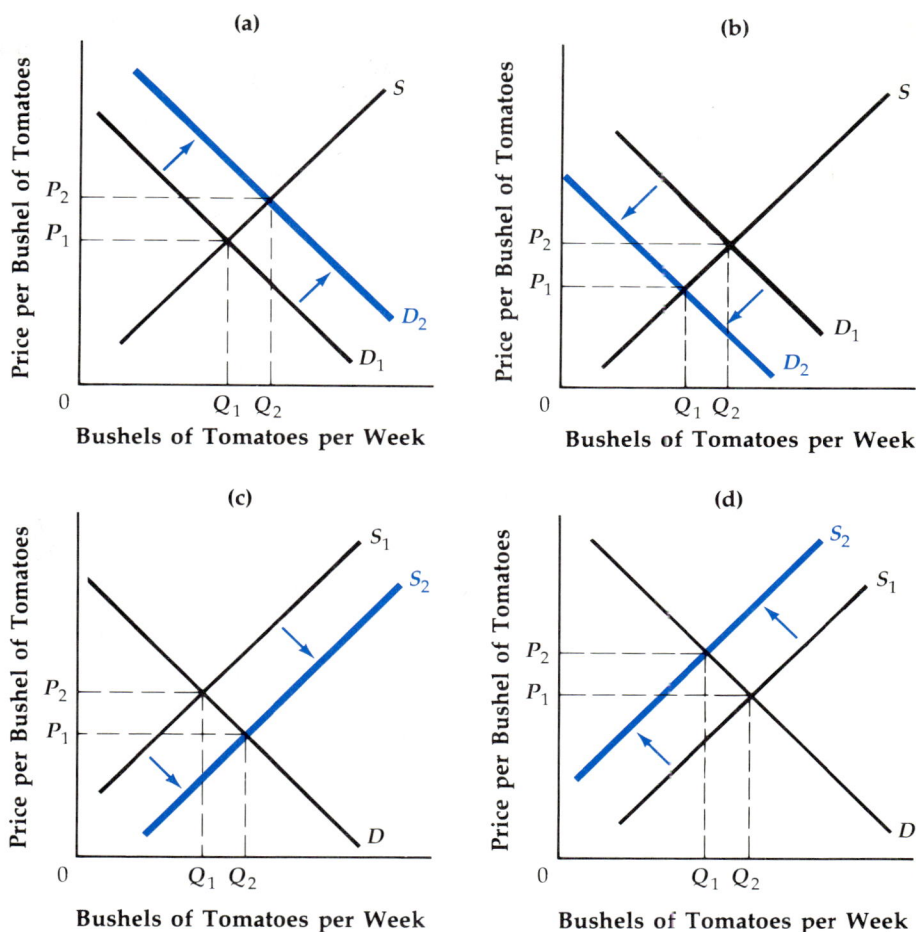

FIGURE 3.7 The Effects of Changes in Supply and Demand
An increase in demand—panel (a)—raises both the equilibrium price and the equilibrium quantity. A decrease in demand—panel (b)—has the opposite effect: a decrease in the equilibrium price and quantity. An increase in supply—panel (c)—causes the equilibrium quantity to rise but the equilibrium price to fall. A decrease in supply—panel (d)—has the opposite effect: a rise in the equilibrium price and a fall in the equilibrium quantity.

raises the equilibrium price from P_1 to P_2 and quantity from Q_1 to Q_2. In panel (b), a decrease in demand from D_1 to D_2 has the opposite effect, lowering price from P_2 to P_1 and quantity from Q_2 to Q_1.

An increase in supply from S_1 to S_2—panel (c)—has a different effect. The equilibrium quantity rises from Q_1 to Q_2, but the equilibrium price falls from P_2 to P_1. A decrease in supply from S_1 to S_2—panel (d)—causes the opposite effect: the equilibrium quantity falls from Q_2 to Q_1, and the equilibrium price rises from P_1 to P_2.

The Efficiency of the Competitive Market Model

3. When does the market operate "efficiently"?

Early in this chapter we asked how Fred Lieberman knows what prices to charge for the goods he sells. The answer is now apparent: he adjusts his prices until his customers buy the quantities that he wants to sell. If he cannot sell all the fruits and vegetables he has, he lowers his price to attract customers and cuts back on his orders for those goods. If he runs short, he knows he can raise his prices and increase his orders. His customers then adjust their purchases accordingly. Similar actions by other producers and customers all over the city move the market for produce toward equilibrium. The information provided by the orders, reorders, and cancellations from stores like Lieberman's eventually reaches the suppliers of goods and then the suppliers of resources. Similarly wholesale prices give Fred Lieberman information on suppliers' costs of production and the relative scarcity and productivity of resources.

The use of the competitive market system to determine what and how much to produce has two advantages. First, it is tolerably accurate. Much of the time the amount produced in a competitive market system tends to equal the amount consumers want—no more, no less. Second, the market system maximizes output.

In Figure 3.8(a), note that all price-quantity combinations acceptable to consumers lie either on or below the market demand curve, in the shaded

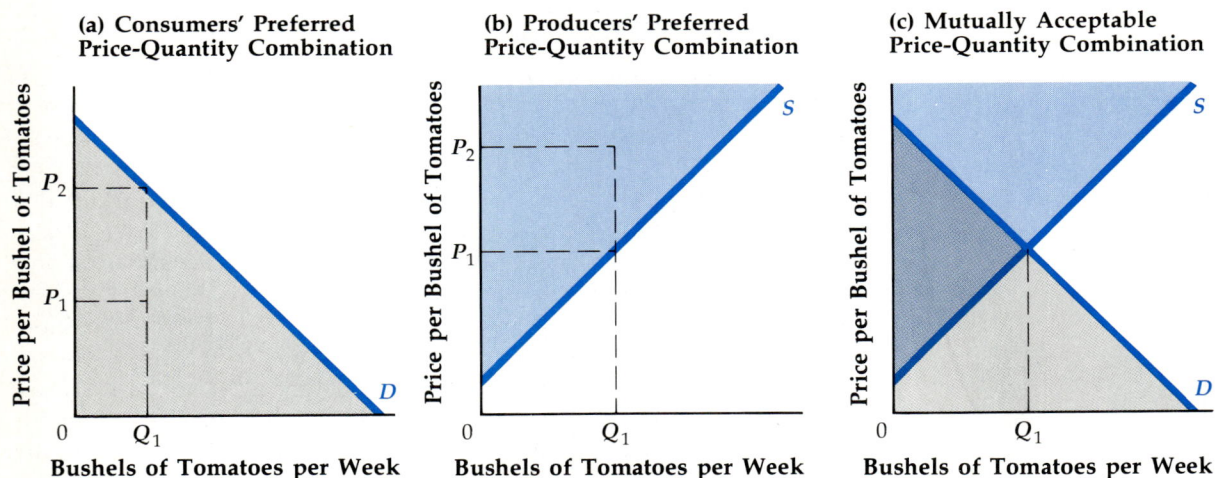

FIGURE 3.8 The Efficiency of the Competitive Market
Only those price-quantity combinations on or below the demand curve—panel (a)—are acceptable to buyers. Only those price-quantity combinations on or above the supply curve—panel (b)—are acceptable to producers. Those price-quantity combinations that are acceptable to both buyers and producers are shown in the darkest shaded area of panel (c). The competitive market is efficient in the sense that it results in output Q_1, the maximum output level acceptable to both buyers and producers.

area. (If consumers are willing to pay P_2 for Q_1 then they should also be willing to pay less for that quantity—for example, P_1.) Furthermore, all price-quantity combinations acceptable to producers lie either on or above the supply curve, in the shaded area shown in Figure 3.8(b). (If producers are willing to accept P_1 for quantity Q_1, then they should also be willing to accept a higher price—for example, P_2). When supply and demand curves are combined in Figure 3.8(c), we see that all price-quantity combinations acceptable to both consumers and producers lie in the darkest shaded triangular area. From all those acceptable output levels, the competitive market produces Q_1, the maximum output level that can be produced given what producers and consumers are willing and able to do. In this respect, the competitive market can be said to be efficient, or to allocate resources efficiently. **Efficiency** is the maximization of output through careful allocation of resources, given the constraints of supply (producers' costs) and demand (consumers' preferences). The achievement of efficiency means that consumers' or producers' welfare will be reduced by an expansion or contraction of output.

Efficiency: the maximization of output through careful allocation of resources, given the constraints of supply (producers' costs) and demand (consumers' preferences).

The market system exploits all possible trades between buyers and sellers. Up to the equilibrium quantity, buyers will pay more than suppliers require (those points on the demand curve lie above the supply curve). Beyond Q_1, buyers will not pay as much as suppliers need to produce more (those points on the supply curve lie above the demand curve). Again the market can be called efficient.

Nonprice Competition

▲ 4. What are the many ways firms compete?

Markets in which suppliers compete solely in terms of price are relatively rare. Table salt is a relatively uniform commodity sold in a market in which price is an important competitive tool. Even producers of salt, however, compete in terms of real or imagined quality differences and the reputation and recognition of brand names. In most industries, competition is through a wide range of product features, such as quality or appearance, design, and durability. In general, competitors can be expected to choose the mix of features that gives them the greatest profit.

In fact, price competition is not always the best method of competition, not only because price reductions mean lower average revenues, but because the reductions can be costly to communicate to consumers. Advertising is expensive, and consumers may not notice price reductions as readily as they do improvements in quality. Quality changes, furthermore, are not as easily duplicated as price changes. Consumers' preferences for quality over price should be reflected in the profitability of making such improvements. If consumers prefer a top-of-the-line calculator to a cheaper basic model, then producing the more sophisticated model could, depending on the cost of the extra features, be more profitable than producing the basic model and communicating its lower price to consumers.

If all consumers had exactly the same preferences—size, color, and so on—producers would presumably make uniform products and compete

PERSPECTIVES

Price Floors and Price Ceilings

Political leaders have occasionally objected to the prices charged in open, competitive markets and have mandated the prices at which goods must be sold. That is, the government has enforced price ceilings and price floors. A **price ceiling** is a government-determined price above which a specified good cannot be sold. A **price floor** is a government-determined price below which a specified good cannot be sold. Supply and demand graphs can illustrate the consequences of price ceilings and floors. For example, some cities impose ceilings on the rents (or prices) for apartments. Such a ceiling must be below the equilibrium price—somewhere below P_1 in Figure 3.9(a). (If the ceiling were above equilibrium, it would be above the market price and would serve no purpose.) As the graph shows, such a price control creates a market shortage. The number of people wanting apartments, Q_2, is greater than the number of apartments available, Q_1. Because of the shortage, landlords will be less concerned about maintaining their units, for they will be able to rent them in any case.

If the government imposes a price *floor*—on a commodity like milk, for example—the price must be above the equilibrium price, P_1 in Figure 3.9(b). (A price floor below P_1 would be irrelevant, because the market would clear at a higher level on its own.) The result of such a price edict is a market surplus. Producers want to sell more milk, Q_2, than consumers are willing to buy, Q_1. Some producers—those caught holding the surplus $(Q_2 - Q_1)$—will be unable to sell all they want to sell. Eventually someone must bear the cost of destroying or storing the surplus—and in fact the government holds vast quantities of grain, cotton, and dairy products because of its past efforts to support an equilibrium price for those products.

through price alone. For most products, however, people's preferences differ. To keep the analysis manageable, we will explore nonprice competition in terms of just one feature—product size. Suppose that in the market for television sets, consumer preferences are distributed along the continuum shown in Figure 3.10. The curve is bell shaped, indicating that most consumers are clustered in the middle of the distribution and want a middle-sized television. Fewer consumers want a giant screen or a mini-television.

Everything else being equal, the first producer to enter the market, Terrific TV, will probably offer a product that falls somewhere in the middle of the distribution—for example, at T in Figure 3.10. In this way, Terrific TV offers a product that reflects the preferences of the largest number of people. Furthermore, as long as there are no competitors, the firm can expect to pick up customers to the left and right of center. (Terrific TV's product may not come very close to satisfying the wants of consumers who prefer a very large or very small television, but it is the only one available.) The more Terrific TV can meet the preferences of the greatest number of consumers, everything else being equal, the higher the price it can charge and the greater the profit it can make. (Because consumers value the product more highly, they will pay a higher price for it.)

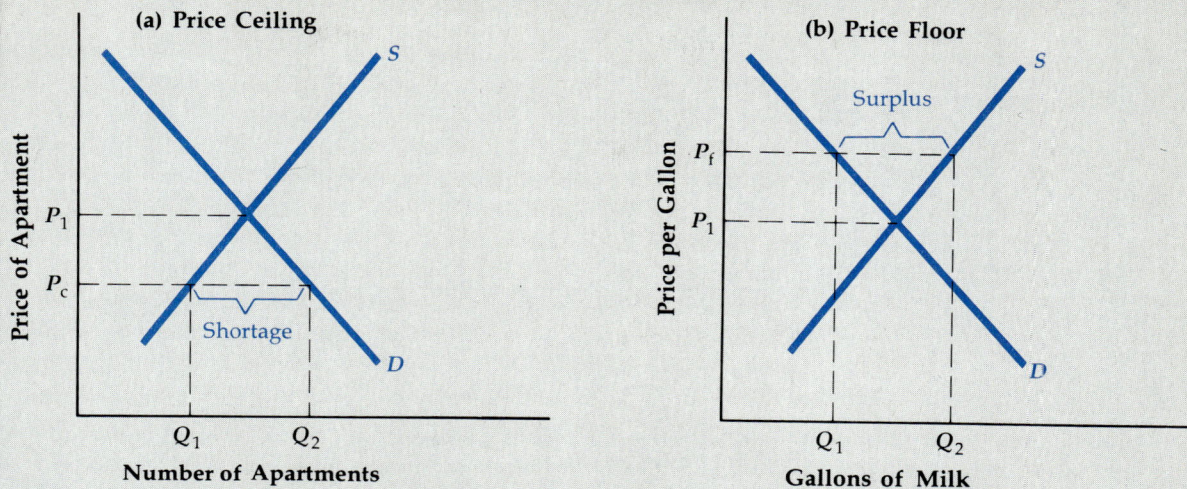

(a) Price Ceiling

(b) Price Floor

FIGURE 3.9 Price Ceilings and Floors
A price ceiling P_c—panel (a)—will create a market shortage equal to $Q_2 - Q_1$.
A price floor P_f—panel (b)—will create a market surplus equal to $Q_2 - Q_1$.

The first few competitors that enter the market may also locate close to the center—in fact, several may virtually duplicate Terrific TV's product. These firms may conclude that they will enjoy a larger market by sharing the center with several competitors than by moving out into the wings of the distribution. They are probably right. Although they may be able to charge more for a giant screen or a mini-television that closely reflects some consumers' preferences, there are fewer potential customers for those products.

To illustrate, assume that competitor Fabulous Focus locates at F, close to T. It can then appeal to consumers on the left side of the curve because its product will reflect those consumers' preferences more closely than does Terrific TV's. Terrific TV can still appeal to consumers on the right half of the curve. If Fabulous Focus had located at C, however, it would have direct appeal only to consumers to the left of C, as well as to a few between C and T. Terrific TV would have appealed to more of the consumers on the left, between C and T, than in the first case. In short, Fabulous Focus has a larger potential market at F than at C.

However, as more competitors move into the market, the center will become so crowded that new competitors will find it advantageous to move away from the center, to C or D. At those points the market will not be as

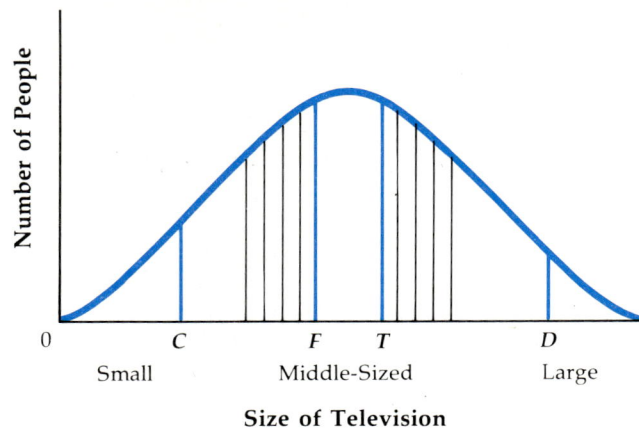

FIGURE 3.10   Consumer Preference in Television Size
Consumers differ in their wants, but most desire a medium-sized television. Only a few want very small or large televisions.

large as it is in the center, but competition will be less intense. If producers do not have to compete directly with as many competitors, they can charge higher prices. How far out into the wings they move will depend on the tradeoffs they must make between the number of customers they can appeal to and the price they can charge.

Like price reductions, the movement of competitors into the wings of the distribution benefits consumers whose tastes differ from those of the people in the middle. These atypical consumers now have a product that comes closer to or even directly reflects their preferences.

Our discussion has assumed free entry into the market. If entry is restricted by monopoly of a strategic resource or by government regulation, the variety of products offered will not be as great as in an open, competitive market. If there are only two or three competitors in a market, everything else being equal, we would expect them to cluster in the middle of a bell-shaped distribution. That tendency has been seen in the past in the broadcasting industry, when the number of television stations permitted in a given geographical area was strictly regulated by the Federal Communications Commission. Not surprisingly, stations carried programs that appealed predominantly to a mass audience—that is, to the middle of the distribution of television watchers. The Public Broadcasting System, PBS, was organized by the government partly to provide programs with less than mass appeal to satisfy viewers on the outer sections of the curve. When cable television companies were permitted to break into local television markets, television programs became more varied.

Even with free market entry, product variety depends on the cost of production and the prices people will pay for variations. Magazine and newsstand operators would behave very much like past television managers if they could carry only two or three magazines. They would choose *Newsweek* or some other magazine that appeals to the largest number of people. Most motel operators, for instance, have room for only a very small newsstand, and so they tend to carry the mass-circulation weeklies and monthlies.

For their own reasons, consumers may also prefer such a compromise. Although they may desire a product that perfectly reflects their tastes, they may buy a product that is not perfectly suitable if they can get it at a lower price. Producers can offer such a product at a lower price because of the economies of scale gained from selling to a large market. For example, most students take predesigned classes in large lecture halls instead of private tutorials. They do so largely because the mass lecture, although perhaps less effective, is substantially cheaper than tutorials. In a market that is open to entry, producers will take advantage of such opportunities.

If producers in one part of a distribution attempt to charge a higher price than necessary, other producers can move into that segment of the market and push the price down; or consumers can switch to other products. In this way, an optimal variety of products will eventually emerge in a free, reasonably competitive market. Thus the argument for a free market is an argument for the optimal product mix. Without freedom of entry, we cannot tell whether it is possible to improve on the existing combination of products. A free, competitive market gives rival firms a chance to better that combination.

The case for the free market becomes even stronger when we recognize that market conditions—and therefore the optimal product mix—are constantly changing.

Competition in the Short Run and the Long Run

▲ 5. How do competitive markets adjust to changes in conditions in the "short run" and "long run"?

One of the best examples of the workings of both price and nonprice competition is the market for hand calculators. Since the first model was introduced in the United States in 1969, the growth in sales, advancement in technology and design, and decline in prices in this market have been spectacular. The early calculators were simple—some did not even have a division key—and bulky by today's standards. By 1976 they had shrunk from the size of a large paperback book to a tiny two by three-and-a-half inches for one model, and sales exceeded 16 million.

While quality improved, prices fell. The first calculator, which Hewlett-Packard sold for $395, had an eight-digit display and performed only four basic functions—addition, subtraction, division, and multiplication. By December 1971 Bowmar was offering an eight-digit, four-function model for $240. The next year, in an attempt to maintain its high prices, Hewlett-Packard introduced a sophisticated model that could perform many more functions, still for $395. By the end of the year, Bowmar, Sears, and other firms had broken the $100 barrier, and firms were offering built-in memories, AC adapters, and 1,500-hour batteries to shore up prices. At the year's end, Casio announced a basic model for $59.95.

In 1973 prices continued to fall. By the end of the year, National Semiconductor was offering a six-digit, four-function model for $29.95, and Hewlett-Packard had lowered the price of its special model by $100 and added extra features. In 1974, six-digit, four-function models sold for as little as $16.95. Eight-digit models that would have sold for over $300 three or four years earlier carried price tags of $19.95. By 1976 consumers could buy a six-digit model for just $6.95. All this happened during a period when prices in general rose at a rate unprecedented in the United States during peacetime. Thus the relative prices of calculators fell by even more than their dramatic price reductions suggest.

Yet the drop in the price of calculators was to be expected. Although the high prices of the first calculators partly reflected high production costs, they also brought high profits and tempted many other firms into the industry. These new firms duplicated and then improved the existing technology and increased their productivity in order to beat the competition or avoid being beaten themselves. Firms unwilling to move with the competition quickly lost their share of the market.

The increase in competition in the calculator market, can be represented visually with supply and demand curves. Such an analysis permits us to observe long-run changes in market equilibrium. Given the limited technology and the small number of firms producing calculators in 1969, as well as restricted demand for this new product, let us assume that the supply and demand curves were initially S_1 and D_1 in Figure 3.11. The initial

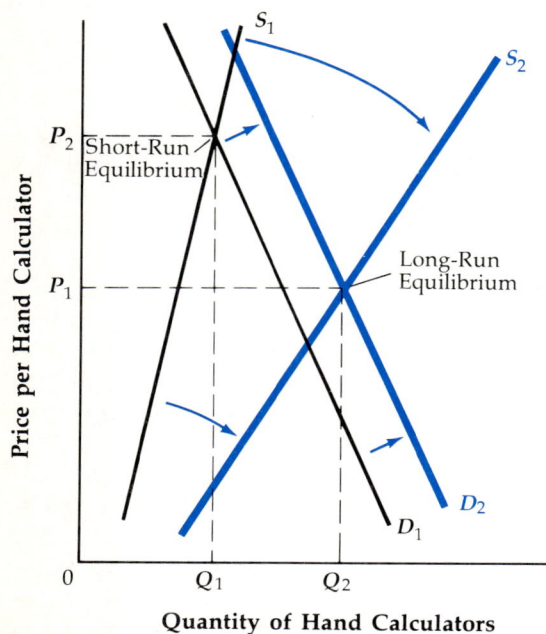

FIGURE 3.11 Long-Run Market for Calculators
With supply and demand for calculators at D_1 and S_1, the short-run equilibrium price and quantity will be P_2 and Q_1. As existing firms expand production and new firms enter the industry, the supply curve shifts to S_2. Simultaneously, an increase in consumer awareness of the product shifts the demand curve to D_2. The resulting long-run equilibrium price and quantity are P_1 and Q_2.

Short-run equilibrium: the price-quantity combination that will exist as long as producers do not have time to change their production facilities (or some other resource that is fixed in the short run).

equilibrium price would then be P_2 and the quantity sold, Q_1. This is the short-run equilibrium. **Short-run equilibrium** is the price-quantity combination that will exist as long as producers do not have time to change their production facilities (or some other resource that is fixed in the short run).

Short-run equilibrium did not last long. In the years following 1969, firms expanded production, building new plants and converting facilities that had been producing other small electronic devices. Economies of scale resulted, and technological breakthroughs lowered the cost of production still further. Several $150 circuits were reduced to very small $2 chips. The increased supply shifted the supply curve to the right, from S_1 to S_2 (see Figure 3.11). Meanwhile, because of advertising and word of mouth, people became familiar with the product and market demand increased, shifting the demand curve from D_1 to D_2. Because supply increased more than demand, the price fell from P_2 to P_1, and quantity rose from Q_1 to Q_2. The new equilibrium price and quantity, P_1 and Q_2, marked the new long-run market equilibrium. **Long-run equilibrium** is the price-quantity combination that will exist after firms have had time to change their production facilities (or some other resource that is fixed in the short run).

Long-run equilibrium: the price-quantity combination that will exist after firms have had time to change their production facilities (or some other resource that is fixed in the short run).

The market does not always move smoothly from the short run to the long run. Because firms do not know exactly what other firms are doing, or exactly what consumer demand will be, they may produce a product that cannot be sold at a price that will cover production costs. In fact, in the mid-1970s prices fell enough that several companies were losing money. Long-run improvements sometimes come at the expense of short-run losses.

In this example, a long-run market adjustment caused a drop in price (because supply increased more than demand). The opposite can occur: demand can increase more than supply, causing a rise in the price and the quantity produced. In Figure 3.12(a), when the supply curve shifts to S_2 and the demand curve shifts to D_2, price increases from P_1 to P_2 and quantity produced rises from Q_1 to Q_2. Supply and demand may also adjust so that price remains constant while quantity increases (Figure 3.12(b)).

Shortcomings of Competitive Markets

▲ **6. What are the shortcomings of competitive markets?**

Although the competitive market may promote long-run improvements in product prices, quality, and output levels, it has deficiencies, and we must note several before closing. (Market deficiencies will be discussed further in later chapters.)

First, the competitive market process can be quite efficient because production is maximized. Consumer demand, however, depends on the way income is distributed. If market forces or government programs distort income distribution, the demand for goods and resources will also be distorted. If, for example, income is concentrated in the hands of a few, the demand for luxury items will be high, but the demand for household appliances and new housing will be low. In such a situation, the results of competition may be efficient in a strict economic sense, but whether these results are socially desirable is a matter of values—of normative, rather than positive, economics.

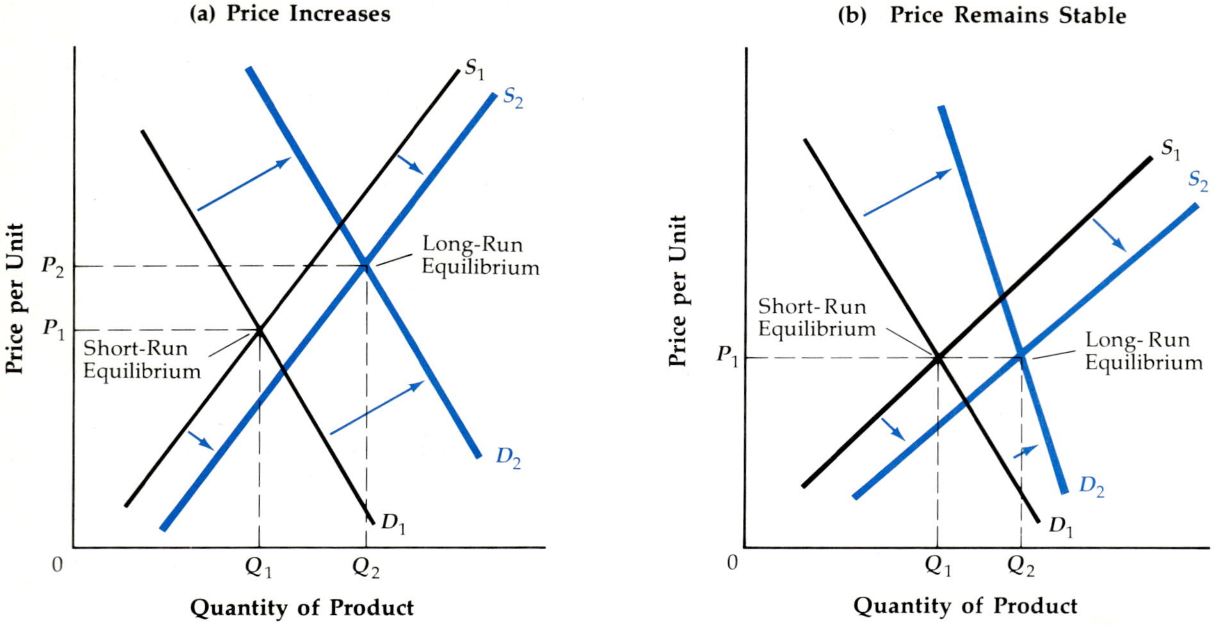

(a) Price Increases

(b)   Price Remains Stable

FIGURE 3.12   Prices in the Long Run
If demand increases more than supply, the price will rise along with the quantity sold—
panel (a). If supply keeps up with demand, however, the price will remain the same even
though the quantity sold increases—panel (b).

Second, the outcome of competition will not be efficient to the extent
that production costs are imposed on people who do not consume a product. People whose house paint peels because of industrial pollution bear a
portion of the offending firm's production cost, whether or not they buy its
product. At the same time, the price consumers pay for the product is lower
than it would be if all costs, including pollution costs, were incurred by the
producer. Because of the low price, consumers will buy more than the
efficient quantity. In a sense, this is an example of overproduction. Because
all the costs of production have not been included in the producer's cost
calculations, the price is artificially low.

Third, in a free market, competition can promote socially undesirable
products or services. A competitive market in an addictive drug like alcohol
or heroin can lead to lower prices and greater quantities consumed—and
thus increase in social problems associated with addiction. Competition can
be desirable only when it promotes the production of things people consider beneficial, but what is beneficial is a matter of values.

Fourth, opponents of the market system contend that competition
sometimes leads to "product proliferation"—too many versions of essentially the same product, such as aspirin—and to waste in production and

PERSPECTIVES
The Effect of Airline Deregulation on Travel Safety
William F. Shughart II, University of Mississippi

Before 1978 airlines in the United States were strictly controlled by government agencies. The safety of airlines was, and remains today, regulated by the Federal Aviation Administration (FAA). In addition, airline fares and routes were controlled by the Civil Aeronautics Board (CAB). The effect of CAB regulations was to restrict the ability of airlines to compete by price and entry into markets. Without CAB approval, for example, Delta Airlines could not lower its air fares or enter new markets to expand its business.

In 1978 Congress passed legislation to eliminate gradually most of the economic controls the CAB had over the domestic airline industry. However, airlines were not totally free to set prices and change routes until 1983.

Many commentators fear that airline deregulation may have resulted in a reduction in the safety of air travel in the United States.[1] From the perspective of economic theory, there are several reasons for believing that air safety may have been compromised. First, airline deregulation has led to reductions in the prices of many popular flights, especially long-distance flights (say, between New York and Los Angeles), and travel by air may have increased. Deregulation may have increased the opportunity for air accidents. Second, with the expansion of air travel, airlines may have had to draw on less experienced, qualified, and careful pilots and mechanics.

Third, with greater competition in the airline industry, several airlines may have become unprofitable and managers may have reduced expenditures on needed plane repairs in order to increase airline profits. Fourth, before air fares were deregulated, airlines may have competed in many nonprice ways—for example, meals and inflight service, movies, interiors of planes, and safety records. When they could compete by price after deregulation, airlines may have sacrificed safety competition for price competition. All of these factors may have led to increased air accidents and deaths.

Economists have statistically investigated the effect of airline deregulation on airline safety. While the debate continues, recent studies show that airline deregulation has in fact led to significantly more air travel but that the number of airline accidents and deaths has not been affected.[2] Airline deaths have been on a downward trend for decades (a point that is made clear in the accompanying Figure 3.13), and airline deregulation does not appear (to date) to have slowed the pace of decrease.[3] Economists have reasoned that the greater freedom given airlines by deregulation may have been held in check by the considerable costs that airlines incur when they do have accidents. Airlines, in other words, may have continued to maintain their safety records because of the fear and cost of liability suits that are brought against them when they do have crashes. In addition, safety was never deregulated by Congress.

Various government policies often have hidden, secondary market effects that economists and policymakers must consider. Airline deregulation is a good case in point. Airline deregulation could have reduced total travel deaths in the country by its indirect impact on highway travel and accidents.

By deregulating airlines fares, Congress increased air travel. At the same time, Congress increased the *relative* cost of travel by car on the

1. See Hobart Rowen, "Bring Back Regulation," *Washington Post* (National Weekly Edition), August 31, 1987, p. 5.
2. See Nancy L. Rose, *Financial Influences on Airline Safety*, no. 1890-87 (Cambridge, Mass.: Sloan School of Management, Massachusetts Institute of Technology, 1987; and Richard B. McKenzie and William F. Shughart II, "The Impact of Airline Regulation on Air Safety," *Regulation* (January 1988), pp. 42–47.
3. Establishing the effect of airline deregulation on air travel and air accidents and deaths is more difficult than it appears. This is because many factors affect air travel and deaths, including the amount of income people in the economy have to spend. The very valuable statistical methods used by economists to separate the impact of airline deregulation from people's income is called econometrics.

continued

The Effect of Airline Deregulation on Travel Safety
continued

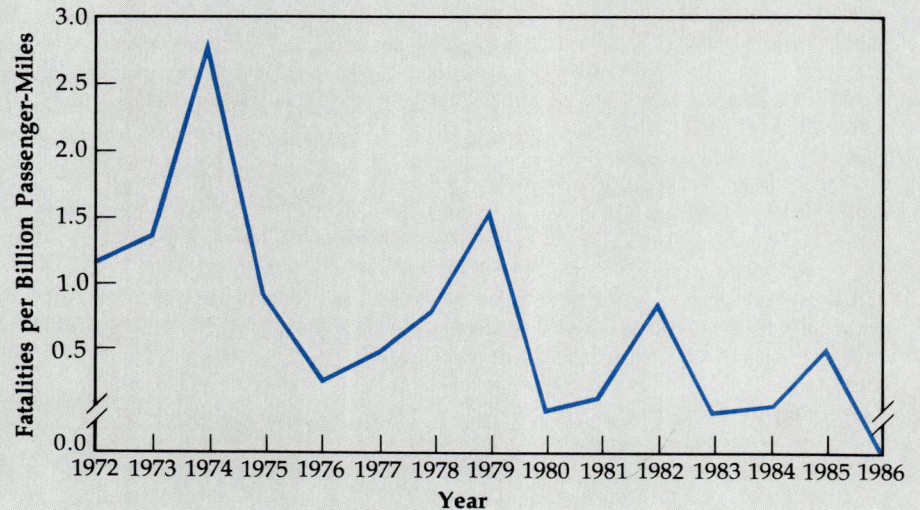

FIGURE 3.13 Fatalities per Billion Passenger-Miles Flown for Scheduled Airlines, 1972–1986[a]

Despite fears that airline deregulation would lead to increased accidents and deaths, recent studies show that this is not the case. Although airline deregulation has led to an increase in air travel, the number of deaths has in fact decreased.

a. Airline deregulation was enacted in 1978.

Source: Federal Aviation Administration

advertisement. Because so many types of the same product are available, production of each takes place on a very small scale, and no plant is fully utilized. This may be true. The validity of this objection, however, hinges on whether the range of choice in products compensates for the inefficiencies in production. The question is whether firms should be forced to standardize their products and to compete solely in terms of price. What about people who want something different from the standard product?

Fifth, unscrupulous competitors can take advantage of customers' ignorance. A competitor may employ unethical techniques, such as circulating false information about rivals or using bait-and-switch promotional tactics (advertising very low-priced, low-quality products to attract customers and to switch them to higher-priced products when they get into the nation's highways. This is because, as noted, after deregulation, air travel became more convenient and often cheaper. Therefore, car travel became relatively expensive relative to air travel.

Airline deregulation has had two distinct effects on automobile travel. It has had a *price (or substitution) effect*. Less automobile travel would be expected with relatively lower air fares. Airline deregulation has also had an *income effect* because greater efficiency in air travel may have led to more national production and income. The greater national income may have led to more travel by air and cars.

Because the price and income effects of airline deregulation on automobile travel are not expected to be in the same direction, theory alone does not give a clear answer to the question, "How has airline deregulation affected automobile travel?" Statistical analysis is required, and the only study currently available on the issue found that airline deregulation has, indeed, reduced travel by automobiles (by an annual average of nearly 4 percent between 1979 and 1985).[4] However, because miles traveled on highways and automotive accidents and deaths are likely to be directly related, the small estimated decrease in automobile travel may have reduced automotive

accidents and deaths by a sizable number. In fact, one of the authors estimates that airline deregulation has probably reduced automobile accidents by an annual average of several hundred thousand and deaths by an annual average of several hundred.[5]

The indirect effects of policy changes, which are revealed through economic analysis, cannot be ignored by policymakers. Policymakers need to be mindful of the fact that efforts to resurrect the type of airline regulation abandoned in the late 1970s may, or may not, improve airline safety records. Re-regulation, however, may cause people to shift from air travel to highway travel. Unfortunately, highway travel remains far more dangerous than air travel, and unless precautions are taken, overall travel deaths can be increased by airline re-regulation. This does not mean that re-regulation should not be undertaken but only that care must be taken in designing any new economic controls on airlines.

4. Richard B. McKenzie and John T. Warner, *The Impact of Airline Deregulation on Highway Safety* (St. Louis: Center for the Study of American Business, Washington University, December 1987).

5. Ibid., p. 4.

store). Competition can control some of these abuses. For instance, competitors will generally let consumers know when their rivals are misrepresenting their products. Still, fraudulent sellers can move from one market to another, keeping one step ahead of their reputations.

Chapter Review

Review of Key Questions

▲   *1. What is the competitive market process?*

The competitive market process can best be defined as a process through which buyers and sellers, pursuing their own interests, attempt to outwit, outdistance, or outmaneuver other buyers and sellers. In the process, market rivals are forced to reveal the limits of what they will accept in terms of price, quantity, quality, and so on.

◢   2. *What are the supply and demand curves and how can they be used to understand the market process?*

The demand curve graphically illustrates the assumed inverse relationship between price and quantity, everything else held constant. The supply curve graphically illustrates the assumed relationship between the price and quantity producers are willing to offer, everything else held constant. The supply curve is normally upward sloping, depicting a positive relationship between price and the quantity of a good sellers are willing to offer on the market. Supply and demand curves help explain how prices and output levels are determined in competitive markets. They help sort out the price/quantity effects of changes in market conditions—for example, an increase in consumer incomes or a decrease in production costs.

Price competition among producers will push the market price and quantity toward the intersection of the supply and demand curves, called the equilibrium point. At the intersection of supply and demand, the market clears, meaning that consumers are willing and able to buy the exact amount producers are willing to offer. Market shortages will occur if a market price is below the equilibrium price. Market surpluses will occur if a market price is above the equilibrium price.

◢   3. *When does the market operate "efficiently"?*

When the market price and quantity move toward and reach the equilibrium price and quantity, the market is said to be operating efficiently. At the intersection of supply and demand, all mutually beneficial trades have been undertaken. Output is maximized at the intersection of supply and demand, given the constraints of consumer preferences (demand) and producer costs (supply).

◢   4. *What are the many ways firms compete?*

Producers seek to sell their goods and services through the creation of attractions other than price—for example, changes in size, flavor, color, texture, and usefulness. These methods of seeking to outdo and outmaneuver sellers is called "nonprice competition." Nonprice competition can lead to a greater variety of goods and services that meet the demands of different buyers.

◢   5. *How do competitive markets adjust to changes in conditions in the "short run" and "long run"?*

Short-run changes in supply and demand can give rise to immediate changes in price and sales. However, short-run changes in market conditions can change the profitability of production and consumer awareness of products. An increase in the profitability of firms in the market can give rise to additional firms that seek to enter the market, increasing the supply in the long run. An increase in short-run supply can lower the market price and increase consumer awareness of the price, increasing the demand in the long run. In response to changes in short-run demand or supply, the long-run equilibrium price can rise, fall, or remain the same, depending on the exact nature of changes in production costs and consumer preferences.

◢   *6. What are the shortcomings of competitive markets?*

Although the competitive market may be efficient, it is not perfect, and criticisms are still leveled against the use of markets. Markets may not be considered "fair" because the community's or nation's income is never equally distributed. Markets may not always be efficient—for example, when firms emit pollution and impose costs on people not parties to the market transactions. Goods produced by markets may be considered socially objectionable, as is the case with street drugs. Markets may also result in much waste of resources tied up in product proliferation. Finally, in an effort to gain profits, producers and consumers may take advantage of their market positions and engage in fraud.

Further Topics

The market is a system that provides producers with incentives to deliver goods and services to others. To respond to those incentives, producers must meet the needs of society. They must compete with other producers to deliver their goods and services in the most cost-effective manner.

A market implies that sellers and buyers can freely respond to incentives and that they have options and can choose among them. It does not mean, however, that behavior is totally unconstrained or that producers can choose from unlimited options. What a competitor can do may be severely limited by what rival firms are willing to do.

The market system is not perfect. Producers may have difficulty acquiring enough information to make reliable production decisions. People take time to respond to incentives, and producers can make high profits while others are gathering their resources to respond to an opportunity. In the electronics industry, three or four years were required to reduce the price of a basic calculator from $300 to $40. Some consumers still may not be getting exactly the kind of calculator they want.

An uncontrolled market system also carries with it the very real prospect that one firm will acquire monopoly power, restricting the ability of others to respond to incentives, produce more, and push prices and profits down.

Review of New Terms

Competition The process by which market participants, in pursuing their own interests, attempt to outdo, outprice, outproduce, and outmaneuver each other.

Decrease in demand A decrease in the quantity demanded at each and every price, represented graphically by a leftward, or inward, shift of the demand curve.

Decrease in supply A decrease in the quantity producers are willing and able to offer at each and every price, represented graphically by a leftward, or inward, shift of the supply curve.

Demand The assumed inverse relationship between the price of a good or service and the quantity consumers are willing and able to buy during a given period, all other things held constant.

Efficiency The maximization of output through careful allocation of resources, given the constraints of supply (producers' costs) and demand (consumers' preferences).

Equilibrium price The price toward which a competitive market will move, and at which it will remain once there, everything else held constant. The price at which the market "clears"—that is, at which the quantity demanded by consumers is matched exactly by the quantity offered by producers.

Equilibrium quantity The output (or sales) level toward which the market will move, and at which it will remain once there, everything else held constant. Reached when the quantity demanded equals the quantity supplied (at the equilibrium price).

Increase in demand An increase in the quantity demanded at each and every price, represented graphically by a rightward, or outward, shift in the demand curve.

Increase in supply An increase in the quantity producers are willing and able to offer at each and every price, represented graphically by a rightward, or outward, shift in the supply curve.

Long-run equilibrium The price-quantity combination that will exist after firms have had time to change their production facilities (or some other resource that is fixed in the short run).

Market shortage The amount by which the quantity demanded exceeds the quantity supplied at a given price. Graphically, the shortfall in supply that occurs at any price below the intersection of the supply and demand curves.

Market surplus The amount by which the quantity supplied exceeds the quantity demanded at a given price. Graphically, the excess supply that occurs at any price above the intersection of the supply and demand curves.

Perfect competition A market composed of numerous independent sellers and buyers of an identical product, such that no one individual or buyer has the ability to affect the market price by changing the production level. Entry into and exit from a perfectly competitive market is unrestricted.

Price ceiling The government-determined price above which a specified good cannot be sold.

Price floor The government-determined price below which a specified good cannot be sold.

Short-run equilibrium The price-quantity combination that will exist as long as producers do not have time to change their production facilities (or some other resource that is fixed in the short run).

Supply The assumed relationship between the quantity of a good producers are willing and able to offer during a given period and the price, everything else held constant.

Review Questions

1. What are the consequences of competition in markets? (◀ 1)
2. Why does the demand curve have a negative slope and the supply curve a positive slope? (◀ 2)

3. The mercantilists argued that a country's wealth consisted of its holdings of "gold bullion" (money). To keep gold in a country, they proposed tariffs and quotas to restrict imported goods and services. How do you react to that argument? (◢2, ◢3)

4. Suppose that supply and demand are represented by the following functions:

$$Q_d = 110 - 10P$$

$$Q_s = 10 + 10P$$

What is the equilibrium price and quantity? (◢2)

5. In what sense can competition in the production of undesirable goods be bad? (◢3)

6. List what you consider to be the deficiencies of the free market system. Do the deficiencies outweigh the benefits? (◢3, ◢6)

7. Why will the competitive market tend to move toward the price-quantity combination at the intersection of the supply and demand curves? What might keep the market from moving all the way to that equilibrium point? (◢2)

8. Suppose the demand for blue jeans suddenly increases. Discuss possible short-run and long-run movements of the market. (◢5)

9. If the government imposes a price ceiling on gasoline, what would be the result? (◢3)

10. If the government imposes a price floor on whole milk and buys the resulting surplus, can it later sell what it has bought and recoup its expenditure? What else can the government do with the milk surplus? (◢3)

The Public Sector

The end of law is not to abolish or restrain but to preserve and enlarge freedom; for in all the states of created beings capable of law, where there is no law, there is no freedom. For liberty is to be free from restraint and violence of others, which cannot be where there is no law; but freedom is not, as we are told: a liberty of every man to do what he lists—for who could be free, when every man's humor might domineer over him?—but a liberty to dispose and order as he lists his . . . actions, possessions, and his whole property, within the allowance of those laws under which he is.
   John Locke

KEY QUESTIONS

▲ 1.   What does government do?

▲ 2.   What are the economic functions of government?

▲ 3.   Under what circumstances will markets "fail"?

▲ 4.   Why are some resources overused and abused?

▲ 5.   How can government-provided income-security programs be justified?

▲ 6.   What can government do to stabilize the economy?

▲ 7.   What are the shortcomings of government actions?

NEW TERMS

Average tax rate
Budget deficit
Budget surplus
Common access resources
Corporate income taxes
Excise taxes
External benefits
External costs
Externalities
Fiscal policy
General sales tax
Macroeconomic policy

Marginal tax rate
Monetary policy
Monopoly
Personal income taxes
Private sector
Progressive tax system
Property rights
Property tax
Proportional tax system
Public sector
Regressive tax system

Our study of markets in the last chapter may have suggested that all economic decisions are made by individuals acting in their own self-interest, constrained by the forces of supply and demand. Nothing could be further from the truth. Many economic decisions are made by government, which allocates tax revenue for various public uses, such as national defense, retirement income, education, and garbage collection. Government decisions also influence the types of products we buy, the quality of the air we breathe and the water we drink, the safety of our workplaces, and the number of goods we can buy from foreign countries. In all these ways, government influences how scarce resources are allocated among competing public and private ends.

Because government is powerful, it must be considered in any economics course. We need to ask why, from an economic perspective, government exists in the first place and how its policies affect private economic activity. After distinguishing the public and private sectors, we will briefly survey the extent of government taxation and expenditure. We will conclude by examining the economic justification for government's various roles.

An Overview of the Public Sector

◢ 1. What does government do?

Private sector: all the economic transactions undertaken voluntarily by individuals, either alone or in association with others.

In most Western nations, economic life from year to year depends critically on trillions of decisions by millions of individuals acting on their own and as members of social and business organizations. This complex private sector, from which most of us draw a substantial portion of our livelihood, is largely an unintended consequence of purposeful individual action. The **private sector** encompasses all the economic transactions undertaken voluntarily by individuals, either alone or in association with others. Some economists have characterized activity in the private sector as "ordered anarchy" (for its myriad individual actions tend somehow toward economic stability). Others have called it "spontaneous order" (because it occurs without direction) or "self-generating order" (because it emerges on its own and is self-perpetuating). Without some help from government, however, the private economy may not be very orderly, spontaneous, or self-generating.

Many crucial decisions are not made by individuals acting independently, but by people acting collectively through government. Government decisions are binding on all citizens, and government activities are paid for by forced taxation. The lack of individual control in the public sector is necessary partly because not everyone agrees with government decisions and partly because the benefits of many government activities, such as highways and national defense, cannot be distributed selectively. Without taxation, those who benefit from government activities would be unlikely to pay for the services voluntarily, and the services might never be provided. (More will be said about this later.) The **public sector** includes the activities of federal, state, and local government. Government decisions are normally made collectively, either by voters in a referendum or by Congress, and are financed primarily by forced taxation.

Public sector: the activities of federal, state, and local government.

At all levels of government—federal, state, and local—government in the United States is big business. All told, it accounts for approximately 35 percent of the nation's total output. In its 1989 budget (see Table 4.1), which was proposed in early 1988, the federal government planned to spend $1.1 trillion in fiscal year 1989; $294 billion (or 27 percent) of this

TABLE 4.1   Federal Government Outlays and Receipts, 1989[a] (in billions of dollars)

Budget Receipts	964.7
Individual income taxes	412.4
Corporation income taxes	117.7
Social insurance taxes and contributions	354.6
Excise taxes	35.2
Estate and gift taxes	7.8
Customs duties	17.2
Miscellaneous receipts	19.8
Budget Outlays	1,094.2
National defense	294.0
International affairs	13.3
General science, space, and technology	13.1
Energy	3.1
Natural resources and environment	16.0
Agriculture	21.7
Commerce and housing credit	7.9
Transportation	27.3
Community and regional development	5.9
Education, training, employment, and social services	37.4
Health	47.8
Social security	233.8
Medicare	84.0
Income security	135.6
Veterans benefits and services	29.6
Administration of justice	9.9
General government	9.5
Central federal credit activities	−6.3
Net interest	151.8
Undistributed offsetting receipts	−41.0

a. Estimates available in 1988.

Source: Executive Office of the President, Office of Management and Budget, *Budget of the United States Government, Fiscal Year 1989* (Washington, D.C.: U.S. Government Printing Office, 1988), pp. 6g–8, 6g–9.

total was to be spent on national defense. Social security and income security outlays, which include retirement benefits, payments to disabled workers, and medical care for a wide range of people, were budgeted at $453 billion (or 41 percent of total federal outlays). The federal government also planned to spend $37 billion on education and $22 billion on agriculture. Billions more were budgeted for energy, international affairs, transportation, and housing.

Of the $965 billion that were expected to be collected in revenues in 1989, most ($412 billion, or 43 percent) were expected to come from individual income taxes. Another $118 billion (or 12 percent) were to come from corporate income taxes, and Social Security taxes were expected to add $355 billion, or 37 percent. Significant revenues were expected to come from excise taxes on products like gasoline, tobacco, and alcohol, and on inheritance.

As Table 4.2 shows, federal receipts have grown substantially, rising from less than $600 million in 1900 to $965 billion in 1989. Most of this growth has occurred since the 1930s. Although inflation has played a large part—dollars are worth much less now than they were in the 1930s—much of the growth is due to an expansion in the federal government's activities. Growth in federal outlays has been even more dramatic than growth in receipts. As a consequence, the federal budget deficit has mushroomed. A **budget deficit** is the amount by which outlays exceed receipts during any given accounting period. It is the opposite of a **budget surplus,** the amount by which receipts exceed outlays during a given accounting period.

Figure 4.1 shows federal outlays and receipts since 1970. Between 1970 and 1989, outlays grew from 20 to 22 percent of total domestic production. The growing reliance on deficit spending is indicated by the shaded area. The federal deficit expanded from 1 to 2 percent of total domestic production in the early 1970s to 5 to 6 percent of total domestic

Budget deficit: the amount by which outlays exceed receipts during any given accounting period.

Budget surplus: the amount by which receipts exceed outlays during a given accounting period.

TABLE 4.2   Federal Government Receipts, Selected Years, 1900–1989

Year	Billion Dollars	Year	Billion Dollars
1900	0.6	1950	39.5
1905	0.5	1955	65.5
1910	0.7	1960	92.5
1915	0.7	1965	116.8
1920	6.6	1970	193.7
1925	3.6	1975	279.1
1930	4.1	1980	517.1
1935	3.7	1985	736.9
1940	6.4	1988	909.2
1945	45.2	1989	964.7

Sources: U.S. Bureau of the Census, *Historical Statistics of the United States* (Washington, D.C.: U.S. Government Printing Office, 1975), pp. 1104–1105; *Economic Report of the President* (Washington, D.C.: U.S. Government Printing Office, 1988, pp. 339–341; Executive Office of the President, Office of Management and Budget, *Budget of the United States Government, Fiscal Year 1989* (Washington, D.C.: U.S. Government Printing Office, 1988), p. 1–5.

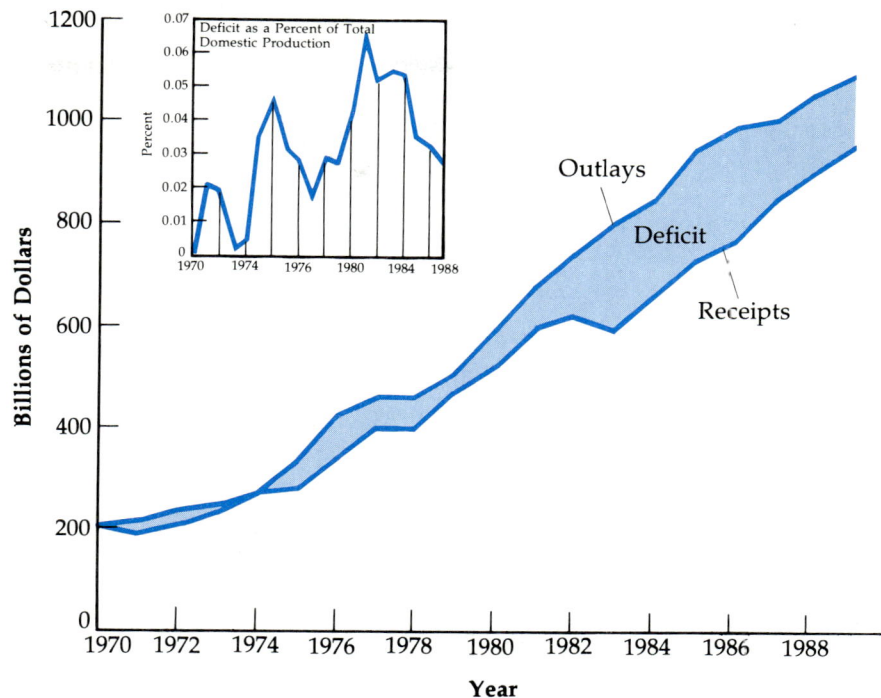

FIGURE 4.1   Federal Budget Receipts and Outlays, 1970–1989
Federal outlays have risen substantially over the past fifteen years. Because they have risen faster than receipts, the budget deficit (shaded area) has also grown.
Source: Executive Office of the President, *Economic Report of the President* (Washington, D.C.: U.S. Government Printing Office, 1988), p. 337.

production in the early 1980s (see inset in Figure). The deficit is expected to be back down to less than 3 percent of domestic production by 1989.

In 1987 the fifty state governments and the 85,000 local (county, city, and town) governments spent a total of $607 billion, most of which went for roads, education, police protection, and local government. They obtained their revenue largely from income, sales, and property taxes. To their revenue from local property taxes and fees for services provided, the state and local governments added $105 billion received from the state and the federal governments. Most local expenditures went for services such as police and fire protection, roads, sewers, and water systems. A relatively small percentage went to welfare programs.

Besides making its own expenditures, government regulates private production. According to one estimate, federal regulation of business activities, including pollution, occupational safety, and product design, costs the private sector over $100 billion annually in added production expenses. State and local regulations increased the bill.

Governments also influence the use of resources through tax exemptions. For example, individuals can deduct the interest paid on money borrowed for houses from their federally taxable incomes. Thus their taxes go down when they take out home mortgages. The economic effect of such a deduction is to reduce the after-tax price of houses and to increase sales of homes. Before the passage of the Tax Reform Act of 1986, businesses could also reduce their federal tax bills, by up to 10 percent of the cost of new plant and equipment. The so-called Investment Tax Credit encouraged the formation of capital and the updating or expansion of industrial equipment. Like government tax and spending decisions, these tax deductions and credits divert resources from private to public uses. Private expenditures made in order to take advantage of tax deductions and credits are called "tax expenditures."

Government decisions loom large in the overall economy, adding to and subtracting from individuals' incentives to work, save, and invest for the future. As government budgets increase, citizens must ask whether all governmental activities are necessary and justifiable.

Several functions traditionally belong to government:

- to define and protect property rights
- to protect the public from crime and bring criminals to justice
- to provide for the national defense
- to educate the general public
- to establish a stable monetary system

In modern times, however, government responsibilities have expanded to include other functions:

- to stabilize the economy—that is, moderate the swings in general economic activity and unemployment
- to control the use of the environment, regulate industry, and protect consumers from perceived abuses of the competitive market process
- to provide income security and health insurance

We will examine most of these governmental functions, starting with the traditional function of protecting property.

Minimal Government: Protection of Property

▲ **2. What are the economic functions of government?**

Property rights: legally defined and permissible uses, both private and collective, of resources, goods, and services.

Although the last chapter's discussion of the market system rarely mentioned government, it was actually based on the existence of some collective authority. In the market system, what is really sold is not tomatoes or hand calculators, but the property rights to tomatoes and hand calculators—and property rights are generally established and protected by government. **Property rights** are legally defined and permissible uses of resources, goods, and services, both privately and collectively.

Property rights are a social phenomenon—a response to the problem of living peaceably in a world where few have everything they want. In places where people are separated from one another by natural barriers, or where resources are abundant, property rights have no meaning. To Robinson Crusoe, shipwrecked on a lonely island, property rights were inconsequential. His behavior was restricted only by the resources he found on the island, the tools he took from his wrecked ship, and his own ingenuity. Although he encountered problems in allocating his time efficiently—between food gathering, shelter building, and so on—the notion of property never restrained his behavior. He simply took from the ship, with impunity, whatever seemed most useful.[1]

With the arrival of Friday, it became necessary to establish some restrictions on behavior. The problem was particularly acute because Friday was a cannibal. Clearly each man had to establish property rights to his body. Then the two had to work out a system of ownership for the various possessions on the island.

The property rights traded in the market system are based ultimately on the need for social order. These rights bring obligations as well as privileges. A person who buys a house is actually buying the right to live in the house under certain conditions—for example, for as long as he or she does not disturb others or does not allow the property to deteriorate so much as to threaten the neighbors' safety. These rights and obligations of property owners draw their legitimacy, to a significant degree, from government enforcement of the law.

Just how much markets depend on government for the protection of private property rights is hard to determine. Markets existed in the Old West, which lacked formally instituted government. Even today, we cannot depend on government to arbitrate all questions of property rights. In college dormitories, disputes over property rights are usually settled before they reach the student council, to say nothing of the dean's office or the police station. In society at large, most conflicts over property are resolved personally, and many never arise because people conform to socially accepted standards of behavior.

Nevertheless government definition of property rights represents an importance difference between the public and private sectors. When government defines or redefines property rights, it changes the economic circumstances—including the wealth—of individuals in the private sector. For instance, when the federal government imposes price ceilings, as it did in 1971, it restrains the freedom of buyers and sellers in the market system. One purpose of economics is to analyze the effects of a government-ordered realignment of property rights on the efficiency of production.

We are inclined to think of property rights as being natural, a part of our birthright. The Declaration of Independence speaks of "certain inalienable rights," and it is hard to imagine a world without rights to property. In addition, government enforcement of property rights has an economic basis.

Recall the imaginary island world of only two people, Fred and Harry. Let's assume that initially, like Crusoe and Friday, they have neither rules

---

1. The absence of other human beings affected Crusoe's idea of what was useful. Discovering a coffer of gold and silver coins on the ship, he exclaimed, "Thou art not worth to me, no, not the taking off of the ground; one of those knives is worth all this heap." On second thought, however—perhaps after considering the possibility of rescue—Crusoe took the coins.

PERSPECTIVES
Sources of Income in the Public Sector

Government at all levels—local, state, and federal—is a major user of the nation's resources and a major buyer of its goods and services. It secures the funds for massive expenditures by borrowing money and by levying taxes on income, sales, and property.

At the national and state levels, most tax revenues come from personal and corporate income taxes. **Personal income taxes** are government revenues collected from individual earnings, after allowance for certain exemptions and deductions. Under federal tax law in 1988, individuals pay taxes on their gross earnings minus exemptions for dependents (taxpayer, spouse, and children) and deductions for certain expenses (interest payments on home mortgages, charitable contributions, and business expenses, among others). **Corporate income taxes** are government revenues collected on a corporation's computed profits, as reported on its profit and loss statements. A corporation's taxable profits are computed by subtracting its business expenses from its sales revenues.

Because of exemptions and deductions many people, including high income earners, pay no federal income taxes. Many other high income earners pay only a small percentage of their income in taxes. Most high income earners who pay little or no tax do so by purchasing municipal bonds, the interest on which is not taxed, or by investing in real estate and taking deductions for depreciation. Other ways of reducing taxes might include charitable contributions, deductions for legitimate business expenses (for example, office supplies and business travel), and personal expenses disguised as business expenses (lunches, home office expenses, and vacations).

Taxes on sales of various commodities also provide income for government. **Excise taxes** are taxes levied on specific products or services, for specific purposes. For instance, an excise tax on gasoline might be used to fund road construction and repair. Sometimes an excise tax is levied to discourage consumption of a product: many liquor taxes serve this purpose. Excise taxes are levied at all levels of government, primarily federal and state. They are normally a percentage of the purchase price. The **general sales tax**, a tax on most, but not necessarily all, consumer purchases, is another type of levy on sales. The tax is usually imposed by states, but in some areas local governments may share its revenues or raise the tax slightly.

The third source of tax revenues, property, is a major source of revenue for local government, as well as a minor source of revenue for most states and the federal government. The **property tax** is a tax on specified assets, usually real estate, cars and boats, household goods, bank account balances, and stocks and bonds.

The economic effect of all these taxes varies according to the way they are administered. In general, tax systems may be described as progressive, regressive, or proportional. A **progressive tax system** is any means of collecting government revenues in which the percentage of income that is paid in taxes rises with income. For example, a tax system in which the tax rate rises from 10 to

nor natural barriers to divide their spheres of interest. Furthermore, each man wants more than he can produce by himself. Each has two fundamental options for increasing his welfare. He can use his labor and other resources to produce goods and services, or he can steal. Fred and Harry can be expected to allocate their time in the most productive way. With no social or ethical barriers restricting their behavior, each man will steal from the other as long as theft is more rewarding than the production of goods and services. Each will then have to divert some of his resources into protecting

30 percent as income rises from $15,000 to $100,000 a year is progressive. Personal income taxes are generally progressive, as are corporate income taxes at the federal level. Property taxes are also progressive, since people with higher incomes tend to save and invest a higher percentage of their income in taxable property.

A **regressive tax system** is any means of collecting government revenues in which the percentage of income that is paid in taxes declines as income rises. Under a regressive tax system, as income rises from $15,000 to $100,000, the tax rate would fall—from 10 to 7 percent, for instance. The general sales tax is considered regressive, because lower income groups tend to spend a higher percentage of their incomes on consumer purchases than higher income groups. If a man earning $10,000 a year spends 98 percent of his income, a 5 percent general sales tax on those purchases constitutes 4.9 percent of his earned income. If a woman earning $100,000 a year spends 75 percent of her income, the same 5 percent sales tax works out to only 3.75 percent of her earned income.

A **proportional tax system** is any means of collecting government revenues in which all income earners pay the same tax rate. Under a proportional tax system, the tax rate might be 10 or 20 percent across the board. At the state level, corporate income taxes are often proportional. In South Carolina in 1988, the corporate income tax was a straight 7 percent.

The economic effect of a tax depends largely on the marginal (as opposed to average) tax rate. A **marginal tax rate** is the percentage of any additional income that is paid in taxation. An **average tax rate** is the percentage of total income that is paid in taxes. It is obtained by dividing total taxes paid by total taxable income. The federal income tax system is founded on progressive marginal tax rates. As income rises, additional earned income is taxed at higher and higher rates, up to a limit of 33 percent as of 1988. Thus the more income a person earns, the more tax he or she is forced to pay.

In all their forms, taxes tend to discourage the economic activity they are levied on. Income taxes, especially if they are progressive, can discourage people from earning a taxable income or from seeking a higher income through education or job training. Generally speaking, the higher the income tax rate, the less the incentive to earn an income, and the more the incentive to avoid taxes. High corporate taxes can discourage investment in corporations and retard the growth of industry. As already mentioned, excise taxes can—and are often intended to—reduce consumption of certain goods and services. General sales taxes can encourage consumer spending on the relatively few products and services—for example, food or clothing—that are not subject to the sales tax. Property taxes can discourage people from accumulating property and can encourage them to consume instead. In all of these ways, government tax policies can have a significant impact on general economic activity.

what he has produced (or stolen). Presumably this approach will eventually become counterproductive, and each will be investing so much in attacks and counterattacks that neither one of them will find further investment in the activity profitable.

In a limited economic sense, the resources Fred and Harry spend on stealing and preventing theft are wasted, for they are taken away from the production of new goods and services. If those resources were applied to production, total output would rise, and both Fred and Harry would be better off. The wastefulness of plunder is the economic principle that underlies the establishment of property rights. Through social contracts people restrict their behavior to avoid the heavier restraints associated with anarchy. The fear of being attacked on the streets at night can be far more confining than laws that restrict people from attacking one another. As John Locke wrote, "The end of law is not to abolish or restrain but to preserve and enlarge freedom."

Even when they recognize the benefits of a social contract, Fred and Harry may be tempted to chisel on the agreement. Fred may find that although he benefits from agreeing to property rights, he benefits even more if he then violates those rights (that is, as long as Harry does not retaliate). By stealing or otherwise ignoring Harry's rights, Fred can redistribute some of Harry's wealth to himself. Of course, if Harry retaliates, the two producers could end up back in a state of anarchy.

Thus the social contract can disintegrate because of individuals' offensive actions as they seek to improve their own positions. Defensive actions can also lead to a return to anarchy. Each citizen must consider what the other might do. Neither would want to be caught upholding an agreement while the other violates it. If Fred thinks Harry might violate his rights, he may violate Harry's rights first, or vice versa. Many wars and battles, both on the street and internationally, have been fought because one party was afraid the other would attack first.

To prevent violations both offensive and defensive, societies have developed police, court, and penal systems to protect the rights specified in the social contract. The costs of such systems may be high, but they are less than the costs of anarchy, in which resources would be diverted to predatory and defensive uses. The costs of making and enforcing the contract will determine just how extensive the contract is.

The social contract that defines property rights establishes only the limits of permissible behavior. Fred and Harry may not be satisfied with the property rights they have, even if they respect them. Both men will try to improve their individual well-being, most likely through socially approved trading arrangements. Suppose the only goods on their island are coconuts and papayas. The social contract specifies the division of fruits between Fred and Harry—whatever each can produce. Suppose also that the additional satisfaction each receives from the last coconut and papaya in his possession is as follows:

	Coconut	Papaya
Fred	10 utils	15 utils
Harry	90 utils	30 utils

Fred receives more satisfaction from his last papaya (15 utils) than from his last coconut (10 utils). He would be better off if he could trade a coconut (sacrificing 10 utils) for a papaya (gaining 15).[2] Harry, on the other hand,

_____

2. A util is the economist's name for a unit of satisfaction. We have no idea what a unit of satisfaction is, but it provides a measure that we need to make our point.

would receive more satisfaction from his last coconut; he would gladly trade a papaya for one more coconut. Thus Fred and Harry can be expected to exchange coconut and papaya rights until they can no longer gain from trade. We can also expect them to specialize in producing the fruit in which they have a comparative advantage (see Chapter 2 for a review of comparative advantage).

Government Production of Public Goods

▲ 3. Under what circumstances will markets "fail"?

The protection of property rights that undergirds Fred and Harry's system of specialization and trade requires certain services, such as police and court systems. These services, called public goods, are generally produced by government. They include goods and services that benefit all members of the community. By their nature, no one can be excluded from the benefits of public goods.

Unlike public goods, private goods benefit only those individuals who possess them. The benefits of a Snickers® bar, for example, are received exclusively by the person who eats it. If someone else wants a Snickers bar, a new one will have to be produced and purchased; it cannot be consumed simultaneously by two people. Because only one person can eat a particular candy bar, the producer can withhold it until payment is made, just as Fred and Harry can withhold fruit from the market until a favorable rate of exchange has been established. That is why private firms are willing and able to sell private goods.

By their very nature, public goods are not suited to private production. National defense is one of the best examples. No citizen can be denied the benefits of national defense; all are protected by it, more or less simultaneously. Thus the benefits of defense cannot be withheld from consumers until payment is made, as is usual in a free market system. Most people would not pay for goods that they could get free. Instead, they would take the free benefits and assume their payment would be so small that it would not be missed. In other words, they would free-ride on the payments of others. Few private firms would be willing to produce under such conditions, for they could not sell enough even to recover their costs. Consequently government must undertake the production and payment for this public good.

National defense is a relatively pure public good, in the sense that almost everyone in the community can benefit from it. Many government services are only partially shared, however, and not necessarily by those who provide the good. Care of the environment, education, and poverty relief would fall into this category. The argument for government provision here is that market exchanges in certain goods and services affect people other than the buyers and sellers. To use an economic term, the benefits (or costs) of such transactions are "externalized." Externalized costs are often referred to as externalities. **Externalities** are the positive (beneficial) or negative (harmful) effects that market exchanges have on people who do not participate directly in those exchanges. Externalities are third-party, or "spillover," effects.

Externalities: the positive (beneficial) or negative (harmful) effects that market exchanges have on people who do not participate directly in those exchanges. Third-party, or "spillover," effects.

External Benefits

External benefits: benefits of production and
consumption that are
received by people not
directly involved in the
production, consumption,
or exchange of a good.
Positive effects on some
third party.

Beneficial externalities are called external benefits. **External benefits** are benefits of production and consumption that are received by people not directly involved in the production, consumption, or exchange of a good. They are positive effects on some third party. Education is a good example of a service that provides external benefits. It helps both students and others in the community. Education equips people for more productive jobs and prepares them for their civic responsibilities.

The effects of external benefits can be illustrated graphically. Suppose the demand curve D_1 in Figure 4.2 reflects parents' private benefit from and demand for their children's education. The supply curve S reflects the supply of places in school. Without government intervention in the education market, the number of children attending school would be Q_1. However, if the external benefits of an education were added to parents' demand, demand would be D_2 instead of D_1. The vertical distance between D_1 and D_2 indicates the external benefits that are not being captured by the market system. Education is being underproduced by $Q_2 - Q_1$ places.

The government could remedy the underproduction by using some of its tax receipts to provide subsidies to parents with children in school. This move would push the demand for education to D_2, thus increasing the number of children in school to Q_2. Such a scheme would spread the cost of the external benefits among the people in the community who receive them.

Notice that government need not become directly involved in the production of education (that is, in running the schools) in order to correct the misallocation of resources. Education can be encouraged through subsidies to private schools or the pupils who attend them. Garbage collection, which

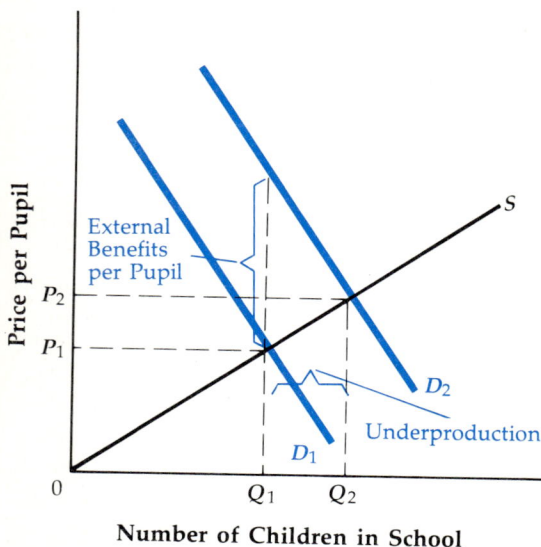

FIGURE 4.2 The External Benefits of Education
Given market supply and demand curves D_1 and S, only Q_1 people will be educated. If the external benefits of education were recognized by the market, demand would be D_2, and the number of people educated would be Q_2. Without government intervention in this market, education will be underproduced. The misallocation of resources can be corrected by a per pupil subsidy equal to the vertical distance between D_1 and D_2.

captures external health benefits, is often procured through contracts with private firms. Fire, police, and even penal correction services can be secured through government contract rather than government production.

External Costs

External costs: costs of production and consumption that are imposed on people not directly involved in the production, consumption, or exchange of a good. Negative effects on some third party.

Harmful externalities are called external costs. **External costs** are costs of production and consumption that are imposed on people not directly involved in the production, consumption, or exchange of a good. These are negative effects on some third party. Smoke pollution is an example of an external cost. It results from a process that benefits the producers of the pollution and consumers but harms others in the area.

The external cost of pollution can be shown graphically. Suppose that in Figure 4.3, the demand curve D represents car owners' demand for gasoline, which depends on their demand for driving, and that S_1 represents the costs refineries incur in producing the gasoline. In the competitive market, the equilibrium price will be P_1 and the equilibrium quantity will be Q_2. When car owners drive, however, they pollute the atmosphere, causing other people discomfort or even ill health. This cost of gasoline use is just as real as refiners' costs of hiring labor and buying crude oil, but *it is not paid by refiners or drivers* and so is not included in supply curve S_1. If it were, the supply curve would shift to S_2, and the equilibrium gasoline price and quantity would be P_2 and Q_1. In other words, consumers of gasoline would have to pay a higher price and would cut back on their use of the product.

Thus if producers and consumers are not required to pay for pollution costs, they will overuse gasoline by $Q_2 - Q_1$ gallons. In this sense, resources have been misallocated. Social welfare would be increased if less gasoline

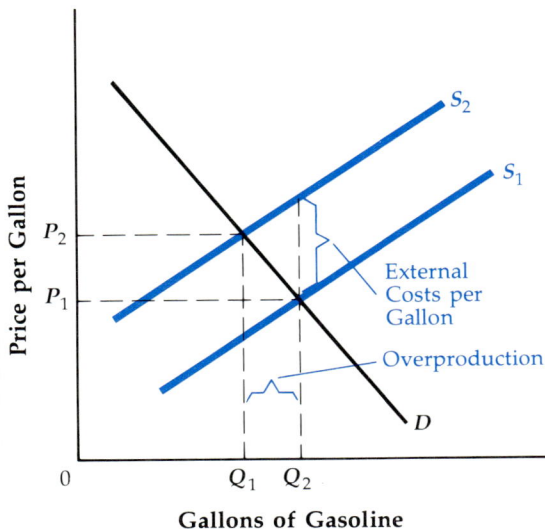

FIGURE 4.3   The External Costs of Pollution
Given market supply and demand curves S_1 and D, the number of gallons of gasoline sold will be Q_2. If producers had to pay the external costs of pollution associated with gasoline use, however, the supply curve would be S_2 and the number of gallons sold would be Q_1. Without government intervention, gasoline will be overproduced. To correct the misallocation of resources, government can impose a tax on each gallon of gasoline sold, which will shift the supply curve to S_2 and reduce the quantity of gasoline sold to Q_1.

The Threatened Social Security System

The Social Security system has enjoyed wide-spread support since its establishment during the Great Depression. Designed originally to provide workers with monthly benefits on retirement at age sixty-five, the program has been expanded over the years to include dependents' and survivors' benefits, and disability and health care insurance. Social Security now covers over 90 percent of the work force. In 1984 nearly $210 billion in cash benefits was paid—about 20 percent of total federal expenditures.

The system is both an insurance and a welfare program. As insurance, Social Security payments were intended to replace part of the earnings workers lost when they retired. The program was therefore financed through a special payroll tax, assessed against part of a worker's income. The payroll tax was essentially an insurance premium, entitling participants to a government annuity in their old age, based to a limited extent on the amount paid into the system.

Social Security benefits are not based solely on taxes, however. Some benefits are paid on the basis of need, regardless of an individual's contributions to the plan. For example, benefits favor low-income workers. And workers with dependents can receive more benefits than single workers with identical employment histories.

Social Security has been criticized on several grounds. First, it is a regressive tax, one that places the heaviest burden on the low-income group it was designed to help. If the Social Security system had never been established, the nation's elderly poor would most likely be provided for through welfare programs, which are financed by the progressive income tax. As it is, elderly poor people who qualify for public assistance in addition to Social Security receive less than they would without the Social Security program. Yet they were taxed heavily in their working years for the privilege of receiving Social Security. And the poor tend to be taxed longer than the rich, who can delay entering the labor force by extending their schooling. And because low-income and minority groups typically have shorter life-spans, they do not collect benefits as long as the rich.

Second, the goals of welfare and insurance are financially incompatible. Social Security cannot provide extensive welfare benefits and still remain a sound insurance program. The taxes collected by the Social Security Administration are not saved and invested, but are paid out almost immediately to those receiving benefits. People who retired in the early days of the program, most of whom were not poor, received enormous windfalls from Social Security, paid for by younger people.

---

were used. The overuse might be corrected with a tax on gasoline production, equal to the vertical distance between S_1 and S_2. If producers have to pay such a tax, the supply curve will shift to S_2, the price will be bid up, and consumers will cut back on their consumption of gasoline.

Government Protection of Common Access Resources

◢ **4. Why are some resources overused and abused?**

It may seem that in the ideal economy everyone would have the right to use all resources, goods, and services, and no one—not even the state—would have the right to exclude anyone from their use. In fact, the rights to many

At first this redistribution of income worked, because many workers were paying into the program and relatively few were collecting benefits. But today the system is threatened by financial insolvency. In 1950, there were sixteen workers for each beneficiary. Today that ratio is just three to one, and it may decline to two to one by the year 2035. The average retiree today receives five times more in benefits than he or she has paid into the program, even after allowing for the interest those payments could have earned if invested. Many younger workers will be less fortunate. They will receive a low rate of return on their taxes, probably less than if they had invested their money elsewhere.

Some economists argue that Social Security discourages working and saving. If individuals view the payroll tax as a form of forced saving, they are likely to reduce their personal saving for retirement. And if Social Security payments raise their marginal tax rate, they are likely to work fewer hours. These adverse effects of Social Security may be overstated, however. Social Security may simply have replaced the private, pay-as-you-go support systems once operated by families. And to the extent that Social Security enables people to retire earlier, it may encourage them to save more to achieve that goal.

Regardless of the system's past effects, Social Security now promises more in future benefits than can be delivered by its expected collections. Various proposals have been advanced to put the system back on a sound footing. In 1983 Congress took steps that will delay bankruptcy of the system until sometime in the twenty-first century. Payroll taxes have been raised; coverage has been extended to new groups of workers; cost-of-living adjustments have been delayed; benefits above certain thresholds will be taxed; and the retirement age will be gradually raised. Future shortfalls might be financed by either slowing the growth of future benefits or finding new sources of revenue. More radical proposals would eliminate the program's welfare function, transferring that responsibility to traditional welfare programs. Some people would even transfer the program's insurance function to private retirement funds, abolishing the government-run Social Security system in the process.

Common access resources: resources owned in common instead of privately by individuals. Thus individuals may not be excluded from their use.

scarce resources are held "in common," or communally, with only minimal restrictions, if any, on their use. When access to resources is open to almost everyone, they are called common access resources. **Common access resources** are resources that are owned in common instead of privately by individuals. Thus individuals may not be excluded from their use. Rights to the use of a college or university's facilities are frequently held in common. As long as a student conforms to certain rules and regulations, he or she cannot be excluded from the use of the library, the parking lots, and other common facilities. The rights to city parks are also held communally. For several millennia before whites immigrated to this continent, Indian tribes held communal rights to hunting grounds. During the early part of the nineteenth century, whites living on the prairie held communal grazing rights. Anyone could let cattle loose on the plains. (The United States government claimed the right to exclude people from the plains but did not exercise it.)

Communal property rights can be employed efficiently if (1) there is more than enough of the resource to go around—in other words, there is no cost to its use; or (2) the people who use the resource account fully for the effects of their use on others. Unless one of these two conditions is met, the resource will tend to be overused.

While a common access resource is being used, it is in effect the temporary private property of the user. Yet the users pay nothing for the privilege. Freeway drivers get a toll-free trip on a well-engineered road. If they are rational, they will use the road until the trip is not worth the cost to them in time and gas. One cost they may overlook, however, especially as it applies to themselves personally, is the alternative use to which their space might have been put by other drivers. (Environmentalists argue that many roads should never have been built. The alternative use in that case would have been scenery.) Increased highway congestion and the discomfort of other drivers are other hidden costs. These external costs, sometimes called social costs, of driving are just as important as other costs. Because drivers do not incur such costs themselves, however, they are effectively subsidized by others. Thus drivers will tend to overuse the road.

To lessen highway congestion the government could impose a tax on gasoline or a toll on road use. Drivers might then have to pay the true cost of their use of the road and would be encouraged to cut back on their driving. The government could turn the road into private property, giving the new owners the right to charge for its use. Such a solution would have essentially the same effect, reducing the use of the road. The main difference is that the revenues collected would go directly to individuals instead of to the government—a result that is either good or bad depending on one's personal values.

Monopoly: a sole seller of a good or service. Because a monopoly has no competitors, it can cut back on production (thus limiting the quantity supplied), charge higher prices, and reap greater profits than other firms.

If the road is privately owned and no alternate mode of transportation is available, the owners may overcharge. In doing so they would be exploiting a monopoly on transportation. A (pure) **monopoly** is a sole seller of a good or service. Because a monopoly has no competitors, it can cut back on production (thus limiting the quantity supplied), charge higher prices, and reap greater profits than other firms. For that matter, the state may also overcharge, acting like a monopolist. Although state agencies may not make a profit in the normal sense of the term, their revenues can be used to improve the salaries and working conditions of state employees. The question is whether the drawbacks of state or private use outweigh the drawbacks of communal use.

Some additional examples will help clarify the problems associated with communal ownership of common access resources.

Air and Water

Although federal and state governments hold the rights to the nation's water and airways, until recently they have not asserted much control over the use of these communal resources. Pollution has been the unhappy result. In dumping waste into the air and rivers, polluters are using a common access resource as if it were their own. Owners of private property generally exact payments for its use, but when polluters draw a common access resource away from an alternative use, like unspoiled scenery, no one reimburses society for the loss. No one compensates the people who live next to a plant with billowing smokestacks for their eye irritation or the additional paint jobs their homes require.

Pollution is often seen as a product of antisocial behavior, as indeed it often may be. Many who pollute simply do not care about what they do to others. However, much pollution results from a failure to recognize that individual behavior has an effect on the environment. The person who drops a cigarette butt to the ground may believe that littering on that scale cannot materially affect anyone's sensibilities. If everyone follows the same line of reasoning, however, the cigarette butts will accumulate into an eyesore. Even then an individual may reason that his own behavior has little effect one way or the other. This type of reasoning, of course, is a powerful argument against communal rights.

Endangered Species

The hunting grounds of the Labrador Peninsula were originally held in common by Indian tribes. All Indians could hunt as they wished without fear of exclusion. Because of the difficulty of hunting and the limited demand for meat, skins, and bones, the area was not overhunted, and wildlife flourished. With the emergence of the European fur trade, however, the value of skins skyrocketed, encouraging the Indians to hunt beyond the area's natural capacity.

Once again communal rights were to blame. Hunters did not have to consider how their actions affected other hunters' ability to trap and hunt. Yet when one hunter killed a beaver, the task of hunting was made more difficult for others. Unlimited hunting imposed a social cost much like the cost imposed by unlimited driving. Moreover, hunters had little incentive to avoid excessive trapping. If one hunter did not kill a beaver, another would. The Labrador Indians solved the problem of overkill by assigning private property rights to portions of their hunting grounds. Because he could exclude others, each hunter had incentive to control his take from the land.

Not all endangered species can be saved so easily. Whales have been hunted for centuries, but the threat of extinction is relatively recent. Until about two hundred years ago people did not have the technology to kill whales faster than the whales could reproduce. Theoretically, the problem could be solved in the same way as the beaver problem, through the establishment of private property rights. Some whales, however, migrate through six thousand miles of ocean annually. Establishing and enforcing private property rights over such a wide expanse, to say nothing of working out the international legal complications, would doubtless prove costly. Whales will probably remain communal property, and the species' survival will continue to be threatened.

Communal property rights can also influence the methods of hunters. In the 1970s the Canadian government in effect declared the first fifty thousand baby seals killed annually to be a common access resource. Rights to the seals were allocated communally on a first-come, first-served basis, a rationing system that encouraged hunters to act quickly and ruthlessly.

> The Canadian government permitted no more than 50,000 animals to be taken, so hunters worked with speed to make their kills before the legal maximum was reached. They swarmed over the ice floes and crushed the babies' skulls with heavy clubs. Government offices received many protests that the seals were unhumanely clubbed (by humans) and often skinned alive.[3]

Public Property

In a condominium development in Blacksburg, Virginia, most of the grounds are held communally by the owners' association. By contract, all owners must become dues-paying members of the association and contribute their share toward the cost of upkeep. Thus no one can free-ride on the groundskeeping efforts of others, and the grounds are reasonably well kept, even though communally owned.

Not all the land in the development is held communally, however. Each unit comes with its own small back yard, which is the unit owner's responsibility. To encourage the upkeep of these yards, the condominium association bought lawn mowers, garden tools, and grass seed and stored them in a communal shed. This communal property was abused. Within a few months the garden tools had mysteriously disappeared. After a year the lawn mowers fell apart from rough use and lack of maintenance. The grass seed too seemed to disappear rapidly, though enough had been purchased to cover the entire community several times.

The argument for the purchase of communally held tools and seed had been economies of scale. It seemed more efficient to have one lawn mower for all than one for each small back yard. The system never achieved the planned economies, however, because residents had no incentive to use communal property with care. Like the whale and seal hunters, the members of the association fell victim to the negative effects inherent in communal property rights.

Communal property rights do not always bring this type of problem. The family is an institution in which much property is owned communally and with tolerably efficient results. In many cases, however, government intervention of some kind is necessary to prevent overuse and abuse of common access resources.

Government Provision of Income Security and Health Insurance

▲ 5. How can government-provided income-security programs be justified?

Government programs to guarantee incomes and provide health insurance are often justified on ethical grounds. If enough people feel that citizens are entitled to a minimum standard of living, income security can be viewed

3. Armen A. Alchian and Harold Demsetz, "The Property Rights Paradigm," *Journal of Economic History* 33 (March 1973), p. 20.

as a good for which there is a demand, like any other good. Government simply produces this good for the same reason a farmer produces apples.

In addition to helping recipients, some argue, income security increases the general social welfare. As income rises, the value of each additional dollar of income diminishes, for people generally satisfy their most pressing needs and wants first. Additional income is used to satisfy less pressing needs and wants. Hence if some income is taken from the well-off and given to the poor, the transferred money will be put to better use. Opponents of income redistribution would counter that the value of income is just as great for the well-off as for the poor. Therefore income redistribution would not improve societal welfare.

Suppose we accept that income security is a worthwhile service. Why should it be provided by government? The answer generally given is that externalities make private provision unworkable. If contributions to welfare programs were private and voluntary, many people might refrain from contributing, reasoning that they would not gain as much benefit from the program as others. Others might reason that they as individuals could abstain without jeopardizing the benefits to others. If enough people withheld support, contributions might not cover the benefits paid out under the program. From this perspective, income security programs can be seen as an effort to overcome the external benefit problem—that is, underproduction in the private sector.

Government Stabilization of the Economy

▲ 6. What can government do to stabilize the economy?

Macroeconomic policy: the manipulation of taxes, federal expenditures, and the money supply to promote a high and stable level of employment and production, price level stability, and economic growth.

Throughout history, the general level of economic activity has fluctuated in business cycles. Sometimes overall economic activity rises, increasing the nation's output and employment. At other times it declines, decreasing production and throwing people out of work. Until recently the U.S. government has generally not attempted to interfere with these economic swings. Since the 1940s, however, the federal government has increasingly tried to use macroeconomic policy to control the overall level of economic activity, including prices, output, and employment and unemployment. **Macroeconomic policy** is the manipulation of taxes, federal expenditures, and the money supply to promote a high and stable level of employment and production, price level stability, and economic growth.

This change in attitude was spurred by the writings of John Maynard Keynes, a British economist whose theory of business cycles was published during the Great Depression. Keynes believed that swings in economic activity were caused by changes in the demand for goods and services by consumers, government, and business. Government could moderate those swings, he taught, by monitoring and if necessary stimulating or restraining demand for goods and services.

Fiscal policy: the manipulation of federal expenditures and taxes to promote a high and stable level of employment and production, price level stability, and economic growth.

Just what the government should do to moderate swings in the economy remains a highly controversial question. Keynesians argue for the manipulation of fiscal policy, meaning taxes and expenditures. **Fiscal policy** (also called budgetary policy) is the manipulation of federal expenditures and taxes to promote a high and stable level of employment and

DIALOGUE

The Rush to "Privatize"

New York Times Editors

"Privatization" means the opposite of "nationalization," but until just a few years ago, the tendency was all one way. Selling or giving away public property was just a gleam in the eye of a few free-market zealots. Nowadays, the idea of privatization is generating enthusiasm from the Potomac to the Ganges.

The British Government has sold off aerospace, communications, oil, hotel and trucking companies and plans to sell British Airways, Rolls-Royce and the London Water Authority. Japan's Government is auctioning off telephone, airline, rail and tobacco companies. Turkey's has sold the bridge across the Bosporus.

In America, coalitions of environmentalists, budget cutters and free-marketeers are pressing for the sale of Federal grazing and timberlands, hydropower and irrigation water. President Reagan urges the sale of Conrail. Budget Director James Miller reportedly favors privatizing Government functions like home mortgage insurance, small-airport traffic control and postal service.

The global trend owes much to the failure of socialism or traditional statism to raise living standards or redress economic injustices. But the wisdom of trying to stimulate growth by converting public ownership to private should be measured case by case. If privatization is not be become a discredited fad, there needs to be an analytic framework for picking potential winners.

Consider what privatization might, and might not, do:

It cannot ease the credit crunch caused by budget deficits. Selling public property for cash does indeed reduce a government's measured deficit. That seems to be why White House budget cutters are tempted to sell off the Federal Housing Administration. But unlike a tax increase or spending reduction, that would not reduce private wealth or income. So it cannot cut consumption and thus would not reduce interest rates or liberate capital for more productive uses.

It can't relieve a government of its social responsibilities. Private enterprise may be able to deliver essential public services like mass transit, sanitation, education or parks, with less waste. Scottsdale,

Ariz., for example, saves $2 million a year by hiring a private firefighting contractor. But the reluctance of people to pay for services they once got "free" should not be confused with an increase in efficiency. For example, the inability of poor people to afford private college tuitions does not mean delivering the service at public expense is not worth the cost. Nor does it justify the recent decision of firefighters in Salem, Ark., to let a house burn because the owner had failed to pay his fire protection dues.

It isn't likely to make monopolies more efficient. State-owned airlines, like British Airways, are typically less well managed and employ labor less productively than private lines. But that is usually due to the lack of competition, not public ownership. Regulated monopolies, public or private, that can easily pass on costs to consumers have little reason to economize.

But privatization may reduce incentives for waste. Government agencies that sell scarce resources, like irrigation water or hydropower, often find it politically impossible to charge private customers for their real value. The result, in cases like the Westlands Water District in central California, is profligate use, even as Los Angeles spends hundreds of millions to develop new sources of water. Letting the Westlands farmers resell the water at market rates would eliminate their incentive to squander the resource.

And privatization may temper political demands for inefficient operations. State-run businesses that depend on government subsidies, like Amtrak, are rarely able to cancel uneconomical services or to dismiss employees. Privatizing such companies doesn't eliminate the public pressure. But in America, where subsidizing money-losing private companies is not traditional, it may shift the burden to those who want to maintain the services.

Privatization is not a cure for every economic ailment. But the spreading skepticism about public enterprises offers opportunities to re-examine them with an eye to raising productivity and paring unjustifiable government subsidies. The tough job ahead is to mold that trendy skepticism into enduring economic improvements.

te">*New York Times*, January 13, 1986. © 1986 by The New York Times Company. Reprinted by permission.

Why Privatize?

Stuart M. Butler, Heritage Foundation

A remarkable trend in recent years has been the enthusiastic embrace by many countries of the policy of "privatization"; that is, the transfer of government functions in whole or in part to the private sector. In places as different as Japan and Jamaica, Britain and the People's Republic of China, governments are reversing the once-common policy of "nationalization," the direct government control or ownership of economic activity.

This privatization trend takes three main forms. The most widespread outside the United States is the *sale of government assets.* Britain, for instance, has sold several nationalized companies to the general public, ranging from the entire telephone system to the Jaguar sports car company. It has also sold more than 1 million public housing units to their existing tenants. The second form, common in the United States, is *contracting* with private companies or organizations to deliver government services, such as garbage pickup or bus services. The third is the use of *vouchers,* where the government provides financial assistance to individuals that is restricted to the purchase of specified goods and services, and then the recipient spends those vouchers in the private sector. In the United States, such vouchers are provided to the poor to help them rent decent housing (the Reagan administration's housing voucher program) and to obtain food (the Food Stamp program, started during the Johnson administration).

Why are so many governments adopting such privatization policies? There are several reasons, but two rank as the most important:

Increasing economic efficiency: Privatization is part of the general worldwide movement away from central planning and public ownership. Government control of key parts of the economy was meant to bring efficiency and democratic control but resulted instead in spiraling subsidies and inefficient bureaucratization. Selling nationalized firms to private investors—or public housing units to tenants—introduces incentives that lead to better economic uses of the assets. Contracting and the use of vouchers allows the government or a subsidized individual to purchase services from private firms on the basis of the best value for money.

The key to improved efficiency, of course, is competition, so needless to say, the benefits of privatization are reduced if only one contractor is available or if a public monopoly is merely turned into a private monopoly (although there *are* still gains in this case since the cost of political interference is removed). For this reason, Britain, which chose in the early 1980s to sell nationwide utilities as regulated monopolies, is now restructuring utilities prior to sale, to ensure a greater degree of effective competition.

Improving public finances: Greater efficiency from contracting or vouchers means lower costs for government-sponsored services and hence budget savings. This makes privatization an attractive strategy for politicians of varying political persuasions. In addition, asset sales can lead to large inflows of cash for a financially strapped government. This has led some economists to criticize asset sales as a "smoke-and-mirrors" budget device with no net economic or public finance impact. That is faulty analysis. Besides the benefits to the national economy of debureaucratization, the taxpayer gains because the market price of the asset up for sale reflects a valuation based on higher potential performance in the private sector. Hence the sales revenue is higher than the present value of the future stream of income from the asset in (less efficient) government hands.

Privatization does not mean that government is abrogating its responsibilities. When a society, through its representative system, instructs government to make sure that a certain goal is achieved, or service provided, that does not mean government itself necessarily is the best vehicle to undertake that action. Increasingly, governments are recognizing that through privatization, the powerful incentives and efficiency of private ownership and markets can be utilized to achieve public purposes much more effectively than by direct government provision.

Stuart M. Butler, Ph.D., is director of Domestic Policy Studies at The Heritage Foundation, a public policy research organization in Washington, D.C.

Monetary policy: the manipulation of the rate of growth of the nation's money supply to promote price level stability and a high and stable level of employment and production.

production, price level stability, and economic growth. Monetarists, in contrast, maintain that business swings are caused largely by changes in the rate of growth of the nation's money stock. These economists recommend that the government moderate the swings through monetary policy. **Monetary policy** is the manipulation of the rate of growth of the nation's money supply to promote price level stability and a high and stable level of employment and production. Much of our study of economics will involve the implications of these and other theories for government policy. Here we need only stress that stabilization of the nation's economic activity has come to be a major function of government.

The Shortcomings of Government Action

◢ **7. What are the shortcomings of government actions?**

In this and the last chapter, we discussed some of the shortcomings of the market system: an inability to provide public goods; the existence of external costs and benefits; and distortion in the allocation of resources by monopolies. The free market system does not always use the economy's scarce resources efficiently, but it does not follow that government should always attempt to correct market failures. Government too has its shortcomings.

All government action requires the use of scarce resources—and they will not necessarily be used more efficiently than in the private sector. A private monopoly may distort the allocation of resources, but the distortion may be slight compared with the cost of an antitrust suit against the monopoly. Cigarette smokers may throw their butts on the ground, but the cost of their pollution may be less than that of an antilitter campaign.

Government is itself a kind of monopoly. Because it faces no competition in many of its activities, it can become quite inefficient, distorting the allocation of resources, reducing the quality of the goods and services produced, or increasing their price. The U.S. Postal Service can afford to charge monopoly prices for first-class mail service precisely because the law prohibits private firms from entering that market.

Chapter Review

Review of Key Questions

◢   *1. What does government do?*

Governments at all levels make a substantial share of all purchases of goods and services produced in the country. The federal government alone spends more than $1 trillion a year (or about a quarter of total domestic production).

◢   *2. What are the economic functions of government?*

The economic functions of government include: defining and protecting property rights; providing public goods like national defense; reducing the inefficiencies associated with external costs and benefits; protecting common access resources; providing for the public's health and security; and stabilizing overall economic activity. Government establishment and enforcement of property rights increases production by

freeing producers from the need to engage in wasteful conflicts over
property. Where property rights are defined and protected, markets will
emerge, and mutually beneficial trades will be made.

◢   *3. Under what circumstances will markets "fail"?*

   Markets will fail to produce efficient levels of public goods and services. This is because people cannot be charged for the benefits received
from public goods and services. (They can be excluded from the consumption of private goods.) Markets will also result in "overproduction"
in the presence of external costs and "underproduction" in the presence
of external benefits. Finally, markets may result in underproduction of
goods and services produced by private firms that have a significant degree of monopoly power.

◢   *4. Why are some resources overused and abused?*

   Markets will fail to operate efficiently when property rights are neither well defined nor firmly enforced. Failure to define property rights
frequently results in overuse and abuse of resources. Common access
resources are inefficiently used partly because no one has the power to
exclude users and to charge for their use.

◢   *5. How can government-provided income-security programs be justified?*

   Government income-security programs are often justified because
they improve the fairness of the income distribution. On economic
grounds, they are justified as a means of providing the public good of
poverty relief. Private payments to aid the poor have external effects;
that is, they improve the welfare of people who do not make the contributions. Without income-security payments from government, poverty-
relief programs would be "underproduced."

◢   *6. What can government do to stabilize the economy?*

   Economists disagree as to whether and how government should try
to stabilize the economy. Some recommend the use of fiscal policy,
others the use of monetary policy. (The controversies surrounding appropriate stabilization policies will be studied under macroeconomics.)

◢   *7. What are the shortcomings of government actions?*

   Like the free market system it sometimes attempts to correct, government is far from perfect in an economic sense. Its actions can be ex-
cessively costly and even monopolistic.

Further Topics

Markets depend on property rights, which form the basis of trade. The
private sector of our economy depends on the government to define and
enforce property rights. In establishing the political and economic framework for trade, government performs an essential economic function.
   Government has many other functions, some more essential than
others. Government sometimes acts as a producer in order to correct for
inefficiencies created by external costs and benefits or to produce public
goods that cannot be provided privately. It may also use its power to tax
to provide goods and services not traditionally among its responsibilities,
such as public welfare services. Although economists are certainly not

opposed to the relief of economic distress, many of them are becoming increasingly concerned with the inefficiencies of government attempts to promote the national well-being.

Review of New Terms

Average tax rate The percentage of total income that is paid in taxes, obtained by dividing total taxes paid by total taxable income.

Budget deficit The amount by which outlays exceed receipts during any given accounting period.

Budget surplus The amount by which receipts exceed outlays during a given accounting period.

Common access resources Resources owned in common instead of privately by individuals. Thus individuals may not be excluded from their use.

Corporate income taxes Government revenues collected on a corporation's computed profits, as reported on its profit and loss statements. A corporation's taxable profits are computed by subtracting its business expenses from its sales revenues.

Excise taxes Taxes levied on specific products or services, for specific purposes. Excise taxes are normally a percentage of the purchase price.

External benefits Benefits of production and consumption that are received by people not directly involved in the production, consumption, or exchange of a good. Positive effects on some third party.

External costs Costs of production and consumption that are imposed on people not directly involved in the production, consumption, or exchange of a good. Negative effects on some third party.

Externalities The positive (beneficial) or negative (harmful) effects that market exchanges have on people who do not participate directly in those exchanges. Third-party, or "spillover," effects.

Fiscal policy The manipulation of federal expenditures and taxes to promote a high and stable level of employment and production, price level stability, and economic growth.

General sales tax A tax on most, but not necessarily all, consumer purchases. Sales taxes are usually levied by states, but some local governments may share its revenues or raise the tax slightly.

Macroeconomic policy The manipulation of taxes, federal expenditures, and the money supply to promote a high and stable level of employment and production, price level stability, and economic growth.

Marginal tax rate The percentage of any additional income that is paid in taxation.

Monetary policy The manipulation of the rate of growth of the nation's money supply to promote price level stability and a high and stable level of employment and production.

Monopoly A sole seller of a good or service. Because a monopoly has no competitors, it can cut back on production (thus limiting the quantity supplied), charge higher prices, and reap greater profits than other firms.

Personal income taxes Government revenues collected from individual earnings, after allowance for certain exemptions and deductions.

Private sector All the economic transactions undertaken voluntarily by individuals, either alone or in association with others.

Progressive tax system Any means of collecting government revenues in which the percentage of income that is paid in taxes rises with income.

Property rights Legally defined and permissible uses, both private and collective, of resources, goods, and services.

Property tax A tax on specified assets, usually real estate, cars and boats, household goods, bank account balances, and stocks and bonds.

Proportional tax system Any means of collecting government revenues in which all income earners pay the same tax rate.

Public sector The activities of federal, state, and local government.

Regressive tax system Any means of collecting government revenues in which the percentage of income that is paid in taxes declines as income rises.

Review Questions

1. What are property rights? Why do they exist? (◢ 1)

2. In economic terms, describe the causes of the pollution of some portion of your environment. (◢ 3)

3. How is the cost of enforcement related to the existence of property rights? What might be the effect of an increase in the cost of enforcement? A decrease? (◢ 4)

4. "Government can correct for inefficiencies due to external benefits by subsidizing producers and/or consumers." Do you agree? Illustrate your answer with supply and demand curves. (◢ 3, ◢ 4)

5. "Government can correct for the external costs of pollution by imposing taxes on the pollutants firms emit or on the products they produce." Do you agree? Explain your answer with supply and demand curves. (◢ 3, ◢ 4)

6. Economists frequently refer to national defense as a public good. What does that term mean? If national defense benefits everyone, why do so many people demonstrate against it? (◢ 2)

7. Name ten government-administered programs and give an economic justification for each. Which if any of those programs could be "privatized"—that is, turned over to private firms or produced by private firms with government subsidies? (◢ 2, ◢ 5, ◢ 6)

8. Why are criticisms of government activity so prevalent? (◢ 7)

PART II

The Macroeconomy

Measurements of the Macroeconomy

"But 'glory' doesn't mean 'a nice knock-down argument,'" Alice objected.

"When I use a word," Humpty Dumpty said in a rather scornful tone, "it means just what I choose it to mean—neither more nor less."

"The question is," said Alice, "whether you can make words mean so many different things."

"The question is," said Humpty Dumpty, "which is to be the master—that's all."

Lewis Carroll

KEY QUESTIONS

▲ 1. Why is GNP the most common measure of economic production for the macroeconomy?

▲ 2. What are the deficiencies of GNP statistics?

▲ 3. What are other non-GNP measures of productive activity in the macroeconomy?

▲ 4. What does the unemployment rate measure?

▲ 5. What are the shortcomings of unemployment rate statistics?

▲ 6. What is inflation and how is it estimated in the macroeconomy?

NEW TERMS

Consumer price index (CPI)
Consumer unit
Disposable personal income
Expenditure approach
Final goods and services
Gross national product (GNP)
Hidden unemployment
Implicit GNP price deflator index
Inflation
Intermediate goods and services
Labor force
Labor force participation rate
Measure of (or net) economic welfare (MEW or NEW)

National income
Net national product (NNP)
Nominal, money, or current dollar gross national product
Personal income
Producer price index (PPI)
Real (or constant dollar) gross national product
Resource cost-income approach
Underemployed workers
Underground economy
Unemployment rate
Value added

Our era is replete with macroeconomic problems. In newspaper headlines and news broadcasts, these problems are referred to as "recession," "unemployment," "inflation," "idle industrial capacity," "retarded economic growth," and "stagflation." In plainer language, they are lost production, lost income, rising prices, quiet factories, a stalled standard of living, and economic stagnation coupled with rising prices.

What can and should be done to correct these problems? That is the central question of the macroeconomic policy debates that greet us almost daily in the news media, and the central question of macroeconomics itself. Twenty years ago, economists generally agreed on the policies the government should follow to reach acceptable levels of national production, employment, and inflation. Years of high inflation and unemployment, both here and abroad, however, have shown how difficult it is for government, constrained by political reality, to achieve its stated policy objectives. In fact, many economists now suspect that government policy has increased unemployment and inflation—that the nation would have been better off without the government's attempts to alter overall economic performance. Others argue that to reduce unemployment and inflation, government must exercise even more powerful and direct control over the economy.

The following chapters attempt to develop an understanding of this issue. First, to appreciate the magnitude and complexity of our macroeconomic problems, we must consider the problem of how to measure macroeconomic activity. This chapter covers macroeconomic measurement, and Chapter 6 outlines macroeconomic problems and policies. Then we must understand how the macroeconomy works, or how conditions in the various parts of the economy affect general economic activity—employment, production, incomes, and prices. Finally, we must appreciate the conflicts and tradeoffs that accompany policymakers' attempts to manipulate the macroeconomy.

Macroeconomic theory and policy are treated in depth in Chapters 8 through 16.

Measurement is important in macroeconomics, for inaccurate or misleading measures can distort the statistics upon which government policy decisions are based. We must be able to track accurately the performance of the economy if we are to have a chance to adopt productive policies. Among the many ways of measuring macroeconomic activity, the most important are: (1) gross and net national product, precise although sometimes arbitrary measures of overall national production; (2) national, personal, and disposable income, measures of consumer buying power before and after taxes; (3) the unemployment rate, a measure of people's inability to find work; and (4) the inflation rate, a measure of any sustained increase in the general price level, with appropriate adjustments made for changes in the quality of the commodities involved.

Gross National Product (GNP)

▲ **1. Why is GNP the most common measure of economic production for the macroeconomy?**

Measuring gross national product, or total production of goods and services, allows economists and policymakers to evaluate a nation's economic progress over a period of years and to monitor the impact of government policy on production and incomes. It also enables economists to test their theories of how the macroeconomy works against real-world data and government officials to develop policies that will increase the nation's production. It is not meant to be a subjective measure of economic welfare. GNP statisticians merely count the output objectively, but make no subjective evaluations of their data.

Businesspeople use general economic data as they plan for future production. They understand that the sales of their product depend in part on the level of production in the economy as a whole. Automobile producers, for example, realize that the income and productivity of workers in other industries will influence the number of cars sold. If production is down elsewhere, people will earn less money and have less to spend on automobiles. With data on recent and current economic activity, businesspeople can estimate roughly how much they should produce to meet future market demand, or how much to spend on raw materials and labor.

Thus, any measurement of the nation's economic pulse does more than record what has happened in the past; it also influences future policy. Figures showing that prices have been rising too fast can create public dissatisfaction, which may well influence future government policy. If figures show that production has dropped sharply in some sectors of the economy, businesses in other sectors of the economy may cut back on their production, thereby contributing to the slump. In short, economic measures like the GNP themselves affect the economy. The methods used in calculating such data are therefore crucial to macroeconomic policy debates.

Definition of GNP

Gross national product (GNP): the current market value in dollars of all final goods and services produced in the economy in a given period.

Although there are many ways to measure the nation's general level of economic activity, the one used most often in developing government policy, and cited most often in the news media, is the gross national product (GNP). **Gross national product (GNP)** is the current market value in dollars of all final goods and services produced in the economy in a given period. Certain key words in this definition must be stressed. First, national production is measured in terms of current market value, which means current market prices. Market prices sometimes overstate (and sometimes understate) the intrinsic value of goods. To that extent, GNP may be distorted as a measure of general social welfare. For instance, the public production of government services such as fire and police protection and schools is reported at cost. Therefore higher-cost, more inefficient government services are assigned a higher output value than lower-cost efficient ones! All goods and services count at their dollar value with no distinction made between schools, hospitals, or cigarettes. GNP also includes the social "bads" that result from production, such as pollution and congestion, as well as goods designed to remedy them.

Final goods and services: those goods and services that are purchased by their ultimate users rather than for further processing or resale.

Second, only final goods and services are included in GNP. **Final goods and services** are those goods and services that are purchased by their ultimate users rather than for further processing or resale. GNP excludes the dollar value of intermediate goods used in the production process. **Intermediate goods and services** are goods and services that are purchased for further processing in producing another good or service for resale. If intermediate goods were included in GNP, the total value of the nation's production would be vastly overstated. All intermediate goods would be counted at least twice—once when they are sold to be used in the production of final goods and again when the final products are sold.

Intermediate goods and services: goods and services that are purchased for further processing in producing another good or service for resale.

Value Added

Value added: amount of additional market value or income created at any stage of production.

Consider the intermediate good wheat, for instance. Wheat is used to make flour, an intermediate good used to make bread. The table below shows sales price (total revenue) and the **value added**—i.e., the amount of additional market value or income created at any stage of production—of given quantities of wheat, flour, and bread. If we add the sales price (total revenue) of all three transactions, our measure of total economic activity will be $600.

Stage of Production	Sales Price (Total Revenue)	Value Added
Wheat sold to the miller	$100	$100
Flour sold to the baker	200	100
Bread sold to the consumer	300	100
	$600	$300

This procedure counts the value of the wheat three times: once by itself, once as part of the flour, and once as part of the bread. Because the value of the bread includes the value of the wheat and flour as well, total production can be measured by the market value of the final product alone—the bread. The price of the final product, bread ($300), is equal to the total value added at all stages ($300).

Furthermore, if intermediate goods were included in GNP, that measure would change with changes in the structure of an industry. For example, if wheat production, flour milling, and baking were originally three separate businesses, but were later consolidated into one firm, our measure of total economic activity would fall from $600 to $300. Yet economic activity would not have changed. The farmer and miller would still be producing their products, but because they were now parts of a single firm, no market value would be attached to their activities.

Computation of GNP

Expenditure approach: the approach to calculating GNP which sums the dollar value of all final products.

Resource cost-income approach: the approach to calculating GNP which sums the dollar income payments to all resources.

GNP can be calculated by the **expenditure approach,** which sums the dollar value of all final products, or by the **resource cost-income approach,** which sums the dollar income payments to all resources. The first method sums expenditures in the household, business, government, and international sectors. It is also important to understand that anything that does not contribute to current output is excluded from GNP by either approach. GNP counts only goods and services produced during the current period. For instance, secondhand sales of used autos, machines, buildings, and so forth are merely transfers of assets that were included in the previous year's GNP. Financial transactions such as the sale of securities also merely transfer ownership and are not new production. Finally, private and public transfer payments, such as your uncle's birthday gift to you or your grandmother's Social Security checks, do not represent current production and are therefore excluded from current GNP.

Gross national product is normally stated in annual terms, although data are also compiled quarterly. The latest national income and product statistics are available monthly in the *Survey of Current Business,* published by the Bureau of Economic Analysis, U.S. Department of Commerce. Table 5.1 shows the gross national product for 1987, along with the figures used to calculate it on both an expenditure and a resource cost-income approach.

Let us look at the expenditure approach first. As in the example of bread production, the value of the nation's final products is stated as their dollar value at the time of sale. Of the $4,486 billion total, over $2,966 billion was consumer purchases ("personal consumption expenditures"). These consumption purchases included durables, nondurables, and services and represent by far the largest component (about two-thirds) of GNP. Another $716 billion was purchased by businesses, in the form of plant and equipment and additions to inventory, and by households, in the form of new houses ("gross private domestic investment"). These expenditures provide future flows of consumption or production services. The major outlays on durable capital assets are called fixed investment, whereas the other smaller, more volatile outlays are on changes in inventories. Both the replacement of worn out capital assets and the expansion of existing capital assets are included in gross investments. While national income statisticians largely separate investment as belonging to business (except for housing) and consumption as belonging to households, this division is arbitrary. Federal, state, and local governments spent about $924 billion on consumption and investment goods and services ("government purchases of goods and services") or about 20 percent of GNP. This does not include transfer payments unrelated to current GNP that would swell the role of government in economic activity.

The negative figure in the last category of expenditures ("net exports") shows that exports from the United States were about $120 billion less than imports into the nation (i.e., net exports = total exports − total imports). Because all exports are a part of U.S. production, you may wonder why only *net* exports are tabulated here. It is because other categories of expenditures include goods imported into the United States. For instance, when imported clothing is purchased by consumers, it is counted as a personal consumption expenditure. Yet imports are not part of U.S. production. They are the output of foreign countries and should be subtracted from any measure of U.S. economic activity. By subtracting imports from exports, the net exports figure does just that.

Because the dollar amount buyers spend on goods and services must equal the dollar amount received by producers, total expenditures must equal the total value of goods produced. When added together, then, the four major categories of expenditures shown in Table 5.1 yield the gross national product. Again, this is the expenditures approach to calculating GNP.

Alternatively, GNP can be calculated by summing the resource-cost income payments made to wages and salaries, the self-employed, rents, interest, corporate profits, and certain nonincome indirect expenses such as depreciation and indirect business taxes. As you can see from Table 5.1, identical values for GNP are produced by either method that is used. The dominance of the wages and salaries paid to labor services for employee compensation in total GNP has been true for as long as GNP records have been compiled. The titles of the various resource cost-income components are self-explanatory, except for proprietors' income, which refers to those risk-taking people who own and work for their own businesses. The last two items in the resource cost-income approach column—indirect business taxes and depreciation—are noncost factors that do generate an income payment to a resource supplier but are included in GNP.

Figure 5.1 shows GNP both with adjustments for price changes (real GNP) and without them (nominal or money GNP) from 1929 to 1987. To a limited extent, this graph, especially real GNP, indicates the nation's economic progress over the long term. We can see, for example, that the Great Depression of the early 1930s was a substantial blow to the nation's economic activity. Real GNP fell roughly 30 percent from 1929 to 1933. Furthermore we can see that production has grown irregularly, rising and then leveling out before rising again. By studying such data, economists can begin to draw some conclusions about the relationship between business and government policy and national production.

TABLE 5.1 Two Methods of Measuring GNP (1987 data, billions of current dollars)[a]

Expenditure Approach			Resource Cost-Income Approach		
Personal consumption expenditures		$2,966.0	Compensation of employees		$2,647.5
Durable goods	$ 413.9		Proprietors' income		327.8
Nondurable goods	980.4				
Services	1,571.6		Rental income of persons		18.5
			Corporate profits		305.3
Gross private domestic investment		$ 716.4			
Fixed investment	670.6		Net interest		336.7
Change in business inventories	45.7		Nonincome indirect cost items		847.0
Government purchases of goods and services		$ 923.8	Indirect business taxes (includes		
Federal	380.6		transfers)	367.6	
State and local	543.2		Depreciation (capital consumption allowances)	479.4	
Net exports of goods and services (exports minus imports)		$−119.9			
Gross national product		$4,486.2	Gross national product		$4,486.2

a. Preliminary estimate. Totals may not add up exactly because of rounding.

Source: Economic Report of the President (Washington, D.C.: U.S. Government Printing Office, 1988), pp. 248–249.

Shortcomings of the GNP

▲ **2. What are the deficiencies of GNP statistics?**

Although the gross national product is probably the best available measure of overall production in the United States, it is by no means perfect. One of its deficiencies—the fact that it omits entirely certain sectors of the economy—is of increasing concern to economists.

Nonmarket Production

With a few exceptions, the gross national product includes only final goods and services that are bought and sold in the market.[1] It excludes people's unpaid activities that benefit themselves, their families, and their friends. For instance, GNP includes the price paid for meat, potatoes, and lettuce but not the value of the work done to prepare a meal. (It does, however, include the price of meals purchased at restaurants.) GNP includes the price paid for landscaping, but not the value of yard work done by home-

---

1. The Department of Commerce assigns a value to the farm products that farmers grow and consume themselves. It also estimates the rental value of homes occupied by their owners. Both those figures are included in personal consumption expenditures.

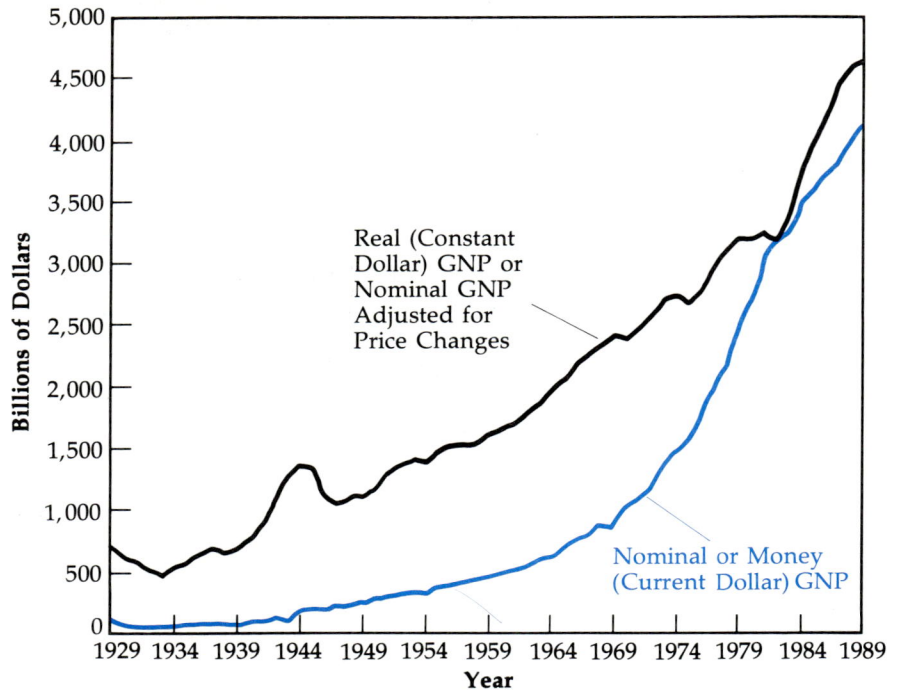

FIGURE 5.1 Nominal and Real Gross National Product 1929–1987

The gross national product in nominal or real terms (1982 dollars) has increased significantly over the past five or six decades as a long-run trend, punctuated by the sometimes volatile short-run ups and downs of business cycles.

Source: Economic Report of the President (Washington, D.C.: U.S. Government Printing Office, 1988), pp. 248, 250.

owners. The same is true for any home repairs, such as to your roof or sink, that you do yourself.

Two reasons have been given for excluding nonmarket activities from GNP. First, it is extremely difficult to assign a value to the services people provide for themselves, because the quality of those services varies greatly from person to person. Because the quality of many paid professionals—lawyers, athletes, professors—also varies enormously, this by itself does not explain the nonexclusion. Second, economists have found it difficult to decide which nonmarket activities should be included. Perhaps dishwashing, clothes washing, and garbage removal should be included, but what about tooth brushing? That service, when performed by a dentist, has a market value—but few of us think we are adding to national production when we brush our teeth.

Because nonmarket activities are excluded, trends in GNP may not accurately reflect changes in social welfare. For example, during the Great Depression, nominal (or money) GNP fell from $103.9 billion in 1929 to

$56.0 billion in 1933. Although people were much worse off in 1933 than in 1929, total production, including both market and nonmarket activity, had not fallen as much as GNP indicates. People who lost their jobs invested more time in maintaining their households. More people kept bigger gardens and did more repair work around the house than they had before the economic downturn. Although such activities could not compensate fully for lost income, people were able to offset their losses in part. This increase in home-related productive activity was not included in GNP.

The Underground, Subterranean, or Irregular Economy

Many goods and services—hard drugs, moonshine liquor, gambling, and prostitution, for instance—are illegal in most areas of the United States. Nonetheless, they are part of the nation's total production—and because they are produced surreptitiously, and are unreported, they escape measurement. Other transactions are not counted because people are trying to evade taxation. To avoid taxes, many people trade rather than sell the goods they produce for the things they want. Thus, orthodontists and lawyers swap services. Medical doctors also extend professional courtesies to one another that escape measurement. Others sell their goods and services for cash, but do not report the income to the Internal Revenue Service. Waiters, taxi drivers, and hairdressers, for example, often report only part of their tips; producers of firewood do not always declare the cash they receive; and many wealthy people store earnings from foreign assets in Swiss bank accounts closed to IRS inspection. The underground economy consists of unreported legal and illegal activities excluded from traditional GNP estimates. Estimates of the size of this underground economy vary. Some economists believe that the value of productive activity in this sector is between 10 and 25 percent per year. In recent years, unreported legal activity has been growing at about 10 to 15 percent per year, while unreported illegal activity has been growing at about 15 to 20 percent per year.

Underground economy: unreported legal and illegal activities excluded from traditional GNP estimates.

Leisure Time

GNP makes no allowances for changes in the amount of time workers spend at their jobs. During this century the length of the work week (the average number of hours worked by each laborer each week) has gradually decreased, from about sixty hours in 1900 to just under forty hours in 1988. The value of today's workers' greater voluntary leisure time, which has unquestionably enhanced human welfare, is not reflected in GNP. If people were still working as many hours as they once did, the total value of the nation's production would be much higher.

Production of "Bads"

In the course of producing goods and services, the economy also produces social costs or "bads"—things that detract from the quality of life. For example, steel mills often pollute the environment. Other industrial processes create solid wastes that are difficult to dispose of. In preparing our meals (a good) we jointly produce garbage (a bad). The negative value of these by-products is not subtracted from the gross national product. Equipment purchased to clean up a pollution problem, however, is counted as part of GNP. Thus a snowfall in New York City or a flood in Lincoln, Nebraska, can lead to greater national production but not greater national welfare.

Measure of (or Net) Economic Welfare

Measure of (or net) economic welfare (MEW or NEW): a measure that adjusts GNP for non-market bads and goods to obtain a better measure of quality of life or social welfare.

Because of the dissatisfaction with GNP in measuring some of the afore-mentioned items, economists (but not national income accounting sources) have turned to an adjusted GNP concept called **measure of (or net) economic welfare (MEW or NEW)** that adjusts GNP for non-market bads and goods to obtain a better measure of quality of life or social welfare. This measure modifies GNP in three ways: (1) by subtracting certain unmet costs (or bads) such as pollution, noise, and litter that are unavoidable joint products with goods in GNP; (2) by excluding some intermediate services such as police and fire protection; and (3) by adding certain items such as home activities, leisure, and so forth. This new measure has grown more slowly than GNP since 1930. GNP also fails to measure the human costs involving the mental and physical strain and safety of economic activity, such as monotony, stress, or danger. The state of civil liberties is also not taken into account.

Prices of Goods and Services

Because GNP is computed in terms of current prices, comparisons over time are distorted by inflation. If prices rise, the GNP will reflect the inflation, exaggerating the increase in production of actual goods and services.

In Table 5.2, column 1 shows the nominal (current-dollar) value of the GNP for selected years from 1929 to 1987. At first glance, it appears that U.S. production was over 43 times greater in 1987 than in 1929. Output appears to have fallen by about 46 percent between 1929 and 1933, and to have risen by about 452 percent between 1970 and 1987. Much of this apparent change in production is actually a change in price, however. Prices fell significantly between 1929 and 1933, magnifying the underlying real drop in output. During the 1970s, prices rose at unprecedented peacetime rates, puffing the rather modest increases in total production out of proportion.

To eliminate distortions caused by price changes, the Department of Commerce adjusts GNP figures against various price indexes. These indexes measure changes in the price levels in particular sectors of the economy—such as lumber, agriculture, and energy—in relation to some base year, such as 1982. For example, if the price of lumber rose 12 percent between 1982 and 1987, the price index for lumber would be 1.12 in 1987. To eliminate the influence of inflation, the Department of Commerce divides the 1987 production figure by 1.12. Similar adjustments are made for all sectors, and the resulting figures are then summed to obtain real, or constant dollar, GNP. **Real or constant dollar gross national product** is the gross national product adjusted for price changes using the implicit GNP price deflator, and is shown in column 2 of Table 5.2. Once such adjustments have been made for all years, changes in GNP over time will reflect

Real or constant dollar gross national product: the gross national product adjusted for price changes using the implicit GNP price deflator.

TABLE 5.2   Nominal and Real, Gross National Product, 1929–1987

Year	Nominal (Current Dollar) GNP (billions) (1)	Real (Constant 1982 Dollar) GNP (billions) (2)	U.S. Population (millions) (3)	Per Capita Real (Constant 1982 Dollar) GNP [(2) ÷ (3)] (4)
1929	$ 103.9	$ 709.6	121.8	$ 5,826
1933	56.0	498.5	125.6	3,969
1940	100.4	772.9	132.1	5,851
1950	288.3	1,203.7	152.3	7,903
1960	515.3	1,665.3	180.7	9,216
1970	1,015.5	2,416.2	205.1	11,780
1980	2,732.0	3,187.1	227.8	13,991
1987	4,486.2	3,819.6	243.8	15,667

Source: Economic Report of the President (Washington, D.C.: U.S. Government Printing Office, 1988), pp. 248, 250, 283.

Nominal, money, or current dollar gross national product: the gross national product with no adjustments made for price changes.

Implicit GNP price deflator index: a price index that shows the cost of buying the final goods and services included in the GNP during some year relative to the cost of buying these same items during a base year (currently, 1982).

changes in actual production, not changes in price. **Nominal, money, or current dollar gross national product** is the GNP with no adjustments made for price changes.

Table 5.3 shows the way real GNP is computed. The *P*s and *Q*s stand for prices and quantities, respectively; the subscripts indicate the year. Notice that the values in column 1 vary with changes in both price and quantity, whereas the values in column 2 vary only with changes in quantity. If such adjustments are made for all the figures in column 1 of Table 5.2, we arrive at column 2 of Table 5.2, GNP in constant 1982 dollars. The **implicit GNP price deflator index** shows the cost of buying the final goods and services included in the GNP during some year relative to the cost of buying these same items during a base year (currently, 1982). This comprehensive

TABLE 5.3   Method of Computing Nominal (Current Dollar) Gross National Product and Real (Constant Dollar) Gross National Product

Year	Nominal GNP in Current Prices (1)	Real GNP in Constant 1982 Prices (2)
1929	$P_{29} \times Q_{29}$	$P_{82} \times Q_{29}$
1933	$P_{33} \times Q_{33}$	$P_{82} \times Q_{33}$
1940	$P_{40} \times Q_{40}$	$P_{82} \times Q_{40}$
1950	$P_{50} \times Q_{50}$	$P_{82} \times Q_{50}$
1960	$P_{60} \times Q_{60}$	$P_{82} \times Q_{60}$
1970	$P_{70} \times Q_{70}$	$P_{82} \times Q_{70}$
1980	$P_{80} \times Q_{80}$	$P_{82} \times Q_{80}$
1988	$P_{88} \times Q_{88}$	$P_{82} \times Q_{88}$

Note: *P* = price; *Q* = quantity.

quarterly index presently tracks about 2,200 goods and services at their first commercial sale. Real or constant dollar GNP figures for 1929 to 1987 are also plotted in Figure 5.1.

Whether you or your parents are better off in real income terms from one year to the next requires a comparison of relative or real values and not absolute or nominal values. Thus, the absolute values of the figures represented in Figure 5.1 and in column 2 of Table 5.2 are less meaningful than their relative value. These real (constant-dollar) figures show that production in the United States was indeed greater in 1987 than in 1929—slightly more than five times greater. They also show that between 1929 and 1933, total production of goods and services fell less than nominal (current-dollar) figures would suggest—by approximately 30 percent rather than 50 percent. Between 1970 and 1987 output grew much less than the price-inflated figures in column 1 suggest. This can be illustrated by comparing the curves in Figure 5.1.

Population Growth

Real gross national product may increase over time, but if population grows faster, people will not be better off. To determine whether production per capita (per person) is increasing, we must divide real GNP by yearly population figures. This procedure yields per capita real GNP, shown in column 4 of Table 5.2. On a per capita basis, U.S. production increased less than threefold between 1929 and 1987, less than the figures in columns 1 and 2 would suggest. Per capita figures offer no insight into how the national output is distributed among the population, however.

Quality of Goods and Services

GNP estimates the money value of goods and services, but prices do not necessarily reflect changes in the quality of goods, especially over a long period of time. The GNP adjusts imperfectly for both changes in the quality of old goods and for the introduction of new ones. For example, since the early 1970s, the prices of calculators have declined while their quality has improved. Prices do not reflect the division of output between consumer goods and government purchases either. If a nation shifts production from consumer goods in peacetime to war equipment in wartime, the average citizen's standard of living may suffer, even though factories are operating night and day. Production increased dramatically during the Second World War, but many consumer goods, such as butter and hosiery, were so scarce that they had to be rationed. Although some people may have benefited because the demand for war materials increased the demand for (and the price of) their services, others—those who paid higher taxes to finance the war—may have been worse off.

Net National Product (NNP)

▲ **3. What are other non-GNP measures of productive activity in the macroeconomy?**

Gross national product includes the current value of all final goods and services, including plant and equipment (sometimes called capital goods) purchased by businesses to replace worn-out plant and equipment. Because replacement plant and equipment is included, GNP overstates the actual

TABLE 5.4 Nominal Gross National Product, Net National Product, and Disposable Personal Income, 1929–1987 (in current dollars)

Year	Gross National Product (billions) (1)	Net National Product (billions) (2)	Disposable Personal Income (billions) (3)	Per Capita Disposable Personal Income (billions) (4)
1929	$ 103.9	$ 94.0	$ 81.7	$ 671
1933	56.0	48.4	44.9	357
1940	100.4	91.1	75.0	568
1950	288.3	264.6	207.5	1,368
1960	515.3	468.9	358.9	1,986
1970	1,015.5	926.6	715.6	3,489
1980	2,732.0	2,428.1	1,918.0	8,421
1985	4,010.3	3,572.7	2,841.1	11,872
1987[a]	4,486.2	4,006.8	3,181.1	13,048

a. Preliminary estimate.

Source: Economic Report of the President (Washington, D.C.: U.S. Government Printing Office, 1988), pp. 272, 279.

increase in total goods and services. Some of the machines used to produce GNP wear out. To estimate the increase more accurately, the Department of Commerce subtracts the value of worn-out plant and equipment—called the capital consumption, or depreciation, allowance—from the gross national product (no direct payment to a resource owner is involved). This adjusted measure is called net national product (NNP). **Net national product (NNP)** equals gross national product minus an allowance for replacement of worn-out plant and equipment (called the capital consumption allowance). Because replacement of old equipment has been subtracted, net national product is a better measure of the real growth of production than gross national product.

Net national product usually amounts to between 89 and 92 percent of gross national product (see Table 5.4, column 2). The two measures are equally good indicators of change in production over time.

Net national product is a reasonably good indicator of national production over time, but it is not the best available measure of social welfare. It does not tell us how much of the rewards of production ends up in people's pockets. To see how much money people have to spend, and therefore how much of the gross national product they can buy, we must look at measures of national income.

Net national product (NNP): gross national product minus an allowance for replacement of worn-out plant and equipment (called the capital consumption allowance).

National Income

National income is another way of measuring productive activity in the macroeconomy. "National income" is one category in national income accounting. This specific concept needs to be distinguished from the generic use of "national income" to refer to all measures of national income. When

PERSPECTIVES

Underground's Hidden Income

Leonard Silk, New York Times

The state of the American economy, with the stock and bond markets swinging back and forth in the last few weeks, has been baffling policy makers and investors. Is it on the verge of recession or is it gaining strength again? Are consumers so deeply in debt that they are bound to cut back their borrowing or spending or are a great many of them really loaded with more cash savings and other financial assets than the national-income accounts disclose?

One of the sources of uncertainty about the actual state of business conditions is what is happening in the "underground economy"—the huge slice of national income that goes unreported to escape taxation. A lot of that underground income comes from drug dealing, burglaries, illegal gambling and other criminal activities, but much of it is unreported or collected "off the books" by all sorts of people who get it from their businesses or professions—ranging from medicine and law to driving taxis, waiting on tables, renting or subletting rooms and a host of other legal occupations.

For obvious reasons, only rough estimates exist of how large the underground economy is. In recent years it has often been estimated at about 10 percent in this country and possibly as much as 20 percent or more in some foreign countries. But new estimates by James J. O'Leary, economic consultant to the United States Trust Company, suggest that the underground economy in the

United States is bigger than earlier studies have found.

According to Mr. O'Leary's method of calculation, disposable personal income on a cash basis (excluding barter deals) in the American underground economy averaged only about 5.7 percent a year of the total disposable income during 1971–75 but nearly tripled to 15.7 percent a year during 1981–85. In 1984, according to his estimates, underground income peaked at nearly 21 percent of personal disposable income but fell to 15.2 percent in 1985.

In current dollars, the amount of unreported cash going underground grew from an average of $52.5 billion a year in 1971–75 to an average of $370.7 billion a year in 1981–85. In 1984 it reached $558.4 billion, before dropping to $431.7 billion in 1985. Despite the seeming precision, these figures can be regarded only as ballpark numbers, based on some educated assumptions.

Mr. O'Leary derives these figures from the conflicting estimates of personal savings calculated by the Federal Reserve Board and those of the Commerce Department, as measured in the national income accounts. The Fed's saving figures, which run substantially higher than the Commerce Department's, are built on the net increase each year in the total amount of financial assets—including currency, checking deposits and time and savings deposits— held by individuals plus their net investment in

National income: the total income payment made to owners of human and physical productive resources for the use of those resources during a given period.

people produce goods and services, they generate wages and salaries that reflect their contribution to production. The rewards of production must ultimately be distributed to these people—employees, managers, or owners of capital assets. Thus total income received must equal the total value of goods and services produced. For instance, if $100 worth of goods is produced, the people who produce the goods must earn a total of $100 in income. The figure for national income is not obtained by summing individual incomes, but rather by making technical adjustments to net national product. **National income** is the total income payment made to owners of human and physical productive resources for the use of those resources tangible assets. By comparison, the Commerce Department's figure for personal savings represents the residual between its estimates of disposable personal income and of personal outlays, including personal consumption expenditures, interest paid by consumers to businesses and net of personal transfer payments to foreigners.

After examining the alternative methods, Mr. O'Leary concluded that the Commerce Department's procedure is "much more vulnerable to error" than the Fed's estimate. In 1984, for example, the Fed's flow-of-funds data reported personal savings $92.7 billion higher than the Commerce Department estimated.

To "guesstimate" the total personal income going underground, Mr. O'Leary made two assumptions: first, that half the difference between the Fed and Commerce data on personal savings results from estimation shortcomings in the Commerce Department's national income accounts; second, that the actual savings rate is two percentage points higher than that calculated on the national-income accounts basis. He then divided the savings rate into the annual volume of underground savings derived from the Fed's data, to get the total annual personal income in the underground economy.

Since the Fed's flow-of-funds data measure only the increase in reported net financial assets, they miss the increase in financial assets clandestinely shifted abroad by Americans and unreported by foreign financial institutions.

Even without counting taxes on those billions of dollars smuggled abroad, Mr. O'Leary figures that the loss of personal income taxes to the Treasury through the domestic underground economy was $56 billion in 1984 and $43 billion in 1985.

There is a chance, he thinks, that we have seen the peaks in the underground economy. The requirement that banks and other financial institutions report interest and dividends to the Internal Revenue Service appears to be forcing the savings of the underground economy into cash or non-earning assets, which costs the tax evaders money.

When combined with a greater fear of detection, the prospective cuts in marginal income tax rates are likely to reduce incentives for many taxpayers to go underground. Thus, the tax revision bill now before Congress could be more of a revenue raiser, and more of a deficit shrinker, than estimated, based only on what the Commerce Department's "above-ground" savings and income data imply.

Finally, as Mr. O'Leary adds, the shrinkage of the underground economy "would mean the reduction of a moral and ethical blot on our society."

during a given period. It is equal to the total cost of producing the goods and services included in the net national product.

Table 5.5 shows the method for computing national income from NNP. The most significant adjustment is the subtraction of indirect business taxes, such as federal excise taxes on liquor or local property taxes, which are not considered to be payments earned in the market by resource owners. These embodied taxes raise the prices of the goods they are levied on, so we must subtract them to get to the true added value of national income. Similarly, business transfer payments such as gifts made to charities and consumer bad debts must be subtracted. On the other hand, we need to add in the inducement subsidy payments to various factors of production. The statistical discrepancy can be positive or negative depending on the situation.

National income does not tell us how much money consumers earn. That figure is called personal income. **Personal income** is the part of national income that is paid to individuals as opposed to businesses.

Personal income: the part of national income that is paid to individuals as opposed to businesses.

Corporate profits, interest payments that do not go directly to individuals, and Social Security taxes must be subtracted from national income to obtain the figure for personal income. Then government transfer payments, interest income, corporate dividend payments, and business transfer payments received by individuals must be added (see Table 5.5). The method of accounting is somewhat arbitrary; Social Security taxes are deducted but personal income taxes are not. (No good reason has been given for the discrepancy. For many years Social Security taxes were deducted from people's paychecks, but income taxes were not. Today both are deducted before the wage earner ever sees a paycheck, but national income compilers haven't changed their method.)

Personal income still does not tell us how much money people have to spend. Because of taxation, people's take-home pay is usually much less than their total income. A better measure of their welfare may be what they take home after taxes (and some minor non-tax payments) for use in the purchase of goods and services. This measure is called disposable personal income. **Disposable personal income** is personal income minus personal tax payments (as well as some minor non-tax payments).

Disposable personal income: personal income minus personal tax payments (as well as some minor non-tax payments).

Disposable personal income in the United States is shown in columns 3 and 4 of Table 5.4, and in Table 5.5. In 1987 Americans received a total disposable personal income of $3,181 billion, or approximately 71 percent of the gross national product for that year. Of that amount, consumers spent $3,061 billion and about $120 billion (3.8 percent) was saved. In 1929, by contrast, Americans received approximately 80 percent of GNP as disposable personal income. The nine percentage-point drop in personal income between 1929 and 1987 is mostly because taxes were higher in 1987 than in 1929.

Disposable personal income figures must be adjusted for price changes and population growth before they can accurately reflect changes in consumer purchasing power. (See column 4 of Table 5.4 for per capita disposable personal income in current dollar terms.)

The Unemployment Rate

▲ 4. What does the unemployment rate measure?

Gross national product and national income are positive measures of the nation's economic activity. The unemployment rate, on the other hand, estimates the absence or nonoccurrence of economic activity. This negative measure indicates the portion of the nation's able labor force that is currently out of work.

Unemployment data are compiled monthly by the Bureau of Labor Statistics in its publication *Monthly Labor Review*. Table 5.6 shows the aver-

TABLE 5.5 Relationship of Gross National Product (GNP), Net National Product (NNP), National Income (NI), Personal Income (PI), and Disposable Personal Income (DPI), 1987 (in billions of dollars)[a]

Gross national product		$4,486.2
Less:	Capital consumption	479.4
Equals:	*Net national product*	4,006.8
Less:	Indirect business taxes and nontax liability	367.6
	Business transfer payments	23.2
	Statistical discrepancy	−6.8
Plus:	Subsidies less current surplus of government enterprises	13.1
Equals:	*National income*	3,635.9
Less:	Corporate profits	305.3
	Net interest	336.7
	Contributions for social insurance (Social Security)	394.4
	Wage accruals less disbursement	.0
Plus:	Government transfer payments to persons	519.8
	Personal interest income	515.8
	Personal dividend income	87.5
	Business transfer payments	23.2
Equals:	*Personal income*	3,745.8
Less:	Personal tax and nontax payments	564.7
Equals:	*Disposable personal income*	3,181.1
Composed of:	Personal outlays	3,060.9
	Personal saving	120.2

a. Preliminary estimate.

Source: Economic Report of the President (Washington, D.C.: U.S. Government Printing Office, 1988), pp. 272–273, 278.

age monthly unemployment rate for selected years from 1950 to 1987. The 1950 unemployment rate of 5.3 percent was considered high at the time. Two decades later, the rate had fallen slightly to 4.8. In 1975 the rate hit an alarming 8.3 percent, and by the early 1980s it had almost doubled its 1970 level.

Like GNP, the unemployment rate is interpreted by the media, by the public, by government officials, and by business people as a sign of how successfully public policy goals are being met. Almost everyone thinks that an increase in the unemployment rate is a sign of worsening economic activity and increasing social hardship. Like a drop in GNP, a rise in unemployment could induce some businesses to curtail their production plans in anticipation of reduced consumer demand—perhaps causing even more workers to be laid off. Worsening unemployment can be a boon to opposition candidates in election years. In 1980, for example, Ronald Reagan scored political points with the unemployed, unions, and other worker groups by stressing the apparent failure of the Carter administration to control unemployment, then at 7 percent.

In evaluating the unemployment rate and the statements of politicians, it helps to remember Humpty Dumpty's remark in Lewis Carroll's *Through the Looking Glass*: "When I use a word, it means just what I choose it to

TABLE 5.6 Number of Civilian People Employed and Unemployed, and the Civilian Unemployment Rate, 1950–1987

Year	Millions of Civilian People Employed (1)	Millions of Civilian People Unemployed (2)	Millions of People in the Civilian Labor Force [(1) + (2)] (3)	Civilian Unemployment Rate (percent) [(2) ÷ (3)] (4)	Civilian Labor Force Participation Rate[a] (percent) (5)
1950	58.9	3.3	62.2	5.9	59.2
1960	65.8	3.8	69.7	5.6	59.4
1970	78.7	4.1	82.8	5.0	60.4
1980	99.3	7.6	106.9	7.1	63.8
1985	107.2	8.3	115.5	7.2	64.8
1987	112.4	7.4	119.9	6.2	65.6

a. Labor force participation rate = adult civilian labor force ÷ adult civilian noninstitutionalized population.

Source: Economic Report of the President (Washington, D.C.: U.S. Government Printing Office, 1988), pp. 284, 289.

mean—neither more nor less." When the Bureau of Labor Statistics uses the term *unemployment rate,* the bureau chooses it to mean something very specific. The rate is computed using precise definitions of *employed* and *unemployed,* which have a significant effect on its numerical value.

Computing the Unemployment Rate

Unemployment rate: the ratio of the number of people estimated to be unemployed to the number of people estimated to be in the labor force, stated as a percentage.

Stated rigorously, the **unemployment rate** is the ratio of the number of people estimated to be unemployed to the number of people estimated to be in the labor force, stated as a percentage, or

$$\text{unemployment rate} = \frac{\text{number of people unemployed}}{\text{number of people in labor force}}$$

Labor force: all persons sixteen years of age or older (i.e., adults) who are willing and able to work and who are counted as either unemployed or employed.

Labor force also has a very specific meaning: the **labor force** consists of all persons sixteen years of age or older (i.e., adults) who are willing and able to work and who are counted as either unemployed or employed,[2] or

$$\text{labor force} = \text{number of people unemployed} \\ + \text{number of people employed}$$

Specifically, the only people who can be counted as employed or unemployed are those adults who are at least sixteen years of age and who are not institutionalized—that is, do not reside in a penal or mental institution or a home for the aged, infirm, or needy. The Bureau of Labor Statistics ex-

---

2. The civilian labor force equals the total labor force minus the members of the armed forces of the United States. The civilian unemployment rate is the number of civilian people unemployed divided by the number of people in the civilian labor force.

cludes persons under sixteen years of age because child labor laws, compulsory education, and general social customs prevent most of them from working.

Subject to the restrictions indicated above, employed persons include

○ All persons who, during the week in which the survey was taken, did any work at all for pay or worked at least fifteen hours without pay in a family-operated business

○ All persons who were not working during the survey week but were temporarily absent from their jobs or businesses because of illness, bad weather, vacation, strikes, or personal reasons

○ Members of the military

Unemployed persons include

○ All persons who did not work at all during the week of the survey but were looking for work and were available for work

○ All persons who had made some effort to find work in the past four weeks (such as filling out an application) and were waiting for the results

○ All persons who (a) were waiting to be called back to a job from which they had been laid off, (b) were waiting to report to a new job within the next thirty days, or (c) would have been looking for work if they had not been sick

Classified as "not in the labor force" are all those who are not considered either employed or unemployed and are not in the military. This group includes people who

○ are under sixteen years of age or are full-time students

○ are homemakers

○ are unable to work

○ are retired

○ work fewer than fifteen hours a week without pay for their family business

○ work without pay for a charitable or religious organization

○ do seasonal work and are idle because it is off season

○ are scheduled to report to a new job in more than thirty days

Columns 1 and 2 of Table 5.6 show the numbers of civilian people employed and unemployed, from which the yearly unemployment rates in column 4 were computed.

Unemployment statistics are gathered from a survey of a representative sample of people in approximately sixty thousand housing units located in counties and cities throughout the nation. They include data on over one hundred thousand people sixteen years of age or older. Each household is interviewed for four consecutive months, dropped for the next eight months, and then interviewed again for four more months. In gathering the data, the Bureau of Labor Statistics relies on the voluntary cooperation of those who are questioned.

PERSPECTIVES
Forecasting the Macroeconomy

The movie tycoon Sam Goldwyn warned us that "forecasts are dangerous, particularly those about the future." Despite the danger, numerous economists and pseudo-economists have made large amounts of money establishing consulting firms to forecast the macroeconomy. Forecasting is a difficult and high risk business with no durable truths. The process requires continuous revision, accommodation, and most of all, change.

We have seen that the macroeconomy is subject to business cycles of expansions and contractions, rising to peaks and falling to troughs. There is little uncertainty in documenting cyclical turning points after they have occurred. The National Bureau of Economic Research (NBER) is the final arbiter on completed cycles; they define a recession as two or more quarters of negative real GNP growth. The difficult issue is predicting these turning points *before* they occur.

How do people estimate the future ebbs and flows of the macroeconomy? You have heard of people reading tea leaves and gazing at crystal balls to make predictions. Haruspex, a class of lesser ancient Roman priests and soothsayers, professed to foretell the future by interpreting the entrails of sacrificial animals—a truly dirty job! Less imaginative, but more accurate econometric techniques are used by academic economists to make projections. In fact, econometric techniques are used by business, industry, and government

forecasters to anticipate the impact of economic change on their own environment. In the past, many noneconomists used to simply assume that last year's experience would be more or less typical for a good many years to come. This simplistic adaptive expectations approach, however, no longer prevails.

The most common task of an economic prognosticator today is to find some reliable and readily available leading indicator that changes directions in advance of general business conditions. Of course, investors, businesspeople, and policymakers are interested in forecasting future GNP in the belief that high GNP translates into higher profits and higher stock prices. In truth, stock prices lead rather than follow GNP; stock prices are in fact the most reliable and accurate single leading indicator available. The monthly *Business Conditions Digest* publishes data on 12 basic leading indicators as well as a composite index of these 12 indices that have been reasonably consistent in leading the business cycle.[1] The composite index performs better than any single index does (perhaps reflecting what Arthur Okun calls the patron saint of economists, St. Offset), in that haphazard excesses in one index may have been neutral-

1. Our discussion of leading indicators draws on Geoffrey A. Hirt and Stanley R. Block, *The Complete Investor: Instruments, Markets and Methods* (Homewood, Illinois: Dow Jones-Irwin, 1987), pp. 116–123.

Shortcomings of Employment and Unemployment Statistics

▲ 5. What are the shortcomings of unemployment rate statistics?

Like any data, employment and unemployment figures are not more reliable than the workers who administer the survey and those who are interviewed. If survey procedures are changed or if survey workers do not follow established procedures—that is, if they vary the wording or emphasis of the questions—the results of the survey will be distorted. If those who are interviewed conceal their true employment status, the results will be distorted further. Small changes in unemployment rates from month to month may reflect errors or procedural changes as much as true changes in the number of people employed and unemployed.

ized by those in another index. The leading indicators of this widely followed composite index include:

- average workweek, production workers, manufacturing (hours);
- average weekly initial claims, state unemployment insurance (thousands);
- new orders for consumer goods and materials in 1972 dollars (billion dollars);
- vendor performance, companies receiving slower deliveries (percent);
- net business formation (index: 1967 = 100);
- contracts and orders for plant and equipment in 1972 dollars (billion dollars);
- new building permits, private housing units (index: 1967 = 100);
- change in inventories on hand and on order in 1972 dollars, smoothed (annual rate, billion dollars);
- change in sensitive materials prices, smoothed (percent);
- stock prices, 500 common stocks (index: 1941–1943 = 10);
- money supply (M2) in 1972 dollars (billion dollars); and
- change in credit—business and consumer borrowing (annual rate, percent).

The composite index has varied widely at peaks, giving as long a lead time as twenty-three months before the peak in 1957 and as short a lead time as three months in 1981. The longest lead time for troughs was eight months before the bottom in 1982; the shortest was one month in 1974–1975.

One difficulty is that the composite index does not provide an identical lead time for peaks as for troughs. The lead time on the peak warning is much longer than the trough warning. In addition to a large variance in lead times, there are occasional unclear or even false signals. Anyone who predicts within 3 or 4 months of a top or bottom is very good, very lucky, or both.

Forecasting, a combination of art and science, is something that is both improving and necessary. Any U.S. president inaugurated into office today inherits an economy. A significant portion of the "grade" given to any president is based on what happened to the macroeconomy during the term of office. For a president to be able to use the full arsenal of monetary and fiscal policies, reasonably tolerable accuracy in predicting the macroeconomy is mandatory. Of course, something must be done once the prediction is made. Contemporary policymakers have a great advantage over their predecessors because econometric models and data continue to improve rapidly. Truly accurate forecasting remains a vital and challenging area.

Unemployment statistics do not measure the hardship borne by the underemployed. Anyone who has worked for pay at all during the survey week is counted as employed—even those who have worked only five or ten hours. If production cuts in the automobile industry drastically reduce the number of days or hours its employees can work, unemployment figures for auto workers will not be affected. These people whose work hours are reduced involuntarily and who work at part-time jobs although they want full-time jobs, along with people working at jobs for which they are overqualified, are called "underemployed" even though they are not officially called "unemployed." **Hidden unemployment** includes underemployed and discouraged workers, who quit looking for jobs after long periods of rejections and are thus not considered unemployed, as they are not actively

Hidden unemployment: underemployed and discouraged workers, who quit looking for jobs after long periods of rejection and are thus not considered unemployed, as they are not actively seeking work.

**Underemployed work-
ers:** those people either
working at part-time jobs
although they would
prefer full-time jobs or
working at jobs for which
they are overqualified in
terms of training, educa-
tion, or experience.

**Labor force participation
rate:** the number of adult
civilian people in the
labor force divided by the
adult civilian noninstitutional population.

seeking work. **Underemployed workers** are those people either working at part-time jobs although they want full-time jobs or working at jobs for which they are overqualified in terms of training, education, or experience.

Finally, unemployment statistics are not adjusted for changes in the relative size of the labor force. One reason for the increase in the unemployment rate over the last three decades is that a growing percentage of the working-age population has been looking for jobs. For a more accurate picture of national employment, we must look at the labor force participation rate. The **labor force participation rate** is the number of adult civilian people in the labor force divided by the adult civilian noninstitutional population. Table 5.6 shows that the labor force participation rate increased over six percentage points from 1950 to 1987, significantly more than the increase in the unemployment rate.

Reducing the Unemployment Rate

For several reasons, the unemployment rate as defined by the Bureau of Labor Statistics can never be reduced to zero. In a dynamic economy people will always be changing jobs. Some people expect to report to a new job within thirty days but are classified as unemployed by the government. Others may decline one job offer in hope of getting a better one. Some who are willingly unemployed may claim they are still job hunting so that their unemployment pay will continue. Those who are employed in the illegal underground economy may not admit they are working. Finally, some people do not have the skills necessary to earn the minimum wage rate for even the most menial jobs. In short, because of government procedures, voluntary unemployment, and unreported employment, the unemployment rate may exaggerate the extent of economic hardship in the nation.

For these reasons, it is doubtful that the unemployment rate, as currently defined, can be reduced much below 5 percent (some would say 6 percent). Others contend that unless some legislative changes are made—like the elimination of the minimum wage law and of union barriers to entry into various labor markets—the unemployment rate will not fall much below 7 percent for very long. Economists like to talk about the natural rate of unemployment that does not include cyclical unemployment—only frictional and structural unemployment. If no more than the natural rate of unemployment is experienced, then full employment is said to exist.

The Consumer Price Index (CPI)

◢ **6. What is inflation
and how is it estimated
in the macroeconomy?**

Another negative measure of the nation's economic well-being is the inflation rate. **Inflation** is a sustained rise in the general level of quality-adjusted prices over a period of time; it causes both costs and benefits (Chapter 9 describes these costs and benefits in detail). If the prices of some goods rise but others fall, the general price level has not necessarily risen, although the relative prices of goods have changed. Inflation occurs when sustained

Inflation: a sustained rise in the general level of quality-adjusted prices over a period of time; it causes both costs and benefits.

Consumer price index (CPI): the ratio of the cost of specific consumer items included in a representative consumer market basket in any one survey year to the cost of those items in the base year (currently, 1967).

Consumer unit: a household of people who pool their money.

rise in the quality-adjusted prices of many goods and services is not offset by a decrease in the prices of other goods and services. In other words, during inflationary times the price level, or weighted average of all prices, rises.

The measurement of price levels and ultimately inflation rates depends on what prices are averaged and how they are weighted. The consumer price index (CPI), computed by the Bureau of Labor Statistics of the U.S. Department of Labor, is the measure of price level most often cited. The consumer price index (CPI) is the ratio of the cost of specific consumer items included in a representative consumer market basket in any one survey year to the cost of those items in the base year (currently, 1967). Because the CPI includes things consumers buy regularly, it is frequently called the cost of living index. The index does not, however, represent everyone's cost of living. It is designed to represent the changes in the prices of specific goods that are bought in large quantities by people who work and shop in cities, like craftspeople, factory supervisors, carpenters, and salespeople.[3]

The CPI provides a reasonably accurate estimate of the price level of thousands of items produced by twenty-four thousand businesses in eighty-five urban areas, however. The so-called market basket, or list of items covered by the survey, includes most goods and services urban consumers buy. Food, fuel, clothing, automobiles, homes, house furnishings, household supplies, drugs, and recreational goods; fees for medical services, legal services, and beauty shops; rent, repair costs, transportation fares, public utility rates, interest rates; and sales, property, and excise taxes are all included. Prices are weighted according to their importance in a typical family budget in the survey years.[4]

In 1987 a new market basket based on census surveys conducted between 1982 and 1984 replaced the previous market basket based on surveys in 1972 and 1974.[5] The market basket is divided into 184 different "item strata" including about 400 items such as college expenses, men's suits, white bread, and sofas. The new item strata include information processing (e.g., smoke detectors and home PCs), video equipment (e.g., video games and VCRs), and home care for the elderly. Thousands of consumer units—households of people who pool their money—were interviewed to obtain a market basket that reflects the purchases of a typical consumer. These consumer units included in the new market basket are on average smaller compared with the old one (in terms of the number of people contained

---

3. The BLS publishes two slightly different indices of consumer prices: (1) a newer all urban consumers index (CPI-U) and (2) and an older urban wage earners and clerical workers index (CPI-W). The more often cited CPI-U covers about 81 percent of all consumer units in the noninstitutional population whereas the CPI-W covers only 38 percent of all consumer units.

4. The Bureau of Labor Statistics found the following average percentage budget allocations: food and beverage 17.8; housing 42.6; clothing 6.5; transportation 18.7; medical care 4.8; entertainment 4.4; and other goods and services 5.1. Housing, clothing, and medical care were up in 1982–1984 from 1972–1973, whereas food, transportation, and medical care were down.

5. Timothy Tregarthen, "Introducing the CPI's New Basket," *The Margin* (September 1987), pp. 12–13.

within a typical unit), poorer in real income terms, and less likely to be headed by a male.

The process of finding cost of living changes based on the random sampling of prices has its limitations. Style and quality changes make price comparisons over time difficult. If a PC is three times more powerful and costs twice as much as before, this is a quality-unadjusted price *increase*, but a quality-adjusted price *decrease*. Historically, the BLS has underestimated quality changes, thereby overstating price increases.

The CPI is very important to our economy. The incomes of over 60 million people, primarily Social Security recipients (38 million) and pensioners, and 20 million food stamp recipients are indexed to it. In addition, roughly 4 million workers have cost-of-living adjustment (COLA) clauses in their contracts. The CPI is not only the most popular general price index, it is also a figure closely watched by policymakers. Much of our countercyclical monetary and fiscal policy is tuned to the movements of the CPI. The CPI differs from the comprehensive quarterly implicit GNP deflator price index mentioned previously. That price index includes all final goods and services produced (consumer, investment, government, and world trade) and not just consumer goods, and it uses current-year market basket weights rather than base-year market basket weights. The two indices do tend to move together. The **producer price index** (PPI, formerly the wholesale price index) is the ratio of nonretail prices in any year to nonretail prices in the base year (currently, 1967). The PPI is done monthly for "all commodities," (1) for stages of processing (by degree of fabrication, finished goods, intermediate or semifinished goods, and crude materials) and (2) for commodity groupings such as farm products and various industrial commodities (textiles, chemicals, lumber, machinery, transportation, etc.). PPI prices are usually a leading indicator for CPI prices.

Producer price index (PPI): the ratio of nonretail prices in any year to nonretail prices in the base year (currently, 1967).

The CPI figure for any year is obtained by dividing the cost of the market basket for that year by its cost in the base year (currently, 1967) and multiplying by 100. For example, the consumer price index for 1988 is figured this way:

$$\text{consumer price index} = \frac{\text{cost of market basket in 1988}}{\text{cost of market basket in 1967}} \times 100$$

The index figure for 1967 is equal to 100 (that is, the cost of the market basket for the base year quantity of goods and services for 1967 divided by the cost of the same basket of goods, which equals 1, multiplied by 100). Because prices were lower in the years before 1967, the index figures for those years are less than 100. Since 1967 prices have been higher, and the index figures are greater than 100. For instance, prices were 3.404 times higher in 1987 than in 1967 for the market basket, so the 1987 CPI is 340.4 (3.404 × 100).

Table 5.7 gives the consumer price index for selected years from 1929 to 1987. Prices fell by around 24 percent between 1929 and 1933, the period of the Great Depression. They nearly tripled in the three decades between 1933 and 1967, and more than tripled again in the two decades between 1967 and 1987. From a yearly rate of 1.6 percent in 1960, inflation

Year	Consumer Price Index (1)	Annual (year-to-year) Percentage Change in Consumer Price Index (2)
1929	51.3	0.0
1933	38.8	−5.1
1940	42.0	1.0
1950	72.1	1.0
1960	88.7	1.6
1967	100.0	2.9
1970	116.3	5.9
1980	246.8	13.5
1987	340.4	3.7

TABLE 5.7 Consumer Price Index, 1929–1987 (base year 1967)

Sources: U.S. Bureau of the Census, *Historical Statistics of the United States* (Washington, D.C.: U.S. Government Printing Office, 1975), pp. 210–211; *Economic Report of the President* (Washington, D.C.: U.S. Government Printing Office, 1988), pp. 313, 318.

jumped to 13.5 percent in 1980 before dropping to 3.7 percent in 1987. From 1939 to 1988 the CPI fell—i.e., there was deflation—in only three years (1939, 1949, and 1954) and each decrease was less than 2 percent.

Chapter Review

Review of Key Questions

1. *Why is GNP the most common measure of economic production for the macroeconomy?*

   Gross national product is a precise, albeit sometimes arbitrary, measure of total production of final goods and services in the United States during a specified period of time—usually one calendar year. It can be calibrated using either an expenditure or resource cost-income approach. GNP does not attempt to measure social or even economic welfare. GNP statisticians are merely "bean counters" who make no value judgments.

2. *What are the deficiencies of GNP statistics?*

   GNP is deficient in several respects: it values goods in terms of their market prices; does not include all production, such as household and unreported (underground) income, in the economy, including instead only market production; adjusts imperfectly for changes in the quality of old products and for the introduction of new products; does not allow for changes in the amount of time people spend at work; is not adjusted for the production of economic "bads" with positive social costs; and does not reflect the impact of changes in the price level and in population. The measure of (or net) economic welfare makes adjustments in GNP for non-market bads and goods to obtain a more accurate assessment of social welfare. The computation of real GNP corrects for price changes through the GNP deflation price index. The calculation of per capita GNP corrects for population changes.

◢   *3. What are other non-GNP measures of productive activity in the macro-economy?*

Net national product (NNP) is obtained by subtracting a capital con-sumption allowance for replacement of old equipment from gross na-tional product. NNP measures real growth in production rather than maintenance of existing productive capacity. National production can be computed by adding up either the total market value of the goods and services sold, or the total expenditures made on those goods and services. Because the market value of goods is determined by the amount of money people spend on goods and services, the two measures must be equal. National income (NI) is a measure of the income received by all resources. Personal income (PI) is a measure of the income people re-ceive before personal taxes are deducted. Disposable personal income (DPI) is a measure of the amount of income people have available to spend after taxes. People can either save or spend their DPI. In recent years, people in the United States have generally saved 5 percent or less of their DPI.

◢   *4. What does the unemployment rate measure?*

The unemployment rate is an indicator of lost production as well as a measure of the economic hardship suffered by workers. The calculated unemployment rate is based on very precise definitions of who is and is not employed and unemployed. Because of the definition of unemployed used by the Bureau of Labor Statistics, the unemployment rate cannot be expected to fall to zero.

◢   *5. What are the shortcomings of unemployment rate statistics?*

Because the unemployment rate does not recognize hidden unem-ployment such as underemployed or discouraged workers, it does not capture the full extent of social hardship and forgone production. The unemployment rate also fails to reflect changes in the size of the labor force. The labor force participation rate, however, measures what frac-tion of the relevant population is in fact active in the labor force.

◢   *6. What is inflation and how is it estimated in the macroeconomy?*

Inflation is a continuing increase in the overall level of quality-adjusted prices over a period of time, causing both costs and benefits. The consumer price index is perhaps the most popular means of mea-suring inflation. Because it is based on a survey of goods and services that are not bought in the same proportions by everyone, the CPI does not give a true indication of changes in the cost of living for all con-sumers. Two other popular measures of inflation are the GNP implicit price deflator index and the producer price index.

Further Topics

The gross national product, the unemployment rate, and the consumer price index measure the performance of the U.S. economy in terms of national production, the percentage of the work force without jobs, and the level of prices. These figures will always be rough approximations of the variables they measure. The method used for determining gross national product dictates that much productive activity will go unmeasured because we lack a reasonable means of estimating the monetary value of the goods and services we produce for ourselves and for the underground economy. The method used for calculating the unemployment and employment rates counts as employed some people who are hard hit by economic decline, whereas others who are working (in the underground economy) are considered unemployed.

Slight inaccuracies like these are unavoidable. All-inclusive surveys of employment and price levels would be prohibitively costly. The Bureau of Labor Statistics cannot interview every potential worker in the United States every month. Nor can it hope to record the monthly prices of all the millions of goods and services produced by the economy. Thus the Bureau has adopted statistically sound sampling procedures based on broad categories of employment status and a representative selection (a market basket) of consumer goods.

As rough as they are, macroeconomic statistics can influence the nation's economic performance. Changes in the gross national product and other indexes can cause businesses to alter their production plans and support or undermine the public's confidence in the economy. If the statistics look bad, politicians may feel compelled to do something to demonstrate their concern, even though their response may be inadequately planned, ill-timed, and perhaps unwarranted. Unless we understand the meaning of these statistics—their sample base, limitations, and deficiencies—they may become our masters, as Humpty Dumpty suggested. People unfamiliar with the definition of *unemployed* may ask why government does not try to reduce unemployment to zero, for instance. They may expect more of government than it can possibly deliver.

Review of New Terms

Consumer price index (CPI) The ratio of the cost of specific consumer items included in a representative consumer market basket in any one survey year to the cost of those items in the base year (currently, 1967).

Consumer unit A household of people who pool their money.

Disposable personal income Personal income minus personal tax payments (as well as some minor non-tax payments).

Expenditure approach The approach to calculating GNP which sums the dollar value of all final products.

Final goods and services Those goods and services that are purchased by their ultimate users rather than for further processing or resale.

Gross national product (GNP) The current market value in dollars of all final goods and services produced in the economy in a given period.

Hidden unemployment Underemployed and discouraged workers, who quit looking for work after long periods of rejection and are thus not considered unemployed, as they are not actively seeking work.

Implicit GNP price deflator index A price index that shows the cost of buying the final goods and services included in the GNP during some year relative to the cost of buying these same items during a base year (currently, 1982).

Inflation A sustained rise in the general level of quality-adjusted prices over a period of time; it causes both costs and benefits.

Intermediate goods and services Goods and services that are purchased for further processing in producing another good or service for resale.

Labor force All persons sixteen years of age or older (i.e., adults) who are willing and able to work and who are counted as either unemployed or employed.

Labor force participation rate The number of adult civilian people in the labor force divided by the adult civilian noninstitutional population.

Measure of (or net) economic welfare (MEW or NEW) A measure that adjusts GNP for non-market bads and goods to obtain a better measure of quality of life or social welfare.

National income The total income payment made to owners of human and physical productive resources for the use of those resources during a given period.

Net national product (NNP) Gross national product minus an allowance for replacement of worn-out plant and equipment (called the capital consumption allowance).

Nominal, money, or current dollar gross national product The gross national product with no adjustments made for price changes.

Personal income The part of national income that is paid to individuals as opposed to businesses.

Producer price index (PPI) The ratio of nonretail prices in any year to nonretail prices in the base year (currently, 1967).

Real or constant dollar gross national product The gross national product adjusted for price changes using the implicit GNP price deflator.

Resource cost-income approach The approach to calculating GNP which sums the dollar income payments to all resources.

Underemployed workers Those people either working at part-time jobs although they would prefer full-time jobs or working at jobs for which they are overqualified in terms of training, education, or experience.

Underground economy Unreported legal and illegal activities excluded from traditional GNP estimates.

Unemployment rate The ratio of the number of people estimated to be unemployed to the number of people estimated to be in the labor force, stated as a percentage.

Value added Amount of additional market value or income created at any stage of production.

Review Questions

1. Are absolute current-dollar GNP figures meaningful? (◢ 1, ◢ 2)

2. Using the definitions of *employed, unemployed,* and *not in the labor force,* classify each of the following:
   a. A person who works twenty hours a week without pay in a family-owned drugstore.
   b. A person who works ten hours a week for a charitable organization.
   c. A person who works six hours a week for pay.
   d. A person who is on strike.
   e. A steel worker who has been laid off because of a strike in the automobile industry.
   f. A person who expects to report back to work within ten days.
   g. A person who is not working but who expects to report to a new job within sixty days.
   h. A person whose hours have been cut from forty to twenty per week.
   i. A person who is not working but who expects to report to a new job within fifteen days.
   j. A full-time college student.
   k. A person out of work because of sickness.
   l. A person fifteen years old who works thirty hours a week for pay.
   m. A person seventeen years old who works fourteen hours a week on his family's farm. (◢ 4)

3. Presuming that the data in question 2 cover the whole labor force, determine the unemployment rate. (◢ 4)

4. Should much importance be attached to small month-to-month changes in the unemployment rate and consumer price index? Why? How may government interpret such changes? How may an opposition party interpret them? (◢ 5, ◢ 6)

5. Do people have sufficient incentive to learn about the limitations and deficiencies of economic statistics? Given your answer, how may these statistics be used by politicians? (◢ 2, ◢ 3, ◢ 5)

CHAPTER

6

Macroeconomic Problems and Policies

What can be done [about inflation]? Before we look for remedies, we must examine the causes. Inflation is like cancer: many substances are carcinogenic, and many activities generate inflation. The sources of inflation can be diagnosed at several levels. . . . Inflation usually is the final link in the chain of well-meant actions. Inflation is the long-run consequence of short-run expediencies. Life, to be sure, is a succession of short runs, but every moment is also the long run of some expedience of long ago. We are now experiencing the long-run consequences of the short-run policies of the past. These consequences are as unacceptable as rain on weekends, and just as easy to change.
    Henry Wallich

KEY QUESTIONS

▲ 1. Is inflation a major macroeconomic problem in the United States?

▲ 2. Is unemployment a major macroeconomic problem in the United States?

▲ 3. Are stagflation and lagging productivity major macroeconomic problems in the United States?

▲ 4. What are business cycles?

▲ 5. What are the major macroeconomic schools of thought?

NEW TERMS

Aggregate demand
Aggregate supply
Business cycle
Classicism
Coincident indicator
Composite index
Cost-push or sellers' or
    suppliers' inflation
Cyclical unemployment
Demand-pull or buyers' inflation
GNP gap
Hidden unemployment
Keynesian
Lagging indicator
Leading indicator
Misery (or discomfort) index
Monetarist
Natural rate of unemployment

Neutrality of money
Okun's Law
Peak
Phillips curve
Potential output (or GNP)
Rational expectations
Real balances or wealth effect
Recession
Recovery
Stagflation
Structural inflation
Structural unemployment
Supply-side
Transitional (frictional or
    search) unemployment
Trend
Trough

The last chapter described several ways economists measure macroeconomic activity—or the lack of it. In this chapter we will use those measures to explore the depth and breadth of the economic problems our nation faces, as well as various theories about the causes and cures of those problems.

A macroeconomic policy to improve the welfare of much or all of a nation's population must pursue goals that have achieved some general consent. Domestic macroeconomic goals on which policymakers and the public generally agree include (1) full and stable employment, (2) reasonable price stability, and (3) high and rising incomes.[1] Attaining these goals is no simple matter, however.

The opening chapters of this book noted that every economic endeavor has a cost. This is certainly the case with macroeconomic policy. The pursuit of stable prices may require that we forgo some jobs. Attempts to stabilize employment may reduce economic growth. The search for macroeconomic stability may also require that we sacrifice some individual freedoms, since no government policy ever enjoys the consent of all citizens. Therefore, in considering our macroeconomic problems and the policies available to us, we might ask

○ How serious is the problem?

○ What can be done about it?

○ At what costs will the problem be resolved?

Macroeconomic Problems

▲ **1. Is inflation a major macroeconomic problem in the United States?**

In recent decades, the United States and most other nations have failed to reach their macroeconomic goals. In varying degrees, they have faced inflation, unemployment, or both of those problems simultaneously—a macroeconomic condition that has been called stagflation. Although the Reagan

---

1. As we shall see in Chapters 34 and 35, macroeconomic policy may also be used to attain international goals such as reasonable stability in the exchange rate and equilibrium in the balance of payments.

Misery (or discomfort) index: the equally weighted sum of the CPI inflation rate and the civilian unemployment rate.

administration improved the **misery (or discomfort) index,** the equally weighted sum of the CPI inflation rate and the civilian unemployment rate (for instance, if the inflation rate is 5 percent and the unemployment rate is 6 percent, then the misery index is 11 percent), it was still at historically high levels until about 1986. Economic growth has been sluggish in many parts of the world. We will examine the effects and suspected causes of each of these problems in turn.

Inflation

The price level has been changing throughout U.S. history. As Figure 6.1 shows, periods of increasing prices (inflation) have alternated with periods of decreasing prices (deflation). Since 1939 there have been only three years of actual deflation (1939, 1949, and 1954), and even then, it was very modest—under 2 percent each year. Most episodes of rapid inflation have occurred during wartime: the War of 1812, the Civil War (1861–1865), the two world wars (1914–1918 and 1941–1945), and the Korean and Vietnam wars (1950–1953 and 1961–1973). The highest year-to-year increase in the CPI in the United States since 1939 was 14.4 percent in 1947, which pales compared to some countries such as Bolivia, whose annual inflation rate was 20,000 percent in 1985!

Persistent growth in the peacetime inflation rate is a recent problem. Over the nineteenth century, prices drifted gradually downward. In 1800 the consumer price index stood at less than 40; one hundred years later, after several periods of ups and downs, it was only 25.[2] Not until the 1920s did the index regain its 1800 level. By 1950 the CPI stood at 72—44 percent higher than it had been just twenty years earlier, and in the next decade alone, the price level rose 23 percent.

The generally upward course of prices over the last twenty-eight years is shown more clearly in Figure 6.2. During the first half of the 1960s the inflation rate was a modest 1.2 percent, but in the second half of the decade, as the war in Vietnam escalated, prices began to move sharply upward. The average rate of inflation for the period 1965 to 1969 was 3.4 percent. For the early 1970s, despite government-imposed price controls, the rate was even higher, 6.1 percent. In 1974 it hit a shocking 11 percent, and for the rest of the decade inflation continued high, at an average of 8.1 percent. Not until the late 1980s—a decade after the end of the Vietnam War—did inflation return to the levels of the late 1960s. While inflation averaged 7.5 percent from 1980–1984 (peaking at 13.5 percent in 1980), it fell to 3.1 percent from 1985–1987. For six years—from 1982 to 1987—CPI inflation averaged a modest 3.8 percent.

The generally rising inflation rate was all the more difficult to deal with because it varied from year to year. It might reach 6 percent in one year and fall to 4 percent the next, and then rise to double-digit levels. At times during 1979 and 1980, the inflation rate rose to 15, even 18, percent.

---

2. The index figures for the years before 1930, when data were not gathered regularly, are rough estimates only.

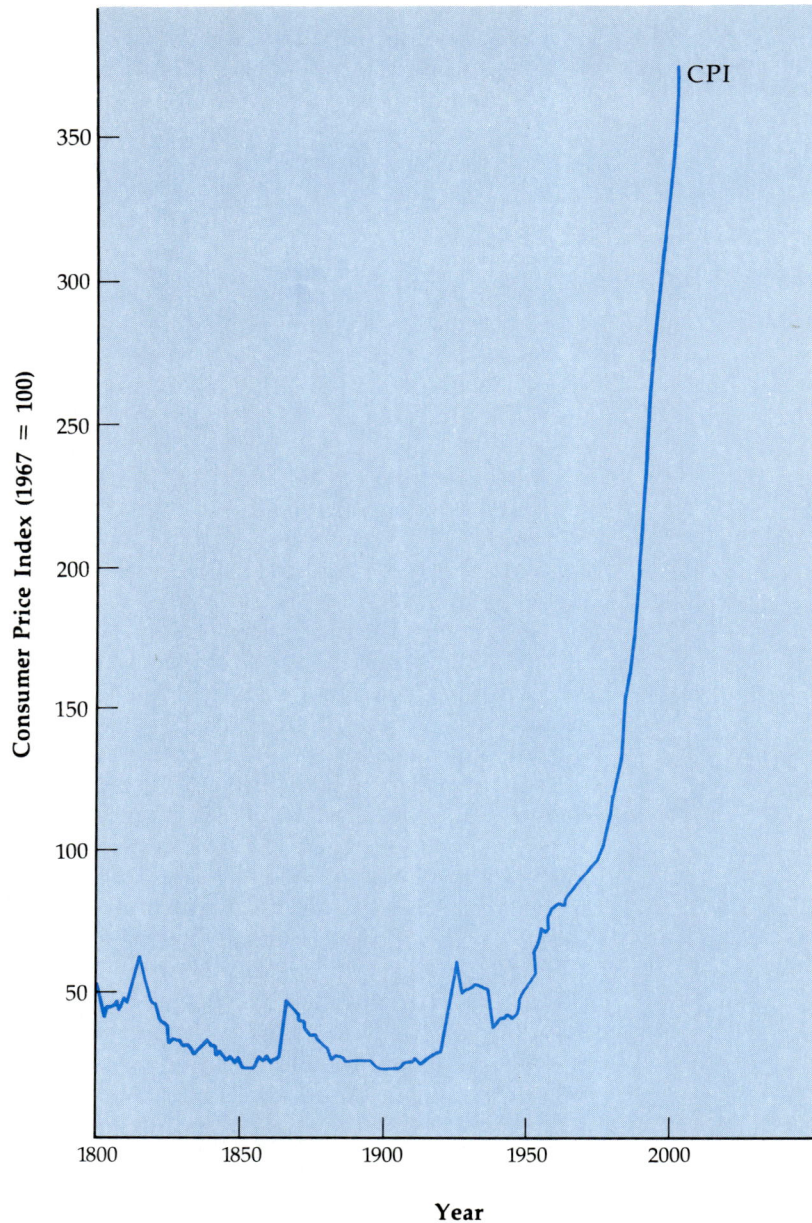

FIGURE 6.1 The Consumer Price Index, 1800–1987

Over the past two centuries the price level has moved both up (inflation) and down (deflation). Many of the fluctuations occurred during times of major change in the nation's
monetary institutions. Since 1939 there have been only three years (1939, 1949, and 1954)
of deflation; deflation was less than 2 percent in each of these years.

Sources: U.S. Bureau of the Census, *Historical Statistics of the United States* (Washington, D.C.: U.S. Government Printing Office, 1975), pp. 210–211; *Economic Report of the President* (Washington, D.C.: U.S.
Government Printing Office, 1988), p. 313.

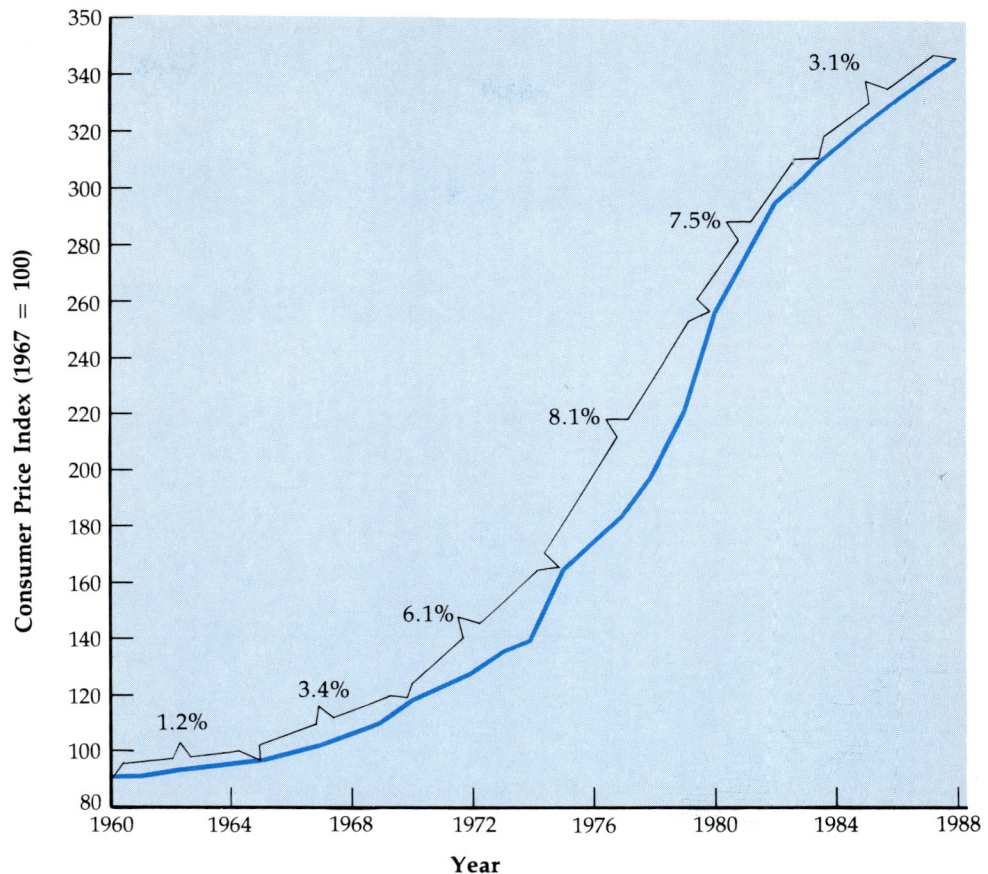

FIGURE 6.2 The Consumer Price Index, 1960–1987

Over the past twenty-eight years the consumer price index measured year to year has moved sharply upward, reflecting rising rates of inflation. From a five-year average of 1.2 percent in 1960–1964, 3.4 percent in 1965–1969, and 6.1 percent in 1970–1974, inflation rose to an average of 8.1 percent in the last half of the 1970s, from 1975–1979. From 1980–1984, however, the rate fell to an average of 7.5 percent, and for the three years 1985–1987 the rate tumbled to 3.1 percent.

Source: Economic Report of the President (Washington, D.C.: U.S. Government Printing Office, 1988), p. 318.

Predicting future inflation rates became an exercise in crystal-ball gazing, and planning future purchases became a risky endeavor for both consumers and business people. The volatile annual U.S. inflation rates are shown in Figure 6.3.

U.S. inflation has been lower than that of many other nations (see Table 6.1). During the late 1950s and most of the 1960s, the United States had one of the world's lowest compound inflation rates, 2 percent. The compound rate was higher in the 1970s, averaging around 7 percent, but it

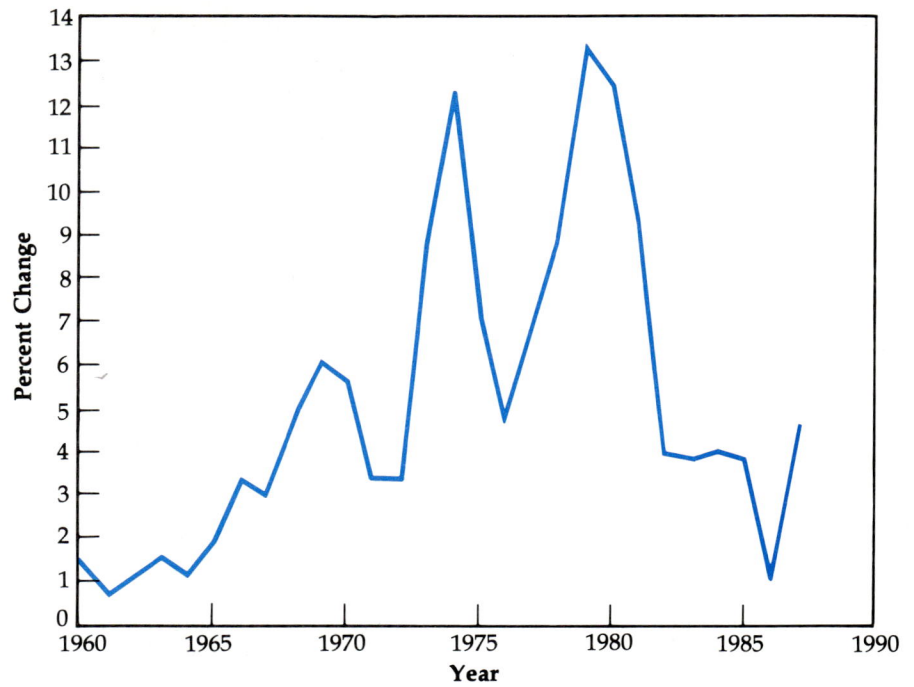

FIGURE 6.3 Percentage of Change Year to Year in the Consumer Price Index, 1960–1987

The inflation rate, as measured by the percentage of change in the consumer price index year to year, generally moved sharply upward during the 1960s and 1970s. However, the pace of price increases was very irregular, especially during the 1970s. On an annual basis, the inflation rate peaked at an average of 11 percent in 1974, only to fall to 5.8 percent in 1976. In 1980 it peaked again at an annual average of 13.5 percent. On a month-to-month basis, the inflation rate in 1980 was even more volatile: it fell from 18.2 percent in January to 1.2 percent in July, and then rose to 14 percent in November. After averaging about 12 percent for 1980–1981, the inflation rate fell dramatically. From 1982 to 1987 it averaged 3.8 percent.

Source: Economic Report of the President (Washington, D.C.: U.S. Government Printing Office, 1988), p. 318.

was still one of the world's lowest. Even the double-digit rate of 1980–1981 was below the rates of most other nations. Over the five-year period 1981–1985 the United States did quite well, averaging 6 percent inflation; only Japan, West Germany, and Switzerland did better, having lower rates.

The record of the past two-and-a half decades nevertheless raises some questions:

○ What causes inflation?

○ Why has inflation risen so dramatically in the last several decades?

○ How does inflation affect our ability to produce and earn a living?

○ What are the costs and benefits of inflation?

○ What roles does government policy play in creating inflation?

○ What can government do to stop or at least moderate inflation?

These questions have no easy answers. If they did, inflation would surely not be such a persistent problem. As the Wallich quotation at the opening of this chapter suggests, part of the difficulty is that inflation has many causes.

Types of Inflation

There are three types of inflation: demand-pull, cost-push, and structural. Each has a different cause. **Demand-pull or buyers' inflation** occurs when total planned expenditures increase faster than total production. That is, people want to buy more than the economy is producing, usually at full employment or full capacity. In bidding for the limited number of goods and services available, they pull prices up. Demand-pull inflation may be stimulated by increases in the supply of money or in government expenditures—a subject to which we will return in later chapters.

Cost-push or sellers' or suppliers' inflation occurs when restrictions are placed on the supply of one or more resources or when the price of one or more resources is increased. The linchpin of this inflation is on the supply side of the market. For example, cost-push inflation may result from a cutoff in oil imports because of war or political disturbances. Competition

Demand-pull or buyers' inflation: a general rise in prices that occurs when total planned expenditures increase faster than total production.

Cost-push or sellers' or suppliers' inflation: a general rise in prices that occurs when restrictions are placed on the supply of one or more resources, or when the price of one or more resources is increased.

TABLE 6.1   Inflation Rates in Selected Countries, 1955–1985

	Compound Annual Rate of Change in Consumer Prices				
Country	1955–1968	1969–1974	1975–1978	1980–1981	1981–1985[a]
Argentina	27	32	244	105	383
Brazil	38	21	36	106	154
Canada	2	5	8	12	7
Chile	28	225	180	20	6
Colombia	10	15	23	28	22
Ecuador	2	11	13	16	27
France	5	7	10	13	10
Italy	3	8	15	18	14
Japan	4	10	7	5	3
Peru	9	9	38	75	105
Switzerland	2	7	7	7	4
United Kingdom	3	9	15	12	7
United States	2	6	7	10	6
West Germany	2	6	4	6	3

a. Unweighted average of annual percentage changes.

Sources: U.S. Congress, Joint Economic Committee, *Industrial Policy Movement in the United States: Is It the Answer?*, 98th Congress, 2nd Session (Washington, D.C.: U.S. Government Printing Office, June 8, 1984), p. 24; U.S. Bureau of the Census, *Statistical Abstract of the United States: 1987* (107th edition) Washington, D.C.: U.S. Government Printing Office, 1986), p. 829.

for the restricted supply pushes oil prices up. It may arise from a curtailment of food supplies, like wheat or soy beans, because of poor weather. Cost-push inflation may also stem from wage increases that are not matched by productivity increases or from price fixing on the part of monopolies and oligopolies. In all these instances, output is restricted—either physically or, as in the last two cases, because a higher price reduces the demand for a resource. Competition among consumers for the limited output then forces the general price level up.

Structural inflation occurs when producers cannot readily shift production in response to changes in the structure of the economy. Changes in the demand for a product, in the technology of its production, and in the competition producers face can all cause structural inflation. Structural inflation may result when the overall composition of what consumers, businesses, and governments want to buy changes and producers cannot readily alter their employment of resources and their product mix. It may also be caused by the introduction of a major production innovation—for example, the advent of trains or the development of assembly-line robots. Changes in the structure of the economy create strategic shortages, or bottlenecks, in production supply lines. If a good like steel is caught in such a bottleneck, its price will rise, and that increase will then be transmitted to the prices of many other goods that use steel.

Structural inflation: a general rise in prices that occurs when producers cannot readily shift production in response to changes in the structure of the economy.

Reducing Inflation

There are two major problems in dealing with inflation. The first is identifying which type of inflation is at work because each type requires a different response. Demand-pull inflation may be tackled by reducing total spending—for example, by cutting government expenditures or increasing income taxes (since higher taxes will reduce consumer spending). Programs to increase the supply of certain key products, such as oil, may relieve cost-push inflation. Structural inflation may be attacked by eliminating the problems workers encounter when moving among different industries.

The second problem is overcoming political objections to implementing the appropriate policies. If inflation is caused by increases in the amount of money in circulation or by excessive government spending, then the obvious solution is to control the money supply and the government's tendency to overspend. Such steps may be politically unpopular, however. As long as citizens believe in the existence of the free lunch, governmental belt tightening—especially when it hits one's favorite government program—is bound to be controversial.

Unemployment

▲ **2. Is unemployment a major macroeconomic problem in the United States?**

During most of the years from 1959 to 1970, unemployment fluctuated between 3 and 7 percent. After 1970, however, the rate moved irregularly upward, peaking above 10 percent in 1982 before falling back to under 6 percent in 1988 (see Figure 6.4).

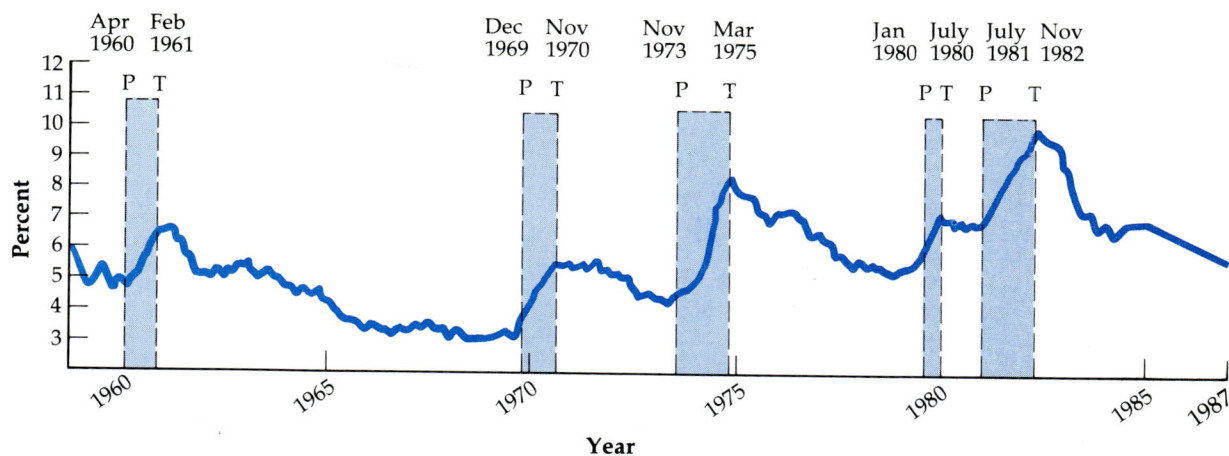

FIGURE 6.4   Unemployment in the United States
Over the past thirty years the unemployment rate has rarely dropped below 4 percent.
Since the late 1960s the rate has gradually increased, rising to unusually high levels during
times of recession (the shaded areas). The *P*s correspond to peaks, the *T*s to troughs.
Sources: U.S. Department of Commerce, Bureau of Economic Analysis, *Business Conditions Digest* (February 1985), p. 18; *Economic Report of the President* (Washington, D.C.: U.S. Government Printing Office,
1988), p. 292.

Unemployment means lost output as well as personal hardship for
those who are out of work. Besides reducing output, unemployment trig-
gers higher government expenditures on unemployment compensation
and welfare programs. Eventually those expenditures are translated into
higher taxes for the reduced working population—a problem in itself. Upward mobility becomes more difficult and discrimination accelerates when
many people are scrambling for few jobs. Investment and innovation also
suffer when unemployment is high.

As in the case of inflation, the data on national production and unemployment raise many questions:

○ Why is the national production level not greater than it is? Why is it
not smaller?

○ Why is the unemployment rate so high? Why has the rate not fallen
below 4 percent more often? Why does the economy seem unable to
operate with unemployment of less than 3 percent?

○ How has government policy affected the nation's unemployment
and production levels?

○ Why has a growing percentage of the labor force sought employment outside the home? Why has the economy not provided all such
people with jobs?

DIALOGUE
Growing Stability in the Twentieth Century

During the twentieth century the real gross national product of the United States has grown at a modest rate of about 3 percent a year. Although the overall trend has been positive, annual growth rates have fluctuated widely (see Figure 6.7). Especially in the first half of the century, the economy swung back and forth between rapid growth and negative growth.

These swings were not random, but related to historical events. The first major downswing of the century, the recession of 1913 to 1914, was due partly to a financial panic that caused a run on the banks. Both the panic and the recession were short-lived. They were followed by a period of inflationary growth, caused by mobilization for the First World War. When the war ended in 1918, the price level fell, and the nation had to convert its factories back to peacetime production. The result was a new downturn, the recession of 1919 to 1921, but the gains made after that recession more than offset its losses.

The 1920s were years of rapid economic growth, but the postwar boom halted abruptly with the onset of the Great Depression of 1929 to 1933—the greatest peacetime cataclysm in American history. In just four years the nominal gross national product fell from $104.6 billion to $56.1 billion. Even allowing for the simultaneous fall in prices, real GNP dropped at a precipitous rate.

Like earlier recessions, the Great Depression was followed by an economic expansion. This recovery, however, did not advance the economy past earlier highs. Its gains almost, but not quite, made up for depression losses. (Figure 6.7 shows that the upswing following 1933 is of almost the same magnitude as the downswing preceding 1933.) In 1938, real GNP was almost the same as it had been in 1929.

The stagnation of the 1930s ended with mobilization for the Second World War (1939–1945), which brought another inflationary boom. Real GNP, the price level, and manufacturing output all rose rapidly after 1940. Once the United States became an active participant in the war (1941),

unemployment virtually disappeared. As had happened after the First World War, the end of the hostilities was followed by deflation and problems of readjustment to peacetime production. The result was a short but severe recession from 1945 to 1947. Recovery was rapid, however, and growth had resumed by the 1950s, aided somewhat by the expansion accompanying the Korean War (1950–1953). Growth remained positive throughout the decade, except for a brief recession in 1954 following the end of the Korean War.

The 1960s witnessed sustained economic growth, leading some economists to conclude that business cycles were a thing of the past. Indeed, the chart shows a moderation of the wide swings of the first half of the century. Although the Vietnam War brought the usual wartime inflation, it did not produce the rapid economic expansion associated with previous wartime eras.

The naive belief that the business cycle was obsolete collapsed in 1974–1975, when the Arab oil embargo plunged the United States and other industrial nations into the most severe recession since the 1940s. Although the ensuing recovery more than offset the losses of that recession, it was accompanied by the century's highest rate of peacetime inflation. In 1980 the consumer price index rose an alarming 13.5 percent. The recession that followed in 1981–1982 may have been caused in part by the adoption of anti-inflationary policies in the early 1980s.

Although events of the 1970s and 1980s have shown that the business cycle is not dead, the rate of change in real GNP has clearly been much steadier since 1950 than before. Why has the business cycle become less extreme? One possibility is that since 1950 the nation has experienced no events as catastrophic as the Great Depression or the Second World War. The U.S. economy may be more stable because the world as a whole is more stable. Another possibility is that the counter-cyclical policies the federal government has pursued in the last few decades have moderated the effects of business cycles. As government policymakers learn more about macroeconomics, their effectiveness may be increasing. Finally, the moderation of business cycles may stem from the increasing size of government itself. Government economic activity tends to be more stable than private economic activity, and the government's share of real GNP has been growing in the latter half of the century.

Whatever the reason, the U.S. economy has become more stable since 1950. Most economists believe that this greater stability will continue through the end of the century.

Continuing Instability in the Twentieth Century

Most economists routinely accept the belief that the macroeconomic stability of the American economy has increased over time. Disagreements arise over why (see previous box), but the general improvement is taken as a fact. Recently, however, the standard belief has been challenged in a provocative series of papers by Christina Romer.[1]

According to Romer, the macroeconomic instability of the pre-1929 economy is a statistical illusion arising from the methods used to calculate national income and other macroeconomic data. The government did not begin to collect data on gross national product and other aggregate measures of economic activity until after World War II. Data for earlier years are statistical reconstructions produced by economic historians. Such reconstructions are, of course, likely to contain more errors than data collected in more recent times. The "bad" data enshrined in the statistical reconstructions of economic historians are full of missing observations, necessitating frequent interpolations between benchmark years and the use of proxies for missing data. Romer contends that the procedures used to create the historical series have confused instability with the errors and limitations of the data. For example, the historical data on industrial production display much greater voltaility before 1914 than after 1947 because the pre-1914 index was based very heavily on the production of materials, which is far more cyclical than overall production.[2] In other words, an error due to the limited and inappropriate nature of the data shows up in the time series as instability. When data collection improved after the war, such errors disappeared and stability apparently increased.

In an ingenious research strategy, Romer compared the pre-1929 and post-1945 macroeconomies by constructing "bad" data for the postwar era. Her aim was to create a series comparable to the historical data by applying the methods of the economic historians to modern data. When she carried out this exercise, she found that the pre-1929 economy was approximately as stable as the post-1945 economy. The real contrast in American economic history is therefore not pre– versus post–World War II, but the Great Depression of 1929–1939 versus the rest of our history. The important question for economic historians, then, is why that one episode of catastrophic instability occurred.

Critics have questioned some of Romer's methods and conclusions. She has nevertheless struck a telling blow against the complacent belief that our increasing economic knowledge and experience have caused a steady increase in the stability of the American economy.

1. Christina Romer, "New Estimates of Prewar Gross National Product and Unemployment," *Journal of Economic History* 46 (June 1986): 341–352.

2. Christina Romer, "Is the Stabilization of the Postwar Economy a Figment of the Data?," *American Economic Review* 76 (June 1986): 314–334.

Types of Unemployment

Unemployment has various causes, each requiring its own remedy. Unemployment may be transitional (frictional or search), cyclical, structural, or hidden. **Transitional (frictional or search) unemployment** occurs when people move from one job to another requiring similar skills. Transitional unemployment is caused by normal shifts in the supply of and demand for products. It is generally temporary, lasting a few days to a few weeks.

Cyclical unemployment is caused by downswings of the business cycle—that is, by a broad-based reduction in the overall spending in the economy. It generally lasts for a period of weeks or months, until something eliminates the insufficient aggregate demand, causing an increase in business activity that raises national output and increases demand for labor.

Structural unemployment is caused by major changes in the skills needed by workers because of technological innovation or changes in the relative competitiveness of an industry. In total, structural unemployment can be caused by technological changes, geographic and demographic factors, changes in the structure of consumer demand, and foreign competition. Structural unemployment can last for years, until workers are retrained for new jobs.

Hidden unemployment involves people not counted in statistics as unemployed because they are either underemployed involuntarily at part-time rather than the desired full-time jobs, or they are working at jobs for which they are overqualified, or they are discouraged and have quit looking for work after a long period of turndowns. This means that true unemployment is worse than statistics indicate. Of course, people may lie about looking for a job—to be unemployed rather than not in the labor force and to keep welfare payments or unemployment compensation payments. This would mean that true unemployment is better than statistics would indicate.

Reducing Unemployment

Different types of unemployment require different solutions. Transitional unemployment may be shortened by providing information on jobs—for example, through Job Service offices. Manipulation of government spending and tax policies can moderate business cycles, thus reducing cyclical unemployment and some forms of hidden unemployment. Relief of structural unemployment may require the introduction of special training programs or changes in the educational system.

Realistically, however, unemployment can never be completely eliminated. The natural rate of unemployment is always higher than zero. The **natural rate of unemployment** is the minimum percentage of the labor force that is unemployed because of structural problems in the economy and transitional movement among jobs. The natural rate of unemployment involves the economy's maximum sustainable rate of **potential output (or GNP)** such that there is no tendency for inflation to accelerate or decelerate. This natural rate is not immutably fixed by nature, but is influenced by both public policy and the structure of the labor force. As we saw in the preceding chapter, the unemployment rate is really a snapshot of the economy at a given point in time. At any particular moment, some people will be

---

Transitional (frictional or search) unemployment: unemployment that occurs when people move from one job to another requiring similar skills.

Cyclical unemployment: unemployment that is caused by downswings of the business cycle—that is, by a broad-based reduction in the overall level of spending in the economy.

Structural unemployment: unemployment that is caused by major changes in the skills needed by workers.

Hidden unemployment: unemployment that involves people not counted in statistics as unemployed because they are either underemployed involuntarily at part-time jobs, or they are working at jobs for which they are overqualified, or they are discouraged and have quit looking for work.

Natural rate of unemployment: the minimum percentage of the labor force that is unemployed because of structural problems in the economy and transitional movement among jobs.

Potential output (or GNP): the maximum sustainable rate of output (i.e., real GNP) that involves no tendency for inflation to accelerate or decelerate, associated with the natural rate of unemployment.

caught changing jobs. Others will be counted as unemployed because of the way the Department of Commerce defines *unemployed*. In a dynamic economy, furthermore, some workers are bound to be out of work because of changes in the structure of the economy. That is, their skills are no longer easily employed where they live. Until they adjust their skills or location, they will be counted among the unemployed.

Economists generally agree that the natural rate of unemployment is several percentage points above zero. They do not agree on exactly what the figure might be and whether or not it has been rising over time. In the 1960s many economists felt that the natural unemployment rate might be as low as 3 or 4 percent. Nowadays, many believe it is probably at between 5 and 7 percent of the labor force. Of course, the actual role of unemployment is normally greater than the natural rate, although on rare occasions (such as 1943–1945) the actual rate (below 2 percent) was less than the presumed natural rate (3–4 percent).

During the 1970s most economists felt that the frictional and structural unemployment that makes up the natural rate of unemployment increased.[3] The three major factors were unfavorable demographics, increasing government transfer payments, and inflationary shocks. The women and baby-boomers who were flocking to the labor force could not be absorbed quickly enough. Frictional unemployment also rose because these groups had less attachment to the labor force. The government's enhanced unemployment compensation, welfare, and social benefits made people choosier about jobs, which augmented the natural rate. Finally, dramatic increases in oil and food prices and tight labor and commodity markets made the government fight inflation more vigorously at the expense of jobs. Happily, by the mid-1980s this trend was arrested, and the natural rate of unemployment dropped as the previously three factors were each moderated. The demographics have been more favorable, and government policy helped to reduce transfer payments and inflation. Also the erosion of the real minimum wage by inflation and the lost market power by unions have helped keep the natural rate down despite the off-setting tendency of rapid technological change to increase it.

GNP gap: the difference between potential GNP (i.e., full employment) and actual GNP.

Okun's Law: for every 1 percent increase in actual unemployment greater than the natural rate there is produced a 2½ percent increase in the GNP gap.

Of course, the major loss to society of unemployment is the loss in GNP. This loss is usually measured in terms of the **GNP gap**—the difference between potential GNP (i.e., full employment) and actual GNP. (Normally this gap is positive, but during World War II and Vietnam it was negative.) Arthur Okun was an economist who estimated the magnitude to society of idle resources. **Okun's Law** states that for every 1 percent increase in actual unemployment greater than the natural rate there is produced a 2½ percent increase in the GNP gap. Thus, if the actual unemployment was 8 percent and the natural rate was 5 percent, this 3 percent difference would generate a 7.5 percent (3.0 times 2.5) GNP gap. There are also noneconomic—social, political, psychological—costs for

---

3. Henry F. Myers, "High Unemployment Is Likely to Linger On," *Wall Street Journal* (February 25, 1985), p. 1.

those unfortunate enough to be unemployed. Of course, the probability of unemployment is not random across the labor force but falls more heavily on blue-collar, teenage, minority, and female workers.

Stagflation

▲ **3. Are stagflation and lagging productivity major macroeconomic problems in the United States?**

As recently as twenty years ago, most economists and government policy-makers believed that high unemployment would be accompanied by low rates of inflation and vice versa. During periods of high unemployment, they reasoned, workers would be competing for a restricted number of jobs and thus would lose much of their ability to drive up wages. (Wage increases would be passed on to consumers as higher prices.) High unemployment would also depress people's incomes and thus the demand for goods and services. Lower demand would mean less upward pressure on prices.

Phillips curve: a graphical representation of the presumed short-run inverse relationship between unemployment and inflation, assuming a certain expected rate of inflation.

This presumed relationship between unemployment and inflation is shown graphically by the Phillips curve, named for the British economist who first observed it (see Figure 6.5). The **Phillips curve** is a graphical representation of the presumed short-run inverse relationship between unemployment and inflation, assuming a certain expected rate of inflation. Since the 1960s much of government policy has been based on the idea that a lower unemployment rate could be traded for a higher inflation rate and vice versa. In other words, using government fiscal and monetary powers, policymakers could move the macroeconomy up or down the Phillips curve at will. The only question facing policymakers was which combination of unemployment and inflation they should seek.

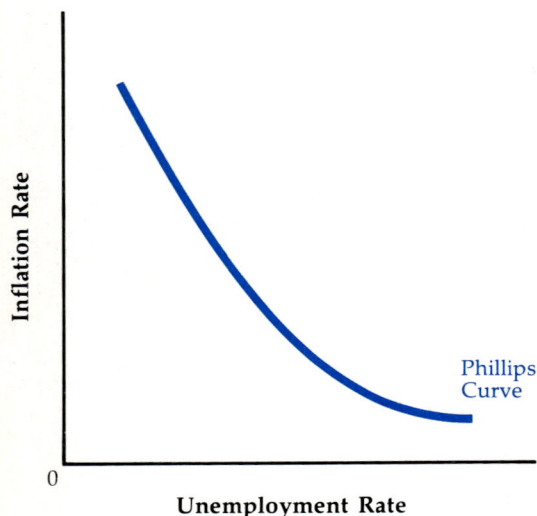

FIGURE 6.5 The Short-Run Tradeoff Between Inflation and Unemployment

The Phillips curve illustrates the presumed short-run inverse relationship between unemployment and inflation, assuming a certain expected rate of inflation. Theoretically, the inflation rate rises when the unemployment rate falls, and vice versa.

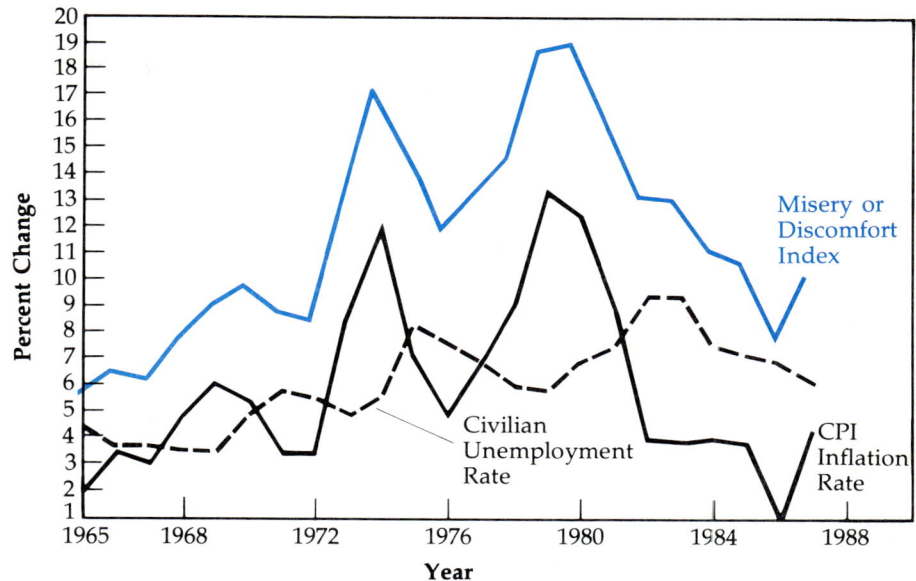

FIGURE 6.6   The Misery or Discomfort Index, 1965–1987

Over the past twenty years or so both unemployment and inflation have generally tended to move upward. The misery (or discomfort) index—the sum of the civilian unemployment and CPI inflation rates—has therefore moved upward as well. The experience of the last two decades suggests that unemployment and inflation may not be inversely related in the long run, as economists once thought.

Source: Economic Report of the President (Washington, D.C.: U.S. Government Printing Office, 1988), pp. 292, 318.

Events of the 1970s and early 1980s disproved that line of thinking, however. Although economists of different persuasions—Keynesian, monetarist, supply side, rational expectations, and so forth—may argue over the short-run validity of the Phillips curve, few economists today believe in its long-run validity. As Figure 6.6 shows, inflation and unemployment were not inversely related in the 1970s and 1980s—at least not for more than a few months. Economists found during the 1970s and early 1980s that the Phillips curve was not stable but shifted to the right, largely based on heightened expectations about the future inflation rate. In the late 1980s it shifted back to the left as these expectations were changed. From 1965 to the early 1980s both unemployment and inflation followed a general upward trend, with lower inflation subsiding significantly after 1982. In fact, in the 1970s the overall relationship between unemployment and inflation may well have been positive. That is, the higher the inflation rate, the higher the unemployment rate and vice versa. The long-run positive tendency is particularly striking if the two rates are summed to obtain the so-called misery (or discomfort) index (see Figure 6.6).

Stagflation: the combination of persistently high rates of unemployment and inflation.

This dual problem of high unemployment and high inflation is often called stagflation. **Stagflation** is a portmanteau word created from *stag*nant and in*flation*. It is the combination of persistently high rates of unemployment and inflation. This economic condition has challenged old remedies and posed a new set of questions:

1. How can high unemployment and high inflation coexist? Is stagflation a peculiarly modern problem? Is it presently a concern?

2. Is there a cause-and-effect relationship between inflation and unemployment? If so, what is it? Is there a tradeoff between unemployment and inflation disguised somewhere in the data for 1970–1987? Can the unemployment part of stagflation be reduced by reducing the inflation rate? If so, how can inflation be lowered, and how long will it take for the lower rate to reduce unemployment?

3. Have government policies contributed to the simultaneous rise of inflation and unemployment? To what extent is stagflation caused by economic forces outside the United States, like the oil price increases of 1974?

Lagging Growth in Productivity and Real Income

Because people's incomes are tied directly to what they produce, increases in the aggregate national income must be tied to increases in productivity. Without an increase in worker output, there can be no increase in worker income. People can be given more dollars to spend. Without an increase in output to spend them on, however, the extra dollars will go up in the smoke of higher prices.

Historically, American workers have increased their productivity gradually through improved skills, better education, the use of greater amounts of physical capital, and the discovery of new and less costly sources of energy. Between 1947 and 1970, for instance, output per workhour in the private sector expanded at an average annual rate of 2.3 percent. After 1970, however, growth in worker productivity dipped below 2 percent per year and almost ground to a halt during the last three years of the 1970s. That slowdown in productivity growth diminished the growth of real purchasing power. Beginning in 1983 worker productivity turned upward again, along with the increase in general economic activity that began then.

Table 6.2 shows the rate of growth in real GNP in several developed countries (including OECD countries, the European Community, the United States, Canada, and Japan) and in developing and communistic nations from 1961 to 1987. In the 1960s, output grew more slowly in the United States than in most other nations, whether developed, developing, or communistic. In the late 1970s, however, only Japan and the developing countries had noticeably higher growth rates than the United States. The baby-boom generation reached working age in the 1970s, and the labor force participation rate rose as more women took jobs outside the home.

TABLE 6.2   Growth Rates in Real Gross National Product, 1961–1987 (percentage of change)

Area and Country	1961–1965 Annual Average	1966–1970 Annual Average	1971–1975 Annual Average	1976–1980 Annual Average	1981–1985 Annual Average	1986	1987[a]
Developed countries							
OECD countries[b]	5.3	4.6	3.0	3.3	2.5	2.7	2.8
European Community[c]	4.9	4.6	2.9	3.0	1.5	2.6	2.3
France	5.9	5.4	4.0	3.6	1.5	2.1	1.6
Italy	4.8	6.6	2.4	3.8	1.6	2.7	2.7
United Kingdom	3.2	2.5	2.1	1.7	1.9	2.3	3.5
West Germany	4.7	4.2	2.1	3.4	1.2	2.5	1.7
Canada	5.3	4.6	5.2	3.7	2.7	3.0	3.7
Japan	12.4	11.0	4.3	5.0	4.0	2.5	3.6
United States	4.6	3.0	2.2	3.4	2.6	2.9	2.9
Developing countries	5.3	5.8	5.7	5.0	1.6	4.0	3.3
Communist countries[d]	4.4	5.0	4.2	2.8	2.4	4.1	(e)
China	−0.2	8.3	5.5	6.1	9.3	7.5	9.5
Eastern Europe	3.9	3.8	4.9	1.9	1.2	2.7	2.0
U.S.S.R.	4.7	5.0	3.0	2.3	1.9	3.8	1.0

a. Preliminary estimates.
b. OECD (Organization for Economic Cooperation and Development) includes Australia, Austria, Belgium, Denmark, Finland, France, Germany, Greece, Iceland, Ireland, Italy, Luxembourg, Netherlands, New Zealand, Norway, Portugal, Spain, Sweden, Switzerland, Turkey, and United Kingdom.
c. Includes Belgium, Denmark, Greece, Ireland, Luxembourg, Netherlands, Portugal, and Spain.
d. Includes North Korea and Yugoslavia.
e. Not available.

Sources: Department of Commerce, International Monetary Fund, Organization for Economic Cooperation and Development, and Council of Economic Advisers; cited in *Economic Report of the President* (Washington, D.C.: U.S. Government Printing Office, 1988), p 374.

The result was a sharp increase in the size of the United States work force. In the 1980s the U.S. economy held its own against everyone and bettered most other economies.

Still more questions arise:

1. What caused the slowdown in the growth of worker productivity during the 1970s and the modest pickup in the 1980s?

2. Is worker productivity affected by the rate of inflation? By tax increases? By government policy? If so, how?

3. What can government do, if anything, to promote growth in productivity? How will policies to promote growth in productivity affect the inflation and unemployment rates?

Alan S. Blinder points out most vividly the poor economic performance of the United States since 1973—he calls it "miserable"—in Table 6.3, which we have updated. All six of the indicators—unemployment, inflation, real GNP, real disposable income per capita, productivity, and real wages—worsened from the 1962–1973 period to the 1974–1986 period. Of course, the United States did not run downhill alone. Most countries, even the vaunted Japanese economy, performed worse in the 1974–1976 period than in the 1962–1973 period.

TABLE 6.3	Indicators of Macroeconomic Performance, United States, 1962–1987		
	1962–1973	1974–1986	1987[a]
Average unemployment rate (percentage of civilian labor force)	4.7%	7.4%	6.1%
Inflation rate (average percentage change, GNP implicit price deflator)	4.1%	6.7%	3.0%
Real GNP (average annual growth rate)	3.9%	2.3%	2.9%
Real disposable income per capita (average annual growth rate)	3.4%	1.4%	0.3%
Average growth rate of productivity (output per hour, business sector)	2.6%	0.9%	0.9%
Real wage rate (average annual growth rate, real compensation per hour, business sector)	2.6%	0.3%	−0.7%

a. Preliminary estimate.

Sources: Economic Report of the President, 1988 and *Economic Indicators.* Slightly adapted from Alan S. Blinder, *Hard Heads, Soft Hearts* (Reading, Mass.: Addison-Wesley, 1987), Table 2, p. 40.

Business Cycles

▲ **4. What are business cycles?**

As Figures 6.3 and 6.4 show, recent economic activity has proceeded in fits and starts. In fact, the history of the U.S. economy has been one of ups and downs, booms and busts. Figure 6.7 shows the irregular path of the nation's annual rates of growth in real GNP from 1910 to 1987. The Great Depression of the 1930s, the rather large shaded area in the middle of the graph, stands out as this century's longest period of economic distress. In recent decades, business activity has been substantially higher than the overall trend. Much of that apparent surge in activity can be ascribed to inflation, however.

Trend: a long-run directional change, up or down, in some economic variable—for example, real GNP.

The long-run upward movement of economic activity seen in Figure 6.4 is called a trend. A **trend** is a long-run directional change, up or down, in some economic variable—for example, real GNP. Because they are long-run measures, trends may be obscured by the small irregularities, or ups and downs, in year-to-year business conditions. These smaller movements, which can last for several years, within the long-term trend are called business cycles. A **business cycle** is a recurring but irregular swing in general economic activity, or a smaller pattern of ups and downs within a major long-term trend.

Business cycle: a recurring but irregular swing in general economic activity, or a smaller pattern of ups and downs within a major long-term trend.

Business cycles have four phases: a recession, a trough, a recovery, and a peak (see Figure 6.8). The cycle begins with a downturn in activity, called a recession. A **recession** is a downward movement in general economic activity, especially in national production and employment. The Department of Commerce defines a recession as a downward movement in real GNP that lasts at least six months (or two quarters). An especially severe

Recession: a downward movement in general economic activity, especially in national production and employment.

Trough: the bottom of the business cycle, the point at which general economic activity ceases to fall.

Recovery: an upward movement in general economic activity, especially in national production and employment.

Peak: the phase of the business cycle that occurs when general economic activity is no longer rising.

recession, with a substantial decline in real production and an unemployment rate of 15 percent or more, is called a depression.

When real GNP stops falling and unemployment stops rising, the trough of the business cycle has been reached. The **trough** is the bottom of the business cycle, the point at which general economic activity ceases to fall. Once the economy hits bottom, it may shift upward almost immediately or languish there for several months. When real GNP begins to rise and unemployment to fall, the economy has entered the recovery phase. A **recovery** is an upward movement in general economic activity, especially in national production and employment. A recovery may continue until full employment is approached, or it may be aborted fairly quickly by another recession.

The business cycle ends when the recovery phase reaches its peak. A **peak** occurs when general economic activity is no longer rising. The peak is

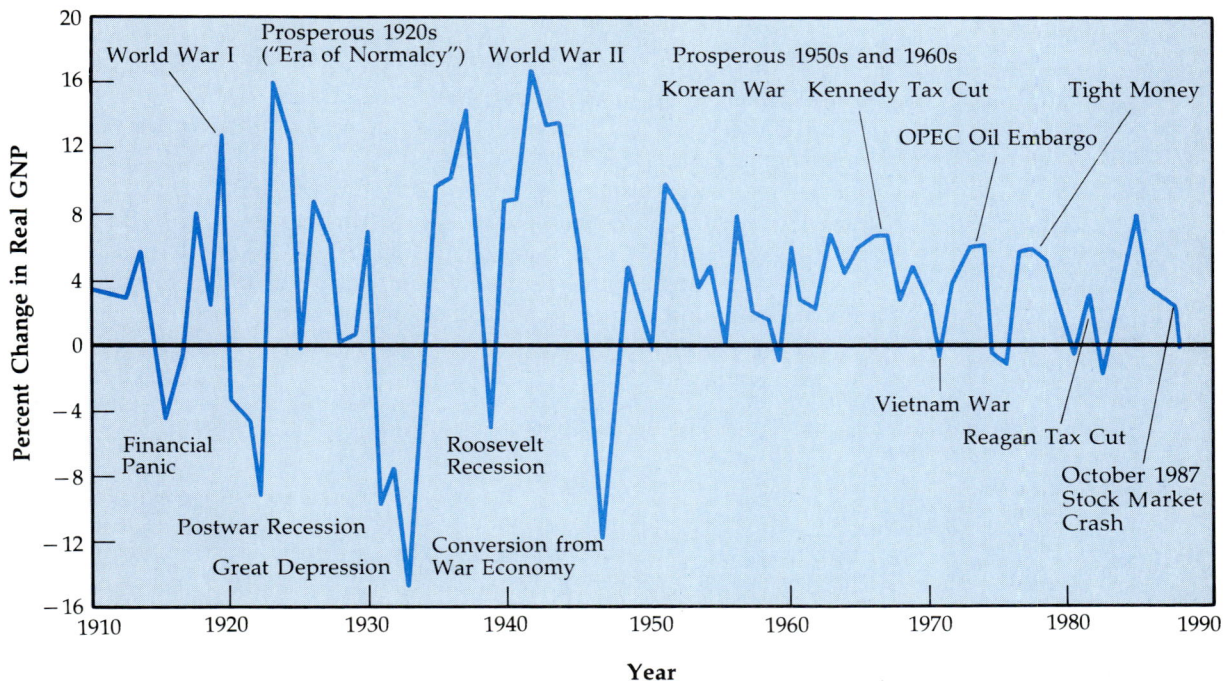

FIGURE 6.7   Business Cycles in the United States, 1910–1987

Overall, economic activity—measured by the percentage of change in real GNP—in the United States has expanded over the last century. The generally upward trend includes many boom-and-bust cycles, however, the most severe of which led to the Great Depression of the 1930s.

Sources: U.S. Bureau of the Census, *Historical Statistics of the United States* (Washington, D.C.: U.S. Government Printing Office, 1975), pp. 226–227; *Economic Report of the President* (Washington, D.C.: U.S. Government Printing Office, 1988), p. 251. Figures from 1939 on use 1982 dollars.

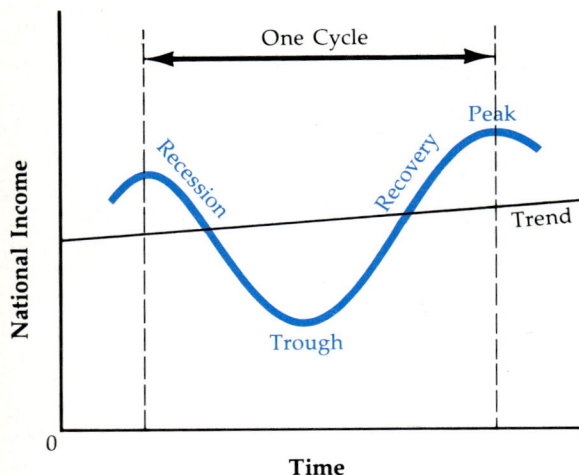

National Income

One Cycle

Recession

Recovery

Peak

Trend

Trough

0

Time

FIGURE 6.8   The Business Cycle
A complete business cycle has four phases: recession, trough, recovery, and peak.

the top of the business cycle, the transition from the recovery phase of one cycle to the recession phase of another. Thus a peak cannot be identified until a new recession has been declared—at least six months after real GNP begins to fall.

The length of a business cycle is measured from peak to peak. As Table 6.4 shows, recent U.S. business cycles have varied significantly in length, from one to several years. Look again at Figure 6.7. No two business cycles are exactly alike in depth or timing. These variations make predicting future business conditions an imperfect science at best.

TABLE 6.4   Business Cycles in the United States, 1926–1988

Peak	Trough	Peak	Length of Cycle from Peak to Peak (in months)
October 1926	November 1927	August 1929	41
August 1929	March 1933	May 1937	34
May 1937	June 1938	February 1945	93
February 1945	October 1945	November 1948	93
November 1948	October 1949	July 1953	45
July 1953	May 1954	August 1957	56
August 1957	April 1958	April 1960	49
April 1960	February 1961	December 1969	32
December 1969	November 1970	November 1973	116
November 1973	March 1975	January 1980	47
January 1980	July 1980	July 1981	62
July 1981	November 1982	Continuing	Continuing

Source: U.S. Department of Commerce, Bureau of Economic Analysis, *Business Conditions Digest* (February 1988 and earlier issues).

Leading indicator: an index of business activity that tends to move up or down several months before measures of general economic activity, like real GNP, move.

Coincident indicator: an index of business conditions that tends to move up or down roughly in line with general economic activity, like real GNP.

Lagging indicator: an index of business conditions that tends to move up or down several months after general economic activity, like real GNP, moves.

Composite index of leading indicators: a combined index of twelve leading economic indicators of business activity that tends to move up or down several months before measures of general economic activity, like real GNP, move.

Among the tools economists use in predicting business conditions are measures called leading indicators, which are published monthly by the National Bureau of Economic Research in *Business Conditions Digest*. A **leading indicator** (stock prices, unemployment) is an index of business activity that tends to move up or down several months before measures of general economic activity, like real GNP, move. A **coincident indicator** (personal income, industrial production, manufacturing, and trade sales) moves roughly in line with the general economy, like real GNP, and a **lagging indicator** (prime rate, unemployment duration, labor costs) tends to move up or down several months after general economic activity, like real GNP, moves. The **composite index of leading indicators** is a combined index of twelve leading economic indicators that tends to move up or down several months before measures of general economic activity, like real GNP, move. The composite index of twelve leading economic indicators for the 1964–1988 shown in Figure 6.9 combines information on stock prices, size of the money stock, unemployment, building permits, housing starts, commercial and industrial loans, and so forth, into a single measure of economic activity that tends to forecast changes in real GNP. The composite index has been a better predictor than any single index, although the notice prior to the peaks is much longer than prior to troughs. Sometimes the indicators give false signals or no clear signal at all. It is interesting to note that stock market prices are the most reliable and accurate of the twelve basic individual leading indicators. However, stock market prices lead peaks by only nine months and troughs by only five months.[4] By watching the index, as well as the individual indexes that go into the composite, economists and policymakers discern clues as to what will happen in the future. If the composite index turns down for several months, economists can predict a recession with some confidence.

Our survey of business cycles raises still more questions about the macroeconomy:

1. What causes the ups and downs in general business activity? Why is the overall upward trend not a smooth one?

2. What can government do to make recessions less likely or less severe?

3. Do government policies contribute to the length and severity of business cycles?

Major Macroeconomic Schools

▲ **5. What are the major macroeconomic schools of thought?**

Economists differ widely on what should be done to remedy the macroeconomic problems we have been discussing. In later chapters we will explain their views in considerable detail. Here we will simply outline them briefly.

---

4. Geoffrey A. Hirt and Stanley B. Block, *The Complete Investor: Instruments, Markets and Methods* (Homewood, Ill.: Dow Jones-Irwin, 1987), Chapter 5.

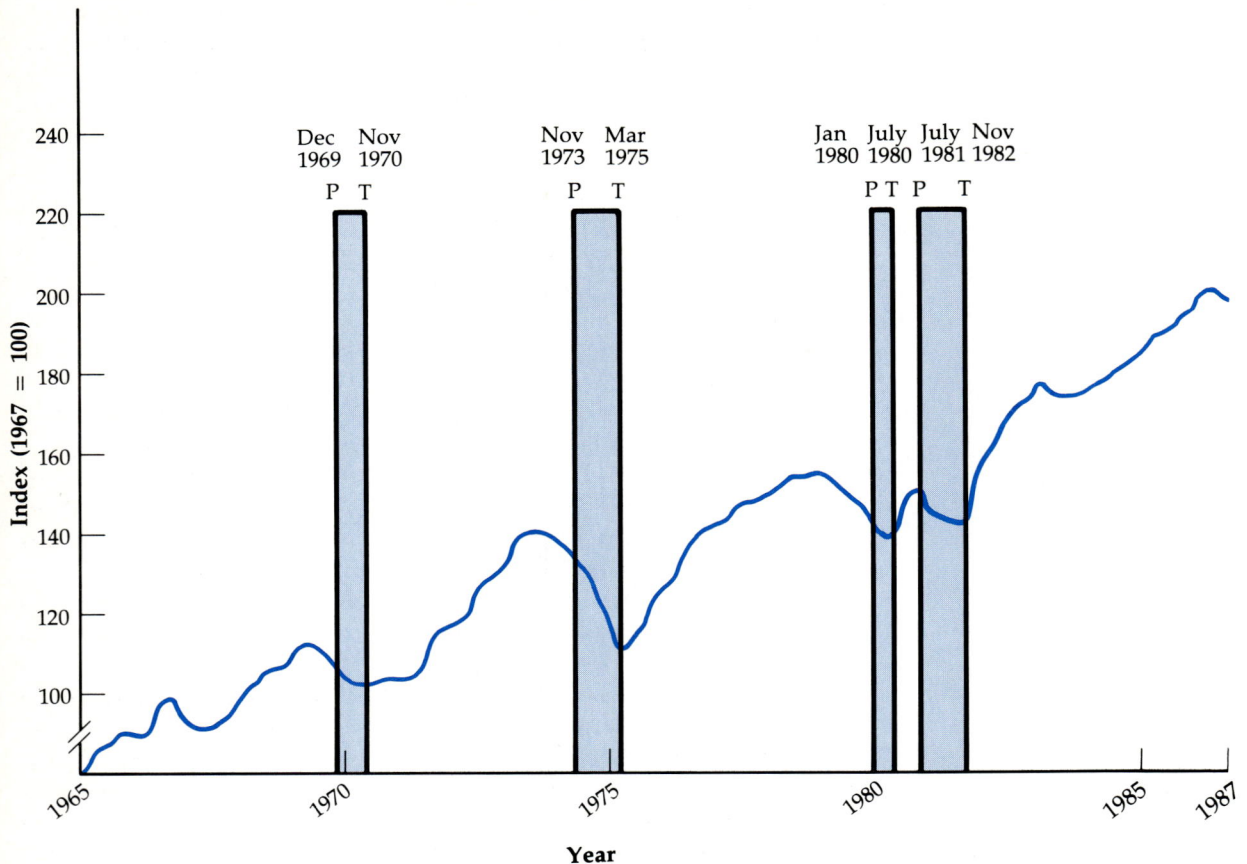

FIGURE 6.9   Composite Index of Leading Economic Indicators

The composite index of leading economic indicators is compiled from indexes that economists find useful as predictors, including indexes of stock prices, size of the money stock, unemployment, building permits, housing starts, and commercial and industrial loans. The composite index tends to change direction several months before a change in general economic activity—for example, a change in real GNP. Thus it aids economists in forecasting future economic conditions.

Note: The shaded areas correspond to recessions, with *P* for the peaks and *T* for the troughs of the business cycles.

Source: U.S. Department of Commerce, Bureau of Economic Analysis, *Business Conditions Digest* (February 1985), p. 10.

Classicism: a macroeconomic theory that emphasises that the economy in the long run will, if unimpeded, achieve equilibrium at full employment and neutrality of money.

The Classical School

Before the 1930s, most economists believed that the forces of supply and demand would eventually remedy problems of unemployment and low levels of production. **Classicism** is a macroeconomic theory that emphasises that one economy in the long run will, if unimpeded, achieve equilibrium and neutrality of money. According to classical theory, a rise in unemployment would depress wage rates because more workers would be competing for fewer jobs. When the price of labor fell, employers would hire more workers, lowering the unemployment rate and boosting production. Classical economists blame temporary factors for short-run disequilibrium problems and blame persistent unemployment and underproduction on unions and laws that prevent wage rates from falling in response to falling demand. Their prescription is straightforward: eliminate all legal impediments to flexibility in prices and wages.

Lagging growth in productivity can also be solved by the free market system, according to classical economists. If people want more goods and services enough to pay for them, then businesses will invest more, and the newer, more efficient equipment will permit a rise in productivity and future output. In the view of classical economists, lagging productivity indicates that consumers are not willing to pay for greater future output by forgoing current consumption. The classicists also opine that money could not change the real magnitudes of economic variables. That is, they believe in **neutrality of money:** that changes in the money supply affect the general price level but not relative prices. (For more on the classical school of economics, see Chapter 10).

Neutrality of money: the classical economists' belief that changes in the money supply affect the general price level, but not relative prices.

The Keynesian School

Keynesian economists—followers of the British economist John Maynard Keynes (1883–1946)—believe that the principal cause of low production and unemployment is inadequate total spending. Together, consumers, businesses, and government do not demand enough goods and services to employ the labor force fully. Keynesians would say that the fluctuations in macroeconomic activity reflect the fluctuations in demand, especially the demand for investment in capital goods. **Keynesianism** is a macroeconomic theory that emphasizes that the economy is inherently unstable and requires an activist discretionary government policy to stop unemployment and inflation. Their solution for unemployment is to increase total spending in any of several ways. One possibility is to reduce taxes, thereby increasing consumer and business purchasing power (and ultimately demand). Another is to increase government spending. A third is to lower interest rates by increasing the money stock, thereby encouraging businesses and consumers to obtain loans for new purchases. In fact, Keynesians believe any policy that stimulates the demand for investment will ultimately increase both production and the rate of growth in worker productivity. For Keynes's followers, both output and prices play an equilibrating role in the short run. Which factor will dominate depends on how many unemployed resources there are. If there are many unemployed resources, output changes more. If there are few unemployed resources, however, prices change more. The classicists put the entire burden of equilibrium in the short run upon prices.

Keynesianism: a macroeconomic theory that emphasizes that the economy is inherently unstable and requires an activist discretionary government policy to stop unemployment and inflation.

Keynesians also tend to see inflation as primarily a demand problem. Consumers demand more in total than the economy can produce, putting upward pressure on prices. The solution: reduce total demand by reversing the policies prescribed to reduce unemployment. Raise taxes, dampening consumer and business spending; or reduce government spending; or raise interest rates, reducing business and consumer loans and purchases. Unfortunately, according to traditional Keynesian theory, policies designed to reduce inflation will tend to raise unemployment and vice versa. (See Chapters 11–13 for more on the Keynesian model of the macroeconomy.)

The Monetarist School

The monetarists tend to see inflation and economic instability as largely a monetary problem. They believe that inflation results when too many dollars are pumped into the economy by government authorities (in the United States, principally the Federal Reserve System, which controls the money stock). The monetarists' solution is to reduce the growth in the amount of money in the economy. **Monetarism** is a macroeconomic theory that emphasizes a nonactivist economic policy; monetarists believe that the economy is inherently stable and will usually return to its natural state after any temporary disequilibrium. Thus, they recommend an "automatic" money supply growth rule (such as 2–4 percent per year) or at least a smoother and slower rate of growth of the money stock, rather than discretionary authority by the Fed. They place a lot of faith in the private sector's ability to right itself and are skeptical about the government's ability to manage the economy. Nobelist Milton Friedman compares the Federal Reserve's policymaking to a car racing through a tunnel, bouncing off the walls. The automobile may get to its destination, but people may get hurt in the process.

> **Monetarism:** a macroeconomic theory that emphasizes a nonactivist economic policy; monetarists believe that the economy is inherently stable and will usually return to its natural state after any temporary disequilibrium.

The monetarists also believe that many irregularities in economic activity stem from the irregular growth of the money stock. This opinion is based on the belief that the velocity of money is stable or at least predictable. They argue that the Great Depression of the 1930s was worsened by the Federal Reserve's contraction of the money stock by as much as a third during the early 1930s. Prices and wages simply could not adjust downward as rapidly as the money stock contracted; the result was severe unemployment.

Although they emphasize variations in the growth of the money stock, monetarists share many of the views of the classical school of economics. Much of modern unemployment, they believe, is due to legal restrictions such as minimum wage laws, which keep wage rates from falling and labor markets from reaching equilibrium. Monetarists also believe that some unemployment must be expected, given people's attempts to find the best jobs available, and given the existence of unemployment compensation and welfare benefits. In fact, if unemployment benefits and the growth of the money stock increase simultaneously, the monetarists would predict a rise in both inflation and unemployment. Monetarists are more concerned about reducing inflation than reducing unemployment. (Details of the monetarist theory are founded on the principles of money creation and control developed in Chapters 7, 8, and 9 and on theoretical points presented in Chapter 14.)

The Supply-Side School

Supply-side: a macroeconomic theory that emphasizes supply management and increased incentives to work, save, and invest over demand management when formulating macroeconomic policy to attain maximum employment, production, economic growth, and price stability.

In the late 1970s and early 1980s, some analysts began to suspect that much of our unemployment and inflation was due to problems with supply (not demand, as the Keynesians would argue). **Supply-side** is a macroeconomic theory that emphasizes supply management and increased incentives to work, save, and invest over demand management when formulating macroeconomic policy to attain maximum employment, production, economic growth, and price stability. Supply-side economists see high income tax rates as an important cause of low production and unemployment. Because government takes a relatively high percentage of what people earn, they reason, people have inadequate incentive to work, save, invest, and create jobs. Supply-side economists also see inflation as partly a supply problem. Price increases, they point out, can be moderated by an increase in production—in the supply of goods and services people want. Supply-side economics was so prominent during the Reagan administration that such economic policies are called *Reaganomics* by some.

Although the ideas and agenda of supply siders tend to "hang loose," a supply-side solution to unemployment, inflation, and productivity problems is to reduce tax rates, increasing people's willingness to work, save, and invest. Reduced unemployment and greater national output should result; and if the number of dollars in circulation stays constant or rises less than output, the increased supply of goods and services should exert downward pressure on prices. Reducing the tax rate may also (but will not necessarily) increase government revenues, for the rise in disposable income may more than offset the lower tax rate. Supply siders also advocated and were successful in 1985 in eliminating "bracket creep." This indexing was designed to eliminate, or at least moderate, "taxflation" on federal income taxes, whereby higher nominal incomes pushed people into higher tax brackets under the progressive tax system. (See Chapter 15 for more information on supply-side economics.)

The Rational Expectations School

Rational expectations: a macroeconomic theory that emphasizes the futility of macroeconomic policy-making, because people acting in their own self-interest will make adjustments to their anticipations or expectations based on what they know.

Although people's expectations of the future play a role in the Keynesian, monetarist, and supply-side models, they are a central element in the rational expectations model of the macroeconomy. **Rational expectations** is a macroeconomic theory that emphasizes the futility of macroeconomic policy-making, because people acting in their own self-interest will make adjustments to their anticipations or expectations based on what they know. Rational expectations theorists assume that people will acquire some rationally determined amount of information on the impact of government policies and will act on that information. For example, if people observe that government deficits and interest rates are positively related, they will try to borrow money when the government deficit goes up, expecting a rise in interest rates.

Unfortunately, the increased demand for borrowed funds will drive interest rates up almost immediately, not some time in the future. Keynes-

The Economic History of the Very Long Run

Economists and historians have long been fascinated with the economic history of the very long run. In the very long run, knowledge, technology, and the amount of resources all change. When everything is variable, prediction becomes extremely hazardous. We simply cannot know what will happen; all we can do is study what has come before in the hope of discerning some pattern. Many prominent scholars have searched for some hidden meaning or key to the grand sweep of economic history. Here we will briefly consider some of the more influential theories of the very long run.

In the 1920s the Russian economist N. D. Kondratieff claimed to have discovered long waves of economic activity. The long wave lasted fifty to sixty years and in turn consisted of several shorter waves or cycles. Kondratieff based his long wave theory on some apparent statistical correlations between economic time series (that is, annual data on prices, interest rates, exports, imports, and outputs of certain agricultural and industrial commodities) in France, Great Britain, Germany, and the United States. Although he had no theory to explain his long waves, Kondratieff believed that they were an inherent part of the development of capitalist economies. After years of neglect, interest in the Kondratieff cycle revived the wake of the business cycles of the 1970s and 1980s. If long waves exist (and the data are by no means clear on their existence), and one can discover their logic, it should be possible to predict the long-term movements of stock prices, bond prices, and a host of other economic variables. The potential payoff to such a discovery has fueled the revival of interest in long waves. Most economists remain skeptical, based on the belief that if human history can indeed be described as a series of Kondratieff cycles, we are still left with far too little historical data to discover the nature of these waves. After another ten waves (six hundred years) or so, mainstream economists will perhaps be more willing to pronounce on the validity of Kondratieff's theory.

The caution of most mainstream economists on the question of long waves notwithstanding, a few bold theorists have speculated on the existence and nature of the phenomenon. In the 1970s James B. Schuman and David Rosenau published a book on the long wave.[1] Based on their interpretation of Kondratieff, they predicted that the stock market would crash in 1980 and plunge the nation into a depression as severe as that of the 1930s. Needless to say, the 1980s have not been a depression decade, although the stock market declined in 1980.

1. James B. Schuman and David Rosenau, *The Kondratieff Wave* (New York: Delata, 1974).

ian theory predicts that an increase in the government deficit will raise national production (because demand rises with greater government spending), but rational expectations theorists would expect a higher deficit to lead to higher interest rates and an offsetting reduction in investment spending. Similarly, government efforts to change the money stock will be offset by people's defensive reaction, based on their expectations of what will happen to interest rates, prices, and production costs. Pushed to its logical limit, rational expectations theory suggests that government is virtually incapable of affecting national production and employment levels, even in the short run, by varying taxes, expenditures, or the money stock. (More will be said about rational expectations theory in Chapter 16.)

More recently, the economist Ravi Batra has proposed his own version of the long wave theory.[2] According to Batra, all human societies evolve according to the law of social cycles developed by the Indian scholar Prabhat Ranjan Sarkar. According to the law of social cycles, human beings can be divided into four basic types: laborers, warriors, intellectuals, and acquisitors. Human societies pass through epochs in which one of the four types dominates. In a society dominated by the acquisitive class, wealth becomes more and more concentrated until an economic crisis occurs, sweeping away the acquisitors and initiating an era of laborers and a new social cycle. American society, according to Batra, is now dominated by the acquisitors. He predicts, based on his belief that economic activity follows predetermined thirty- and sixty-year cycles, that in the 1990s the United States will experience a depression as severe as that of the 1930s. The stock market crash of October 19, 1987, seemed to bear out his prediction of a crash; we must wait to see if the depression follows.

Economic historians, as well as economists, are skeptical of long wave theories. To the historian, history—especially economic history—does not repeat itself. This is not to say that similar forces do not operate at different times. What historians believe is that humankind is not locked into some continually repeating historical pattern. The most influential theories of history portray it as a secular progress toward some desirable or undesirable end. For example, in Karl Marx's theory of history, class struggle based on the mode of production characterizes every historical stage. Yet the class struggle that takes place in feudal society differs from the class struggle that takes place in capitalist society. Other theories of history stress the increasing sophistication of technology and business organization. Others believe that the story is one of the growth of freedom and that economic freedom is one of several basic human rights.

It is, of course, altogether possible that economic history has no pattern other than that imposed by the historian. Any series of unique, random events will generate some correlations purely by chance. The historian may notice those correlations and build a theory to explain them, even though the events are not necessarily related. Perhaps people need to believe in some determinate pattern of events, even though none exists. The role of the historian of the very long run, then, may be to construct imaginative patterns that help people make sense out of an otherwise bewildering human past.

2. Ravi Batra, *The Great Depression of 1990* (New York: Simon and Schuster, 1987).

Common Ground Among Theories

Our discussion of the various schools of macroeconomic thought has emphasized the differences among the classical, Keynesian, monetarist, supply-side, and rational expectations theories. Those differences explain why economists often disagree about the policies government should adopt toward unemployment, inflation, and lagging growth. They disagree because they subscribe to different theories.

Discussing schools of thought separately has allowed us to highlight macroeconomic variables and their probable effects. Keynesian economics focuses on the impact of demand on production, income, and employment.

Monetarism considers how growth in the money supply influences inflation. Classical and supply-side economics stress factors that affect aggregate supply, and rational expectations theory emphasizes the influence of people's expectations on interest rates, inflation, and unemployment.

Readers should not conclude, however, that Keynesians are unconcerned with prices and expectations, that monetarists do not recognize government budgets' effect on prices, that supply-side economists ignore the effect of demand on production, or that rational expectations theorists do not recognize influences other than people's expectations. Almost all macroeconomic theories allow for the interplay of a combination of economic forces. Those forces invariably include money, aggregate demand, aggregate supply, and expectations. Theories differ primarily in their relative emphasis on these forces.

Aggregate Demand and Supply: A Macroeconomic Model

Chapter 3 showed how the laws of supply and demand determine the prices and quantities of particular goods in a market economy. Similar concepts can be applied to macroeconomics. In future chapters, we will see how aggregate (total) demand and aggregate (total) supply determine the general price level, national output, and national income. The aggregate demand and supply model will prove a useful tool for analyzing the various schools of macroeconomic thought.

Aggregate Demand

Graphically, aggregate demand can be described as a downward sloping curve, like the curve labeled *AD* in Figure 6.10. It looks much like the demand curve for individual products. The market demand curve and the aggregate demand curve are two different concepts, however. The market demand curve relates the price of a given good to its consumption level; the aggregate demand curve relates the general price level to total desired spending on national output. **Aggregate demand** is the presumed negative relationship between the general price level and the total quantity of goods and services consumers, business, and government want to buy in the economy during a given period of time.

The two curves slope downward for different reasons. The individual demand curve slopes downward because changes in price cause income and substitution effects. The aggregate demand curve slopes downward because changes in the general price level affect people's wealth (not because the market demands for individual products slope downward). When the price level falls, people can buy more with their cash, stocks and bonds, and other monetary assets; their aggregate real wealth rises, and they will buy more goods and services. Conversely, when the general price level goes up,

Aggregate demand: the presumed negative relationship between the general price level and the total quantity of goods and services consumers, business, and government want to buy in the economy during a given period of time.

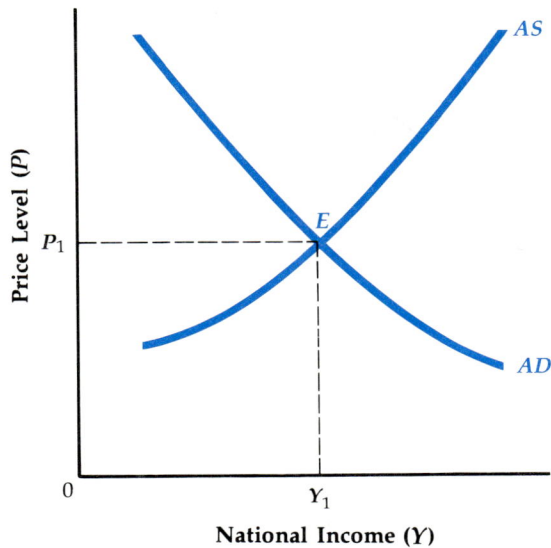

FIGURE 6.10 Aggregate Demand and Aggregate Supply
Aggregate demand and supply relate the nation's price level to its output. Here the macroeconomy will be in equilibrium (E) at a price level of P_1 and a national output level of Y_1. At any price level above P_1 the goods and services available will exceed the quantity demanded by households, firms, and government. Competitive pressure will force the price level back down to P_1. At any price level below P_1 the quantity of goods and services demanded will exceed the quantity supplied. Competitive pressure will force the price level back up to P_1.

Real balances or wealth effect: the change in real wealth resulting from a change in the purchasing power of nominal wealth.

aggregate purchases will decline along with aggregate real wealth. The change in real wealth resulting from a change in the purchasing power of nominal wealth is called the **real balances or wealth effect.** The aggregate demand curve shifts to the right or left if there are changes in real income, interest rates, the anticipated rate of inflation, future business activity that may cause changes in planned spending, or tastes. In addition, as the price level changes there is an interest-rate effect on consumption and investment spending. For instance, with the money stock fixed, a lower price level will lower the demand for money (and hence lower the interest rate) causing a greater consumption of interest-rate-sensitive goods and services—cars, houses, computers.[6]

Aggregate Supply

Aggregate supply: the presumed positive relationship between the general price level and the total quantity of goods and services produced in the economy during a given period of time.

Aggregate supply relates national output to the general price level. **Aggregate supply** is the presumed positive relationship between the general price level and the total quantity of goods and services produced in the economy during a given period of time. The short-run aggregate supply curve slopes upward, like the curve labeled *AS* in Figure 6.10. In the short run, production may be expected to rise with an increase in the price level, because

_____

6. In later chapters we will learn that one could add a foreign net export effect because a decline in the U.S. price level will increase exports relative to imports infusing net foreign spending into the United States.

price increases may take time to be translated into cost increases. Until costs catch up, producers will expand production to reap extra profits. In the long run, cost increases usually do catch up with price increases and supply contracts; aggregate supply becomes vertical, constrained by the natural rate of unemployment. The aggregate supply curve shifts in both the short run and the long run if there are changes in resource supplies, technology or productivity, or institutions that affect resource efficiency and productivity. It will also shift in the short run if there are unanticipated supply shocks and changes in the expected rate of inflation.

Aggregate Demand and Supply

Analysis of aggregate demand and supply resembles analysis of market supply and demand in one important respect: equilibrium (E) occurs at the intersection of the supply and demand curves. In Figure 6.10 at the equilibrium E_1, national output level is Y_1, the equilibrium price level P_1. If the price level is higher than P_1, the aggregate quantity of goods and services demanded will not meet the quantity producers offer on the market. The price level will fall, increasing the quantity business, government, and consumers will buy and decreasing the quantity producers will offer. If the price level is lower than P_1, all sectors of the economy will demand more than producers offer. Total production will expand; and the total amount that all sectors want to buy will contract.

The apparatus of aggregate demand and supply can be used to analyze many contemporary problems. For instance, it can be used to study infla-

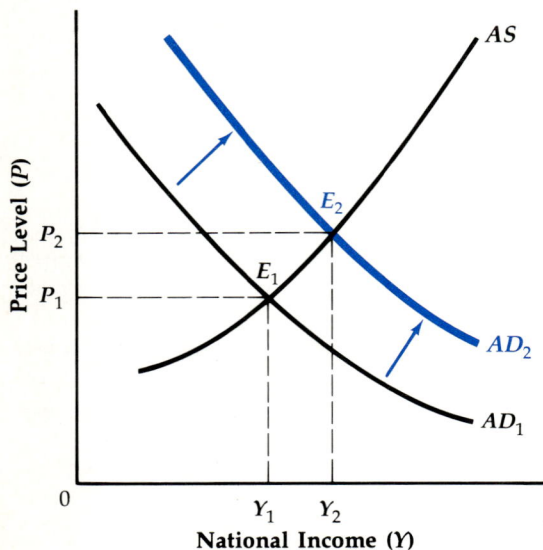

FIGURE 6.11 Effects of an Increase in Aggregate Demand
If aggregate demand rises from AD_1 to AD_2, the equilibrium will rise from E_1 to E_2 associated with new equilibrium price and national output levels. This level rises from P_1 to P_2 and the national output level rises from Y_1 to Y_2.

tion. In Chapter 9 we take up in detail both the costs and the benefits of inflation.

The following chapters will discuss the details of how price and output levels adjust, and how changes in aggregate demand and supply affect production, employment, and the price level. Economic policies designed to influence aggregate demand are likely to also influence aggregate supply and vice versa, thereby moderating their effectiveness. Briefly, an increase in government demand for goods and services (unless offset by a reduction in consumer and business demand) can cause an expansion in equilibrium national production and possibly an increase in the price level. The increase in government demand will shift the aggregate demand curve out—say, from AD_1 to AD_2 in Figure 6.11. At the initial price level, total planned spending will be greater than total supply; the price level will rise, prompting producers to expand production to the new equilibrium, E_2, from the previous equilibrium at E_1. A decrease in taxes could cause the same result. If disposable income rises, increasing aggregate demand, then price levels and national output will increase.

The price level may also fall, as a result of an increase in aggregate supply. If tax rates are reduced, increasing people's willingness to work and produce, the aggregate supply curve will shift outward to the right—say, from AS_1 to AS_2 in Figure 6.12. A higher national output level, Y_2, but a lower price level, P_1, will result at the new equilibrium, E_2, compared to the previous equilibrium at E_1.

Just how and why aggregate demand and supply change is the subject of considerable dispute among economists. Many suspect that business cycles are caused by these shifts in aggregate demand and supply. When

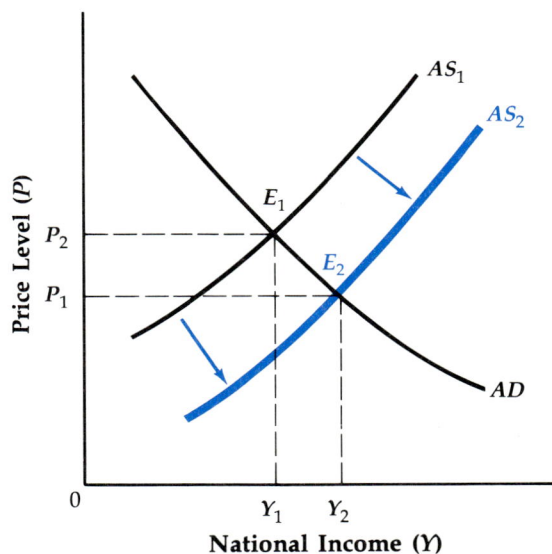

FIGURE 6.12 Effects of an Increase in Aggregate Supply
If aggregate supply increases from AS_1 to AS_2, the equilibrium will fall from E_1 to E_2 associated with a fall in the price level from P_2 to P_1 and a rise in the national output level from Y_1 to Y_2.

aggregate demand or supply shifts back and forth, everything else held constant, general economic activity will pick up or slow down. In fact, macroeconomics is largely the study of how broad sectors of the economy affect one another through their effect on aggregate demand and supply. Economists also disagree on the shape of the aggregate demand and supply curves. For instance, classical economists and some of the present offshoots of their philosophy believe that the aggregate supply curve is vertical, whereas Keynesian economists believe that it is horizontal. More will be said about aggregate demand and supply in Chapter 13.

Chapter Review

Review of Key Questions

◢   *1. Is inflation a major macroeconomic problem in the United States?*

Persistent high peacetime inflation is a relatively recent phenomenon in the United States. Although the inflation rate has varied considerably from month to month and year to year, over the last two decades the overall trend has been upward. The factors causing inflation can come from demand, supply, or structural factors.

◢   *2. Is unemployment a major macroeconomic problem in the United States?*

Since the Second World War, the U.S. economy has operated below capacity much of the time. The gap between actual real GNP and potential real GNP (full employment) reflects the unusually high rates of unemployment during this period. Unemployment comes in many sizes and shapes, including transitional, cyclical, structural, hidden, and natural. The actual unemployment rate is normally greater than the natural rate of unemployment (i.e., the structural and frictional), although on rare occasions it has been less.

◢   *3. Are stagflation and lagging productivity major macroeconomic problems in the United States?*

In the last two decades, policymakers have confronted the problem of stagflation, or high inflation combined with high unemployment. Economists disagree on the causes of stagflation. Over the last twenty years the misery or discomfort index has generally worsened, although there has been some relief in recent years.

◢   *4. What are business cycles?*

Business cycles involve recurrent, generally periodic fluctuations of economic activity around the long-run average or trend. Although each cycle differs in some respect from others, the common features include recession, trough, recovery, and peak. Forecasters often use the composite index of leading indicators to predict business cycles.

◢   *5. What are the major macroeconomic schools of thought?*

Economists differ on what should be done about inflation and unemployment. The classical, Keynesian, monetarist, supply-side, and rational expectations schools of thought stress different factors as the primary cause of economic difficulties.

Further Topics

Inflation, unemployment, and lagging growth in productivity affect almost all of us to some extent. We must all cope with uncertainty about future prices. To the extent that unemployment means lost output—that is, unsatisfied wants—it also affects everyone. Reductions in productivity growth will make us all less well off in the future than we might have been. What should we do about these problems? Economists disagree not only on which theory should guide policy, but on what goals government should pursue. Some believe government should do virtually nothing aside from creating a stable monetary system. They contend that, despite good intentions, government action has left us worse off on balance.

Most economists believe government bears some responsibility for promoting full employment, high productivity, and price stability. They do not always agree on how those goals should be achieved, however, because they base their policies on different theories. We would all be happier if the solutions to macroeconomic problems could be presented in a few pages. Unfortunately, the policy debate is not yet resolved, and probably will not be for some time.

Review of New Terms

Aggregate demand The presumed negative relationship between the general price level and the total quantity of goods and services consumers, business, and government want to buy in the economy during a given period of time.

Aggregate supply The presumed positive relationship between the general price level and the total quantity of goods and services produced in the economy during a given period of time.

Business cycle A recurring but irregular swing in general economic activity, or a smaller pattern of ups and downs within a major long-term trend.

Classicism A macroeconomic theory that emphasizes that the economy in the long run will, if unimpeded, achieve equilibrium at full employment and neutrality of money.

Coincident indicator An index of business conditions that tends to move up or down roughly in line with general economic activity, like real GNP.

Composite index of leading indicators A combined index of twelve leading economic indicators of business activity that tends to move up or down several months before measures of general economic activity, like real GNP, move.

Cost-push or sellers' or suppliers' inflation A general rise in prices that occurs when restrictions are placed on the supply of one or more resources, or when the price of one or more resources is increased.

Cyclical unemployment Unemployment that is caused by downswings of the business cycle—that is, by a broad-based reduction in the overall level of spending in the economy.

Demand-pull or buyers' inflation A general rise in prices that occurs when total planned expenditures increase faster than total production.

GNP gap The difference between potential GNP (i.e., full employment) and actual GNP.

Hidden unemployment Unemployment that involves people not counted in statistics as unemployed because they are either underemployed involuntarily at part-time jobs, or they are working at jobs for which they are overqualified, or they are discouraged and have quit looking for work.

Keynesianism A macroeconomic theory that emphasizes that the economy is inherently unstable and requires an activist discretionary government policy to stop unemployment and inflation.

Lagging indicator An index of business activity that tends to move up or down several months after general economic activity, like real GNP, moves.

Leading indicator An index of business activity that tends to move up or down several months before measures of general economic activity, like real GNP, move.

Misery (or discomfort) index The equally weighted sum of the CPI inflation rate and the civilian unemployment rate.

Monetarism A macroeconomic theory that emphasizes a nonactivist economic policy; monetarists believe that the economy is inherently stable and will usually return to its natural state after any temporary disequilibrium.

Natural rate of unemployment The minimum percentage of the labor force that is unemployed because of structural problems in the economy and transitional movement among jobs.

Neutrality of money The classical economists' belief that changes in the money supply affect the general price level, but not relative prices.

Okun's Law For every 1 percent increase in actual unemployment greater than the natural rate there is produced a 2½ percent increase in the GNP gap.

Peak The phase of the business cycle that occurs when general economic activity is no longer rising.

Phillips curve A graphical representation of the presumed short-run inverse relationship between unemployment and inflation, assuming a certain expected rate of inflation.

Potential output (or GNP) The maximum sustainable rate of output (i.e., real GNP) that involves no tendency for inflation to accelerate or decelerate, associated with the natural rate of unemployment.

Rational expectations A macroeconomic theory that emphasizes the futility of macroeconomic policy-making, because people acting in their own self-interest will make adjustments to their anticipations or expectations based on what they know.

Real balances or wealth effect The change in real wealth resulting from a change in the purchasing power of nominal wealth.

Recession A downward movement in general economic activity, especially in national production and employment.

Recovery An upward movement in general economic activity, especially in national production and employment.

Stagflation The combination of persistently high rates of unemployment and inflation.

Structural inflation A general rise in prices that occurs when producers cannot readily shift production in response to changes in the structure of the economy.

Structural unemployment Unemployment that is caused by major changes in the skills needed by workers.

Supply-side A macroeconomic theory that emphasizes supply management and increased incentives to work, save, and invest over demand management when formulating macroeconomic policy to attain maximum employment, production, economic growth, and price stability.

Transitional (frictional or search) unemployment Unemployment that occurs when people move from one job to another requiring similar skills.

Trend A long-run directional change, up or down, in some economic variable—for example, real GNP.

Trough The bottom of the business cycle, the point at which general economic activity ceases to fall.

Review Questions

1. Can you think of a macroeconomic problem not mentioned in this chapter? (◢1, ◢2, ◢3, ◢4)

2. Look up aggregate business expenditures in the most recent issue of *The Statistical Abstract of the United States,* published by the Department of Commerce, or in the *Economic Report of the President.* Then graph investment expenditures over the last twenty years. Do the same for the prime interest rate. Do the two measures seem to be related? (◢4)

3. Find several articles on macroeconomic problems in recent issues of the *Wall Street Journal.* Classify the statements of the economists quoted in those articles by school of thought. Do the articles represent a variety of theories? (◢5)

4. What actions has the government taken recently to deal with inflation, unemployment, and low productivity? How are those actions supposed to affect the economy? (◢3)

5. Are there tradeoffs in dealing with inflation, unemployment, and low productivity? If so, explain how the problems may be interrelated. (◢1, ◢2, ◢3)

PART III

Money and Monetary Policy

CHAPTER
7

The Meaning and Creation of Money

Money is a contract—the freest, most gorgeous contract of them all. Money is somebody else's promise to pay, to give me what I want, when I want it. What a magnificent conception! . . . Whatever else history may ultimately record of the Western Bourgeoisie, this honor most certainly must be accorded them: They perfected modern money, which is a contract with parties unknown for the future delivery of pleasures undecided upon.
   David Bazelon

KEY QUESTIONS

▲ 1.   What is money?

▲ 2.   What determines the value of money?

▲ 3.   What are the three types of demand for money?

▲ 4.   What are our major forms of money?

▲ 5.   What constitutes our banking system?

▲ 6.   How do checks transfer money?

▲ 7.   How do banks create money?

▲ 8.   What causes the money stock to fluctuate?

NEW TERMS

Asset demand for money
Checkable deposits
Depository institutions
Excess reserves
Federal funds rate
Fiat money
Financial intermediary
Full-bodied commodity money
L
Liquidity
Money stock
M1
M2

M3
Precautionary demand for
   money
Representative commodity
   money
Reserve deposits
Reserve requirement ratio
Reserves
Speculative demand for money
Target
Transactions demand for money
Velocity (V)

You may not think the dollar is very valuable, but you are likely to be more concerned about losing one than about losing a plain piece of paper. Have you ever wondered why dollars have value—why, for example, you are willing to buy a wallet to protect them? Do you know how they are created? What form does the money in your bank account take, and what are you actually giving when you hand someone a check? How can banks make loans to some people at the same time others are withdrawing their deposits?

Although superficially there is nothing baffling about money, its effects on the macroeconomy are sufficiently mysterious to occupy the time of a great many economists. (More will be said on that subject in Chapters 8 and 9.)

The Meaning of Money

▲ **1. What is money?**

Money is a social phenomenon that has taken different forms in different cultures, running the gamut from animals and minerals to vegetables. In the United States, we think of money in terms of dollars. In Great Britain, it is the pound sterling; in France, the franc. At other times and in other places, money has been anything from silver to cigarettes, beads, or seashells. Today in some parts of Tanzania, the monetary unit is the cow or the bull, and cattle are used in exchange just as we use dollar bills. Thus, money is anything that is generally acceptable as a means of payment for the direct purchase of goods and services, and in the discharge of debts. It is also evidence of a future claim on society's goods and services. No unique set of assets has ever served throughout history as *the money*.

Money can be traded to obtain the things we want or held until we decide we want to use it: that is its essence. Because it is used so widely, however, money also serves as a unit of account. It is, in other words, a kind of common denominator in which the relative values of most other goods and services can be expressed. Money simplifies comparability valuations and bookkeeping because it functions as a standard of value. In all its different forms, money is both a readily acceptable medium of exchange (means of making payment) and a financial asset—a form of savings that represents a store of readily usable purchasing power.

Money is so commonplace in our society that people take for granted the convenience it bestows. As we have stressed before, in a barter economy—one that uses no money—goods trade only for other goods, and people are paid for their labor with the goods they and others produce. In barter, the buyer must find a seller who not only offers the desired goods but also wants the goods the buyer has to trade. For instance, the person who has turkeys to sell and wants pigs must find someone who has pigs to sell and wants turkeys. The person who is paid in corn must trade it to people who are paid in the goods and services he or she wants. Needless to say, the coincidence of wants mandated in barter is a very complicated, time-consuming, and costly way to trade.

When money is used as a medium of exchange, it facilitates trade and contributes to national production. If money is readily accepted by others, people with money need only find the things they want to buy. Those who receive money for what they sell can in turn use money to buy the things they want. The cost (time and effort) of searching for mutually beneficial trades is reduced, and the time saved can be used to produce goods and services. Money functioning as a medium of exchange avoids the coincidence of wants necessitated under a barter system.

In this indirect way, money contributes to national production. If money is used less frequently in an economy for some reason, we would expect people to spend much more time consummating trades and much less time producing goods. That is what happened in Germany in the years after both world wars. National output fell dramatically, in part because of the destruction of plant and equipment, but also because the German currency was less acceptable in trade. When output rose again, it was partially because the government instituted a new, more acceptable currency.

As a store of purchasing power, money gives its owner another kind of convenience, called liquidity. **Liquidity** is the ease with which any asset can be converted on short notice into spendable form with little or no loss of value. The owner of money can quickly and inexpensively convert it into other assets, like furniture, a loaf of bread, or even stock in a corporation. At little or no transaction cost, money can be traded for practically anything else. Other financial assets, such as corporate bonds, cannot be as easily converted. To exchange a bond for a car, the owner must typically sell the bond for money and then use the money to buy the car. The extra transaction takes time, and the seller may have to pay a fee to the agent or brokerage house that sells the bond. A house is even less liquid than a corporate bond; it may take weeks or months to sell. Thus, liquidity has to do with ease of marketability, high stability of value, and low or no conversion costs. By serving as a storehouse of value, money allows its holder to pay off debts that are normally stated in fixed money terms.

For money to be a good means of storing purchasing power, its value—that is, how much it will buy—must be reasonably stable. If prices rise rapidly, the purchasing power of stored money will deteriorate rapidly. Instead of holding on to their money, people will use it to buy goods and services, like gold, jewels, and stocks, before its purchasing power deteriorates even further. Conversely if prices fall rapidly, people will want to hold on to more money than usual. They will delay their purchases, hoping to buy things at lower prices.

Liquidity: the ease with which any asset can be converted on short notice into spendable form with little or no loss of value.

The Value of Money

▲ 2. What determines the value of money?

Why does money have value, in the sense that people will accept it in exchange for goods and services? Obviously, dollar bills themselves have no intrinsic value. Dollars in bank accounts cannot have intrinsic value—they are just figures on computer tape. Although the paper used for dollar bills is tough and relatively expensive, the purchasing power of the dollar is far greater than the value of the paper used. Similarly, all coins in the United States are token money in that the intrinsic or bullion value is less than the face value of the coins. This reduces the profitability to people of melting down the coins for sale as bullion when bullion values rise.

Furthermore, the dollar's value is not based on some kind of "gold backing"—there is no such thing. Contrary to popular belief, the government no longer holds gold in Fort Knox to back the dollar. Until 1971, the government was required to hold $0.25 in gold for every dollar outstanding. Even then, however, the gold did not determine the value of the money, since $0.25 in gold cannot give a dollar bill a dollar's worth of value.

From an individual standpoint, trading goods for dollars and vice versa is quite sensible. The dollars received can always be traded to someone else. Dollars are valuable simply because people have confidence that others will accept them for the purchase of goods and services and in the discharge of debts. The same was true of gold and silver coins when they were used as money. Although silver and gold have always had intrinsic value, in the sense that they can be used for jewelry and dental fittings, they would have been worth much less if they had not been used as money. The reason that coins were valued so highly was that people were willing to accept them readily in exchanges.

Although it may seem a little like magic, confidence in its general acceptability is the stuff money is made of. The message printed on a dollar bill—"This note is legal tender for all debts public and private"—gives a dollar some contrived commercial value. The value of money, however, ultimately depends on the unwritten social agreement that it is valuable. There are good reasons for demanding money. At any rate, most of our money stock—checkable deposits—is not legal tender, nor are certified checks. All coin and currency are legal tender. Thus, whether something is legal tender does not determine whether it is money. Like any commodity, money is valuable because of its relative scarcity and utility. It is subject to the same laws of supply and demand as any commodity. Its major difference compared to other commodities such as shoes, corn, and haircuts is that it has almost no "cost" to manufacture and thus has no self-disciplining supply restraint. The supply can be limited by quantity or price restraints.

The Demand for Money

▲ 3. What are the three types of demand for money?

Because of the utility or benefits of using and holding on to money, there is a demand for money, just as there is a demand for other utility-yielding goods. Holding money also involves an opportunity cost: the forgone benefits or return on some other asset not acquired—for example, the furniture

Transactions demand for money: the desire to hold money balances in order to carry out anticipated purchases of goods and services.

Precautionary demand for money: the desire to hold money balances in order to finance unexpected or emergency purchases of goods and services.

Speculative demand for money: the desire to hold money in anticipation of a decrease in the price of other assets and in anticipation of future profits.

Asset demand for money: the combined precautionary and speculative reasons for holding money.

one could have purchased or the profits one could have earned by investing in a business. Despite the costs, there are three good reasons for holding on to or demanding money. One is the need for money as a medium of exchange; this is called the transactions demand for money. The **transactions demand for money** is the desire to hold money balances in order to carry out anticipated purchases of goods and services. A second is the need for security; this is called the precautionary demand for money. The **precautionary demand for money** is the desire to hold money balances in order to finance unexpected or emergency purchases of goods and services. A third reason for demanding money is the desire to be able to take advantage of future opportunities; this is called the speculative demand for money. The **speculative demand for money** is the desire to hold money in anticipation of a decrease in the price of other assets and in anticipation of future profits. The combined precautionary and speculative reasons are sometimes called the **asset demand for money**.

The demand for money is influenced by personal income and wealth, interest rates, the general price level, and expectations about future prices, as well as other economic variables to be considered later.[1] Specifically:

A rise in people's incomes or wealth will generally increase the transactions demand for money. Higher incomes or more wealth mean more purchases, and hence a greater need for money balances to finance those purchases.

A rise in interest rates—the rental cost of money—or more generally, a rise in the rates of return on various financial assets will raise the opportunity cost of holding on to money, discouraging people from maintaining large money balances for any purpose. People will try to economize on their use of money. Empirical studies have shown that the demand for money is responsive to interest rate changes and is relatively stable over time.

An increase in the price level will increase the demand for money to finance transactions, which now require more dollars.

If people expect prices to rise, they will buy now to avoid higher prices in the future, reducing the money balances they individually seek to hold. If people expect prices to fall, they will hold on to money so as to take advantage of lower prices later.

The Money Stock

▲ 4. What are our major forms of money?

In a modern society, money is basically the debts of the government and financial institutions. Aside from dollar bills and coins, several other financial assets serve as mediums of exchange and stores of purchasing power. Demand deposits, or money in checking accounts, are highly liquid. So are

1. An excellent summary of the theoretical and empirical work on the demand for money is in David Laidler, *The Demand for Money: Theories and Evidence*, 3rd ed. (New York: Harper and Row, 1985).

Money stock: the sum of all identified forms of money held by the public (as opposed to the financial institutions) at a given point in time.

M1: the total of the public's (as opposed to the financial institutions') holdings of currency (paper bills and coins), demand deposits at commercial banks, traveler's checks, and other bank accounts against which checks can be written, such as NOW (negotiable order of withdrawal) and ATS (automatic transfer services) accounts.

Checkable deposits: any deposits against which checks or their equivalent can be written.

M2: M1 plus savings accounts and small-denomination (less than $100,000) time deposits and certificates of deposit, plus money market accounts and other highly liquid assets.

savings accounts and certificates of deposit, which are like government savings bonds but are issued by banks.

How do economists measure the amount of money that exists in the economy at any point in time? The answer depends on how one defines the money stock. A broad definition is easily given. The **money stock** is the sum of all identified forms of money held by the public (as opposed to the financial institutions) at a given point in time. Actually measuring the money stock is a more complicated problem. How many dollars are there? Which dollars should be counted? These questions are still subject to much debate. Different groups of economists measure the money stock in different ways, and how one calculates the total amount of money in the economy changes with changes in the method of measurement.

Two measures of the money stock are used widely in economics journals and the financial sections of newspapers and magazines. The better known is M1, which includes cash and checking accounts. **M1** is the total of the public's (as opposed to the financial institutions') holdings of currency (paper bills and coins), demand deposits at commercial banks (bank accounts against which withdrawals can be made on demand, or by check), traveler's checks, and other bank accounts against which checks can be written, such as NOW (negotiable order of withdrawal) and ATS (automatic transfer services) accounts. NOW accounts differ from regular demand deposits in that they earn interest. ATS accounts permit the automatic transfer of funds from savings accounts to checking accounts; this allows depositors to earn interest on the idle money in their checking accounts. **Checkable deposits** are a broad classification that includes any deposits against which checks or their equivalent can be written. Thus, in simple terms M1 = currency plus checkable deposits. If M1 is used as a measure of money, in December 1987 the money stock was $753.2 billion (see Table 7.1). Of that total, $199.7 billion (27 percent) was held in currency and $553.5 billion (73 percent) in demand deposits and other checkable deposits.

M1 includes savings as well as cash and checking accounts. **M2** is M1 plus savings accounts and small-denomination (less than $100,000) time deposits (bank accounts that generally are not subject to transfer by check, and sometimes not to withdrawal on demand) and certificates of deposit, plus money market accounts and other highly liquid assets. For example, if M2 is used as a measure of money, in December 1987 the money stock was $2,894.8 billion—more than four times the size of M1 (see Table 7.1). Note that credit cards are not in any of the definitions of the money supply, as they are merely a short-term loan by the issuer when utilized.

M1 and M2 reflect the two basic uses for money. M1 emphasizes the medium-of-exchange role. It consists of only those types of money that are used directly in trade—coin, paper bills, and demand deposits. M2 measures money as a store of purchasing power. When paper bills, coins, and demand deposits are not being used actively in exchange, they are being held as a store of purchasing power. Adding savings accounts, small certificates of deposit, and money market funds to M1 yields a measure of the nation's total store of purchasing power. The Federal Reserve also routinely publishes statistics on two broader, less widely used money stocks

TABLE 7.1 Two Measures of the Money Stock, December 1987[a]
(in billions of dollars)

	M1	M2
Currency (paper bills and coins)	$199.7	$ 199.7
Travelers checks	7.0	7.0
Demand deposits	291.7	291.7
Other checkable deposits	254.7	254.7
Overnight repurchase agreements (RPs) net plus overnight Eurodollars		77.6
Money market mutual fund (MMMF) balances		221.2
Money market deposit accounts (MMDAs)		523.7
Savings accounts		410.6
Small-denomination time deposits		913.4
Totals	$753.2	$2,894.4

a. Preliminary estimate. Totals may not add up because of rounding.

Source: Economic Report of the President (Washington, D.C.: U.S. Government Printing Office, 1988), p. 325–327.

M3: M2 plus large-denomination time deposits and other relatively minor components.

L: M3 plus other liquid assets not included in other aggregates such as bankers' acceptances, commercial paper, and Treasury bills.

called **M3** (M2 plus large-denomination time deposits and other relatively minor components) and **L** (M3 plus other liquid assets not included in other aggregates such as bankers' acceptances, commercial paper, and Treasury bills). The M2, M3, and L aggregates contain successively larger percentages of nontransaction balances. As shown in Figure 7.1, M2 is roughly four times larger than M1, M3 is five times larger than M1, and L is six times larger than M1. A fourth concept, debt, defined as the outstanding credit market debt of the United States government, state, and local governments

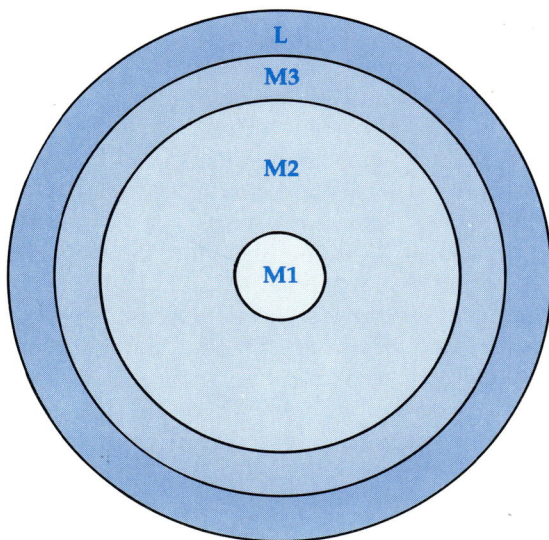

FIGURE 7.1 Major Money Aggregates
The Federal Reserve System reports aggregations of four measures of money. The M1 measure is the transaction balance aggregate. The M2, M3, and L aggregates contain successively larger percentages of the nontransaction balances. Thus by definition, M1 < M2 < M3 < L.

and private nonfinancial sectors, is also computed by the Fed. The Fed has the most control over M1 and the least over L. In recent years, the Fed has focused more on M2 and M3 and less on M1, which has historically been their main target. These definitions can be found in any *Federal Reserve Bulletin* (published monthly) or any recent money and banking textbook.

Measurements of the money stock are extremely interesting to economists studying how the size of the money stock affects prices, national production, and unemployment. (In following chapters we will develop that subject in detail.) The particular measure an economist uses in statistical studies of these questions depends in part on his or her perception of money. Those who view money as something that is held, as opposed to something that is traded, will use M2 in their studies. Those who view money primarily as a medium of trade will use M1.

It is worth noting that families use currency for about 34 percent of their expenditures, savings accounts, money market accounts, and money orders for about 10 percent, checks for 48 percent, and credit cards for 8 percent.[2] Eventually, electronic fund transfers will replace checks used in payments.

The Banking System

▲ **5. What constitutes our banking system?**

Demand deposits are an important part of M1 and time deposits an important part of M2. Both kinds of accounts are held at banks, which are an integral part of the monetary system. Broadly speaking, the U.S. banking system may be divided into profit-oriented, private depository institutions and financial intermediaries (commercial banks and savings and loan associations, and credit unions) and the quasi-public Federal Reserve System ("the Fed"), a national institution.

Depository Institutions and Financial Intermediaries

Depository institutions: privately owned profit-seeking financial institutions, including commercial banks and thrift institutions such as credit unions, mutual savings banks, savings banks, and savings and loan institutions (S&Ls) that handle transaction accounts and checkable deposits.

Depository institutions are privately owned profit-seeking financial institutions, including commercial banks, and thrift institutions such as credit unions, savings and loan associations (S&Ls), savings banks, and mutual savings banks, that handle transaction accounts and checkable deposits. In 1988 there were approximately 14,500 commercial banks, 20,000 credit unions, 450 mutual savings banks, and 4,000 S&Ls. They hold deposits and checking and savings accounts for individuals and firms. They also make loans in return for interest payments on the amount of the loan. It is crucial to understand that these depository institutions are profit-maximizing entities that seek to enhance the wealth of their owners, such as is true of manufacturing, mining, agriculture, services, utilities, wholesale, and retail businesses. Commercial banks, for instance, retail and manufacture

2. *Federal Reserve Bulletin* (March, 1987), p. 180.

"money" in their quest for wealth, subject to the prevailing governmental and market constraints and regulations.

Transaction accounts include all deposits on which the account holder is permitted to make withdrawals by negotiable or transferable instruments, payment orders of withdrawal, and telephone and preauthorized transfers in excess of three per month for the purpose of making payments to third persons or others. Transactional deposits that can be withdrawn by the depositor or transferred to someone else at any time (usually by check) without any prior notice to the banks, and that generally pay no interest are called demand deposits by banks. Other transactional accounts pay interest, but are restricted as to transferability. Checkable deposits include deposits on which a depositor can write checks, such as demand deposits, NOW deposits, and share draft accounts in depository institutions' different accounts. Demand deposits or checkbook money usually do not earn interest, are available without delay either to be withdrawn or made payable to a third party by a check, and are offered only at commercial banks. Negotiable order of withdrawal (NOW and Super NOW) and share draft accounts are interest-earning checkable deposits, although legally the withdrawal is not by a "check." Since deregulation intensified in 1980, interest-bearing transaction accounts have mushroomed; NOW accounts make up about one-third of our M1 money stock. People use these accounts as combination checking and savings accounts, keeping opportunity costs down by receiving interest. In general, time and savings deposits are interest-earning deposits, where the redemption may be subject to a specified waiting period. Nonpersonal time deposits are time deposits, including savings deposits, that are not transaction accounts and in which a beneficial interest is held by a depositor that is a business entity or corporation rather than a person.

Before 1981 banks could be categorized according to the types of deposits they received. Only commercial banks were permitted to accept demand deposits, funds that could be withdrawn "on demand," or without notice, by way of checks. Government regulation prohibited the payment of interest on demand deposits. Commercial banks also held some savings accounts, or time deposits, on which they paid a modest interest rate. Savings institutions (savings and loan associations, credit unions, and savings banks) concentrated on time deposits, on which they were allowed to pay a slightly higher interest rate than commercial banks.

These distinctions were obliterated by the Depository Institutions Deregulation and Monetary Control Act of 1980. Savings institutions can now carry what are in essence checking accounts. All institutions can now pay interest on accounts with checking privileges. The act was intended to increase competition among banks by giving them greater flexibility.

To help you better understand a typical commercial bank, Table 7.2 shows what percentages the various assets and liabilities comprise for all banks. A consolidated balance sheet shows assets, liabilities, and net worth. The assets of a business are the things of value that it can claim or that it owns. Liabilities are the claims against the business or the amount it owes. Net worth is the difference between assets and liabilities. For any business, assets will always equal liabilities plus net worth. It is important to recognize

TABLE 7.2 Consolidated Balance Sheet for All Commercial Banking Institutions[a]

Assets	Percentage of Total	Liabilities and Net Worth	Percentage of Total
Loans	66.0%	Time deposits	32.6%
Investment securities	7.6	Transaction or demand deposits	20.1
Cash items in process of collection	2.6	Savings deposits	18.7
Demand balances with U.S. depository institutions	1.3	Borrowings	14.8
		Other liabilities (net)	7.3
Trading account assets	1.3	Total capital accounts	6.5
Cash in vault	1.0		
Reserves with Federal Reserve banks	0.9		
Other assets (net)	9.3		
Total	100.0%	Total	100.0%

a. Commercial banking institutions include insured domestically chartered commercial banks, branches and agencies of foreign banks, Edge Act and Agreement corporations, and New York State Foreign investment corporations.

Source: Federal Reserve Bulletin (April 1986), p. A18. These figures (1) include interbank claims of commercial banks against each other and (2) are Last-Wednesday-of-Month series for January 1986.

Financial intermediary: a financial institution that assembles the funds of savers or lenders to lend to borrowers at interest rates that generally cover at least the cost of operation (including normal profit).

that two-thirds of the banks' assets are loans and that their major liabilities—deposits of various types—are dominated by time deposits, with demand and savings deposits each about 60 percent as large as time deposits. As recently as 1960, commercial banks held over 60% of their total liabilities in demand deposits. A bank is a **financial intermediary**—a financial institution that assembles the funds of savers or lenders to lend to borrowers at interest rates that generally cover at least the cost of operation (including a normal profit). These financial expediters include commercial banks, mutual savings banks, savings and loan associations, credit unions, life insurance companies, pension funds, mutual funds, charitable foundations, finance companies, and government credit agencies.

Before 1981, banks came under the regulatory control of either a state banking commission or the Federal Reserve System, which is in effect the central bank of the United States. In 1980 only the largest banks, about 35 percent of the nation's fourteen thousand banks, belonged to the Federal Reserve System. (By 1988, 40 percent were part of the system.) Nationally chartered banks had to join the Federal Reserve, but state-chartered banks had a choice. Those private member banks, which own the Federal Reserve in theory but not in practice, held about 80 percent of all demand deposits. As of 1981, however, all depository institutions—commercial banks, savings banks, savings and loan associations, and credit unions—became subject to partial or complete control by the Federal Reserve System. Efficiency, technology, and competition have replaced safety and stability as the watchwords of depository institutions. Distinctions among financial institutions are blurring at an exponential rate as the vigor of competition has intensified dramatically, helped by electronic funds technology and deregulation. In addition, the historical restrictions on depository institutions operating across state lines are crumbling.

While the debate continues on the social desirability of this interstate banking, it is proceeding by leaps and bounds. The restrictions on branch banking—i.e., a bank operating more than one office—is also changing. While some states prohibit branching and others allow it on a limited or complete basis, branching is growing and is generally regarded as beneficial, although it has its drawbacks. To understand how banks operate, then, and how the money stock is controlled, we must examine the structure and powers of the Federal Reserve System.

The Federal Reserve System

The Federal Reserve System, created by an act of Congress in 1913, is made up of twelve Federal Reserve District Banks scattered throughout the nation. Figure 7.2 shows the geographical areas covered by the district banks and their branch territories. The Far West, for example, is served by the Federal Reserve Bank of San Francisco (district 12), which covers Alaska, Hawaii, Washington, Oregon, California, Idaho, Nevada, Utah, and most of Arizona. Each district bank has one or more branch offices: there are twenty-five branches in all.

The Federal Reserve System is headed by a seven-member Board of Governors. Each governor is nominated by the president of the United States and confirmed by the Senate for a term of fourteen years. Terms are staggered, with one term expiring every two years. The chair of the Board of Governors, like the chairperson of any collective organization, has limited powers, restricted to persuasion and administration. Nevertheless the chair, presently Alan Greenspan, is one of the most influential people in the nation when it comes to determining economic policy.

It has been estimated by a former Board member that in setting monetary policy, the chair exercises 45 percent of the power, the staff 25 percent, other governors 20 percent, and the Federal Reserve Banks 10 percent.[3]

The governors meet several times a week. Twice a year, the Board submits a written report to Congress on the state of the economy and the direction of monetary policy. The chair and others may be called to consult with Congress on this report and also appear frequently before congressional committees to speak on various matters involving our financial system. The governors are in continuous contact with officials of other government agencies such as the Treasury, the Council of Economic Advisers, and the Office of Management and Budget to help evaluate the economic climate and to discuss objectives.

---

3. Sherman J. Maisel, *Managing the Dollar* (New York: W. W. Norton, 1973).

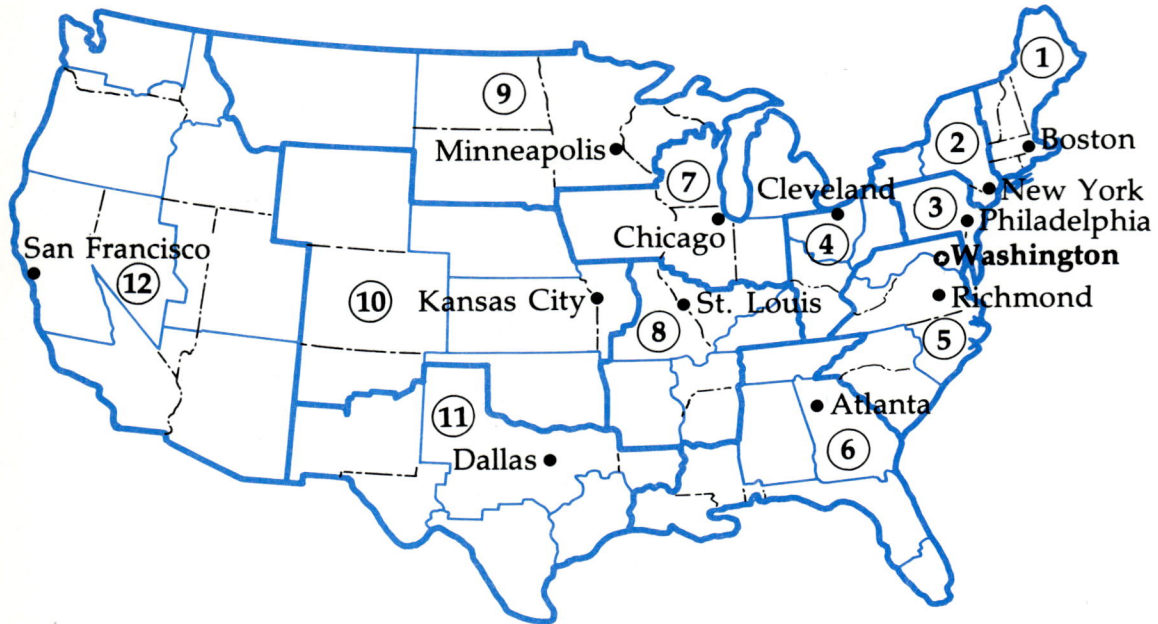

FIGURE 7.2 The Federal Reserve System: Boundaries of Federal Reserve Districts and Their Branch Territories

The Federal Reserve System has twelve district banks throughout the nation. They are (1) Boston, MA, (2) New York, NY, (3)Philadelphia, PA, (4) Cleveland, OH, (5) Richmond, VA, (6) Atlanta, GA, (7) Chicago, IL, (8) St. Louis, MO, (9) Minneapolis, MN, (10) Kansas City, MO, (11) Dallas, TX, and (12) San Francisco, CA. Look at the face of any one dollar bill—Federal Reserve Note—that you have. The roseate at the left with a letter of the alphabet tells you what Federal Reserve Bank the note belongs to. The number of the Federal Reserve district (e.g., 6 for Atlanta) is also shown four times on the front of the bill. Each Reserve Bank supervises the banks in its district. District Reserve Banks also hold reserve deposits for member banks, provide them with currency, and lend them money when necessary. The headquarters of the Federal Reserve System is in Washington, D.C.
Source: Federal Reserve Bulletin (March 1988), p. A80.

At the district level, each Reserve Bank has a president and is supervised by a board of directors made up of representatives from the district. Each district bank board submits nominations for president of its district bank to the Fed's Board of Governors. The Board of Governors then appoints the twelve district bank presidents.

The primary function of the Federal Reserve System is to establish and conduct the nation's monetary policy. As discussed in Chapter 4, formulating and executing monetary policy involves the manipulation of the rate of growth of the nation's money stock and interest rates to promote a high and stable level of employment and production without excessive inflation. More specifically, monetary policy is the management of the growth rate of various monetary aggregates.

Major monetary policy decisions are made by the Board of Governors and a group called the Federal Open Market Committee (FOMC). This latter twelve-person group consists of the seven governors and the presidents of five of the twelve Federal Reserve Banks selected on a rotating basis, except for the New York president, who is automatically selected. The FOMC meets on the third Tuesday of every month to review the Fed's monetary policy. Members study the latest figures on GNP, unemployment, prices, and other pertinent variables before determining whether to increase or decrease the money stock, by how much and by what action. Most decisions are implemented by ordering the purchase or sale of government securities on the open market, actions that result in a change in the money stock.

The Federal Reserve also serves as the central bank of the United States, a "banker's bank," or perhaps more accurately since 1981, a "depository institution's depository." The Fed offers depository institutions many of the same services that they provide to their customers. However, the Fed does not hold the deposits of the public nor does it ordinarily lend directly to the public. When depository institutions such as banks get deposits from their customers, they are entitled to claim an equal amount of reserves at the Fed. **Reserves** are the cash that a depository institution has in its vault plus its deposits at the Federal Reserve Bank. No reserves are required against the Fed's deposits. As explained in detail on pages 189–192, reserves rise and fall with a bank's deposits. When banks gain customer deposits, their reserves rise, and vice versa. Reserves also change with loans to a bank's customers. They fall when the bank makes a loan, and they rise when the loan is repaid. The Federal Reserve System manages the reserve deposits for banks in its jurisdiction. **Reserve deposits** are the accounts that depository institutions hold in Federal Reserve Banks. (A depository institution's reserve deposit balance plus its vault cash equals its total reserves.)

The Fed attempts each year by targeting to keep the growth of some selected monetary aggregate—M1, M2, or M3—within a certain tolerable range, such as 6 to 8 percent growth per year, in order to promote its economic goals for that year. Thus, a **target** is any economic variable—usually some monetary aggregate—that the Fed manages in the attempt to attain certain macroeconomic goals. Targets were first set publicly in 1975. There has always been a controversy over which measure of money is best to target for policy purposes. While some economists prefer using interest rates as the target, most prefer using monetary aggregates, as they are more closely and reliably related to most economic goals of the Fed.[4] Because the

Reserves: the cash a depository institution has in its vault plus its deposits at the Federal Reserve Bank.

Reserve deposits: the accounts that depository institutions hold in Federal Reserve Banks. (A depository institution's reserve deposit balance plus its vault cash equals its total reserves.)

Target: any economic variable—usually some monetary aggregate—that the Fed manages in the attempt to attain certain macroeconomic goals.

---

4. In fact, interest rates rather than the money stock were targeted by the Fed until October 1979. In October 1979 the Fed decided to control monetary aggregates and let the interest rates fluctuate over wider limits. In October 1982 the Fed decided to look somewhat at both interest rates and the money stock. The Fed cannot control strictly both simultaneously.

PERSPECTIVES
A Short History of Money
Dennis Placone, International Trade Commission

At various times in history, different forms of money have been used in trade. The very first monies were full-bodied commodity money. A **full-bodied commodity money** is a medium of exchange or store of value that has some intrinsic value as a consumer good or factor of production. In other words, it has some economic use apart from its monetary role. In parts of the ancient Roman Empire, rock salt was used as a form of money. Barley and silver served as monies three hundred years before the birth of Christ; seashells and tobacco, in colonial times in North America. Gold, cattle, woodpecker scalps, corn, and cigarettes have all been used as a medium of exchange.

All these goods were common to the communities or societies that used them. Therefore their market values were generally well known. People would accept such goods in trade, even if they did not have an immediate use for them, because they could always be sold at a known price. And if for some reason a commodity money lost part of its value as a money, it could always be used as a good instead. Barley could be ground into meal; cattle could be butchered; woodpecker scalps could be fashioned into ornaments; cigarettes could be smoked. Gold and silver monies, in particular, gradually became common around the world, because they were more useful, portable, divisible, durable, and recognizable in value than other commodity monies.

Full-bodied commodity monies were generally not created by government. Governments have sometimes attempted to influence or control the value of commodity monies, however. In 1791 the U.S. government sought to establish a bimetallic money standard by buying and selling gold and silver at official fixed prices. The task was not as simple as it had imagined, however. The price of gold was set at fifteen times the price of silver, even though the market price of gold was 15.5 times the price of silver. As a result people bought gold from the federal treasury and sold it at a profit on the world market. Because silver was officially undervalued and gold officially overvalued, gold was driven out of circulation in the United States and sent abroad, where it was more highly valued.

Such an outcome was to be expected. People will always attempt to use money that is overvalued, because they expect that its relative market value may fall. They will tend to horde undervalued money, expecting that its value will rise. The U.S. government tried to halt the outflow of gold in 1834 by readjusting the official price to be sixteen times the price of silver. But at the new official price, silver was undervalued and gold overvalued. Soon silver was driven out of circulation and replaced by gold.

As economic systems became more complex, new, more convenient forms of money emerged. The transactions costs of using gold and silver were high, because substantial resources had to be invested to mine and protect them. To cut those costs, banks developed representative commodity monies. **Representative commodity monies** are certificates or notes that can be converted into given quantities of a specific commodity, like gold or silver. Banks found that people would accept such notes in the belief that they could be redeemed for the gold banks held in their vaults. At first banks backed the notes fully, holding a dollar's worth of gold for every dollar note outstanding. But banks soon found they could issue notes

growth rates of the monetary aggregates can diverge sharply in the short run, it is a remote possibility that targets for all aggregates (M1, M2, M3, and L) could be achieved simultaneously. Hence, priority is usually given to one aggregate. Historically, the transaction balance aggregate M1 was felt by the Fed and many outsiders to be the most reliable way to influence economic activity, as it was most easily controlled by the Fed.

for more than the value of the gold in their vaults. People would continue to circulate the notes in trade, confident they could be redeemed when desired.

So long as people felt secure in using notes as money, the representative commodity monetary system worked. But problems eventually emerged. From 1834 to 1860, over sixteen hundred state-chartered banks, most of them largely unregulated, issued notes. Many banks issued so many notes that they could not always redeem them at full face value. Runs on banks, in which panicked noteholders attempted to cash in their notes for gold, became common. Some banks collapsed when they could not redeem all the notes presented to them. Counterfeiting sometimes provoked a run on a bank. Because each of the sixteen hundred banks issued notes of its own design, the average trader could not always tell a counterfeit or worthless note from a genuine one. Counterfeit bills increased the information cost of using notes and reduced their general acceptance.

Because of these difficulties, governments began to issue paper money. In the United States, the federal treasury issued gold and silver certificates that could be redeemed for metal coin, and "greenbacks"—unbacked paper currency issued to finance the Civil War. The general acceptance of these monies was encouraged by the treasury's willingness to accept them in payment of taxes and by the requirement that creditors accept them in payment of debt. (If creditors refused to accept greenbacks and gold and silver certificates as payment, debtors were legally absolved of their obligations.)

When the Federal Reserve System was established in 1913, private bank notes became illegal and were replaced by Federal Reserve Notes, the paper money we use today. At first Fed notes were backed by a government pledge to redeem the notes in gold and silver. The number of notes in circulation was determined partly by the amount of gold held by the government. These notes were considered so sound by foreigners that they tended to be in short supply in the United States. To increase the money stock and raise prices, President Franklin Roosevelt took the United States off the gold standard in 1933. Roosevelt declared that dollars would no longer be redeemed in gold at the Treasury or the Federal Reserve. Indeed, he outlawed private hoarding of gold and required people who held it to sell it to the government for $22.50 an ounce. (Later the price of gold was set officially at $35 an ounce.) In 1968 Congress revoked the Fed's obligation to redeem silver certificates in silver.

The U.S. monetary system is now based entirely on inconvertible paper currency, or fiat money. **Fiat money** is a medium of exchange or store of value that cannot be redeemed for anything other than a replica of itself. A fiat dollar can be exchanged only for another dollar. The general acceptability of fiat money does not depend on either its intrinsic market value (as was the case with corn), or its redemption value (as was the case with silver certificates). It depends entirely on people's confidence in its continued usefulness in trade.

Velocity (V): the rate of turnover or circulation of the money stock (M) relative to GNP; thus, $V = GNP/M$.

Since 1987, the Fed no longer targets or specifies annual growth rates in M1 (currency in circulation, checkable deposits, and traveler's checks). M1 was changed from a "targeted" to a "monitored" variable. Although the Fed still considers M1 to be a predictor of future changes in national income, it now targets only M2 and M3. The problem with M1 was that it had lost its reliability because of unstable velocity. **Velocity (V)** is the rate of turnover or circulation of the money stock (M) relative to GNP; thus, $V = GNP/M$. For instance, if GNP is $6,000 and M is $1,000 in some year, the income velocity of money is said to be 6 that year. If velocity fluctuates unpredictably, the Fed will have considerable trouble administrating monetary policy. A given change in a monetary aggregate based on a certain velocity may over- or undershoot the market if velocity is higher or lower than expected. The problem with the M1 velocity was that the responsiveness of the demand for money to interest rates had increased so significantly as to distort predictions based on older relationships. The Fed perceived that there was no longer a stable relationship between M1 and GNP. For most of the period from the end of World War II until the 1980s, velocity was reasonably stable, increasing along a 3 percent growth trend. Starting in 1981, M1 became more variable and the velocity trend reversed itself. People demanded more money to hold as a fraction of GNP. M1 velocity started showing a stronger systematic relationship with interest rates.

Disinflation (slowing of the inflation rate), which requires people to hold less money, and deregulation are the two most likely explanations for the heightened interest-rate sensitivity. Declining interest rates such as happened in 1984–1986 lowered the opportunity cost of holding or "parking" money. M1 velocity contains NOW accounts that involve a significant component of true savings not held for immediate outlays. As this savings component increases, M1 increases—but national income does not increase because these unspent funds lower the velocity. Financial deregulation changed the composition of monetary aggregates as various interest-bearing transaction accounts were permitted, and interest-rate ceilings on all types of accounts were eliminated. The increased interest-rate sensitivity since the proliferation of new interest-bearing deposits is certainly responsible for at least part of the change in velocity, as interest-bearing deposits were almost one-third of M1 in 1986 compared to a negligible share in 1978.

How long the lessening emphasis on M1 will continue is anyone's guess. Many monetarists, such as Milton Friedman, have long advocated that the Fed concentrate on the broader, more stable M2 money stock that adds money in money market funds, small savings accounts, and overnight repurchase agreements to M1. M2 is less volatile than M1 because M2 includes M1 plus the kind of deposits that people might shift to M1 accounts when the opportunity cost changes. Shifts out of M1 affect the magnitude of that particular aggregate, but they do not affect the magnitude of M2 because the latter includes both M1 (*from* which the shift occurred) and alternative deposits (*to* which the shift occurred). Shifts from one component of M2 to another component leave the total of M2 unchanged. If people shifted from currency (M1) to savings accounts (M2), M1 would change but not M2. M2 is therefore less affected by changes in the market rate of interest. However, there is still debate among economists as to which measure, M1 or M2, contains the more "noise" or influence by extraneous factors.

Around 1987, the Fed also began to put more emphasis on the foreign exchange rate (i.e., the price of U.S. dollars relative to the price of other foreign currencies) as a constraint on monetary policy. If interest rates are lowered in the United States, foreigners are more reluctant to buy U.S. securities and prefer to buy higher-yielding securities elsewhere. This pushes down the demand for dollars. Also, with lower interest rates in the United States, U.S. residents start buying higher-yielding foreign securities. This increases the supply of dollars. As a result of a falling demand and a rising supply of dollars, the price of the U.S. dollar (i.e., the exchange rate of the dollar) falls, or the U.S. dollar depreciates in value.

Federal Reserve Banks were considered "lenders of last resort" historically, but could in one sense be considered "lenders of first resort" today if they lend reserves cheaply at below-market interest rates, as is sometimes done. They make loans to all depository institutions and provide currency when needed. For instance, if a bank needs more currency to meet daily withdrawals, the manager can call the district Reserve Bank or one of its branch offices and order some from the "discount window," a department of each district Federal Reserve bank responsible for lending reserves to banks. The bank pays for the currency with a reduction in its reserves. (The switch of funds from reserves to currency does not by itself reduce total bank reserves because both currency and reserve deposits count as reserves. Bank reserves are reduced, however, when more cash is taken out of the bank than is deposited.) Like some large commercial banks, the Federal Reserve Banks also provide check-clearing services for banks. They collect, sort, and distribute checks to their banks of origin.

The Fed regulates, supervises, and examines financial institutions, and serves as the fiscal agent for the U.S. Treasury and other federal government agencies as well. The Fed earns revenues by charging for services, such as check clearing, and by the interest earned on its U.S. government securities. The huge surplus it earns after paying dividends to member banks is turned over to the Treasury. This is not something a private corporation would do by choice. Thus, we regard the Federal Reserve as a quasi-public (or quasi-private) entity. It is neither a pure private entity nor a pure public entity, but rather a hybrid with more public than private leanings, as it does focus its efforts on controlling the supply and cost of money regardless of profitability.

To understand better how the Fed operates, look at the consolidated balance sheet for all Federal Reserve Banks, shown in Table 7.3. As the table shows, over three-fourths of the Federal Reserve Banks' main assets are investments are in U.S. government securities. Over three-fourths of their total liabilities are in Federal Reserve notes—the paper currency circulating in our economy. Other major liabilities include reserves of depository institutions and U.S. Treasury deposits. Also, there is very little paid-in capital.

Checks and the Transfer of Money

▲ **6. How do checks transfer money?**

The Fed is involved with clearing checks and providing certain other financial services—since 1980 largely on a cost-benefit basis—to the nation's financial institutions. How does check clearing work?

TABLE 7.3 Consolidated Balance Sheet of All Federal Reserve Banks

Assets	Percentage of Total	Liabilities	Percentage of Total
U.S. government securities	78.7%	Federal Reserve notes	76.6%
Gold certificate account	4.9	Depository institutions deposits	10.3
Loans to depository institutions	4.3	U.S. Treasury—General account deposits	7.1
Items in process of collection	2.9	Deferred credit items	2.6
Special Drawing Rights (SDR) certificate account	2.1	Foreign and other deposits	0.3
Coin	0.3	Other liabilities and accrued dividends	1.1
Other	6.9	Capital accounts:	
		Paid-in capital	0.8
		Surplus	0.8
		Other capital accounts	0.3
Total	100.0%	Total	100.0%

Source: Federal Reserve Bulletin (April 1986), p. A10 (End-of-Month Series for January 1986).

When you write a check to your sister you know that eventually your bank balance will fall and hers will rise. How does your money move from one bank to another? Actually nothing tangible ever moves. The figures on the banks' books are simply adjusted to account for your check.

To see how the process works, we must look at some simplified bank records called T accounts (so called because they look like a large T). Each side of the T represents one half of an accounting statement, or balance sheet, listing the bank's assets and liabilities (see Figure 7.3). The assets half includes all properties the bank owns. The liability half includes all claims that nonowners have against the bank. Assets are recorded on the left side of the T, liabilities on the right side. As the name balance sheet implies, the two sides of the T must balance. According to standard bookkeeping technique, an equal asset exists for every liability.[5]

Suppose you write a check for $100 to your university bookstore. Figure 7.3 shows the bookkeeping entries that will result. When the bookstore deposits your check, its demand deposits go up. Since the bookstore's checking account represents a legal claim that the bookstore has against its bank, Citizens and Southern National Bank, we classify the increase in the bookstore's deposits as a liability of Citizens and Southern. Thus we enter $100 in the name of the bookstore on the right side of Citizens and Southern's balance sheet. This is entry *a*.

---

5. Actually, the balance sheet also includes an additional set of entries, called capital accounts, which represent the net worth or claims of the owners against the assets.

How does Citizens and Southern collect the money it has just received from your university's bookstore? The simplest way is to send your check to the Federal Reserve. At the Fed, Citizens and Southern's reserve deposit rises (entry *b*), and the reserve deposit of your bank, Northwestern National, falls (entry *c*). While Citizens and Southern's reserve deposit is a liability to the Fed, it is an asset to Citizens and Southern. Thus the check you wrote to the bookstore also results in a $100 increase in the assets column of Citizens and Southern's own bookkeeping records (entry *d*).

Once the appropriate entries are made on the Fed's accounting records, your check is returned to your bank. Only when the check reaches your bank, perhaps three or four days after you wrote it, is your checking account balance reduced (entry *e* on Northwestern's balance sheet). Because your bank's reserve deposit with the Fed is down by $100 (entry *c*), Northwestern National must also deduct $100 from its own assets (entry *f*).

Citizens and Southern National Bank

Assets	Liabilities
Reserve deposits: + $100 (entry *d*)	University bookstore's demand deposit + $100 (entry *a*)

Federal Reserve Bank

Assets	Liabilities
	Citizens and Southern's reserve deposit + $100 (entry *b*) Northwestern National's reserve deposit − $100 (entry *c*)

Northwestern National Bank

Assets	Liabilities
Reserve deposits: − $100 (entry *f*)	Your demand deposit − $100 (entry *e*)

FIGURE 7.3 Money Transfers in T Accounts
If you write a check on your Northwestern National Bank account to your university bookstore, your demand deposit at Northwestern (bottom) will fall by the amount of the check. At the same time the bookstore's demand deposit at Citizens and Southern (top) will rise by the same amount. Northwestern's reserve deposit at the Federal Reserve will fall, while Citizens and Southern's reserve deposit will increase.

Several points should be made about these transactions.

1. The check causes your bank balance to fall and the bookstore's bank balance to rise (entries *e* and *a*).

2. The check causes an adjustment in the Fed's reserve deposits. Your bank's reserve deposit goes down; the other bank's reserve deposit goes up (entries *c* and *b*).

3. The Fed's reserve deposits are not the same as the deposits you and your bookstore maintain at your local banks. They are bookkeeping entries based on the demand deposits of member banks. Thus reserve deposits are not money. They are not used directly in trade, as demand deposits are.

4. Reserve deposits are assets to the member banks that maintain them (that point will become clearer in the next section). Thus any check you write causes your bank's assets at the Fed to fall, and the assets of another bank to rise (entries *f* and *d*). (This statement assumes that the person who writes the check and the person who receives it maintain accounts in different banks. If the two parties have accounts with the same bank, one person's deposit will go up and the other's down, but the bank's assets at the Fed will remain the same.)

5. Most important, when anyone writes a check, the nation's money stock does not change. Money is simply moved from one account to another.

The Creation of Money

▲ 7. How do banks create money?

When gold was used as a medium of exchange, the creation of money was much like the production of jewelry. Gold ore was mined from the ground and smelted, and the pure metal was molded into coins. How much money was created depended primarily on the amount of gold in the ground and the cost of getting it out. Today, in industrial nations like the United States, money is created principally through the commercial banking system. Banks create money; they create it every time they make a loan.

How is it done? Simply lending out someone else's money would amount to transferring money already in existence from one person to another. When banks create money it is by writing checks to, or increasing the deposits of, borrowers. Suppose you have negotiated a $5,000 car loan with Northwestern National Bank. You sign the necessary papers and the bank gives you a check to deliver to the car dealer. When the dealer deposits the check, money is created.

It is money's general acceptability in trade that enables your bank to create money out of thin air, as it were. As long as the car dealer is willing to accept the bank's check, and other people are willing to accept the checks the dealer writes, something has been created that has general acceptability: money.

The Reserve Requirement

Banks are not allowed to create unlimited amounts of money. Legally, the amount of money a bank can create depends on the level of its customer deposits. The more customer deposits it has, the more money it can lend and the more money it can create. Even if there were no legal restrictions, a bank would need to maintain sufficient liquidity to satisfy its customers' needs. If the bank's customers were uncertain about its solvency, there could be a run on the bank, whereby a significant percentage of its customers withdraw their deposits over a short period of time.

The money-creating capability of banks is further restricted by the Federal Reserve, which imposes reserve requirements, branch limitations, restraints on interstate banking, and the like. The most important of these is reserve requirements. When a bank receives a customer's deposit, its reserve deposit with the Federal Reserve bank increases. When you ask for a loan, your bank writes its check against this reserve account, and its reserve deposit decreases. The bank cannot write checks indefinitely against its reserve deposit, however. It must maintain a minimum deposit, called the reserve requirement, at the Federal Reserve Bank in its district, as vault cash (or in the case of nonmember banks, balances with a Federal Reserve Bank indirectly on a pass-through basis with certain approved institutions). In any event, the funds are idle in the sense that they cannot be put into interest-earning loans or investments. The **reserve requirement ratio** is that portion of a depository institution's (such as a bank's) reserves that by law cannot be used to create money. A bank's total legal reserves are all assets held by the bank that the law permits to be used in meeting reserve requirements.

The reserve requirement ratio is expressed as a percentage of the depository institution's (such as the bank's) total demand deposits. For example, if the reserve requirement is 15 percent, the bank must maintain a reserve deposit equal to at least 15 percent of its demand deposits. That is, through loans the bank can create money equal to 85 percent of its demand deposits. Thus the amount of money a bank can create depends on its excess reserves. **Excess reserves** equal the amount of a depository institution's (such as a bank's) total reserves minus the required reserves:

Excess reserves = total legal reserves − required reserves

Excess reserves are any reserves above and beyond the minimum required by law.

A bank can lend out safely the amount of its excess reserves even if the "homing power" on new loans is zero and all the money goes to different banks. If, however, it retained part of its newly created deposits, the bank could lend out a bit more than that amount. A banking system that operates with banks acting independently can end up lending many times the amount of excess reserves, even if each bank in the system lends only the amount of its excess reserves. A bank's excess reserves depend on the reserve requirement (as shown in the table on page 194) and on its total legal reserves, or funds that according to law may be counted as part of the

Reserve requirement ratio: the portion of a depository institution's (such as a bank's) reserves that by law cannot be used to create money.

Excess reserves: the amount of a depository institution's (such as a bank's) total reserves minus the required reserves.

reserves that the bank must keep against its deposits. A decline in the reserve requirement increases a bank's excess reserves and its money-creating capability. When the reserve requirement goes up, excess reserves and money-creating capabilities go down.

Reserve Requirement (percentage)	Loans Can Be Equal to: (percentage of demand deposits)
10	90
15	85
17	83
20	80

A bank with a total demand deposit of $10 million and a reserve requirement of 10 percent can make loans of up to $9 million (90 percent of $10 million). If the reserve requirement is 17 percent, the bank can make loans of only $8.3 million (83 percent of $10 million). The purpose of reserve requirements is to restrain credit expansion.

Many people have the impression that the reserve requirement is a means of ensuring that banks have some money on hand to meet the public's withdrawals. In fact, it is illegal to use reserves to meet unanticipated cash withdrawals. Even if the reserves were available, they would be insufficient under fractional reserves if there were a serious bank run. Thus, the reserve requirement is not intended to serve that purpose or to maintain the financial soundness of the banking system. The purpose of the reserve requirement is simply to restrict the amount of money that banks can create. If banks want security against customer withdrawals, they must maintain reserves above and beyond their required reserves, which are bookkeeping entries only. Banks do not really lend out other people's money when they make loans. Although reserve deposits are calculated on the basis of a bank's demand deposits, they are not the same thing. If they were, banks would not be able to create money. Loans would merely transfer money from depositor to borrower. Banks create money by lending their excess reserves.

The Multiple Effects of Loans

So far we have considered only the immediate effects of creating money by loan. The process extends beyond the addition of a specific amount of money to the economy in the form of a loan check, however.

Assume Bank A has total customer deposits of $10 million and a reserve deposit of an equal amount. Its accounts and those of the Federal Reserve are shown in Step I of Figure 7.4 (pp. 196–197). Assume also that the reserve requirement is 20 percent. Bank A can therefore lend against 80 percent of its $10 million in reserves, or as much as $8 million. Bank A decides to lend all $8 million to a local firm that needs new equipment. The firm buys the equipment, handing over Bank A's check to the supplier, who deposits it at Bank B.

Bank A's check increases Bank B's total customer deposits, a change shown on Bank B's balance sheet in Step II of Figure 7.4. Bank B's reserve deposit increases by $8 million, a change recorded in the Fed's liability column (entry b). At the same time, Bank A's reserve deposit falls from $10 million (Step I) to $2 million (Step II, entry c).

Bank A's assets are still worth $10 million, but they are rearranged because of the loan. Total loan assets increase by $8 million (entry d), and the reserve deposit decreases to $2 million (entry e). Bank B records in its own assets column the $8 million increase in its reserve deposit (entry f).

Total demand deposits rise from $10 million in Step I to $18 million in Step II ($10 million of demand deposits in Bank A plus $8 million in Bank B). In other words, the total money stock has increased. This is the reason we say that banks create money when they extend loans.

The money-creating process does not stop with the increases in Bank B's balance sheet. With its newly acquired reserves of $8 million, Bank B can also create money through a loan. It can lend against 80 percent of its additional reserves, or up to $6.4 million. Bank B's loan ends up as a deposit in Bank C, as shown in Step III (entry g). Bank B's reserve deposit decreases by $6.4 million to $1.6 million, both in its own records and in the Federal Reserve's (entries h and i). Bank B's loan account rises by $6.4 million (entry j). Finally, Bank C's reserve deposit increases by $6.4 million, both in its own records and in the Federal Reserve's (entries k and l). As a result of Bank B's loan, total demand deposits in the banking system rise to $24.4 million ($10 million in Bank A plus $8 million in Bank B plus $6.4 million in Bank C). Again the money stock has increased because of a bank loan.

Bank C can now extend loans based on its newly acquired demand and reserve deposits. Like Banks A and B, Bank C can lend against 80 percent of its reserve. As Bank C and successive banks extend new loans up to the legal maximum, the money stock continues to expand. It will not rise indefinitely, however. Each new loan is smaller than the one before it; each adds less to the money stock. Given the reserve requirement of 20 percent and initial excess reserves of $8 million, we can determine the maximum increase in the money stock through a simple formula:

$$= \text{Bank A's excess reserves} \times \frac{1}{\text{reserve requirement ratio}}$$

$$= \$8 \text{ million} \times \frac{1}{0.20} = \$40 \text{ million}$$

Theoretically, once all banks have extended their loans to the legal maximum, the money stock cannot expand further without a change in total reserves or the reserve requirement. In Chapter 8 we will see how the Federal Reserve can change the total reserves and reserve requirement to increase or decrease the money stock.

Step I

Bank A		Federal Reserve Bank	
Assets	Liabilities	Assets	Liabilities
Reserve deposits: $10 million	Total deposits: $10 million		Reserve deposit of Bank A: $10 million

Step II

Bank A		Bank B	
Assets	Liabilities	Assets	Liabilities
Reserve deposits: $2 million (entry e)	Total deposits: $10 million	Reserve deposits: $8 million (entry f)	Total deposits: + $8 million (entry a)
Loans: $8 million (entry d)			

Federal Reserve Bank

Assets	Liabilities
	Reserve deposit of Bank A: $2 million (entry c)
	Reserve deposit of Bank B: + $8 million (entry b)

FIGURE 7.4   The Creation of Money Through the Banking System
In Step I, assuming a reserve requirement of 20 percent, Bank A has excess reserves equal to $8 million. In Step II, a loan of $8 million from Bank A ends up as a deposit in Bank B. Bank A's loan also shifts reserves from Bank A to Bank B at the Federal Reserve Bank. In Step III, Bank B can now make a loan for as much as $6.4 million (again, assuming a 20 percent reserve requirement). Bank B's loan ends up as a deposit in Bank C and shifts $6.4

Fluctuations in the Money Stock

◄ **8. What causes the money stock to fluctuate?**

Federal funds rate: the interest charged by one depository institution to another for a temporary loan based on the use of unneeded balances at Federal Reserve banks.

The foregoing description of the creation of money was based on several assumptions made to simplify the analysis. Money creation does not actually proceed as smoothly as this theoretical model suggests. Day-to-day changes in business conditions cause temporary fluctuations in the money stock. For instance, banks are continually receiving payments on loans. Because they earn their income from such arrangements, they will attempt to relend the payments they receive as quickly as possible. Banks often loan their excess reserves to other banks for periods as short as a day or less, charging what is called the federal funds rate. The **federal funds rate** is the interest charged by one depository institution to another for a temporary loan based on the use of unneeded balances at Federal Reserve banks. A bank's loan payments do not always match its loan requests; at times they exceed requests. At such times, a bank will have idle excess reserves. Because it has not made as many loans as possible, it will not have created as

Step III

Bank A

Assets	Liabilities
Reserve deposits: $2 million	Total demand deposits: $10 million
Loans: $8 million	

Bank B

Assets	Liabilities
Reserve deposits: $1.6 million (entry *h*)	Total demand deposits: − $8 million
Loans: $8.4 million (entry *j*)	

Bank C

Assets	Liabilities
Reserve deposits: $8.4 million (entry *l*)	Total demand deposits: $8.4 million (entry *e*)

Federal Reserve Bank

Assets	Liabilities
	Reserve deposit of Bank A: $2 million
	Reserve deposit of Bank B: $1.6 million (entry *i*)
	Reserve deposit of Bank C: $8.4 million (entry *k*)

FIGURE 7.4 *Continued*

million in reserves from Bank B to Bank C at the Fed. Bank C now has excess reserves equal to $5.1 million that it can loan. This money expansion process can continue as long as excess reserves exist. The maximum addition to the money stock from Bank A's initial $8 million loan would be $40 million.

much money as it can create. If all banks have problems of this kind, the total money stock will not be as great as it could be.

Moreover, not all bank loans end up as demand deposits in other banks. Part of the money created by banks may end up as currency held in the pockets of the public. Although currency is money, it is not the kind of money that permits banks to claim reserve deposits—not, therefore, the kind of money on which additional loans can be made. To the extent that bank loans end up as currency, the ability of banks to expand loans and increase the money stock is reduced.

For instance, suppose the firm that received the $8 million check from Bank A deposited only $7.5 million in Bank B, taking $500,000 in currency. Bank B would then have been able to lend only $6 million (80 percent of $7.5 million) instead of $6.4 million. Bank C would have received this smaller deposit and would have been able to lend less to Bank D. The total increase in the money stock would have been only $37.5 million instead of $40 million.

The public's willingness to hold money in the form of both currency and demand deposits will influence the overall level of the money stock. If the public reduces its demand deposits and increases its currency holdings, banks will have lower reserves and will not be able to make as many loans. Unless there are compensating changes (to be discussed in the next chapter), the money stock will fall. Similarly, if the public reduces its currency holdings by depositing currency in its demand accounts, bank reserves will rise. Banks will increase their loans, thereby increasing the money stock.

The simple formula assumes that all banks are subject to the same regulations and same reserve requirements. It also assumes that the lending bank does not retain any of its loan-created deposits. Since a lending bank ordinarily retains some of these deposits, it could, *ceteris paribus,* loan out a bit more than its excess reserves. It is also important to remember that banks do not slavishly follow a mechanical formula. Bankers do what they think is best, regardless of any formulas, to maximize their banks' long-run profits, within the legal and market constraints imposed upon them.

Chapter Review

Review of Key Questions

◢   *1. What is money?*

Money consists of those assets that can be used as a medium of exchange, standard of value (unit of account), and a store of purchasing power or value. Money that functions as a means of payment is more efficient than a barter system that mandates a coincidence of wants, and money lowers transaction costs. Money is manufactured and retailed by depository institutions such as banks. Financial institutions—except for the Federal Reserve, which is a quasi-public institution that seeks to influence economic activity regardless of profitability—are profit-seeking, just like other types of businesses.

◢   *2. What determines the value of money?*

Money has value not because it is backed by gold, but because of people's confidence—an unwritten social agreement—in its general acceptability and its stability. Legal tender is a contrived value given to our coins and currency. The biggest portion of our money stock—checkable deposits—is not legal tender. Like any commodity, money is valuable because it is both useful and relatively scarce. It is subject to the laws of supply and demand, although it has very low marginal costs.

◢   *3. What are the three types of demand for money?*

People hold money balances to finance transactions (the transactions demand for money); to cover unexpected expenditures (the precautionary demand); and to take advantage of anticipated increases in interest rates (the speculative demand). The last two combine to form the asset demand for money. The demand for money is positively related to people's income and wealth and the present price level (and expected future price level if expected to be higher), and inversely related to yields (or rates of return) of various financial assets and the interest rate.

◢   *4. What are our major forms of money?*

The two most widely used measures of the money stock in the United States are M1 and M2. M1 includes currency and checkable deposits and mainly involves transaction accounts. M2, M3, and L are successively broader aggregates with larger proportions of nontransaction balances. M2 includes M1 plus savings account deposits and small-denomination certificates of deposit. M3 includes M2 plus large-denomination time deposits and some minor items. L is M3 plus other assets such as bankers' acceptances, commercial paper, and T-bills.

◢   *5. What constitutes our banking system?*

Our banking system includes depository institutions (commercial banks, credit unions, mutual savings banks, and savings and loan associations). Deregulation has blurred the previous distinctions among these institutions. Competition, technology, and efficiency are now rampant over safety and stability in these institutions. The quasi-public Federal Reserve's primary goal is to control the cost and supply of money regardless of profitability.

The Federal Reserve System is composed of twelve district banks and is headed by a Board of Governors, which is primarily responsible for the conduct of the nation's monetary policy. In addition, the Federal Reserve moves currency and coin into and out of circulation according to demands of depository institutions (and therefore the public). The Fed also allows eligible depository institutions to borrow at its discount windows, and safekeeps securities for them. The Fed collects, processes, and clears checks. It performs fiscal agency services for the U.S. Treasury, such as providing checking accounts and issuing and redeeming government securities. It supervises, examines, and regulates depository institutions for safety and soundness. Since the Monetary Control Act of 1980, the costs of the Fed's various services are costed out to member banks and other eligible depository institutions. The reserve requirements are uniformly set for all depository institutions.

◢   *6. How do checks transfer money?*

When one person writes a check to another, the demand deposit of the person who receives the check increases, while the deposit of the person writing the check decreases. The bank that pays the check loses reserve deposits, and the bank that receives the check gains reserve deposits. The total stock of money remains the same, however. The continuing operation of the payment mechanism requires the important and expensive process of check-clearing.

◢   *7. How do banks create money?*

When banks make loans, they create money in the form of demand deposits. Demand deposits are the biggest portion of our M1 money stock. A bank's ability to create money is restricted approximately by its excess reserves, which depend on the legally mandated reserve requirement. If a bank tried to loan more than the reserve requirement, it would suffer adverse clearing balances, because a good proportion of the checks drawn would have low "homing power"; i.e., they would therefore be deposited in other banks. In the case of a pure monopoly bank—one and only one bank—this constraint would not be true. The maximum money multiplier of the whole banking system would be relevant, since all checks drawn would have to return to the sole bank in that system. The maximum amount of money that can be created by the entire depository institution system equals the excess reserves in the system times the reciprocal of the reserve requirement (that is, one divided by the reserve requirement), assuming no currency drain or idle excess reserves. Thus, the entire depository institution's system can lend a multiple of its excess reserves because there is no threat of adverse clearing balances. The homing power is 100 percent. Only individual banks can lose reserves. For the entire banking system, reserves are a zero-sum game; their total can never be increased or decreased by the private banks themselves.

8. What causes the money stock to fluctuate?

The money stock tends to fluctuate because of unevenness in the granting and repayment of bank loans and changes in the amount of currency held by the public. Banks make money by providing loans at higher interest rates than they pay to attain and maintain deposits. They therefore dislike idle, non-interest bearing, unloaned excess reserves. Because of currency drains—currency held by the public from bank-created loans—and because of the desire of some banks to hold idle some excess reserves for liquidity or other reasons, the banking system seldom creates money to its maximum potential.

Further Topics

Money is a medium of exchange that facilitates trade. In the form of currency and financial assets that can be stored or used to buy goods and services, money is productive. It reduces the time people must spend searching out mutually beneficial trades and increases the time they can spend producing goods and services. Currency, demand deposits, and savings deposits also provide liquidity, or ease of conversion into other assets.

Holding money involves costs as well as benefits. When people hold money, they forgo the goods and services that money could buy. People will not hold money unless the benefits of doing so are at least equal to the benefits of the goods and services it could buy.

Paper money and checks have value simply because they are used as money. People are willing to accept and hold them because they are confident that others will do so. For this reason, modern money is relatively easy to produce. The amount of money that can be created is not limited, for example, by the amount of gold beneath the earth's crust. It is figuratively created with the stroke of a pen or a blip of the computer by governments, commercial banks, and the Federal Reserve System.

Government may be tempted to use its money-creating authority to produce money too fast. In recent history, many governments have succumbed to the impulse to inflate the money stock, and the result has been a continuing increase in price levels—that is, inflation—sometimes of runaway proportions. One of the most pressing problems of monetary economics is the question of how to control the money stock wisely. It is no simple problem, as we will see in the next two chapters.

Review of New Terms

Asset demand for money The combined precautionary and speculative reasons for holding money.

Checkable deposits Any deposits against which checks or their equivalent can be written.

Depository institutions Private, profit-seeking financial instutions, including commercial banks and thrift institutions such as credit unions, mutual savings banks, savings banks, and savings and loan institutions (S&Ls) that handle transaction accounts and checkable deposits.

Excess reserves The amount of a depository institution's (such as a bank's) total reserves minus the required reserves.

Federal funds rate The interest charged by one depository institution to another for a temporary loan based on the use of unneeded balances at Federal Reserve banks.

Fiat money A medium of exchange or store of value that cannot be redeemed for anything other than a replica of itself.

Financial intermediary A financial institution that assembles the funds of savers or lenders to lend to borrowers at interest rates that generally cover at least the cost of operation (including normal profit).

Full-bodied commodity money A medium of exchange or store of value that has some intrinsic value as a consumer good or factor of production. It has some economic use apart from its monetary role.

L M3 plus other liquid assets not included in other aggregates such as bankers' acceptances, commercial paper, and Treasury bills.

Liquidity The ease with which any asset can be converted on short notice into spendable form with little or no loss of value.

Money stock The sum of all identified forms of money held by the public (as opposed to the financial institutions) at a given point in time.

M1 The total of the public's (as opposed to the financial institutions') holdings of currency (paper bills and coins), demand deposits at commercial banks, traveler's checks, and other bank accounts against which checks can be written, such as NOW (negotiable order of withdrawal) and ATS (automatic transfer services) accounts.

M2 M1 plus savings accounts and small-denomination (less than $100,000) time deposits and certificates of deposit, plus money market accounts and other highly liquid assets.

M3 M2 plus large-denomination time deposits and other relatively minor components.

Precautionary demand for money The desire to hold money balances in order to finance unexpected or emergency purchases of goods and services.

Representative commodity money Certificates or notes that can be converted into given quantities of a specific commodity, like gold or silver.

Reserve deposits The accounts that depository institutions hold in Federal Reserve Banks. (A depository institution's reserve deposit balance plus its vault cash equals its total reserves.)

Reserve requirement ratio The portion of a depository institution's (such as a bank's) reserves that by law cannot be used to create money.

Reserves The cash a depository institution has in its vault plus its deposits at the Federal Reserve Bank.

Speculative demand for money The desire to hold money in anticipation of a decrease in the price of other assets and in anticipation of future profits.

Target Any economic variable—usually some monetary aggregate—that the Fed manages in the attempt to attain certain macroeconomic goals.

Transactions demand for money The desire to hold money balances in order to carry out anticipated purchases of goods and services.

Velocity (V) The rate of turnover or circulation of the money stock (M) relative to GNP; thus, $V = GNP/M$.

Review Questions

1. Suppose you head the government in a nation involved in an unpopular war. You can pay for the war by increasing taxes or by printing more money. Which option would you take? What would be the consequences of your action? (◢2)

2. Dollar bills are elaborately engraved to prevent counterfeiting. Why? If dollar bills could be easily duplicated, what would happen to the money stock? To the nation's production and price levels? To the value of the dollar? (◢1, ◢2, ◢8)

3. Do S&H Green Stamps qualify as money? Why or why not? (◢1, ◢2, ◢4)

4. Suppose you receive a $15 check from a friend who has an account at another bank. You deposit the check in your account. Using T accounts, sketch the entries that will be made on the books of your bank, your friend's bank, and the Federal Reserve Bank. What happens to the money stock because of the transaction? What happens to the ability of the two banks to make loans? (◢5, ◢6, ◢7, ◢8)

5. Suppose that your bank has total demand deposits of $20 million; that the reserve requirement is 10 percent; and that the bank has already made loans worth $5 million. How much more money can your bank lend to those who want to borrow? (◢7)

6. If the reserve requirement is 100 percent, will banks be able to make loans? Will they be willing to handle the public's demand deposits? (◢7)

7. Would anyone demand money to cover an event such as a change in the price of bonds? (◢3)

The Federal Reserve and the Money Stock

Do changes in the quantity of money matter? . . . There is massive historical evidence that they do. Every economic recession but one in the U.S. in the past century has been preceded by a decline in the rate of growth of the quantity of money. And the sharper the decline, the more serious the subsequent recession—though this tendency is far from uniform.
  Milton Friedman

KEY QUESTIONS

▲ 1. What are the Federal Reserve's three quantitative money stock controls and how do they work?

▲ 2. How does monetary policy affect the rate of inflation?

▲ 3. What is the effect of change in the money stock on aggregate demand and supply?

▲ 4. What are the politics of monetary policy?

NEW TERMS

Discount rate
Equation of exchange
  $(MV = PQ)$
Federal funds rate

Open market operations
Reserve requirements
Velocity of money (V)

Commercial banks are profit-maximizing firms that produce financial services. As the last chapter discussed, the amount of money that over 14,500 commercial banks in the United States can create depends on their reserves and the reserve requirement. This chapter describes how the Federal Reserve uses its powers to change the total reserves and the reserve requirement to control the money stock. Since the major deregulation legislation of 1980 this power now extends to all depository institutions, but commercial banks are still the protagonists. This extension means that the Fed has a greater ability to conduct monetary policy because it has a greater percentage of depository institutions under its reserve requirement control. The blurring of the distinction between banks and other financial institutions continues daily as deregulation rolls on.

The Federal Reserve cannot control the money stock with precision. Its controls resemble the farmer's controls over crop size. The farmer who uses specific quantities of seed and fertilizer has a rough idea of how large his harvest will be. Because natural forces like the weather can change suddenly, however, the farmer can never be quite sure of the size of the harvest. Similarly, because of the many forces constantly interacting in the national economy, the governors of the Federal Reserve cannot always be sure exactly what will happen to the money stock when they employ one of the Fed's monetary controls. They know the approximate range within which change may occur, and the general direction the change should take, but no more.

Control of the Money Stock

1. What are the Federal Reserve's three quantitative money stock controls and how do they work?

The Federal Reserve tries to stabilize the economy and promote economic growth through monetary policy.[1] The Federal Reserve exercises control over the money stock in three ways: (1) by imposing the reserve require-

1. Although the Fed as a whole opines that it can in both the short run and the long run influence both nominal and real factors, monetarists believe that in the long run the Fed can influence only prices and not real factors. The two Federal Reserve Banks that emphasize monetarism are in St. Louis and Richmond.

ment; (2) by making loans to depository institutions and charging a discount rate for the service; and (3) by purchasing and selling government securities (mainly bills, notes, and bonds issued by the U.S. Treasury). In Keynesian analysis, these policy decisions work because they affect interest rates directly or indirectly by changing reserves that change the money supply. Changes in interest rates affect investment, and to a lesser extent consumption spending, and therefore affect the equilibrium GNP.

The Fed cannot directly influence its ultimate goals. The three means of control discussed above are used to attain certain operating targets and intermediate targets in the hope of ultimately influencing macroeconomic goals and objectives such as reducing unemployment and inflation rates, increasing real GNP, or stabilizing the balances of payments. These targets must not only be strongly linked to these macroeconomic goals, but must be such that the Fed can actively and accurately control them as well. Unfortunately, most suitable targets are not independent of other non-Fed forces in the economy. The Fed can influence its macroeconomic goals only indirectly through the supply of money, depository institution's credit, and interest rates. Hence, these are considered intermediate targets. However, intermediate targets are not directly and completely under the Fed's control either. What the Fed shoots for are certain identifiable, achievable, and verifiable operating targets such as reserve aggregates and money market conditions, hoping they will affect the intermediate targets and in that way ultimately achieve its goals. For example, the Fed might specify an intermediate growth target for some monetary aggregate—M2, for instance—of 6 to 8 percent per year and set an operating target for nonborrowed reserves of 2 to 4 percent per year that is consistent with the intermediate target.

The Reserve Requirement

Reserve requirements: the amount of reserves, expressed as a percentage of deposits, held by depository institutions in the form of cash holdings in their own vaults or on deposit at the Federal Reserve Bank (or at another depository institution for nonmember banks) that cannot be used to create money through loans.

The reserve requirement is the amount of reserves, expressed as a percentage of deposits, held by depository institutions in the form of cash holdings in their own vaults or on deposit at a Federal Reserve Bank (or at another depository institution for nonmember banks) that cannot be used by law to create money through loans. The bank's reserves, which include both its deposits at the Fed in its district and the currency in its vault, can drop no lower than the specific percentage of its demand deposits.

Actually, the reserve requirement is not a single figure, but a set of figures that apply to different types of accounts—i.e., transaction versus time—and to different levels of deposits or dates of maturity. Table 8.1 shows the reserve requirements on demand and nonpersonal time deposits as of July 1988.

The general effect of a change in the reserve requirement is fairly simple. Suppose banks have loaned all the money they can, given the reserve requirement. If the requirement is reduced, they will be able to make more loans. As they do, the money stock will rise. The additional loans will end up as negotiable bank deposits or currency (see Chapter 7), which will supplement the existing money supply.

TABLE 8.1   Reserve Requirements of Depository Institutions[a]

Type of Deposit and Deposit Interval	Reserve Requirement Percentage of Deposits[b]
Net transaction or demand deposit accounts	
$0–$41.5 million	3%
More than $41.5 million	12
Nonpersonal time deposits (by original maturity)	
Less than 1½ years	3
1½ years or more	0

a. Depository institutions include commercial banks, mutual savings and loan associations, credit unions, and agencies and branches of foreign banks, and Edge Act corporations.
b. Required reserves must be held in the form of deposits with Federal Reserve Banks or vault cash. Nonmembers may maintain reserve balances with a Federal Reserve Bank indirectly on a pass-through basis with certain approved institutions.
Source: Federal Reserve Bulletin (February 1989), p. A8.

If the reserve requirement is increased, banks will have to increase their reserves. They will therefore make fewer loans. If banks cannot relend the money they gain when people repay their loans, the money stock must fall. Eventually the ratio of reserves to demand deposits will rise to the new required level.

Although we know that a decrease in the reserve requirement tends to increase the money stock, and vice versa, it is difficult to calculate when or how much the money stock will change. If the Fed lowers the reserve requirement, banks may not expand their loans immediately. Unfavorable business conditions may lead them to hold excess reserves. For instance, suppose banks expect interest rates to rise in the very near future. Instead of increasing their loans immediately, at relatively low interest rates, many banks may wait. Conversely, if the Fed increases the reserve requirement, some banks may not have to contract their loans immediately if they already have on hand all the reserves they need.

At different times, confronted with different market forces, the banking system will respond differently to a change in the reserve requirement. Sophisticated statistical procedures (called econometric model building) can increase the accuracy of the Fed's predictions. Even those methods are not always reliable, however. If a change in reserve requirements fails to produce the desired effect, the Fed may have to take corrective measures. Because a very small change in the reserve requirement can result in large changes in the money stock, and because banks have difficulty responding to changes in the reserve requirement, the Fed makes such changes infrequently—rarely more than once a year.

Loans to Depository Institutions

The Federal Reserve can increase or stabilize the money stock through loans to depository institutions. Just as individuals and business firms borrow from depository institutions, a depository institution can borrow from the Federal Reserve Bank that serves its region. In return for its IOU, the bank receives an increase in its reserve deposit. This type of transaction is illustrated in Figure 8.1. Suppose Northwestern National Bank wants to borrow $1 million in reserves from the Federal Reserve Bank of San Francisco. Northwestern commits itself to repaying the loan plus interest and receives a $1 million increase in its reserves. The loan is listed as a liability on Northwestern's books (entry *a*) and, because interest is collected on it, as an asset on the Federal Reserve Bank's books (entry *b*). The $1 million reserve deposit that Northwestern acquires is an asset to it (entry *c*) and a liability to the Federal Reserve (entry *d*).

Northwestern can use its reserves either to make interest-bearing loans to the public or to ensure that it meets the reserve requirement. If it makes loans, they will increase the money stock. If it uses the new reserves to meet its reserve requirement, it will not have to reduce its outstanding loans, which would contract the money stock.

For example, suppose Northwestern's demand deposits are $10 million and its reserves $1 million. If the reserve requirement is 20 percent, Northwestern has $1 million less than it needs to meet the requirement. It could get the extra reserves by reducing its outstanding loans, but that procedure would reduce the money stock. If it borrows $1 million in reserves from the Fed, Northwestern will not have to reduce its loans, and the money stock will not be reduced.

Banks borrow from the Fed for very short periods of time, usually a matter of days. When they pay back their loans, they reduce their reserves, and thus their ability to create money. Usually some banks are borrowing from the Fed while others are repaying their loans. Until late 1984, loans from the Fed hovered around $1 billion. For reasons that were not immediately clear, Fed loans shot up to $8 billion in early 1985. Even then, they amounted to less than 4 percent of total reserves.

Where does the Fed get the reserves that it loans to commercial banks? It creates them. The Fed simply accepts the bank's IOUs and increases its reserve deposits, which exist only as bookkeeping entries.

Northwestern National Bank		Federal Reserve Bank of San Francisco	
Assets	Liabilities	Assets	Liabilities
Reserve deposits: + $1 million (entry *c*)	Loan from Federal Reserve: + $1 million (entry *a*)	Loans to member bank: + $1 million (entry *b*)	Reserve deposit of Northwestern: + $1 million (entry *d*)

FIGURE 8.1 Federal Reserve Loan to a Depository Institution
A Federal Reserve loan to Northwestern National Bank increases Northwestern's reserve deposit. Northwestern can use its new reserves to make loans to its customers, which will ultimately increase the money stock.

The Fed can control the number and amount of the loans it grants in two ways. It can refuse to grant a loan (borrowing from the Fed is considered a privilege, not a right). It can also control the level of its lending by changing the interest rate it charges—the so-called discount rate. The **discount rate** is the interest rate the Federal Reserve charges on loans to depository institutions such as commercial banks. A decrease in the discount rate will encourage banks to borrow because it makes loans less costly. An increase in the discount rate will make loans more costly, discouraging borrowing. A financial institution may prefer to borrow reserve funds from other financial institutions rather than from the Fed. Such loans are ordinarily made for a single day, in multiples of $1 million, charging the **federal funds rate**—the interest rate one financial institution charges on loans to another financial institution.

In practice, changing the discount rate is not an important tool for controlling the money stock, for the number of loans the Fed makes to depository institutions is not an especially influential factor. Economists and financial analysts for major banks and brokerage firms often view changes in the discount rate as an "announcement effect" that the Fed plans to take other actions that will significantly change depository institution reserves—open market operations, for example. In 1986, two reductions in the discount rate were taken as signals that the Fed intended to increase the growth rate of the money stock.

Open Market Operations

By far the most important of the Fed's tools is its ability to sell government securities through its open market operations. **Open market operations** are the purchase and sale by the Federal Reserve of U.S. government securities, which can be bills (91 days–1 year), notes (1–10 years), or bonds (10–40 years). When the Fed buys government securities, it increases bank reserves and the money stock. When it sells government securities, bank reserves and the money stock decline.

Suppose the Fed buys a government bill from a private firm. The manager of the Fed's open market account, who works at the Federal Reserve Bank of New York, first asks dealers in the government securities market for the selling price on the bills they hold. Assume the Fed agrees to pay $1 million for the bill. It is delivered to the Federal Reserve, which issues a check for $1 million to the securities firm. The check ends up as a demand deposit in the firm's bank, increasing the money stock. The bank receiving the deposit can claim an increase in its reserves at the Fed.

Figure 8.2 shows the resulting entries on the books of Northwestern National Bank, which receives the deposit, and of the Federal Reserve. The Federal Reserve's U.S. Treasury Bill holdings, an asset, increase (entry *a*), while the reserve deposit of Northwestern National, an offsetting liability, also increases (entry *b*). Similarly, Northwestern National records an increase in its demand deposits (entry *c*) and in its reserve deposit (entry *d*). Northwestern can now increase its loans up to the limit set by the reserve

---

Discount rate: the interest rate the Federal Reserve charges on loans to depository institutions such as commercial banks.

Federal funds rate: the interest rate one financial institution charges on loans to another financial institution.

Open market operations: the purchase and sale by the Federal Reserve of U.S. government securities, which can be bills, notes, or bonds.

Northwestern National Bank		Federal Reserve Bank	
Assets	Liabilities	Assets	Liabilities
Reserve deposits:	Demand	Holdings of U.S.	Reserve deposit
+ $1 million	deposits:	government	of Northwestern:
(entry *d*)	+ $1 million	securities:	+ $1 million
	(entry *c*)	+ $1 million	(entry *b*)
		(entry *a*)	

FIGURE 8.2 Purchase of a Government Bill by the Federal Reserve
The Fed's purchase of a government bill from a private firm increases the firm's deposit at Northwestern National Bank. It also increases Northwestern's reserve deposit at the Federal Reserve. By acquiring a government security, that is, the Fed increases Northwestern's ability to make loans and expand the money stock.

requirement. In short, it can start the process of money expansion described in Chapter 7 (see pages 194–197).

Where does the money to buy the bill come from? The Fed creates it. As long as people are willing to accept checks written by the Federal Reserve in exchange for their government securities, and as long as banks are willing to accept those checks as demand deposits, what the Federal Reserve creates is money.

The Federal Reserve can just as easily reduce the money stock, by selling some of the government securities it holds. (In 1988, the Fed held over $220 billion worth of government securities.) When it sells a bill, the Fed receives a check drawn on someone's demand deposit, and the reserves of that person's bank fall. The Fed does not increase its accounts with the money represented by that check, however. It figuratively destroys the money by entering a zero on its books.

This transaction is shown in Figure 8.3. Assume that payment for the bill is made by a check written on an account with Northwestern National.

Northwestern National Bank		Federal Reserve Bank	
Assets	Liabilities	Assets	Liabilities
Reserve deposits:	Demand	Holdings of U.S.	Reserve deposit
− $1 million	deposits:	government	of Northwestern:
(entry *b*)	− $1 million	securities:	− $1 million
	(entry *a*)	− $1 million	(entry *d*)
		(entry *c*)	

FIGURE 8.3 Sale of a Government Bill by the Federal Reserve
The sale of a government bill by the Federal Reserve decreases the buyer's deposit at Northwestern National Bank. It also decreases Northwestern's reserve deposit at the Fed. Thus the sale of a security by the Fed reduces Northwestern's ability to make loans and create money.

Northwestern's demand deposits fall by the amount of the purchase price, $1 million (entry *a*). At the same time its reserve deposit falls by $1 million (entry *b*). The Federal Reserve loses an asset in the form of the government security (entry *c*) and dispenses with an equal liability in the form of a decrease in Northwestern's reserve deposit (entry *d*). One million dollars has disappeared from the money stock—but that is not all. Assuming that Northwestern has loaned up to its legal maximum before the sale of the bill, it must now reduce its loans in order to build its reserve deposit back up to the legal requirement. The money stock thus decreases further.

Summary of Monetary Controls

The members of the Open Market Committee of the Fed have several ways of exerting control over the money stock. If they want to increase the money stock, they may:

1. Reduce the reserve requirement.
2. Increase the loans made to depository institutions.
3. Buy government securities on the open market.

If they want to decrease the money stock, they may:

4. Increase the reserve requirement.
5. Reduce the loans made to depository institutions.
6. Sell government securities held by the Fed.

If the committee takes any of the first three actions and the growth of the money stock accelerates, the Fed is said to be following an expansionary or loose monetary policy. If it takes any of the last three actions and the money stock decreases or slows its rate of growth, the Fed is said to be following a contractionary or tight monetary policy.

The Fed's controls over the money stock are powerful, but it is difficult to apply them precisely within narrow limits. Various forces may work against—or in concert with—monetary controls. For instance, banks may choose not to lend against all their excess reserves. Even if they do, the money expansion process takes time to work through the banking system. In addition, changes in the demand for money may offset changes in the supply of money, thereby frustrating monetary policy. For instance, a stimulative expansion of the money stock may not expand GNP if money demand drops significantly. Furthermore, while the Fed is trying to increase reserves, the public may be increasing its currency holdings and reducing its demand deposits, in turn reducing reserves and the potential to create money. Moreover, the U.S. Treasury has demand deposits both at the Fed and in depository institutions around the nation. If the Treasury decides to move some of its deposits from depository institutions to the Federal Reserve, it will reduce reserves. Also, if the interest rate does not change much as the supply of money is changed, or if investment is insensitive to shifts in the interest rate, then monetary policy can be frustrated. Finally, monetary policy and fiscal policy are more effective against demand-pull inflation than against cost-push inflation.

In short, the Fed's attempts to increase the money stock may simply offset opposing forces that tend to reduce the money stock. Indeed, the Fed often buys government securities (or reduces the reserve requirement, or increases loans to depository institutions) simply to keep the money stock from falling, rather than to increase it. Similar difficulties may frustrate attempts to contract the money stock.

Monetary policy is thought by some to be superior to fiscal policy—i.e., government altering its spending and taxes to control the economy—as it applies quickly with few lags. For instance, the Federal Open Market Committee is much more flexible than a congressional committee. Monetary policy is also more impersonal, subtle, and therefore somewhat more politically acceptable, applying to almost everyone instead of a select few.

A Monetary Explanation of Inflation and Deflation

▲ 2. How does monetary policy affect the rate of inflation?

The ultimate purpose of monetary policy is not simply to change the money stock, but to influence the nation's production, employment, and price levels. In recent years the Federal Reserve has been particularly concerned with the effect of its monetary policy on the rate of inflation.

Size of the Money Stock and the Value of Money

The value of anything is measured by what it can get in trade. Thus the value of money is what money will buy. If a dollar will buy a regular hamburger at the local McDonald's restaurant, the exchange value of the dollar is one regular hamburger. (Contrary to the opinion frequently quoted by the press, the value of the dollar is not about 30 cents. Very few people would trade a dollar for 30 cents.)

In general, the value of the dollar depends on the supply of dollars relative to the supply of goods and services people have to sell. If the supply of dollars people are willing to spend rises faster than the quantity of goods offered on the market, prices will rise. (Competition for the limited number of goods will drive prices up.) As prices rise, the dollar will buy fewer goods, and its value declines. That is why an increase in the money stock is normally associated with a decrease in the value of the dollar. However, an increase in the money stock only decreases the value of the dollar if the increase in the money stock is in excess of any associated increase in real output.

This relationship between the size of the money stock and the value of the monetary unit has been observed throughout history. When Alexander the Great conquered the Persian Empire and took its capital, Persepolis, he found an immense hoard of gold that the Persian emperors had been accumulating for generations. He spent the gold immediately, partly on his

PERSPECTIVES
What Economists Do at the Richmond Fed
Thomas M. Humphrey, Federal Reserve Bank of Richmond

The Federal Reserve Bank of Richmond employs fifteen Ph.D economists in its research department, about the same number employed by most of the other regional Feds. Richmond economists spend most of their time analyzing issues in bank regulation, the payments mechanism, financial markets, and monetary theory and policy. Like their counterparts in academia, they communicate the results of their research through a variety of channels—at professional meetings and Fed conferences, in scholarly journals, in the Bank's own publications, in briefings to the Bank's directors, in newspaper articles, and in speeches to the public. Staff economists also prepare detailed comments on regulatory proposals emanating from the Board of Governors in Washington. Most importantly, they help the Bank's current president,[1] himself a Ph.D economist, prepare for the periodic Federal Open Market Committee (FOMC) meetings that take place in Washington, D.C. approximately every six weeks. The FOMC determines current monetary policy, which it conducts through the purchase and sale of govern-

ment securities (open market operations). In these ways, the Federal Reserve System regulates the quantity of money in the economy.

The president presents his policy views at these meetings. With nineteen FOMC members to be heard from, his policy statement must be crisp, clear, and to the point.[2] At the same time, it must contain the right mix of insight, originality, and credibility to convince other FOMC members of its validity. Monetary policy is always a contentious subject, even in a relatively collegial body such as the FOMC. The statement must be crafted in a way that takes account of differences of opinion within the committee if it is to be persuasive.

Pre-FOMC preparation begins on a Friday, roughly two-and-one-half weeks before the meeting itself. Richmond's research director calls the staff together to identify the key issues likely to be discussed by the FOMC. Perhaps a recent *Wall Street Journal* article has pointed to a potential flaw in the Fed's policy procedures. Perhaps the Fed Chairman has made a recent speech touching on topics of current interest. Perhaps the trade deficit has worsened, or the stock market has collapsed, or the monetary aggregates have been exceeding

1. Regional Bank presidents are nominated by the Banks' boards of directors and approved by the Board of Governors. Each Federal Reserve Bank has a nine-member board of directors that oversees its operations under the general supervision of the Board of Governors. Three Class A (representing member banks) and three Class B (representing the public) directors are elected by the member banks, and three Class C directors (also representing the public) are appointed by the Board of Governors.

2. The FOMC consists of the 7 members of the Board of Governors plus the 12 regional Fed presidents, 5 of whom are voting members at any one time on a rotating basis except for the President of the New York Fed who serves on a continuous basis. However, all twelve presidents attend each of the meetings and present their respective views on issues discussed.

army and partly on himself. As a result, prices all over the Greek world rose sharply. When the stock of money suddenly increased in relation to the supply of goods and services, so many people wanted to spend their newly acquired gold pieces that the prices of goods and services rose, driving the value of the gold down.

There have been other instances of inflation in metallic currencies. Several centuries ago the Spanish discovery of gold and silver mines in the Americas increased the European supply of those metals, depressing their

their target paths, or interest rates, capacity utilization indexes, and the foreign exchanges have been signaling the resurgence of inflation. All such events are likely to be grist for the FOMC's mill and all therefore need to be analyzed by the Richmond staff. Once the staff has clarified each issue, five or six economists are assigned to write policy memos on the issues of their choice. Their assignments once made are rarely changed, and then only in response to a drastic and completely unforeseen shock to the economy. For example, after October 1987's stock market crash, the economists were instructed to abandon their memos on inflation and to concentrate instead on the causes and policy implications of the crash.

Drawing on an extensive base of statistical data and aided by a staff of research assistants who are proficient in statistical analysis and computer programming, the economists complete their memos, which they then send to the president by Wednesday of the week before the FOMC meeting. Two days later, on Friday afternoon, the president meets with the economists and the research chief to discuss the memos and to hammer out a policy statement. These sessions, although often hectic and tending to last for at least 3 hours, are always informal, friendly, and even a bit exhilarating. The procedure followed at these meetings is generally the same: One economist reviews and critiques the Board staff's forecast of the real economy. This forecast is contained in the so-

called *Greenbook*. A second economist then reviews the financial situation, focusing chiefly on the recent behavior of the federal funds rate, nonborrowed and borrowed reserves, and the various monetary aggregates ranging from the monetary base to M2. There follows a no-holds-barred discussion of the policy memos with the authors answering questions posed by the president and the staff. After two or three hours of this, the research chief finally announces that it is time to crystallize the results of the proceedings into a policy statement that (1) enunciates the principal policy issue as Richmond sees it, and (2) specifies the Bank's position on the issue.

The meeting breaks up around 5 PM, but the research director's work is hardly finished. For the next two or three hours he will revise, rewrite, and polish the policy statement drafted in the meeting. Then he will meet with the president on Sunday afternoon for further revision of the statement. Early Monday afternoon, he and the president will drive to Washington in time to review the policy statement once more before the FOMC meeting, which begins typically at 9 AM on Tuesday.

Meanwhile, back in Richmond the economists will have resumed work on their ongoing projects. With policy preparation over, they can devote their attention to longer-term research and writing until pre-FOMC week rolls around again.

value. The California Gold Rush had much the same effect throughout the world. The most recent example of a gold-backed inflation occurred between 1890 and 1910, when the development of the cyanide flotation process of extracting gold from ore increased the supply of gold and decreased its value.

Modern monies are substantially different from the metallic currencies of the past, but the relationship between the money stock and the price level is the same. The German government financed the First World War largely by borrowing. After the war, instead of raising taxes to pay off its debt, the government printed new money in an effort to inflate it away. The sudden dramatic rise in the money stock caused prices to soar. By 1923, prices were a trillion times higher than their prewar levels. The value of German money diminished so rapidly that people were increasingly reluctant to accept it in trade or even to hold on to it. Although it was only during the last few days or weeks of the hyperinflation money was not used, the pace of economic activity was still sharply curtailed.

In recent years, governments in Italy, Great Britain, and several South American nations have also printed more money than their economies could absorb. In 1985 the following staggering inflation rates, in percentages, prevailed: Brazil, 220 percent; Israel, 407; Argentina, 851; and Bolivia, 3,408!

In the United States the story has been less dramatic. During the 1950s, both the money stock and the price level increased at an average annual rate of slightly less than 2 percent. In the first half of the 1960s, the average rate of growth of the money stock rose to 3 to 4 percent, and inflation followed at approximately the same rate. In the late 1960s and early 1970s, the average annual growth rate of money increased again to 6 percent, but inflation rose only to 5 percent, partly because of government price controls. In the mid-1970s, price controls were effectively discarded, the annual growth rate of money rose to 7 percent, and inflation accelerated to 9 percent.

Both the money stock and prices hit alarming double-digit rates late in the 1970s. In the early 1980s the Fed sharply reduced money growth. This dramatic drop in the growth rate of money—indeed, the sudden reversal of policy from a rising to a decreasing rate of growth—was accompanied by two recessions. Real GNP dropped and unemployment increased sharply. When the Fed expanded money growth to roughly 10 percent between 1982 and 1983, however, price increases of the same magnitude did not follow. In fact, from 1982 to 1984, prices increased less than 5 percent, in part because production expanded along with prices. In mid-1983, the Fed again began to tighten up on money growth. Yet the CPI inflation rates were only 3.6 percent in 1985, 1.9 percent in 1986, and 3.7 percent in 1987. For the eight years from 1980 to 1987, the four monetary aggregates—M1, M2, M3, and L—increased roughly 10 percent per year while CPI inflation averaged about 6 percent and the civilian unemployment rate about 8 percent per year.

Although inflation has been the general rule in recent history, deflation—a general decrease in prices—has also occurred, usually after wars. Just as nations may be tempted to increase the money stock as a means of financing war-related expenditures, they often try to reduce war-inflated prices afterward by reducing the money stock. The result is deflation. England underwent a long period of mild deflation after the Napoleonic wars; so did the United States after the Civil War. Prices also dropped significantly in the United States in 1920–1921, following the First World War. In each case deflation was caused by a reduction in the money stock. Since 1939, prices have fallen in three years (1939, 1949, and 1955), but even then by less than 2 percent.

The Equation of Exchange

Equation of exchange ($MV = PQ$): a statement of mathematical equality between the product of the money stock (M) and the velocity of money (V) and the product of the price level (P) and the national output level (Q).

Velocity of money (V): the average number of times a dollar is used during a given period. It is the circulation or turnover ratio for money (M) relative to GNP (PQ) or $V = PQ \div M$

The relationship between the money stock and the price level is expressed by the formula $MV = PQ$, called the equation of exchange. The **equation of exchange ($MV = PQ$)** is a statement of mathematical equality between the product of the money stock (M) and the velocity of money (V) and the product of the price level (P) and the national output level (Q). That is, the money stock (M) multiplied by the velocity of money (V) equals the prices of goods and services (P) multiplied by the quantity of goods and services produced (Q). (Prices are normally measured in terms of some recognized index of the price level, such as the Consumer Price Index.) **Velocity of money (V)** is the average number of times a dollar is used during a given period. It is the circulation or turnover ratio of money relative to GNP (PQ) or $V = PQ/M$. Thus, if $M = \$1,000$ and $PQ = \$6,000$ in a given year, $V = 6$ for that year.

In a sense, velocity represents the demand for money. The basic problem with monetary policy is that the Fed can control—and imperfectly at that—only the supply of money, but not the demand for it.

On one level, the equation of exchange means simply that the dollar value of people's expenditures (MV) must equal the dollar value of what they buy (PQ). The equation also relates changes in the money stock to changes in the price level. If V is held constant, an increase in the money stock, M, on the left side of the equation must result in an increase in either P or Q on the right side of the equation. If the economy is at full employment—producing all the goods and services (Q) it can—then an increase in M must be largely if not fully translated into an increase in the price level, P.

Effects of a Change in the Money Stock

The equation of exchange enables us to draw other conclusions about the relationship between production, the money stock, and the price level. Suppose that the nation's production level, Q, is continuously expanding as a result of increases in productivity. If the money stock and velocity remain constant, the price level, P, must fall. Otherwise PQ could not remain equal to MV. To keep the price level from falling when production is rising, either M or V (or both) must rise. In other words, during times of rising production, increases in the money stock can lead to price stability. Inflation will result only if the money stock, velocity, or both grow faster than the level of production. If production falls while the money stock rises (and velocity remains constant), too many dollars will be chasing too few goods, and prices will rise.

What will happen if the money stock decreases? If V is held constant, a drop in M on the left side of the equation must be offset by a drop in either prices or production on the right side. Generally prices will fall when the money stock falls, because fewer dollars will be competing for the nation's goods and services. The decrease in demand will cause producers to compete with each other through lower prices. Unless the costs of production fall along with prices, unemployment will result. If businesses must pay constant wages while receiving lower prices for their products, they cannot employ as many workers as before. Even if wages decline during times of deflation, they usually do not adjust rapidly enough to prevent unemployment from rising. The extent of the unemployment problem depends on how much and how fast the money stock is reduced and how rapidly wages and prices adjust downward.

Effects of a Change in Velocity

The equation of exchange also tells us that if M is held constant, a decrease in velocity (V) will lead to a decrease in P or Q, with the same general result: unemployment. Conversely, an increase in velocity (V) can cause prices to rise. That is, assuming that M remains constant, an increase in V on the left side of the equation must lead to an increase in P (the price level), in Q (output), or in both on the right side of the equation.

Increases in velocity, however, are not likely to cause long periods of continuous price increases. Velocity increases because people are using their money more rapidly, holding on to lower and lower money balances. But institutional constraints on velocity, such as regular pay periods, determine the minimum amount of money people must hold. Thus there are limits to how far and how fast velocity can increase—and to how much inflation it can cause.

Still, short-run changes in the velocity of money are possible. The rule is that the velocity of money varies inversely with the amount of money people want to hold. The more money people want to hold, the lower the rate of turnover. As we noted in the previous chapter, people want to hold money for three reasons: to cover expected and unexpected transactions, and in anticipation of higher interest rates. If economic conditions change—for example, if interest rates rise, changing the amount of money demanded—the velocity of money will change. Shifts in the velocity of money are readily seen in Figure 8.4, which shows quarterly data from 1960 to 1987 of both M1 velocity and the three-month U.S. Treasury bills.[2] Note how velocity since 1980 has moved more closely with short-term interest rates.

Effects of a Change in the Money Stock on Aggregate Demand and Supply

◢ 3. What is the effect of change in the money stock on aggregate demand and supply?

The effects of a change—say, an increase in the money stock—can also be analyzed in terms of aggregate demand and supply, which were introduced in Chapter 6, and will be described in detail in Chapter 13. If the economy

---

2. Figure 8.4 shows one measure of velocity V_1 = GNP divided by M1. Other velocities such as V_2 = GNP divided by M2, M3, or L showed no upward trend from 1960 to 1987. All measures varied from quarter to quarter. (See the current issue of the Federal Reserve's *Historical Chart Book* or the *Economic Report of the President*.)

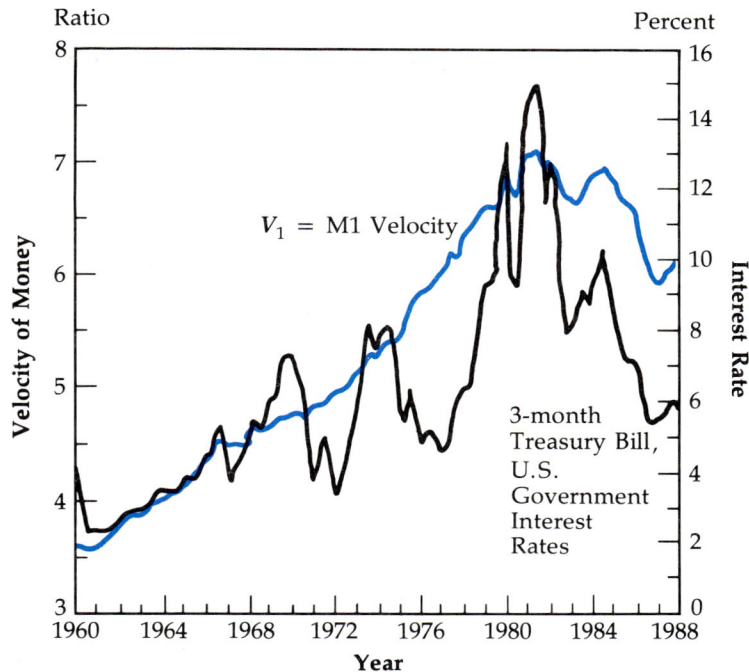

FIGURE 8.4   The Velocity of M1 Money (*V*1) and Short-term Government 3-Month Treasury Bills Interest Rates

The M1 velocity of money, defined as GNP divided by M1, rose gradually from 1960 to 1984 and declined modestly from 1985 to 1987. On a quarterly basis, however, it fluctuated considerably. The short-term interest rate on three-month U.S. Treasury bills also fluctuated widely. After 1980 velocity and short-term interest rates moved in tandem with one another.

Source: Board of Governors of the Federal Reserve System as shown in Federal Reserve Bank of Cleveland, *Economic Trends* (February 1988), p. 18.

is at full employment, additional output cannot be produced to compensate for a rise in *M* or *V*. In effect, the aggregate supply curve is vertical, as shown in Figure 8.5. Aggregate demand, however, will take on its normal downward sloping shape. With a given money stock, the price level will be P_1 and the output level Q_1 in Figure 8.5. If the money stock expands, people will have more money than they want to hold. As they try to use up their money balances, they will push aggregate demand up from AD_1 to AD_2. This shifts the equilibrium from E_1 to E_2. Because output cannot rise past Q, the price level will be pushed up to P_2. Although the output level stays at Q_1, the monetary measure of GNP rises with the increase in prices (GNP goes from $P_1 \times Q_1$ to $P_2 \times Q_1$).

If the economy is not at full employment, output can expand with the price level, and the aggregate supply curve will slope upward as in Figure

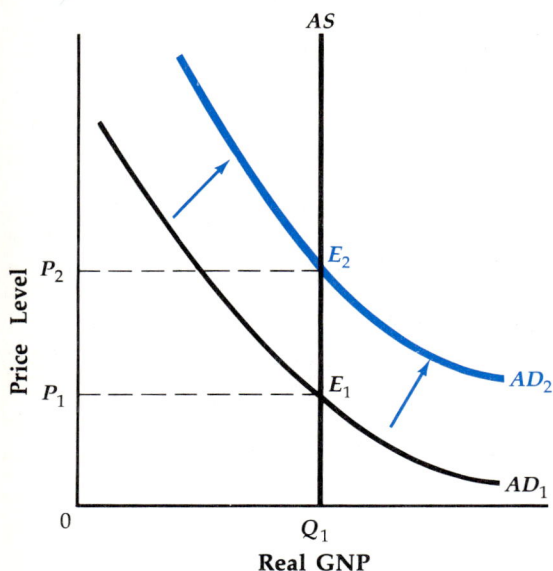

FIGURE 8.5 Effects of an Increase in the Money Stock on Aggregate Demand, Full Employment Assumed

If the economy is at full employment—the aggregate supply curve is vertical—an increase in the money stock will shift the aggregate demand curve from AD_1 to AD_2, shifting the equilibrium from E_1 to E_2. The price level will rise from P_1 to P_2, but output will remain the same: Q_1.

8.6. The increase in the money stock increases the aggregate demand curve from AD_1 to AD_2 and shifts the equilibrium from E_1 to E_2. This will still push the price level up, from P_1 to P_2, reducing the velocity of money. More important, output will expand in response to the change in the price level, from Q_1 to Q_2. In this case, the increase in the money stock increases both production and the price level.

The Politics of Monetary Policy

◢ 4. What are the politics of monetary policy?

To the extent that increases in the money stock cause inflation, the Federal Reserve can be blamed for higher prices. It has sometimes increased the money stock more than was warranted by the nation's production level. Monetary policy is not created in a vacuum, however. The Fed operates in a system in which government fiscal policy often runs counter to monetary policy. It is subject to political pressure from government, and it must deal with competing economic objectives, such as the reduction of both inflation and unemployment. According to monetarists, this is where the Fed goes wrong. They feel that the Fed should have but *one* objective—to stabilize prices, for prices are the *only* variable the Fed can permanently influence. Unfortunately, the Fed tends to look at (and attempts to manipulate) a number of other variables, such as output and employment, over which it has no long-run influence. Some other macroeconomic schools disagree with this harsh position.

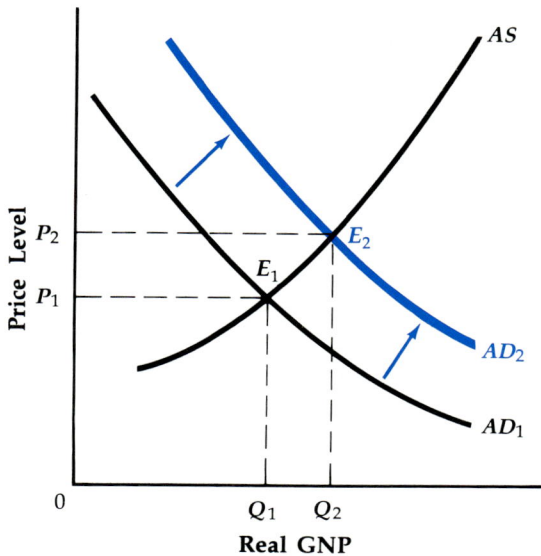

FIGURE 8.6   Effect of an Increase in the Money Stock on Aggregate Demand, Some Unemployment Assumed If the economy is not at full employment—the aggregate supply curve is positively sloped—an increase in the money stock will raise output. The aggregate demand curve will shift from AD_1 to AD_2, as it would under full employment. The equilibrium shifts from E_1 to E_2, resulting in a rise in prices from P_1 to P_2 and encouraging producers to raise output, from Q_1 to Q_2.

Federal Government Deficits

One of the most troublesome influences on the Fed in recent decades has been the tendency of the government to overspend. Suppose that while the Federal Reserve is attempting to control inflation, the federal government is running up a budget deficit. To make up the difference between what it spends and what it collects in taxes, the government must borrow money by selling bonds in the bond market. This increases the demand for borrowed funds and perhaps the interest rates that businesses, households, and government at all levels have to pay. (The extent to which interest rates are raised by government deficit spending, if at all, is for many economists and policy makers an unsettled issue.)

In such situations, members of the House Banking Committee and the administration often accuse the Federal Reserve of adopting an unreasonably tight monetary policy. They will support their claim by citing rising interest rates on loans for everything from houses and cars to school construction and road improvements. Under political pressure, the Fed may then attempt to counteract heavy federal government borrowing by entering the market as a buyer of bonds, in effect increasing the money stock (see pages 208–210). The Fed's purpose is to keep interest rates down. As we saw earlier, purchases of bonds by the Fed can raise prices. If inflation occurs, is the Fed responsible? In a sense it is—but Congress and the administration must also be held accountable for adopting inflationary spending policies. In the sense that the Fed is forced to monetize budget deficits to keep interest rates from rising, the Fed's independence is a myth. In principle, the Fed and the U.S. Treasury are different institutions with different purposes, although they frequently cooperate on a number of fiscal matters. The Fed focuses on achieving various macroeconomic goals by controlling the money stock, but has other less crucial functions as well. The U.S. Treasury emphasizes budgetary matters, seeking to finance the national or public debt that arises when tax revenues fall short of government spending. The Fed cannot issue U.S. Treasury securities, and the U.S. Treasury cannot issue currency or create money.

Political Pressures on the Federal Reserve

Theoretically, the Federal Reserve is an independent agency. It is not required to seek the advice or consent from the administration or from Congress, but only to inform Congress of its immediate plans. Congress confirms nominees to the board of governors and retains the power to change the Federal Reserve charter, however, and thereby to curtail its independence—members of Congress frequently threaten such action. If it wishes to remain independent, then, the Fed cannot completely ignore administrative and congressional wishes. Thus, the Fed is quasi-independent, as it operates in a democratic society.

There are pros and cons to having greater Fed independence. In the last decade the Federal Reserve has sometimes resisted political pressure from both parties with unusual vigor. (Its resistance was no doubt fortified by the unusually high inflation rates of the 1970s.) At other times, however, it has expanded the money stock as if its primary purpose were to assure the president's reelection. This was especially true in the early 1970s when the Fed opened the monetary floodgates and contributed to Richard Nixon's reelection. The result has been an erratic monetary policy, with accompanying fluctuations in the inflation rate. For instance, in the quarter-century from 1962 to 1987, growth in both monetary aggregates and prices fluctuated widely, averaging 8.5 percent per year for M2 and 5.5 percent for the GNP price deflator. We had severe recessions in 1972 to 1975 and 1980 to 1982 and inflation of more than 15 percent during the 1970s. In the prior decade, 1952 to 1962, the average annual rate of growth of M2 was 5.5 percent and of prices 2.3 percent. It is because of such activities over the Fed's 75-year lifetime that Milton Friedman has remarked that "no major institution has so poor a record of performance over so long a period as the Federal Reserve, yet so high a public reputation."[3]

Some people believe in a "political business cycle," wherein fluctuations in GNP, employment, and inflation are related to the attempts of politicians to get reelected at periodic intervals.[4] For instance, the theory suggests an

3. Milton Friedman, "The Fed Has No Clothes," *Wall Street Journal* (April 15, 1988), p. 30.
4. See, e.g., David R. Kamerschen, *Money and Banking,* 9th ed. (Cincinnati: South-Western, 1988), pp. 553–554, for a review of the debate.

PERSPECTIVES
Should the Fed Be Independent?

The Federal Reserve Act of 1913 established the Federal Reserve System (see Chapter 7). The legislation creating the Federal Reserve embodied the Progressive approach to government intervention in the economy. Progressive era reformers believed that scientific management should replace partisan politics in the making of economic policy. The goal of much of the legislation of that era was to replace politicians with experts. The purpose of the Fed, then, was to turn the management of the nation's banking system over to experts armed with the latest principles of sound banking.

To ensure that the Federal Reserve was nonpartisan, its operations were made independent of president and Congress. Members of the Board of Governors serve for fourteen years; the chairman serves for four years. The long tenure, in theory, prevents the president (and the Senate, which confirms appointments to the Board) from exerting political pressure on members by threatening to withhold reappointments.

In practice, the Fed has not operated according to the Progressive vision. Its independence has varied according to the chairman. (Alan Greenspan, who succeeded Paul Volcker in August 1987, is the Fed's thirteenth chairman.) Some past chairmen have indeed followed independent courses; others have adopted policies based on the political priorities of the president or Congress. The Fed's independence is limited because Congress always has the power to repeal or amend the Federal Reserve Act. Also, members of the Board of Governors rarely serve for more than a small part of their fourteen-year terms, creating frequent opportunities for the president to influence policy through the appointment of new members.

The Fed, then, is only partly independent. Should it be fully independent? Opponents of Fed independence argue that in a democracy, monetary policy should be made by the elected representatives of the people, not by a Board of Governors accountable to no one for its mistakes. They argue that the Fed should be forced to operate according to policy guidelines set by the president and Congress.

Supporters of the independence of the Fed, by contrast, consider the nation's monetary system to be part of the basic institutional structure of the economy, analogous to the legal system. It therefore must be stable and should not be allowed to change with every political change. The monetary system is the stable framework within which economic policies are made but should not itself be subject to economic policy.

Debates over Fed policy and performance continue. The long survival of the system in its current form, however, implies that change is more likely to come through changes in the membership of the Board of Governors than through changes in the laws governing the Fed's basic powers and functions. In other words, the Federal Reserve System will probably remain semi-independent.

incumbent government pushes an expansionary monetary policy to lower interest rates and unemployment before the election. The later increases in prices and interest rates come after the election and presumably are soon forgotten. The validity of both the motives and the facts of this theory are currently being debated. One defect is that the political business cycle theory assumes that politicians can perpetually fool the public.

Cost-Push or Sellers' Inflation

Another problem for the Fed is the tendency of unions to seek wage settlements that cannot be supported by current market conditions. Such wage increases mean that employers cannot afford to hire as many workers as before. The result will be a rise in unemployment. Again, the Fed may be pressured by the administration and Congress to do something to alleviate the problem. Increasing the rate of growth of the money stock will enable businesses to hire more workers at the new wage rates. Such a policy will also contribute to inflation. Once again, the Open Market Committee of the Federal Reserve is only partially to blame, for it did not negotiate the inflationary wage settlements. This same argument could be made for any factor of production—labor, land, capital, or entrepreneurs—that seeks nonmarket returns. However, the cost-push argument is flawed if there is not continually rising market power. Otherwise, you would just get a one-time rise in wages or prices and not the continually rising prices that inflation requires. Thus, you must have a continuing rise in the degree of market power to get continuing cost-push or seller's inflation.

In fact, inflation has no one clearly defined cause. Rather the inflationary process is a set of interconnected causes, some related directly to technical control of the money stock and others related to political and market pressures. Asked what can be done about inflation, Henry Wallich, governor of the Federal Reserve, responded

> The familiar debate about the sources of violence provides an analogy. Do guns kill people? Do people kill people? Does society kill people? Some assert that money, and nothing but money, causes inflation—the "guns kill people" proposition. Some assert that the entire gamut of government policies, from deficit spending to protectionism to minimum wage to farm supports to environmental safety regulations, causes inflation—the "people kill people" proposition. Some argue, finally, that it is social pressures, competition for national product, a revolution of aspirations, which are at the root—the "society kills people" proposition. The first view holds primarily responsible for the inflation the central bank, the second the government, and the third the people that elect and instruct the government.[5]

Chapter Review

Review of Key Questions

1. *What are the Federal Reserve's three quantitative money stock controls and how do they work?*

The Federal Reserve has three fundamental means of controlling the operating targets (e.g., reserves) and the intermediate targets (e.g.,

---

5. Henry C. Wallich, "Honest Money," *Macroeconomics 1979: Readings on Contemporary Issues* (Ithaca, N.Y.: Cornell University Press, 1979), p. 43.

the money stock and perhaps interest rates) and ultimately its GNP objectives or goals (e.g., low inflation and unemployment rates and high and growing GNP). The three means are: (1) the reserve requirement, (2) loans to depository institutions, and (3) open market operations. The reserve requirement is the ratio of minimum reserves to deposits that legally a depository institution must hold on deposit at the district Federal Reserve Bank or in its vault cash. The discount rate is the interest rate that Federal Reserve Banks charge on loans to depository institutions. If the discount rate is too high, depository institutions can borrow temporarily unneeded Federal Reserve Bank balances from each other at the federal funds rate. Open market operations involve the purchase and sale of U.S. government securities by the Fed. The Federal Reserve can increase the money stock by (a) reducing the reserve requirement, (b) increasing loans to depository institutions (which can be accomplished by lowering the discount rate), and (c) purchasing government securities. The Federal Reserve can reduce the money stock by (a) increasing the reserve requirement, (b) decreasing loans to depository institutions (which can be accomplished by increasing the discount rate), and (c) selling government securities. The Fed's open market operations are the most important and frequently used control over the money stock. The 12-person group in control of these operations is the Federal Open Market Committee. It meets approximately eight times a year to determine the nation's stock of money and credit. The Fed's attempt to control the stock of money can sometimes be frustrated by the demand for money or by velocity that is outside its control.

◢ *2. How does monetary policy affect the rate of inflation?*

The purpose of monetary policy is not simply to influence the money stock, but to influence some ultimate macroeconomic variable such as inflation as well. The equation of exchange, $MV = PQ$, states the relationship between the money stock and the price level. A change in either the money stock (M) or velocity (V) on the left side of the equation will be reflected in an equal change in prices (P) or output (Q) or both on the right side. If V is relatively stable as the monetarists suggest, changes in M will influence P and/or Q. In the United States, M1 velocity rose gradually from 1960 to 1984 and declined modestly from 1985 to 1987.

◢ *3. What is the effect of change in the money stock on aggregate demand and supply?*

The extent to which prices or production levels are changed by an increase in the money stock depends on how close the economy is to full employment. Under conditions of effective full or nearly full employment (that is, when the aggregate supply curve is vertical), any action by the Fed that increases the money stock is likely to increase prices, with little or no effect on output. When unemployment exists, however (that is, when the aggregate supply curve slopes upward to the right), any action by the Fed that increases the money stock is likely to affect both price and production levels. At times, the Fed uses its monetary controls to offset changes in velocity, which would otherwise affect prices and national output.

◢   *4. What are the politics of monetary policy?*

The Fed may increase the growth rate of the money stock in response to pressure from Congress or the White House to reduce interest rates and unemployment. In the long run, however, such increases in the growth rate of the money stock will probably lead to higher interest and inflation rates. There are pros and cons to having an independent Federal Reserve that controls the money stock and manages our financial and monetary system. One problem for the Fed is that cost-push or sellers' inflation (if it truly exists) is difficult to handle with conventional monetary policy.

Further Topics

The specific actions the Federal Reserve can take to expand or contract the money stock, and their impact on the price level, are technical matters. Its decisions, however, are very much influenced by the political setting in which it operates. The Fed is often pressured into taking actions contrary to its long-run policy objectives.

Occasionally the Fed's actions have been misguided. For instance, its attempts to keep interest rates low by buying government securities have increased the growth rate of the money stock, fueling inflation. As we will see in the chapters that follow, an increase in the inflation rate can also increase interest rates. Those who lend their money will require a higher interest rate to compensate for the depreciation of the dollar. Thus attempts to keep interest rates low can be self-defeating.

Review of New Terms

Discount rate The interest rate the Federal Reserve charges on loans to depository institutions such as commercial banks.

Equation of exchange ($MV = PQ$) A statement of mathematical equality between the product of the money stock (M) and the velocity of money (V) and the product of the price level (P) and the national output level (Q).

Federal funds rate The interest rate one financial institution charges on loans to another financial institution.

Open market operations The purchase and sale by the Federal Reserve of U.S. government securities, which can be bills, notes, or bonds.

Reserve requirements The amount of reserves, expressed as a percentage of deposits, held by depository institutions in the form of cash holdings in their own vaults or on deposit at the Federal Reserve Bank (or at another depository institution for nonmember banks) that cannot be used to create money through loans.

Velocity of money (V) The average number of times a dollar is used during a given period. It is the circulation or turnover ratio for money (M) relative to GNP (PQ) or $V = PQ/M$.

Review Questions

1. Suppose people decide to withdraw more money than usual from their demand deposits and convert it into currency. How would this shift affect banks' ability to make loans? What effect would it have on the money stock? (◢ 1)

2. What can the Fed do to increase the money stock? What can it do to offset an increase in currency holdings? On the basis of your answers, does it follow that when the Fed buys bonds on the open market, it is always attempting to increase the money stock? (◢ 1)

3. What is the relationship between people's willingness to hold money in currency and demand deposits and the velocity of money (the average number of times each dollar is used)? What is the relationship between the rate of interest and people's willingness to hold money? On the basis of your answers, what is the relationship between the interest rate and the velocity of money? (◢ 2)

4. Suppose that we reestablish gold and silver coins as the medium of exchange in the United States. Under such a monetary system, would the nation still experience periods of inflation and deflation? Suppose that dimes are made of silver, and that the amount of silver in the dime varies from coin to coin. Which dimes would tend to be used in trade? (◢ 2)

5. The Federal Reserve conducts monetary policy in part through the purchase and sale of government bills. If the Federal Reserve bought and sold private bills instead of government bills, would the effect be any different? (◢ 1)

6. Suppose all the nation's power groups—large unions, corporations, and governmental units—pushed prices up and held them there, dramatically increasing the price of almost everything. Assume also that the money stock was held constant. What would be the effect on the economy? Explain your answer in terms of the equation of exchange. (◢ 2, ◢ 4)

7. If a nation's central bank increases the money stock too often and too much, causing high rates of inflation, what can be done to counteract the problem? Why might the central bank take such actions? (◢ 4)

8. How would an expanding money stock affect aggregate demand? (◢ 3)

The Costs and Benefits of Inflation

In a full-employment situation money creation is strictly equivalent to taxation: Normal methods of taxation can be supplanted by the government's money creation, which . . . will cause inflation and a tax on people's average cash balances.
    Roger Leroy Miller and
    Raburn M. Williams

KEY QUESTIONS

▲ 1. What are the costs of inflation?

▲ 2. What are the benefits of inflation?

▲ 3. Should inflation be slowed down or even eliminated?

NEW TERMS

Bracket creep (or taxflation)
COLA
Fisher effect
Hyperinflation

Inflation premium
Variable-rate or adjustable-rate
    mortgage (ARM)

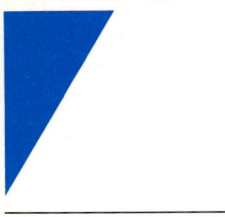

As we have emphasized in this book, all economic activity has both costs and benefits. Moreover, the costs and benefits of any change in economic activity are not shared equally by all members of our society. Inflation is no different. Inflation is a persistent increase in the average or general level of prices that is not matched by an equivalent increase in the average quality of the goods and services consumed. Alternatively, you may think of it as a continuing decline in the value of the monetary unit. It is crucial to recognize that inflation (1) is a continuing process (rising prices) and not a once-and-for-all change (high prices) and (2) occurs only in monetary, but not barter, economies.

The costs of inflation are widely recognized, and often exaggerated. When people think about inflation, they tend to consider only the reduction in the purchasing power of their dollar. They often fail to recognize that their wages rise along with prices during inflationary times. Many readers, then, may be puzzled by the reference to the benefits of inflation in the title of this chapter—but people both gain and lose from inflation. Indeed, if it benefited no one and hurt everyone, including government, the political opposition to inflation would probably be overwhelming.

Because government and some segments of the population benefit from rising prices, inflation is difficult to stop once started. Even if the rate of inflation is reduced, as it was between 1980 and 1987, government may find it difficult to hold inflation down, as explained later in this chapter. Before discussing the benefits of inflation—including the incentives government has to inflate prices—we will review its more familiar costs.

The Costs of Inflation

◢ 1. What are the costs of inflation?

There are two effects of inflation. One effect results from the redistribution of income from losers to gainers, with potentially no overall harm to the macroeconomy. The second and more serious effect is the misallocation of resources that diminishes productivity and economic growth by distorting the aggregate demand and aggregate supply for the economy as a whole. The damage done by inflation depends primarily on two factors: (1) whether it is anticipated or unanticipated and (2) what the rate of inflation is. We will begin by considering the effects of unanticipated inflation, a condition experienced in the United States in the mid-1960s and mid-1970s.

As noted in Chapter 8, inflation ran between 1 and 4 percent per year in the United States throughout the 1950s and early 1960s. Americans became accustomed to only moderate price increases. When prices started to rise at rates of 4 to 6 percent during the late 1960s, most people were caught off guard. Disgruntled grocery shoppers demonstrated against escalating prices. Richard Nixon railed against the "exorbitant" 5 percent rate of inflation in his campaign for the presidency in 1968. In August 1971, as public concern about inflation mounted, President Nixon froze wages and the prices of practically all goods and services.

At the time of the wage-price freeze the rate of inflation was 3.5 percent—relatively modest compared with the double-digit rates of 1974 and 1979 to 1980. The unanticipated inflation of the late 1960s imposed costs that people were not prepared for, however. For that reason its consequences were perhaps more serious than the results of the later round of price increases. One of the most noticeable consequences, from the average citizen's point of view, was the decline in the relative value of cash savings.

Losses to Cash Holders

Unanticipated inflation hurts people with dollars in their pockets or in demand and savings accounts. The value of the dollars they are holding goes down, for the dollar buys less at today's prices than it did yesterday. The losses to cash holders are so clear that if people anticipate a high rate of inflation, they will convert their dollars into goods and services at present prices, before their purchasing power goes down. One might argue, then, that people who hold on to their dollars are wagering that the benefits of holding money will exceed the costs. Whether they should be expected to make such bets is an emotional issue. From an economic perspective, the movement of financial resources into goods and services as a result of anticipated inflation reduces investment and ultimately lowers national production.

Losses to Institutional Creditors

Institutional creditors, like banks and insurance companies, also lose from unanticipated inflation. Assume that during noninflationary times a bank lends $30,000 to someone who agrees to repay the principal at the end of the year, with 6 percent interest. The bank expects $31,800 [$30,000 + (0.06 × $30,000)] on the termination date. If prices rise unexpectedly by 10 percent, however, the *real* value of the dollars the bank receives (that is, what they will buy) will be less than the original value of the loan: $28,620 rather than $30,000. The creditor would have done better to invest the $30,000 in land or some other real good, whose price would have risen along with the prices of other goods and services. In that case, the asset purchased for $30,000 would now be worth $33,000 [$30,000 × (0.10 × $30,000)]. The *real* value, or purchasing power, of the $33,000 piece of property would be no greater than the original purchasing power of the $30,000. The bank would not have gained anything, but it would not have lost anything either.

If inflation is anticipated, banks and other creditors can demand—and borrowers will be willing to pay—a higher rate of interest on the money they lend, to compensate for the expected lost purchasing power of the dollars they receive in payment. That is why interest rates tend to rise with the inflation rate. High interest rates are generally a consequence rather than a cause of inflation.

Losses to Bond Buyers

Like banks that make loans, people who buy government and corporate bonds are creditors. When they buy bonds, they lend money to the bond issuer. In return they expect to be paid interest at regular intervals. They also expect to receive the principal (that is, the face value of the bond) on the date of maturity. Because both the interest payments and the principal are normally stated in terms of dollars, an unanticipated increase in the inflation rate can mean an unexpected drop in the purchasing power of the interest and principal. If the inflation is anticipated, bond buyers' demand recompenses for it. In fact, if lenders and borrowers expect identical rates of inflation, they should take into account the **Fisher effect,** which states that the nominal (market) rate of interest is equal to the real rate of interest (based on the real productivity of capital) plus the rate of anticipated inflation. If the real interest rate is 3 percent and the anticipated inflation rate is 6 percent, the nominal interest rate must be 9 percent. Thus, nominal interest rates include an inflation premium (in our example, 6 percent) to compensate for any erosion of purchasing power.

Like banks, individuals can protect themselves against anticipated inflation by seeking a premium in the interest rate that compensates them for the expected loss of purchasing power. Unless they receive such a premium, they will tend to withhold their funds from the bond market, pushing interest up.

Fisher effect: an economic principle which states that the nominal (market) rate of interest is equal to the real rate of interest (based on the real productivity of capital) plus the rate of anticipated inflation.

Losses to Businesses and Workers

Inflation means that quality-adjusted prices in general are on the rise, not necessarily that all prices rise by the same amount.[1] Some prices may not rise at all, and some may even fall.

---

1. In both microeconomics and macroeconomics, prices are always measured in constant-quality units; otherwise, comparisons over time and space would be meaningless.

Some prices tend to change rather rapidly and smoothly, reflecting changes in market forces, like the quantity and velocity of money. The prices of agricultural commodities such as wheat and beef tend to mirror changes in their auction markets with reasonable rapidity, but the prices of many other goods take time to adjust upward. Price increases may be delayed when there are long time lags between the placement of an order and the delivery of the product, or when contracts specify the price at the time of delivery. Commercial airplanes, heavy electrical equipment, and many buildings are constructed and sold under these conditions. For the producers of these products, unanticipated inflation can mean cost increases and narrower-than-expected profit margins, or even losses, as well as payment in devalued dollars.

If the prices of products rise at different rates, then wages are likely to follow at different rates, for workers' wages depend in part on the prices charged for their products. In addition, some workers' wages are restrained by contracts that extend over a period of one or more years. In short, some workers' pay may keep pace with inflation; other workers' wages may lag behind price increases. The latter group will suffer a loss.

Not all reductions in the purchasing power of wages can be attributed to inflation, however. In any dynamic economy, there will always be groups of workers whose real wages decline because of the market forces affecting their industries. A decrease in the demand for a particular good, or an increase in the supply of workers in a particular industry, can cause such a decline in wages. Because more people are seeking college teaching positions, for instance, the real salaries of many college professors have declined in recent years. The fairly high rate of inflation in the past decade only quickened the downward adjustment. In short, inflation can mean temporary losses in purchasing power for some groups, but not all.

Losses to Taxpayers

Because of the way income tax systems are structured, almost every income earner is hurt by inflation as their nominal (but not necessarily real) income rises. Most tax systems are arranged so that they take a higher percentage of a person's money income as it rises. Thus if Ms. Sue Jones's money income rises with inflation, the government will take a greater percentage of it in taxes—even if its real purchasing power merely remains constant. The purchasing power of Ms. Jones's after-tax income declines with inflation.

Suppose, for instance, that the marginal tax rate rises from 15 percent on the first $18,000 of taxable income to 28 percent on the next $25,000, and so on up to 33 percent on incomes over $43,000 (see Table 9.1). If Sue Jones earns $43,000 of taxable income, her tax bill for the year is $9,700 (15 percent of $18,000, or $2,700, plus 28 percent of $25,000, or $7,000). Her after-tax income is $25,000.

Over the following year prices rise by 10 percent, and Sue Jones receives a 10 percent increase in taxable income. While her dollar income rises to $47,300, her real income before taxes remains basically the same

TABLE 9.1 Hypothetical Income Tax Schedule	
Income	Marginal Tax Rate (percent)
$0 to $18,000	15%
$18,001 to $43,000	28
$43,001 and up	33

Bracket creep (or taxflation): the loss of purchasing power that occurs if progressive tax brackets are not indexed: people are pushed into higher tax brackets by inflation as money incomes (but not real incomes) rise, and pay a higher percentage of their incomes to the government.

(since $47,300 will buy the same goods and services that $43,000 could buy a year earlier). The extra $4,300 that permits her to keep pace with inflation, however, puts Sue in a higher tax bracket. It is taxed at the higher marginal rate of 33 percent, increasing her tax bill to $11,119 (15 percent of $10,000, or $2,700, plus 28 percent of $25,000, or $7,000, plus 33 percent of $4,300, or $1,419). After taxes Sue has $36,181 ($47,300 − $11,119) to spend—$2,881 more than she had the previous year. Her purchasing power is only $32,563 ($36,181 × 0.90), however, after adjustment for the 10 percent inflation rate. In short, Sue loses $737 in purchasing power through what is called bracket creep. **Bracket creep (or taxflation)** occurs if progressive tax brackets are not indexed: people are pushed into higher tax brackets by inflation as money incomes (but not real incomes) rise, and pay a larger percentage of their incomes to the government. The government gains the taxpayers' lost purchasing power.

In 1981 the Reagan administration pushed through Congress the Economic Recovery Tax Act (ERTA) requiring the Internal Revenue Service to adjust, or index, income tax rates for inflation. Tax indexing became effective in 1985 although on a scaled-back version from that called for in the ERTA. Because indexing reduces the gains government can expect from inflation, it may reduce the government's incentive to inflate the money stock.

Losses to Pensioners

Retired people who depend on fixed periodic payments from their company pension plans are hurt by rising prices. Congress addressed the problem by providing for cost-of-living adjustments in Social Security checks.

General Losses from Inflation

During inflationary times, losses in the purchasing power of the dollar can encourage people to hold less money and more real assets, such as land, houses, gold, and collectibles (such as jewelry, artwork, and stamps). Scarce managerial talent is detoured *from* managing production, seeking efficiency and economy, and innovating, *to* maneuvering, speculating, and searching for protection against or benefit from inflation.

Anticipated inflation can also lead to an overheating of the economy, or unrealistically high production levels. By encouraging purchasing now instead of later, inflation moves consumption and investment forward in time. If business people expect higher rates of inflation in the future, this increases expected future prices of output relative to the current costs of capital goods and encourages investment. Businesses will also build up their inventories now, to avoid paying higher prices later. At some point, having accumulated more inventory than necessary, business will cut back on orders for goods. Then production will fall, leading to unemployment and lost income for workers.

In periods of anticipated modest inflation, creditors can adjust their interest rates to compensate for the expected decrease in the value of the dollar. Similarly, workers can increase their wage demands. During periods of **hyperinflation,** when there is an abrupt and substantial rise in prices (e.g., 50 percent or more per month), the value of currency deteriorates so quickly that people become reluctant to accept and hold money.[2] To avoid significant economic losses, they tend to spend the dollars they receive as fast as they can. Although hyperinflation perhaps can lead to a moneyless economy—a return to the barter system in which resources are devoted as much to searching out mutually beneficial trades as to production—it never has. In such circumstances production levels can fall significantly, as they did in Germany after the First World War. Even in the last stages of the German hyperinflation, however, people continued to use money. Even though money was plummeting in value, it was still much more efficient than bartering.

In the 1980s economic growth slowed in Argentina, Brazil, Bolivia, Peru, some other Latin American countries, and Israel, in part because of inflation rates that exceeded several hundred percent a year. Such economic downturns are felt not just in the nations where they occur, but in creditor nations like the United States, whose banks finance investments throughout the world.

Hyperinflation: an abrupt and substantial rise in prices (e.g., 50 percent or more per month) that causes the value of currency to deteriorate so quickly that people become reluctant to accept and hold money.

The Benefits of Inflation

▲ **2. What are the benefits of inflation?**

When one person loses from an unanticipated increase in prices, someone else usually gains. (The obvious exception is when inflation contributes to a downturn rather than a redistribution in total production, in which case almost everyone can lose.) Like the costs of inflation, benefits emerge largely because some people do not anticipate the rise in prices or cannot adjust readily to it. In such situations, people who do foresee rising prices and move to counteract them will gain at the expense of others. They can buy early, at relatively low prices, and sell later at much higher prices. The

2. Ivan C. Johnson and William W. Roberts, *Money and Banking: A Market-Oriented Approach,* Second Edition (New York: Dryden Press, 1985), page 30, page 598.

PERSPECTIVES
Inflation and the Inflated Demand for Housing
Dwight R. Lee, University of Georgia

Home ownership is the American dream, and a vibrant housing industry is associated with a healthy economy. However, home ownership was boosted in the 1970s for reasons that were harmful to the economy. Recently home ownership has become a more costly dream and the result will be good for the economy.

The 1970s saw both a record number of housing starts and a steady increase in the size of houses. This occurred despite the fact that real after-tax income increased very little and average family size decreased. The explanation for the boom in housing was explained by the twin economic culprits of the 1970s: high marginal tax rates and inflation. High marginal tax rates and inflation combined to make investment in housing artificially profitable. Besides increasing the nominal value of housing, when combined with high tax rates inflation reduces the cost of carrying a mortgage. High tax rates and inflation thus subsidize the purchase of a house.

Suppose you are in the 40 percent marginal tax bracket. Since every dollar you pay in mortgage interest is deducted from your taxable income, the interest rate you actually pay is 40% less than what is stated on the mortgage. If there were no inflation, the stated interest rate would be about 4 percent and your after-tax interest rate would be 2.4 percent (60 percent of 4 percent).

Now assume that the inflation rate is 10 percent (an inflation rate that was exceeded at times during the 1970s). The stated interest rate on your mortgage is now 14 percent (4 percent plus the 10 percent inflation rate) and the after tax interest rate is 60 percent of that, or 8.4 percent. Since inflation is decreasing the value of the money you owe by 10 percent per year, however, your real after-tax interest rate is not 8.4 percent but negative 1.6 percent. This negative interest rate is in effect a subsidy on the purchase of a new house, a subsidy that increases with inflation and the marginal tax rate.

This subsidy not only artificially increased the number of houses purchased, but had an inverse effect on the type of houses that were built as well. By any realistic standard, the size of newly constructed houses in the 1970s should have decreased. The average family size declined from 3.24 people in 1970 to 2.76 in 1980. The price of energy skyrocketed, dramatically increasing the cost of home heating and cooling. Median family

possibility of reaping such gains is one factor that tends to draw resources away from production in inflationary times. People use their resources for speculation in the hope that they may be among the gainers from inflation.

Gains to Debtors

Probably the largest single group of people who gain from unanticipated inflation are debtors who owe money at the time inflation begins. The largest subgroup (not including the government) in this category is homeowners who are paying mortgages with fixed interest charges. They are a significant part of the population, since historically most single-family dwellings have been financed this way. Homeowners benefit because the income, after adjusting for inflation and taxes, was $436 less in 1980 than in 1970. Yet in this same period, the size of the average new house increased to 1,760 square feet from 1,510 square feet, an increase of nearly 17 percent. Rather than expanding the nation's productive capital, Americans were putting their saving into larger houses for smaller families.

In a recent study, economist Edwin S. Mills has estimated that perverse investment incentives favoring housing over plant and equipment has resulted in a housing stock that, as a fraction of total capital stock, is 32.5 percent greater than it ideally should be. This does not mean that if investment had been allocated properly the housing stock would be over 30 percent less than it is. Because of this over-investment in housing, Mills also estimates that real GNP is approximately 9 percent smaller than it otherwise would be; about $3.28 trillion instead of $3.61 trillion in 1983 dollars. If this output had not been lost because of excessive investment in housing relative to plant and equipment, much of it would have been spent on housing. Under an ideal investment mix, the relative amount spent on housing would have

been far less than it was, but the absolute amount spent on housing would have probably been only a little less than it was.

Fortunately for the economy, the inflation rate was down to a little under 5 percent in 1987, and marginal tax rates have been significantly reduced by the 1981 and 1986 tax reform acts. While this is good for the economy, it has increased the cost of home ownership. For example, according to a recent study, tax reform alone, assuming a 5 percent inflation rate and a 9.9 percent interest rate, has, for a family with a $40,000 annual income, increased the first year costs of home ownership by 18.1 percent.

This does not necessarily mean that fewer people will be able to afford home ownership. While tax reform along with the decline in inflation has increased the cost of buying a house, it has also increased the after-tax income of many lower-income families. What the increased cost of buying a house will do is reduce the average size of the houses people buy. This may not be good for the housing industry in the short run, but it is good for the economy. In the long run, it will be good for the housing industry as well.

real value of their debts shrinks. Thus the person with a mortgage during an inflationary period is paying off the loan in dollars that are worth less than the dollars that were borrowed.

Consider Jennifer and Michael, who purchased a house for $30,000 in 1960, putting $1,000 down and taking out a mortgage for the remaining $29,000 at 6 percent interest. Today the dollar will purchase less than a third of what it could buy in 1960. Therefore the $29,000 mortgage is worth much less today to the bank that holds it than it was in 1960. Because the price of housing has risen slightly faster than other prices, however, the real or relative value of the house to the buyers has increased. Today the house could probably be sold for over $120,000. Thus while the dollar asset held by the mortgage company has shrunk, the debtor's real asset has appreciated.

The homeowners who have gained on their mortgage may not have gained overall from inflation, however. The homeowners may have some dollar assets, perhaps a government bond that pays 3 percent interest. The decline in the bond's real value because of inflation will partially if not entirely offset the decline in the value of the mortgage.

In periods of unstable prices, as we have seen, creditors charge higher interest rates to compensate for expected inflation. Because the rate of inflation tends to be variable and unpredictable, banks have moved away from fixed-rate mortgages to loans with variable rates. A **variable-rate or adjustable-rate mortgage (ARM)** is one whose interest rate is adjusted periodically to agree with some market interest rate—for example, the rate on a specific type of government or corporate bond. If the designated market interest rate rises, the mortgage interest rate also rises and vice versa. Market interest rates make good benchmarks for mortgage rates because they tend to move up and down with the inflation rate—as lenders adjust their asking price to the expected rate of inflation, borrowers demand loans that bid up the interest rate so that it incorporates the inflation premium. The **inflation premium** is the additional interest required by, and thus included in, the nominal or market interest rate as compensation and protection against erosion of real purchasing power due to inflation.

The variable-rate mortgage does not eliminate the risks associated with inflation. It merely shifts them from the creditor to the debtor, whose mortgaged assets appreciate with inflation. Although debtors can still obtain fixed-rate mortgages, creditors are likely to charge a higher interest rate that incorporates a risk premium. This "risk cost" is another example of how inflation reduces the efficiency of the economy by increasing the cost of doing business. If too low a risk premium is charged on fixed rate mortgages, borrowers will snap them up and there will be—with apologies to Ernest Hemingway—a farewell to ARMs.

Gains to Businesses and Workers

Not all prices adjust upward in times of inflation. Because of institutional barriers to the adjustment of wages and prices, such as lengthy production procedures and long-term labor contracts, some wages and prices rise less rapidly than others. Just as the people whose wages and prices adjust sluggishly are hurt by inflation, those whose wages and prices adjust quickly receive temporary benefits from unanticipated inflation. In particular, statistics show that business profits tend to rise in the early phases of a new and higher inflationary cycle because product prices tend to rise faster than wages. In such a situation, business owners gain at the expense of workers, who may not anticipate the increase in prices soon enough to incorporate it into their wage demands. In a minority of cases, workers are protected by special clauses in their contracts, called **COLAs** (cost-of-living adjustment clauses). COLAs compensate workers in part or in full for erosion of their real purchasing power by inflation (as measured by the CPI).

Variable-rate or adjustable-rate mortgage (ARM): a mortgage whose interest rate is adjusted periodically to agree with some market interest rate—for example, the rate on a specific type of government or corporate bond.

Inflation premium: the additional interest required by, and thus included in, the nominal or market interest rate as compensation and protection against erosion of purchasing power due to inflation.

COLA: a cost-of-living adjustment clause found in some wage contracts to compensate workers in part or in full for erosion of their real purchasing power by inflation (as measured by the CPI).

Gains to Politicians and Government Employees

Not surprisingly, those who are responsible for increasing the money stock and contributing to inflation tend to benefit from it. This observation holds true whether money is made of gold or paper, although the benefits tend to be smaller with metal-based currencies. The discovery of gold in California in the nineteenth century benefited the gold miners who produced and sold it. The miners' benefits were limited to the difference between the cost of mining the gold and the price it commanded when sold, however. To the extent that mining increased the demand for equipment like shovels and pans, some product suppliers also benefited from the increase of the gold supply. The cost of the inflation was shared among everyone who was holding gold at the time because the new discovery reduced the value of existing gold.

Because paper money is much less difficult and expensive to produce than metal-based currencies, the profits to the producers can be much greater. Modern governments often take advantage of inflation, particularly in wartime. Government can produce paper money in two ways. First, it can increase the money stock directly, either by printing new currency or by raising its bank balance at the central bank (in the United States, the Federal Reserve). The government then uses this newly created money to buy new roads or military bases. As long as people are willing to accept new currency or checks drawn on the Federal Reserve account, the money stock will increase, and government will benefit from the increase. Politicians who promote government programs, workers who staff them, and people who benefit directly from them will all gain from inflation. The losers will be those who hold dollar assets and those who must pay higher prices for goods and services because fewer resources are available for nongovernment uses.

The United States government does not increase the money stock in this direct manner, but often takes a more circuitous approach. The federal government runs a budgetary deficit, borrowing the difference between its tax receipts and its expenditures. First the U.S. Treasury sells bonds on the open market, which tends to decrease the price and increase interest rates. The Fed may then come under political pressure to keep interest rates from rising. In response, the Fed orders the Open Market Committee to buy bonds on the open market, which tends to increase the bonds' prices and decrease interest rates. Although the Fed is not bound by law to accommodate the Treasury's wishes, its directors are sometimes under a good deal of political pressure to keep interest rates from rising. If the pressure is great enough, the Fed will cooperate by expanding the money stock.

When the Fed accommodates the Treasury and buys federally issued bonds, the effect on prices is virtually the same as the effect of printing more dollars. The government gains at the expense of everyone who holds financial assets valued in dollars and at the expense of taxpayers, who must pay a higher percentage of their real income to the government as taxes.

Historically the Fed has made only sparing use of its power to monetize the federal debt. Still, since the Second World War the government has

TABLE 9.2   The Federal Debt in Current and Constant (1967) Dollars Selected Years, 1929–1987

Year	Current Dollar Debt (Billions)	Constant (1967) Dollar Debt[a] (Billions)
1929	$ 16.9	$ 32.9
1940	50.7	120.6
1945	260.1	482.6
1950	256.9	356.3
1955	274.4	342.1
1960	290.9	328.0
1965	323.2	342.0
1970	382.6	329.0
1975	544.1	337.5
1980	914.6	370.6
1985	1,827.2	567.1
1986	2,130.0	648.6
1987	2,355.3	691.9

[a] Computed with year-to-year consumer price index.

Source: Economic Report of the President (Washington, D.C.: U.S. Government Printing Office, 1988), p. 337.

benefited significantly as inflation eroded the value of the federal debt. Table 9.2 shows that the federal debt in current dollars (column 1) rose from about $17 billion in 1929 to $260 billion in 1945 to $544 billion in 1975 and $2.355 billion in 1987. In constant 1967 dollars, the debt fell from $483 billion in 1945 to $463 billion in 1983, before rising beyond its 1945 level in 1984 and increasing thereafter, reaching $692 billion in 1987. The federal government gained from inflation at the expense of holders of government securities.

From 1980 to 1986, inflation fell from double-digit levels to less than 2 percent. Yet real interest rates remained high by historical standards. In 1986, for example, home mortgage interest rates exceeded 10 percent in many parts of the nation despite the fact that CPI inflation was under 2 percent. It is often argued that the expectation of continued high federal deficits (sometimes more than $220 billion annually) kept interest rates high. According to this theory, lenders feared the government would increase its credit demands, pushing up interest rates, and then repudiate the growing debt by monetizing it, as in the past. Creditors attempted to protect themselves from an anticipated new round of inflation by asking higher interest rates on their money.

Thus, by creating money, the government can redistribute resources from private to public use. Directly or indirectly, inflating the dollar increases the government's purchasing power. Because taxes also redistribute purchasing power from the public to the government, inflation can be considered taxation in disguise. Tax collected in this way is obscured by the complex mechanisms of money creation. However, inflation distributes the cost of government programs more haphazardly than normal taxation, and inflation is a kind of taxation without representation because it is never officially approved by Congress. For politicians who want to vote for public programs but not the taxes to pay for them, inflation may be the ideal tax system.

Should Inflation be Stopped?

▲ **3. Should inflation be slowed down or even eliminated?**

Many people are hurt by inflation, particularly long-term creditors who live on fixed incomes. Some benefit, particularly debtors and the government. The costs in terms of lost production and employment are lower for preventing inflation than for curing it once it is under way. Once inflation has been under way for some time, it becomes hard to stop without harming those who have made rational adjustments to the condition. If it appears that inflation will continue, home buyers will be willing to take on mortgages at a high rate of interest, on the assumption that the loans can be repaid with depreciated dollars. If the inflation rate is reduced, they will have to make high mortgage payments with dollars that do not depreciate as rapidly as expected. Mortgages can be refinanced or paid off with funds from a new mortgage written at a lower rate. When long-term rates began to fall in 1984, many homeowners refinanced their mortgages, but refinancing often involves a penalty.

The predicament of farmers is more pressing. Many took out loans to buy land and machinery in the late 1970s and early 1980s. They anticipated that rising inflation rates would push up land and crop prices. They expected to cover their debt payments with devalued dollars. When the inflation rate dropped dramatically in the early 1980s, many farmers found themselves saddled with debts that had to be paid off with dollars that were more valuable than expected. The farmers' problems were compounded by falling land and crop prices, caused partly by the reduced profitability of farming and partly by the drop in demand for land as a hedge against inflation. Many farm bankruptcies were due at least in part to the unexpected reversal of the inflationary spiral.

The normative question raised by inflation is whether people should be expected to cope with such changes in the rate of price increase—changes that no individual can control. Monetary stability can be thought of as a public good, a benefit to the general population that the government can produce if the electorate demands it. Because inflation ultimately is related to excessive money creation, the government working with the Fed has the potential to control it. Thus, in the long run, an increase in the money stock is a necessary, but not sufficient, condition for the continuation of inflation. Rapid inflation is always associated with rapid money creation, but rapid money creation may not always result in rapid inflation. Because unanticipated inflation has both its costs and benefits, a rigorous evaluation of the impact of welfare on society is complex and difficult. In recent years excessive money creation has been the result of deficit financing by the federal government to stimulate the economy and conduct various welfare programs, and not to fight a war as in the past.

Chapter Review

Review of Key Questions

▲   *1. What are the costs of inflation?*

Inflation is a quality-adjusted rise in the general price level. In the long run, excessive money creation is a necessary, but not sufficient, condition for inflation. Those who stand to lose from unanticipated inflation include (a) holders of demand and savings deposits, (b) creditors, (c) bond buyers, (d) businesses and workers tied to long-term price and wage agreements, and (e) taxpayers.

▲   *2. What are the benefits of inflation?*

Those who stand to gain from unanticipated inflation include (a) debtors, (b) businesses and workers who are free to adjust their prices and wages faster than others, and (c) government. It is primarily unexpected inflation that has redistributional effects and harms the overall economy by its effects on aggregate demand and supply. Government creation of money can be interpreted as a hidden tax on the public. An increase in the rate of money creation can lead to an unanticipated increase in the rate of inflation, as well as to increased tax collections.

▲   *3. Should inflation be slowed down or even eliminated?*

Because inflation has its winners and losers, a rigorous assessment of the total welfare effects from slowing it down or stopping it entirely is quite difficult and complex.

Further Topics

Inflation can be harmful to some individuals through its redistribution effects even if society's real output is unchanged. Even more important, inflation can be harmful to society as a whole through misallocated resources, arrested productivity and economic growth. The complex process of inflation affects both aggregate demand and aggregate supply. Inflation causes problems mainly when the rate of price increase changes unexpectedly, and if the inflation rate is so high people do not as readily accept dollars in trade. If inflation is anticipated, people can make adjustments in their financial and real assets and in the wages they demand for their labor. Creditors can require higher interest rates for the funds they lend. Laborers can incorporate expected price increases into their labor contracts. Even institutional barriers to price and wage adjustment—fixed salary schedules and contract periods, for example—can be changed to allow for regular adjustment for inflation. Inflation need not redistribute income from creditor to debtor, from employee to employer. As long as the rate of price increase is steady enough that people can expect a similar rate in the future, the costs of inflation will not be prohibitive.

Review of New Terms

Bracket creep (or taxflation) The loss of purchasing power that occurs if progressive tax brackets are not indexed: people are pushed into higher tax brackets by inflation as money incomes (but not real incomes) rise, and pay a higher percentage of their incomes to the government.

COLA A cost-of-living adjustment clause found in some wage contracts to compensate workers in part or in full for erosion of their real purchasing power by inflation (as measured by the CPI).

Fisher effect An economic principle which states that the nominal (market) rate of interest is equal to the real rate of interest (based on the real productivity of capital) plus the rate of anticipated inflation.

Hyperinflation An abrupt and substantial rise in prices (e.g., 50 percent or more per month) that causes the value of currency to deteriorate so quickly that people become reluctant to accept and hold money.

Inflation premium The additional interest required by, and thus included in, the nominal or market interest rate as compensation and protection against erosion of purchasing power due to inflation.

Variable-rate or adjustable-rate mortgage (ARM) A mortgage whose interest rate is adjusted periodically to agree with some market interest rate—for example, the rate on a specific type of government or corporate bond.

Review Questions

1. How has inflation affected your real income, or your parents', during the last few years? List your gains and losses, and indicate the net effect. (◢1, ◢2)
2. Who gains and who loses from deflation? (◢1, ◢2)
3. Why do the effects of anticipated inflation differ from those of unanticipated inflation? (◢1, ◢2)
4. If everyone anticipated the rate of inflation perfectly, and could adjust his prices and wages freely to the new rate, would inflation do any harm? (◢1, ◢2)
5. The federal government currently increases the money stock through the sale of government bonds to the Fed. Would the effect on the economy be different if the government printed new dollar bills and dumped them out of airplanes? (◢1, ◢2)
6. Can inflation be stopped? Explain. (◢3)

PART IV

National Income and Fiscal Policy

Unemployment and the Equilibrium Income Level: An Introduction

Revolutions occur infrequently in the United States. Or else, when these uprisings happen, there are few observers sufficiently alert to recognize them. Relative unobtrusiveness is only one reason that the "new" economics is so remarkable; with hardly a shot fired, it was named an "economic" revolution in its own time.
    E. Ray Canterbery

KEY QUESTIONS

▲ 1.   What was the pre-Keynesian perspective on macroeconomics?

▲ 2.   What is the Keynesian perspective on macroeconomics?

▲ 3.   Why is macroeconomic equilibrium not necessarily at full equilibrium?

▲ 4.   How does the government fit into the Keynesian paradigm?

NEW TERMS

Circular flow of income	Leakage (outflow)
Equilibrium income level	Planned investment
Full employment	Real wage rate
Injection (inflow)	Saving
Investment	Say's law
Keynes's law	Unplanned investment

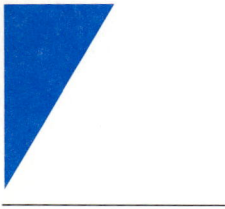

In this and the following six chapters we will cover macroeconomic theory, past and present. In particular, we will focus on the causes and cures of cyclical changes in national income and employment. To put the so-called Keynesian revolution into historical perspective, this chapter begins with a brief consideration of several earlier theories of unemployment. Then we will develop the basics of what has become known as the Keynesian macroeconomic model—not as its architect John Maynard Keynes developed them (see the brief biography on page 253), but as his followers have. Chapter 11 will extend and qualify that basic model, and Chapter 12 will show how the Keynesian model has been applied in government fiscal policy.

Unfortunately, economic theory—especially macroeconomic theory—does not always provide undisputed policy solutions to the macroeconomic problems of inflation, unemployment, and stagflation. Many of the policy recommendations drawn from Keynesian macroeconomic models are controversial. Alternative theories, discussed in the following section, offer conflicting policies. The debate will not be settled for many years, if ever; we certainly cannot offer conclusions here. Instead we will outline the framework economists use to think about unemployment and inflation, and in that way isolate the points of contention.

Before Keynes

◢ 1. What was the pre-Keynesian perspective on macroeconomics?

There is perhaps no better example of how economics is basically a reactive science developed almost entirely in response to prevailing economic situations and to the frailties of prevailing economic theories than Keynesian economics. John Maynard Keynes (1883–1946) developed his theory of how to moderate economic fluctuations in the midst of the worst depression in world history. Even then, Keynes's proposal of *intentional* budget deficits as part of a program for economic recovery was not accepted wholeheartedly until the 1960s with the Macmillan administration in England and the Kennedy-Johnson administrations in the United States. Lord Keynes did not singlehandedly bring about the Keynesian revolution. A number of economists who were studying unemployment during the Great Depression of the 1930s made many of the same recommendations as Keynes—including the suggestion that in times of heavy unemployment, the government should run a budgetary deficit to stimulate the economy and create jobs. Their theories may not have been as precisely developed as Keynes's, but their conclusions were identical. For instance, Jacob Viner (1892–1970) wrote, "When business activity is declining, or is stagnant and at a low level, reduced taxation, and budget deficits are, from the point of view of the national economy as a whole, sound policy rather than unsound."[1] Frank Knight (1885–1972) wrote, "As far as I know, economists are completely agreed that the government should spend as much and tax as little as possible at a time like this—using the expenditure to do the most good in itself and also to point toward relieving the depression."[2]

To these and other economists, the politics proposed in Keynes's *The General Theory* was nothing new, and they may have been surprised when the book became the manifesto for the new economics. For an idea to become widely accepted, however, it must be effectively presented and promoted. Keynes's contribution probably lies more in the presentation of his theory—in a relatively simple, straightforward manner that attracted both professional and public attention—than in its originality.

One scholar suggests six primary reasons for the success of Keynes's *General Theory*: "Keynes's reputation and activities, the book's theoretical content, its relevance for policy, its relationship to national income accounting and econometrics, its stylistic brilliance, and its incorporation of detailed knowledge of economic institutions and business practices."[3]

To appreciate the impact of the Keynesian revolution on people's thinking, we will look briefly at some theories that were in vogue before Keynes. The most influential was the classical explanation for unemployment. This theory is important not only for its historical significance, but for its crucial role in modern supply-side economics and to a lesser extent in monetarism and modern-day Keynesianism.

The Classical Model of the Labor Market

Equilibrium in the classical labor market occurs at the intersection of the demand and supply of labor. Equilibrium is the nonnormative position that once attained (or achieved), tends to be maintained. The downsloping demand for labor is derived from labor's marginal revenue productivity, calculated by determining the extra dollar or revenue that the firm obtains when it sells the output that labor produces. The more dollars of revenue

---

1. As quoted in J. Ronnie Davis, *The New Economics and the Old Economists* (Ames: Iowa State University Press, 1971), p. 40.

2. Ibid., p. 16.

3. Donald A. Walker, "Why Keynes's General Theory Was a Success," *Economic Notes* 3 (1986): 29.

Real wage rate: the nominal or money wage rate (the number of dollars a person earns per hour or day) adjusted for inflation or deflation. The real wage rate measures a worker's actual purchasing power.

that labor can bring to the firm from the sale of that labor's physical output of goods or services, the more valuable that labor is to the firm. The upsloping supply of labor is based on the fact that resource owners choose the employment that provides the greatest net advantage to them, including both monetary and nonmonetary factors.

Classical economists assumed that the number of workers employers will hire is inversely related to the wage rate, specifically the real or price-adjusted wage rate. The **real wage rate** is the nominal or money wage rate (the number of dollars a person earns per hour or day) adjusted for inflation or deflation. The real wage rate measures a worker's actual purchasing power. Because the general price level determines how much a given money wage will buy, the real wage rate can be expressed as the ratio W/P, where W is the money wage and P is an index (like the consumer price index) representing the general price level:

$$\text{real wage} = \frac{\text{money wage}}{\text{price index}} = \frac{W}{P}$$

Mathematically, the real wage rises with an increase in the money wage and falls with an increase in the price level.

If the real wage rate rises, the quantity demanded of labor and hence number of available jobs falls, and vice versa. Classical economists also assumed a direct relationship between the real wage rate and the number of laborers willing to work. That is, if the real wage rate rises, the quantity supplied of labor will rise and hence more workers will give up their leisure time and spend more time at work. Hence an increase in the real wage rate will cause the quantity of labor supplied to rise, and vice versa. The labor supply curve, like other supply curves, slopes upward.

The supply and demand curves for the classical model of the labor market are shown in Figure 10.1. As in other competitive markets, the equilibrium point E_1 falls at the intersection of the two curves, defined as being equal to the natural rate of unemployment and consisting of frictional and structural unemployment (which differs from full employment according to the Bureau of Labor Statistics). At the real wage rate $(W/P)_1$, everyone who is willing to work (N_1) can find a job. In this limited sense, the competitive market process tends toward full employment. In classical theory, **full employment** occurs when the quantity of labor demanded equals the quantity of labor supplied at a competitive market-determined real wage rate.

Full employment: the employment level that occurs when the quantity of labor demanded equals the quantity of labor supplied at a competitive market-determined real wage rate.

Of course, if anything destroyed wage or price flexibility, equilibrium would not necessarily be at full employment. Business, labor, or government can have some monopolistic control over price. Alternatively, rigid wages might simply result from custom or (misplaced?) sympathy by employers.

According to classical theory, if some workers are unemployed, it is because the going real wage is artificially or temporarily high. In that case the market is not in equilibrium: the real wage is above the intersection of supply and demand. In Figure 10.1, any real wage rate above $(W/P)_1$, such as $(W/P)_3$, will produce unemployment. The number of workers supplied

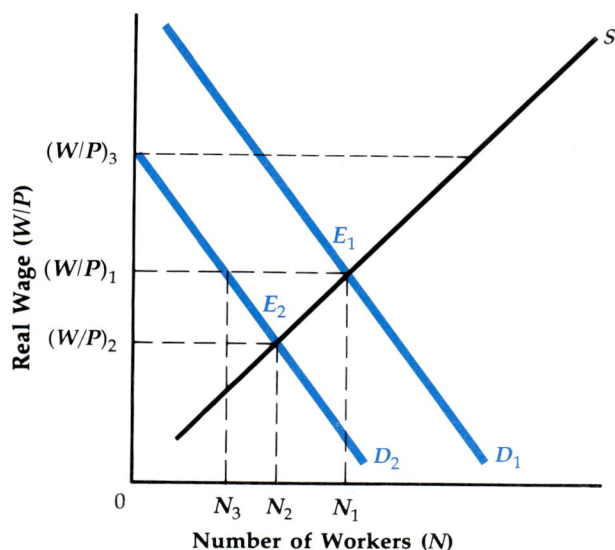

FIGURE 10.1 The Labor Market: The Classical Model
With supply and demand for labor represented by
curves S and D_1, equilibrium (E_1) will be achieved at full
employment with a real wage rate of $(W/P)_1$. If the
demand for labor in this market falls to D_2, the number
of workers willing to work (N_1) will at first exceed the
number demanded (N_3) at wage $(W/P)_1$. Until the real
wage rate adjusts downward to the equilibrium E_2 at
$(W/P)_2$, some unemployment will persist.

will be greater than the quantity demanded. Union wage rates, legislative
wage laws, and other market restrictions can cause such an effect.

Even in a competitive market unhampered by a government- or union-
fixed wage rate, unemployment can arise temporarily as a result of changes
in supply and demand. Unemployment will persist until the real wage rate
adjusts to a new equilibrium point. For instance, suppose the demand for
labor in Figure 10.1 falls from D_1 to D_2 as the result of a change in consumer buying habits. The product made by the workers in this market is
now less desirable than a product made by other workers. This jarring
change in demand will eventually throw the market from equilibrium E_1 to
E_2. The quantity of labor that employers demand at the initial real wage
rate, $(W/P)_1$, will fall to N_3. Thus $N_1 - N_3$ people will be out of work. In a
perfectly competitive labor market, the real wage rate (along with the
money wage) may fall very quickly to $(W/P)_2$, eliminating this gap between
the number of jobs available and the number of people seeking them going
to N_2. When the price is above equilibrium, workers will take cuts in their
money wages; because prices fall by a smaller amount, the real wage falls,
restoring the economy to full employment. In the real world, however,
markets never work that smoothly. Adjustment requires time—months or
even years—and during that period, some people will be unemployed.

An increase in the supply of labor—that is, the number of people
willing to work at any given wage—can have a similar effect on unemployment, again temporarily. The supply curve shifts rightward or outward,
lowering the point of intersection with the demand curve. If the real wage
adjusts downward in a competitive manner, the gap between the old real

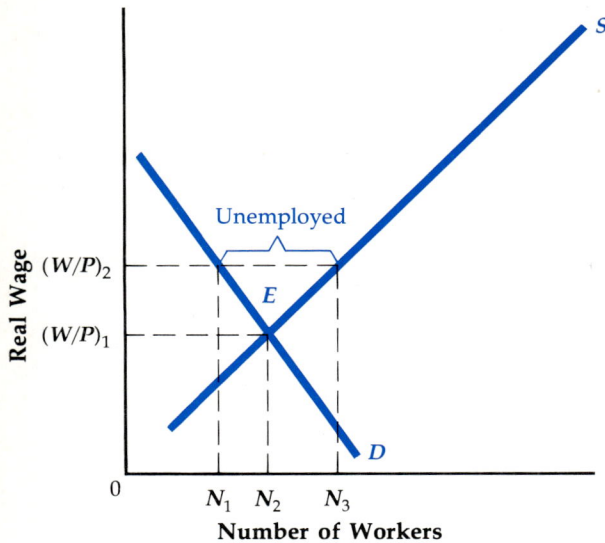

FIGURE 10.2 Obstruction in the Labor Market
In a free competitive market, the equilibrium is at point E and the real wage rate will settle at $(W/P)_1$ with N_1 workers employed. If the money wage is established at the artificially high level of $(W/P)_2$, however, it will push the real wage rate above equilibrium, causing unemployment equal to the difference between N_1 and N_3.

wage rate and the new equilibrium wage will be closed. As before, there will be unemployment during the transition.

If unemployment persists beyond a transitional period, classical economists would argue that it is because obstructions in the labor market are preventing the real wage rate from falling. Suppose the equilibrium is at point E, with the real wage rate at $(W/P)_1$ and employment at N_1 (see Figure 10.2). If the money wage is raised by union contract to an artificially high rate while the price level remains unchanged (real wage $(W/P)_2$), unemployment equal to the difference between N_1 and N_3 will persist. As we saw in Chapter 8, the government can solve this unemployment problem by increasing the money stock—and with it an increase in the general price level. With an increase in the price level (the denominator in $(W/P)_2$), the real wage rate will fall—assuming, of course, that the money wage rate remains constant. If the real wage rate falls, the gap between the quantity of labor demanded (N_1) and the quantity of labor supplied (N_3) will evaporate. If unions are able to negotiate perpetual wage increases, however, a government intent on pushing the real wage rate down to the equilibrium point will have to inflate the price level continually. If money wages and prices rise together, the real wage will never reach equilibrium, and unemployment will never disappear.

Classical economists reasoned that an economy would never be completely free from unemployment. Continuing adjustments in the labor market as well as restrictions that prevent the real wage from adjusting—minimum wage laws and union contracts—would keep unemployment from falling to zero. They also recognized that "monetary policy"—inflating the money stock—could be used to solve unemployment under the condition of "sticky" money wages.

Early Theories of the Business Cycle

Modern economic history has been a continuing series of business cycles, or alternating periods of recession and recovery. Before Keynes, economists explained these swings in national income and employment as the result of unfavorable growing conditions, excessive production of goods and services, or overexpansion and eventual contraction or collapse of the banking system.

Agricultural Theories

Economic life has always proceeded irregularly. There have always been good years and bad years, as measured, for example, by the gross national product. When a large proportion of the population was engaged in farming, economic ups and downs were caused by changes in the weather. Poor rainfall or an early frost altered farm production and hence the level and distribution of income. These changes would in turn affect the demand for various goods and various types of labor. For instance, bad growing conditions hurt merchants who made their living by trading with farmers, and the new supply and demand conditions caused transitional unemployment while wage rates adjusted. During poor weather people moved out of the farm labor market, and unemployment increased among suppliers of agricultural equipment and household goods.

Because agriculture still dominated people's lives in the eighteenth and early nineteenth centuries, social scientists of that time looked to natural causes for an explanation of economic instability. One hundred years ago, for instance, the sunspot theory was a favorite explanation for changes in economic activity. Observers had noticed that sunspots were frequently followed by poor growing seasons. Today, of course, agriculture is much less important to national production, and causes other than sunspots must be sought for cyclical unemployment.

The Theory of General Glut

As commerce and industry developed, people realized that economic fluctuations are not necessarily connected to agriculture. Merchants observed that in some periods business was bad in all lines of merchandise, and they could not dispose of their goods at the usual prices in the usual volume. They reasoned that the problem was overproduction. Too much of all goods had been produced, leading to a general glut of merchandise. The resulting cutbacks in production caused unemployment.

This theory now seems unsophisticated, for the modern economy produces several times more than the level the early theorists considered excessive. In fact, the theory of general glut was attacked almost immediately by Jean Baptiste Say (1767–1832), a French economist of the late eighteenth and early nineteenth centuries. Say argued that in a barter economy the production of one good for sale represented the demand for another because its production was a means of gaining purchasing power. That is, we produce more than we want to consume so that we may trade with others to

Say's law: the macroeconomic belief that supply creates its own demand—that is, that the production of a supply of goods and services creates an equal demand for these goods and services.

acquire what we want but do not produce. This proposition led to the formulation of Say's law. According to **Say's law,** supply creates its own demand—that is, the production of a supply of goods and services creates an equal demand for these goods and services.

In other words, an increase in the quantity of a good produced must mean that people are demanding more of other goods. Their motive for producing more is to be able to trade for more of something else. At times the wrong goods may be produced for sale, or the wrong quantities of goods. The result will be changes in the relative prices of goods and in the supply and demand for various types of labor, as well as transitional adjustments in employment. That does not mean, however, that a general glut exists, or that demand for all goods and services is insufficient.

Monetary Theories of the Business Cycle

In a barter economy, Say's law is the correct answer to the theory of general glut. Although Say considered hoarding to be irrational because people would only hold money for transaction purposes, he hinted that his line of reasoning ran into difficulties when money was introduced into an economic system. If producers hold on to the money they receive from the sale of goods, rather than spending it immediately, the total supply of goods will be greater than the total demand. If people sell a product of their labor for $100, for instance, but do not spend the money, $100 worth of other goods will be left on the market. Thus for the period of time people hold money, overproduction and a reduction in economic activity will result. If there were wage and price flexibility, overproduction could be eliminated, according to Say's law. Keynes attacked Say's law on the theoretical basis that hoarding was rational behavior because of people's speculative demand for money, and on the empirical basis that wages and prices are "sticky" in a downward direction.

Most early monetary theorists blamed fluctuations in economic activity on the structure of the banking system—specifically, contractions of the money supply that occurred during times of financial panic. In the eighteenth and nineteenth centuries, the money stock consisted of gold, silver coins, and paper money printed by banks, called bank notes. If a customer took a bank note to a bank and demanded payment, he would receive gold coins. Because banks made money by extending loans through the issuance of bank notes, there was always a risk of overextension—the banks might create too much money. From time to time, a bank would find itself unable to meet depositors' demands for gold and it would go "bankrupt." Bankruptcy might be the result of bad management or extraordinary circumstances, like poor weather, that made it impossible for people to repay loans. Because banks held deposits in other banks, one bank's financial problems could spread throughout the banking system.

The process of contraction proceeded as follows: A bank under pressure to pay off its customers would withdraw its deposits from other banks. Seeing the run on that bank, customers of other banks would lose confidence in the security of their deposits, and they too would attempt to

PERSPECTIVES
John Maynard Keynes (1883–1946)

Perhaps no individual has had a more profound influence on modern economic thought than John Maynard Keynes. His reputation rests primarily on a book published in 1936, *The General Theory of Employment, Interest, and Money.* In this work, he attacked the conventional, or "classical," explanation for unemployment. According to the classical theory, wage rates in a market economy would adjust so as to prevent unemployment. Temporary imbalances could occur, but in the long run the economy necessarily generated as many jobs as there were people willing to work. Unemployment could persist only if some artificial interference—such as labor unions or minimum wage laws—prevented wage rates from reaching their equilibrium level. At equilibrium, full employment would necessarily hold.

Although he had begun his career as an adherent of classical economics, Keynes came to believe that the world of classical equilibrium constituted a special case. The economic events of his time no doubt contributed to the change in Keynes's thought. Between 1921 and 1939 the rate of unemployment in Britain averaged more than 14 percent, never falling below 10 percent. Keynes concluded that high unemployment, not full employment, might well be the usual result in a free market economy. In the *General Theory* he explained why.

Keynes believed that planned expenditure would not necessarily be equal to output; it would often fall below output because of insufficient planned investment. According to the classical economists the shortfall presented no problem because the rate of interest would fall, stimulating expenditure so as to bring it into equality with output. Other classical models assumed that decreases in the price level could encourage consumption expenditures enough to carry off output. The equilibrating factor in the classical model was always some price, whether the rate of interest or the price level of all output. According to Keynes, in the short run prices would not adjust so as to bring about macroeconomic equilib-

rium. Instead, output would adjust. If planned expenditures fell short of output, output would fall so as to bring about the necessary equality between income and expenditure. As business firms reduced output, unemployment rose.

The problem of insufficient planned expenditure, or aggregate demand, was likely to recur in a capitalist economy because businesspeople were naturally timid. By timid, Keynes meant that they tended to underestimate the opportunities for profitable investment and therefore invest too little. The only way to maintain an adequate level of planned expenditure was for the government to take up the slack. Government fiscal and monetary policy must be expansionary in order to maintain full employment. Keynes did not specify what the government should purchase; he believed that it did not matter as long as the money got spent. Indeed, he facetiously suggested emulating the pharoahs and building pyramids. What Keynes did not suggest was extensive microeconomic intervention in the economy. If aggregate demand were sufficient, the rest of the economy would get on quite well.

The influence of Keynes has waxed and waned since his death in 1946. It seems a safe bet that economists will still be debating the merits and demerits of Keynesian economics fifty years from now. To some, he is the theorist who rescued market capitalism. To others, he diverted economics from the path of truth. Part of our continuing fascination with Keynes the economist stems from our fascination with Keynes the man. Book collector, patron of the arts, biographer, civil servant, teacher, currency speculator, member of the Bloomsbury circle—he differed from the typical economist of today in that he excelled in many fields. He also appears to have been personally acquainted with every major artistic, intellectual, and political figure of the first half of the twentieth century. As Keynes himself might have said, anyone he didn't know was probably not worth knowing.

withdraw their deposits. Banks did not (and still do not) hold sufficient reserves under fractional reserve banking systems to meet their depositors' demands in times of widespread panic. As a result all banks within a city or perhaps even a nation would collapse at virtually the same time, causing a dramatic decrease in the money stock and in the prices of goods and services. (Remember that $MV = PQ$. With V held constant by institutional constraints, a decrease in M on the left side of the equation must lead to a decrease in P and/or Q on the right side, as discussed in Chapter 8. The classical economist argued that a decrease in M would have an immediate impact on P.)

During widespread bank failure, businesses found that the real value of their financial obligations had risen. The price of their assets fell along with their incomes, yet their debts remained the same in dollar terms. (Debtors also lose during a deflationary period.) Unable to cope with such financial pressures, many businesses also collapsed, further disrupting the flow of economic activity. At the same time, the dramatic decrease in prices increased real wages. (If the numerator of the real wage, W, remains constant or falls slightly while the denominator, P, falls substantially, the real wage, W/P, increases.) The result was a decrease in the quantity of labor demanded and an increase in unemployment. Although in a competitive labor market, nominal and real wages will eventually move toward equilibrium, during a period of bank failure and contraction of the money stock, unemployment tends to persist. This periodic pattern—a collapse of the banking system followed by a rise in unemployment—prompted the classical economist Irving Fisher (1867–1947) to suggest that depressions and booms were merely a consequence of "the dance of the dollar." Attempts were made to correct the instability of the early banking system. In the United States, the Federal Reserve System was created in 1913 to ensure that banks would be able to obtain additional money when they needed it. In times of financial panic, banks can get all the currency necessary to satisfy depositors' demands from the Fed. Ideally, by squelching bank runs and preventing the collapse of the banking system, the Fed could prevent periods of major depression and unemployment.

The Keynesian Perspective: The Essentials

▲ 2. What is the Keynesian perspective on macroeconomics?

The philosopher Thomas Kuhn has hypothesized that scientific knowledge is advanced in two distinct ways. New discoveries may be made gradually, in a relatively methodical and orderly procedure. Occasionally, however, there is a sudden radical change in the basic paradigm, or world view, held by scientists. Sir Isaac Newton (1642–1727) caused such a paradigm change in physics. Later, Albert Einstein (1879–1955) and the quantum physicists brought about others.[4]

---

4. Thomas S. Kuhn, *The Structure of Scientific Revolutions*, 2nd ed. (Chicago: University of Chicago Press, 1970).

Keynes brought about such a paradigm change in economists' view of recessions and unemployment. Instead of taking the classical labor supply and labor demand curves as his frame of reference, Keynes focused on the interrelationship between the overall real national income level (and therefore employment, since the two are closely related) and the aggregate, or total, demand for goods and services. These two macroeconomic factors interact to form the basis of the circular flow of income. Lord Keynes stood Say on his head by suggesting implicitly **Keynes's law,** the macroeconomic belief that "demand creates its own supply"—that is, that the demand for goods and services creates an equal production of these goods and services—the inverse of Say's law.

Keynes's law: the macroeconomic belief that "demand creates its own supply"—that is, that the demand for goods and services creates an equal production of these goods and services.

The Circular Flow of Income

To see the connection between national income level and aggregate demand in the simplest terms possible, imagine an economy without government, without international economic relations (a "closed" economy), and without business saving (all saving is personal saving done by households). (These assumptions are highly unrealistic, but allow us to develop the basic principles of Keynesianism. We will bring government and the international sector into the analysis later.) This private economy is divided into two sectors, households and firms, as in Figure 10.3. In this simplified macroeconomic model, households perform two roles. They supply resources such as labor and capital to firms, and they consume the goods and services produced by the firms. Similarly, firms perform two roles. They receive labor and capital from households and sell their goods and services to them. This model is called the **circular flow of income,** the real and money flows of resources and goods and services between firms and households.

Circular flow of income: the real and money flows of resources and goods and services between firms and households.

The two arrows shown in Figure 10.3 would be sufficient to describe a barter economy in a classical or Keynesian model. Resources go from households to firms, which in turn supply goods and services to households in exchange for resources. In a monetary economy, however, the system is more complicated. Resources are supplied to firms in exchange for money or income in the form of wages, dividends, and interest. Households then use that money to buy goods and services from the firm. The flow of money is added to the flow of goods, services, and resources in Figure 10.4.

The money received by households (on the left side of the outer flow) mirrors household earnings. It reflects the contribution of household members to the production of goods and services. If firms produce $100 worth of goods and services, households must earn an aggregate or national income of $100, simply because the full value of anything produced must ultimately be attributed to someone (including the return to the entrepreneur that is called profits). On a conceptual level, income and the value of what is produced are equal (although in practice workers generally take home less than the full value of their earnings). In future discussions, the terms *national output* and *national income* will be used interchangeably.

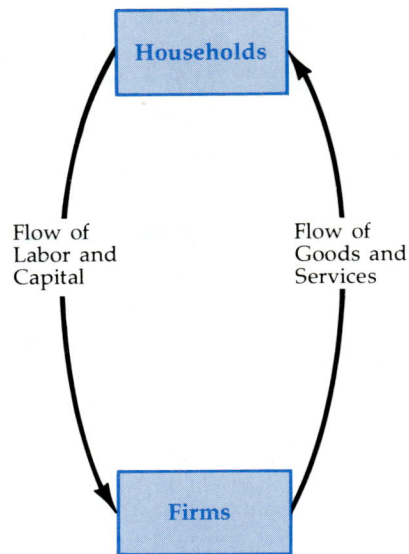

FIGURE 10.3 The Circular Flow of Income in a Barter Economy
The macroeconomy can be divided into two sectors, households and firms. In a barter economy, resources like labor and capital flow from the households to the firms. Goods and services flow back from the firms to the households.

The circular flow model shows that the ability of firms to sell their products depends on the willingness of households to buy what is produced. Obviously the tendency of households to buy is influenced by the income they earn. Because they determine household income, firms' production plans influence how much households will buy, and thus how much firms will sell. If firms do not produce, households will not have the purchasing power to buy goods and services. Similarly, households' employment opportunities and income depend in part on their aggregate buying decisions. If households in the aggregate refuse to buy goods and services, there will be no basis for employment or paychecks.

Because income and output are by definition equal in value, if households spend all their income on firms' output, all the output will be purchased. What if firms fail to pay households all they have earned, or households fail to spend what they earn on the goods firms produce? Either households will not receive enough income to buy what has been produced, or firms will not be able to sell all they have produced. In either case, if firms keep producing at full-employment level—that is, at the point where everyone who wants a job can have one—and households continue to spend less than they earn, not all goods will be taken off the market. Unwanted inventory (unsold goods) will pile up. To stop the accumulation of unwanted inventory, firms will cut back on production, reducing household income (since fewer work-hours are needed to produce the lower output). To the extent that consumption depends on total income, consumers will reduce their expenditures. The result will be unemployment. If there were price flexibility, the market would "solve" the unemployment problem. If we make the Keynesian assumption of fixed or slow-to-adjust wages and prices, the unemployment problem can persist.

Saving: A Leakage from the Circular Flow

Saving: that portion of income not spent. Represents forgone expenditures on real goods and services.

Leakage (outflow): a withdrawal of income from the circular flow.

The process of income contraction we have been discussing is illustrated in Figure 10.5. Suppose firms pay households $100, but households choose to spend only $90 of their earnings and to save $10. Saving is that portion of income not spent; it represents forgone current expenditures on real goods and services. Because saving does not go back to firms in the form of purchases, it represents a leakage from the circular flow of income. A leakage (outflow) is a withdrawal of income from the circular flow. (If government and international trade are considered, taxes and imports are also leakages.) As a result of the $10 saving leakage, firms will sell only $90 worth of what they have produced and will be left with $10 worth of unwanted inventory. If they continue to produce $100 worth of goods and services, and households continue to save $10, inventory will mount by $10 each time $100 worth of goods and services is produced.

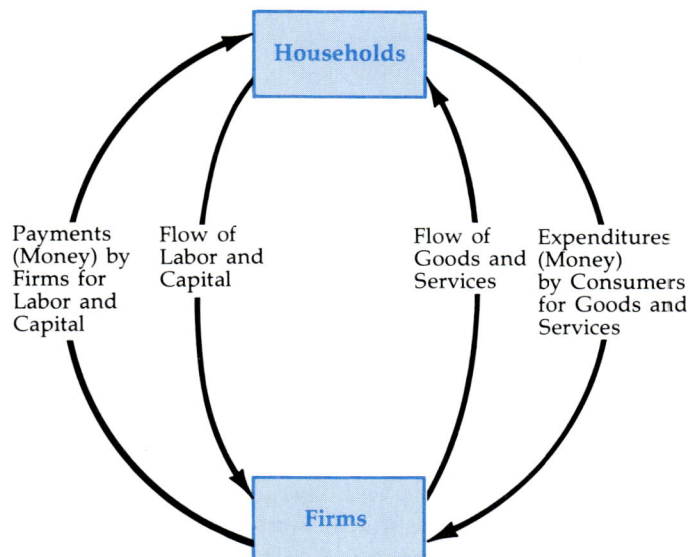

FIGURE 10.4 The Circular Flow of Income in a Money Economy
In a money economy, firms make money payments to households for the resources they provide. Households then spend the money payments on goods and services produced by the firms.

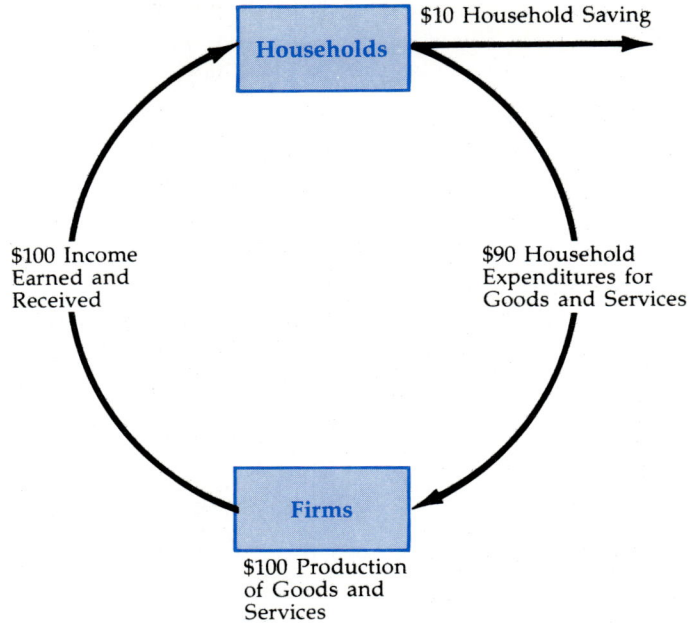

FIGURE 10.5 Leakage from the Circular Flow

If households save $10 of each $100 they earn, they will buy only $90 of the $100 worth of goods and services produced. If firms then continue to produce at the level of $100, unwanted inventory will pile up. At some point firms will have to curtail production, and unemployment will rise.

Firms must eventually try to bring their production level in line with their sales. At that point they will reduce both employment and household income—depressing consumer expenditures as well as household saving. To take up this new slack, firms may have to reduce production still further. For example, if producers reduce production to $90 (because households have been spending only $90 out of $100), people may in turn reduce their saving from $10 to $7—but they will still be spending only $83 ($90 of income minus $7 of saving). Goods and services will continue to go unsold, and production will have to be reduced still further.

At this point you may ask why prices do not fall in response to the surplus of goods and services. In practice they may very well fall. In its most basic form, however, the Keynesian model of the macroeconomy assumes constant prices—a controversial assumption, as you can imagine. We will sidestep the difficulty for the moment by stating the rationale for the assumption of constant prices. First, the Keynesian model is intended to describe the short run, a period during which prices are more or less inflexible and adjustments in economic activity are expressed at least as much in output as in price. Income, in other words, is assumed to adjust faster than prices.

Second, as prices fall, wages and other payments to households must fall as well. Although a given number of dollars will now buy more, there are fewer dollars in income to buy with. Thus lower prices may not stimulate greater sales. Eventually, prices and wages may decline enough to induce consumers to buy more, if only because their savings are worth more after deflation. As prices fall, the purchasing power of assets fixed in money terms such as bank account deposits rises, creating the real balances or real wealth effect discussed in Chapter 6. That is, because people feel wealthier at lower price levels, they tend to spend more. If prices eventually fall enough, anyone who has a dollar becomes a millionaire in real terms and can buy any good or service, such as a Rolls-Royce, as befits the new situation. Again, the Keynesian model is designed for the short run. During the time it takes for wages and prices to fall, production and employment can also decline. Although economic problems may eventually work themselves out, that prospect provides small comfort to people who are unemployed during the weeks and months, or even years, of the sticky adjustment process.

Investment: An Injection into the Circular Flow

Injection (inflow): an introduction of income into the circular flow.

Investment: the purchase of capital goods—plant and equipment, residential structures, and changes in inventory— that can be used in the production of other goods and services.

Planned investment: anticipated, scheduled purchases of plant and equipment, residential homes, and inventory.

Unplanned investment: unanticipated, unscheduled purchases of plant and equipment, residential construction, and inventory.

The damaging effects of leakages from the circular flow can be partially offset by corresponding injections. An injection (inflow) is an introduction of income into the circular flow. Investment is an injection into the circular flow (if government and international trade are considered, governmental expenditures and exports are also injections). By investment we do not mean the purchase of stocks and bonds by individuals, but the purchase of investment goods by businesses. Investment is the purchase of capital goods—plant and equipment, residential structures, and changes in inventory—that can be used in the production of other goods and services. The durable assets of business, plant and equipment, and construction of residential homes along with changes in inventory provide a future flow or stream of services unlike consumption expenditures that are immediately used.

Investment may be planned (and therefore desired) or unplanned (undesired). Planned investment includes anticipated, scheduled purchases of business plant and equipment, residential homes, and business changes in inventory. Unplanned investment includes unanticipated, unscheduled purchases of business plant and equipment, residential construction, and business changes in inventory. Unplanned investment is purchase by default. It represents goods and services that were produced to be sold, but ended up as inventory because no one bought them.

Figure 10.6 shows a planned investment expenditure of $10. If this inflow into the circular flow equals the saving outflow, all the goods and

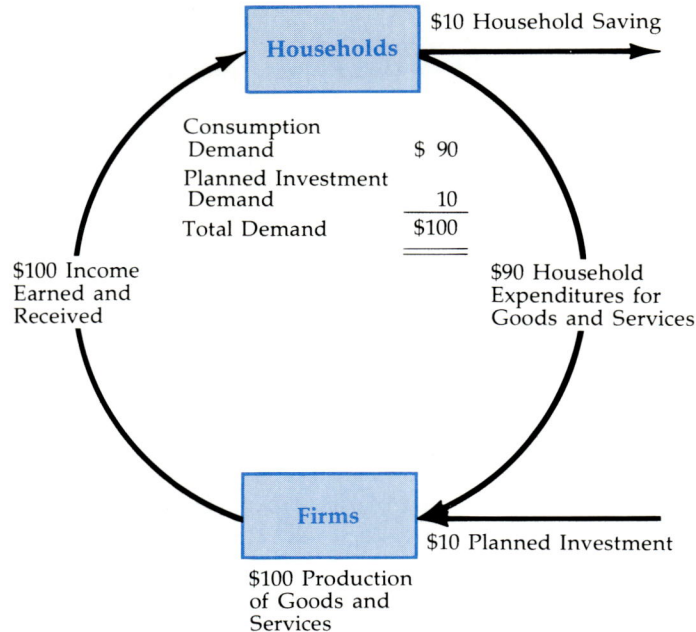

FIGURE 10.6 Injection into the Circular Flow
When the planned saving outflow exactly equals the planned investment inflow, the macroeconomy is in equilibrium. The total demand for goods and services exactly equals the quantity of goods and services produced, and firms have no reason to expand or contract production.

services the economy has produced will be purchased. Households will buy $90 and save $10. Firms will buy the remaining $10 worth of goods and services in the form of capital goods (plant and equipment) and perhaps some additions to inventory. Total planned expenditures by consumers and investors (*TPE*) will exactly equal the national income-output level (*Y*) at $100. The economy, in other words, will be in equilibrium. Firms will have no reason to produce more or less than they are already producing because households and firms together will demand no more or less. Equilibrium is achieved when total planned spending equals national income or output. That is precisely the case in Figure 10.6. Planned investment equals planned saving at $10, and national income and output do not change.

To Keynesians, the economy can be at equilibrium at less than full employment; therefore, planned saving and planned investment may be equal at less than full employment. If an economic system is at full employment, it will tend to remain so, as long as the levels of planned investment and saving remain constant. If discrepancies between planned saving and planned investment arise, however, aggregate income and employment will be affected. For instance, if saving rises to $15 while planned investment falls to $5, households and firms will spend a total of only $90 ($85 in consumption and $5 in planned investment). As a result $10 worth of goods will go unsold, ending up as an unplanned addition to inventory or unplanned investment. Firms will then seek to reduce their unplanned inventory by cutting back on production. The result will be a rise in unemployment.

Actual (or realized) saving is *always* equal to actual (or realized) investment by definition, but planned saving is equal to planned investment *only* at equilibrium. In other words, actual saving always equals actual investment at any time, while planned saving is equal to planned investment only at equilibrium. Actual saving or investment includes both a planned and an unplanned component. For example, actual investment is obtained by adding changes in unplanned inventory or unplanned fixed investment to planned investment. Only in equilibrium is unplanned investment equal to zero.

Maintaining the Equilibrium Income Level

3. Why is macroeconomic equilibrium not necessarily at full equilibrium?

Keynes saw two problems in achieving and maintaining a full-employment national income level. The first had to do with getting wages and prices to adjust enough so that everyone who wanted to work would be employed. The second had to do with ensuring that demand would be sufficient to take off the market all the goods and services produced by the fully employed labor force. In terms of the circular flow model, planned saving must equal planned investment at the full-employment income level. Keynes questioned the classical theory that interest rates would adjust to bring planned saving in line with planned investment because savers and investors are substantially different groups with different motives that may be largely unrelated to the interest rate.

Equalizing Saving and Investment: The Classical Theory of Interest Rates

Figure 10.7 shows the relationship of planned investment and planned saving to interest rates. The investment curve slopes down, reflecting the inverse relationship between planned investment (reflecting the expected net rate of return from investment) and real interest rates (i.e., nominal interest rates adjusted for inflation). The saving curve slopes up, indicating the direct relationship between saving and real interest rates. People save more (and invest less) as the real interest rate rises.

Is there a way to equalize planned saving and planned investment at the full-employment level of national income? Classical economists thought that a change in the market real interest rate would bring planned saving in line with planned investment. That is, people will decide how much to save according to the interest rate. If the interest rate rises, they will save more, and vice versa. With higher interest rates, people will give up more goods and services today in anticipation of even greater quantities in the future.

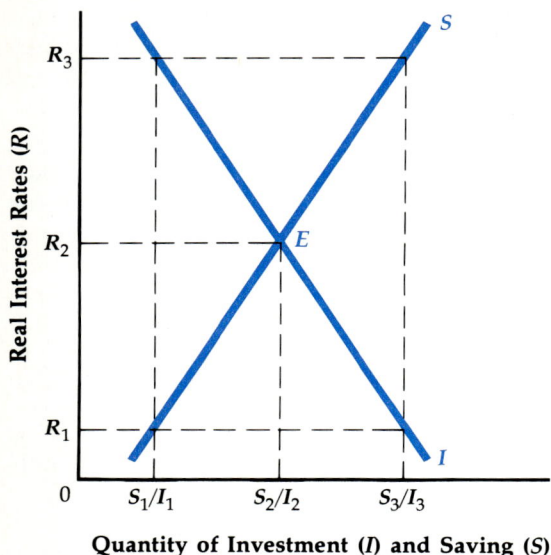

FIGURE 10.7 The Relationship of Planned Saving (S) and Planned Investment (I) to Real Interest Rates (R): The Classical Theory

Classical economists assumed that real interest rates (i.e., nominal interest rates adjusted for inflation) would adjust to maintain equality between planned saving (S) and planned investment (I). If saving falls short of the demand for investment, as at interest rate R_1, the rate will move up to R_2 to bring saving and investment into equilibrium at E. If saving exceeds investment demand, as at R_3, the rate will adjust down to R_2. In the extreme version of Keynesian income theory, the saving (S) curve would be or almost be a vertical or a perfectly inelastic curve.

Planned investment, on the other hand, decreases as the rate of interest increases—and vice versa. Obviously, firms will want each project to earn a rate of return at least as high as the cost of borrowing to finance it. At a 10 percent interest rate, for instance, firms will not want to invest in any project that yields a return of less than 10 percent. Thus if interest rates are low, firms can afford to undertake a variety of projects, some of which may earn only a modest return. At high interest rates, however, they can justify investing only in lucrative projects.

Just how is the interest rate adjusted to bring planned saving and planned investment into line? Classical economists argued that in a competitive market, the interest rate will move automatically toward the intersection of the saving and investment curves—R_2 in Figure 10.7. If the interest rate is below that level—say, R_1—the demand for funds to invest (I_3) will be greater than the amount of money made available for investment through saving (S_1). The interest rate will rise, causing investors to cut back on their planned investment and households to save more. At R_2, saving (S_2) will equal planned investment (I_2). Likewise, if the interest rate is above R_2, firms will want to borrow less (I_1) than people will want to save (S_3), and the interest rate will fall. Again, at R_2, the levels of saving and investment are equal. In terms of the circular flow of income, the economy will be in equilibrium at E. Then, classical theory indicates, unless obstacles in the capital or labor market prevent adjustments in the wage rate and the prices of other resources, the economy will move toward full employment.

Workers would take a cut in their real wage either because of "money illusion" or because a rise in the price level affected all workers in the same way (in the classical model). Because the supply of labor depends on the money wage in the Keynesian model, equilibrium could occur in the labor market at less than full employment. Because labor will resist money wage reductions, thereby keeping real wages above the full employment level, unemployment problems occur. Unemployment can occur in the Keynesian labor market at equilibrium because actual GNP can be less than potential GNP.

Keynesian Objections to the Classical Theory of Interest Rates

Keynes believed that interest rates cannot be expected to adjust quickly to close a gap between planned saving and planned investment. Moreover, he argued, the interest rate depends on other forces besides the demand for investment and the supply of savings. People need to hold part of their incomes as cash or bank balances, both to carry out day-to-day transactions and to have some precautionary reserve for unexpected purchases or emergencies. To Keynes, saving depended on the level of income more than the interest rate. Therefore, the interest rate did not equate saving and investment. Keynes felt that the level of income equilibrated saving and investment. Thus, in the extreme version of Keynes's income theory, the saving curve in Figure 10.7 would be vertical (or almost vertical).

Some people also hold on to money in hopes that its value will rise in the future. This speculative motive for holding money requires additional explanation. If people expect interest rates to go up, they will want to maintain larger-than-usual money balances: if they lend their money out now, they will be stuck with a low rate of interest in the future, but if they are correct in their expectations, they will be able to lend it at a higher rate later. While speculators wait for a better interest rate, they are neither spending their funds nor lending them to investors. Their speculation keeps the rate above the intersection of the investment and saving curves in Figure 10.7 and causes a leakage from the circular flow that is not offset by a corresponding injection.

Figure 10.8 shows the impact of this discrepancy on the national income level. Planned investment is only $5, while $15 is being saved. Consumers will buy $85 worth of goods and services ($100 in income minus $15 in saving) and investors will buy $5. Total planned spending will therefore be $90, $10 short of the value of the goods and services produced ($100). Because the planned investment inflow does not fully offset the planned saving outflow, producers will eventually cut back on production, to stop the accumulation of excess inventory. Production, income, and employment will spiral downward. With reduced production, fewer workers will be needed and household income will fall, reducing consumption and causing further cutbacks in production and employment.

This downward spiral, fortunately, will not continue indefinitely. Assuming (to simplify the analysis) that planned investment remains constant as saving and income fall, at some point planned saving and planned invest-

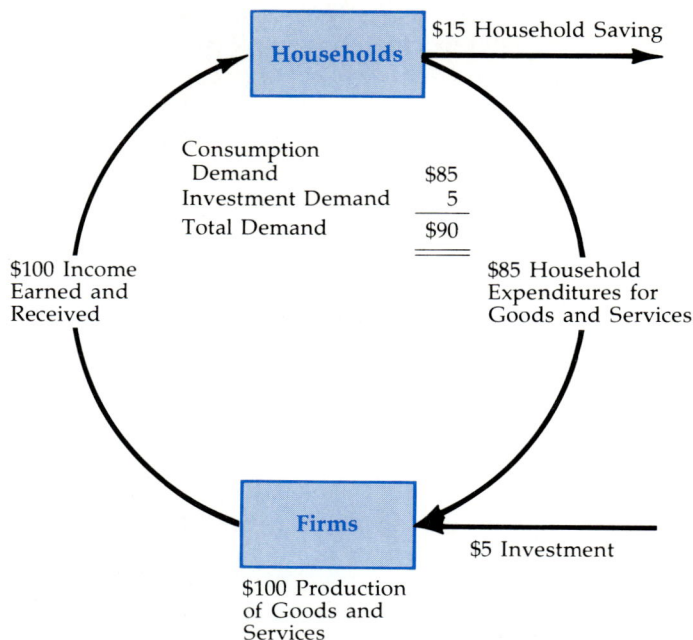

FIGURE 10.8 Disequilibrium in National Income

When planned household saving ($15) is greater than firms' planned investment expenditures ($5), aggregate demand ($90) falls short of the level of production ($100). Unwanted inventory will build up and eventually production will be cut back, reducing national income and raising the unemployment level.

Equilibrium income level: the income level (not necessarily at full employment) at which producers have no reason to change their output level because leakages equal injections.

ment will become equal. This point is called the equilibrium income level. The **equilibrium income level** is the income level (not necessarily at full employment) at which producers have no reason to change their output level. It is reached when leakages (outflows) equal injections (inflows). There is nothing desirable per se about an equilibrium. The U.S. economy may have been in equilibrium in the 1930s, yet a quarter of the labor force was out of work!

Keynes believed that the supply of labor depended on the money wage and not the real wage. Thus, workers looked at their money wages when they offered their services for hire on the market. Workers would not take a cut in their money wages because they were either under a "money illusion" or they looked at their money wages relative to other workers in other occupations. Thus, the classical wage and price flexibility does not exist to stop the spiral of falling economic activity.

The process by which planned saving falls to meet planned investment is shown in Figure 10.9. In one version of Keynes, as income decreases, the saving curve shifts to the left—from S_1, associated with income level Y_1, to

S_2, associated with a lower income level, Y_2,—reaching equality with planned investment at the higher interest rate of R_2 (although in the simplest and most naive Keynesian model the interest rate is fixed). A new equilibrium income level (E_2) is established—but at a lower national income (Y_2) and a higher unemployment rate. In another version of Keynes, the savings curve is (or is close to) vertical. In this extreme version, saving depends entirely on the level of income and not at all on the interest rate.

We can now state the central difference between the classical and the Keynesian models. In the classical model, the theoretical focus is on how interest rates adjust to eliminate discrepancies between saving and investment. In the Keynesian model, the theoretical focus is mainly (but not exclusively) on how income adjusts to alleviate those discrepancies. Whereas the classical economists argued that the saving curve would not shift because interest rates would adjust downward rapidly, Keynes insisted that speculation would slow down interest rate adjustments. Equilibrium would be reached only after production levels—and income—had fallen. In the simplest but unlikely Keynesian case of fixed interest rates due to a liquidity trap, the less than full employment conclusion is even easier to understand.

In the Keynesian model, the interest rate usually does adjust downward over the long run, as people alter their expectations about future interest rates. If workers believe that increasing unemployment and a falling national production level will cause interest rates to fall, for instance,

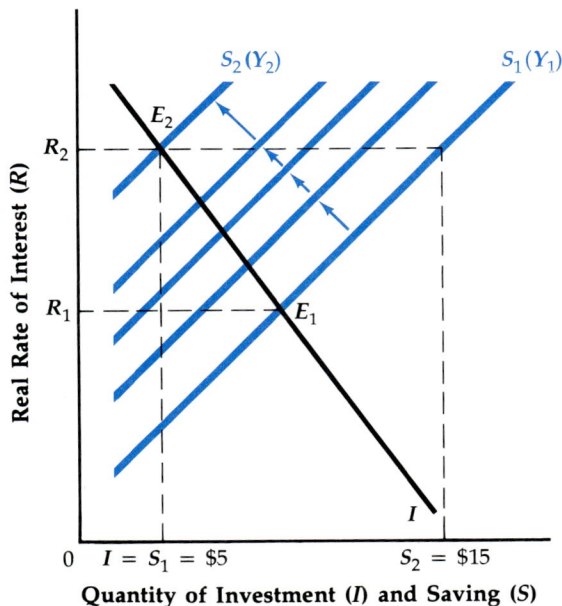

FIGURE 10.9 The Relationship of Saving (S) and Investment (I) to Interest Rates: The Keynesian Theory According to one version of the Keynesian theory, the speculative demand for money may prevent interest rates from falling to bring saving into line with investment. If saving exceeds investment at interest rate R_1, total planned expenditures will fall short of national production. Firms will cut back on production, causing further drops in income and saving (see Figure 10.8). As saving falls, the saving curve will shift inward, from S_1 (associated with income level Y_1) to S_2 (associated with the lower income level Y_2). Equilibrium (E_2) will be restored at the higher interest rate R_2. In another more extreme version of the Keynesian theory, the planned saving (S) curve is, or is close to, vertical. In this version, saving depends entirely on the level of income and not at all on the interest rate.

they will lend their money at present interest rates rather than holding on to it. In doing so, they will reduce interest rates (because they will be increasing the supply of funds for hire). The lower interest rates will stimulate investment, production, and the demand for goods and services, increasing the need for labor. In the long run, a decline in wages and prices may cause a drop in the real wage rate and an increase in wealth held in dollars. It may bring additional increases in planned consumer and investment expenditures and additional reductions in unemployment. In the meantime, however, unemployment can be a significant social problem. The Keynesian prescription for government spending during a recession was directed at these short-run cyclical unemployment problems. Keynes was fully aware that his policy recommendations would not begin to solve long-run unemployment problems, which can last for decades.

Adding Government to the Circular Flow

4. How does the government fit into the Keynesian paradigm?

So far we have seen that if households receive from firms an amount of income equal to their earnings, and spend all they receive on goods and services produced by firms, the income flow will remain constant and the macroeconomy will be at equilibrium. Saving, however, constitutes a leakage from the circular flow. Unless planned saving is offset by planned investment, the national income level will fall. If investment exceeds saving, the income level will rise—provided, of course, that unemployed resources can be used in production.

What can government do to modulate swings in economic activity that result from discrepancies between saving and investment? Like saving, government taxes are a diversion of consumer purchasing power away from the circular flow.[5] Taxes may eventually reenter the circular flow in the form of planned government expenditures. At the moment government extracts them from the flow, however, taxes have essentially the same effect as personal saving. For this reason, taxes are shown as an outflow in Figure 10.10. At the same time, government expenditures on goods and services (such as defense systems, buildings, and roads) are paid to firms, and constitute an inflow to the economy. Because they resemble business purchases of capital equipment (investment), planned government expenditures are also represented by an arrow pointing toward the circular flow.

Once government has been introduced into the analysis, we can see that equality in planned saving and investment is not enough to ensure that national income will be at equilibrium. National income equilibrium occurs when total planned outflows (planned saving plus taxes) equal total planned inflows (planned investment plus government expenditures), as in Figure 10.10. Assume again that the economy produces $100 worth of goods and services. Households earn that amount in income, but they pay

_____

5. Corporate income taxes, property taxes, and sales and excise taxes also divert funds from businesses and stockholders to the government. To keep the analysis as simple as possible, we shall ignore these forms of taxation. Their exclusion will not affect the general argument or the conclusions drawn.

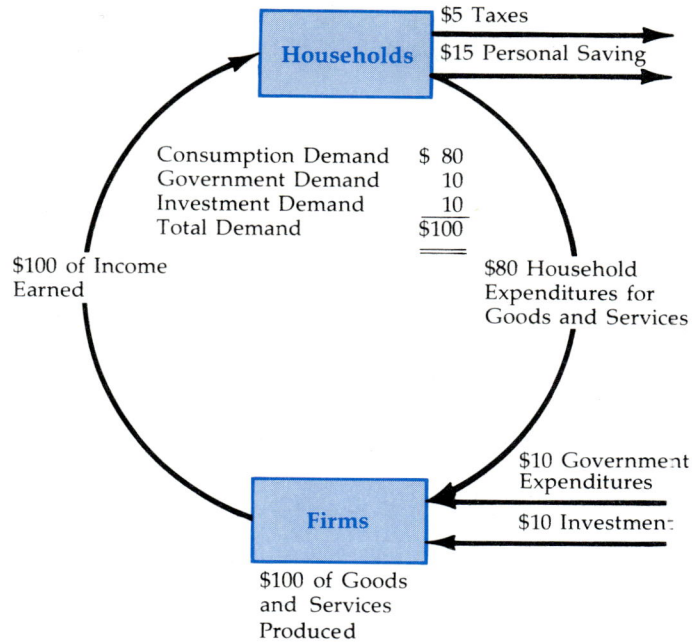

FIGURE 10.10 The Circular Flow of Income, Government Included

If government is introduced into the circular flow model, equilibrium in national income occurs when total planned outflows—planned saving plus taxes—exactly equal total planned inflows—planned investment plus government expenditures. Here taxes at $5 plus saving at $15 equal government expenditures at $10 plus investment at $10.

$5 in taxes and save $15. Planned government expenditures and planned business investment are each $10. The planned consumption demand of households is therefore $80 [$100 − ($5 + $15)]; business and government demand is $20 ($10 + $10). Total planned expenditure equals national income at $100. Because all the goods firms have produced are sold to investors, consumers, or the government, firms have no reason either to raise or to lower production.

Total planned expenditures (*TPE*) are now composed of three types of expenditure: planned consumption (*C*), planned investment (*I*), and planned government spending (*G*).[6]

$$TPE = C + I + G$$

6. For the moment we will neglect the possibility of international economic relations. Their addition would not be difficult, however, because the dollars coming into the United States from selling exports would be an injection (inflow) into the circular flow for the United States and the dollars going out of the United States from buying imports would be a leakage (outflow).

Similarly, people can do three things with the income they earn (Y); they can spend it (C), save it (S), or pay taxes with it (T).

$$Y = C + S + T$$

Since in equilibrium, total planned expenditure must equal national income ($TPE = Y$), the components of total planned expenditure must equal national income.

$$Y = C + I + G$$

In Figure 10.10, this condition is met. One hundred dollars of income is earned. Consumers in the aggregate spend $80 on goods and services; firms spend $10 on investment goods; and government spends $10.

$$TPE = \$80 + \$10 + \$10 = \$100 = Y$$

If total planned expenditures equal national income, the components of total planned expenditure must equal the components of national income.

$$C + I + G = C + S + T$$

This equation reduces to $I + G = S + T$, because the Cs on either side of the equal sign cancel out. In terms of the circular flow model, $I + G = S + T$ simply means that in equilibrium, planned inflows must equal planned outflows. That is the case in our example.

$$\$10 + \$10 = \$15 + \$5$$

The Function of Deficits

In this section we examine the impact of governmental budget deficits, in which government outlays exceed receipts, on income determination. In the last example, planned saving is greater than planned investment. In our earlier model, when planned saving exceeded planned investment, the income level fell and unemployment rose. In this case, however, government expenditures offset the difference between planned saving and planned investment. Government planned expenditures exceed taxes by the same amount that saving exceeds investment, $5. The government runs a budgetary deficit in this example, borrowing $5 from savers to make up the difference between taxes and expenditures. In doing so, it keeps the national income level from falling.

According to Keynesian theory, budget deficits should not always be feared or avoided. The equilibrium income level achieved with a deficit exceeds the income level to which the economy might fall without a deficit. In our example, if taxes and government expenditures both equaled $10 (that is, if the budget were balanced), consumption demand would be only $75: $100 in income minus $10 in taxes and $15 in saving. Total demand would be $95: $75 in consumption plus $10 in government expenditures and $10 in investment. Five dollars worth of goods and services would not

be sold, and firms would have to cut back on production. The national
income level would decline in a process of lower consumption and lower
income.

If some resources remain unused, government can raise the national
income level by increasing outflows over inflows. It can reduce taxes or it
can increase expenditures on roads, schools, and hospitals, or it can reduce
taxes and increase expenditures at the same time. Regardless, the Keynesian prescription for unemployment is to run a budgetary deficit—or if the
government is enjoying a budgetary surplus, to run a smaller surplus. The
overriding goal is to bolster total planned expenditures, which may or may
not mean deficit spending.

Suppose, for instance, that the government increases expenditures
from $10 to $15, as in Figure 10.11. Consumption demand is still $80, but
with the increase in government spending, total planned expenditures rise
to $105. Consumers, investors, and government are now demanding more
than firms are producing, giving firms an incentive to raise their production levels. Increased production means a higher income level and increased consumption, which in turn induces firms to produce even more

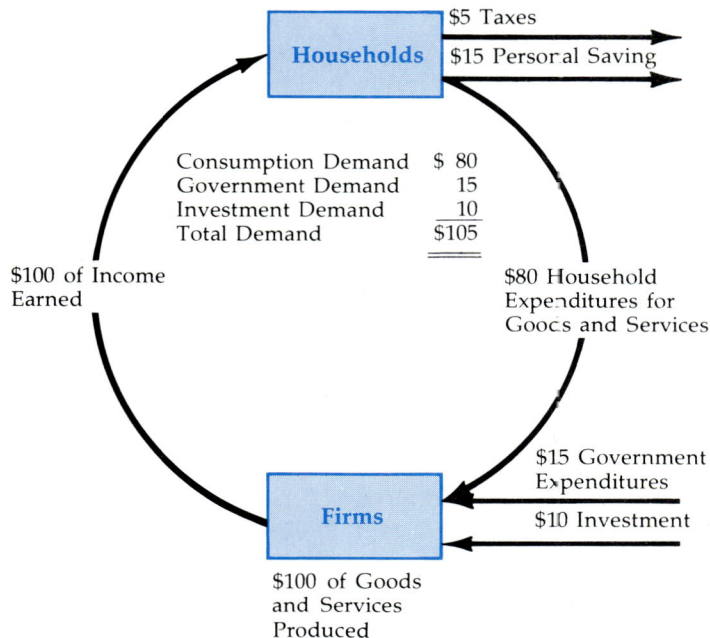

Consumption Demand	$ 80	
Government Demand	15	
Investment Demand	10	
Total Demand	$105	

FIGURE 10.11 Rising National Income
When the total planned inflows exceed total planned outflows, total planned expenditures
will exceed national income. If some resources, capital, and workers are still unemployed,
the national income level will rise.

goods and services and generate more income. In this way, the national income level moves up.

As the economy moves upward toward the new, higher equilibrium income level, however, planned saving will rise in response. Taxes will also rise if income tax rates are tied to household income levels. For instance, if national income increases from $100 to $110, saving may rise from $15 to $16, and taxes may rise from $5 to $5.25. When the sum of planned saving and taxes equals the new, higher level of planned investment and government expenditure ($25), a new equilibrium income level will be achieved.

Reducing taxes can produce virtually the same increase in national income as increasing government expenditures. The main difference in this case is that people may put a portion of their tax reduction into saving. A $5 reduction in taxes may mean a $1 increase in saving, and as a result total outflows will fall by only $4 instead of $5. Therefore an increase in government expenditures will tend to have a slightly greater effect on the national income level than would an equal decrease in taxes.

Chapter Review

Review of Key Questions

1. *What was the pre-Keynesian perspective on macroeconomics?*

Before Keynes, economists attributed unemployment to normal shifts in the supply and demand for goods and services, and to obstacles in the labor market that prevented wage rate adjustments. Unemployment was also thought to result from changes in the money stock, which affect the real wage rate paid to labor and therefore the quantity of labor supplied and demanded. However, it was felt that automatic free-market forces propelled the economy toward full employment. Classical economists believed in Say's law: that supply creates its own demand.

2. *What is the Keynesian perspective on macroeconomics?*

The essentials of the Keynesian perspective can be shown in a simple circular flow of income diagram showing the real and money flows between inputs and outputs between businesses and households. Keynes's law states that demand creates its own supply. Keynesian equilibrium occurs when planned inflows are equal to planned outflows.

3. *Why is macroeconomic equilibrium not necessarily at full equilibrium?*

Keynes argued that unemployment could result from the failure of consumers and businesses to demand all the goods and services produced by the economy. If businesses and consumers do not plan to buy all that is produced, firms will accumulate excess inventory and will have to cut back on production, increasing the unemployment level. In classical theory, the interest rate adjusts to equalize saving and planned investment. In the Keynesian model, the national income level adjusts to bring planned saving and planned investment into line. In the Keynesian model of the circular flow of income, the conditions for macroeconomic equilibrium can be stated in two ways. First, the macroeconomy will be in equilibrium when total demand for goods and services exactly equals total output. Second, leaving government out of the analysis, the macroeconomy will be in equilibrium when the planned saving of households and firms exactly equals the planned investment expenditures of firms (the purchase of plant and equipment and changes in inventories). The equilibrium income level is not necessarily the full-employment level. According to Keynesian theory, as long as some unemployment exists, government can expand national income and employment by increasing total spending. It can do so either by increasing its own expenditures on goods and services or by lowering taxes, thus increasing household and business expenditures.

▲   *4. How does the government fit into the Keynesian paradigm?*

According to the Keynesian model, government budgetary deficits are not necessarily bad. As long as some unemployment exists and planned saving exceeds planned investment, government can raise the national income level by increasing its expenditures or by cutting taxes. Whether it must run a deficit to do so is not important. If planned saving does not equal planned investment, the government can cool off the economy by decreasing its expenditures or by raising taxes. The use of discretionary government spending and tax collections to steer the economy in a desired direction is called fiscal policy. The Fed can also use discretionary monetary policy—for example, changing the money supply—to try to achieve a maximum production, full-employment, noninflationary level of economic activity. While Keynesians believe that activist policy of both forms can be useful, they prefer fiscal over monetary policy.

Further Topics

The Keynesian revolution must be seen in historical context. The classical approach to reducing unemployment is to speed up the flow of information to workers who are transitionally unemployed and reduce restrictions on wage and labor movements, such as legislative wage laws, union shops, and race and sex discrimination. Keynes and his followers, however, accepted such restrictions as a political reality. They also accepted as practical reality that workers would not take a cut in their money wages. In both cases Keynes assumed little could be done about them in the short-run. Instead he suggested another means of correcting unemployment—an increase in total demand for goods and services.

According to the Keynesian model of the circular flow of income, periods of low production and high unemployment result from a discrepancy between saving and planned investment. Investment includes spending on business equipment, machinery, and tools; spending on all business and household construction; and business changes in inventories. With everything else held equal and assuming for the moment no government activity, the national income level will fall and unemployment will rise when planned investment expenditures are less than the level of planned saving. (If planned investment expenditures exceed the level of planned saving, the national income level will rise and unemployment will fall.)

To restore national income and production to their former levels, government must somehow increase total demand, offsetting the gap between planned saving and planned investment. Government can boost total demand by increasing its expenditures while holding taxes constant, or it can reduce taxes while holding government expenditures constant. A rise in government expenditures increases total demand directly. Reducing taxes achieves the same effect indirectly. If people take home more pay, they can be expected to spend more, increasing the level of total demand. In the next chapter we will explore these policies in more detail, as we examine a more complicated version of the Keynesian model.

Review of New Terms

Circular flow of income The real and money flows of resources and goods and services between firms and households.

Equilibrium income level The income level (not necessarily at full employment) at which producers have no reason to change their output level because leakages equal injections.

Full employment The employment level that occurs when the quantity of labor demanded equals the quantity of labor supplied at a competitive market-determined real wage rate.

Injection (inflow) An introduction of income into the circular flow.

Investment The purchase of capital goods—plant and equipment, residential structures, and changes in inventory—that can be used in the production of other goods and services.

Keynes's law The macroeconomic belief that "demand creates its own supply"—that is, that the demand for goods and services creates an equal production of these goods and services.

Leakage (outflow) A withdrawal of income from the circular flow.

Planned investment Anticipated, scheduled purchases of plant and equipment, residential homes, and inventory.

Real wage rate The nominal or money wage rate (the number of dollars a person earns per hour or day) adjusted for inflation or deflation. The real wage rate measures a worker's actual purchasing power.

Saving That portion of income not spent. Represents forgone expenditures on real goods and services.

Say's law The macroeconomic belief that supply creates its own demand—that is, that the production of a supply of goods and services creates an equal demand for goods and services.

Unplanned investment Unanticipated, unscheduled purchases of plant and equipment, residential construction, and inventory.

Review Questions

1. According to the classical model of the labor market (see Figures 10.1 and 10.2), how will a rapid rise in the price level affect employment? What will happen to the money wage rate? To the real wage rate? (◀ 1)

2. Suppose investment increases. What will happen to the equilibrium level of income, according to classical theory? According to Keynesian theory? (◢ 1, ◢ 2)

3. The graph below shows saving and investment as a function of the interest rate. Suppose the interest rate is held above the E_1 equilibrium at R_2. If the equilibrium income level falls, as Keynesian theory suggests it should, what will happen to saving? Why? (◢ 3)

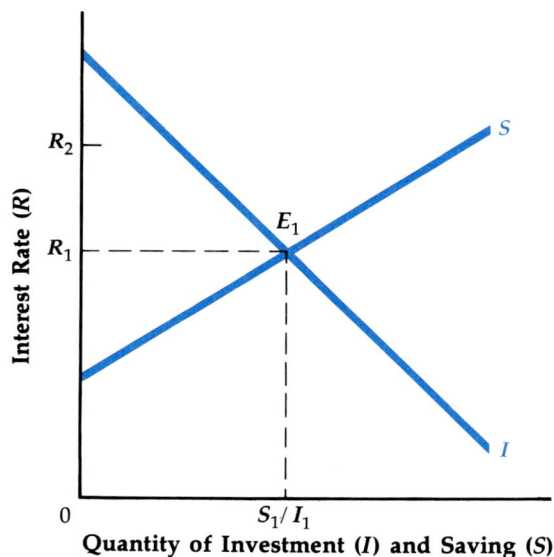

Quantity of Investment (I) and Saving (S)

4. Given the information in the graph for question 3, assume that the interest rate declines slowly when saving exceeds investment. Will the equilibrium income level fall by as much as if the interest rate were held rigidly at R_2? Explain your answer using both a graph and a circular flow diagram like the one in Figure 10.6. (◢ 2, ◢ 3)

5. Suppose that saving and investment are equal and the government runs a budgetary deficit. What will happen to the national income level in the Keynesian model? (◢ 4)

Unemployment and the Equilibrium Income Level: A More Complicated Model

It is too early to say, but it does not now appear an extravagant statement, that Keynes may in the end rival Adam Smith in his influence on the economic thinking and governmental policy of his time and age. Both lived at profound turning points in the evolution of the economic order. Both were products of their times. Yet both were also powerful agents in giving direction to the unfolding process of institutional change.
   Alvin Hansen

KEY QUESTIONS

◢ 1.   What is the planned investment and planned saving approach to income equilibrium?

◢ 2.   What is the total spending approach to income equilibrium?

◢ 3.   What effects do changes in planned total expenditures have on equilibrium income?

NEW TERMS

Consumption function
Contractionary (expansionary) gap
Dissaving
Frills multiplier (f)
Investment function
Marginal efficiency of investment (MEI)

Marginal propensity to consume
Marginal propensity to save
Multiplier (m)
Paradox of thrift
Potential GNP
Saving function
Simplest multiplier (m)
Total expenditure function

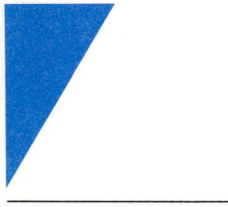

The circular flow model developed in the preceding chapter provided a broad picture of the Keynesian macroeconomy. The equilibrium national income level and its relationship to savings and consumer expenditures were only lightly sketched, however. While the model demonstrated the direction in which national income will move when planned saving and investment are unequal, it did not indicate the extent of the change.

This chapter attempts to add precision to the Keynesian analysis of how the national income and employment levels are determined. First we will develop more fully the concepts of planned (or desired) saving and investment and their role in determining the equilibrium national income level. Then we will examine national income from the perspective of total spending, using the concept of planned consumption. To keep the analysis simple, government will be excluded from the model. In the next chapter, however, we will reintroduce government in connection with the question of possible remedies for high unemployment and low production levels. We shall also assume in our Keynesian model that wages, prices, and interest rates are fixed and that we have a no-trade closed economy. Eventually all of these assumptions will be relaxed.

The Planned Investment and Saving Approach to Income Equilibrium

1. What is the planned investment and planned saving approach to income equilibrium?

Chapter 10 presented three essential conclusions of the governmentless Keynesian analysis. First, if the level of planned saving exceeds the level of planned investment during any given period, total spending on goods and services by households and firms will fall short of the national production level. Unable to sell all they have produced, firms will accumulate unplanned inventory and will eventually have to cut back on production. When production is curtailed, the national income level will fall. Because less is produced, total earnings (also called national income) must also be less.

Second, if planned investment expenditure exceeds planned saving, total spending for goods and services will exceed the quantity of goods and services produced. Production will fall short of sales, and inventory will dwindle to undesirably low levels. If some workers and other resources are unemployed, firms will hire them and expand production. The national income level will rise.

Third, when planned saving equals planned investment, the producing sector of the economy has no reason to expand or contract production. As long as planned saving and planned investment remain equal, the circular flow of income will remain constant and the macroeconomy will be at equilibrium, which may or may not be at full employment. We can now refine the Keynesian analysis by adding detail to these fundamental conclusions.

In formal national income accounting, investment includes expenditures on the production of new durable assets such as (1) equipment; (2) business, farm, or residential structures; and (3) expenditures on additions to inventories. Since additions by business to plant and equipment is far bigger (about two-thirds of total investment) than residential investment in new housing or business investment in stocks of goods for inventory, we focus on business spending.

The Investment Function

Marginal efficiency of investment (MEI): the expected yield or expected rate of net profit on additions to the capital stock or investment.

The planned investment expenditures of businesses on plant, equipment, and inventory are influenced by many variables, including the real interest rate; the national income level; expectations regarding the profitability of future production; government tax policies; the discovery of new ways of producing goods; and the development of new goods and services themselves. As we saw in Chapter 10, planned investment expenditures are likely to be directly related to the expected yield or expected rate of net profit on additions to the capital stock—called the **marginal efficiency of investment (MEI)**—and inversely related to anticipated real interest rates. The marginal efficiency of investment depends on the level of technology and innovation, the expected level of production (acquisition, maintenance, and operating) costs, taxes, the expected demand for the goods and services that the new investment will produce, and the existing stock of capital available to serve extant and future market demands.

The most important interest rate influencing investment is the expected real interest rate, which is equal to the expected nominal or market interest rate minus the expected rate of inflation. Thus, if the expected nominal rate is 10 percent, and the expected inflation rate is 4 percent, then the expected real rate of interest is 6 percent. Investment will rise as anticipated real interest rates fall and decline as anticipated real interest rates rise.

There are at least two possible explanations for the inverse relationship between investment and the real interest rate. First, when interest rates are low, firms are better able to justify borrowing to expand their plant and equipment. A larger number of investment projects will meet their profitability criteria when the cost of borrowed funds is relatively low. Second, a rise in interest rates may persuade some firms to postpone investment until interest rates decline again.

The level of planned business investment tends to increase or decrease along with the level of national income and with the utilization of the nation's productive capacity. During prosperous periods, when national income is on the rise, businesses are more profitable and thus have more funds on hand to invest. Many businesses will expand their facilities to meet the rising demand for their products. Furthermore, entrepreneurs tend to project present business conditions into the future. Their confidence in future investments rises in prosperous times and falls during depressed periods. Planned investment can therefore be expected to rise and fall with current economic conditions, for it represents plant and equipment that can be used only in the future.

The introduction of new technology can significantly affect the general level of planned investment. The development of the automobile, for instance, stimulated considerable investment in roads, service stations, tourist facilities, and assembly lines. In the future, solar and wind technologies may have a similar effect on the level and distribution of planned investment expenditure. Government tax policies also influence the profitability of current investment. An increase in business taxes will generally reduce planned investment, for firms will have less after-tax income to devote to new plant and equipment. The present stock of capital goods available is also important. In addition, if the cost of acquiring, operating or maintaining capital goods changes, this influences investment demand.

Investment function: the assumed relationship between national income and total planned expenditures on new equipment, construction, and inventory.

National income is probably one of the most important factors affecting investment. Its relationship to investment is called the investment function. The **investment function** is the assumed relationship between national income and total planned expenditures on new equipment, construction, and inventory. For the moment, however, we will assume that planned investment does not vary, not even with income. Keynes himself assumed that investment (I) was an *autonomous* expenditure, independent of national income (Y).[1] Later in our discussion we will discard this simplifying assumption of a constant level of planned investment expenditure and consider the effect of a change in interest rates or tax policy on investment and national income. For now, given our assumption, the investment function can be represented by a horizontal line, as in Figure 11.1(a), where planned investment is constant at I_1, or $400 billion.

The Saving Function

The level of saving is influenced by many variables. They include current and expected future interest rates on bonds and savings accounts; previous, current, and expected future income; the stock of assets, wealth, and durable goods; subjective tastes and preferences; income tax rates; the price

---

1. In this text the capital letter Y represents nominal or money national income at current dollars and lower case y represents real national income adjusted by price level changes.

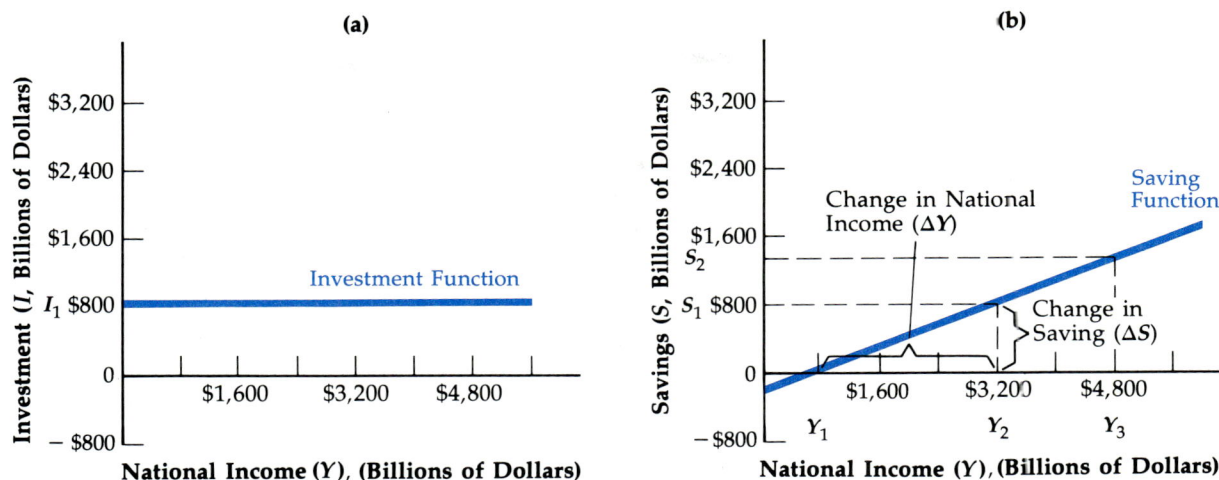

FIGURE 11.1 Planned Investment and Saving
If it is assumed that planned investment is completely autonomous and unaffected by the nominal national income level (Y), the investment function can be drawn as a horizontal line, as in part (a). Investment remains constant at I_1 at all income levels. If it is assumed that planned saving is directly related to national income, the saving function must be drawn as an upward-sloping curve, as in part (b). At an income level of Y_1, total saving is assumed to be zero. At income levels of Y_2 and Y_3, saving is S_1 and S_2, respectively.

level; levels of consumer credit and indebtedness; job security; levels of advertising by business; and current demand for goods and services (since saving is defined as the unspent portion of disposable income). High interest rates increase the relative price of current consumption, for a failure to save means forgoing relatively more future income. During times of rising interest rates, then, people tend to reduce their consumption, save more of their incomes, and postpone some spending.

When personal income rises, people are encouraged to buy more security (among other normal goods and services). People purchase security by adding to their savings, thus increasing their financial reserves for less advantageous times. Because personal and corporate income taxes significantly affect workers' take-home pay and firms' after-tax profits, tax rates have an indirect influence on personal saving and corporate dividends and investment. Planned saving generally moves in the opposite direction from taxes. As taxes rise, saving falls, and vice versa.

Expectations about future inflation rates and income levels also influence current planned saving. If people expect prices to rise sharply in the future, they will tend to buy more and save less now, to avoid relatively high future prices. If they expect their future income to drop significantly, they are likely to save more now, to build up the cash reserves they will need.

To keep the discussion simple, we will assume that except for income, all variables that influence the level of saving are given. Like Keynes, we will assume that planned saving varies directly with the national income level. In the aggregate, people will save a portion of any increase in their income. This tendency, known as the marginal propensity to save, can be stated as a ratio. The **marginal propensity to save** (*MPS*) is the percentage of any change in national income that consumers are inclined to save.

Marginal propensity to save: the percentage of any change in national income (ΔY) that consumers are inclined to save (ΔS), stated as a ratio, $MPS = \Delta S/\Delta Y$.

$$MPS = \frac{\text{change in saving } (S)}{\text{change in national income } (Y)} = \frac{\Delta S}{\Delta Y}$$

where Δ = change in

To illustrate, if the marginal propensity to save is 10 percent (*MPS* = 1/10), people as a group will be inclined to change their level of planned saving by 10 percent of any increase or decrease in their income. If their incomes rise by $100, they will be inclined to save $10 more than before (10 percent of $100). Likewise a $100 decrease in total income will reduce planned saving by $10. The higher the marginal propensity to save (say, 12 instead of 10 percent), the greater the change in planned saving that results from any given change in national income.

The upward-sloping curve in Figure 11.1(b) represents this assumed direct relationship between saving and income, called the saving function. The **saving function** is the assumed direct relationship between nominal national income (Y) and the amount of income saved (not spent on goods and services). As it is drawn, the saving function incorporates the assumption that there is some income level at which people save nothing—in Figure 11.1(b), level Y_1. The U.S. economy operated on the zero-saving income level for several years during the 1930s, when Americans as a group saved nothing. At income levels higher than Y_1, the planned saving level is positive—that is, people are adding to their financial assets. For instance, at an income level of Y_2, people plan to save a total of $800 billion ($S_1$). At an income level of Y_3, they plan to save $1,332 billion ($S_2$). When their income is less than Y_1, people engage in planned dissaving, also called negative saving. **Dissaving** is any net withdrawal from accumulated past savings, or any net increase in borrowing. For instance, in 1933 the U.S. economy had dissaving or negative saving of $1.6 billion. In Figure 11.1(b), at levels below Y_1, people as a group are withdrawing funds from their savings accounts or borrowing to meet their financial obligations. Regardless of the particular income and planned saving levels, the upward-sloping curve reflects the fundamental assumption that income and saving are directly related.[2]

Saving function: the assumed direct relationship between nominal national income and the amount of income saved (not spent on goods and services).

Dissaving: any net withdrawal from accumulated past savings, or any net increase in borrowing.

---

2. Geometrically, the slope of a curve like the planned saving function is equal to the opposite side of the triangle Y_1Y_2E divided by the adjacent side, or the change in S divided by the change in Y, which is also the marginal propensity to save. Letting Δ represent a (small) change, we can define

$$\text{slope of saving function} = \frac{\text{change in saving}}{\text{change in national income}} = \frac{\Delta S}{\Delta Y} = MPS$$

As the curve is drawn, the change in saving is substantially less than the change in income; the marginal propensity to save is much less than 1. In other words, people are assumed to save only a minor fraction of any change in income—an assumption supported by real-world experience.

The Equilibrium National Income Level

Potential GNP: the total amount of output that could be produced under full employment.

Contractionary gap: when actual GNP is less than potential (i.e., full employment) GNP.

Expansionary gap: when actual GNP is more than potential (i.e., full employment) GNP.

Equilibrium income means the only income that the economy will be able to sustain, in that there is a balance of forces consistent with the actions of demanders and suppliers. It does not necessarily mean full employment income. The total amount of output that could be produced under full employment is called **potential GNP** When actual and potential GNP differ, there is a GNP or income gap. When actual GNP is less than (more than) potential (i.e., full employment) GNP a **contractionary (expansionary) gap** exists. Gaps are only defined relative to full employment. Figure 11.2(a) shows both the saving and investment functions. Given the information summarized, we can determine that the economy will move toward an equilibrium national income level of Y_2, of $3,200 billion at point E.

Suppose the economy is generating an income of Y_3, or $4,800 billion. Planned investment will be at its assumed constant level of I_1, or $800 billion, but planned saving will be at the higher level of S_2. Rather than purchasing all Y_3 goods, then, people will be saving part of their income,

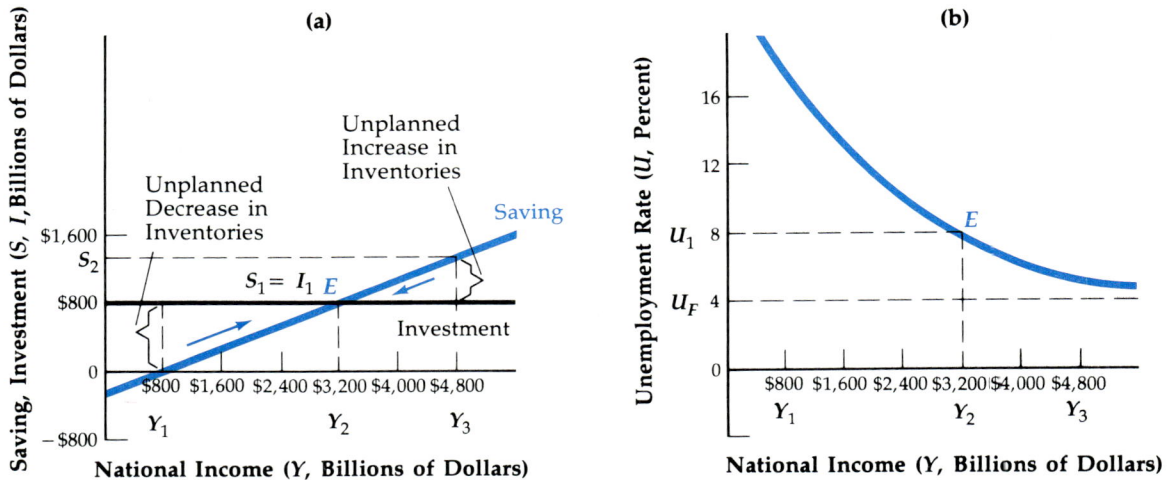

(a)

(b)

FIGURE 11.2   Determining the National Income: The Planned Investment and Saving Approach

In part (a) the equilibrium national income level is Y_2, or $3,200 billion, the point where planned saving equals planned investment at E. At national income levels above Y_2, saving will exceed investment, the national income level will fall and there will be an unplanned increase in inventories. At national income levels lower than Y_2, planned investment will exceed planned saving, the national income level will rise and there will be an unplanned decrease in inventories.

The equilibrium income level may or may not be the full-employment income level. In part (b), the equilibrium income level corresponds to an unemployment rate of 8 percent. If the full employment level of national income was $3,200, then at $2,400, there would be an expansionary gap; at $4,000, there would be a contractionary gap.

causing a gap between planned saving and investment. At an income level of Y_3, firms will produce more than they will sell. They will pile up unplanned additions to inventory, and at some point will have to cut back on production, thus reducing total income.

This reduction in total income will reduce planned saving. As Figure 11.2(a) shows, the movement back from Y_3 will eventually make up the difference between planned saving and investment. At Y_2 the two will be equal. Once at Y_2, firms may try to expand production. If they do, planned saving will increase and unplanned investment (inventory) will again pile up, causing firms to move back toward Y_2 again.

If, on the other hand, the economy is operating below Y_2—say at Y_1— firms in the aggregate will have an incentive to expand production. At Y_1, planned saving is zero, but planned investment is at the higher level of I_1. Consumers are intentionally spending all they earn, but still firms want to buy additional capital goods. The total spending of households and investors is greater than the level of production. To satisfy the excess demand for goods and services, firms must produce more. In the process they will increase household income; assuming a positive marginal propensity to save, the level of saving will rise with the increase in income. Eventually planned saving will reach the level of planned investment (assumed to remain constant). This will happen at the national income level of Y_2, or $3,200 billion. At any point in time, actual saving (planned + unplanned), will always, by definition, be equal to actual (planned + unplanned) investment. Equilibrium is not required to reach that equality. In contrast, equilibrium requires that planned saving equals planned investment. When they are equal, and only when they are equal, there will be equilibrium.

This previous numerical example illustrates a basic point of Keynesian economics. There is some income level toward which the economy will gravitate, and at which it will tend to remain unless economic conditions change. This income level may or may not be the full-employment income level. Given an equilibrium level of $3,200, if the full employment level of national income was at, say, $1,600, there would be an expansionary gap; if it were at, say, $4,800 there would be a contractionary gap.

As more goods and services are produced, more resources, including workers, are needed for production. As national income rises, therefore, the unemployment rate falls. In Figure 11.2(b), the equilibrium at point E is associated with a national income level Y_2 that corresponds to an unemployment rate of U_1 (8 percent). That rate is higher than the lowest possible unemployment rate, U_F, or 4 percent here.[3]

Here Keynesians depart from the classical notion that the economy will continue to move toward the minimum unemployment level. According to classical theory, if unemployment rises above that minimum rate, a reduc-

---

3. At any moment, some workers will be changing jobs. Therefore many economists do not believe that unemployment will ever fall below 4 percent. The 1978 Humphrey-Hawkins or Full Employment and Balanced Growth Act considered 4 percent unemployment as full employment. Many do not believe that an unemployment rate below 6 percent can be sustained.

tion in wage rates will cause the national income level to rise and unemployment to fall. Keynesians, on the other hand, stress that the economy may fail to achieve full employment in the short run because households are saving too much and consuming too little—or because firms are not investing enough.

The Total Spending Approach to Income Equilibrium

▲ 2. What is the total spending approach to income equilibrium?

Another way to arrive at the equilibrium-level national income is through the equation of national output with national income.[4] In the preceding section we noted that when the equilibrium income level is achieved, planned saving (an outflow from the circular flow of income) is equal to planned investment (an inflow to the circular flow).

planned saving = planned investment

or

planned outflow = planned inflow

Chapter 10 showed that when saving equals investment, total planned expenditures by households and firms exactly equal national output. That is, the equilibrium national income level is achieved when firms sell in the aggregate exactly what they have produced.

total planned expenditures = national output

With all firms selling exactly what they produce, business has no reason either to expand or to contract production.

These two different conditions for equilibrium are mathematically consistent. We know that nominal national income (Y) is a mirror image of national output. National income is simply a reflection of what is produced in the economy, for without production there is no income. Furthermore, in our simple model, from which government has been excluded, households can do only two things with their income. They can use it for planned consumption (C) or for planned saving (S). Therefore income must equal consumption plus planned saving:

$$Y = C + S$$

If planned saving is equal to planned investment ($S = I$), we can rewrite this equation to read:

$$Y = C + I$$

Because national income and output measure the same thing, and since in our model consumption and saving make up total planned spending, the

4. Remember that for simplification, we are assuming (1) no government so there are no taxes or transfer payments and (2) no depreciation, interest payments, foreign trade, or retained earnings.

equations above mean that when planned saving and planned investment are equal, total national output equals total planned expenditure (*TPE*):

$$Y = C + I = C + S = TPE$$

In an economy at equilibrium, then, what is produced by firms is bought either by consumers (as consumer goods) or by businesses (as investment goods).

Thus the equilibrium national income level can be discussed in terms of the forces that determine total planned expenditures. That is the approach Keynes himself emphasized. His theory was built on three relatively simple propositions. First, he argued that the nominal national income level (*Y*) depends on the level of total planned expenditures (*TPE*). That is, the amount of goods and services produced in the economy, and therefore the amount of income earned, depends on the amount of goods and services households and firms in the aggregate want to buy. Second, as we have just demonstrated, the equilibrium income level is the point at which total planned expenditures equal national income. Third, he assumed that prices were given and constant in the economy, so that aggregate demand intersects with the horizontal aggregate supply to determine equilibrium output and income.

The Consumption and Investment Functions

Like planned saving, households' planned consumption expenditures, or total demands, are influenced by a number of variables. Among them are the interest rates people receive on their savings; personal wealth; the expected rate of inflation; income taxes; and the current and expected future national income level. Interest rates are likely to be inversely related to planned consumption expenditures. As interest rates rise, people will be inclined to save more and borrow less in order to buy things like furniture and cars. Expected inflation has the opposite effect. If people expect the inflation rate to increase, they are likely to buy more now, to avoid paying higher prices in the future. If income tax rates rise, on the other hand, people will reduce their planned consumption expenditures, for they will have less after-tax income to spend. Finally, an increase in the national income level is likely to increase planned consumption expenditures, simply because more income will enable people to satisfy more of their wants.

Among these variables, special attention must be paid to national income, whose relationship to consumption demand is called the consumption function. The **consumption function** is the assumed direct relationship between the national income level and the planned or desired consumption expenditures of households. Keynesians make three intuitively plausible assumptions about the consumption function.

First, as income rises, planned consumption expenditures will rise by a lesser amount. That is, people will not spend all of their extra income; they will save part of it. This inclination of consumers to spend only part of an increase in their income is called the marginal propensity to consume. The **marginal propensity to consume (*MPC*)** is the percentage of any change in

Consumption function: the assumed direct relationship between the national income level and the planned or desired consumption expenditures of households.

Marginal propensity to consume (*MPC*): the percentage of any change in income (ΔY) that consumers are inclined to spend (ΔC). Stated as a ratio, $MPC = \Delta C/\Delta Y$.

income that consumers are inclined to spend. Like the marginal propensity to save, the marginal propensity to consume can be expressed as a ratio.

$$MPC = \frac{\text{change in consumption}}{\text{change in national income}} = \frac{\Delta C}{\Delta Y}$$

If the marginal propensity to consume is 90 percent, for instance ($MPC = 9/10$), consumers will be inclined to spend 90 percent of any change in their income. If national income rises (or falls) by $100, planned consumption expenditures will rise (or fall) by $90. (The actual figure for MPC in the United States is about 90 to 95 percent.)

The marginal propensity to consume and the marginal propensity to save are complementary concepts. Indeed, in our simplified model, whatever portion of an increase in income consumers do not spend, they must save, for $Y = C + S$. If the marginal propensity to save is 0.10, therefore, the marginal propensity to consume must be 0.90. Together, $MPC + MPS = 1$.

Second, Keynesians assume that there is some national income level—a very low one—at which consumers will plan to spend all the income they earn. At that level, consumers may simply be unable to save; they may have to spend everything they earn for subsistence.

Third, at even lower national income levels, consumers will plan to spend more than they earn—to dissave. If people's income levels are seriously depressed for a short period, they will withdraw funds from their savings accounts to meet their current obligations. If collectively people plan to spend more than they are earning, in effect they are planning to buy more goods than are currently being produced. (Income and output must always be equal.) For a while firms will be able to meet the excess demand by reducing their inventories. Consumption expenditures cannot exceed income indefinitely, however; firms will eventually run out of inventory.

Figure 11.3(a) shows the upward-sloping consumption function curve, which summarizes graphically the relationship between the national income level and household consumption expenditures. The 45-degree line with a slope of 1 is drawn for convenience. At any point on this 45-degree line the values of consumption are equal to the values of national income. At a national income level of $800 billion ($Y_1$), the consumption level is also $800 billion ($C_1$). This is the income level at which people spend all they earn. At a higher income level, $3,200 billion ($Y_2$), the consumption level is also higher, $2,400 billion. The increase in consumption expenditures ($1,600 billion) is less than the increase in national income that caused it ($2,400 billion). As we saw above, the marginal propensity to consume is less than 1—in this case, 2/3.

$$MPC = \frac{\Delta C}{\Delta Y} = \frac{\$1,600}{\$2,400} = \frac{2}{3}$$

At all national income levels over $800 billion ($Y_1$), consumers in the aggregate will save some part of their income. The 45-degree line that extends out of the origin shows what the consumption function curve would look like if consumers spent all they earned. At a national income

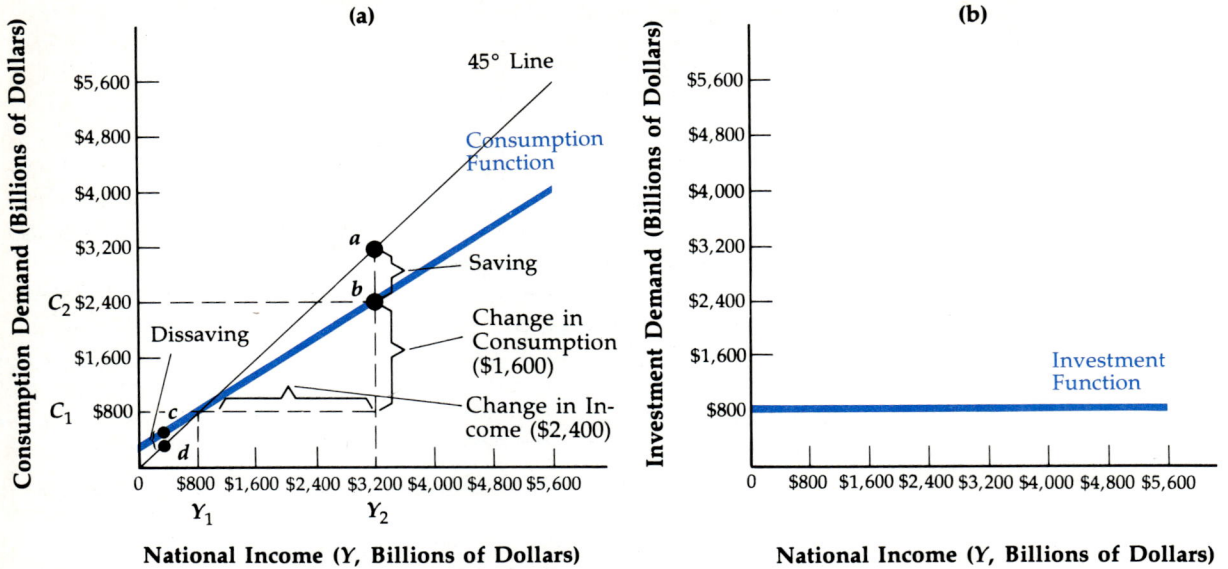

(a)

(b)

FIGURE 11.3   Planned Consumption and Investment

Assuming that household consumption expenditures are directly related to national income, the consumption function may be drawn as an upward-sloping curve. The 45-degree line with a slope of 1 is drawn for convenience. At any point on this line the values of consumption are equal to the values of national income. At national income level Y_1, consumers are spending all they earn and saving nothing. At higher income levels consumption rises, but not as much as national income does. Consumers, in other words, are saving part of their income. For example, at a national income level of $3,200 billion, the consumption level is $2,400 billion; saving is $800 billion, or the distance between points a and b. Dissaving occurs at income levels below Y_1. Investment—part (b)—is assumed to be constant at $800 billion.

level of $3,200 billion, for instance, $3,200 billion would be spent. If consumers are spending only $2,400 billion at an income level of $3,200 billion, they must be saving the rest, namely $800 billion. This planned level of saving is represented in the figure by the vertical distance between points a and b. At higher national income levels, the vertical gap between the consumption function and the 45-degree line is larger, and the level of planned saving is greater. The growth of saving is consistent with our definition of the saving function, which specifies that the level of consumer saving is directly related to national income.

At national income levels below Y_1, the consumption function curve lies above the 45-degree line. Consumption exceeds the national income level. Consumers are spending more than they are earning, drawing down their savings accounts to meet current expenses. The amount of their dissaving is equal to the vertical distance between the 45-degree line and the consumption function. For example, at a national income level of $400 billion, the planned level of dissaving is $132 billion, or the vertical distance between points c and d in the graph. If consumers are spending more than they earn at these low income levels, they must be buying more than is currently being produced. Businesses must also be drawing down their inventories to meet consumer demand.

According to our simplified model of the macroeconomy, planned investment and consumption are the only components of total spending ($TPE = C + I$). We have already discussed investment demand; nothing more need be added here. For the moment, we continue to assume that planned investment does not vary with national income. We can therefore represent the investment function as a horizontal line, as in Figure 11.3(b)

The Equilibrium National Income Level

We have demonstrated that equilibrium in national income and employment is established where total planned expenditures equal national income (or output). In our model, total planned spending is composed of two variables, planned consumption and planned investment expenditures. To describe total planned spending graphically, therefore, we must add the investment function from Figure 11.3(b) to the consumption function of Figure 11.3(a). The resulting combined curve, shown in Figure 11.4(a), represents the total expenditure function. The total expenditure function is the relationship of total planned expenditures to national income. This is normally assumed to be a direct relationship.

Total expenditure function: the relationship of total planned expenditures to national income, normally assumed to be a direct relationship.

In Figure 11.4(a), the line labeled $C + I$ is the total expenditure function. It is the graphical summation of the consumption function curve, C, which lies slightly below it, and the horizontal investment function curve. Investment demand is represented by the vertical difference between the consumption function curve, C, and the total expenditure function curve, $C + I$. The vertical space between the two curves, $800 billion, is equal to the value of the investment demand curve in Figure 11.3(b).

Given the total expenditures curve in Figure 11.4(a), we can deduce that the equilibrium national income level is $3,200 billion—the point where the $C + I$ curve crosses the 45-degree line. At that income level (Y_2), consumers will buy $2,400 billion worth of goods and services (that is, their consumption demand will be C_1) and firms will buy $800 billion worth of plant, equipment, and inventory. Total expenditures will equal national income at $3,200 billion.

$$TPE = \$3,200 \text{ billion} = Y$$

Consumers and firms will be buying all that is produced.

If the economy is producing either more or less, it will move toward a level of $3,200 billion. For instance, suppose the national income level is $5,600 billion ($Y_3$). Consumers in the aggregate plan to buy $4,000 billion worth of goods and services (C_2). Businesses plan to buy $800 billion worth.

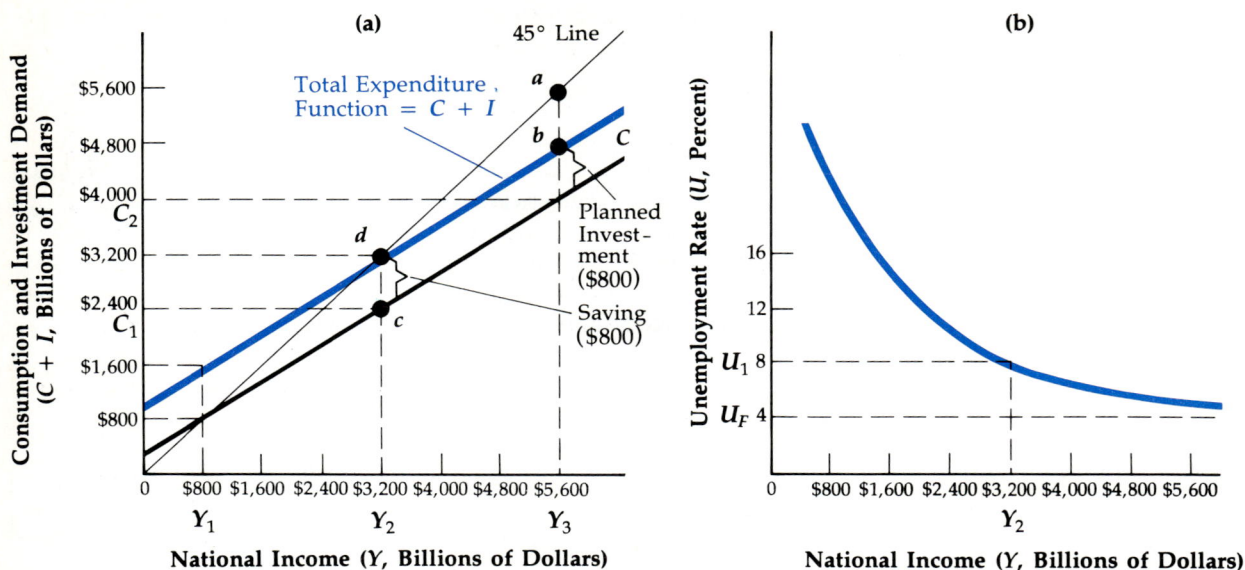

FIGURE 11.4 Determining the National Income Level: The Total Spending Approach
The equilibrium national income level is Y_2, or $3,200 billion, the point where consumption plus investment or total expenditures equals national income. At income levels above Y_2, not all that is produced will be bought. At income levels below Y_2, consumers and businesses will want to buy more goods and services than are produced.
      In part (b), the equilibrium income level corresponds to the unemployment rate U_1 (8 percent).

Total planned spending by consumers and firms will therefore equal only $4,800 billion, or $800 billion less than is being produced. As long as firms continue to produce $5,600 billion worth of output and to sell only $4,800 billion worth, unwanted inventory (unplanned investment) will accumulate. The vertical distance between points *a* and *b* represents this $800 billion of unwanted inventory.

Instead of continually adding to their inventories, firms will at some point reduce their production levels. When they do, the national income level will fall, and planned consumer expenditures will fall with it, although not by as much as national income. If national income initially exceeds total planned spending and falls faster than consumption demand, at some point it must become equal to total demand for goods and services ($C + I$). This equality is achieved, as stated above, at a national income level of $3,200 billion ($Y_2$).

If the national income level is below Y_2, it will rise until it reaches that level. Suppose firms in the aggregate are generating only $800 billion worth of goods and services. At that income level, Y_1 in Figure 11.4(a), consumers are inclined to spend $800 billion and businesses are inclined to spend another $800 billion. Obviously total planned spending will exceed the quantity of goods and services produced.

$$TPE = C + I = \$800 \text{ billion} + \$800 \text{ billion} = \$1,600 \text{ billion}$$

To satisfy this high level of demand, firms must draw down their inventories and/or expand production. At some point they are likely to exhaust their inventories and will have to expand production. When they do, more national income will be generated, increasing planned consumption. If demand at first exceeds production, but production (national income) rises faster than planned consumer expenditures, at some point producers will be able to meet total demand. Again, the national income level at which they will be able to do this is Y_2, or $3,200 billion.

Note that Y_2 is the equilibrium income level arrived at by the saving-investment approach described in Figure 11.2. At Y_2, planned saving is equal to planned investment. That fact can be seen in Figure 11.4 as well. At Y_2, the vertical distance between the C and $C + I$ curves is the planned investment level ($800 billion). The vertical distance between point c on the C curve and point d on the 45-degree line is the planned saving level ($800 billion). If both investment and saving are $800 billion, then planned saving is equal to planned investment. Figures 11.2(a) and 11.4(a) are both representations of the same Keynesian model, then, each emphasizing a different aspect of the model.

As Figure 11.4(b) shows, the equilibrium national income level (Y_2) is consistent with an unemployment rate of 8 percent (U_1). That is higher than the assumed minimum unemployment rate (U_F) of 4 percent, which can be achieved at a higher production level. Before more is produced, firms and consumers must be inclined to buy more. Thus Keynesian analysis concludes that national income and employment depend on the level of total planned expenditures. In the classical model, unemployment results principally from shifts in the supply and demand for labor and from labor market obstructions to wage adjustments. In the Keynesian model, unemployment is caused by insufficient demand.

The information shown in Figure 11.4 can also be expressed in tabular form. Column 1 of Table 11.1 lists some possible national income levels, from $0 to $5,600 billion. Column 2 shows consumption, reflecting the three Keynesian assumptions described in Chapter 10. At an income level of $0, planned consumption is $266 billion—more than income. At an income level of $800 billion, consumption equals income. Above $800 billion in income, consumption falls short of income. Thus, below $800 billion, consumers are dissaving; above it they are saving (column 3).

Under our simplifying assumption, planned investment is held constant at $800 billion for all income levels (column 4). Total planned expenditures is shown in column 5. By comparing it with column 1, we see that equilibrium with national income is achieved at an output of $3,200 billion. At income levels above $3,200 billion, total planned expenditures fall short of total output. Below $3,200 billion, expenditures exceed output.

National Income (Y) (1)	Consumption (C) (2)	Saving (+) or Dissaving (−) (S) (3)	Investment Expenditures (I) (4)	Total Planned Expenditures (TPE) (5)
$ 0	$ 266	$− 266	$800	$1,066
400	532	− 132	800	1,332
800	800	0	800	1,600
1,200	1,066	+ 134	800	1,866
1,600	1,334	+ 266	800	2,134
2,000	1,600	+ 400	800	2,400
2,400	1,866	+ 534	800	2,666
2,800	2,134	+ 666	800	2,934
3,200	2,400	+ 800	800	3,200
3,600	2,666	+ 934	800	3,466
4,000	2,934	+1,066	800	3,734
4,400	3,200	+1,200	800	4,000
4,800	3,466	+1,334	800	4,266
5,200	3,734	+1,466	800	4,534
5,600	4,000	+1,600	800	4,800

TABLE 11.1 National Income Equilibrium (in billions of dollars)

Changes in Total Planned Expenditures

▲ **3. What effects do changes in planned total expenditures have on equilibrium income?**

If, with no government and no foreign trade, the levels of planned investment and consumption determine the equilibrium national income level, then changes in the levels of planned investment and consumption will produce a different equilibrium income level. This section discusses the rather complicated effects that changes in planned investment and consumption can have on the equilibrium national income level.

Changes in Planned Investment

In the simplest Keynesian model, investment is assumed to be fixed and independent of the interest rate, which is also fixed. All investment is said to be autonomous or independent of national income. In truth, a change in any of the forces that influence investment decisions—real interest rates, the national income level, expectations regarding the profitability of future production, and so forth—can change the planned level of investment and thus national income. Consider the assumed inverse relationship between the market interest rate and the planned level of investment, shown by the downward-sloping curve ID_1 in Figure 11.5. If the interest rate is initially R_3, planned investment will be I_1. If this level of planned investment is constant, it can be represented by the planned investment curve I_1 in Figure 11.6(b). That level of investment corresponds to an equilibrium national income level of Y_2 (part (a) of Figure 11.6) and an unemployment rate of U_2 (part (c) of Figure 11.6).

If the interest rate falls to R_2 in Figure 11.5, the level of planned investment will rise to I_2 in Figure 11.6(b). Total planned expenditures will rise to $C + I_2$ in Figure 11.6(a). At the initial income level of Y_1, total planned expenditures $(C + I_2)$ will exceed output. In simple terms, firms will face a greater demand for goods and services than they can satisfy with current production schedules. Given this excess demand, firms will expand production, employing more workers and causing the unemployment rate to fall. Household incomes will rise, and people will save more. Eventually the economy will move toward the new equilibrium income level Y_2, where planned saving and investment are once again equal (Figure 11.6(b)). The new lower unemployment rate of U_1 is still above the minimum employment rate, however (Figure 11.6(c)).

If investment depends on the interest rate, and income and unemployment on investment, it follows that each interest rate in Figure 11.5 is related to a specific income and unemployment level in Figure 11.6. The minimum level of unemployment (U_F, the full-employment rate) will not be achieved until the equilibrium income reaches a much higher level than Y_2. Thus investment must rise higher than I_2, and the interest rate must fall lower than R_2, to achieve the full employment rate U_F.

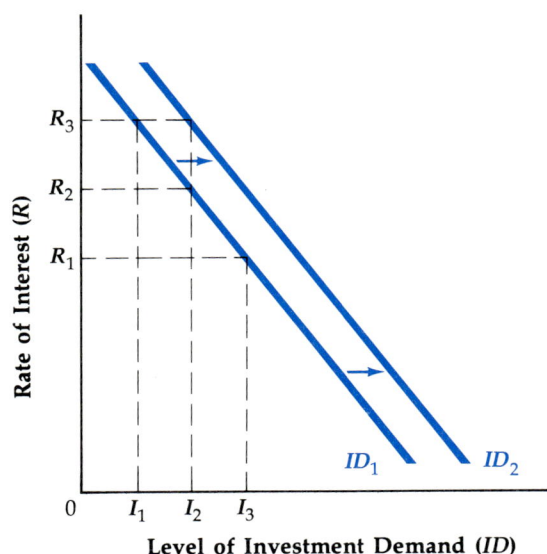

FIGURE 11.5 The Effect of Interest Rates (R) on Planned Investment Demand (ID)
Planned investment is inversely related to the rate of interest firms have to pay on borrowed money. If the interest rate falls from R_3 to R_2, the level of planned investment will rise from I_1 to I_2. An outward shift in the investment demand curve has the same effect. If the interest rate remains constant at R_3 but the investment demand curve shifts from ID_1 to ID_2, the level of investment will rise from I_1 to I_2.

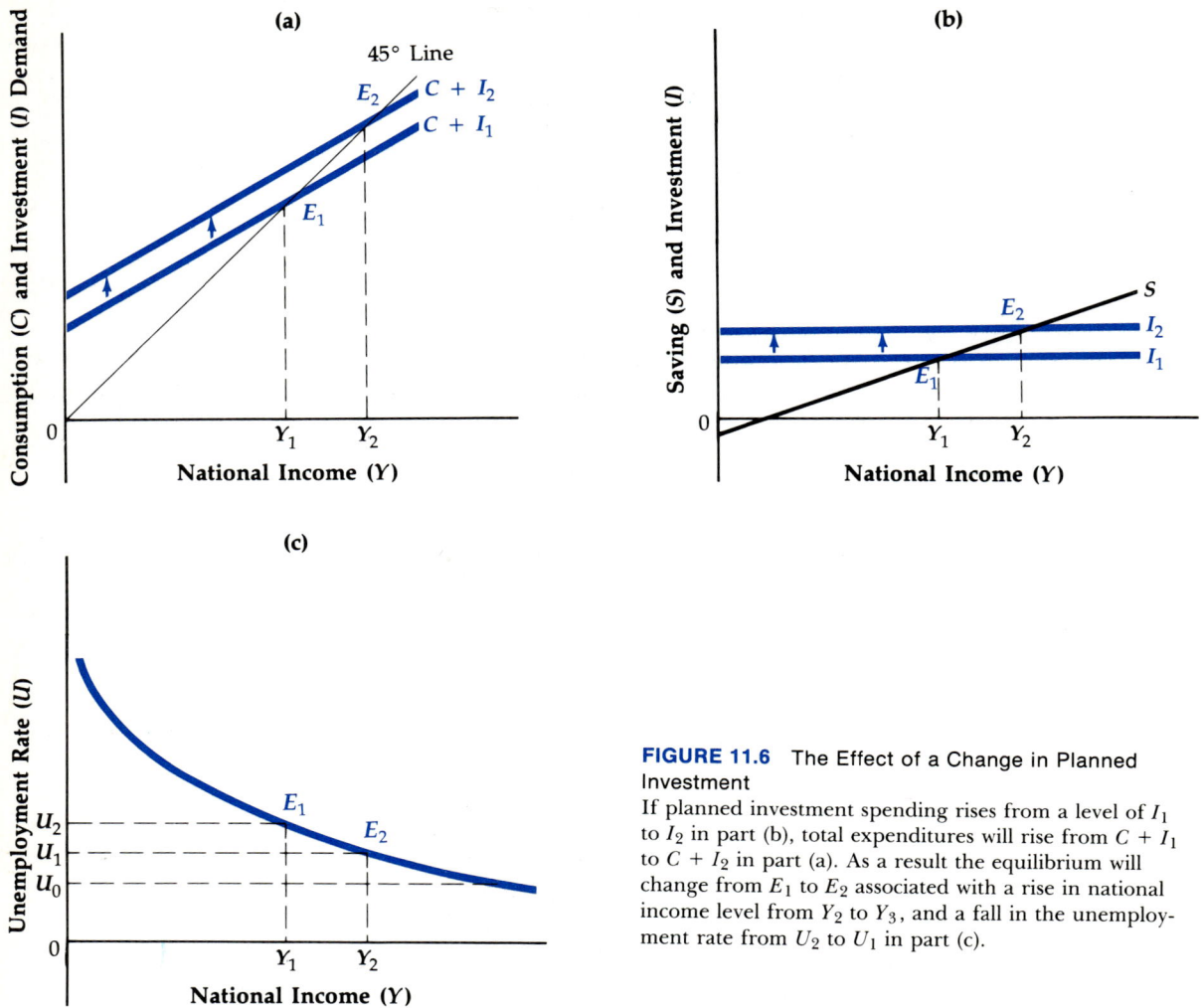

(a)

(b)

(c)

FIGURE 11.6 The Effect of a Change in Planned Investment
If planned investment spending rises from a level of I_1 to I_2 in part (b), total expenditures will rise from $C + I_1$ to $C + I_2$ in part (a). As a result the equilibrium will change from E_1 to E_2 associated with a rise in national income level from Y_2 to Y_3, and a fall in the unemployment rate from U_2 to U_1 in part (c).

An upward shift in the investment demand curve in Figure 11.5 can have an effect similar to a reduction in the interest rate. Such a shift might be caused by an increase in the expected profitability of an investment, perhaps because of an increase in the productivity of capital goods or a reduction in property taxes. If investment demand shifts from curve ID_1 to curve ID_2, for instance, and the interest rate remains constant at R_3, the level of planned investment will rise from I_1 to I_2. The equilibrium income level will rise from Y_1 to Y_2 in Figure 11.6(a), and unemployment will drop from U_2 to U_1 (Figure 11.6(c)).

A reduction in the level of planned investment expenditures—say, from I_2 to I_1—will have exactly the opposite effect. The equilibrium income level will fall and the unemployment rate will rise. The level of planned investment can be reduced through either an increase in the interest rate or a downward shift in the investment demand curve in Figure 11.5.

As the economy moves toward a new equilibrium income level, a peculiar phenomenon occurs. In Figure 11.6, planned investment expenditures increase by the difference between I_2 and I_1, but the national income level increases a great deal more—by the difference between Y_1 and Y_2. In fact, the increase in national income is *three times* the increase in planned investment. The explanation of this phenomenon involves one of the most significant contributions of Keynesian analysis, the concept of the multiplier.

The Multiplier

Multiplier (m): the ratio of the final change in national income to the initial change in total planned expenditures that stimulated it:

$$m = \frac{\text{final change in } Y}{\text{initial change in } TPE}$$
$$= \frac{\Delta Y}{\Delta TPE}$$

Simply stated, the **multiplier (m)** is the ratio of the final change in equilibrium national income to the initial change in total planned expenditures that stimulated it:

$$m = \frac{\text{final change in } Y}{\text{initial change in } TPE} = \frac{\Delta Y}{\Delta TPE}$$

Thus, m is the numerical coefficient expressing how much final equilibrium national income will change as a result of an initial change in autonomous or exogenous spending. It is always greater than 1 because any initial change, whether positive or negative, in planned spending induces further changes in consumption.

In the example just given, the change in total planned expenditures is simply the change in planned investment. The concept of the multiplier is applicable to *any* change in total planned expenditures, however—to consumer and government spending as well as to planned investment. A multiplier of 3 means that the national income level will rise (or fall) eventually by three times the increase (or decrease) in total planned autonomous spending—whether the change in *TPE* is due to a change in investment, in consumer demand for goods and services, or in government demand for goods and services. Rearranged slightly, the equation reads:

$$\text{change in } Y = m \times \text{change in } TPE \text{ or } \Delta Y = m \times \Delta TPE$$

The formula for the multiplier is derived as follows. We know that at the initial equilibrium income level of Y_2, planned saving and investment are equal. We also know that planned saving and investment must again be equal at the new equilibrium income level of Y_3. Therefore any increase in planned autonomous investment that causes firms to produce more must eventually be matched by an equal increase in planned saving. If planned autonomous investment goes up by $10 billion, for instance, causing a movement away from the equilibrium income level, a new equilibrium level will not be reached until planned saving has also risen by $10 billion.

If we know the marginal propensity to save, we can figure the increase in national income from the increase in saving. Suppose the marginal propensity to save is one-third (that is, people will save one-third of any change in their incomes). We can predict that income will rise by three times the change in saving. If planned saving must rise by $10 billion in order to equal planned investment, then national income must rise by $30 billion. At

DIALOGUE
A Keynesian Explanation of the Great Depression

In 1929, along with much of the rest of the world, the United States began to slide into the worst depression in its history. In that year the gross national product totaled $103 billion. By 1933, at the bottom of the Great Depression, GNP had fallen to $56 billion. During the intervening four years, practically all prices fell sharply. After adjustment for price reductions, the nation's measured output level fell by 31 percent. At the same time unemployment rose to 25 percent of the civilian labor force. Many more people who were underemployed as part-time workers were not counted in the unemployment statistics. The level of private business investment plummeted from $16 billion in 1929 to a little over $1 billion in 1933. The nation was wearing out its plant and equipment faster than it was replacing them. The stock market crashed. At the peak of the boom in 1929, the total dollar value of stocks listed on the New York Stock Exchange was $90 billion. At the bottom of the market collapse three years later, it was $15 billion—83 percent less.

What caused it all? Keynesian economists point to the decrease in demand, particularly consumption and investment demand, that began in the late 1920s. In the first half of the decade, the demand for plant and equipment had been bolstered by several factors. The First World War had left much of Europe's industrial and agricultural plant and equipment in ruin. European nations looked to the United States for many of the capital goods and consumer products they could not supply themselves. Moreover there was a backlog of domestic demand for new and improved housing and consumer goods of all kinds because during the war the United States had given priority to the production of war-related goods. Many industries had to expand and retool to meet this shift in domestic demand.

Third, during the 1920s the use of the automobile expanded considerably, and new products such as the radio, the electric stove, and the refrigerator became part of the American way of life. The demand for these new products created a demand for increased capital in the expanding

industries that produced them. Finally, people were caught up in a wave of optimism. Some people believed the stock market would continue to rise indefinitely—and planned their expenditures accordingly. Businesses, ignoring a deterioration in underlying economic conditions, continued to base investment decisions on an assumption of sustained growth in demand and profit.

By the middle of the decade, however, most European industries had rebuilt and were able to satisfy their region's demand for many consumer products and capital goods. At the same time the productive capacity of many American industries had caught up with the backlog in consumer demand. In some industries, capacity had obviously been overextended. Table 11.2 shows the pattern in the housing industry. The construction of new housing fell from its 1925 peak of 937,000 units to 509,000 units in 1929—a drop of 46 percent. Until 1928 this decline in residential construction was more than offset by the rise in nonresidential construction. In 1929, however, total construction declined significantly, and purchases of automobiles and electrical appliances fell too.

All these downward trends in demand caused a significant drop in investment demand during the late 1920s. If productive capacity had caught up with consumer demand, there was no need for

---

TABLE 11.2 Urban Residential Construction in the United States, 1920–1929

Year	Dwelling Units	Year	Dwelling Units
1920	247,000	1925	937,000
1921	449,000	1926	849,000
1922	716,000	1927	810,000
1923	871,000	1928	753,000
1924	893,000	1929	509,000

Source: U.S. Bureau of the Census, *Historical Statistics of the United States* (Washington, D.C.: U.S. Government Printing Office, 1975), p. 393.

further investment, either in production or in new plant and equipment. According to Keynesian theory, such a reduction in planned investment will lead to a reduction in production, and thus to lower incomes and further reductions in consumer demand. Through the multiplier process, the economy headed downward into the Great Depression.

Thus the stock market collapse did not cause the Great Depression. The drastic fall in stock prices merely reflected investors' sudden recognition that the economic boom of the twenties was over—but the Great Crash, as it was called, worsened the problem. It dramatically shattered business confidence, causing a further decline in business investment. It also substantially reduced many people's personal wealth. To rebuild their lost security, Americans had to try to save more in times that were already hard. Even those with income resisted buying consumer goods out of fear that the Depression would eventually touch them. Consumers' reductions in planned expenditures also contributed to the downward spiral. Many banks collapsed, causing a sharp reduction in the money supply and the demand for goods based on credit. Finally, because of the growing riskiness of loaning money, interest rates rose to historically high levels, further suppressing investment. Given all these calamities, one might wonder why the Depression, which imposed considerable hardship on many Americans, was not even more severe.

Non-Keynesian Explanations of the Great Depression

Explaining the Great Depression of 1929 to 1939 remains one of the unfinished tasks of modern economics. At one time Keynesian explanations held sway (see previous box). In the last twenty-five years or so, however, various non-Keynesian explanations have been gaining adherents.

In *A Monetary History of the United States, 1867–1960,* probably the most influential book on macroeconomics published since Keynes's *General Theory,* Milton Friedman and Anna Jacobson Schwartz put forth the hypothesis that a severe contraction of the supply of money caused the Great Depression. Between August 1929 and March 1933 the nation's stock of money fell by over a third, the largest decline in U.S. history. The short-run effect of the massive monetary contraction was the contraction of real output and employment. The Great Depression, then, was a monetary phenomenon. If there is a villain in the Friedman and Schwartz story, it is the Federal Reserve Board, which allowed the precipitous drop in the stock of money.

Another explanation for the Great Depression is that real wages were too high. In the standard supply and demand framework, unemployment occurs when the wage rate is above equilibrium. The unemployment disappears when the wage falls to its equilibrium level. With the onset of the recession in 1929, unemployment began to rise. Instead of allowing the wage rate to fall, however, the government and labor unions worked to keep money wages at their 1929 level. Indeed, President Hoover called in leading industrialists and extracted pledges from them to maintain money wages. Money wages eventually fell, but not rapidly enough to prevent mass unemployment. Furthermore, from 1934 on real wages rose despite substantial unemployment. Similar policies were

Non-Keynesian Explanations of the Great Depression
continued

continued under President Roosevelt. Although the aim of such policies was to keep up consumer spending, the unintended result may have been the high rates of unemployment of the 1930s.

One of the more puzzling aspects of the Depression was its length. Previous recessions had been followed by rapid expansions and recoveries. The expansions of the thirties failed to regain the ground lost during the contractions. Unemployment remained unbelievably high. Why were the 1930s different from (say) the 1890s or the 1980s? One possible difference is that the 1930s were subject to the New Deal. The set of policies instituted to end the Depression may well have inadvertently prolonged it. The New Deal failed to generate sufficient macroeconomic expansion, while at the same time it saddled the economy with massive microeconomic interferences.[1] In other words, it handicapped the market's ability to

respond to economic forces without providing a sufficient substitute for markets.

Some students of the period believe that the Smoot-Hawley Tariff of 1931 and corresponding measures in other countries might be the key to the Depression.[2] The Great Depression, it must be remembered, occurred throughout the Western world. Its long duration may have been due to the collapse of world trade as one nation after another put up protectionist trade barriers. The retreat from relatively free trade could have produced a downward "multiplier" effect on the world economy. The volume of world trade declined dramatically after 1929. The adjustments and cutbacks following such a massive dislocation of productive activity could well have generated the world's longest depression.

Other explanations for the Great Depression exist. Indeed, there are almost as many explanations as economists. We may never really know what caused the catastrophe. What we hope is that we have learned enough to prevent its ever happening again.

---

1. The failure of the New Deal to generate an expansion was first demonstrated in E. Cary Brown, "Fiscal Policy in the Thirties: A Reappraisal," *American Economic Review* 46 (December 1956): 857–879. The microeconomic effects of the New Deal are the subject matter of Gary Walton, ed., *Regulatory Change in an Atmosphere of Crisis; Current Implications of the Roosevelt Years* (New York: Academic Press, 1979).

2. See Allan H. Meltzer, "Monetary and Other Explanations of the Start of the Great Depression," *Journal of Monetary Economics* 2 (1976): 455–471.

Simplest multiplier (m): the reciprocal of the marginal propensity to save. Stated as an equation:

$$m = \frac{1}{MPS} = \frac{1}{(1 - MPC)}$$

this point the *MPS* (1/3) times $30 billion equals $10 billion, the increase in saving that is necessary to reestablish equilibrium in national income.

Thus the size of the simplest multiplier is related to the marginal propensity to save.[5] Stated precisely, the **simplest multiplier (m)** is the reciprocal of the marginal propensity to save, or

$$m = \frac{1}{MPS} = \frac{1}{(1 - MPC)}$$

Since the *MPS* and the *MPC* must add up to one (MPS = 1 − MCP) the multiplier can be stated either of the above two ways.

---

5. It is the simplest multiplier because there is no government, no world trade, no upsloping investment function, etc. Unless otherwise indicated, in the rest of this textbook, *m* will always refer to the simplest multiplier.

Given a specific change in expenditures, the change in national income can be computed by multiplying the reciprocal of the marginal propensity to save times the change in total planned expenditures, or

$$\Delta Y = \frac{1}{MPS} \times \Delta TPE$$

A concrete example may help explain why a change in planned investment (or consumer demand, or government demand) has a multiplying effect on national income. If businesses buy more plant and equipment—I_2 instead of I_1 in Figure 11.6—during a given period, their purchases result in higher output and greater income for the suppliers of those investment goods (construction workers and the owners of firms making heavy equipment). Suppliers will spend part of their increased incomes on personal consumption, including such goods as automobiles and refrigerators. The producers of automobiles and refrigerators will then have more income to spend on other items, such as groceries and clothes. In this way, an increase in expenditures for capital goods will affect incomes throughout the economy. There is a limit to how much an increase in planned investment will raise the national income. As the income level rises, people tend to save more. Eventually the planned saving level will equal the new higher level of planned investment, at which point equilibrium will be attained. In a sense, m can be thought of as the consumer spending effect because any initial change in spending has a magnified effect on equilibrium income as every round of changed income changes consumption.

Both the size of the multiplier and the potential change in the national income level are critically related to the value of the marginal propensity to save (or, geometrically, to the slope of the outflow curve). Compare the following sample values for the MPS with their associated simplest multipliers.

$$MPS = 0.4 \qquad m = \frac{1}{0.4} = 2.5$$

$$MPS = 0.5 \qquad m = \frac{1}{0.5} = 2$$

$$MPS = 0.6 \qquad m = \frac{1}{0.6} = 1.66$$

Although these hypothetical values are much higher than the real-world MPS, they illustrate the inverse relationship between the MPS and the multiplier. As the marginal propensity to save rises, the value of the multiplier falls. Since the multiplier determines how much national income will rise with an increase in planned investment (change in $Y = m \times$ change in TPE), we can see the impact of MPS. The higher the MPS, the smaller the change in income with any change in investment—and vice versa. Thus, if a nation's marginal propensity to save is very small—say 0.05—only a slight change in planned expenditures is required to cause a sharp change in the nation's income level.

Also remember that the multiplier takes time to work out—about half of its final impact coming in the first six months—even in the best of situations. Realistically, some of its power will be dissipated into changed prices rather than entirely in changed output. For instance, if there was a considerable amount of idle resources, the standard multiplier, which assumes the price level is constant, will provide a good estimation of the final change in equilibrium output. Finally, the multiplier operates on both increases and decreases in planned spending. A decrease has a negative multiplier effect. The national income level will fall by some multiple of any decline in planned investment. Unemployment will rise.

If we assume an upward sloping instead of a horizontal investment function, the new multiplier (the **frills multiplier (f)**) would be greater, as we would have:

$$f = \frac{1}{(1 - MPC - MPI)}$$

where

MPI = the marginal propensity to invest.

Thus, by adding an additional source of responding at each round, the ultimate change in GNP is greater. Still more frills, such as taxes, may be added. Roughly speaking, the more complex multipliers come out to be one divided by all pertinent marginal leakages or outflows. (See the Chapter Appendix for a more complete discussion of the multiplier.)

Changes in Planned Consumption and Saving

To many people, saving is a virtue. On an aggregate level, however, and within the confines of the Keynesian model of the macroeconomy, saving can have a detrimental short-run effect on income and employment. Suppose the economy is at equilibrium at a national income level of Y_2 and an unemployment rate of U_1 in Figure 11.7. Total expenditures are $C_1 + I$—part (a)—and saving is S_1—part (b). Now suppose people become more thrifty. Anticipating a recession, they decide to set aside more income. The saving curve shifts upward to S_2, reflecting this greater saving at each and every level of income. The level of planned saving now exceeds planned investment (I_1 in part (b)).

This shift in the saving curve is counterbalanced by a downward shift in the consumption curve in part (a). At the initial income level of Y_1, national production now exceeds total expenditure. Firms will not be able to sell all they produce. As their inventories pile up, they will reduce production, laying off workers in the process. Thus as national income falls, unemployment will rise (part (c)). In all three of the panels in Figure 11.7 the initial equilibrium is E_1 and the new one is E_2.

As income falls, however, saving will fall with it. At the lower national income level of Y_2, planned saving will again equal planned investment, and total planned expenditure will again equal national income. In the process of lowering the nation's income level, the movement toward greater thrift has raised unemployment to U_2 (part (c)). Furthermore, at the new equilibrium income level, people can save no more than they could before, at the initial income level of Y_1. This perverse result is known as the para-

Frills multiplier (f): the value of f is greater than the simplest multiplier (m), as it adds an additional source of respending at each round. Stated as an equation,

$$f = \frac{1}{(1 - MPC - MPI)},$$

where MPC is the marginal propensity to consume and MPI is the marginal propensity to invest.

(a)

(b)

(c)

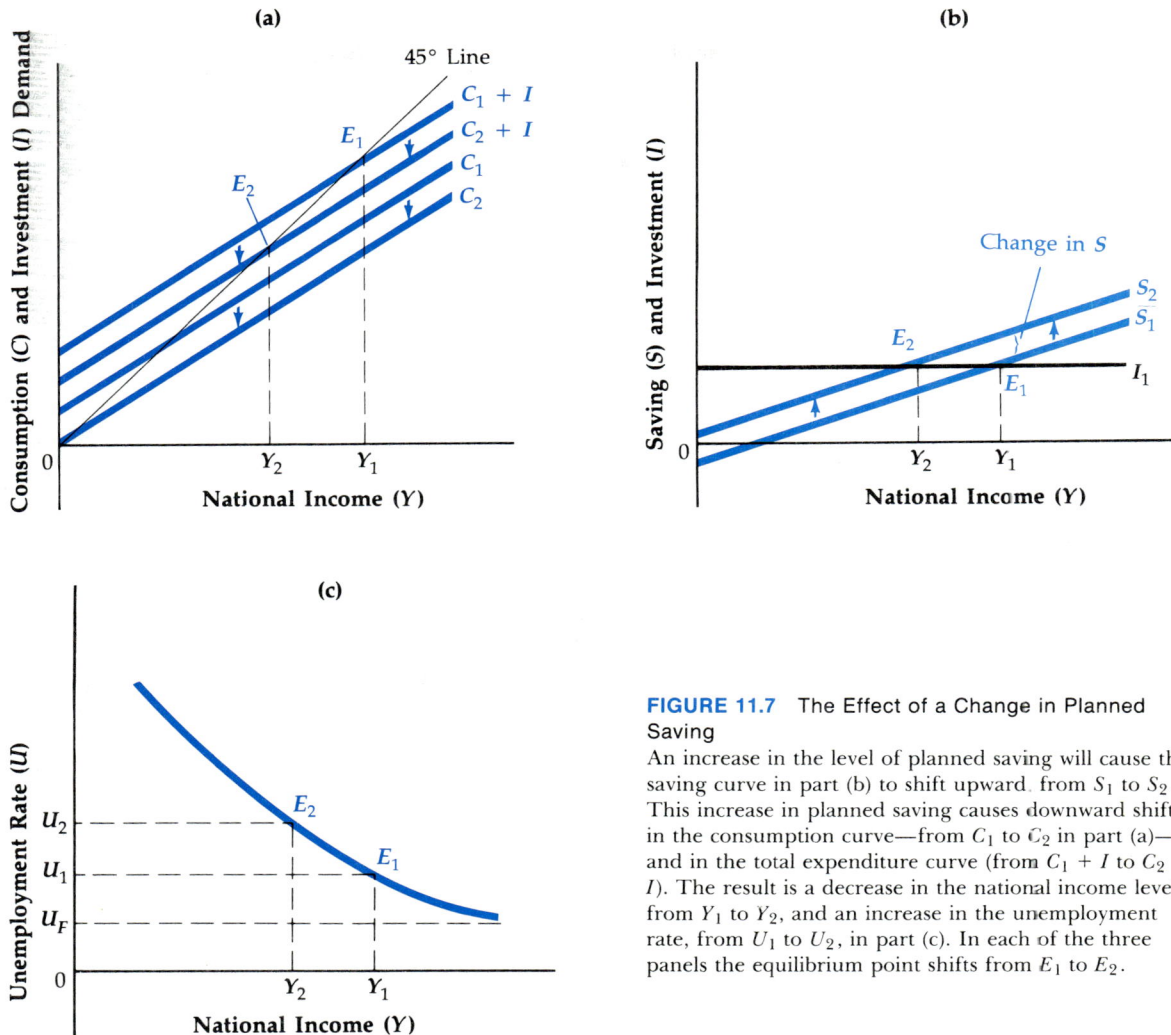

FIGURE 11.7 The Effect of a Change in Planned Saving

An increase in the level of planned saving will cause the saving curve in part (b) to shift upward, from S_1 to S_2. This increase in planned saving causes downward shifts in the consumption curve—from C_1 to C_2 in part (a)—and in the total expenditure curve (from $C_1 + I$ to $C_2 + I$). The result is a decrease in the national income level, from Y_1 to Y_2, and an increase in the unemployment rate, from U_1 to U_2, in part (c). In each of the three panels the equilibrium point shifts from E_1 to E_2.

Paradox of thrift: the theory that if people attempt to save more at every level of income, they will end up earning less in the aggregate and saving no more (and possibly less) than before.

dox of thrift. According to the **paradox of thrift,** if people attempt to save more at every level of income, they will end up earning less in the aggregate and saving no more (and possibly less) than before. For this reason, Keynesian economists argue that efforts to save can be counterproductive, at least in the short run.

The national income level falls because people consume less when they try to save more. In fact, an increase in planned saving has the same negative multiplying effect on the income level as an equivalent drop in planned investment. In Figure 11.7, planned saving rises by the vertical distance between the two saving curves, S_1 and S_2. The national income level falls by a much greater amount—three times as much, to be precise. As before, the marginal propensity to save (the slope of the saving curve) is 0.33, and the multiplier is 3.

Any *decrease* or any *increase* in planned consumption will have a multiplying effect on the economy. The important point is that the multiplier effect moves in the direction of the change in *total* planned expenditures.

Chapter Review

Review of Key Questions

1. *What is the planned investment and planned saving approach to income equilibrium?*

Using the planned investment and saving approach, one can show that equilibrium in national income and employment in an environment without government or foreign trade is established where the level of planned saving equals the level of planned investment. Investment includes spending on new equipment, construction, and inventory. Businesses make investments by comparing the expected net rate of profit (marginal efficiency of investment) with the expected cost of capital or the expected real rate of interest. The investment (saving) function shows the relationship of investment (saving) to national income (Y). A GNP or income gap occurs when the actual equilibrium output is less than the full-employment potential GNP. When actual GNP is greater (less) than potential GNP, a contractionary (expansionary) gap exists.

2. *What is the total spending approach to income equilibrium?*

Using the total planned spending approach, one can show that equilibrium in national income and employment is established where total planned expenditures for goods and services ($C + I$) equals national income. (At this equilibrium income level, planned saving will equal planned investment.) The consumption function relates planned consumption (C) to national income (Y). The $MPC = \Delta C/\Delta Y$. The saving function relates planned saving (S) to national income (Y). The $MPS = \Delta S/\Delta Y$. By definition, $MPC + MPS = 1.0$.

3. *What effects do changes in planned total expenditures have on equilibrium income?*

Planned investment is influenced by many factors, but most important are the real rate of interest firms pay on borrowed money and the expected rate of net return. Investment will be pushed until the expected net rate of profit is just equal to the real interest rate. A decrease in the interest rate will cause an increase in the level of planned investment and therefore in national income and employment, and vice versa. In the Keynesian model of the macroeconomy, each interest rate is associated with a specific national income level. Equilibrium national income will increase or decrease ultimately by some multiple of any change in total planned expenditures. An increase in autonomous investment demand, for example, will eventually cause a magnified increase in the national income level greater than the increase in the investment demand. This increase in national income will be largely in output and not prices if there are abundant idle resources, as the traditional multiplier assumes. In the Keynesian macroeconomic model, the simplest multiplier (m) is equal to the reciprocal of the marginal propensity to save: $m = 1/MPS = 1/(1 - MPC)$. According to the paradox of thrift, if people try to save, they may, under certain conditions, save the same or less if income falls.

Further Topics

Many policymakers use the Keynesian macroeconomic model developed in this chapter to explain the business cycle, or the intermittent swings between rising and falling levels of national income and employment. A decrease in planned investment or an increase in planned saving initiates a decrease in the national income level, which is magnified by the multiplier effect. A drop in planned investment, for instance, will lead to cumulative reductions in income and consumption and to further drops in production and income. An increase in planned investment and a decrease in planned saving will have a multiplicative effect in the opposite direction. The smaller the marginal propensity to save, the greater the value and effect of the multiplier.

Keynesian theory contradicts classical prescriptions for dealing with unemployment. To alleviate unemployment, classical economists recommended letting the free market work by the elimination of labor market restrictions, such as legislative wage laws and union barriers to wage reductions. The Keynesian model suggests that unemployment may be decreased by a reduction in the level of saving, and therefore increasing consumption. Through tax and expenditure policies, Keynesians believe that government can actively guide the economy toward the full-employment income level—a topic we will pursue in the next chapter.

Review of New Terms

Consumption function The assumed direct relationship between the national income level and the planned or desired consumption expenditures of households.

Contractionary gap When actual GNP is less than potential (i.e., full employment) GNP.

Dissaving Any net withdrawal from accumulated past savings, or any net increase in borrowing.

Expansionary gap When actual GNP is more than potential (i.e., full employment) GNP.

Frills multiplier (f) The value of f is greater than the simplest multiplier (m), as it adds an additional source of respending at each round. Stated as an equation, $f = 1/(1 - MPC - MPI)$ where MPC is the marginal propensity to consume and MPI is the marginal propensity to invest.

Investment function The assumed relationship between national income and total planned expenditures on new equipment, construction, and inventory.

Marginal efficiency of investment (MEI) The expected yield or expected rate of net profit on additions to the capital stock or investment.

Marginal propensity to consume The percentage of any change in national income (ΔY) that consumers are inclined to spend (ΔC). Stated as a ratio, $MPC = \Delta C/\Delta Y$.

Marginal propensity to save The percentage of any change in national income (ΔY) that consumers are inclined to save (ΔS). Stated as a ratio, $MPS = \Delta S = \Delta Y$.

Multiplier (m) The ratio of a final change in national income (ΔY) to the initial change in total planned expenditures (ΔTPE) that stimulated it:

$$m = \frac{\text{final change in } Y}{\text{initial change in } TPE} = \frac{\Delta Y}{\Delta TPE}$$

Paradox of thrift The theory that if people attempt to save more at every level of income, they will end up earning less if the aggregate and saving no more (and possibly less) than before.

Potential GNP The total amount of output that could be produced under full employment.

Saving function The assumed direct relationship between nominal national income and the amount of income saved (not spent on goods and services).

Simplest multiplier (m) The reciprocal of the marginal propensity to save. Stated as an equation,

$$m = \frac{1}{MPS} = \frac{1}{(1 - MPC)}$$

Total expenditure function The relationship of total planned expenditures to national income, normally assumed to be a direct relationship.

Review Questions

1. Suppose the nation's marginal propensity to save is 0.2; the level of consumption expenditures increases by $15 at each and every income level; and investment expenditures increase by $10. What will be the amount and direction of the resulting change in national income? What will happen to the unemployment rate? (◀ 1, ◀ 2, ◀ 3)

2. Given the following values for the marginal propensity to save and for changes in investment, compute the multipliers and the resulting changes in national income:

MPS	Multiplier	Change in *I*	Change in *Y*
1/10	_____	+$10	_____
1/15	_____	−$20	_____
3/10	_____	+$5	_____

(◀ 3)

3. Suppose that saving rises by $10 at the same time that investment rises by $10. What happens to the national income level? (◢ 3)

4. The following graph reproduces the saving curve from the other figures in this chapter. The investment function, however, has been drawn as an upward-sloping curve instead of a horizontal line. The implied assumption is that investment is directly related to the national income level. That is, as national income increases, so does investment, and vice versa.

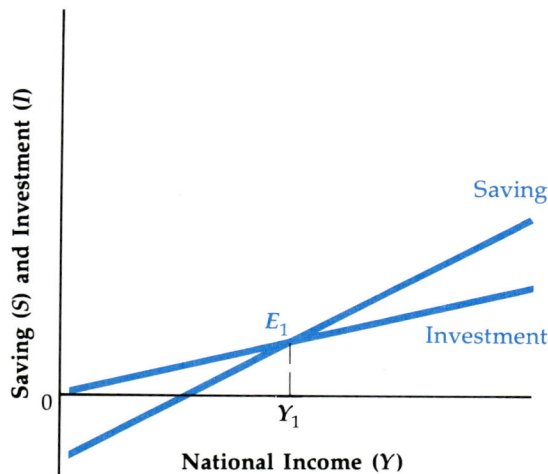

Given this information, suppose that the level of saving increases at each and every income level. (a) What will happen to the national income level and the unemployment rate? (b) What will happen to the actual level of saving? Explain the sequence of events on which your answers are based. (◢ 3)

APPENDIX

Derivation of the Multiplier

We noted on page 296 that the simplest multiplier (m) is related to the size of the marginal propensities to save and to consume. If investment expenditures rise by \$10 billion, to use the example cited there, then planned saving must rise by an equal amount to reestablish equilibrium in national income. If the marginal propensity to save is one-third, then the national income level must rise to \$30 billion before planned saving again equals investment. The multiplier in this example is therefore 3 (\$30 billion ÷ \$10 billion = 3).

The formal derivation of the simplest multiplier is as follows. To begin, we know that the change in national income (ΔY) will equal the simplest multiplier (m) times the change in total planned expenditures (TPE):

$$\Delta Y = m \times \Delta TPE$$

Furthermore, in the example on page 297, the change in total planned expenditures equals the change in investment. We can therefore substitute change in investment for change in total planned expenditures:

$$\Delta Y = m \times \Delta I$$

We also know that in an economy in equilibrium, planned saving must equal investment:

$$S = I$$

Before equilibrium in national income can be reestablished, then, any change in planned investment must be matched by an equal change in planned saving:

$$\Delta S = \Delta I$$

Again, we can substitute one variable for another—ΔS for ΔI—in the multiplier equation:

$$\Delta Y = m \times \Delta S$$

The equation $\Delta Y = m \times \Delta S$ can be rearranged as follows:

$$\frac{1}{m} = \frac{\Delta S}{\Delta Y}$$

Notice that the right side of this equation is the formula for the marginal propensity to save. Thus:

$$\frac{1}{m} = MPS \quad \text{or} \quad m = \frac{1}{MPS}$$

Stated verbally, the simplest multiplier is the reciprocal of the marginal propensity to save.

If we know what the marginal propensity to save is, we can find the value of the simplest multiplier. If the marginal propensity to save is one-third, as in our example, the multiplier must be 3:

$$m = \frac{1}{MPS} = \frac{1}{\frac{1}{3}} = 3$$

Since the marginal propensity to save is equal to 1 minus the marginal propensity to consume, the simplest multiplier can also be stated as:

$$m = \frac{1}{1 - MPC}$$

Thus the value of the simplest multiplier can also be computed from the marginal propensity to consume:

$$m = \frac{1}{(1 - MPC)} = \frac{1}{(1 - \frac{2}{3})} = \frac{1}{\frac{1}{3}} = 3$$

Of course, this number, 3, is unrealistically large. Moreover, the consumer respending effects take many months, even years, to finally work themselves out, and some of the impact may be channeled into changes in prices rather than real output as idle resources become less abundant.

On the other hand, to the extent that we recognize that investment may be positively sloped rather than horizontal, this introduces a new source of potential respending effects that would increase the final effects in the frills multiplier as $f = 1/(1 - MPC - MPI)$, where MPI is the marginal propensity to invest. Introducing international economic relations would also effect the value of the simplest multiplier by introducing additional elements of injections or outflows (exports) and leakages or inflows (imports) that would have to be netted out. Similarly, introducing taxes will complicate the value of the multiplier. As a very crude generalization, the more complex multipliers with more injections (inflows) and leakages (outflows) tend to be equal to one divided by the pertinent marginal leakages or outflows.

Keynesian Fiscal Policy

"Fiscal responsibility" is not synonymous with "fiscal restraint." Rather, it calls for an intelligent fitting of tax and spending positions to the needs of the economy.
    Walter Heller

KEY QUESTIONS

▲ 1. What can the government do to promote economic stability through fiscal policy?

▲ 2. How does deliberate fiscal policy compare with nondiscretionary built-in automatic fiscal stabilizers?

▲ 3. Is deficit spending a problem?

▲ 4. Why is monetary policy subordinate to fiscal policy for Keynesians?

NEW TERMS

Action (administrative) lag
Automatic fiscal stabilizer
Balanced-budget multiplier
Crowding out
Expansionary gap
Fiscal drag

Impact (operational) lag
Liquidity trap
Lump-sum tax
National or public debt
Political business cycle
Recognition lag

The preceding chapter showed how, in the Keynesian model of the macroeconomy, changes in the demand for goods and services can affect national income and employment through the multiplier process. According to that model, the economy's equilibrium income level may not necessarily be its full-employment level. If changes in demand move the economy away from full employment, furthermore, the forces of supply and demand will not necessarily move the economy back toward full employment in the short run.

In this chapter we will consider how, theoretically at least, government fiscal policy can be used to counteract the negative effects of a change in demand. In Chapter 4, fiscal policy was defined as a government's use of tax and expenditure actions to achieve economic goals, such as full employment of the labor force or stable prices. Specifically, we will see how government can move the economy out of a recession by expanding aggregate demand (through a larger budgetary deficit or a smaller budgetary surplus). Conversely, it can reduce inflationary pressures by suppressing aggregate demand (through a larger budgetary surplus or a smaller budgetary deficit). Because such goals have shaped much of our government's economic policy over the past two decades, we will also be able to see the results of Keynesian theory in some real-world situations.

Even the philosopher Adam Smith, who, according to Blinder, showed how the free market "miraculously harnesses greed toward constructive ends . . . led by capitalists motivated only by self-enrichment" recognized that unfettered markets cannot do everything—they cannot "eliminate the scourge of unemployment."[1] In macroeconomic theory, economic stability and full employment are considered public goods that can be attained only through collective government action. In the midst of a recession, for instance, the national income level can be increased only if firms as a group increase their

1. Alan S. Blinder, *Hard Heads, Soft Hearts* (Reading, Mass.: Addison-Wesley, 1987), p. 27.

planned expenditures on plant and equipment, or consumers as a group reduce their planned saving level. Individual households and firms have little incentive to contribute to the production of a public good like economic stability or full employment. A single household or firm is too small by itself to make a significant contribution to such an end or to realize any substantial benefits from it. Firms and households do not operate in the common interest, but in their own private interest. All tend to become free riders. Thus government action is required for the production of economic stability as it is for the production of national defense.

Government as Economic Policymaker

▲ **1. What can the government do to promote economic stability through fiscal policy?**

The long-run trend in the United States has been for real GNP to increase—averaging about a 3.2 annual increase from 1890 to 1988. There have been enormous fluctuations around this trend, however. Since World War II the "great smoother"—the federal government—has had moderate success in tempering those cyclical swings around the long-run trend. To see how government attempts to produce economic stability, we will use graphs (like those in Chapter 11) that relate the various inflows (injections) or outflows (leakages) to the national income level. For the moment, we will continue our simplifying assumption that wages, prices, and interest rates are fixed in our closed (i.e., no-trade) economy.

In our model economy, tax payments and savings are directly influenced by the national income level. As income rises, people save more. Beyond some minimal level, people are required to pay taxes, and to pay more taxes the higher their income. If the government imposes a constant tax that produces the same amount of tax revenue at each level of national income, it is called a **lump-sum tax.** In some of our graphical analyses, we will assume that tax changes are of the lump-sum type. The relationship between taxes, saving, and income is described in Figure 12.1(a). At the nominal national income level Y_1, planned saving and taxes together are assumed to be zero. As income increases, however, planned saving and taxes rise. Any taxes that are collected inevitably reduce the saving outflow. The two outflows, in other words, are not independent. Still, this combined outflow (leakage) curve has a steeper slope than the outflow curve in the last chapter, which included only saving.

Lump-sum tax: a constant tax that produces the same amount of tax revenue at each level of national income.

The effect of taxation on consumption is illustrated in part (b) of Figure 12.1. There the consumption curve has a slightly lower slope than the one in Chapter 11 because taxes reduce consumer expenditures. People simply have less disposable personal income to spend after taxes. Although disposable personal income is not shown directly in Figure 12.1 this means that at a national income level of Y_2, total planned consumer expenditures are C_1, less than they would have been without the tax outflow. Planned

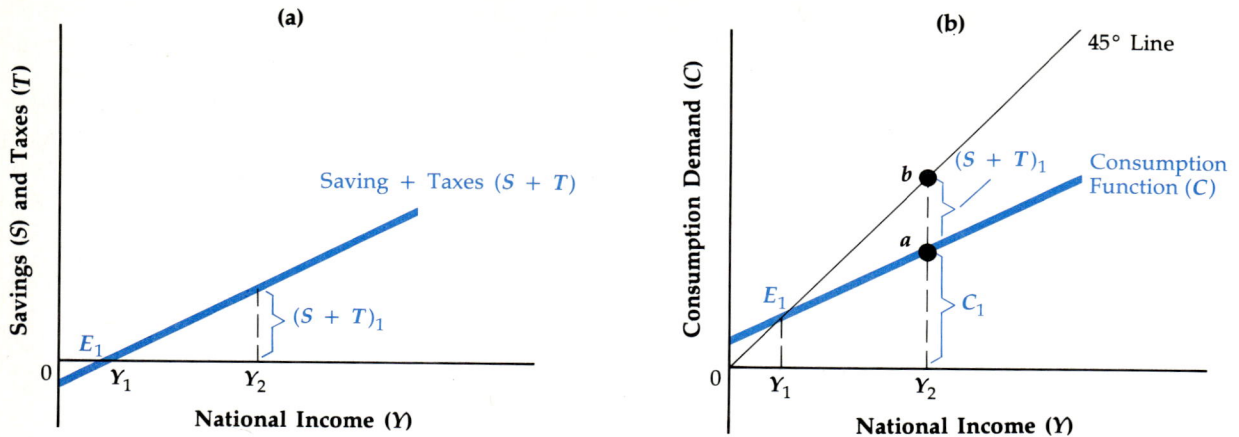

FIGURE 12.1   The Relationship of Planned Saving (S), Taxes (T), and Consumption (C) to Nominal National Income (Y)

Planned saving and taxes, shown by the upward-sloping curve in part (a), both increase with national income. The slope of this combined outflow curve is steeper than the slope of the outflow curve shown in the last chapter, which included only saving. After taxes, the consumption curve—part (b)—still slopes upward, but less than the consumption curve in the last chapter, for taxes reduce consumption. The vertical distance between the consumption function and the 45-degree line is equal to the combined total of planned saving and taxes shown in part (a). With no government or investment spending the equilibrium would be at E_1.

saving and taxes are shown here by the vertical distance between the consumption curve and the 45-degree line (*ab*). With no government or investment spending the equilibrium would be at E_1.

Government spending may well be influenced by the national income level. To keep the analysis simple, however, we will assume that neither planned government expenditures nor planned investment expenditures change with a change in national income. The planned government and investment expenditure curves are therefore horizontal, as in Figure 12.2(a) and (b). Combining these two curves in part (c) yields a higher horizontal curve than the investment curve or government curve alone.

Figure 12.3(a) combines the saving and taxes (outflow) curve from Figure 12.1 with the government spending and investment (inflow) curve from Figure 12.2. Figure 12.3(b) combines the consumption curve from Figure 12.1 and the government spending and investment curve from Figure 12.2 into a single total planned expenditure curve, $TPE = C + I + G$. With these two graphs we can see the equilibrium national income level.

From our discussion in the last chapter, we know that the equilibrium national income level—not necessarily a full employment level—will be reached where outflows (leakages) equal inflows (injections) or where total planned expenditures (*TPE*, or sometimes called aggregate expenditures) equal national income. (In the diagrams in this chapter we will not show the consumption function separately, such as in Figure 12.3(b), but will show only the combined *TPE* function, to keep our figures as uncluttered as possible.) These equilibrium conditions are met at a nominal national income level of Y_2 in Figure 12.3(a) and (b) associated with an unemployment rate in panel (c) of U_2. Again, the 45-degree line in Figure 12.3(b) means that the value of the variable on the vertical axis is equal to the value of the variable on the horizontal axis. At any income level other than Y_2, firms will want to cut back or expand production as there are unplanned inventories (investment). For instance, at an income level of Y_3 (and unemployment rate of U_3), outflows (saving plus taxes) are greater than inflows (planned

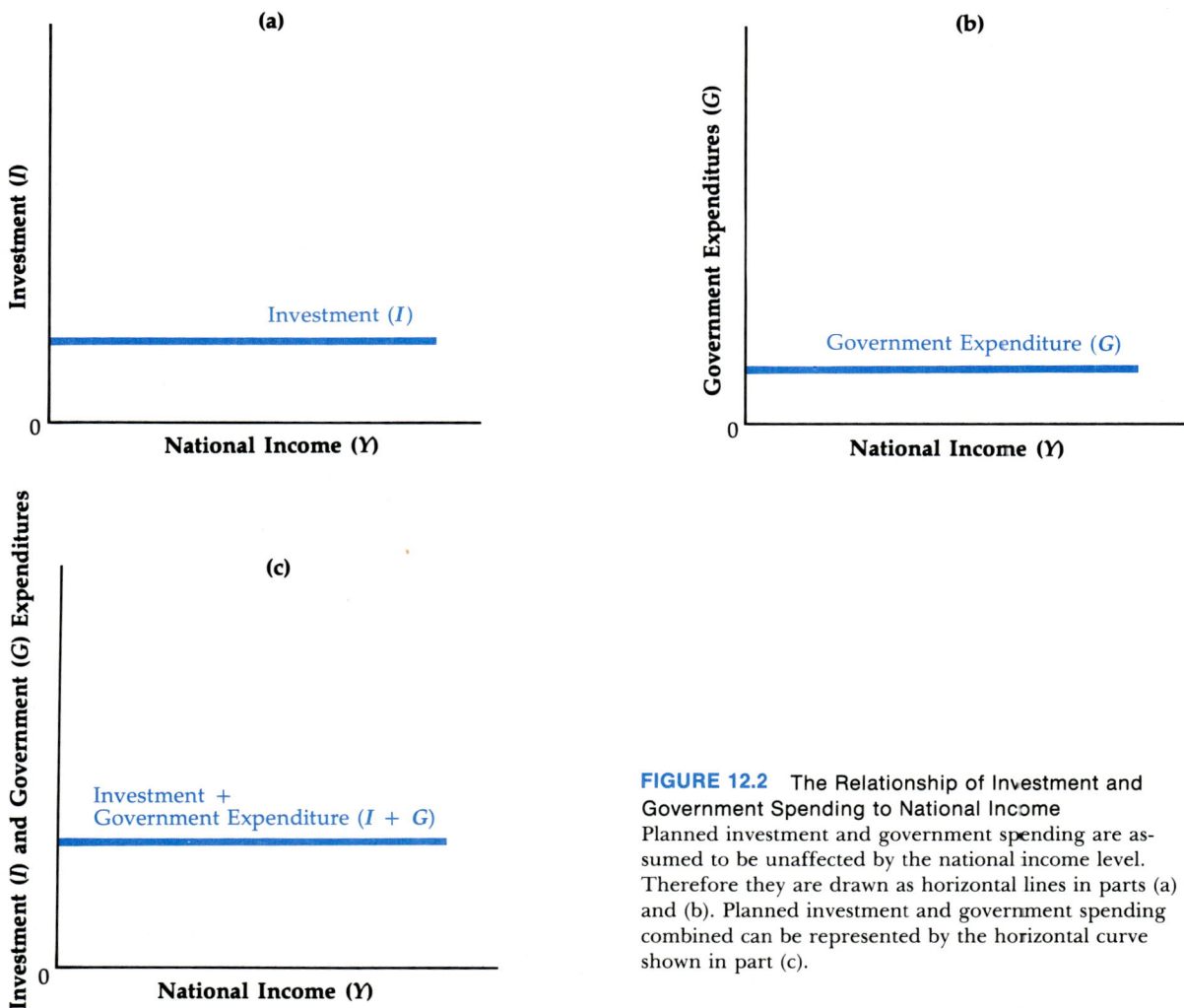

FIGURE 12.2   The Relationship of Investment and Government Spending to National Income
Planned investment and government spending are assumed to be unaffected by the national income level. Therefore they are drawn as horizontal lines in parts (a) and (b). Planned investment and government spending combined can be represented by the horizontal curve shown in part (c).

(a)

(b)

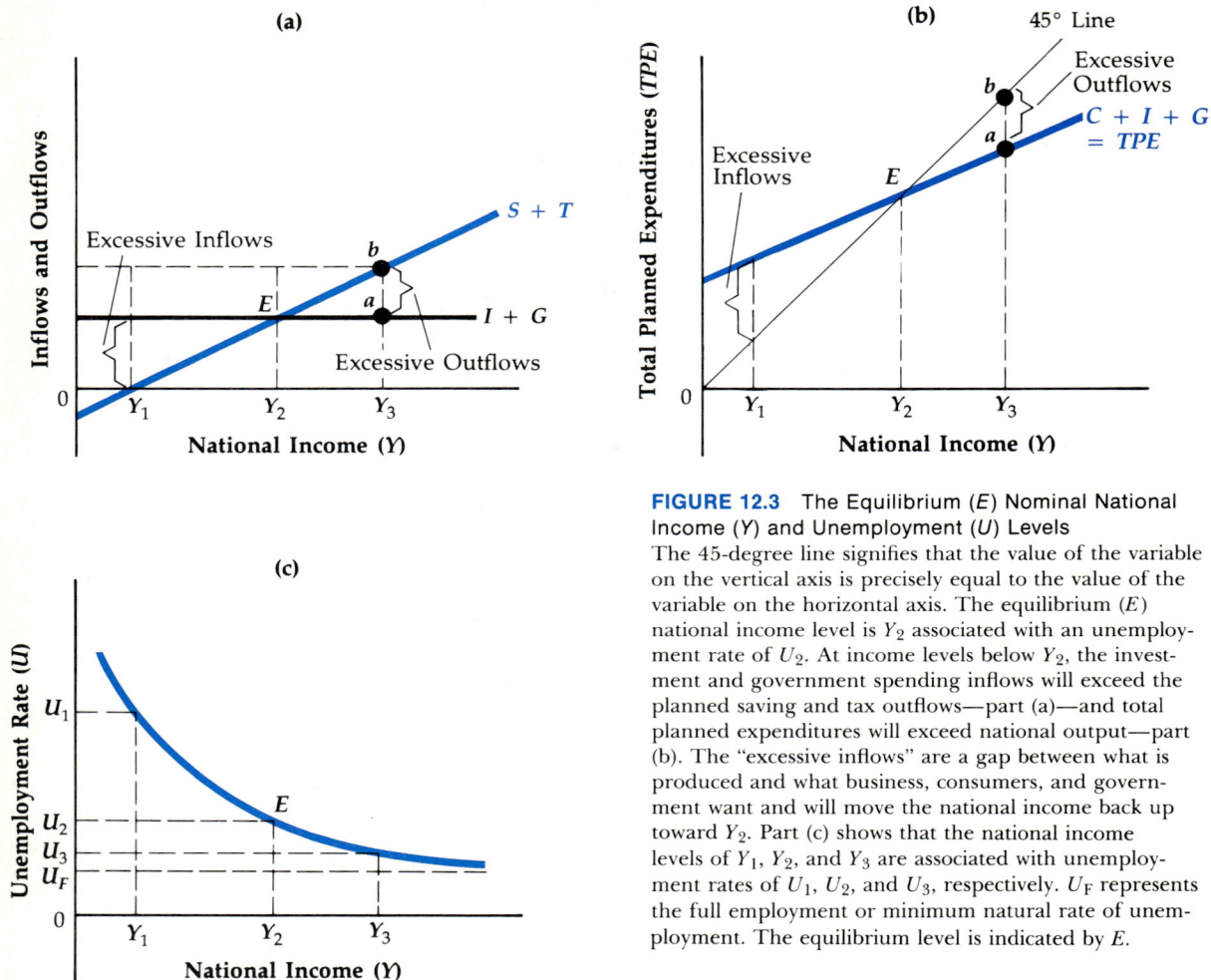

FIGURE 12.3 The Equilibrium (*E*) Nominal National Income (*Y*) and Unemployment (*U*) Levels
The 45-degree line signifies that the value of the variable on the vertical axis is precisely equal to the value of the variable on the horizontal axis. The equilibrium (*E*) national income level is Y_2 associated with an unemployment rate of U_2. At income levels below Y_2, the investment and government spending inflows will exceed the planned saving and tax outflows—part (a)—and total planned expenditures will exceed national output—part (b). The "excessive inflows" are a gap between what is produced and what business, consumers, and government want and will move the national income back up toward Y_2. Part (c) shows that the national income levels of Y_1, Y_2, and Y_3 are associated with unemployment rates of U_1, U_2, and U_3, respectively. U_F represents the full employment or minimum natural rate of unemployment. The equilibrium level is indicated by *E*.

(c)

investment plus government expenditures). These "excessive outflows" or gaps between outflows and inflows is indicated by the vertical distance between points *a* and *b* in Figure 12.3(a) and (b). This is not a contractionary gap as we have not assumed that Y_2 or U_2 represents full employment. You will recall from Chapter 11 that a contractionary (expansionary) gap exists when actual GNP is less than (greater than) potential or full-employment GNP. Because firms will not sell all they have produced under such conditions indicated at Y_3, they will reduce production. The equilibrium national income level will thus contract toward Y_2, along with saving and taxes.

At income levels lower than Y_2, planned investment and government expenditure will be greater than planned saving and taxes, producing "excessive inflows" or a gap between the inflow and outflow curves. (This is not an expansionary gap because we have not assumed that Y_2 represents full employment.) Firms will be producing less than consumers want, and the excess demand will encourage them to increase production. As they do they will increase the national income and employment levels, as well as the outflows of saving and taxes. Eventually outflows will match inflows, at the equilibrium income level Y_2. At that level, total planned expenditures also will equal nominal national income—Figure 12.3(b). The full employment or minimum natural rate of unemployment is represented by U_F in panel (c).

Changes in Planned Government Expenditures

We can now examine, in Figure 12.4, how government changes the national income and employment levels. Suppose the government's budget is balanced (taxes equal expenditures) at equilibrium E_1, where outflows equal inflows. If the government then increases expenditures while holding taxes constant, the national income and employment levels will rise. Figure 12.4 illustrates the impact of such an increase in planned government expenditure, achieved in this case by running a budgetary deficit. With the increase in expenditures, the total planned expenditures curve, $TPE_1 = C + I + G_1$, shifts upward to $TPE_2 = C + I + G_2$ as shown in part (b). The equilibrium shifts from E_1 to E_2. This shift is mirrored in part (a) by an upward shift of the inflow curve, from $I + G_1$ to $I + G_2$. An excessive inflow gap now exists between total planned inflows and total planned outflows. At income level Y_1, businesses are not producing enough to satisfy total demand. As they increase production, the national income and employment levels rise along with the saving and tax outflows. The economy reaches a new equilibrium at E_2, where the national income level is Y_2, outflows again equal inflows, and total planned expenditures equal national income. Significantly, unemployment has dropped in the process, from U_1 to U_2. It is still less than the full employment or minimum rate of unemployment of U_F.

Notice that the change in national income ($Y_2 - Y_1$) is greater than the change in government expenditure that initiated it (measured by either $(C + I + G_2) - (C + I + G_1)$, or $TPE_2 - TPE_1$, or $G_2 - G_1$). Here we see the influence of the multiplier effect (see pages 293–298). When the government spends more, production goes up and employment and people's incomes increase.

In short, income will increase by some multiple (greater than 1) of the increase in government spending.[2] The income multiplier (m) is the numer-

2. With the tax outflow added to the saving outflow, the multiplier is not quite as large as it was in the examples in Chapter 11. Like saving, taxes drain off consumers' purchasing power, limiting the effect of any change in government or investment spending. As we pointed out previously, the simplest multiplier equals the reciprocal of the marginal propensity to save. In that analysis, the marginal propensity to save was the same as the slope of the outflow curve, since saving was the only outflow. With taxes added, the slope of the outflow curve is higher; hence the multiplier is lower. How much lower depends on how much the tax drain affects the saving outflow.

(a)

(b)

(c)

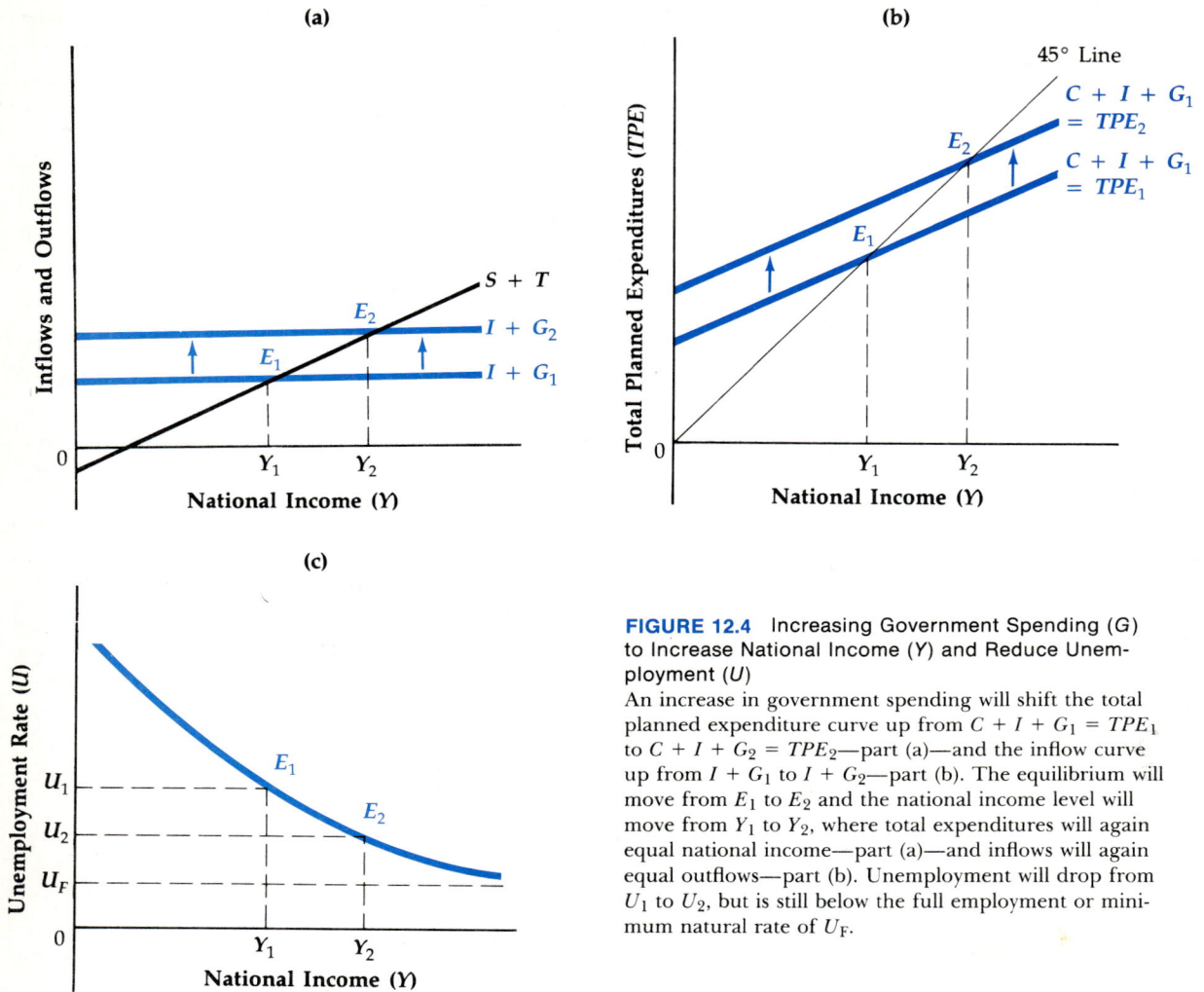

FIGURE 12.4 Increasing Government Spending (G) to Increase National Income (Y) and Reduce Unemployment (U)

An increase in government spending will shift the total planned expenditure curve up from $C + I + G_1 = TPE_1$ to $C + I + G_2 = TPE_2$—part (a)—and the inflow curve up from $I + G_1$ to $I + G_2$—part (b). The equilibrium will move from E_1 to E_2 and the national income level will move from Y_1 to Y_2, where total expenditures will again equal national income—part (a)—and inflows will again equal outflows—part (b). Unemployment will drop from U_1 to U_2, but is still below the full employment or minimum natural rate of U_F.

ical coefficient that shows how much we multiply an initial change in autonomous total planned spending (ΔTPE) to get the final magnified change in national income (ΔY). We know from Chapter 11 that the change in national income equals the multiplier times the change in total planned expenditures.

$$\Delta Y = m \times \Delta TPE$$

Because the change in total spending equals the change in government spending, we can restate our equation to read:

$$\Delta Y = m \times \Delta G$$

Conversely, if the government decreases expenditures while holding taxes constant, the national income level will fall. If the government spends less, firms will produce less, workers will receive less income, consumers will consume less, and so forth. The national income level will decline by some multiple of the decrease in government expenditures, and unemployment will rise. In this case the government's fiscal policy causes or contributes to a recession.

Of course no government is likely to cause a recession intentionally, but government policymakers may very well reduce spending in an attempt to control the rate of inflation. In Figure 12.5, for instance, planned government expenditures and investment add up to $I + G_1$. The equilibrium income level is Y_1, where the outflow and inflow curves intersect (part (a)). Part (c) shows that the economy reaches the full employment or minimum natural rate of unemployment, U_F, at a much lower national income level, Y_F.

In this case the nation simply does not have a labor force sufficient to produce at an output level of Y_1. Yet people are demanding that the economy produce at that level (part (b)). An expansionary gap exists between what consumers, investors, and government demand—point b in part (b)—and what the economy can produce (point a). This excess demand should produce inflation, since consumers will bid up the prices of goods that are in short supply. To eliminate the inflationary pressures, government policymakers may decide to reduce government expenditures, thereby reducing total planned expenditures to $TPE_2 = C + I + G_2$. The equilibrium national income level will then be Y_F, the full-employment level for this economy.

Crowding Out the Effectiveness of Fiscal Policy

Not all economists accept Keynesian doctrine on the effect of government spending, as it neglects some secondary effects. Some maintain that if the government has to create a deficit or increase its deficit in order to increase spending, the multiplier effect will be significantly weakened. When government borrows, it becomes a competitor in the loanable funds market, driving up real interest rates and crowding private borrowers out of the market. This is called **crowding out**: in theory, an increase in government spending tends to cause—working through an increase in the real interest rate—a partial or total offset in total planned expenditures of decreased private spending, thereby making fiscal policy less effective or totally ineffective. If the government borrows funds that would otherwise be used elsewhere, critics charge, any increase in government spending may be partially or totally offset by a decrease in private business ventures, or in state and local government spending.

In the case of full employment of resources, every dollar of increased government spending may crowd out a dollar of private spending, resulting in complete crowding out. The crowding out would be complete if the

Crowding out: the theory that an increase in government spending tends to cause—working through an increase in the real interest rate—a partial or total offset in total planned expenditures of decreased private spending, thereby making fiscal policy less effective or totally ineffective.

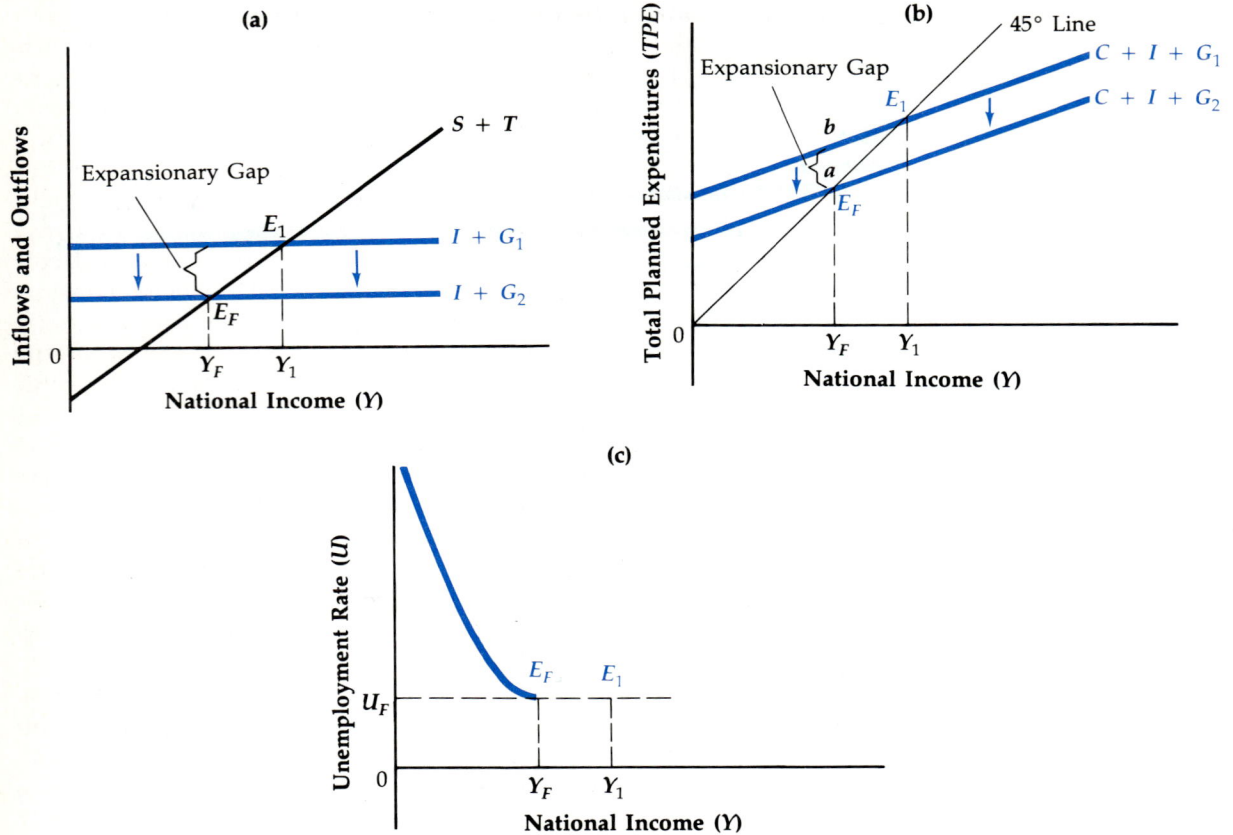

FIGURE 12.5 Decreasing Government Spending (G) to Control Inflation

If consumers, investors, and government together demand more goods than the economy can produce at full employment (Y_F), the gap between demand and output—points b and a in part (b)—will create inflationary pressure on prices at the equilibrium E_1. By reducing government expenditures, policymakers can reduce total planned expenditures TPE_2 to $C + I + G_2$, moving the economy away from the inflationary equilibrium income level of Y_1 to the noninflationary income level Y_F. In part (c) we see that U_F is the full employment or minimum natural rate of unemployment. Once income level Y_F is reached no further reduction in unemployment and hence no further increase in real production and real GNP is possible. Any pressures from excessive aggregate expenditures can only result in inflation.

supply of loanable funds was unchanged, causing the real interest rate to increase. This would in turn reduce private spending, thus offsetting public spending. If there are idle resources, the demand stimulus from an increase in government spending will increase real output and income; that will increase saving, moderating increases in the real interest rate, resulting in incomplete crowding out. Any crowding out—partial or complete—will reduce the effectiveness of fiscal policy.

If the government stimulates demand by spending more than it collects in taxes, it must either increase the money stock or borrow the difference between spending and taxes. The usual method is to borrow the money by selling bonds. Keynes argued that during a severe recession, the government would be borrowing funds that would otherwise remain idle. In a particularly serious recession, he felt, people tend to hold on to their money, fearing that loans to businesses are unsafe or anticipating that interest rates will rise. In that case government borrowing would not lead to a drop in private investment. Any increase in government spending would be fully reflected in the multiplier process.

Not all recessions are severe enough to scare lenders out of investing in private enterprise. What if private investment were to fall at the same time, and by the same amount, as government expenditures increase? Total planned expenditures would not change, and there would be no net multiplier effect, since the positive multiplier effects of increased government spending are exactly offset by the negative multiplier effects of reduced private investment spending. There would no increase in the national income level, and fiscal policy would be ineffective. Even if private investment fell by less than the increase in government spending—say, by $7 billion when government expenditures rose by $10 billion—the net change in total planned expenditures would be much reduced (in this example, to $3 billion). The multiplier effect would still occur, but it would be much smaller than predicted by our earlier analysis.

Especially since the late 1960s, this question has been the subject of considerable controversy. Keynesians cite statistical studies that support the strength of the multiplier effect. Economists of the monetarist, supply-side, and rational expectations schools disagree, as we will see in later chapters. A synthesis on the impact of fiscal policy has begun to emerge, however. The economists who adhere to it acknowledge a modest short-run multiplier effect. They contend that after six months or possibly a year, however, fiscal action is largely ineffective in influencing aggregate demand and national income.

Changes in Planned Taxes

A change in tax rates can have similar effects on the equilibrium national income level.[3] If people's saving habits were not affected by the taxes they pay, a reduction in taxes might cause a sizable downward shift in the outflow curve ($S_1 + T_1$), to the dotted line ($S_3 + T_3$) in Figure 12.6(a) on page 320. The equilibrium national income level would then climb all the way to Y_3. In fact, however, people tend to save some part of a tax reduction, particularly if it is a large one. The drop in the tax outflow is partially offset

---

3. We shall assume that the change is a lump-sum or autonomous tax that shifts the intercept of the saving function but not the slope, as would be the case with a shift in the marginal propensity to tax.

PERSPECTIVES

Microeconomic Foundations of Macroeconomics

Many students come away from their study of economics feeling that macroeconomics (big picture) and microeconomics (little picture) are two distinct and hermetically sealed divisions in economic theory. It is true that macroeconomics or income theory focuses on the major aggregates involved in the attempt to measure, explain, and mitigate temporary economic fluctuations from a long-run growth path dictated by technology and resource growth. In contrast, microeconomics or price theory focuses on how individual economic agents—individuals, firms, and government units—behave and allocate scarce resources in a market setting with little concern for temporary fluctuations. "But it is a mistake to isolate macroeconomics from microeconomics . . . Macroeconomics is only as good as the microeconomics that underlies it."[1] Thus to explain fluctuations, the behavior of economic agents such as consumers, firms, or resource owners operating in consumption, investment, government, financial, or international trade markets must be analyzed closely.

In a sense the real world can be thought of as a continuum or spectrum. At one extreme is pure microeconomics and at the other is pure macro-

economics. All real-world economic problems fall somewhere in between these two extremes and therefore contain elements of both microeconomics and macroeconomics. For instance, an analysis concerned with what would happen if minimum wages were raised in the United States might involve a richer mixture, but still a mixture, of microeconomics than macroeconomics. Another analysis concerned with what would happen to inflation if taxes were cut might involve a heavier combination of macroeconomics than microeconomics. Focusing on inflation for a moment, it is only by a thorough investigation of the microeconomic aspects of people's behavior that we can determine the costs and benefits of inflation and how people will react to stimuli such as tax cuts. For instance, it is only by examining behavior closely using traditional microeconomics that we can understand how inflation is bad: it makes people hold too little money, hurts them through tax distortions if the system is unindexed, and makes them suffer greater uncertainty (such as surprise losses to holders of fixed dollar claims) in nonadapting economic institutions that interfere with optimal resource allocation.

We have tried in this book to take great care in developing the microeconomic foundations of aggregate demand analysis, involving individual

1. Robert E. Hall and John B. Taylor, *Macroeconomics: Theory, Performance, and Policy,* 2nd ed. (New York: W. W. Norton, 1988), p. 4.

by the resulting increase in the saving outflow. The combined outflow curve shifts only part way, to $S_2 + T_2$. What is not saved is spent, for a reduction in taxes represents an increase in disposable income. Thus the total expenditures curve shifts up from TPE_1 to $TPE_2 = C_2 + I + G$, as shown in part (b). The national income level rises only to Y_2, and the unemployment level falls from U_1 to U_2, which is still below the full employment or minimum natural rate of U_F.

How much of a tax cut taxpayers will spend can be estimated by multiplying the change in taxes by the marginal propensity to consume:

$$\Delta C = (MPC \times -\Delta T)$$

behavior in consumption, investment, foreign trade, government, and the monetary system. We have likewise spent a good deal of time laying bare the microeconomic foundations of aggregate supply analysis, involving individual behavior in short-run and long-run labor and capital markets with rational expectations, imperfect information (new classical theory), wage and price rigidities, and dynamics.

The rational and maximizing economic agents portrayed in microeconomics keep right on coming in macroeconomics. For instance, consider the macroeconomic aggregate supply analysis of the productive factors labor and capital. These factors are represented in a production function. Aggregate supply then considers how the demand for factors depends on marginal productivity and the real factor price, and how the supply of factors depends on both monetary and nonmonetary factors. These same representations of productive factors were used in the microeconomic analysis of the theory of the firm and output pricing and the theory of distribution and input pricing. Thus, it is important to remember that all goods and services in the macroeconomic concept of GNP are produced by people—whether self-employed or hired by firms. To understand changes in GNP we need to understand as well how financial incen-

tives affect people in the microeconomy who produce the goods and services with machines, tools, computers, and communication systems.

The macroeconomy is in equilibrium when the four macroeconomic markets of the aggregate demand-aggregate supply framework—the bond market, commodity market, labor market, and money market—are in balance, and employment and output at the natural rate.[2] To understand these macroeconomic markets is to know the workings of the underlying microeconomic agents.

It is of course a formidable assignment to require that macroeconomic analysis always be rooted deeply and widely in sound microeconomic theory. We no doubt will make some slips along the way. But in the end we will have a stronger and more fecund theory for having attempted the slippery slope. So what if we do, on occasion, make some mistakes? As Harvard Professor Emeritus John K. Galbraith has said: "the experience of being disastrously wrong is salutary; no economist should be denied it, and not many are."[3]

2. Walras's law tells us that if there are n markets (say 4) and if n − 1 markets (3) are in equilibrium, then the nth (4th) market must also be in equilibrium. We can thus ignore one of the markets, such as the bond market, in our analysis.

3. John Kenneth Galbraith, A Life In Our Times (Boston: Houghton Mifflin Company, 1981), p. 163.

The minus sign is added to the right side of the formula because consumption is expected to change in the opposite direction from taxes. If the marginal propensity to consume is nine-tenths and taxes are reduced by $30 billion, for example, consumption will rise by nine-tenths of $30 billion, or $27 billion. The remaining portion of the tax cut, $3 billion, will therefore be saved.

A planned tax increase will reduce people's disposable incomes, lowering both saving and consumption. Lower consumption will mean lower production, and eventually still lower incomes. Like a reduction in planned government expenditures, then, a tax increase is often (but not always) intended to reduce the inflationary pressures that arise when total planned

(a)

(b)

(c)

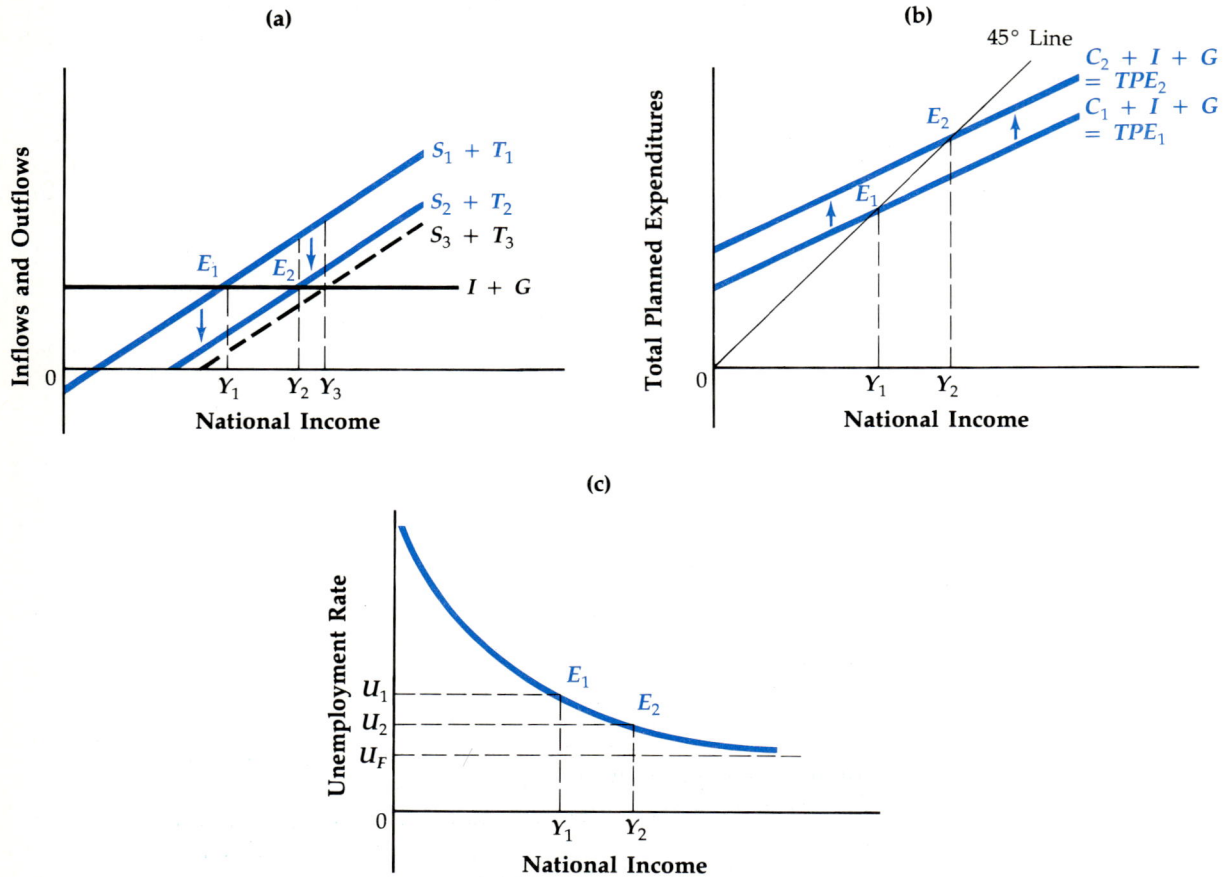

FIGURE 12.6   Decreasing Taxes (T) to Reduce Unemployment (U)

Starting at the equilibrium point E_1, a reduction in taxes shifts the combined original outflow curve ($S_1 + T_1$) downward—part (a)—although not by the full amount of the tax cut, as shown by the dotted line. That is, if some of the tax were not saved, the new outflow curve would be the dotted line $S_3 + T_3$ associated with an income level of Y_3. Some of the cut is saved, increasing the saving outflow at the same time the tax outflow decreases, shifting the combined curve to $S_2 + T_2$. The equilibrium in 12.6(a) goes from E_1 to E_2. Total planned expenditures shift up from TPE_1 to TPE_2 as shown in part (b). The equilibrium moves from E_1 to E_2 with national income level rising from Y_1 to Y_2 and the unemployment rate falling from U_1 to U_2 in part (c), but remains below the full employment (or minimum natural unemployment) rate of U_F.

expenditures exceed the economy's ability to produce. Lowering the demand for all goods and services dampens competition for scarce resources and slows price increases.

A comparison of this method of altering national income with the change-in-expenditure method discussed earlier leads us to two important conclusions. First, either a reduction in planned taxes or an increase in planned government expenditures will raise the equilibrium national income level. A decrease in government expenditures or an increase in taxes will lower the equilibrium national income level, exerting downward pressure on inflation.

Second, a change in planned government expenditures will have a greater effect on the national income level than an equal change in taxes. For instance, suppose the government increases its expenditures by $10 billion. If the multiplier is 3, the change in the equilibrium national income level will be $30 billion (the multiplier times the change in planned government expenditures). If the government reduces taxes by $10 billion, on the other hand, not all of the reduction will be spent by consumers. If $3.33 billion (*MPS* × $10 billion) of the cut goes into saving, consumption expenditures will rise by only $6.67 billion. Because the multiplier process is keyed to the increase in planned consumer expenditures, not to the tax reduction, the change in income will be only $20 billion (the multiplier times the change in planned consumption expenditures). Thus if government policymakers want to increase the national income level by reducing taxes, they will have to reduce them by an amount greater than the increase in expenditures needed to achieve the same effect.

The Balanced-Budget Multiplier

Assume the government's budget is balanced. Now suppose the government increases both its expenditures and the taxes it collects by the same amount, thus keeping its budget balanced. Will such an action affect the national income and employment levels? On the surface, it may seem that the two increases will offset each other. The rise in expenditures would increase national income by the same amount as a tax increase would reduce it. Keynesians argue that a simultaneous increase in government expenditures and taxes should have a small positive effect on national income.

To see why, assume that the marginal propensity to consume is ⅔. An increase of $10 billion in taxes will produce a $6.67 billion reduction in consumer expenditures:

$$\Delta C = (MPC \times -\Delta T)$$
$$= (\tfrac{2}{3} \times -\$10 \text{ billion})$$
$$= -\$6.67 \text{ billion}$$

If the multiplier is 3, this decrease in consumption demand will lead to a decrease in national income of $20 billion:

$$\Delta Y = m \times \Delta TPE$$

In this case, since the change in total spending is equal to the change in consumption,

$$\Delta Y = m \times \Delta C$$
$$= 3 \times -\$6.67 \text{ billion}$$
$$= -\$20 \text{ billion}$$

The increase of $10 billion in government spending will increase national income by $30 billion, for the same reason:

$$\Delta Y = m \times \Delta TPE$$

$$= m \times \Delta G$$
(since $\Delta TPE = \Delta G$)

$$= 3 \times \$10 \text{ billion}$$

$$= \$30 \text{ billion}$$

The net change in national income, then, will be $10 billion ($30 billion − $20 billion). This $10 billion rise in national income equals the increase in government expenditures and taxes that caused it. Thus when government expenditures and taxes are increased by the same amount, the combined multiplier, called the balanced-budget multiplier, is 1. Thus, the **balanced-budget multiplier** states that equal and same sign changes in government spending and taxes result in a net change in aggregate demand and national income of that same magnitude. For example, equal dollar increases in government spending and in taxes will cause an increase in aggregate demand and national income and output of that same amount. The reason is that government spending increases goes undiluted in an increase in the next round of consumer respending, but the tax increase will not decrease the next round of consumer respending by its full amount for part of the taxes will be paid out of savings.

Balanced-budget multiplier: equal and same sign changes in government spending and taxes result in a net change in aggregate demand and national income of that same magnitude.

The Kennedy Tax Cut: A Real-World Case

When President John F. Kennedy took office in 1961, the economy was in a mild recession. He and his economic advisers concluded that the best way to fulfill his campaign promise to "get the economy moving again" was to reduce personal and business taxes by approximately $12 billion. The Kennedy-Johnson administration accomplished both the tax cut and an easy money policy in 1964.

Given that an equal increase in expenditures would have had a greater impact, why did Kennedy choose to reduce taxes? Political considerations probably played an important role in the decision. In either case the government would have to run a larger budgetary deficit, and no previous president had ever proposed to run a deficit or increase one simply to stimulate the economy. Indeed deficits had always been equated with fiscal irresponsibility. They were thought to impose a burden on future generations and to court national bankruptcy. In 1961, increasing government expenditures to stimulate the economy was too radical a move politically. Although the tax cut too was controversial, it was more acceptable to the public because it put extra money into the pockets of taxpayers.

There was a technical as well as a political reason for choosing a tax cut, however. Kennedy's economic advisers argued that tax rates were so high they would prevent the achievement of full employment. If the economy started to recover and national income to rise, tax revenues would become so high that people would lack the income necessary to raise consumption. The economy would stop moving upward at some point before reaching full employment. In short, the tax system would impose what the advisers called "fiscal drag" on the recovery. **Fiscal drag** refers to the possible restrictive effect on the economy of the automatic increase in tax revenues arising from an increase in national income, where such tax revenue is not matched by corresponding increases in expenditures or decreases in taxes. If a tax cut reduced this drain on personal purchasing power, Kennedy's economists argued, the extra money people had to spend would help to speed and extend the recovery.

Keynesian economists argue that the Reagan-backed tax package of 1981, which cut tax rates over the period 1981–1984, stimulated the economy in much the same way as Kennedy's tax cut. There is some debate over whether this more recent tax cut actually had the expected positive effect on national income, however. If the rise in Social Security tax rates and the impact of bracket creep are taken into account, the overall tax rate may not have been cut very much, if at all. Some economists have offered supply-side explanations for the recovery that began in late 1982—an issue that we will take up in Chapter 15. Others attribute the recovery to the rapid rate of increase in the money stock that began late in 1982, not the tax cut. We will consider this monetary explanation for the recovery in Chapter 14.

Although all policymaking contains this possibility, because fiscal policy is more directly under the control of politicians than monetary policy, some economists believe in the notion of a **political business cycle.** Such cycles occur when politicians destabilize the economy to gain short-run voter support by manipulating macroeconomic policy to stimulate the economy before elections and contract it after elections. Politicians are often accused of manipulating economic policy to increase short-run voter support regardless of the long-run destabilizing consequences. This scenario has politicians using stimulative macroeconomic policies near election time to get a hospitable economic environment followed by contractive policies in nonelection years. The empirical evidence is inconclusive as to whether economic policy—especially fiscal—gets perverted in this way.

Fiscal drag: possible restrictive effect on the economy of the automatic increase in tax revenues arising from an increase in national income, where such tax revenue is not matched by corresponding increases in expenditures or decreases in taxes.

Political business cycle: when politicians destabilize the economy to gain short-run voter support by manipulating macroeconomic policy to stimulate the economy before elections and contract it after elections.

Fiscal Policy in the Context of the Business Cycle

◢ **2. How does deliberate fiscal policy compare with nondiscretionary built-in automatic fiscal stabilizers?**

We have seen how Keynesians use changes in government spending and taxes to counteract the negative effects of recession and inflation. Eventually, through the multiplier process, a small change in government spending or taxation will be translated into a much larger change in national income. This sort of corrective fiscal policy cannot be expected to eliminate all ups and downs in economic activity, however. Economic recovery takes time; and timing is one of the most crucial aspects of fiscal policymaking.

Difficulties in the Timing of Fiscal Actions

If policy changes could be put into effect as soon as they were needed, and if they worked almost immediately, fiscal action might be a relatively simple proposition. Almost inevitably the hoped-for increase in national income and employment, or decrease in prices, is slow in coming. Time is lost at several points along the way, starting with the lag in recognizing a problem.

Recognition Lag

Recognition lag: the time elapsed between the initial occurrence of a problem and the recognition of that problem.

Before fiscal action can be taken, government must recognize that a recession or a period of inflation is under way. The recognition lag is the time elapsed between the initial occurrence of a problem and the recognition of that problem. This process may take several months, given the way some economic data are collected. In the beginning of a recession, signals are likely to be mixed. Some measures, like the number of housing starts per month, may indicate a decline in economic activity. Yet an upward trend may persist in others, like the number of new orders for heavy industrial equipment. Thus government policymakers may not begin to address an economic problem for some time—and then they may not be able to agree immediately on the appropriate fiscal actions. Fiscal policy has roughly the same recognition lag as monetary policy (about three months).

Action (Administrative) Lag

Action (administrative) lag: the time elapsed between the general recognition of a problem and the implementation of a policy to correct it.

After policymakers have concluded that the economy has changed direction, they will have to convince Congress that a change in taxes or expenditures is needed. The action (administrative) lag is the time elapsed between the general recognition of a problem and the implementation of a policy to correct it. Members of Congress may bargain for special benefits for their home districts. Thus policy action is further delayed by politicking. The Kennedy tax cut took sixteen months to go through Congress. The Reagan tax package took almost a year.

Impact (Operational) Lag

Impact (operational) lag: the time elapsed between the implementation of a corrective policy and when the economic impact of that policy is felt.

If Congress approves an action, several more months will pass before its impact is felt. The impact (operational) lag is the time elapsed between the implementation of a corrective policy and when the economic impact of that policy is felt. A tax cut will take effect as soon as people's take-home pay increases. An increase in government expenditures tends to work more slowly—new projects must be bid on, and contracts negotiated. All in all, the economy can be well on its way to the bottom or top of a cycle before the effects of a fiscal action become evident.

Unfortunately, if an action comes too late, it is likely to make the problem worse. If a fiscal stimulus is passed late in the recovery phase of a recession, it can add to the inflationary pressures that accompany the approach to the peak of a business cycle. Only in a world in which information is readily available and unambiguous can appropriate action be taken at the appropriate time. Because fiscal policies must be formulated in the political arena, appropriate timing is even more unlikely. If Congress uses Keynesian prescriptions to increase political support at home, a political business cycle—one that moves in accord with elections—may develop.

Use of Automatic Fiscal Stabilizers

Automatic fiscal stabilizer: a built-in tax or expenditure that increases total planned spending in times of recession and lowers it in times of economic expansion, without special explicit action on the part of the administration and Congress.

There is an alternative to the use of deliberate policy actions by government, one that does not involve the risk of poor timing. Some taxes and government expenditures vary automatically with changes in the national income level, and generally in the desired direction. These fiscal instruments are called automatic stabilizers. An **automatic fiscal stabilizer** is a built-in tax or expenditure that increases total planned spending in times of recession and lowers it in times of economic expansion, without special explicit action on the part of the administration and Congress. In a sense, automatic fiscal stabilizers are a form of nondiscretionary fiscal policy. Thus, these mechanisms automatically reduce the impact on GNP of changes in aggregate demand. This means that both prosperity and recession are shorter and less intense than when these stabilizers were few or nonexistent, as they apply restraint in good times and a stimulus in bad times. Among the more important automatic fiscal stabilizers are income taxes, unemployment and welfare benefits, and corporate dividend payouts. These stabilizers reduce the size of economic fluctuations but cannot do the job alone. A good estimate is that they can reduce fluctuations by about one-third. Other explicit discretionary policies are needed to do the rest.

Personal Income Taxes

Through the tax rate structure, personal income taxes are tied directly to the national income level. As their personal incomes rise, people are required to pay an increasing percentage of their taxable incomes to the government. When national income begins to fall, therefore, the government's tax collections decline as well. This drop in tax revenues partly offsets the drop in consumer purchasing power.

Corporate Income Taxes

Like individuals, corporations must pay a percentage of their profits in taxes to the government. Like personal income taxes, corporate income taxes vary with corporate income, or profits. This stabilizer has a particularly powerful effect on total spending, for corporate profits move dramatically in response to a change in national income. They fall considerably during recessions and rise steeply during economic expansions.

Unemployment Compensation and Welfare Benefits

When the national income level falls, the unemployment level rises. There is then an increase in unemployment compensation, as well as many welfare benefits—food stamps, rent subsidies, and aid to dependent children—increasing the level of government spending. Conversely, a rise in national income reduces unemployment, curtailing these social programs and lowering government spending.

Corporate Dividend Policy

Corporations tend to be quite sluggish in raising or cutting dividends when profits fluctuate. By maintaining fairly stable dividends in the short run, consumers can spend more than they could if dividends were raised in good times. This dividend policy tends to cushion a recession and curb inflation by stabilizing consumer spending.

The Pros and Cons of Deficit Spending

▲ **3. Is deficit spending a problem?**

National or public debt: the total amount owed by the Federal government in the form of outstanding U.S. Treasury securities as a result of past net budget deficits.

Before Keynes it was generally agreed that government should try to restrict its expenditures to the level of its tax receipts—in other words, balance its budget. Deficit spending during peacetime was equated with fiscal irresponsibility. An underlying assumption was that the federal government was like an individual household. It could not continually incur budgetary deficits without risking bankruptcy. Moreover, because individual debts must be paid back at some point, deficit spending resulting in a national or public debt was seen as a burden on future generations. Thus, the **national or public debt** is the total amount owed by the Federal government in the form of outstanding U.S. Treasury securities as a result of past net budget deficits.

Keynesian theory undermined the popularity of the balanced budget. Keynesians argued that during periods of slack demand and high unemployment, deficit spending creates no present or future costs. On the contrary, because of the implied increase in total spending, deficits allow more people to work, more income to be generated, and more products to be produced. These resources, both people and equipment, would otherwise remain idle. Since the real cost of any government action must be measured against what is forgone, it follows that the real cost of running a deficit during a recession is virtually zero. Of course, to the extent that people do not save more as deficits increase, the debt is a problem.

Furthermore, to the extent that deficit spending is used to build roads, schools, and national parks, or to encourage private investment through government subsidies, future generations actually benefit from it. They have more capital assets to use in the production of new goods and services. Although they will have to meet the interest payments on the debt, they also have higher incomes with which to meet them. Besides, to the extent the interest is paid to U.S. citizens, such payments do not represent a loss of resources to the nation as a whole. Because we effectively owe the debt to ourselves (less than 20 percent of the national debt is held externally by foreign investors), we pay the interest to ourselves—or so the argument goes. This is all fine if the political problems with raising the money to service the debt are not too severe.

During times of full employment, a government deficit does impose a cost on the private sector, because there are no idle resources to be taken up. Resources must be diverted from private to government use. At such times, the cost of a deficit can be measured by what must be given up in the

PERSPECTIVES
The Political Effects of Keynesian Economics

When Keynes wrote his *General Theory,* British economic policy was formulated by a small group of intellectuals. Keynes developed his arguments for government spending with such a system in mind. He assumed that given good policy recommendations, good men will do good things. He probably did not foresee that his ideas would be taken up by politicians in Washington, who keep one eye on the economy and the other on the opinion polls.

Those who follow the politics of economics have observed that politicians tend to vote for spending programs and against the taxes to pay for those programs.[1] Government expenditures benefit many. To the extent that they benefit a politician's constituency, they increase his or her political support. Taxes, on the other hand, impose costs on political constituencies. They tend to reduce a politician's support. If politicians accept the idea that government budgets must be balanced, some

economists argue, they will vote for government expenditures only if the political support they generate exceeds the support lost by raising taxes to pay for the programs. If politicians do not believe in the balanced budget, they will court political support by voting consistently for government expenditures and against taxes. Given widespread acceptance of deficit spending, even politicians who are opposed to deficits may feel forced to accept them in order to survive politically.

In times of inflation, when the government should reduce total planned expenditures and run a budgetary surplus, the political appeal of a deficit becomes even more obvious. Politicians have an understandable aversion to budget surpluses, since they can be created only by raising taxes but not spending—or reducing spending but not taxes. For politicians, surpluses can spell a net loss in political support. Even during periods of excessive demand and inflation, politicians are more likely to vote for a lower surplus, or even a deficit, than for a higher surplus. Keynesian policy may be effective, but it cannot always be productively employed in the political arena.

1. James M. Buchanan and Richard E. Wagner, *Democracy in Deficit: The Destructive Legacy of Lord Keynes* (New York: Academic Press, 1977).

private sector. Most Keynesians agree that deficit spending is generally appropriate only during periods of relatively high unemployment.

Keynesians also question the analogy between government and household finances. They point out that even an individual household's debt can grow over time, as the family becomes better able to pay interest and to repay the principal. While a household is paying off some debts, it can incur new ones. People who are paying off a car loan, for instance, can still buy furniture on credit. As people's incomes grow over time, their ability to handle more debt increases.

This is just what has happened in the United States since World War II. In 1950 consumer debt (not including home mortgages) totaled $25 billion; by the end of 1987 it had risen to $756 billion. Even allowing for inflation, the increase in private debt had been substantial. Yet personal

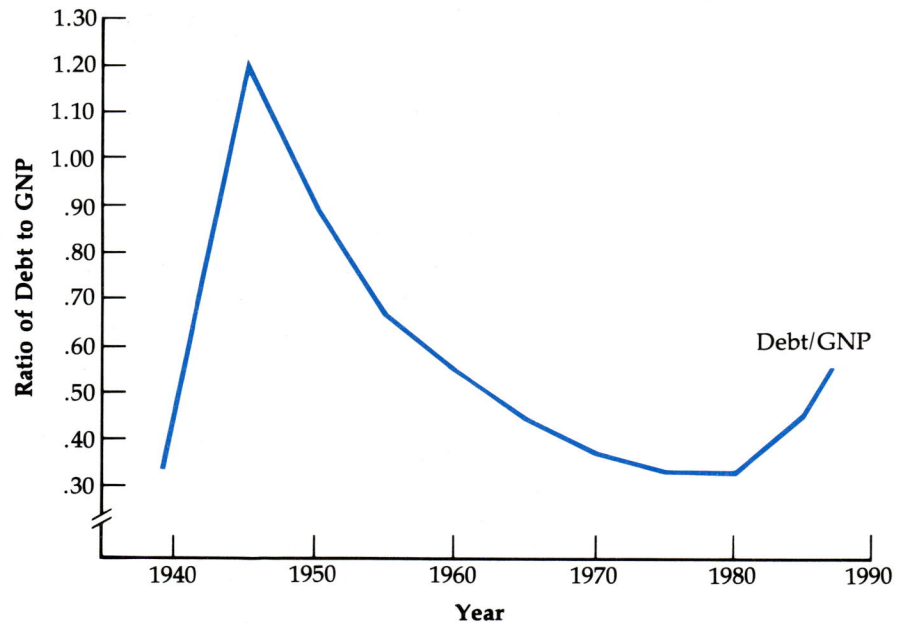

FIGURE 12.7 Measure of Debt Burden: Ratio of Debt/GNP

One measure of the burden of the national debt is its ratio to GNP. The debt ratio peaked during World War II, fell continuously until the 1980s then started rising. Another measure of burden of the debt, the debt/federal receipts ratio follows almost exactly the same path as the debt/GNP ratio.

Source: William R. Bryan, "Perspectives on the Federal Debt: 1791–1987," *Illinois Business Review* (December 1987), p. 6.

income has grown with it. Personal income increased from $228 billion to $3,746 billion between 1950 and 1987.[4] If members of households can increase their indebtedness over time, why not the government? In fact, government debt as a percentage of GNP fell from 1950 to 1982 and started rising after that. The debt reached its peak in World War II, and drifted downward continuously until again rising in the 1980s. Figure 12.7 shows the path of the debt as a percentage of GNP. The federal debt rose more rapidly since 1974 than during any other peacetime period of this century. Another measure of the burden of the debt, debt as a percentage of federal receipts, follows almost exactly the same path as the debt-to-GNP ratio.

Furthermore, the idea that all debts will eventually come due cannot really be applied to government. Because people's lives are limited, mem-

---

4. *Economic Report of the President* (Washington, D.C.: U.S. Government Printing Office, 1988), pp. 273, 336.

bers of an individual household must pay off all their debts—if necessary, through their estates, after death. For all practical purposes the government can expect perpetual life. Granted, government bonds do carry maturity dates, on which bondholders must be repaid the stated amounts. Government can refinance its debt by issuing new bonds and using the funds collected from them to pay off the old debt. Taken collectively, the debt of consumers is never paid off. So why should the government's debt be paid off?

The major constraint on the government's ability to expand its debt is citizens' willingness to buy bonds and their willingness to pay taxes to finance the payment of interest rates. The borrowing limit depends on both the stability of the government and people's propensity to save. If a government is in danger of being overthrown, people will of course be reluctant to lend it money. As long as the government is stable and can pay the going market interest rate out of its tax collections, government bonds will be just as attractive as private bonds, if not more so. U.S. government bonds are generally considered to be safer investments than most corporate bonds, as evidenced by the higher interest rates borne by the latter. Finally, Keynesians would argue, if through deficit spending the government can raise the national income level, and therefore the nation's tax revenues, why worry about increasing the national debt?

We will return to this issue in following chapters, for economists from other schools of thought take issue with the Keynesians' benign view of government deficits.

Monetary Policy from the Keynesian Perspective

▲ 4. Why is monetary policy subordinate to fiscal policy for Keynesians?

Monetary policy is the Fed's use of the money supply's growth rate to achieve economic goals. Proponents of monetary policy argue that its major advantages over fiscal policy are: its flexibility; its ease of implementation and changeability; and its impersonality (since the market and not the Fed determines who is affected).

Critics of monetary policy, however, contend that its primary disadvantages are: that it may not have substantial impact on investment or aggregate demand; that any impact it has may in fact be destabilizing because of various lags; that it is inflexible; that it is asymmetrical, affecting certain types of firms more than others (i.e., interest-sensitive and small firms); and that it may possibly cause conflict between the Fed and the President, and between domestic and international policy goals.

Although modern Keynesians advocate the use of both fiscal and monetary policy to relieve unemployment, Keynesian economics has historically been associated with the management of aggregate demand through fiscal policy. Keynes and his followers doubted that monetary policy would be able to pull the economy out of a particularly severe recession like the Great Depression.

The Federal Reserve During the Depression

During the Great Depression banks were hit hard on both sides of their balance sheet. While borrowers became less capable of paying back their loans, depositors became skeptical of the solvency of banks and withdrew their deposits. Thousands of banks failed (almost 4,000 in 1933 alone!) and many others came close to bankruptcy.

The banks' predicament was made more difficult by the Federal Reserve. The Fed was established to ensure that banks could borrow the reserves they needed whenever their customers made heavy withdrawals. Yet during the 1930s the Fed severely discouraged banks from borrowing at the discount window. Many banks failed simply because they could not obtain the necessary reserves from the Fed. Bank officers soon became extremely cautious about lending money, and worked to build up their reserve deposits with the Fed and other banks. When the Fed later attempted to increase the money stock, banks held on to part of the newly created reserves for their own protection.

To Keynesians, this buildup of excess reserves demonstrated that during a severe depression, people have a highly elastic demand for money. Even very small decreases in interest rates will cause banks to hold on to whatever reserves they can, and individuals to hold on to whatever money the Federal Reserve creates. The money simply will not be spent. And without an increase in spending, the economy will remain depressed.

Thus Keynesians concluded that monetary policy could not alleviate a severe depression. The only way to stimulate the economy in such circumstances, they argued, was to increase spending or reduce taxes.

The Liquidity Trap

Keynesians deemphasize monetary policy not just because of its history during the Depression, but because of its role in Keynesian theory. Keynesians reject the classical theory that interest rates adjust to bring the demand for investment goods into line with the supply of saving. Instead they stress the demand for money versus the stock of money.

According to Keynesian theory, the demand for money is rooted primarily in the transactions demand and the speculative demand. (In Keynesian terms the transactions demand for money includes both the transactions and precautionary demands.) The transactions demand is determined primarily by the national income level. Money is needed to carry on trade, and the greater the national income level, the greater the need for trade. The direct relationship between the national income level and the transactions demand for money is illustrated in Figure 12.8(a).

The speculative demand for money is determined principally by expectations regarding future interest rates. If people think current interest rates are low, they will hold on to their money, waiting for rates to rise. If interest rates are falling, more and more people will begin to expect rates to rise in

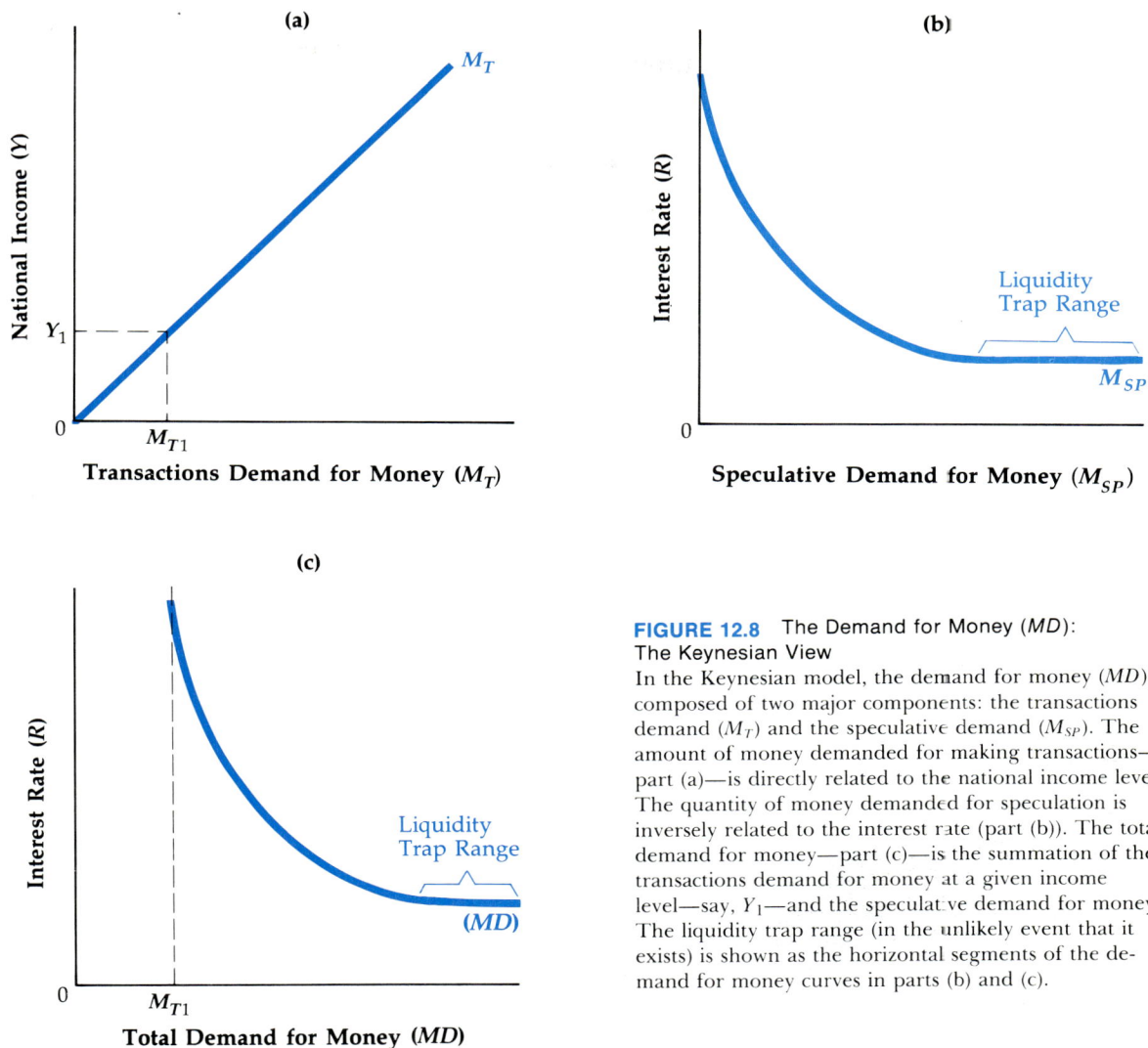

(a)

National Income (Y)

Y_1

0   M_{T1}

Transactions Demand for Money (M_T)

M_T

(b)

Interest Rate (R)

Liquidity
Trap Range

0

Speculative Demand for Money (M_{SP})

M_{SP}

(c)

Interest Rate (R)

Liquidity
Trap Range

(MD)

0   M_{T1}

Total Demand for Money (MD)

FIGURE 12.8   The Demand for Money (*MD*):
The Keynesian View
In the Keynesian model, the demand for money (*MD*) is
composed of two major components: the transactions
demand (M_T) and the speculative demand (M_{SP}). The
amount of money demanded for making transactions—
part (a)—is directly related to the national income level.
The quantity of money demanded for speculation is
inversely related to the interest rate (part (b)). The total
demand for money—part (c)—is the summation of the
transactions demand for money at a given income
level—say, Y_1—and the speculative demand for money.
The liquidity trap range (in the unlikely event that it
exists) is shown as the horizontal segments of the demand for money curves in parts (b) and (c).

the future and will hold on to their money for the present. The quantity of
money demanded for speculative purposes will rise. This inverse relationship between interest rates and the speculative demand for money is illustrated in Figure 12.8(b).

Given an income level like Y_1 in Figure 12.8(a), the total demand for
money will look something like the curve in Figure 12.8(c). Keynes argued
that during severe depressions, the interest rate may fall so low that everyone will believe it is going to rise, and everyone will hold on to all the cash

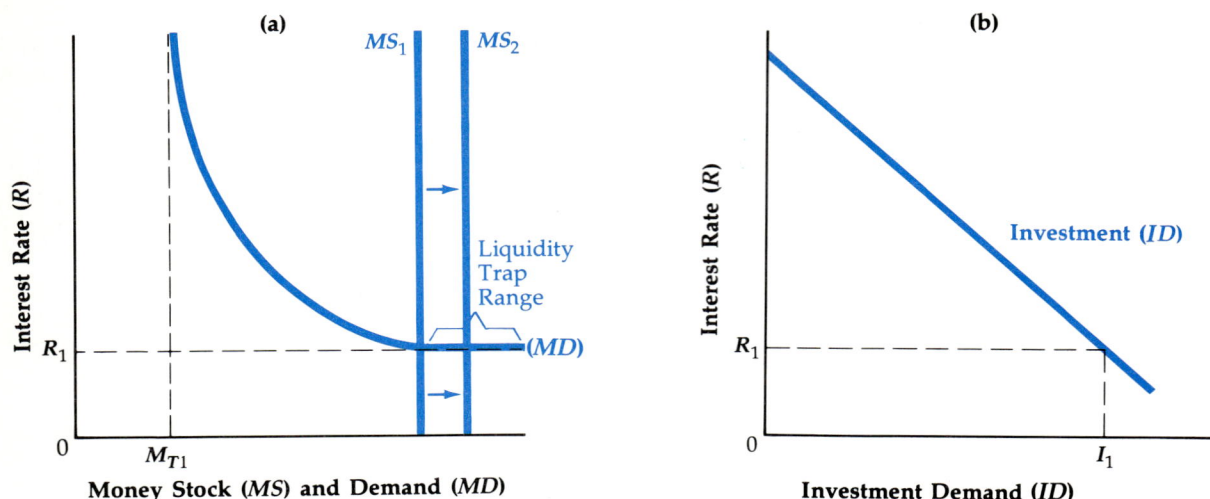

FIGURE 12.9 The Liquidity Trap: People Hoarding All Increases in the Money Stock
If the money demand curve (MD) flattens out at a low interest rate, as in panel (a), and the money stock curve intersects it in its horizontal range, the macroeconomy is said to be in a liquidity trap. An increase in the money stock from MS_1 to MS_2 will not result in a lower interest rate, and therefore will not increase the level of investment (ID)—panel (b). There is little theoretical or empirical support now or in the past for the concept of a liquidity trap.

Liquidity trap: when people under certain unlikely conditions hoard all increases in the money stock so that the demand for money curve is horizontal.

they can get.[5] An economy in such circumstances has fallen onto a "liquidity trap." A **liquidity trap** occurs when people under certain unlikely conditions hoard all increases in the money stock so that the demand for money curve is horizontal. The usual monetary policy remedy—expansion of the money stock—can offer no relief. The horizontal segments of the money demand schedules in Figure 12.8 parts (b) and (c) depict the unlikely case of a range with a liquidity trap.

Suppose, for instance, that the demand for money looks like the downward-sloping curve in Figure 12.9(a), and that the money stock is fixed at MS_1. The equilibrium interest rate will be R_1, where the demand for money and money stock curves intersect. Notice that with this curve, an increase in the money stock, say from MS_1 to MS_2, will not lower the interest rate any further, as it normally would be expected to do. If the interest rate remains at R_1, the investment level will stay at I_1 in Figure 12.9(b). With no increase in investment, the national income level must remain depressed.

5. Keynes thought the logical assumptions for a liquidity trap were unlikely to occur and he personally knew of no actual examples of it. A spate of empirical testing since Keynes has validated its statistical insignificance. For an excellent survey of these studies see David E. Laidler, *The Demand for Money: Theories and Evidence,* 3rd ed. (New York: Harper & Row, 1985).

The Effect of Changes in the Money Stock

Thus Keynesians explained the apparent ineffectiveness of monetary policy during the Great Depression. They concluded that in severe economic conditions, fiscal policy actions are the only means of stimulating the economy. Many Keynesians now recognize that monetary policy can be a useful means of fighting recession. In fact, the demand for money never flattens out completely, as it does in Figure 12.9(a) and Figures 12.8(b) and (c). Rather, it slopes downward all the way, as in Figure 12.10(a). Hence an

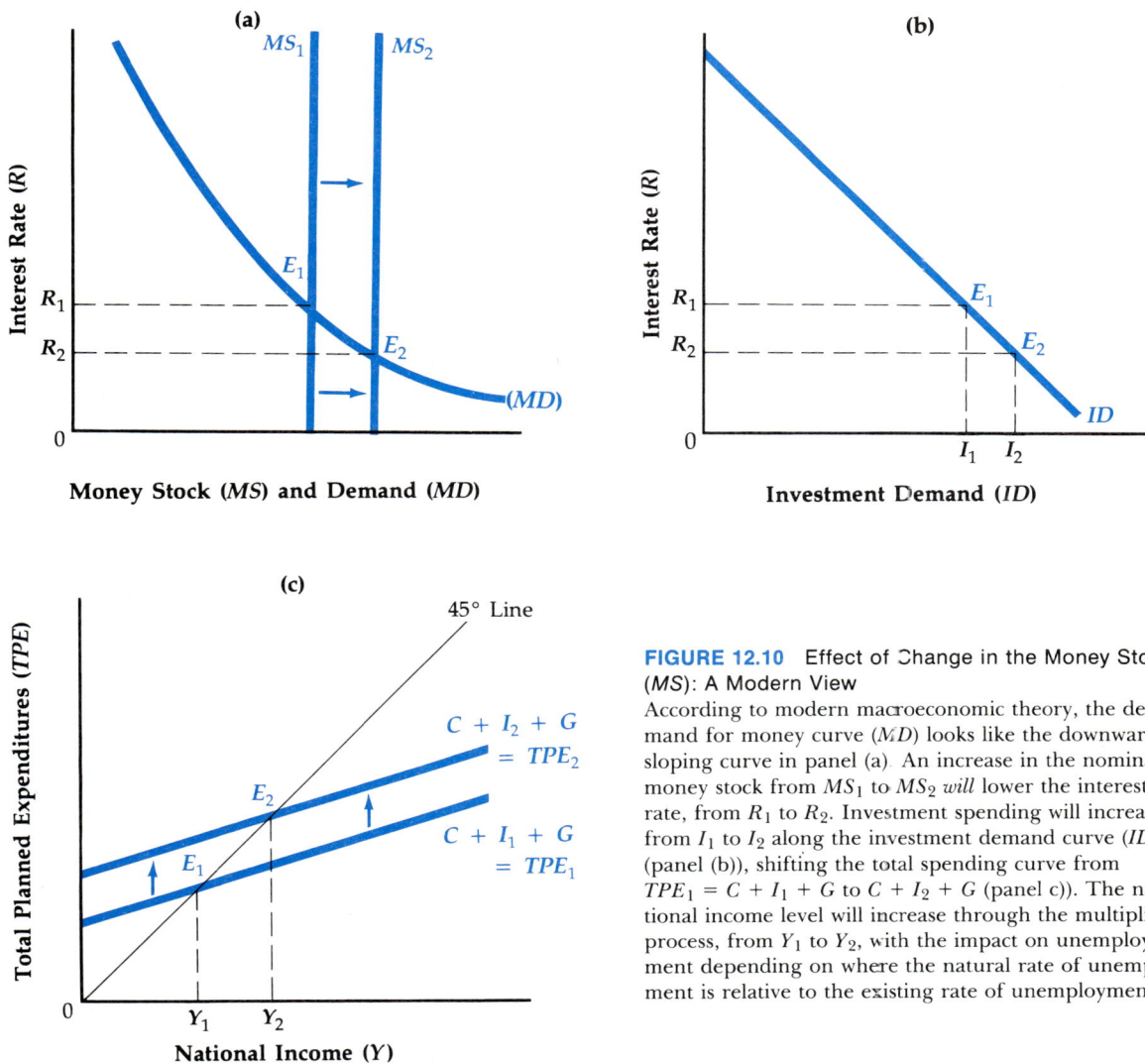

(a)

Money Stock (MS) and Demand (MD)

(b)

Investment Demand (ID)

(c)

National Income (Y)

FIGURE 12.10   Effect of Change in the Money Stock (MS): A Modern View

According to modern macroeconomic theory, the demand for money curve (MD) looks like the downward-sloping curve in panel (a). An increase in the nominal money stock from MS_1 to MS_2 will lower the interest rate, from R_1 to R_2. Investment spending will increase from I_1 to I_2 along the investment demand curve (ID) (panel (b)), shifting the total spending curve from $TPE_1 = C + I_1 + G$ to $C + I_2 + G$ (panel c)). The national income level will increase through the multiplier process, from Y_1 to Y_2, with the impact on unemployment depending on where the natural rate of unemployment is relative to the existing rate of unemployment.

increase in the nominal money stock, say from MS_1 to MS_2, will lead to a lower interest rate and an increase in investment spending, as in Figure 12.10(b). Through the multiplier process, this increase in investment will be translated into a much larger increase in national income, as in Figure 12.10(c). The impact on unemployment will depend on where the natural rate of unemployment is relative to the present rate.

Though economists now agree on the general effect of an increase in the money stock, debate continues over the magnitude of the effect. The size of the change in national income depends on several factors.

1. How far the interest rate will fall as the money stock rises depends on how people's money holdings respond to a change in the interest rate.

2. How much investment spending will increase as the interest rate declines depends on how investment spending responds to a change in the interest rate.

3. How much the national income level will change as a result of a change in investment spending depends on the size of the spending multiplier. The size of the spending multiplier likewise depends on the marginal propensity to consume and on income tax rates.

Keynesians believe that the fiscal spending multiplier is greater than the monetary policy multiplier. The jury is still out, though, since there is conflicting evidence on which policy is more effective, and on the precise impact of fiscal and monetary policy multipliers.

Chapter Review

Review of Key Questions

1. *What can the government do to promote economic stability through fiscal policy?*

Fiscal policy is the government's deliberate exercise of its taxing and spending power to help moderate the swings of the business cycle and to promote the public welfare by encouraging greater production and employment and stable prices. Government can increase total planned expenditures (and thus the national income level) by increasing government spending while holding taxes constant, by reducing taxes while holding government spending constant, or by increasing government spending and decreasing taxes at the same time. Government can reduce total planned expenditures (and thus inflation) by reducing government spending while holding taxes constant, by increasing taxes while holding government spending constant, or by reducing government spending while increasing taxes.

According to Keynesian theory, increases and decreases in government spending or taxes have a multiplier effect on the national income level. The government should thus adjust its expenditures or its taxes by only a fraction of the desired change in national income. An increase in government spending will have a greater effect on the national income level than a tax reduction of equal size. To increase the national income level through a tax cut, the government must reduce taxes by more than it would have to increase government spending to achieve the same effect. The balanced-budget multiplier means that equal and same direction changes in government spending and taxes result in a net change in aggregate demand and national income and output. It has a value of 1.0.

When government borrows money to cover a deficit caused by an increase in its spending, the market interest rate may rise and businesses may reduce their investment spending. This reduction in planned business investment can partially (if not totally) offset the effect of higher government spending on the national income level. This is called "crowding out," and reduces the effectiveness of fiscal policy. Government budgetary deficits should not be incurred needlessly, but they may be acceptable if they emerge from a purposeful fiscal policy designed to stimulate the economy and raise the national income level.

◢   *2. How does deliberate fiscal policy compare with nondiscretionary built-in automatic fiscal stabilizers?*

Delays in the implementation of fiscal policy should be expected because a recognition lag (delay in recognizing the need for a change in fiscal policy), action or administrative lag (delay in getting Congress to take the necessary action), and impact or operational lag (delay in realizing the effects of the policy change). Automatic or built-in fiscal stabilizers are fiscal changes triggered automatically by changes in the national income level, without special action on the part of the administration or Congress. They include personal and corporate tax receipts, unemployment and welfare benefits, and corporate dividend policy. Although they moderate fluctuations, fiscal stabilizers alone are incapable of offsetting them entirely, at most lessening fluctuations by one-third.

◢   *3. Is deficit spending a problem?*

There are both pros and cons to deficit spending. The national or public debt is the total debt owed by the federal government as a result of past net budget deficits through time. The national debt does not have to be paid off; it can be refinanced. When a portion of the national debt comes due, the government can issue new bonds to acquire the funds needed to pay it off. The debt is likely to be a problem only if the capital stock is depleted, the debt is owned to a significant extent externally, and interest payments on the debt are rising and politically difficult to refinance. The burden of the debt measured as a percent of GNP peaked in 1944 and fell continuously until the 1980s when it again started rising.

◢   *4. Why is monetary policy subordinate to fiscal policy for Keynesians?*

Fiscal policy may involve deficit spending. Deficit spending benefits politicians seeking reelection, for their constituents receive more government goods and services without having to pay for them directly through higher taxes. Politicians can thus be expected to support larger deficits than may be necessary to achieve full employment and stable prices. Monetary policy can also influence the national income level. Monetary policy refers to steps taken through the monetary mechanisms and institutions in our society to bring about a desired state of the economy thought to be in the general public interest. It has its major advantages and disadvantages compared to fiscal policy. An increase in the money stock will reduce the interest rate, increasing planned investment and total planned expenditures. Like fiscal actions, the increase in total planned expenditures will be translated by the multiplier process into an increase in the national income level. The notion of a liquidity trap (wherein people hoard all increases in the money stock, thereby preventing the interest rate from falling and investment spending from rising) has received little if any support. Keynesians still feel that the fiscal policy multiplier is more certain and larger than the monetary policy multiplier, especially in severe recessions or depressions. The available evidence suggests that both monetary and fiscal policy have significant impact on economic activity. There is little agreement as to which of these two policies is more powerful or what the precise magnitude of their impact is.

Further Topics

The Keynesian prescription to remedy extremely high unemployment is to increase total planned expenditures, either by increasing government spending or by decreasing taxes. Both methods will increase national income. Either way, though, the government must be willing to create or increase a budgetary deficit or to reduce a budgetary surplus. In times of excessive demand and inflation, the Keynesian prescription is to increase taxes or reduce government expenditures, thus lowering the equilibrium national income level. Such action may require the government to run a budgetary surplus or a smaller deficit.

These same basic effects can be obtained by increasing or decreasing the money stock. An increase in the money stock will tend to lower interest rates, encouraging investment. A decrease in the money stock will do the opposite. Modern-day Keynesians feel that both monetary and fiscal actions can be used effectively, either separately or together, to relieve unemployment and inflation. As we will see in later chapters, however, there is considerable debate about the appropriateness of Keynesian policies. Part of that debate concerns the extent to which fiscal and monetary policy actions affect prices, which we have held constant in the foregoing analysis. That simplifying assumption will be dropped in the next chapter.

Suffice it to say that the present difference between Keynesians and monetarists is much narrower than previously. Both camps agree that money is important, money affects things other than prices, price changes are not proportional to money changes, and the demand for money is influenced by interest rates. Yet on the policy level there is still disagreement in that the monetarists favor monetary policy over fiscal policy in the short-run and feel that no policy has any permanent effect on employment and output in the long run. As we shall discover later, rational expectationists—who feel that people consider all available information including policy actions in forming opinions of future economic activity—share the monetarists' view that monetary policy is impotent in consistently affecting employment and output in the long run.

Review of New Terms

Action (administrative) lag The time elapsed between the general recognition of a problem and the implementation of a policy to correct it.

Automatic fiscal stabilizer A built-in tax or expenditure that increases total planned spending in times of recession and lowers it in times of economic expansion, without special explicit action on the part of the administration and Congress.

Balanced-budget multiplier Equal and same sign changes in government spending and taxes result in a net change in aggregate demand and national income of that same magnitude.

Crowding out The theory that an increase in government spending tends to cause—working through an increase in the real interest rate—a partial or total offset in total planned expenditures of decreased private spending, thereby making fiscal policy less effective or totally ineffective.

Expansionary gap The gap that occurs when actual GNP is greater than potential (i.e., full employment) GNP.

Fiscal drag Possible restrictive effect on the economy of the automatic increase in tax revenues arising from an increase in national income, where such tax revenue is not matched by corresponding increases in expenditures or decreases in taxes.

Impact (operational) lag The time elapsed between the implementation of a corrective policy and when the economic impact of that policy is felt.

Liquidity trap When people under certain unlikely conditions hoard all increases in the money stock so that the demand for money curve is horizontal.

Lump-sum tax A constant tax that produces the same amount of tax revenue at each level of national income.

National or public debt The total amount owed by the Federal government in the form of outstanding U.S. Treasury securities as a result of past net budget deficits.

Political business cycle When politicians destabilize the economy to gain short-run voter support by manipulating macroeconomic policy to stimulate the economy before elections and contract it after elections.

Recognition lag The time elapsed between the initial occurrence of a problem and the recognition of that problem.

Review Questions

1. Will an increase in government expenditures of $10 billion have the same effect on the national income level as a $10 billion decrease in taxes? Explain. (◀ 1)

2. Will a decrease in the money stock reduce or increase the national income level? Explain your reasoning. (◀ 4)

3. If a $10 billion increase in government expenditures causes a $10 billion decrease in investment expenditures, what will happen to the national income level? (◢ 1)

4. In recent years, government has allowed a tax credit for investing in new plant and equipment. That is, businesses have been permitted to reduce their tax payments by a percentage of the value of new plant and equipment purchased during the year. Using the Keynesian model of income and employment, explain the possible effects of such an investment tax credit. (◢ 1, ◢ 2)

5. Does Keynesian theory promote unnecessarily high budgetary deficits? Explain your answer. (◢ 3)

Aggregate Supply and Demand

Can the United States have high-unemployment prosperity without inflation? For some time, the American people have been asked to tune in tomorrow and find out; but the last episode of the serial has not yet been produced. In no period during the past forty years has the American economy been free of excessive unemployment and inflationary tendencies simultaneously. Nor has any other industrial nation found the happier combination; hitting the dual target of high utilization and essential price stability remains the most serious unsolved problem of stabilization policy throughout the Western World.
  Arthur Okun

KEY QUESTIONS

▲ 1. What is the nature and slope of the aggregate demand function?

▲ 2. What is the nature and slope of the short-run and long-run aggregate supply functions?

▲ 3. What is the aggregate demand and supply approach to equilibrium income?

NEW TERMS

Aggregate demand
Econometric model
Econometrics
Linear regression
Long-run aggregate supply

Money illusion
Natural rate of unemployment
Real balances or real wealth
  effect
Short-run aggregate supply

So far we have focused almost exclusively on how changes in total spending affect the national income and employment levels. Little has been said about what happens to the price level when government fiscal or monetary policies change. We have ignored the price level for two reasons. First, Keynesian theory initially assumed that prices (and wages) do not change very much, or change very rapidly with changes in total spending. A central point of Keynesian macroeconomics is that changes in total planned spending will be reflected in output and unemployment—a point that can be illustrated most clearly by holding prices constant. Second, the assumption of constant prices has helped us to keep the analysis relatively simple.

This chapter will extend Keynesian macroeconomic theory in two ways. First, we will introduce prices. To explain how price changes can absorb some of the impact of a change in planned expenditures, we will return to the aggregate demand and supply model introduced in Chapter 6. Second, we will show how changes in the conditions of production can affect national income, employment, and prices.

Aggregate Demand

▲ 1. What is the nature and slope of the aggregate demand function?

In Chapter 6 the aggregate demand function was defined as the presumed negative relationship between price levels and the total quantity of goods and services consumers, businesses, and the government (and foreigners) want to buy during a given period of time.[1] Aggregate demand is not the same as the market demand for a given product or service. Market demand is the relationship between the price of a given product and the quantity consumers are willing and able to buy during a given period of time. **Aggregate demand** is a function or curve that shows the relationship between the

Aggregate demand: a function or curve that shows the relationship between the general price level (an index of the prices of all products and services) and the total quantity of all goods and services demanded during a given period of time.

1. More technically, the aggregate demand curve shows the alternative price and real national income (y) combinations that generate simultaneous equilibrium in markets for both money and commodities for given money and fiscal parameters. (Note that in Chapters 13 and 14, lower case y refers to real national income in constant dollars, whereas in earlier chapters, an upper case Y referred to nominal or money national income at current prices.)

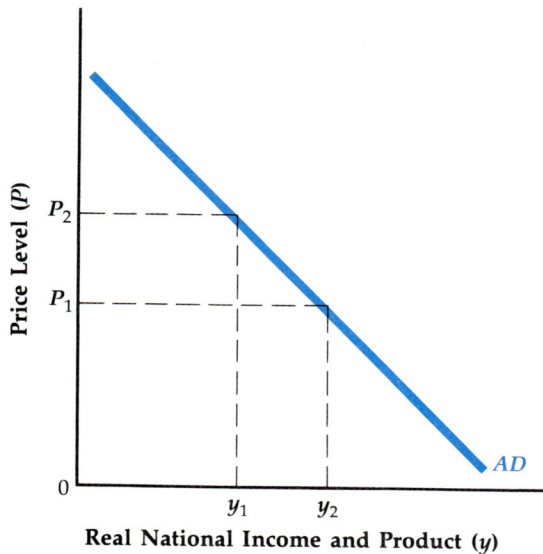

FIGURE 13.1** Aggregate Demand
Aggregate demand (AD) is the assumed inverse relationship between the price level and the real national income (y) of the total output demanded during a period of time. If the price level falls from P_2 to P_1, for example, the total quantity of goods and services demanded by consumers, investors, and government rises from y_1 to y_2.

general price level (an index of prices of all products and services) and the total quantity of goods and services demanded during a given period of time.

Aggregate demand also differs from the total planned expenditures function we discussed in Chapters 10, 11, and 12. That function is the relationship between the national income level and total planned expenditures. Aggregate demand is the relationship between the price levels and the total amount of goods and services, or national output, that people want. Aggregate demand permits us to monitor the influence of the price level on total planned expenditures. To say it another way, the total planned expenditures curve represents a point on the aggregate demand curve.

Usually aggregate demand is drawn as a downward-sloping curve, like the one shown in Figure 13.1. Its downward slope reflects the negative relationship between prices (P) in general and total product demanded, or real national income (y). As the price level goes down, from P_2 to P_1, total real national income and product demanded rises, from y_1 to y_2. All market demand curves slope downward, but that is not why the aggregate demand curve does so. Its shape is a result of the effects of a change in the price level on interest rates and on people's real wealth.[2]

---

2. There is a third explanation that draws on the international economic relations discussed in Chapters 34–35. Briefly, a decrease in the domestic price level leads ultimately to an increase in net exports. It works this way because a lower price level makes domestic goods less expensive and foreign goods more expensive, thereby inducing an increase in net exports (or decrease in net imports). As we will discover, aggregate demand reflects purchases of U.S. goods from all sources, domestic and foreign.

The Effect of a Change in Price Level on Interest Rates

In our discussion of the Keynesian theory of interest rates in Chapter 12, the interaction of the demand for money and the stock of money determines the interest rate. If the demand for money and the real money stock are represented as MD and MS_1/P_1 in Figure 13.2(a), the interest rate will be R_2. Planned investment demand will be I_1 (part (b)), and the real national income level will be y_1 (part (c)).

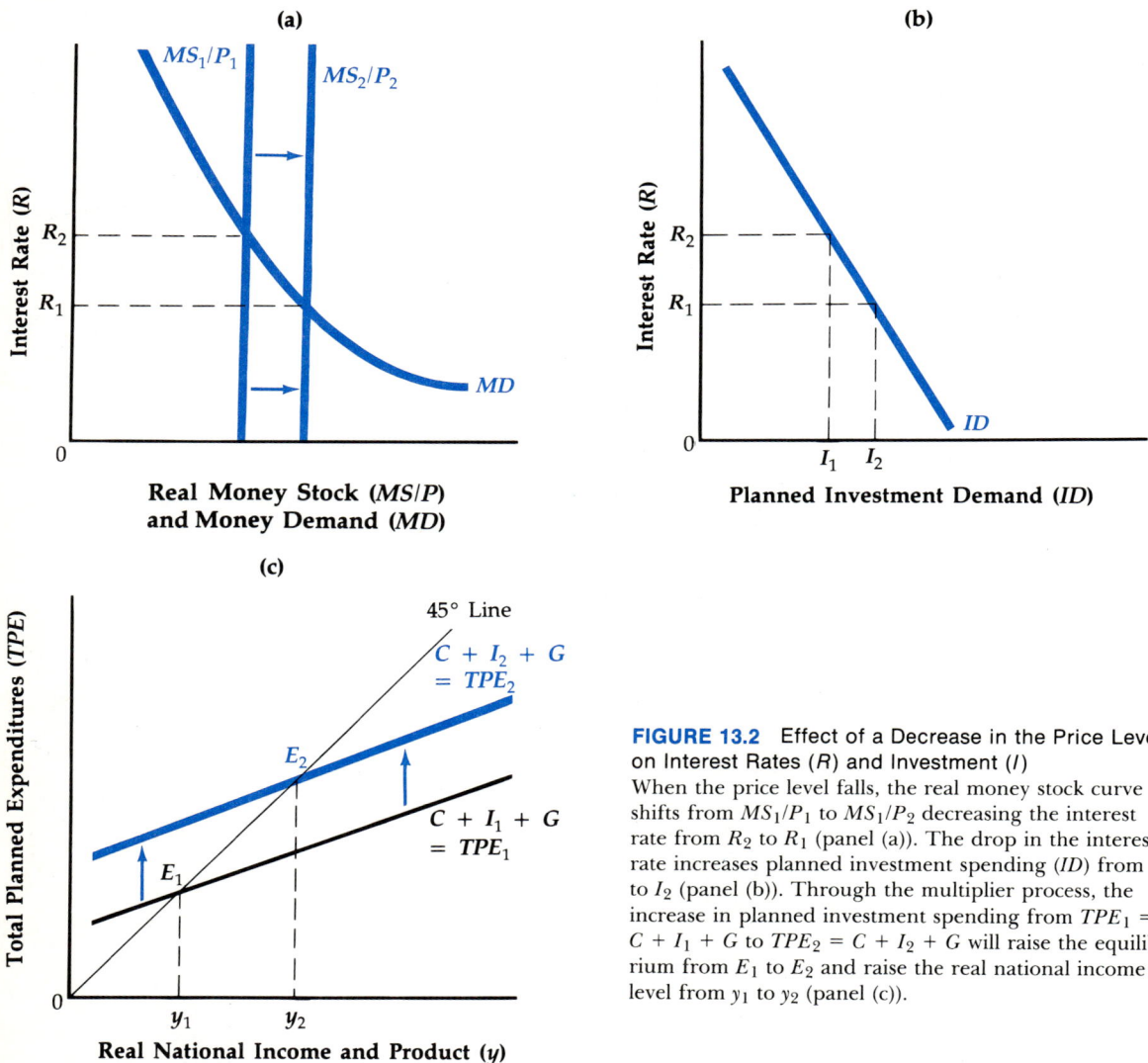

(a)

(b)

(c)

FIGURE 13.2 Effect of a Decrease in the Price Level on Interest Rates (R) and Investment (I)

When the price level falls, the real money stock curve shifts from MS_1/P_1 to MS_1/P_2 decreasing the interest rate from R_2 to R_1 (panel (a)). The drop in the interest rate increases planned investment spending (ID) from I_1 to I_2 (panel (b)). Through the multiplier process, the increase in planned investment spending from $TPE_1 = C + I_1 + G$ to $TPE_2 = C + I_2 + G$ will raise the equilibrium from E_1 to E_2 and raise the real national income level from y_1 to y_2 (panel (c)).

A decline in the price level amounts to an increase in the purchasing power of the nominal money stock. Because the amount of money in existence will now cover more transactions, the real money stock has expanded. A reduction in the price level (P) therefore increases the real money stock. Thus, if the price level falls from P_1 to P_2, given the nominal money supply (MS_1), the real money stock rises from MS_1/P_1 to MS_1/P_2 in Figure 13.2(a). This fall in the price level with the money stock constant is the same as if the nominal money stock increased with the price level constant. After the real money stock increases, the interest rate will drop from R_2 to R_1, increasing planned investment spending from I_1 to I_2. The increase in planned investment will then be translated, through the multiplier process, into a much greater increase in the real national income level, from y_1 to y_2. Think of it this way: A decline in the price level decreases the demand for money, causing—with a fixed money stock—a desire by businesses and households to borrow less in order to draw down their money balances. This reduced borrowing causes lower interest rates, which encourages spending on interest-rate sensitive goods such as automobiles, homes, public utility plants, and the like. From here on, the multiplier again takes over.

We have just deduced an important principle: a reduction in the price level causes an increase in the national income level. Conversely, an increase in the price level will reduce the real money stock, increasing the interest rate and decreasing planned investment and national income. Thus we can say that price level P_1 in Figure 13.1 is associated with a real national income level of y_2, and price level P_2 with a lower real national income level, y_1. That is, the price and national income levels are inversely (negatively) related.

The Effect of a Change in Price Level on Real Wealth

A reduction in the price level can also make people who hold assets valued in dollars—bonds and bank accounts, for example—feel wealthier.[3] With lower prices, people's dollar assets will purchase more goods and services. As their real wealth increases, people may feel less need to save and more freedom to spend their money. A reduction in the price levels tends to have a real balances or real wealth effect on planned consumption: deflation tends to increase the real value of financial assets with fixed money values (i.e., bonds and savings accounts) held by private economic agents, and thus increases the consumption function and increases aggregate spending and national income in the economy. The real wealth effect is illustrated in Figure 13.3. The total planned spending curve shifts from $C_1 + I + G$ to

Real balances or real wealth effect: the manner in which deflation tends to increase the real value of financial assets with fixed money values held by private economic agents, and thus increases the consumption function and increases aggregate spending and national income in the economy.

---

3. It is only the part of the assets that are privately held, but government-issued, that produce a wealth effect. The part of the money stock held by depository institutions as transaction balances is wealth to the owners but a liability to the issuer. Only private economic agents and not the government can experience wealth effects.

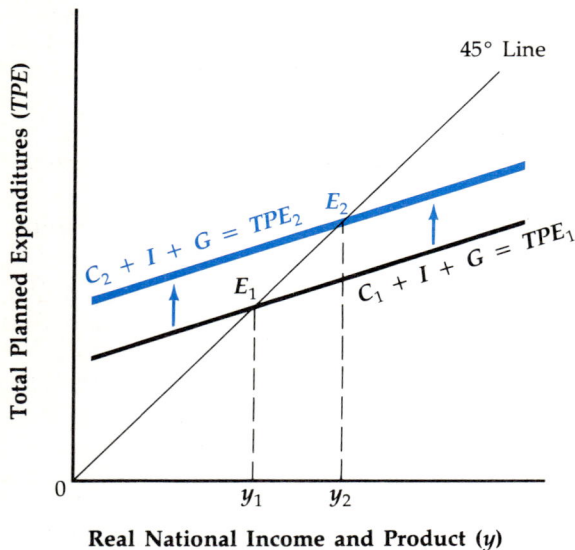

FIGURE 13.3 Effect of a Decrease in the Price Level on Consumption (C)

When the price level falls, wealth valued in dollars rises, reducing the need for saving and increasing total planned expenditures from $TPE_1 = C_1 + I + G$ to $TPE_2 = C_2 + I + G$. The result is a shift in the equilibrium position from E_1 to E_2 and an increase in the national production and income level, from y_1 to y_2.

$C_2 + I + G$, and real national income rises from y_1 to y_2.[4] Here again we can deduce that the aggregate demand curve is downward-sloping. As the price level goes down, from P_1 to P_2 (Figure 13.1), the real national income level goes up, from y_1 to y_2. Conversely, an increase in the price level will make people feel less wealthy, encouraging them to save more. The resulting drop in consumption will shift the total planned spending curve down, reducing the national income level.

In summary, the aggregate demand is downsloping because when the price level decreases (1) investment (and consumption) spending increases as the real money stock rises and interest rates fall; (2) consumption increases due to rising real wealth; and (3) government spending remains constant.[5]

The Size of the Effect of a Change in Price Level

While economists generally agree that the price and national income levels are inversely related, the strength of the relationship remains in dispute. Just how much of an increase in national income can be expected from a

---

4. Some writers call the real balances or real wealth effect the "net claims," "new real balances," or "Pigou effect." It is not considered to be significant empirically, although it does enable non-Keynesians to refute the Keynesian belief in equilibrium at less than full employment. Sufficient price deflation would eventually shift aggregate demand until full employment was restored.

5. As mentioned earlier, net foreign exports may rise as well.

decrease in the price level? In practice the size of any change in national
income is hard to predict. A reduction in the price level may have a substantial impact on national income, as in Figure 13.4. If aggregate demand is
AD_1, a reduction in the price level from P_2 to P_1 will increase real national
income from y_1 to y_3. Much depends on the slope of the aggregate demand
curve. If it is a much steeper slope—for instance, like AD_2 in Figure 13.4—
the same reduction in price level will cause a much smaller increase in real
national income, from y_1 to y_2.

How much a given change in price will change real national income
depends on several factors, including

○ how interest rates respond to a change in the real money stock
○ how investment expenditures respond to a change in interest rates
○ how consumption expenditures respond to a change in people's real
  wealth
○ how much the transactions demand for money changes with a
  change in the national income level

The more interest rates respond to an increase in real wealth, the more
investors respond to a drop in interest rates, and the more consumers
respond to a change in their real wealth, the greater will be the increase in
the real national income level. If interest rates do not fall very far when the
price level falls, and consumers do not increase their expenditures very
much when their real wealth increases, the aggregate demand curve in
Figure 13.4 may look more like AD_2 than AD_1. Although lower prices increase the real wealth of consumers, they decrease the real wealth of creditors, limiting the wealth effect of a drop in the price level. A fall in interest

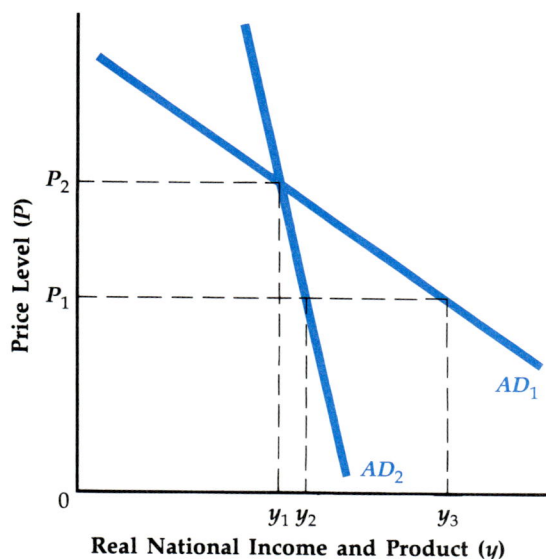

FIGURE 13.4 Size of the Effect of a Decrease in the
Price Level (P)
A decrease in the price level from P_2 to P_1 may cause a
large or a small increase in the total quantity of goods
and services demanded and produced. If the aggregate
demand curve looks like AD_1, the total quantity of goods
and services demanded may rise from y_1 to y_3. If the
curve looks like AD_2, the quantity of goods and services
demanded may rise only to y_2. How much the quantity
demanded will increase with any change in the price
level depends on several factors, including how the
interest rate responds to a change in the real money
stock and how investment spending responds to a
change in the interest rate.

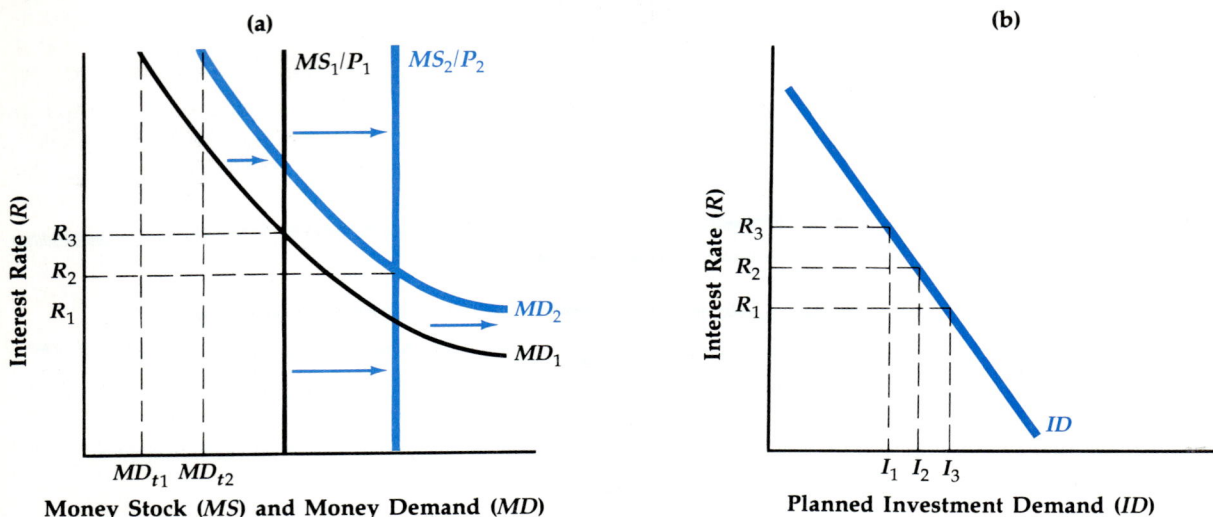

(a)

MS_1/P_1 MS_2/P_2

Interest Rate (R)

R_3
R_2
R_1

MD_2
MD_1

MD_{t1} MD_{t2}

Money Stock (MS) and Money Demand (MD)

(b)

Interest Rate (R)

R_3
R_2
R_1

ID

I_1 I_2 I_3

Planned Investment Demand (ID)

FIGURE 13.5 Effect of an Increase in the Transactions Demand for Money (MD_t)
An increase in the real money stock from MS_1/P_1 to MS_1/P_2 (panel (a)) as the price level falls can decrease the interest rate from R_3 toward R_1 and increase planned investment from I_1 toward I_3. The resulting increase in national income, however, will increase the transactions demand for money, shifting the total demand for money curve outward from MD_1 to MD_2. The shift in the demand for money curve will moderate the fall in the interest rate stopping it at R_2. As a result, the rise in investment spending will stop short at I_2 (panel (b)), tempering the expansion in national income.

rates may be partially offset by an increase in the transactions demand for money—the need to hold more money to finance the greater quantity of goods and services produced and consumed.

Suppose, for example, that the price level falls and the real money stock expands from MS_1/P_1 to MS_1/P_2, as in Figure 13.5 (part (a)). The interest rate, R_3, will begin to fall toward R_1. The reduction in the interest rate will spur investment spending (part (b)), increasing national income and with it the transactions demand for money. The money demand curve will shift outward from MD_1 to MD_2, reflecting this increase in the transactions demand (from MD_{t1} to MD_{t2}). As a result, the interest rate falls only to R_2, not R_1 and planned investment spending rises only to I_2 instead of I_3. Of course the rise in the national income level is limited as well.

Although few economists dispute that the slope of the aggregate demand curve is negative, its exact slope is controversial. For the responsiveness of interest rates, investment, and consumption to a fall in the price level all influence the steepness of the curve. Most economists agree that the aggregate demand curve is flatter in the long run than in the short run. With more time, people are better able to respond to changes in the price level.

Changes in Aggregate Demand

We need to distinguish carefully between a movement along an aggregate demand curve and a shift in the entire curve. The factors that shift the entire aggregate demand curve include changes in real income, inflationary expectations, real interest rates, consumer and business optimism regarding future economic activity, and monetary and fiscal policy. In all these cases, those shifts that are deemed permanent are likely to have a greater impact than those deemed temporary or transitory. The position of the aggregate demand curve in Figure 13.1 reflects a critical unstated assumption. We held constant all the economic factors that can affect the demand for goods and services—consumer and investment spending, fiscal and monetary policies. If planned consumer and investment spending increase, they can shift the aggregate demand curve, say from AD_1 to AD_2 in Figure 13.6. An expansionary fiscal or monetary policy can have the same effect. Conversely, decreases in consumer and investment spending and contractionary fiscal and monetary policies will shift the aggregate demand curve inward. In general, a shift in any outside factor, such as the nominal money supply or government fiscal policy, will shift the *entire* aggregate demand curve. This is quite different than a movement along an aggregate demand curve that occurs because a change in the price level affects real wealth, interest rates, or net exports.

Economists disagree about the effectiveness of fiscal policy actions in shifting the aggregate demand curve. As we saw in Chapter 12, greater government spending may crowd out private investment and consumption, so that the net effect is a small shift in aggregate demand or none at all.

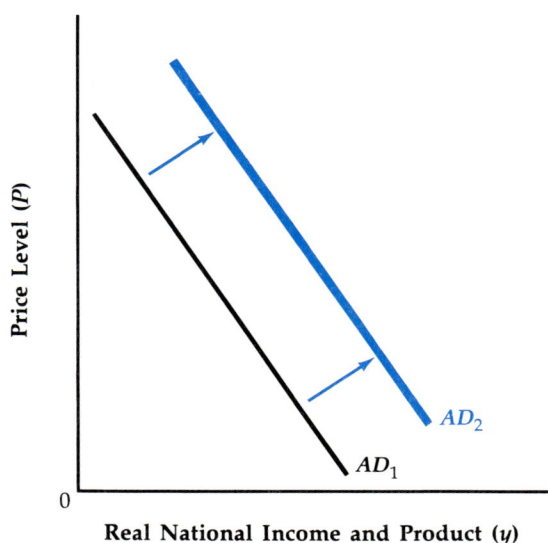

FIGURE 13.6 Change in Aggregate Demand (*AD*)
An increase in aggregate demand, represented by an outward shift in the aggregate demand curve from AD_1 to AD_2 can be caused by an expansionary fiscal or monetary policy. A contractionary fiscal or monetary policy will shift the aggregate demand curve inward.

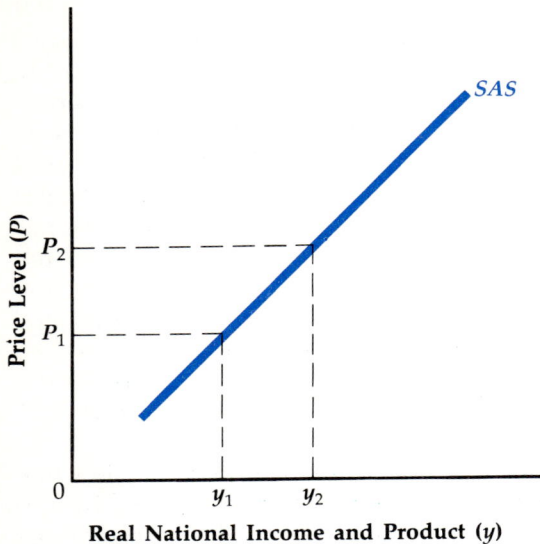

FIGURE 13.7 Short-Run Aggregate Supply (*SAS*)
Short-run aggregate supply (*SAS*) is the assumed positive relationship between the price level and total production or real income over a given period of time. If the price level rises from P_1 to P_2, real national income rises from y_1 to y_2.

Likewise the Federal Reserve's attempts to increase the money stock may be largely absorbed by increases in the public's money balances. Thus interest rates may not fall very much and investment spending may not rise very much in response to a calculated increase in the money stock.

Aggregate Supply

2. What is the nature and slope of the short-run and long-run aggregate supply functions?

In Chapter 6 the aggregate supply function was defined as the presumed positive relationship between the general price level and the total quantity of goods and services that will be produced in the economy during a given period of time.[6] Aggregate supply was shown graphically as an upward-sloping curve, like the one in Figure 13.7. If the price level rises from P_1 to P_2, the nation's real output of goods and services rises from y_1 to y_2—and vice versa. To be more precise, we should say that the aggregate supply curve slopes upward in the short run. Most economists believe that the long-run aggregate supply curve is, or is close to being, vertical because it is closely related to the natural rate of unemployment that depicts the maximum sustainable rate of output. We will take up what happens in the long run in more detail later.

_____

6. More technically, aggregate supply is determined by the economic behavior of buyers and sellers in the resource market. It takes as givens the resource base, the level of technology, and the economic, social, and political institutions existing in the economy.

Short-Run Aggregate Supply (*SAS*)

Early Keynesians did not pay much attention to changes in the price level because they did not believe price increases were a major threat during times of severe recession. They thought the aggregate supply curve resembled the curve in Figure 13.8 (without any systematic distinction between the long and short run). Up to a full-employment national output level of y_F, no price increase was needed to induce greater production. At full employment, however, greater demand for output would be reflected in higher prices, as competitors bid up the price of the economy's limited labor resources.

Economists no longer think of the aggregate supply curve in this way. Modern aggregate supply theory assumes that output will increase only if people have some real or imagined incentive—like a price increase—to expand production. The short-run aggregate supply curve in Figure 13.7 illustrates this assumption.

In the short run, a phenomenon called money illusion provides the incentive needed to expand production. **Money illusion** is the mistaken belief that an increase in market price, stated in dollars, represents an increase in real price. When people find they can sell their labor or their products for a higher price, they initially believe they have received a real increase in payment. Not recognizing that their wage increases were offset by an increase in the prices of the products they buy, workers may work harder and longer hours to take advantage of the apparent increase in

Money illusion: the mistaken belief that an increase in market price, stated in dollars, represents an increase in real price.

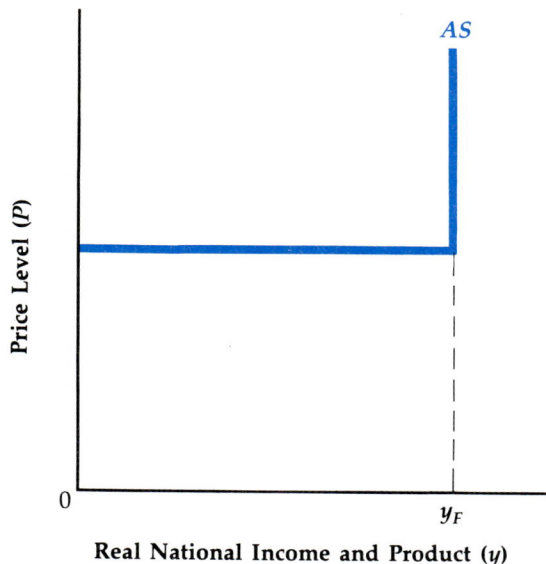

FIGURE 13.8 Early Keynesian Aggregate Supply Curve
Early Keynesian theory assumed a constant price level up to the full-employment output level, y_F. As long as some workers remained unemployed, additional output could be achieved without raising prices. After full employment, any further increase in aggregate demand could be realized only at a higher price level.

real wages. Business owners may expand production. This burst of activity can raise national output, producing an upward-sloping aggregate supply curve like the one in Figure 13.7.

Some of these price increases may indeed be real. Many wage rates, for instance, are set by union contract and cannot be raised with the price level. In the short run, an employer may be able to raise the price of its finished product without having to pay more for labor. The employer will hire more workers, and production will go up. Such an arrangement will not be possible for all employers, however.

How much output will expand in response to an increase in the price level (how steep or flat the aggregate supply curve is) will depend on several factors:

- the availability of unemployed resources
- the ease with which unemployed resources can be put into use when prices rise
- the extent of the money illusion
- the extent to which labor contracts fix wages in current dollar terms

A short-run aggregate supply curve that reflects all these variables can have a slope that changes over the business cycle, as in Figure 13.9. **Short-run aggregate supply** is a curve or function that shows the assumed positive

Short-run aggregate supply: a curve or function that shows the assumed positive relationship between the total production of goods and services and the price level over a given fixed period of time.

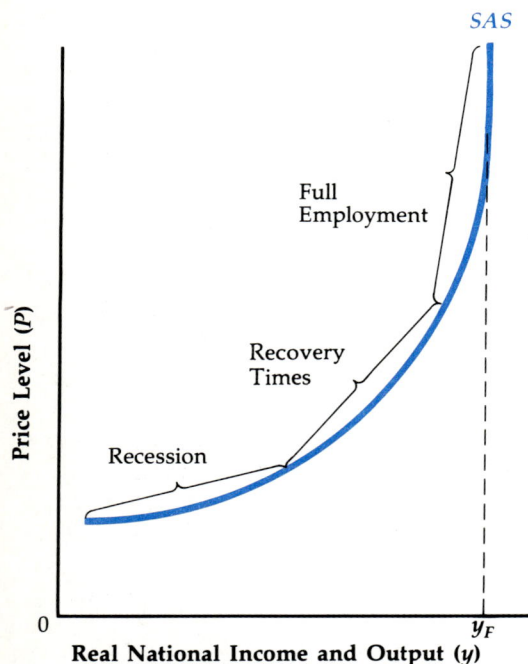

FIGURE 13.9   Short-Run Aggregate Supply (SAS) in the Context of the Business Cycle

Producers' ability to respond to changing prices depends in part on the availability of unemployed resources. During a recession, when there is substantial unemployment of workers, plant, and equipment, a relatively small increase in the price level may bring a substantial rise in national output. During recovery times, when the economy is operating near full employment (y_F), a much larger increase in the price level may be necessary to increase national production. When the economy is at or close to full employment (y_F) national production may respond very little to an increase in prices.

relationship between the total production of goods and services and the price level over a given fixed period of time.

During a recession or depression, the curve can be almost flat. Even a small increase in the price level will cause a significant expansion in national production. During recovery times, when the economy is operating near full capacity, the slope is likely to be much steeper. A greater rise in prices will be needed to cover the high cost of drawing into the production process the last few unemployed (and possibly ill-suited) resources. Beyond full employment the aggregate supply curve will become practically vertical. When resources are, for all practical purposes, fully employed, little additional output can be produced, even if prices do rise.

When the recovery phase of the business cycle begins, expansion in output is likely to be relatively rapid and price increases modest. Such was the case with the recovery that began during the first term of the Reagan administration. Real GNP expanded nicely, while the price level rose only moderately. Generally those favorable conditions do not persist as an economy continues to move out of the recession.

Long-Run Aggregate Supply (LAS)

The money illusion on which the short-run aggregate supply curve is founded will not persist indefinitely. With the passage of time, people come to realize that increases in their dollar wages are not necessarily real increases. They will cease to work extra hours to take advantage of those dollar increases. As soon as they can, workers will adjust their labor contracts to reflect higher prices. In the process, the short-run aggregate supply curve—and the level of production—will shift backward.

It is not clear just how far back aggregate supply will shift. Many economists argue that the long-run aggregate supply curve is vertical—that an increase in the price level will not affect the long-run national output level. In Figure 13.10, suppose the price level rises from P_1 to P_2 because of an increase in aggregate demand following an expansion in the money stock. Production may expand for a while along the short-run aggregate supply curve SAS_1, from y_1 to y_2, but people will eventually adjust to the change in the price level. At that point the aggregate supply curve will fall back toward SAS_4, going progressively from SAS_1 to SAS_2 to SAS_3 and finally to SAS_4 and toward the original real national output level of y_1. The new price level will be P_3, however. So the long-term effect is the same as if the economy had moved straight up the vertical curve LAS. Prices have increased, but real national output has not. The reasoning behind the vertical LAS curve involves the **natural rate of unemployment** that describes the maximum sustainable rate of output consistent with equilibrium in the structure of real wages at any point in time. The equilibrium occurs when the anticipated and actual inflation rates coincide for all market participants so that there is a nonaccelerating rate of inflation. **Long-run aggregate supply** is a function or curve that shows the assumed fixed relationship between the total production of goods and services and the price level over an extended period of time. The classical long-run aggre-

Natural rate of unemployment: the maximum sustainable rate of output consistent with equilibrium in the structure of real wages at any point in time.

Long-run aggregate supply: a function or curve that shows the assumed fixed relationship between the total production of goods and services and the price level over an extended period of time.

gate supply curve was vertical, as flexible wages ensure continuous employment at the natural level with full employment or potential output always
maintained. Although some—most notably Keynesian—economists believe
that the *SAS* curve is horizontal or slightly upsloping so that shifts in aggregate demand affect mainly output, most economists believe that the *LAS*
curve is exactly or nearly vertical so that shifts in aggregate demand affect
mainly prices.

Changes in Aggregate Supply

A change in aggregate supply shifts the entire curve. The factors that shift
both short-run and long-run aggregate supply include changes in technology and productivity, supplies (and hence prices) of resources, expectations
about future inflation, and institutional factors that affect resource efficiency, such as government regulation. Any factors regarded as temporary
that do not alter the long-run economic capacity of the economy, such as
supply shocks or a transitory shift in anticipated inflation, do not have an
impact on long-run aggregate supply. The aggregate supply curve responds not only to price changes, but to anything that affects the availability
of resources or people's incentive to work harder and produce more goods
and services. For example, sudden cutbacks in oil production can cause
energy shortages, crippling the production of a vast array of goods and
services. Such "supply shocks" can shift the short-run aggregate supply
curve backward from SAS_1 to SAS_2 as in Figure 13.11, reducing real national production from y_3 to y_1 and increasing the price level from P_1 to P_3.

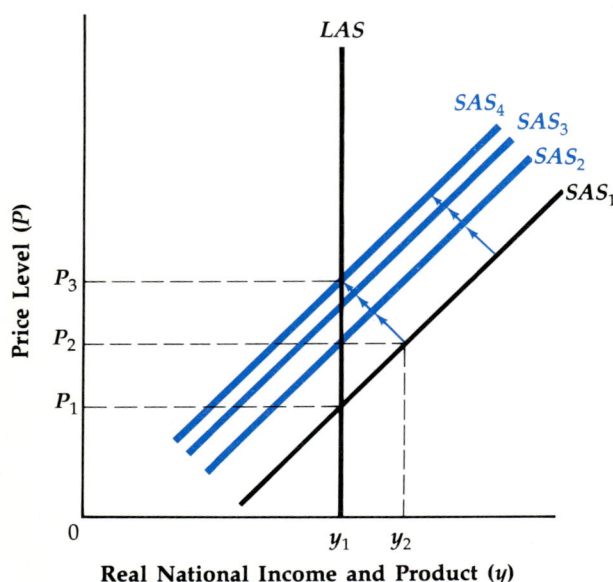

FIGURE 13.10   Long-Run Aggregate Supply
(*LAS*) Curve
An increase in the price level from P_1 to P_2 may temporarily raise real national output from y_1 to y_2. In the long
run, however, after people realize that their real wages
have not risen, the supply of labor and other resources
may contract, shifting the short-run aggregate supply
curve upward from SAS_1 to SAS_4. The end result may be
a price level of P_3 and no long-run expansion in national
production. In other words, the long-run aggregate
supply curve (*LAS*) is vertical.

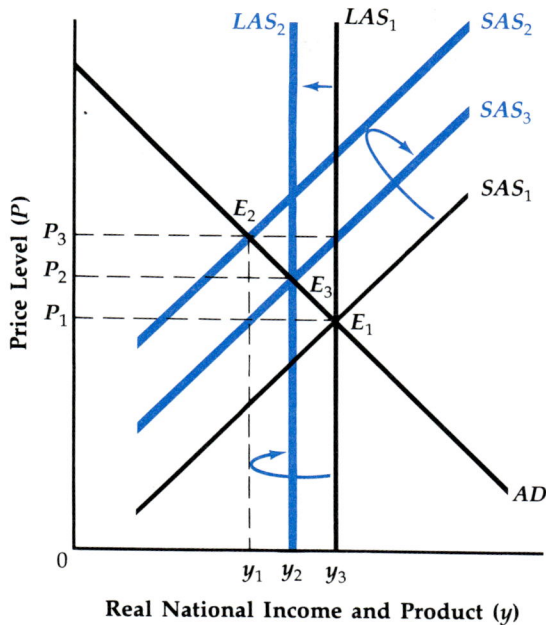

FIGURE 13.11 Supply Shock
A sudden reduction in the availability of an important resource, such as oil, can cause the short-run aggregate supply curve to shift to the left, from SAS_1 to SAS_2. The price level will increase from P_1 to P_3, and the real national output level will fall from y_3 to y_1. Substitute resources may be developed because of the shock, however, so that the short-run aggregate supply curve shifts to the right again to SAS_3. In the long run, then, national production may climb back to y_2 and the price level may drop back to P_2. Thus, the long-run aggregate supply curve does not shift as far to the left as the short-run curve, going from LAS_1 to LAS_2. The equilibrium position started at E_1 shifted to E_2 and finally settled at E_3.

The cutback in energy will not necessarily bring such a dramatic shift in the *long-run* aggregate supply (LAS_1) curve, however. The higher price level, and the higher price of energy in particular, will encourage the discovery of alternative energy sources. The short-run aggregate supply may shift to SAS_2 and the long-run aggregate supply curve may shift back only to LAS_2 from LAS_1, where the increase in price level (to P_2) and the decrease in national income (to y_2) will be more moderate. We should not expect the national income level to return all the way to y_3, however. New energy sources will probably be more costly to use, if only because resources will have been consumed just to make them available. Thus, after starting from equilibrium point E_1, shifts in the aggregate supply move the equilibrium to E_2 and finally to E_3.

The Equilibrium National Income and Price Levels

▲ **3. What is the aggregate demand and supply approach to equilibrium income?**

By putting the aggregate supply and aggregate demand curves in the same graph, as in Figure 13.13 (page 356), we can see that in the short run the economy will gravitate toward the equilibrium position E involving the real national income and price levels of y_2 and P_1. At price levels above P_1—for example, P_2—the total quantity of goods and services producers want to offer (y_3) will exceed the total quantity of goods and services consumers, businesses, and governments want to buy (y_1). The price level will fall back

PERSPECTIVES
Econometrics
N. Keith Womer, University of Mississippi

The real economic world is highly complex. Every day millions of agents make billions of economic decisions. Goods are bought and sold, wages are paid, and investments are made in countless numbers. This daily market is so complicated that economists cannot study it directly. Instead, they must attempt to understand specific aspects of the market by developing and testing economic theories.

Economic theories are based on observations of the real world formalized into precisely stated assumptions. They are not conclusions but tentative hypotheses whose predictive power must be tested scientifically.

Econometrics is the science of the statistical testing of economic theory and predictions. The *metric* in *econometrics* signifies measurement—the measurement of economic relationships. Using economic theory, relevant economic data, and

FIGURE 13.12   Estimated Consumption Function
The relation between consumption and income is linear. If data on consumption and income are plotted on a graph, the points will fall approximately on a straight line. Mathematically, the relation shown here may be expressed as $C = 68.7 + 0.89\,Y$.
Source: Economic Report of the President (Washington, D.C.: U.S. Government Printing Office, 1985), pp. 248 and 254.

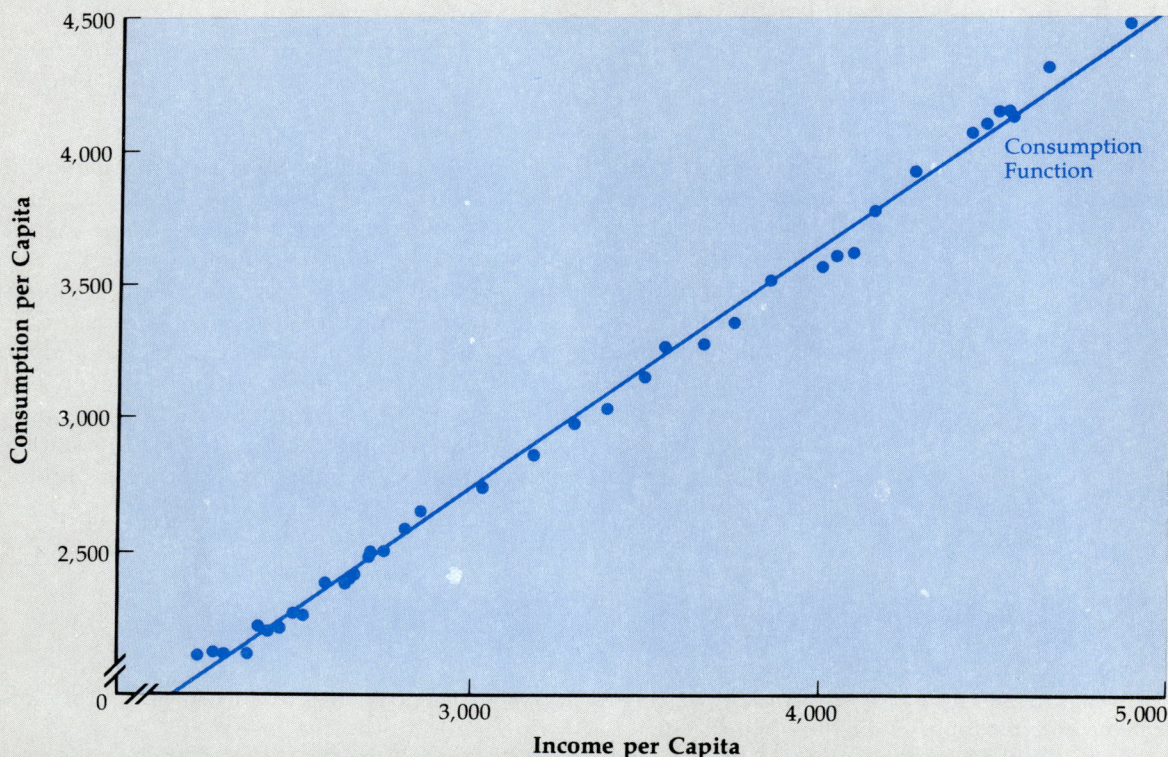

statistical methods, econometricians construct and test econometric models. An **econometric model** is a statistical equation or set of equations that describes economic data.

The data econometricians use are sometimes collected directly, but are more often derived from data that have been collected for other purposes. From these data economic relationships must be carefully estimated through statistical analysis. Then the hypotheses about those relationships can be tested.

This approach can be used to reject or tentatively accept hypotheses. Rejected hypotheses form the basis for revisions of economic theory. Tentatively accepted hypotheses have not been proved. At best, they have been shown to be consistent with observed data. Much of the econometrician's work involves uneasy compromises among economic hypotheses, available data, and the requirements of statistical technique.

Consider the problem of estimating and testing the consumption function, for instance. Keynes stated, "The fundamental psychological law . . . is that men are disposed, as a rule and on the average, to increase their consumption as their income increases, but not by as much as the increase in income." The testable hypothesis derived from Keynes's theory is that the marginal propensity to consume (*MPC*) is positive but less than one.

Statistical technique requires that the relation between two variables be specified precisely. The relation between consumption and income is hypothesized to be linear. That is, if observations of consumption and income were plotted on a graph, the points would fall approximately on a straight line. If the consumption function is linear, the technique of linear regression can be used to estimate it. **Linear regression** is a statistical technique used to find the equation describing the straight line that comes closest to the plotted points of a curve.

Random samples of accurate data on individual consumption and income are difficult to obtain. Econometricians usually use yearly data on aggregate consumption and income together with population statistics to estimate per capita income and consumption. Then they often divide their data by a price index, to adjust for the effects of inflation. An aggregate consumption function derived from such constructed data is illustrated in Figure 13.12. Each point shows the level of consumption associated with a particular income level; the line shows the consumption function derived from the data. Mathematically, that line or function may be expressed as $C = 68.7 + 0.89\,Y$. C equals the consumption function. The estimated intercept (constant term) of the consumption function is $68.70, and 0.89 is the estimated marginal propensity to consume.

This estimate seems to support Keynes's theory. Our computed marginal propensity to consume, 0.89, is positive and less than one, just as he argued. Such a computation may have been generated by chance, however.

To be confident that our computed *MPC* is a close approximation of the true *MPC*, we must run additional statistical tests.[1] If those tests yield the expected results, we can conclude with a high degree of confidence that the true *MPC* is not very different from our computed *MPC*. Though we have not *proved* Keynes's hypothesis, it has survived a challenge. If repeated tests yield the same findings, we will become even more confident that Keynes was correct.

---

1. To test the estimated marginal propensity to consume, an econometrician would first compare the errors around the consumption function (in the figure, the vertical distance between the data points and the straight line) with randomly selected data. If the errors appear to be random, then the econometrician will measure the precision of the estimate by computing a statistic called the standard deviation.

toward P_1 as firms compete to get rid of their unwanted inventory. The price decline will stimulate spending by increasing the real money stock. Interest rates will fall, the level of planned investment will increase, and planned consumption expenditures will rise. Total planned expenditures will climb from y_1 to y_2. At the same time, recognizing that the rewards of their labor have shrunk, people will cut back on production. National output and income will drop from y_3 to y_2.

Similarly, at price levels below P_1, such as P_3, the total planned expenditures of consumers, businesses, and government (y_3) will exceed the total quantity of goods and services produced (y_3). The prices of goods and services will be bid up, reducing the real money stock and hence people's real wealth. Interest rates will rise, reducing planned investment expenditures. Consumption expenditures will fall as people attempt to rebuild their real wealth by saving. Because of fixed wages and money illusion, production will rise as producers and workers try to exploit the price increase.

The Real Effect of Expansionary Fiscal and Monetary Policies

What does the combined aggregate supply and demand model suggest about the likely effect of Keynesian fiscal and monetary policies to increase total planned expenditures? Starting from an equilibrium point, if government reduces taxes, increases its expenditures, or expands the money stock—all steps that should cause total planned spending to rise—the ag-

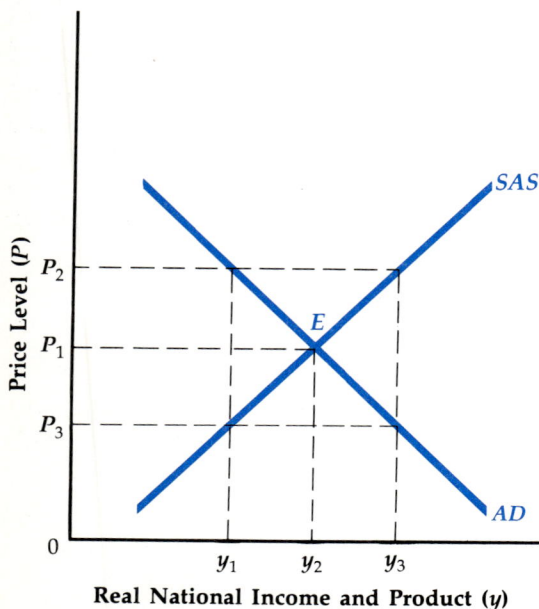

FIGURE 13.13   Short-Run Equilibrium (E) in Real National Income (y) and Prices (P)
Given these aggregate supply and aggregate demand curves, the macroeconomy will move toward an equilibrium at E involving a price level of P_1 and a national production level of y_2. At a price level above P_1—for example, P_2—the total quantity of goods and services produced (y_3) will exceed the total quantity of goods and services demanded (y_1). The price level will fall. As it falls, more goods and services will be demanded while fewer will be produced. At any price level below P_1—for example, P_3—the total quantity of goods produced (y_1) will be less than the total quantity of goods demanded (y_3). Therefore, the price level will rise until the equilibrium point E is reached.

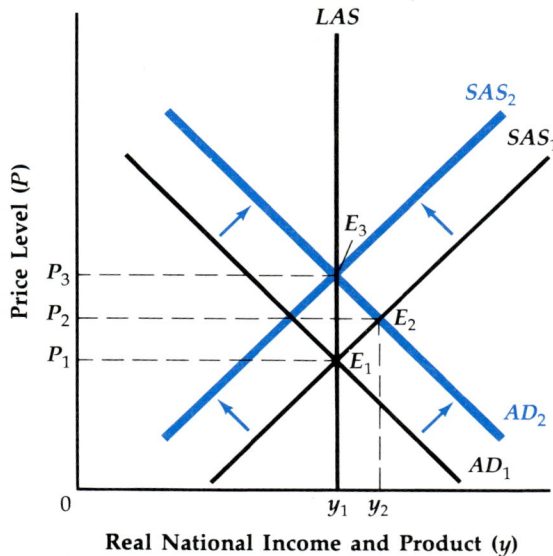

FIGURE 13.14 The Effect of an Expansionary Fiscal or Monetary Policy on Real National Income (y) and Prices (P)

Starting from an equilibrium point at E_1 an expansionary fiscal and monetary policy can shift the aggregate demand curve upward, from AD_1 to AD_2. In the short run the shift in aggregate demand will cause a shift in the equilibrium from E_1 to E_2 involving an expansion in national production, from y_1 to y_2, and an increase in the price level, from P_1 to P_2. In the long run the aggregate supply curve will shift up from SAS_1 to SAS_2. Long-run equilibrium (E_3) will be achieved at an even higher price level, P_3, and national production will return to its original level, y_1.

gregate demand curve will shift outward. The result of the shift from AD_1 to AD_2 is shown in Figure 13.14. The equilibrium shifts from E_1 to E_2 and the real national income level expands from y_1 to y_2. And the price level increases from P_1 to P_2.

In the long run, however, the aggregate supply curve will shift inward to SAS_2 as people adjust their work efforts to the price increase. If the long-run aggregate supply curve is vertical, the end result will be a shift from E_2 to E_3 involving a return to the original equilibrium real national income level of y_1, but at a higher price level: P_3 instead of P_1. In fact, over a period of months or years, expansionary fiscal and monetary policies can produce a business cycle of their own. First a recovery period of expansion in production and employment is stimulated by monetary or fiscal policy. Then the resulting drop in short-run aggregate supply causes a new contraction in production and employment.[7]

The Real Size of the Multiplier

The Keynesian economic models used in Chapters 10 to 12 assumed that prices would remain constant. Under that assumption, we can expect a change in total planned expenditures to be fully reflected, through the

---

7. In addition, over the long run the aggregate demand curve can shift back toward AD_1, reflecting the reduced investment demand caused by the increase in government spending. The effect of such a reduction in investment spending will be a price level lower than P_3.

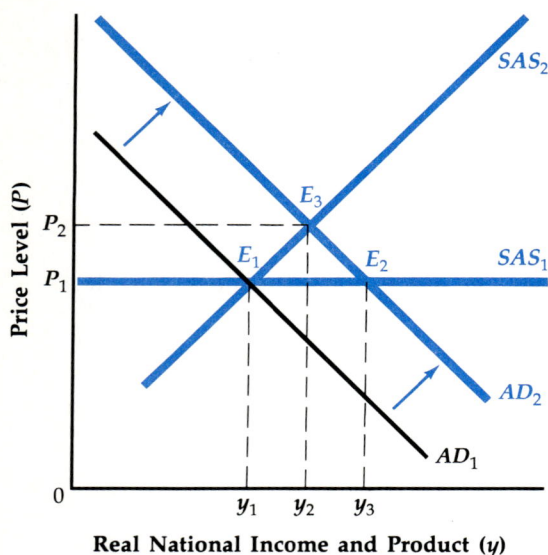

Price Level (P)

P_2

P_1

0   y_1 y_2 y_3

Real National Income and Product (y)

SAS_2

E_3

E_1 E_2 SAS_1

AD_2

AD_1

FIGURE 13.15 The Multiplier Effect on Real National Income (y) and Prices (P)
Starting from an original equilibrium position of E_1, with no change in price level—that is, with a horizontal aggregate supply curve like SAS_1—an increase in aggregate demand from AD_1 to AD_2 will shift the equilibrium from E_1 to E_2, causing national production to rise from y_1 to y_3. If prices rise with aggregate demand—that is, if the aggregate supply curve slopes upward, as SAS_2 does—the same increase in aggregate demand will raise national production only to y_2. That is, the equilibrium shifts from E_2 to E_3. The increase in the price level absorbs part of the impact of the expansion of aggregate demand and reduces the size of the multiplier.

multiplier process, in a change in national income and production. In that case, however, the aggregate supply curve would have to be horizontal, like curve SAS_1 in Figure 13.15. Given such a supply curve, an increase in aggregate demand from AD_1 to AD_2 would make the equilibrium shift from E_1 to E_2, causing national income and production to rise from y_1 to y_3. If prices must adjust upward to create an incentive for increased production and income, as modern theorists believe, then the aggregate supply curve will look like SAS_2, shifting the equilibrium from E_2 to E_3. In that case the shift in aggregate demand from AD_1 to AD_2 will yield a smaller increase in national income and production, from y_1 to y_2.

If prices rise, then, the multiplier effect will be weaker, for the increase in the price level will absorb part of the stimulus to demand. The higher price level will reduce the real money stock, causing interest rates to rise and planned investment spending to fall, and by reducing consumers' real wealth, it will reduce consumption demand. In short, if prices adjust to changes in demand, expansionary fiscal and monetary policies will not be as effective in relieving production and employment problems as early Keynesian theory would suggest. (Conversely, decreases in total planned expenditures will not depress the economy as much as early Keynesian theory would imply.)

It has been estimated that dynamic multipliers in response to government (nondefense) spending, using the leading econometric models of our economy, reach a peak of between 1.5 and 2.8 and start to fall after 4 to 7 quarters, but may continue in diminished form for several years.[8] This raises the problem that a stimulus may occur in the future when it is not needed.

Economic research has shown that both monetary and fiscal policy can be effective. The evidence is not definitive regarding which policy is more powerful, or the exact quantitative impact of either policy's multipliers.

Chapter Review

Review of Key Questions

▲   *1. What is the nature and slope of the aggregate demand function?*

The aggregate demand curve shows the desired flow of aggregate spending on new goods and services at different price levels during some period of time. The aggregate demand curve slopes downward because of the way prices affect interest rates and consumption. When the price level falls, the real money stock rises and the interest rate falls, increasing investment demand. Consumers' real wealth also increases, fueling consumer demand. There is no reason for the federal government spending (G) to be affected much by the real balances or real wealth and interest rate effects. Thus G is assumed to be fixed in response to these effects. Aggregate demand also slopes down because of international trade considerations. The slope of the aggregate demand curve depends on the extent to which a drop in the price level reduces the interest rate and increases planned investment spending, planned consumption, and the transaction demand for money. Factors that shift the entire aggregate demand curve, as opposed to movements along a given aggregate demand curve, include changes in real income and interest rates, optimism, inflationary expectations, and monetary and fiscal policymaking. Expansionary fiscal and monetary policies will shift the aggregate demand curve outward, while contractionary policies will shift it inward.

▲   *2. What is the nature and slope of the short-run and long-run aggregate supply functions?*

The aggregate supply curve shows the flow of aggregate real output that firms are willing to sell at different price levels during some period of time. The short-run aggregate supply curve slopes upward partly because of money illusion and partly because resource owners cannot raise prices immediately when the general price level increases. Factors that shift the entire aggregate supply curve, as opposed to movements along a given aggregate supply curve, include changes in technology and productivity, supplies (and hence prices) of resources, expectations about future inflation, and institutional factors such as government regulations. The long-run aggregate supply curve is steeper than the short-run aggregate supply curve. It may actually be vertical at the natural rate of unemployment associated with the maximum sustainable output. Most

---

8. Robert Gordon, *Macroeconomics,* 4th ed. (Boston: Little, Brown, 1986), pp. 377–378. The multiplier for government (nondefense) spending for the monetarist Federal Reserve Bank of St. Louis model never even reached 1.0!

economists today believe it is vertical in the long run, but there is debate over its short-run shape. Over time, people learn that a rise in the dollar price of resources does not necessarily represent a real increase in price. They adjust resource prices upward to match the increase in the price level. Changes in tax rates can affect aggregate supply as well as aggregate demand, for they affect people's incentives to work, save, and invest. If both curves shift, the price level may go up or down, depending on the relative size of the shifts.

◢ *3. What is the aggregate demand and supply approach to equilibrium income?*

The equilibrium national income level is established by the intersection of the aggregate supply and demand curves. The price level adjusts upward or downward to bring supply and demand into balance. A shift in the aggregate demand curve has a greater effect on national income in the short run than in the long run. Expansionary fiscal and monetary policies therefore have a greater impact in the short run than in the long run. Changes in the price level will moderate the multiplier effect of a shift in total planned spending. Economists have found that both monetary and fiscal policies are effective. They have not been able to determine for certain which policy is more powerful or the precise quantitative value of the multiplier of either monetary policy or fiscal policy.

Further Topics

The aggregate demand and supply model offers a more realistic picture of the economy than the traditional Keynesian model because it includes the effect of price changes on the supply of goods as well as on the quantity demanded. Changes in the price level can lower the value of the multiplier, though the effect may not be dramatic. If the aggregate demand curve has a steep slope, the effect of price changes on total planned spending may be modest.

Changes in aggregate supply may also have a limited effect. The short-run aggregate supply curve slopes upward only to the extent that people mistake a nominal increase in the price of their labor or products for a real one. Money illusion can wear off fast, for workers and producers soon learn that an increase in the overall price level will raise the prices of things they buy as well as the prices of things they sell. They will adjust their contracts accordingly. The long-run aggregate supply curve, then, is likely to be steeper than the short-run aggregate supply curve. It may be practically vertical—reflecting the constraints of the natural rate of unemployment—so that output ultimately changes very little with changes in total planned spending.

Review of New Terms

Aggregate demand A function or curve that shows the relationship between the general price level (an index of the prices of all products and services) and the total quantity of all goods and services demanded during a given period of time.

Econometric model A statistical equation or set of equations that describes economic data.

Econometrics The science of the statistical testing of economic theory and predictions.

Linear regression A statistical technique used to find the equation describing the straight line that comes closest to the plotted points of a curve.

Long-run aggregate supply A function or curve that shows the assumed fixed relationship between the total production of goods and services and the price level over an extended period of time.

Money illusion The mistaken belief that an increase in market price, stated in dollars, represents an increase in real price.

Natural rate of unemployment The maximum sustainable rate of output consistent with equilibrium in the structure of real wages at any point in time.

Real balances or real wealth effect The manner in which deflation tends to increase the real value of financial assets with fixed money values held by private economic agents, and thus increases the consumption function and increases aggregate spending and national income in the economy.

Short-run aggregate supply A curve or function that shows the assumed positive relationship between the total production of goods and services and the price level over a given period of time.

Review Questions

1. Explain the difference between the market demand curve and the aggregate demand curve. (◢ 1)

2. Explain the difference between the total planned spending function and the aggregate demand curve. (◢ 1)

3. In each of the following cases, explain what will happen to the price and national income levels:
   a. Aggregate demand increases.
   b. Aggregate supply decreases.
   c. The expected profitability of investment rises.
   d. The money stock expands.
   e. Tax rates rise. (◢ 3)

4. Why will an increase in aggregate demand have a greater effect on national income in the short run than in the long run? (◢ 3)

5. Suppose a major new energy source is discovered. What will happen to the national income and price levels in the long run? (◢ 2)

6. Explain how the size of the multiplier is affected by an adjustment in the price level. (◢ 3)

7. How does the responsiveness of planned investment to a change in the interest rate affect the slope of the aggregate demand curve? (◢ 1)

8. What can government do to shift the long-run aggregate supply curve outward? (◢ 2)

PART V

Alternative Views of the Macroeconomy

The Monetarist View of Inflation and Unemployment

If we cannot trust economists guided by Keynesian doctrine to direct the fortunes of our economy, whom can we trust?
Robert E. Lucas, Jr.

KEY QUESTIONS

▲ 1. What are the basic doctrines of monetarism?

▲ 2. How do monetarists explain unemployment?

▲ 3. What is the basic cause of inflation?

▲ 4. What are the effects of an increase in the stock of money?

▲ 5. What effect does inflation have on interest rates?

▲ 6. What macroeconomic policy do monetarists propose?

▲ 7. What are the problems with monetarism?

NEW TERMS

Cambridge equation
Demand for money
Fisher effect
Monetarism

Phillips curve
Quantity theory
Velocity

We have stressed that Keynesian theory is controversial. Many of the objections to Keynesian theory come from economists of the monetarist school, itself the center of much controversy. This chapter will examine the monetarist interpretation of the macroeconomy.

Some caution is advised in classifying economic thought as monetarist or Keynesian (or supply-side or rational expectations). Economists from different schools often agree with each other on particular points, while economists from the same school of thought often disagree. Keynesians have disputed the fine points of macroeconomic theory and policy among themselves, although they generally agree that the proper way to study the macroeconomy is to focus on planned total expenditures and the variables affecting them. Similarly, although monetarists do not agree on all particulars, they share a common belief that changes in the stock of money cause most macroeconomic fluctuations. In this chapter, we will study the theories and policy proposals of the monetarists.

The Basis of Monetarism

▲ 1. What are the basic doctrines of monetarism?

Quantity theory: the theory that a change in the stock of money will, in the long run and other things being the same, lead to a proportional increase in the price level.

The theory underlying monetarist thought is the quantity theory of money. The basic proposition of the **quantity theory** of money is that a change in the stock of money will, *in the long run and other things being the same,* lead to a proportional increase in the price level. In other words, the only permanent effect of increasing the quantity of money is to increase the price level. The quantity theory can be explained within the framework of the equation of exchange (introduced in Chapter 8), which states that

$$MV = PQ$$

If Q is real national income (or real gross national product), the symbol y can be substituted into the equation, to give

$$MV = Py$$

According to the quantity theory, in the long run changes in the stock of money (M) lead to proportional changes in the price level (P). Money has no permanent effect on velocity (V) or real gross national product (y).

Velocity: the number of times the average dollar is spent in a year.

Velocity is the number of times the average dollar is spent in a year. Note that the quantity theory does not assume that velocity and real output never change; the theory assumes only that long-run changes in those two variables are caused by forces other than changes in the stock of money. Velocity and real output might be highly variable, but they do not vary systematically with the quantity of money.

The quantity theory is often illustrated using the Cambridge cash balance version of the equation of exchange. The Cambridge equation is

$$M = (1/V)Py, \text{ or}$$

$$M = kPy$$

where $k = (1/V)$. Although it is simply an algebraic reformulation of the basic equation of exchange, the cash balances approach has the advantage of focusing on k, the percentage of nominal income held in the form of money, rather than its inverse, the velocity.

Whatever version of the equation of exchange is used, the long-run proportionality of money and prices is the defining feature of the quantity theory. Differences among quantity theorists arise over what happens in the short run.[1] Modern monetarism is distinguished from other versions of the quantity theory by the assumption that velocity is relatively stable in the short run. The short-run effects of changes in the stock of money therefore fall entirely on Py. The question then becomes one of the division of effects between P and y. Although a host of factors can affect that division, most monetarists place great emphasis on expectations. That part of the monetary expansion (or contraction) that is unanticipated will cause output to change; that part that is anticipated will cause the price level to change. Because all changes will eventually be known and therefore anticipated, in the long run we are left with the quantity theory result that changes in the money stock affect prices alone.

Monetarism: the quantity theory of money combined with the assumption that the velocity of money is highly stable.

Monetarism, then, can be described as the quantity theory of money combined with the assumption that the velocity of money is highly stable. Simple as that may sound, the theory nevertheless generates wide implications for macroeconomic theory and policy.

The Monetarist View of Unemployment

◢ **2. How do monetarists explain unemployment?**

The monetarists base their theory of unemployment on the microeconomic analysis of employment and unemployment. The basic model is illustrated in Figure 14.1. The demand for labor is inversely related to the real wage rate (the money wage rate divided by the price index), while the supply of labor is directly related to the real wage rate. Note that the real wage, not the nominal wage, matters to the labor market. The real wage can be thought of as the real purchasing power of wages or as the real opportunity

---

1. Indeed, Keynes himself can be thought of as a quantity theorist in that he believed that money and prices would change in proportion in the long run. He criticized the quantity theory on the grounds that the economy was rarely if ever in the long run; Keynes therefore concerned himself with the short run.

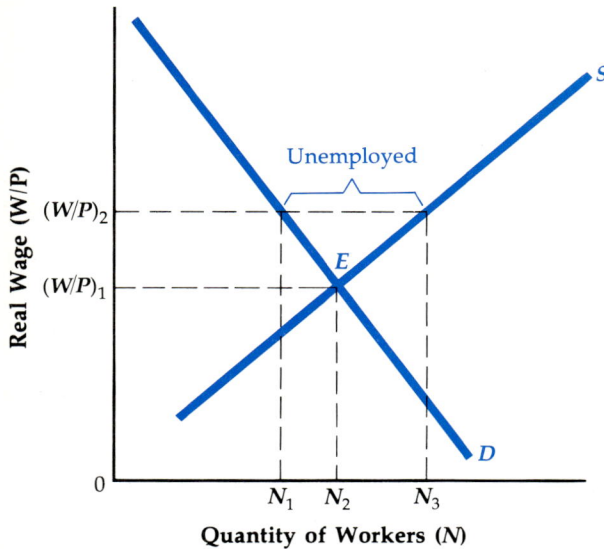

FIGURE 14.1 The Influence of the Price Level (*P*) on Unemployment
Assuming that the demand for labor slopes downward, the supply of labor slopes upward, leading to equilibrium at *E* and the real wage rate is fixed at $(W/P)_2$, $N_3 - N_1$ workers will be unemployed. As long as the money wage rate and the price level remain constant, unemployment will not fall.

cost of labor. If the real wage is prevented from falling below $(W/P)_2$, N_3 workers will want to work, but only N_1 workers will be hired. The difference between N_1 and N_3 is the number of people unemployed. According to monetarist theory, if the money wage rate and the price level remain constant or increase at the same rate, the real wage will not change and $N_3 - N_1$ unemployment will persist. If the price level rises while the money wage stays the same, then real wages fall, reducing or eliminating unemployment.

Monetarists believe that in the long run only real factors affect the rate of unemployment. In other words, only (W/P) matters in the long run. Furthermore, in a free labor market, excessive unemployment will push the wage rate down to $(W/P)_1$ in long-run equilibrium (point *E* in Figure 14.1). Note that some unemployment will necessarily persist because of the normal turnover in the labor market. Also, obstacles to the free movement of wages and workers can cause continuing unemployment. Some of the major obstacles include minimum wage laws, union contracts, discrimination, and restrictions on labor mobility created by a lack of information and transactions costs. The long-run rate of unemployment, then, is the outcome of the interaction of supply and demand in the labor market, as modified with the various restrictions on that market.

Phillips curve: a curve that shows the relationship between the rate of inflation and the rate of unemployment.

The Phillips Curve

The monetarist view of unemployment can be combined with the basic monetarist model of the short-run effects of a change in the money stock to yield the monetarist interpretation of the Phillips curve. The **Phillips**

curve, first presented in Chapter 6, shows a relationship between the rate of inflation and the rate of unemployment. On a typical Phillips curve diagram, the rate of inflation is shown on the vertical axis and the rate of unemployment on the horizontal axis, as in Figure 14.2. The diagram shows that when the rate of unemployment is U_1, the rate of inflation is IR_2. In order to achieve a lower rate of inflation, IR_1, the rate of unemployment must rise to U_2. In the simplest Phillips curve analysis, the problem facing policy makers is to find the optimal combination of inflation and unemployment along the Phillips curve.

Monetarists base their interpretation of the Phillips curve on the belief that in the short run, changes in the stock of money lead to changes in both the price level and real output, or real GNP. Changes in real output are accompanied by changes in employment. Thus, an increase in the rate of growth of the money stock leads to an increase in the rate of inflation and a decrease in the rate of unemployment. A decrease in the rate of growth of the money stock leads to a decrease in the rate of inflation and an increase in the rate of unemployment. Hence, the Phillips curve is a monetary phenomenon.

The phenomenon is necessarily short-run; the Phillips curve exists solely because workers and business firms are fooled into confusing a change in the price level with a change in real prices and wages. How are firms and workers fooled? As the increase in the rate of growth of the money stock begins to push up prices, business firms cannot tell how much of the increase in the price of their products is due to a rising price level and how much is due to an increase in consumer demand for their

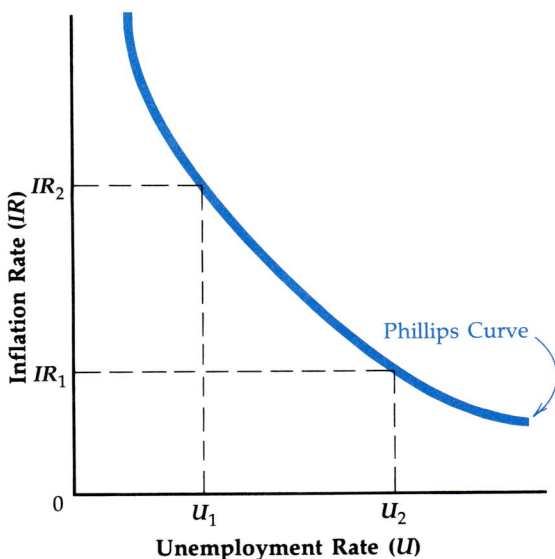

FIGURE 14.2 The Phillips Curve
Keynesian economists have argued that the unemployment and inflation rates are inversely related. Thus an unemployment rate lower than U_2 can be achieved only at the cost of an inflation rate higher than IR_1. An unemployment rate of U_1, for example, could be obtained only at an inflation rate of IR_2.

product. Moreover, since the ratio W/P is falling, firms are willing to hire more workers, causing unemployment to decrease. Real output and employment thus rise as a result of the monetary expansion.

This happy situation cannot last. As workers realize that real wages are falling, they begin to ask for increases in money wages. Labor unions bargain for cost of living increases. As business firms realize that the relative prices of their products have not risen and as real wages return to previous levels, the firms cut back on output and employment. As expectations begin to catch up with the reality, the Phillips curve shifts to the right, as shown in Figure 14.3. Basically, the short-run Phillips curve (SPC) exists because people are fooled. Along a given short-run Phillips curve, the anticipated rate of inflation is a constant. In Figure 14.3, the anticipated rate of inflation along SPC is IR_1. When the actual inflation is IR_2, people are fooled and unemployment is reduced. As anticipations catch up with reality, the short-run Phillips curve shifts to the right. When the anticipated rate of inflation equals the actual rate of inflation, the economy returns to the initial rate of unemployment, U_2. Because expectations will correspond to actual conditions in the long run, there can be no tradeoff between unemployment and inflation in the long run. The long-run Phillips curve, LPC in the figure, is therefore vertical.

The Phillips curve model thus predicts that unemployment can be reduced by inflation only to the extent that it is unanticipated. It is also true that an unanticipated *decrease* in inflation will affect unemployment. In that

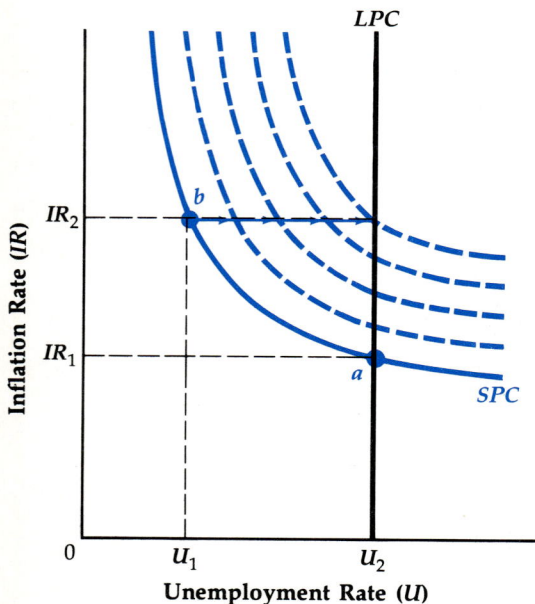

FIGURE 14.3 Short-Run (*SPC*) and Long-Run (*LPC*) Phillips Curves

The rate of unemployment can be temporarily reduced by an unexpected increase in the price level. The economy will move up its short-run Phillips curve (*SPC*), from point *a* to point *b*. In the long run, however, money wages will catch up with the higher prices, and the short-run Phillips curve will shift outward. Unemployment will climb back to U_2, but at a higher rate of inflation. In the long run, the Phillips curve is vertical (*LPC*).

case, however, unemployment will rise. Consider Figure 14.3. The economy is in long-run equilibrium with the actual and anticipated rates of inflation equal to IR_2. If the actual rate drops to IR_1, people will be fooled. Business firms will cut back on output and employment as the real wage rises and the apparent prices of their products fall. Unemployment rises to some level greater than U_2. As anticipations catch up to the reality of diminished inflation, the short-run Phillips curve shifts to the left until the rate of unemployment returns to its natural level, U_2.

The heart of the monetarist position on unemployment is that there is no long-term tradeoff between unemployment and inflation. In the long run, the rate of unemployment is determined by real, not monetary factors. Another way to put it is to say that long-run unemployment is determined by microeconomic, rather than macroeconomic forces. Those microeconomic forces, which include structural and institutional barriers to wage adjustments, generate a natural rate of unemployment that is impervious to conventional macroeconomic policies.

The Historical Evidence

The past few decades have supplied considerable evidence to support the monetarist claim that no long-run tradeoff between inflation and unemployment exists. Figure 14.4 plots U.S. inflation and unemployment rates from 1953 to 1987. The pattern bears no resemblance to a neatly downward sloping Phillips curve; it looks more like a contrail left by a stunt plane. It would be easier to argue for a positive than for a negative relationship between inflation and unemployment on the basis of the historical evidence.

One conclusion nevertheless emerges from the data. The long-run or natural rate of unemployment apparently increased during the 1970s. The rise has been variously attributed to rising unemployment benefits, increasing rates of labor force participation, and rapid structural change. As we would expect, monetarists look to the microeconomics of labor markets (see Chapters 26 and 27) for explanations of the phenomenon.

The Monetarist View of Inflation

▲ 3. What is the basic cause of inflation?

The monetarist view of inflation, as we have seen, is that inflation is caused by an overly rapid increase in the stock of money. To the monetarist, then, inflation is almost always a monetary phenomenon. Their position can be illustrated by returning to the equation of exchange,

$$MV = PQ, \text{ or } MV = Py$$

Inflation is the rate of change of P, the price level. Real output or GNP, y, changes slowly on an annual basis. Moreover, it usually rises and therefore tends to reduce the rate of inflation. In order for changes in y to cause a

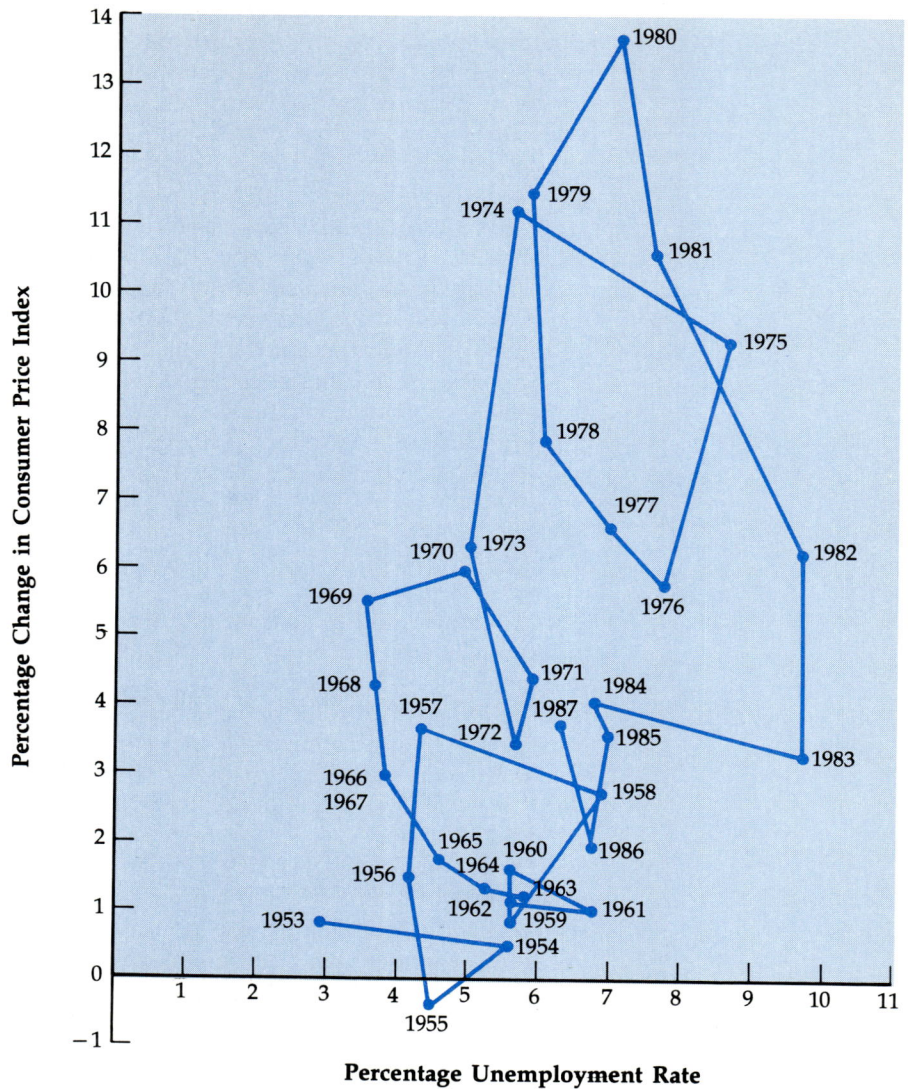

FIGURE 14.4 Inflation and Unemployment in the United States, 1953–1987
Between 1953 and 1987, the unemployment rate fluctuated between 3 and 9.5 percent, while inflation varied annually between practically zero and 14 percent. If a downward-sloping Phillips curve exists, it lasts only a few years. It appears to have shifted up and down over time.

rapid inflation, it would have to fall rapidly, an unlikely event. If velocity, V, is relatively stable, then only money, M, is left to cause inflation. Is velocity stable? That depends on the demand for money.

The Demand for Money

Cambridge equation: $MD = kPy$, where k represents the fraction of income people wish to hold in the form of money.

Demand for money: the willingness of people to hold money.

The monetarist theory of the demand for money can best be illustrated with the Cambridge cash balances approach to the equation of exchange: $M = kPy$. The **Cambridge equation** can be interpreted as the demand for money, where k represents the fraction of income people wish to hold in the form of money. (The **demand for money** is the willingness of people to hold money.) We then write the equation as

$$MD = kPy$$

where MD is desired money balances. People demand money for a variety of reasons, including the convenience of money for carrying out transactions and as a temporary store of value. The money stock, MS, is set by the monetary authorities—the Federal Reserve System in our economy. The equilibrium occurs as in all markets, where the quantity demanded equals the quantity supplied, or

$$MD = MS$$

Let us now consider the demand for money in more detail. Monetarists treat money as an asset that is demanded for the services it yields. The great virtue of money is its liquidity—the ability to trade it easily for other assets and goods. How much money is held by the individual depends on the relative returns to money and to alternative assets. The five major factors that affect the demand for money are (1) wealth, (2) the rates of interest on money and other assets, (3) the price level, (4) the expected rate of inflation, and (5) institutional factors.

1. *Wealth.* An individual's demand for money is directly related to his or her wealth. Rich people hold more assets than poor people. Money is just one type of asset. The demand for money to carry out transactions will be greater, the greater the amount of transactions carried out. Because the rich spend more than the poor, they require more money for transactions purposes.

2. *Rates of interest.* Money held in the form of currency and coin earns no interest. Money held in the form of checkable deposits earns less interest than less liquid assets. In deciding how large a part of one's personal wealth to hold in the form of money, one compares the rate of return on money to the rate of return on other assets. The cost of holding money is the interest forgone by not holding other assets. As the rate of return on bonds and equities rises, the cost of holding money rises; the demand for money is therefore inversely related to the rate of interest on non-money assets.

3. *The price level.* If the price level goes up, people will need to hold larger nominal money balances in order to carry out the same

amount of transactions. Consequently the demand for money balances rises when the price level rises and declines when the price level declines. In essence, people adjust their nominal money balances, M, in order to achieve their desired level of real money balances, M/P.

4. *The expected rate of inflation.* Inflation reduces the value of money balances. If the rate of inflation exceeds the nominal rate of interest on money, it will reduce the purchasing power of their current money holdings. People will therefore reduce their holdings of money if the expected rate of inflation goes up. They will convert money either into consumption goods or into assets whose real value will not be affected by inflation.

5. *Institutional factors.* Many variables come under this heading. The prevailing pattern of wage payments and bill payments affects the demand for cash balances. The expected future stability of the economy will influence the demand for money. Beliefs about political stability also enter here. Although political instability is not a problem in the United States, in many countries it is endemic.

The demand for money is thus affected by many variables. Monetarists nevertheless claim that it is highly stable. The assumption of stability follows from various assumptions about the variables affecting the demand for money. Wealth and the price level both have large potential effects, but both change slowly (on average) in the American economy. Institutional factors also tend to change slowly (although, as we shall see, the 1980s were an apparent exception). Monetarists believe that the demand for money is not highly sensitive to the rates of interest on other assets. With few exceptions, the rate of inflation has not been high enough to have large short-run effects on the demand for money balances. For all these reasons, then, monetarists believe that the fraction of wealth held in the form of money, k, changes slowly. It is by no means a numerical constant, but it is highly stable. If k (in the Cambridge equation) is highly stable, it follows that the velocity (remember that $k = 1/V$) is also highly stable. Under the assumption of stable velocity, the monetarist belief that inflation is a monetary phenomenon follows directly because changes in M must be matched by changes in P to keep the equation of exchange in balance.

The Effect of Changes in the Stock of Money

4. What are the effects of an increase in the stock of money?

Monetarists believe that inflation is caused by expansionary monetary policy. How does an expansion of the money stock get transformed into a rising price level? Suppose that the economy is initially in equilibrium, with

$$MD = MS$$

If the Federal Reserve increases the money stock to MS', then desired money balances will be less than actual money balances, or

$$MD < MS'$$

There is an excess supply of money. People will therefore try to convert money into other assets. Now, an individual can always reduce his or her money holdings by spending the money. The economy as a whole, however, cannot do so. The stock of money is determined by the Federal Reserve and can be changed only by the Federal Reserve. If one person reduces his or her money balances, those balances go to someone else in the economy; the nation's money stock does not change. The simplest way to describe what then happens is that as everyone tries to spend more money, they force up the price of all goods because in the short run total output, y, if fixed. The price level rises, reducing real money balances, M/P. The rising price level increases the demand for money balances until people become willing to hold the new, higher stock of money (recall that the quantity of money demanded varies positively with the price level). In terms of the Cambridge equation, P is pushed up until $MD = kPy$ is once again equal to the stock of money, or

$$MD = kPy = MS'$$

In the actual economy, the transmission from money to prices is somewhat more complex. What happens is that in the first instance people and businesses try to reduce their money balances in more ways than simply increasing purchases of goods and services. They will also purchase other financial assets. The increased demand for financial assets pushes down the rates of interest on those assets and thereby increases planned investment spending. This increase leads to a temporary increase in output and employment. As firms attempt to purchase more labor and other factors of production, however, wage rates and other input prices are bid up. The rise in input prices leads to a rise in output prices—inflation. The economy reaches long-run equilibrium when $MV = Py$ at the original level of real national income. The rise in M ultimately leads only to a rise in P.

The argument is symmetrical with respect to declines in the rate of monetary expansion. When the stock of money is lower than the desired stock, people attempt to increase their money balances by spending less. As the entire economy spends less, the price level falls. Fewer dollars are chasing goods and services, forcing sellers to lower the money prices of goods and services until monetary equilibrium is restored. In the short run, of course, output and employment may decline, but there is no long-run effect.

The Historical Evidence

To support their theory of inflation, monetarists cite extensive evidence on the relationship between the rate of growth of the money stock and the rate of inflation. Whenever the rate of growth of the money stock has exceeded the rate of growth of real national income, inflation has occurred. Whenever the rate of growth of the money stock has fallen short of the rate of growth of real national income, deflation has occurred. Monetarists argue that most business cycles have been initiated by some abrupt change in the

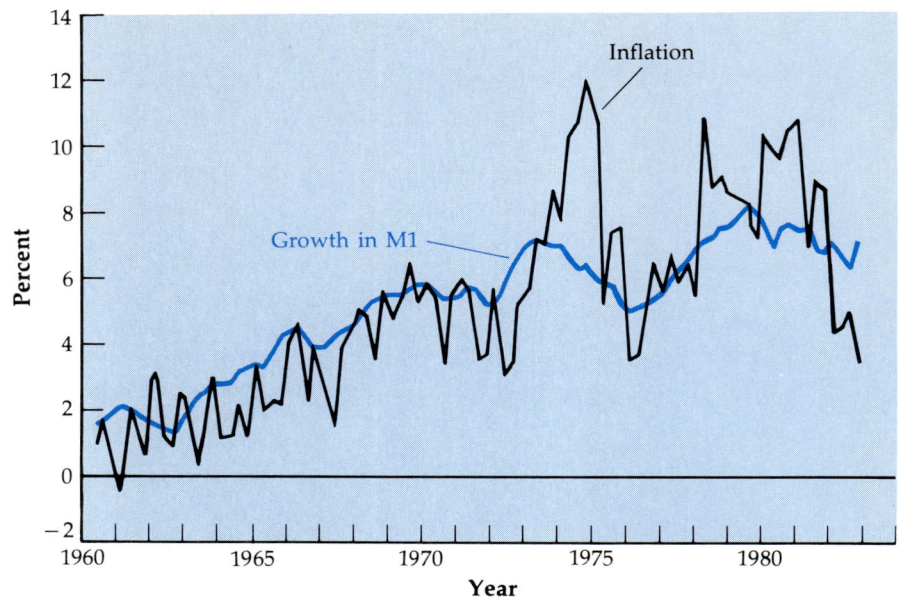

FIGURE 14.5   Inflation and the Rate of Growth of the M1 Money Stock, 1960–1982
The M1 growth line represents a twelve-quarter moving average of M1 growth. The inflation line represents a quarter-to-quarter rate of change in the GNP deflator. The vertical
line between the third and fourth quarters of 1979 indicates a change in the Federal Reserve operating procedures. In the short run the rate of inflation has diverged from the
rate of growth in the money stock. Over the long term, swings in the rate of inflation have
tended to follow swings in the rate of growth in the money stock.
Source: Federal Reserve Bank of St. Louis *Review* 65 (May 1983): 11.

rate of growth of the money stock. The correlation between money and
prices shows up again and again throughout economic history.[2]

Recent evidence on the relationships between money and inflation and
money and income are illustrated in Figures 14.5 and 14.6. Although the
growth path of the money stock does not exactly match the patterns for
inflation and GNP, swings in the growth of the money stock appear to be
reflected in shifts in the growth rates of the price level and GNP. Deviations
among the three patterns can be attributed to time lags between growth in
the money stock and its effects, to fluctuations in real output, and to random changes in the velocity of circulation.

---

2. See Milton Friedman and Anna J. Schwartz, *Monetary Trends in the United
States and the United Kingdom* (Chicago: University of Chicago Press, 1982), for
detailed evidence on money and prices in Britain and America. For a general
survey of the evidence supporting the monetarist theory of inflation, see Michael
D. Bordo, "Explorations in Monetary History: A Survey of the Literature,"
Explorations in Economic History 4 (October 1986): 339–415.

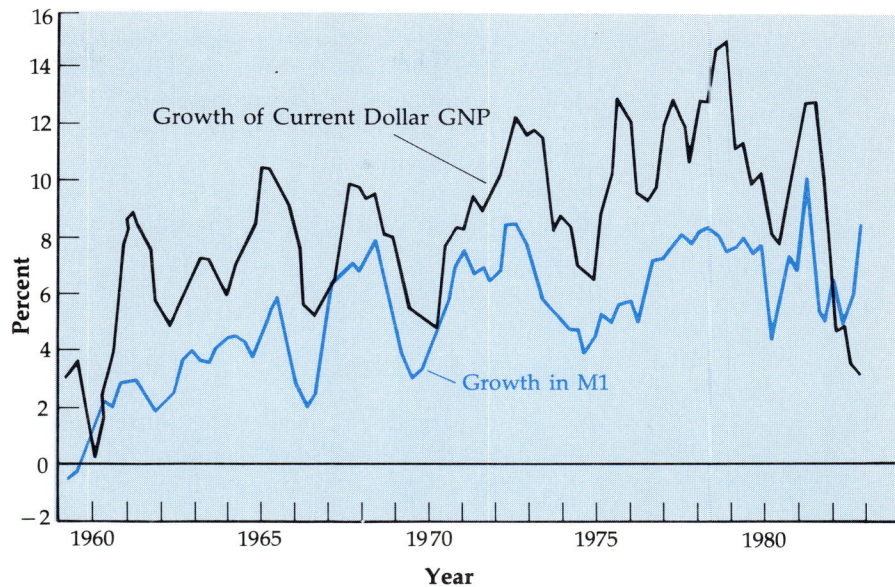

FIGURE 14.6 Growth Rates of the Nominal Gross National Product and the Money Stock, 1960–1982

Each line represents a four-quarter growth rate. The vertical line between the third and fourth quarters of 1979 indicates a change in Federal Reserve operating procedures. Over the long run, the growth paths of the money stock and current dollar GNP have tended to move together. Short-run discrepancies have occurred, however.

Source: Federal Reserve Bank of St. Louis *Review* 65 (May 1983): 10.

The support for the monetarist version of the quantity theory does not rest on recent correlations between money and prices. Rather, centuries of evidence point to the validity of the monetary theory of inflation. Indeed, every major historical inflation has been accompanied by an increase in the money supply. For example, the so-called Price Revolution of seventeenth-century Europe took place in the wake of the expansion of the European money stock brought about by the import of silver and gold from Spanish America. The increased gold supplies resulting from the California and Australia gold discoveries of the mid-nineteenth century were followed by worldwide inflation. The inflation that plagued the Confederate states during the American Civil War clearly had a monetary accompaniment.[3] The money stock increased from $94.6 million in January 1861 to $268.1 million in January 1864. An index of commodity prices increased from 100 to 2,776 over the same three-year period.

---

3. Much of what follows is based on Milton Friedman, ed., *Studies in the Quantity Theory of Money* (Chicago: University of Chicago Press, 1956).

The most striking support for the quantity theory comes from the experience of extremely rapid inflations. During the German hyperinflation of 1922–1923, the price level rose an average of 322 percent *per month*. The quantity of currency increased an average of 314 percent per month. The hyperinflation in Greece between 1943 and 1946 saw rates of monetary growth and inflation peak at several thousand percent per month. Those nations that suffer above-average inflations today invariably have rapidly increasing money stocks. The accumulated evidence, then, leads monetarists to conclude that the quantity theory approach to inflation is essentially correct.

Money, Prices, and Employment

We are now ready to consider the entire sequence of events that follows an increase in the money stock from the perspective of monetarism. The Federal Reserve begins the process by, say, buying government securities on the open market. Although more money has been put into circulation, desired money balances have not changed. Rather than holding the extra money that comes their way, people and business firms will use it to buy more real goods and securities, including bonds. The increased demand for bonds will reduce interest rates, stimulating planned investment.

Combined with increased consumer spending, the increase in investment will increase aggregate demand for goods and services. In terms of Figure 14.7, the aggregate demand curve shifts up from AD_1 to AD_2, and the price level rises from P_1 to P_2. As we saw in Figure 14.1, higher prices will temporarily reduce the real wages paid to labor. As unemployment falls, real national production increases from y_1 to y_2.

The increased output and employment are, as we have seen, only temporary. In the long run, workers will demand higher wages because of the higher cost of living. The real wage rate will return to its previous level, reducing the amount of labor demanded and increasing unemployment. The adjustments in labor supply and output will be reflected in a leftward shift of the short-run aggregate supply curve, from SAS_1 to SAS_2. As aggregate supply shifts, the price level will rise further to P_3, and the level of real national income will fall back to y_1. The shifts of aggregate supply are caused by changes in the anticipated price level. As the anticipated price level rises, the short-run aggregate supply curve shifts to the left. The shifts in aggregate demand and supply combine to establish a new long-run equilibrium at the original output but a higher price level. The long-run aggregate supply curve, *LAS*, like the long-run Phillips curve, is vertical.

The sequence of events following a decrease in the money stock is exactly the opposite. If the initial equilibrium is at P_3 and y_1, a decrease in the money stock reduces aggregate demand from AD_2 to AD_1. As the price level begins to fall, employment and output will decline in the short run. (When the real wage rate rises, employers hire fewer workers.) In the long run the high unemployment will produce greater competition for jobs,

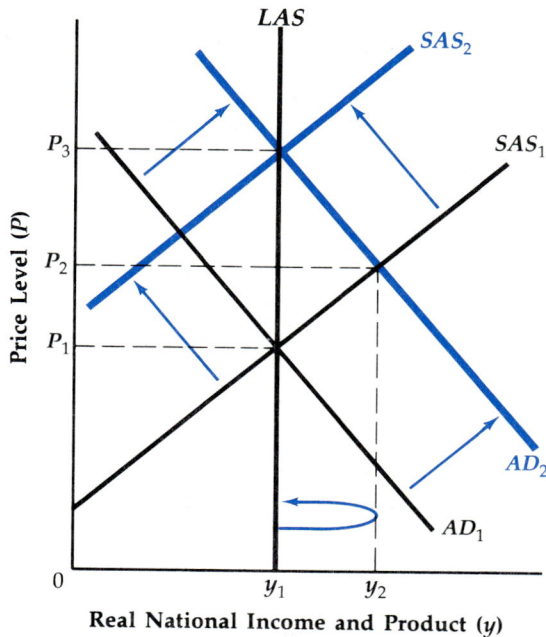

FIGURE 14.7 The Impact of an Increase in the Money Stock on Aggregate Supply and Demand
An increase in the money stock will shift the aggregate demand curve up from AD_1 to AD_2, temporarily increasing the real national income and price levels. When money wages adjust to the higher living cost, however, the aggregate supply curve will shift down from SAS_1 to SAS_2. In the long run the real national income level will return to y_1, but at a higher price level, P_3. The opposite sequence of events will occur if the money stock declines.

pushing down the wage rate and increasing employment and output. The aggregate supply curve will shift rightward, from SAS_2 to SAS_1. Long-run equilibrium will be established when real national income reaches y_1 at price level P_1.

We have carried out the analysis in terms of changes in the price level and the money stock. It is more realistic to think in terms of changes in the rate of growth of the money stock and the rate of inflation. Suppose that an established rate of growth of the money stock has produced an established rate of inflation. Under these conditions, at a moment in time people have an anticipated price level based on the anticipated rate of inflation. An increase in the rate of growth of the money stock will increase the price level faster than anticipated. Prices will rise faster than wages, the real wage will decrease, and employment and production will go up—temporarily, until workers can adjust the rate of wage increases. The aggregate demand and short-run aggregate supply curves are both shifting, but the aggregate demand curve is shifting more rapidly because of the unexpectedly rapid monetary expansion. As expectations catch up, the short-run aggregate supply curve begins shifting as rapidly as aggregate demand, leading to a higher rate of inflation but no changes in the long-run rate of growth of national income.

Henry Calvert Simons (1899–1946)

Henry Simons taught economics at the University of Chicago from 1927 until his death in 1946. He published few works during his lifetime and never achieved a rank higher than associate professor. Few economists outside Chicago took much notice of his death (by suicide). Nevertheless, he profoundly influenced the development of modern monetarism.

At a time when the economics of Keynes was beginning to dominate the way economists thought about the world, Simons vigorously defended an older approach based on the quantity theory of money. Simons recognized the seriousness of the economic problems of the 1930s and agreed with the Keynesians that government needed to take action. He differed from the Keynesians in that he did not believe expansionary fiscal policy (reduced taxes and increased spending) to be the solution to the nation's woes. Rather, he believed that monetary policy alone could return the economy to full employment. Because many Keynesians also believed in expansionary monetary policy, the differences between Simons and the Keynesians superficially appear small. In fact, the differences were profound and irreconcilable. The reason lies in *how* countercyclical policy was to be carried out; the crucial issue to Simons was whether policy would be determined by individuals acting according to their own discretion or according to predetermined rules that left no room for individual discretion. Simons believed that appropriate rules for the conduct of monetary policy could make the Keynesian policy prescriptions unnecessary.

Simons proposed that the monetary authority (the Federal Reserve Board) should be bound by a rule forcing it to use monetary policy to maintain a constant price level. In other words, rules would compel the monetary authority to prevent inflation. Nor would the authorities be allowed discretion on how to enforce the monetary rule. Instead,

strict regulations would govern how the authorities responded to changes in the price level. When the price level rose, the money stock would contract; when the price level fell, the money stock would expand. No deviations from the rules would be necessary because

> Once established . . . they should work mechanically, with the chips falling where they may. To put our present problem as a paradox—we need to design and establish with the greatest intelligence a monetary system good enough so that, hereafter, we may hold to it unrationally—on faith—as a religion, if you please.[1]

The emphasis on rules stemmed from Simons' deep distrust of concentrated power, a distrust that led him to formulate a comprehensive program to preserve individual liberty by keeping power diffused. His monetary proposals were coupled with proposals to eliminate private monopoly, redistribute income, eliminate tariffs, and restrict advertising. All this, argued Simons, was necessary to defend liberty from both public and private abuses of power.

Contemporary monetarists do not advocate the same rule that Simons proposed in the 1930s. The continuing influence of Simons, then, stems less from the particular rules he espoused than from his emphasis on the superiority of rules to authorities. Also, his adherence to the then-unpopular belief that changes in the quantity of money would have real effects on the economy in the short run has been vindicated many times over. The enduring legacy of Henry Simons is to be found in many current proposals that rules adopted through the democratic political process, rather than the judgment of politicians and bankers, should determine monetary policy.

1. Henry C. Simons, *Economic Policy for a Free Society* (Chicago: University of Chicago Press, 1948), p. 169.

A decrease in the rate of monetary expansion leads to a situation in which money wages are rising more rapidly than prices. Unemployment will be higher than normal until long-run adjustments bring the real wage rate back to its original level. The adjustment could, however, take several years if wage and other contracts have been written based on a higher anticipated rate of inflation. Note that it is the unanticipated changes in money and prices that cause unemployment and real national income to differ from their long-term levels. The monetarist prescription, then, is to eliminate unanticipated changes in the money stock by instructing the Federal Reserve to expand the money stock at a constant rate.

The Monetarist View of High Interest Rates

▲ 5. What effect does inflation have on interest rates?

According to the original Keynesian theory, an increase in the rate of growth of the money stock will reduce interest rates because more funds become available for loans. Another way to put it is that the rate of interest must fall in order to induce people to hold the increased money balances. Monetarists agree, but argue that the decrease in interest rates will be temporary. In the long run, greater growth of the money stock will increase rather than decrease interest rates.

The monetarist argument goes as follows: When the interest rate drops, many lenders will refuse to make loans because the nominal return does not compensate them for the higher rate of inflation caused by the increase in the money stock. For example, if a lender can receive only 5 percent and the rate of inflation is 6 percent, the money the borrower pays back will have less real purchasing power than the money that was lent. If the lender invests in real assets (like land) whose nominal value is rising at a rate of 7 percent, he can make a small profit. Unless interest rates rise, lenders will withhold their funds from the loan market and invest them in assets whose real value is not expected to diminish.

The higher rate of inflation, then, decreases the supply of lendable funds. At the same time, households, businesses, and governments will speed up their purchases of goods and services to avoid paying higher future prices. Consumers will buy cars and appliances now in order to avoid paying higher prices when new models come out. Businesses will increase current investment in plant and equipment. Governments will build schools and roads now in order to avoid higher construction costs in the future. To accomplish these goals, individuals, businesses, and governments will want to borrow more money.

The increased demand for lendable funds occurs at a time when lendable funds are in short supply because lenders are unwilling to make loans at the prevailing low rates of interest. The excess demand for lendable funds pushes up the rate of interest. Together, faster growth of the money stock and a higher inflation rate should push rates up above where they were before the increased growth. The increase in nominal interest rates during a period of inflation is known as the **Fisher effect.** The higher rates

Fisher effect: the increase in nominal interest rates during a period of inflation.

PERSPECTIVES
The Fed Has No Clothes

Milton Friedman, Hoover Institution

Every now and then a reporter asks my opinion about "current monetary policy." My standard reply has become that I would be glad to answer if he would first tell me what "current monetary policy" is. I know, or can find out, what monetary actions have been: open-market purchases and sales and discount rates at Federal Reserve Banks. I know also the federal funds rate and rates of growth of various monetary aggregates that have accompanied these actions. What I do not know is the policy that produced these actions.

Many alternative policies have been proposed. For example, undertaking monetary actions directed at attaining a specified steady numerical rate of growth of: (1) seasonally adjusted or (2) unadjusted monetary base, or (3) one or another broader monetary aggregate or (4) nominal gross national product. Or: stabilizing at a specified numerical level (5) one or another price index or (6) exchange rate or (7) index of exchange rates or (8) one or another nominal or real interest rate or (9) rate of unemployment.

However, the closest I can come to an official specification of current monetary policy is that it is to take those actions that the monetary authorities, in light of all evidence available, judge will best promote price stability and full employment—i.e., to do the right thing at the right time. But that surely is not a "policy." It is simply an expression of good intentions and an injunction to "trust us."

Examining Some Gobbledygook

The accuracy of this description can be readily documented. Consider the following excerpts from the nearly 1,000-word statement of "Monetary Policy Plans for 1988" in the Federal Reserve's Monetary Policy Report to Congress, submitted Feb. 24, 1988, in accordance with legislated requirements:

"For 1988, the [Open Market Investment] Committee set ranges of 4% to 8% for growth of M2 and M3. . . . [W]hile the Committee at this time expects that growth of M2 and M3 will be around

the middle of their ranges, the outcome could differ if significant changes in interest rates are required to counter unanticipated weakness in aggregate demand or an intensification of inflation. In carrying out policy, the Committee will continue to assess the behavior of the aggregates in light of information about the pace of business expansions and the source and strength of price pressures, with attention to the performance of the dollar on foreign-exchange markets and other indicators of the impact of monetary policy."

Is it inaccurate to summarize this gobbledygook as "doing the right thing at the right time"? Indeed, the one specific element—the numerical ranges for M2 and M3—is there only because Congress mandated it in 1975 over the vigorous objections of the Fed.

Such a "policy" can be used to judge present actions or anticipate future actions only through informed conjecture based on empirical extrapolation of past reactions of the Fed to a variety of stimuli, and analysis of the beliefs and attitudes of the participants in the decision-making process—that is, by statistical extrapolation and psychoanalysis. And, of course, there is a sizable and remunerative industry in the financial community engaged in reading the Federal Reserve tea leaves.

Contrast such a process with, at the one extreme, a policy of steady growth in the monetary base or of buying and selling gold at fixed prices; or, at the other, of stabilizing an index of basic commodity prices. The first two would yield precise predictions of monetary actions; the third would not, but at least it would provide a ready means of judging the success or failure of the monetary authorities in carrying out their stated policy and of anticipating their future actions.

I hasten to add that the present situation is not unique. On the contrary, it has persisted for nearly the entire 74-year life of the Federal Reserve System. The only exception was from the outbreak of World War II to 1951, when the Fed followed an announced policy of pegging interest rates on federal government securities. For the rest, the Fed has consistently resorted to statements of good intentions both with respect to the future and with respect to its past actions. It has claimed credit for good results and blamed forces beyond its control—generally fiscal policy—for any bad outcomes. And this avoidance of accountability has paid spectacular dividends. No major institution in the U.S. has so poor a record of performance over so long a period as the Federal Reserve, yet so high a public reputation.

To come down to cases, consider the past quarter-century, from 1962 to 1987. Growth in both monetary aggregates and prices fluctuated widely, averaging 8.5% a year in M2 and 5.5% in the GNP deflator; severe recessions occurred from 1972 to 1975 and again from 1980 to 1982; accelerating inflation reached more than 15% during the 1970s and was accompanied by stagflation, followed by drastic disinflation and wild gyrations in interest rates and economic activity.

During the prior decade (1952 to 1962), M2 grew at an average annual rate of 5.5%, and prices of 2.3%, suggesting, in line with much other experience, that monetary growth at about 3% a year was consistent with stable prices. Suppose that in 1962 the Fed had adopted a policy of increasing M2 at an annual rate of 3% to 5% year after year. It could not have stayed within that range week by week or even month by month. However, it clearly could have done so on a semi-annual or annual basis, if it had taken steady monetary growth as its overriding objective.

If monetary growth from 1962 to 1987 had averaged 4% a year instead of 8.5%, M2 currently would be roughly one-third its present level and so would the price level, implying that inflation would have averaged about 1% a year instead of 5.5%. Even more important, the country (and the world) would never have suffered the accelerating inflation of the '70s and the accompanying stagflation, or the subsequent disinflation and erratic movements in interest rates and exchange rates.

Ups and downs in the economy, in prices, interest rates and employment would still have occurred, but they would have been far milder. President Nixon would never have had occasion to impose price controls or President Carter to impose credit controls. Departure from Bretton Woods would at the very least have been postponed. When it did occur, it would not have been followed by the revolution that occurred in financial markets and institutions.

Not a Fanciful Story

You can readily add to this story. And, though hypothetical, it is by no means fanciful—as is suggested by the experience of Japan, which adopted a very similar policy in 1971 under much less favorable circumstances. (Japan, under pressure from us, now appears to be departing from that policy in an inflationary direction, with, as usual, favorable initial effects. It remains to be seen whether it will revert to its earlier policy soon enough to avoid the later bad effects.)

The hypothetical alternative policy would have had one other result: The news media would have paid far less attention to the Federal Reserve System. No poll would have designated the Chairman of the System as the second most powerful person in the country and far fewer people would know his name or the names of the other members of the board. The able people now earning high salaries reading the Fed tea leaves would be earning equally high salaries engaged in more productive activities. Similarly, it would be hard to attract individuals of the caliber of Arthur Burns or Paul Volcker or Alan Greenspan to serve as chairman. Why not, they might well say, turn such a boring job over to a computer? And, indeed, why not? It's my own favorite recipe for improving monetary performance.

do not necessarily discourage investment; firms may pay a higher rate of interest for the money they borrow, but part of their interest payment is returned to them in the increased prices of the goods they sell. During a period of double-digit inflation, for example, a business may have to pay interest of 15 percent or more on the funds it borrows to purchase its raw materials. It can justify such a high rate because it knows that the price of the final goods it produces will rise over time, enabling it to meet its interest payments.

According to the Fisher effect, then, the nominal, or market, rate of interest includes both the real rate of interest, which reflects the real rate of return on capital, and the expected rate of inflation (borrowers and lenders cannot know what the rate of inflation will be next year):

nominal rate of interest = real rate of interest

+ expected rate of inflation

The way to reduce nominal interest rates, contend the monetarists, is to reduce the rate of inflation. To reduce the rate of inflation, the rate of growth of the money stock must be reduced. As always, monetarists point to control of the money stock as the key to dealing with macroeconomic problems.

The Importance of a Stable Rate of Monetary Growth

◢ 6. What macroeconomic policy do monetarists propose?

Because they believe that a predictable monetary policy is crucial to the health of the macroeconomy, monetarists contend that the government should establish a constant rate of growth of the money stock—say, 3 percent a year. That is, the Federal Reserve should establish a policy of expanding the money stock at a fixed rate year in and year out. The rate should be well known to the public so that it will be properly anticipated. Most macroeconomic problems, according to monetarists, arise because of unanticipated monetary growth and inflation. Unpredictable swings in monetary policy generate business cycles. If a known and stable rate of monetary growth is established, business cycles would be far less severe if not eliminated.

The critical need, say the monetarists, is to establish a known and stable rate of increase for the money stock; the exact rate of increase is far less important than that some rule be established. An annual rate of growth of 3 percent would allow for the average annual rise in the production of goods and services (2 to 3 percent), while generating little or no inflation (0 to 1 percent). Other rules would, however, serve as well.

The money stock should increase rather than remain constant or decrease. If the money stock were fixed, an increase in real national income would cause the price level to decline (remember $MV = Py$). Deflation is thought to be something of a problem because of the potential redistribution involved. Anticipated deflation would cause no problems, but moving to a world of deflation from our world of inflation could cause severe short-run disruptions.

Monetarists support rules over authorities not because they believe it is impossible for Keynesian-type policies to work. Rather, they believe that in practice it is so difficult to successfully "fine-tune" the economy that the attempt to do so is more likely to exacerbate the problem than to cure it. The problems in attempting to manipulate the economy through monetary policy are numerous. Monetarists contend that monetary officials do not know enough about how changes in the growth rate of the money stock will affect the economy in the short run. Monetary policy often has long and highly variable lags between the recognition of the problem, the implementation of the policy, and the taking effect of the policy. For example, the Fed may try to help fight a recession by increasing the rate of growth of the money stock. By the time the need for action is recognized, the action is carried out, and the policy takes effect, the recession could be over and the Fed may be adding monetary fuel to an inflation. The attempt to help has only made matters worse.

Steady growth of the money stock and a predictable rate of inflation would reduce the risk attached to holding wealth in the form of money or other assets fixed in dollar amounts. Velocity would therefore be less susceptible to change. Monetarists believe that the discipline and stability introduced by adopting a monetary rule would far outweigh the potential costs of the inflexibility introduced by such a policy. Moreover, monetarists believe that a market economy is inherently stable; leaving it (mostly) alone may be the best way that the government can promote macroeconomic stability.

Criticisms of Monetarism

▲ 7. What are the problems with monetarism?

Critics of monetarist theory make several counterarguments. First, it is difficult to decide which measure of the money stock—M1 or M2 (or M3, not considered here)—should be controlled. Current measures of the money stock are largely arbitrary, and new forms of money not included in the official estimates are constantly being created. Indeed, no one can say for sure what is and is not money. The problem this situation creates for monetarism can easily be imagined. Suppose that the Federal Reserve reestablishes a policy of targeting M1 by increasing it at a rate of 5 percent. If people begin using money market accounts (not included in M1) as a temporary store of purchasing power, the result could be an increase in the velocity of circulation of M1 and a higher-than-expected rate of inflation. The "true" money stock would be increasing more rapidly than M1, the official measure.

Second, critics maintain that the growth of the money stock depends only partly on the growth of currency and required bank reserves—the variables directly controlled by the Fed through open market operations and manipulation of reserve requirements and the discount rate (see Chapter 8). Many other variables, such as the public's demand for currency and

PERSPECTIVES
Solving the Velocity Puzzle
Courtenay C. Stone and Daniel L. Thornton, St. Louis Fed

For over a third of a century—from 1946 to 1981—the growth of the velocity of money, measured as the ratio of gross national product (GNP) to the narrow money stock (M1), was stable. Its stability contributed to the rise of monetarism and the adoption of monetary aggregate targets by the Federal Reserve and other central banks around the world. Its stability also resulted in two empirically based rules of thumb that came to be used fairly successfully as guides to money growth's effects on income and inflation. Now, however, analysts believe that these rules have failed to explain the course of income and inflation during the 1980s, due to a relatively sudden and unanticipated drop in velocity. (See Figure 14.8.)

Numerous attempts have been made to explain the recent changes in velocity. Here, these explanations are grouped loosely into three categories: misspecification, a portmanteau category we call "structural shifts," and cyclical factors.

Misspecification

The most widely used velocity measure, the income velocity of M1, is calculated by dividing nominal GNP by the nominal stock of M1. Both GNP and M1 are empirical counterparts to theoretical concepts that appear in various theories of the demand for money. One explanation for the shift in velocity is that GNP or M1 or both have become less reliable proxies for their correspond-

FIGURE 14.8 Velocity of Money, 1946–1986

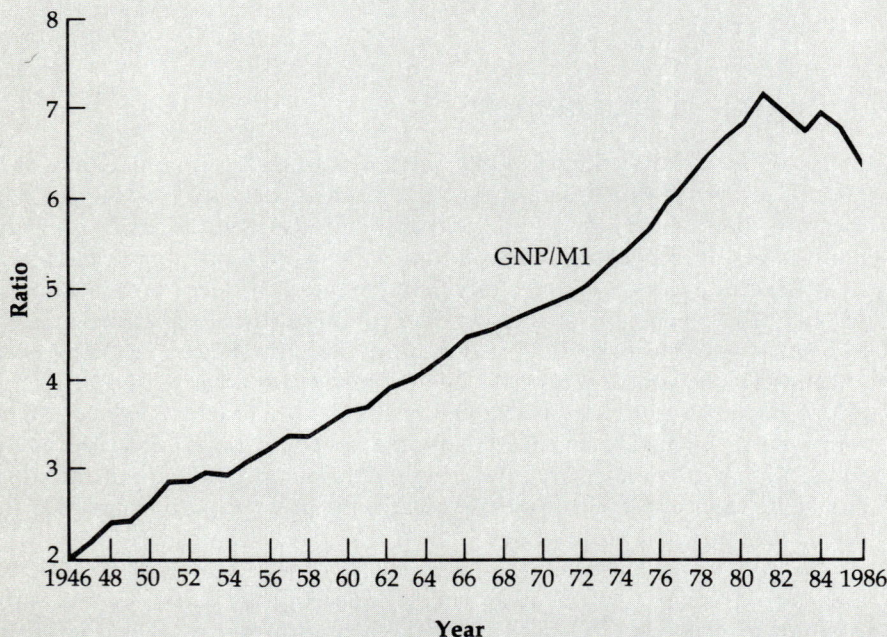

ing theoretical concepts. This problem is called a specification problem.

GNP vs. Transactions Measures

A specification problem could arise if money is held primarily to make daily transactions. If these include intermediate and financial transactions, the usual velocity measure could vary with changes in the proportion of such transactions relative to transactions on final goods and services. Because GNP measures only final output, it will differ widely from the level of expenditures on all transactions. GNP is therefore a useful proxy for total transactions only if the proportion of GNP to total transactions remains relatively constant.

This problem can manifest itself in several ways. For example, suppose consumers purchase more goods and, as a result, increase their money holdings in proportion to their increased desire to spend. If these newly purchased goods are imported or drawn from domestic inventories of previously produced goods, GNP will remain unchanged while the demand for money rises. Consequently, the usual measure of velocity will decline, while an alternative measure based on total transactions will remain unchanged. Thus, using GNP as the transactions measure to calculate velocity may produce sizable swings in velocity whenever there are large swings in inventories or net exports.

Recently, economists have offered another variant of the specification problem. They too argue that the demand for money is based on expenditures instead of current income or GNP. In their view, the 1980 tax cut initially increased disposable personal and business income relative to GNP and, hence, raised desired expenditures relative to GNP; consequently, the tax cut increased the demand for money, resulting in a fall in velocity.

Others have argued that the recent velocity decline is related to a sharp rise in financial transactions relative to total output. According to this view, the rise in financial transactions cause an increase in the demand for money relative to GNP.

Potential Problems with Using M1

Some have suggested that using M1 as the money stock measure when calculating velocity causes significant problems. They argue that the relevant monetary measure cannot be obtained simply by adding together the stocks of various "monetary" assets (currency, checkable deposits, and so on), because each component may provide different quantities of monetary services per unit. Consequently, critics have suggested that an index of the monetary "services" provided by the stock of all relevant financial assets is preferable to the use of M1 for evaluating the relationship between money and spending or prices. If this criticism is valid, changes in "simple-sum" monetary aggregates like M1 and M2 may deviate markedly from changes in their underlying monetary services whenever substantial shifts among various monetary assets occur. In such cases, the usual measure of velocity may show sizable variations, while those based on the underlying monetary services measures should be relatively stable.

Financial Innovation and Deregulation

Several analysts have suggested that the introduction of NOWs, Super NOWs and money market deposit accounts (MMDAs) and the removal of regulation Q interest rate ceilings in recent years have produced a shift in the relationships between M1 and both spending and inflation. In particular, the redefinition of M1 to include interest-bearing checkable deposits (NOWs and Super NOWs) as well as non–interest-bearing demand deposits and currency is alleged to have altered significantly its "moneyness"; now M1 is presumed to include a significant amount of savings balances. Consequently, changes in M1 resulting from changes in these savings balances are likely to have a smaller

Solving the Velocity Puzzle
continued

impact on output and prices than previously. Specifically, there may be extended periods when significant increases in M1 produce little or no associated growth in spending or inflation; on such occasions, velocity would decline substantially. Moreover, if the savings portion of M1 is related to GNP differently than its transaction components, the relationship between the growth rates of M1 and GNP may be permanently altered.

Cyclical Explanations of the Velocity Puzzle

Until now, we have assumed implicitly that measured velocity is independent of the supply of money. Another interpretation argues that substantial exogenous changes in the supply of M1 can induce cyclical swings in measured velocity because of their lagged effects on the economy. For example, an acceleration in the growth rate of M1 initially may produce a less than proportionate rise in the level of nominal GNP and thus an initial decline in velocity. Eventually, however,

when the monetary change has worked its way throughout the economy fully, the longer-run relationship between M1 growth and the rate of spending is reestablished, and velocity returns to its long-run path.

Summary and Conclusions

Alone, none of the explanations for the puzzling downturn in M1 velocity during the 1980s can account for the behavior of M1 velocity. Perhaps, instead, several influences have combined to produce the anomalous velocity behavior that has puzzled researchers. In our opinion, financial innovations and cyclical variations in measured income offer two of the best explanations for the strange behavior of velocity.

Condensed and reprinted with permission from "Solving the 1980's Velocity Puzzle: A Progress Report," Federal Reserve Bank of St. Louis *Review* (August–September 1987): 5–23.

the banking system's desire to hold excess reserves, can also affect the size of the money stock. As a consequence, the Fed may not be *able* to increase the money stock at a constant rate. Keeping monetary growth within a given range may be the best the monetary authorities can do.

Third, many critics question the stability of velocity. Estimates of velocity have shown wide variation during the 1980s. Some critics of monetarism treat velocity as perfectly unstable, amounting to nothing more than the number necessary to make $MV = Py$ come out right. Without stable velocity, the short-run and long-run relationships between money, prices, and output will not conform to monetarist predictions.

Monetarists have responded to their critics. Some—although by no means all—monetarists have recognized the problems in defining and controlling the money stock and have begun to advocate control of the monetary base (bank reserves plus currency in circulation) rather than control of the money stock (as defined by M1, M2, or M3). The Federal Reserve directly controls the size of the monetary base (currency plus Federal Reserve deposits held by commercial banks). Some monetarists now advocate expanding the monetary base at a constant rate while ignoring other measures of "money." The money supply as conventionally measured will not expand at a constant rate under such a rule, but it may well be that a stable relationship exists between the "true" money stock and the monetary base. If such is the case, a rule based on the monetary base (sometimes called "high-powered money") may be the best we can do.

The instability of measured velocity is less easily dealt with by monetarists. Most, however, would argue that the instability exhibited during the 1980s was a temporary phenomenon caused by the deregulation of banking and finance. (See the adjoining "*Perspectives.*") As previously illegal forms of liquidity came into general use, the official measures of money did not immediately pick them up and measured velocity displayed instability. Over time, however, the economy will adjust to the new situation and the stability of velocity will reappear. To put it another way, velocity is stable when institutional conditions are stable. The 1980s were a decade of rapid change in monetary and financial institutions.

The final argument in favor of monetarism is that even if the critics are correct about the problems of monetarism, no one has suggested a better alternative. Monetarism is not proposed as a preferable alternative to policy made by authorities with perfect knowledge of the macroeconomy and full power to act on that knowledge. Rather, it is proposed as an alternative to policies made by authorities with imperfect knowledge and uncertain powers. Monetarists believe that government intervention in the macroeconomy has in most instances made matters worse rather than better. To institute rules that would prevent the government from stepping in and making a bad situation worse strikes monetarists as sufficient justification for their proposals. In an imperfect world, monetarism offers a way to limit the harm we do to ourselves.

Chapter Review

Review of Key Questions

◢   *1. What are the basic doctrines of monetarism?*

Monetarism is based on the quantity theory of money, which states that a change in the stock of money will, in the long run and other things the same, lead to a proportional increase in the price level. In addition, monetarists believe that the velocity of circulation of money (V in the $MV = Py$ identity) is highly stable.

◢   *2. How do monetarists explain unemployment?*

Unemployment is determined by conditions in the labor market. The economy tends to settle at the long-run or natural rate of unemployment. In the short run, unanticipated changes in money and prices can cause unemployment to rise or fall. The Phillips curve embodies this short-run relationship. Monetarist theory and historical evidence indicate that there is no long-run Phillips curve.

◢   *3. What is the basic cause of inflation?*

An excessive rate of growth of the money stock causes inflation. The rate of growth of the money stock is excessive if it exceeds the rate of growth of real output. Monetarists believe that inflation is inherently a monetary phenomenon; they point out that inflations throughout history have been accompanied by increases in the money stock.

4. *What are the effects of an increase in the stock of money?*

In the short run, both the price level and real output increase. The increase in output is accompanied by an increase in employment. In the long run, output and employment fall back to their initial levels. The only long-run effect of a monetary expansion is inflation.

5. *What effect does inflation have on interest rates?*

Inflation increases nominal interest rates. During inflations the nominal rate of interest increases because both lenders and borrowers add the anticipated rate of inflation to the rate of interest.

6. *What macroeconomic policy do monetarists propose?*

Monetarists argue that a monetary rule should replace discretionary monetary policy. The rule monetarists prefer is that the Fed be directed to maintain a constant rate of growth of the money stock.

7. *What are the problems with monetarism?*

Monetarists and other economists are no longer sure what does or does not constitute "money." If we do not know what money is, it is difficult for us to control it. Also, many critics question the Fed's ability to control the money stock. Another problem is that velocity has apparently been unstable in recent years.

Further Topics

Money is not the sole determinant of national income in the monetarist model. Real factors, such as the amount and productivity of resources, the level of technology, and the microeconomic efficiency of markets play an important role in the determination of national income. Indeed, in the long run real factors are the only determinants of real national income and the natural rate of unemployment. The rate of growth of money determines the long-run rate of inflation but has no other long-run effects. In the short run, however, changes in the rate of growth of the money stock cause cyclical swings in employment and income. Many monetarists believe that changes in monetary growth have caused (or at least contributed to) business cycles.

Whereas the Keynesian model of the macroeconomy provides a strong argument for government intervention in the economy, the monetarist model provides a strong argument against government intervention—except for control of the money stock. The monetarist opposition to activist macroeconomic policies is based on two basic beliefs. The first is that government attempts to improve the performance of the macroeconomy may well make macroeconomic performance worse. For example, government attempts to lower interest rates and reduce unemployment may increase both. The second basic belief of monetarists is that once provided with a stable, predictable monetary policy, the macroeconomy will perform quite well if we simply leave it alone.

Review of New Terms

Cambridge equation $MD = kPy$, where k represents the fraction of income people wish to hold in the form of money.

Demand for money The willingness of people to hold money.

Fisher effect The increase in nominal interest rates during a period of inflation.

Monetarism The quantity theory of money combined with the assumption that the velocity of circulation of money is highly stable.

Phillips curve A curve that shows the relationship between the rate of inflation and the rate of unemployment.

Quantity theory The theory that a change in the stock of money will, in the long run and other things being the same, lead to a proportional increase in the price level.

Velocity The number of times the average dollar is spent in a year.

Review Questions

1. In the monetarist model of the macroeconomy, why will an increase in the rate of growth in the money stock not permanently reduce unemployment? (◢ 2)

2. Suppose that the stock of money begins to grow faster. What will happen to market rates of interest in the short run? In the long run? (◢ 5)

3. What will be the effect on the price level of an increase in the velocity of circulation of money (V)? (◢ 1, ◢ 3)

4. In the monetarist model, how does the Federal Reserve contribute to business cycles? (◢ 2, ◢ 4, ◢ 6)

5. What policies would a monetarist recommend to solve the nation's long-run unemployment problem? (◢ 6)

6. According to Milton Friedman and other monetarists, the Board of Governors of the Federal Reserve could be replaced by a computer. What would monetarists program the computer to do? (◢ 6)

7. If the definition of money changes frequently, how can the monetarist policy of constant monetary growth be carried out? (◢ 7)

Supply-Side Economics

No doubt, the issues raised by supply analysts will be of central importance for some time to come as policymakers face the continuing challenges to break the inflation-supply linkage, as well as to stay ahead of the deterioration in incentives to work, save and invest due to the cumulative effects of past fiscal, regulatory and monetary policy. It is likely that, when the smoke clears, it will be impossible to say that one can disregard the supply effects of policy any longer. But then the exaggerated claims or hopes of some supply analysts will be forgotten as well. Over a decade ago, Milton Friedman noted that, "In one sense, we are all Keynesians now; in another, no one is a Keynesian any longer." It is likely that a similar characterization will soon be an apt description of supply-side economics.

    John A. Tatom

KEY QUESTIONS

▲ 1.   What are the basic propositions of supply-side economics?

▲ 2.   What are the basic criticisms of supply-side economics?

▲ 3.   What variables determine the actual impact of supply-side policies?

NEW TERMS

Laffer curve
Supply-side economics

Keynesian economics was spawned during the Great Depression of the 1930s, when a substantial portion (almost 25 percent) of the labor force was unemployed and prices were actually falling. It achieved academic and public prominence during the 1960s, when the inflation rate, at least for the first part of the decade, was a modest 2 to 3 percent, and the nagging social concern was unemployment. Keynesianism suggested that unemployment and inflation could be alleviated, if not eliminated, by government management of total spending. Unemployment could be reduced by an increase in total spending. Inflation could be reduced by a decrease in total spending (see Chapter 13).

If the goals of reduced inflation and reduced unemployment conflict, many Keynesians would say that policymakers should seek some socially acceptable short-run compromise. That is, they should aim for some combination of inflation and unemployment rates lying on the economy's Phillips curve. In the long run unemployment can be alleviated by education, on-the-job training, and poverty relief programs—and as improved labor skills and mobility increase production, the inflation rate will gradually go down. Monetarists would recommend controlling inflation by a gradual downward adjustment in the growth of the money stock.

Such was the general wisdom until the 1970s, when stagflation suddenly cast Keynesian theory into doubt. As one administration after another was foiled in its attempt to reduce inflation and unemployment simultaneously, many economists came to suspect that Keynesian theory was not the answer to all economic ills. The search began for new ways of analyzing and solving macroeconomic problems. Monetarism was questioned as the solution because it shared with Keynesianism an emphasis on aggregate demand management in its fiscal policies. Of course, both camps have advocates of some restrained form of aggregate supply management. Conversely, supply-siders do not ignore demand management or consider it unimportant.

This chapter examines briefly one of the alternative schools of thought that arose from the crisis of the 1970s. Supply-side theorists see high tax rates as a major source of stagflation. Their overriding theme is that reductions in marginal tax rates will give people greater incentives to work, save, and invest. Their extra effort will raise productivity and national income, reducing unemployment and inflation. In short, supply-side economists offer microeconomic, or market, solutions to macroeconomic problems. The proponents of supply-side economics think of it as "incentive economics," whereas its critics consider it "voodoo economics." Demand and supply policies are not necessarily incompatible. The 1981 and 1986 tax cuts had both demand and supply impacts with a richer admixture of the latter.

Tax Rates and Supply-Side Incentives

◢ **1. What are the basic propositions of supplyside economics?**

Supply-side economics: the macroeconomic theory that emphasizes aggregate supply management over aggregate demand management, and long-run growth over short-run cyclical swings.

Supply-side economics is the macroeconomic theory that emphasizes aggregate supply management over aggregate demand management, and long-run growth over short-run cyclical swings. It focuses on the major determinants of aggregate supply: the resource quantities, qualities and prices, state of technology, expected rate of inflation, and any institutional factors that influence productivity, such as income taxes and various government regulations.

Much Keynesian economics implicitly assumes a positive relationship between tax rates and tax collections. Lower tax rates will produce lower tax revenues, allowing total spending to rise—thus stimulating production and employment by increasing demand. Supply-side economists, on the other hand, emphasize the effect of tax rates on the supply of goods and services produced. Tax rates affect people's willingness to earn a living and to report their income to the Internal Revenue Service. Thus many macroeconomic problems should be solved by reducing government impediments to production and increasing people's incentives to work, save, and invest in productive activities.

Three major propositions underlie supply-side theory. As you may surmise, and as supply-side economists—many with conservative predilections—freely admit, these propositions are based on the work of much earlier classical economists, including Adam Smith.

Basic Propositions of Supply-Side Theory

The first and most basic proposition of supply-side economics is that beyond some point, high marginal tax rates on personal income can reduce people's willingness to work and hence reduce aggregate supply. We have

The Impact of Tax Rates Across Countries

Alan Reynolds, Polyconomics, Inc.

Tax revenues are often expressed as a percentage of GNP, but governments cannot pay their bills with percentages. To finance real increases in spending, governments need real increases in tax revenues.

The table [Table 15.1] shows what happened to the growth of real revenues, from 1975 to 1982, among countries where taxes were a relatively high or low percentage of gross domestic product (GDP). The tax percentage is a static snapshot; the growth of real revenue over several years is a dynamic motion picture.

Without exception, countries with persistently high tax rates have sustained an actual loss of real tax revenues over the entire seven-year period. Those that attempted to counter this loss with even steeper tax rates, such as Belgium, had even larger revenue losses.

Countries in which taxes extracted the smallest share of GDP—Japan and Spain—have experienced by far the most rapid increase in real tax revenues. The reason, of course, is that real GDP (or GNP) is the tax base for real revenues, and production invariably grows most rapidly in low-tax countries, as Keith Marsden of the World Bank recently observed . . . last December 18 [1984].

The United Kingdom alone appears to have obtained sizable real revenue gains despite fairly high tax rates. But the seven-year average hides what really happened. British taxes dropped to 33.3% from 35.3% of GDP from 1976 to 1979, and real revenues increased 39%. The average tax rate then rose to 39.6% by 1982, with real revenues falling 20% from 1980 to 1982. Industrial production in the U.K. is now barely higher than it was in 1982 and unemployment is near 13%, so high tax rates undoubtedly continue to depress real revenue.

Revenues as a share of GNP or GDP measure an average tax rate, or "tax ratio," at any moment in time. But an increase in that tax rate implies an increase in the marginal tax rate on added out-

put and income. When that happens, economic growth stagnates or contracts. Inflation may nonetheless continue to raise nominal tax revenues, but it inflates government spending, too. Meanwhile, the tax suffocation of real output raises real government spending to alleviate the added poverty. With real spending up and real revenues flat or down, budget deficits become large and chronic. Deficits of 10% to 13% of GDP have become routine in places like Belgium and Sweden, and will remain that way until they cut marginal tax rates.

Japan also runs perpetual deficits, with a government debt nearly as large as that of Belgium and Sweden. Yet Japan is able to finance that debt at long-term interest rates that are half those of the overtaxed nations, including France (whose debt is only half as large as Japan's). Monetary stability in Japan is part of the explanation though

TABLE 15.1 Rates and Revenues (1975–82; Percentage Change in 1972 Dollars)

	Average Tax Rate (% of GDP)	Change in Real Tax Revenues[a]
Sweden	49.2%	−12.4%
Netherlands	44.6	− 6.8
Belgium	44.6	−15.7
Denmark	43.4	−10.6
France	40.7	6.2
Austria	40.5	7.0
Germany	37.0	7.6
United Kingdom	35.7	29.1
Canada	32.8	6.7
Switzerland	30.9	5.4
United States	30.0	20.1
Portugal	27.9	12.1
Japan	24.3	54.1
Spain	22.7	59.8

[a] Adjusted by deflator for U.S. government purchases. Includes state and local government taxes.

Belgium, too, is quite intolerant of inflation or deflation. Perhaps a better explanation of Japan's high credit rating is that its seemingly large deficits and debt are actually small relative to the rapid growth of real tax revenues. Just as a growing company can easily handle a growing debt, so can a growing national economy. Overtaxed nations, particularly the troubled developing countries, are an inherently bad credit risk, because the ultimate source of real revenues—added GNP—is limited by punitive tax rates.

Those who are proposing a tax increase for the U.S. do not seem to realize that the U.S. is already having an enormous tax increase. Since tax rates were reduced to 18.6% from 20.2% of GNP in 1983, federal tax collections rose almost 7% in real terms last year and are expected to rise an additional 6% to 7% this year. That is an increase in real revenues of almost Japanese proportions.

Such significant revenue effects from economic growth are typically delayed a year. In the first year of recovery, many companies have accumulated losses that initially reduce their taxes, and individual taxes, too, are often paid on the unexpected increases in the previous year's earnings.

A 6% to 7% increase in the U.S. government's real earnings can scarcely be the subject of great public sympathy. Most households and companies expect to get by with a much smaller increase in their own revenues. Attempts to improve the government's budget at the expense of the budgets of the private sector invariably fail, as the European welfare states are learning the hard way.

From 1963 to 1965, federal taxes in the U.S. dropped to 17.7% from 18.5% of gross national product, and real tax revenues soared (with the usual lag) by 19% in the following two years. That was better than we are doing in 1984–85, but the Kennedy tax cuts were more dramatic, and nobody in those days thought 7.2% unemployment constituted an argument for brutal monetary policy. From 1978 to 1981, by contrast, federal taxes rose to 20.8% from 19.1% of GNP, and real tax

revenues fell 12% in the following two years. It may be objected that the rising tax rates of 1979–81 just happened to be followed by stagnation and recession. But that was also true of the rising tax rates in 1974, 1969, 1958–59, 1953–54 and 1937–38. What we are missing is a single example of high or rising tax rates that were not followed by stagnation or recession, here or abroad.

When taxes rise as a percentage of GNP, it may simply mean that GNP slowed down even more than tax revenues. Indeed, this is what should be expected when taxes claim a rising share of added output. Robert Barro's revolutionary new text, "Macroeconomics," concludes that "an increase in the marginal tax rate . . . leads in the short run to less work, output and investment. Further, in the long run, there are reductions in the stock of capital, as well as in the levels of output and consumption."

With lower real GNP, we should expect much lower real tax revenues. Barro estimates that "a decline by 1% in real GNP causes real federal revenues to decrease by 1.8%." For any government to attempt to acquire a larger percentage of a small real GNP, it must move toward the top of the table, losing real revenue in the process. A 40% share of nothing is nothing.

In the back of every U.S. budget, federal spending is shown in real, inflation adjusted terms. But taxes are only shown in nominal terms, as a percentage of nominal GNP.

Those who demand a "tax increase" must make up their minds. If they want a big increase in real tax revenues, we already have that. If instead they want taxes to be a larger percentage of any remaining GNP, then that must be recognized as a well-tested plan to shrink real revenues, increase real transfer payments, and double the budget deficits.

already defined the marginal tax rate as the percentage of any additional income that must be paid to the government. Marginal tax rate normally indicates the tax rate applied to the last increment of taxable income.

Historically, the U.S. federal tax system has been progressive, meaning that the marginal tax rate on additional income rises as earned income rises. However, beginning in 1988 federal personal income taxes became more like a flat-rate tax—but not exactly—with three basic rates: 15, 28, and 33 percent.[1] The top corporate rate on income fell from 46 to 34 percent. A taxpayer with a modest income may have a 15 percent marginal tax rate bracket; if he or she earns one more dollar, they must pay an additional fifteen cents in taxes. A taxpayer with a higher income can face a marginal tax rate of 28 or even 33 percent. Because of taxes, people's take-home pay is less than their earned income. Taxpayers must consider how much their additional earned income will be taxed in deciding whether to work more or harder.

Supply-side theorists propose that lower marginal tax rates on personal income should encourage people to enter the labor force and work longer hours as the opportunity cost of leisure is increased and the wedge between before- and after-tax income is narrowed. Lower marginal tax rates on business income should increase business demand for labor by increasing the after-tax return on labor. A reduction in marginal tax rates thus should increase both the supply of labor and the demand for it. Employment will expand in response to conventional microeconomic forces—that is, to a reduction in the after-tax price of labor. (The use of any other resource would also be expected to increase if its price declined.)

The second basic proposition of supply-side economics is that high marginal tax rates discourage people from investing in education and improving their work-related skills. They can also encourage businesses to invest abroad, where tax rates are lower, rather than in domestic operations. Again, high tax rates reduce the after-tax return on investments, lowering the nation's capital stock, both human and nonhuman. Growth in productivity will slow, depressing future national income levels. A reduction in marginal tax rates, therefore, should produce a more forward-looking, dynamic economy, in which more is invested in education, job training, and plant and equipment. The result will be a higher future national income level achieved through greater productivity.

The third basic proposition is that high marginal tax rates encourage people to work in the underground economy, where their incomes cannot be traced by the Internal Revenue Service. Barter and trade for cash, the clandestine sale of illegal goods and services such as drugs and prostitution, and the nonreporting of legitimate income all flourish under such conditions. High marginal tax rates also encourage people to spend considerable

---

1. The Economic Recovery Tax Act of 1981 and the Tax Reform Act of 1986, widely hailed by supply-siders, reduced personal income tax rates from progressive values ranging from 14 to 70 percent to basic rates of 15, 28, and 33 percent. At the same time, these acts eliminated various deductions that high-income earners use to lower their taxable incomes. A true flat rate tax does not have personal exemptions, deductions, or loopholes and has a single constant tax rate at all income levels.

sums of money in search of tax loopholes, shelters, and avoidances. To the extent that efforts to avoid taxes use up otherwise productive resources, they reduce the efficiency and increase the waste of the economy. So a reduction in tax rates should increase not only the amount of income people report, but the nation's total income. The high marginal rates also involve a substitution from nondeductible to tax deductible goods as relative prices are distorted. People select the personally low cost deductibles, since society picks up some of the tab.

The Effects of a Reduction in Tax Rates

Because high marginal tax rates retard growth in the nation's productive capacity, supply-side economists contend they heighten the inflationary effect of an increase in the money stock. If $MV = PQ$ and Q is retarded, a rise in M must be matched mostly by a rise in P. If tax rates are reduced, then, and the supply of goods grows more rapidly in relation to the money stock, inflationary pressures should subside. As employment opportunities rise with the increase in production incentives, fewer people will find it desirable to work in the underground economy. Most people will be better off—earning more and able to keep a large share of their earnings.

Furthermore, a reduction in marginal tax rates need not reduce tax collections. Tax revenues are a function of two key variables, national income and tax rates. Stated mathematically, tax revenues (TR) equal the tax rate (t) times the money national income (Y). In other words, $TR = tY$. If a given percentage decrease in tax rates is accompanied by a larger percentage increase in national income, the government's tax collections will rise. Suppose, for example, that the national income is $3.5 trillion, and the average tax rate is 40 percent. Suppose further that if tax rates are reduced from 40 to 36 percent, the national income will rise from $3.5 trillion to $4.2 trillion. Total tax revenues rise from $1.4 trillion (40 percent of $3.5 trillion) to $1.51 trillion (36 percent of $4.2 trillion). Under these circumstances, government spending can actually be expanded—or so the argument goes.

The effect of supply-side proposals can also be described in terms of aggregate demand and supply. As we have seen in previous chapters, a reduction in tax rates will raise aggregate demand, shifting the aggregate demand curve outward, from AD_1 to AD_2 and shifting the equilibrium from E_1 to E_2, in Figure 15.1. This shift in aggregate demand works through the multiplier, which is larger the greater the increase in consumption is that takes place when after-tax income rises. The price level will rise from P_1 to P_2, and the real national production level will climb from y_1 to y_2. In the long run, however, national production will probably return to y_1, because the long-run aggregate supply curve is vertical or nearly so, because the natural rate of unemployment dictates the maximum sustainable output.

Supply-side economists add that the aggregate supply curve will also be affected by the tax rate reduction. In the short run, because people have a greater incentive to work, save, and invest, the aggregate supply curve will shift outward, from SAS_1 to SAS_2, in Figure 15.2. This increase in aggregate supply will tend to dampen, if not totally offset, the price effect of the

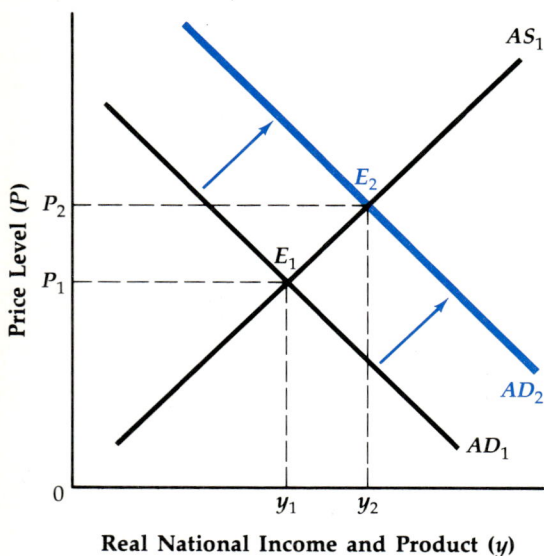

FIGURE 15.1   The Effect of a Cut in Tax Rates: The Keynesian Model
According to Keynesian theory, a cut in tax rates will increase aggregate demand from AD_1 to AD_2 shifting the equilibrium from E_1 to E_2. As a result, the price level will rise from P_1 to P_2, and the real national income level will climb from y_1 to y_2.

increase in aggregate demand. A tax rate reduction, in other words, will not be as inflationary as Keynesian theory might suggest.

If the tax rate reduction is perceived as permanent, it can also shift the long-run aggregate supply curve outward, from LAS_1 to LAS_2, in Figure 15.2. Again, the shift occurs because people have greater incentives to work and add to the nation's capital stock. The outward shift in the long-run aggregate supply curve means that some or all of the income effect of the tax rate cut can be permanent. It also means that the money stock can be expanded more than Keynesian theory might suggest. Whether the price level rises or falls, and by how much, depends on the relative impact of the cut on aggregate supply versus aggregate demand, and on the extent to which the money stock is increased when tax rates are lowered. In summary, an increase in aggregate supply increases output and decreases prices in both the short and the long run. An increase in aggregate demand increases output in the short run, but not the long run, and it increases prices in both the short run and the long run. Thus, we know for certain there will be an increase in potential output, but the price effect is uncertain depending on the size of the relative shifts including the magnitude of the multiplier effect on aggregate.

Does this scenario sound too good to be true? As you can imagine, many economists have serious reservations about some of the supply-side predictions. Nevertheless, the Reagan administration based its economic recovery strategy partly on such thinking. In 1981 and 1986, it pushed through Congress a substantial cut in personal income tax rates, with the top marginal rate falling from 70 to 33 percent.

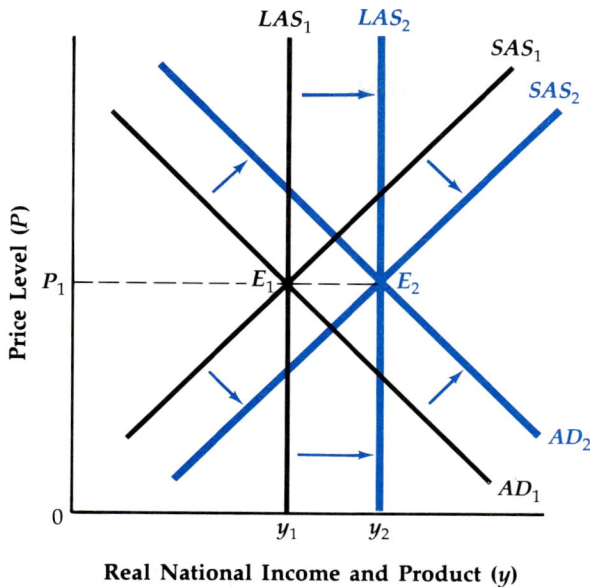

FIGURE 15.2 The Effect of a Cut in Tax Rates: The Supply-Side Model
According to supply-side theory, a cut in tax rates shifts both the aggregate demand curve and the short-run aggregate supply curve outward. At the new equilibrium point E_2 (the intersection of AD_2 and SAS_2) instead of E_1, national income will be higher (y_2 instead of y_1), but the price level will be the same. If the tax cut is perceived as permanent, the long-run aggregate supply curve will also shift, from LAS_1 to LAS_2. In that case the increase in national income will be permanent.

A Critique of Supply-Side Theory

2. What are the basic criticisms of supply-side economics?

One of the more serious criticisms of supply-side theory has to do with the proposition that lower tax rates encourage people to work harder. Critics of supply-side economics charge that high marginal tax rates do not necessarily reduce the number of hours people work. In fact, they can actually increase the amount of time spent at work. Thus a tax cut could reduce production.

The Labor-Leisure Tradeoff

Figure 15.3 shows the critics' view of the labor-leisure tradeoff. Assume the typical citizen-taxpayer has sixty hours to use for work or play each week. Time spent on work yields money income, as shown on the vertical axis. At an hourly wage rate of $10, a worker can earn a maximum of $600 per week. To earn money income, the worker must give up the direct benefits of leisure time, shown on the horizontal axis. In other words, the worker has a production possibilities curve that extends from a point somewhere on the horizontal axis to another point somewhere on the vertical axis.

The tax rate structure will affect the slope of the production possibilities curve. Without any income taxes, the worker's curve may look like Y_4T_1. Assume that the worker chooses point a on that curve. In doing so, she gives up thirty hours of leisure for $300 a week in income. She could move further up the curve and earn more money income, but presumably she

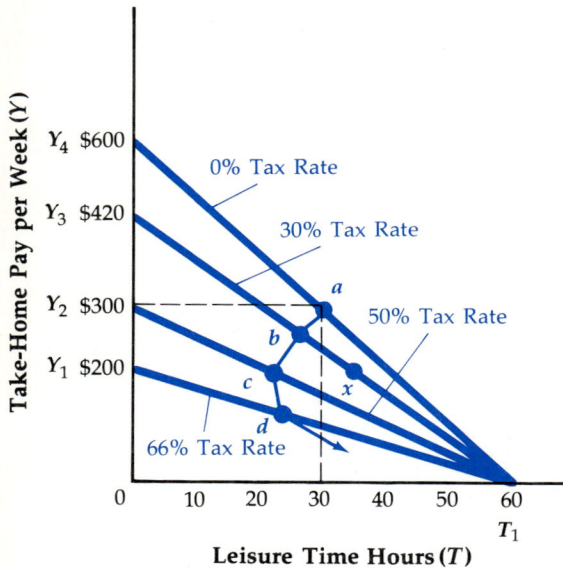

FIGURE 15.3   The Labor-Leisure Tradeoff
At a tax rate of zero, a worker can consume along transformation curve Y_4T_1. A worker making $10 an hour might choose to consume at point a, earning $300 a week and taking thirty hours of leisure time. As the tax rate increases, however, the worker's transformation curve pivots downward. On curve Y_3T_1, the worker might choose point x, which offers less disposable income but more leisure time, or she could move to point b, which minimizes the loss in income but at the cost of less leisure time. The higher the tax rate, the lower the transformation curve, and the more leisure time the worker will have to give up to maintain her income.

values her leisure time more than the additional goods she could purchase with the additional money. In short, combination a maximizes the worker's utility.

Now suppose the government imposes a 30 percent tax on personal income. The worker will take home only $7 out of the $10 she earns for each hour of work. The relative cost of leisure, then, has gone down. Each hour now spent talking with friends means only $7 worth of goods forgone. At the same time the relative price of goods purchased with money has gone up. More leisure time must now be forgone for each good that is purchased. Thus a 30 percent tax rate pivots the production possibilities curve, from Y_4T_1 to Y_3T_1. The worker's maximum take-home pay is now $420 ($7 × 60 hours).

Supply-side economic theory suggests that when a 30 percent income tax is imposed, a worker will move from point a to a point like x on the new curve, choosing more leisure time and less work. Others argue that the worker may just as well move to point b, taking less leisure time and working more. Such a choice seems reasonable, at least for low tax rates. The person who has less take-home pay can be expected to buy less of most goods and services—including recreation. In short, lower tax rates do not necessarily mean greater national income. People may decide to work harder and longer to make up for the purchasing power lost because of a tax increase.

At very high tax rates a tax cut would probably increase the number of hours worked. Suppose the income tax rate is raised gradually, pivoting the transformation curve downward, from Y_4T_1 to Y_1T_1. At some point (in Figure 15.3, when the tax rate is higher than 50 percent) the worker's tendency to work longer hours to make up for lost income is bound to halt. Consider the extreme case. If the income tax rate is 100 percent, the worker's consumption transformation curve will be perfectly flat, overlapping the horizontal axis. The rational individual can then be expected to work zero hours. (Would you work if all your income were taxed away?) At such an extreme rate, a tax cut could only encourage a worker to work more.

No government levies a 100 percent income tax, however. At lower rates, the effect of a tax cut is harder to predict. The outcome depends on both the actual level of the tax rate and the individual's personal preferences. A reduction in a very high tax rate may cause a worker to trade or substitute leisure for income, moving from point d to point c. Supply-side theory is based on this kind of response. Actual tax rates, however, may be lower. If the taxpayer's choice lies in the c to b range, she may decide to take more leisure and work less.

From a strictly theoretical perspective, we cannot know whether a tax cut will cause people to work more. The question is an empirical one. A great deal of empirical evidence suggests that the labor supply curve slopes upward and that workers respond positively to increased compensation.[2] We might also agree that people will be better off if they are free to dispose of their own income—regardless of how many hours they work. The actual effects of implementing supply-side policies cannot be predicted in the abstract.

Unfortunately, supply-side theorists' arguments about the impact of tax cuts on saving and investment are also inconclusive. Lower tax rates can encourage greater saving and investment, but they can also discourage it. Critics of supply-side economics point out that after the Reagan tax cut of 1981, the saving rate in the United States actually fell. Furthermore, even if a tax cut has a positive effect on saving and investment, it may not be very large.

Regardless of the actual outcome, many policymakers may continue to favor supply-side policy, reasoning that lower tax rates minimize government's distorting effects on the market process.

The Laffer Curve

Critics also take issue with the idea that tax rate cuts inevitably increase tax revenues. Tax revenues may go up or down, depending on the responsiveness of workers, savers, and investors to the tax rate cut.

_____

2. More of the upslope is due to people entering the labor force than from a greater amount of work from those already in the labor force, although married women and unmarried people respond more to enhanced recompense than do married men. See Jerry Hausman in Henry Aaron and Joseph Pechman, eds., *How Taxes Affect Economic Behavior* (Washington, D.C.: Brookings Institution, 1981).

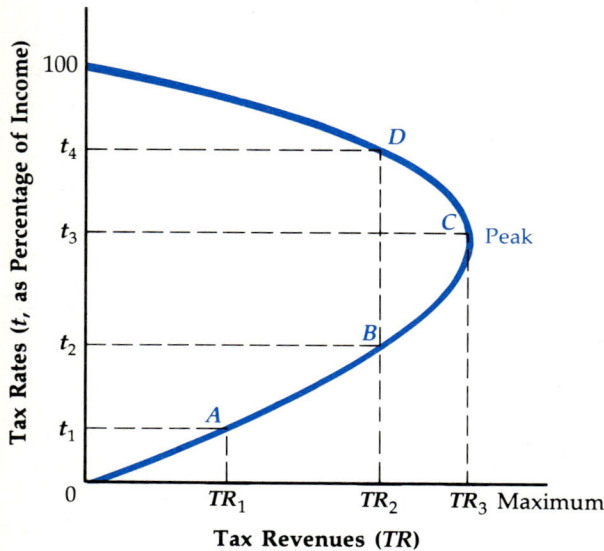

FIGURE 15.4 The Laffer Curve
At low tax rates, represented by the lower half of the Laffer curve, an increase in tax rates, say from t_2 to t_3, can produce an increase in tax revenues (from TR_2 to TR_3). Beyond the peak of the Laffer curve at C, however, an increase in tax rates will lower tax revenues. For instance, an increase in the rate from t_3 to t_4 will decrease revenues from TR_3 to TR_2. Note that the same tax revenues TR_2 are collected with either low (t_2) or high (t_4) tax rates. Thus, the government finds it can increase tax revenues by raising tax rates between A and B and by lowering them from D to C. Going from C to D tax revenues fall as tax rates are increased.

Laffer curve: a diagram that shows the relationship between tax revenues collected and tax rates.

At the bottom of this controversy is the so-called Laffer curve, named after the supply-side economist Arthur Laffer. The **Laffer curve** is a diagram that shows the relationship between tax revenues collected and tax rates. In some ranges, decreases (increases) in marginal tax rates can increase (decrease) tax revenues as incentives to work, save, and invest are altered. Assuming taxes are a disincentive, the Laffer curve relates total tax revenues to tax rates, as in Figure 15.4 and shows that after a point tax increases are counterproductive and will eventually lower income.[3] At low tax levels, an increase in tax rates produces an increase in tax revenues. For example, an increase in the tax rate from t_1 to t_2 would expand tax revenues from TR_1 to TR_2. Beyond some point, however, an increase in tax rates can be expected to reduce tax revenues. For example, an increase in the tax rate from t_3 to t_4 would reduce tax revenues from TR_3 to TR_2. Except for 0 and 100 percent there are no specific numbers on a Laffer curve. Government tax revenues are zero at both these extreme values.

Why does the Laffer curve have the shape it does? At low tax rates, so the argument goes, people have little incentive to avoid taxes. Trading off income for leisure or saving and investment for consumption is not profitable. Finding ways to escape taxes or to move productive activity underground is not worth the trouble. At high tax rates it is costly not to avoid taxes, however. The result is that beyond some peak point (not necessarily at 50 percent), as shown in Figure 15.4, the reported tax base falls off enough that total tax collections go down if the tax rates are increased.

---

3. Initially, if taxes are used for social overhead capital and essential public goods, income may increase.

The general shape of the Laffer curve can also be deduced from demand analysis. Because income buys goods, people have a demand for it. How much income they demand depends partly on its price, which is called the tax price in supply-side economics. The more taxes take out of earned income, the less income people will earn—a proposition that yields the downward-sloping income demand curve in Figure 15.5. At a tax rate of zero, citizens will earn a national income equal to Y_2. If the government raises its tax rate to t_1, tax revenues will rise from zero to t_1Y_1. This movement from zero to t_1 tax rate in Figure 15.5 is equivalent to a movement up the bottom half of the Laffer curve in Figure 15.4.

If the tax rate is raised indefinitely, at some point tax revenues will fall. If the tax price is raised all the way to t_2, people will earn nothing, and again the government will collect no taxes. In short, as long as the amount of income people demand varies inversely with the tax rate, the Laffer curve must have a backward-bending portion.

Whether a particular tax cut will reduce tax revenues depends on three factors: where the present tax rate places the nation on the Laffer curve; how much people respond to a change in the tax rate; and the size of the tax rate cut. If tax rates are above t_3 in Figure 15.4, for example, a tax rate cut will expand tax revenues. At tax rates below t_3, the effect of a cut will be just the opposite. A drop in tax rates all the way from t_4 to t_1 will also lead, on balance, to a reduction in tax collections.

Most economists accept the general shape of the Laffer curve. But many dispute the supply-side claim that marginal tax rates in the United States are so high, at least for high-income groups, that the nation is on the upper D portion of the Laffer curve. There, of course, a tax rate cut would

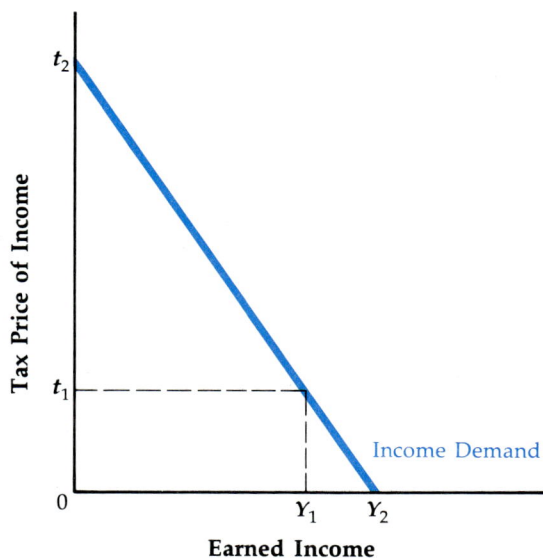

FIGURE 15.5 Effect of the Tax Price or the Demand for Income

At a tax price, or rate, of zero, the amount of earned income demanded by workers is Y_2. The revenues collected by government are also zero. A tax rate of t_1 will lower earned income to Y_1, but increase government revenues from zero to t_1Y_1. Beyond some tax price, however, an increase in the tax rate will mean lower tax revenues. At a tax price of t_2, workers will demand no earned income, and government revenues will again be zero.

PERSPECTIVES
Flat Tax Proposals
Thomas M. Humbert, Office of Congressman Jack Kemp

According to a January 1985 *New York Times*/CBS poll, the American public believes that the U.S. tax system is grossly unfair. An estimated half of all Americans believe they pay more than their fair share in taxes. Two out of three feel that income tax rates should be lowered and most deductions eliminated.

The current attack on the income tax system comes from throughout the political spectrum. Agreement appears widespread that loopholes in the current system, including numerous credits, deductions, exclusions, and exemptions, allow some Americans to escape paying what they should, while others face extremely high tax rates. The system may be considered unfair on two counts. First, loopholes, deductions, and credits violate the principle of horizontal equity—that taxpayers of similar income and circumstances should pay the same taxes. At the same time, they violate the principle of vertical equity—that persons of different circumstances should be taxed according to their differing ability to pay.

Supply-side economists believe that the current system is also inefficient and counterproductive. Because of all the special provisions in the tax code, marginal tax rates are much higher than they otherwise would have to be. These high marginal rates reduce the after-tax return on economic activity. They discourage work, saving, and investment and encourage taxpayers, especially those with high incomes, to seek out tax shelters and loopholes or participate in the underground economy. Business deductions, credits, and loop-

holes may also divert investment from heavily taxed to lightly taxed activities, distorting the flow of resources to their most productive uses. The end result is not only a less productive economy, but lower tax revenues than could be had under a more equitable tax system.

Most reformers seek a tax system that does not alter individual economic behavior. All activities would be taxed equally, so that the relative prices of leisure and labor or of savings and consumption would not change appreciably. In effect, the system would be neutral. A neutral tax system is a system that does not alter the relative prices of goods and services or of work and leisure.

Not everyone agrees on what constitutes a neutral income tax system, but many see it as a flat tax system. A flat income tax system is one in which the marginal income tax rate is constant, or the same for all income levels. It is a proportional tax system. A pure flat tax would eliminate all deductions, exemptions, and loopholes, and tax all income at the same low tax rate. Reformers estimate that a flat tax of 12 percent on all income would produce the same amount of revenue as the current system (1985), in which marginal tax rates range from 14 to 50 percent. Many supply-side theorists believe that such a tax would produce less distortion in the allocation of the nation's resources. It would also make the tax system substantially less complex and more equitable, and stimulate economic growth.

In January 1985, President Ronald Reagan responded to public criticism of the tax system by

increase tax revenues. Without more empirical evidence, many economists will regard this claim with skepticism. Why indeed would politicians ever have raised taxes to such a level? By reducing personal income so much that total government spending (and benefits to their constituencies) declined, they would surely have jeopardized their chances of reelection. The critics contend that no one gains from being on the upper half of the Laffer curve. Although overall tax revenues fell when tax rates were decreased in the early 1980s, taxpayers in the highest marginal brackets may have been in announcing his support for a "modified flat" income tax system. The modified system he proposed significantly lowered marginal income tax rates, but did not equalize tax rates. It was a progressive tax system. By early 1985, two modified flat tax plans had been introduced in Congress, and one had been recommended by the Department of the Treasury. All three plans increased both the standard deduction and exemptions for dependents, to eliminate taxation of the poor. All three retained deductions that were politically popular or promoted activities considered socially desirable, like home ownership and charitable giving. And all three plans retained the graduated tax schedule characteristic of the old tax code.

The Bradley-Gephardt plan, introduced by Senator Bill Bradley (D.-N.J.) and Congressman Richard Gephardt (D.-Mo.), broadened the tax base by eliminating many loopholes and credits. But it retained deductions for charitable giving, a limited amount of home mortgage interest, state and local income and property taxes, payments to IRA and Keogh accounts (retirement plans), and business expenses. And it proposed three marginal tax brackets: 14, 26, and 30 percent.

The Kemp-Kasten plan, introduced by Representative Jack Kemp (R.-N.Y.) and Senator Robert Kasten (R.-Wisc.), eliminated most loopholes, except deductions for home ownership, charitable giving, savings and investment, and private health insurance. Unlike the Bradley-Gephardt plan, it levied a single 24 percent tax rate on all taxpayers. But it gave lower-income families a break by doubling the size of their personal exemptions, increasing their standard deduction, and excluding 20 percent of their wages and salaries from taxation. (This exclusion would gradually be phased out.)

Why did no one propose a pure flat tax, especially when supply-side economists believed that it would stimulate economic growth? First, legislators feared that the adoption of a pure flat tax would cause a massive redistribution of the tax burden, greatly favoring the wealthy at the expense of the poor and middle classes. Second, any attempt to eliminate deductions for mortgage payments or interest on tax-exempt municipal bonds would most assuredly have been politically unpopular. It would have inflicted considerable hardship on home buyers, who had incurred heavy mortgage payments on the assumption the interest would be tax-deductible. And it would have penalized buyers of municipal bonds, who had accepted lower-than-normal rates in return for the bonds' tax-exempt status.

Thus the various modified flat tax plans proposed so far represent compromises among the conflicting goals of efficiency, simplicity, and equity. Proponents of tax reform in Congress recognize that the ideal of the flat tax is both politically difficult and economically controversial. Many strongly believe that a modified flat tax would be a substantial improvement over the current system, as well as a stimulant to the nation's economic growth.

the D to C range as the inflation-adjusted tax revenues from the top 1.36 percent of taxpayers increased from 1981 to 1983.[4]

4. James D. Gwartney and Richard L. Stroup, "Tax Cuts: Who Shoulders the Burden?," Federal Reserve Bank of Atlanta, *Economic Review* (March 1982): 19–27. Also Lawrence Lindsey, *Estimating the Revenue Maximizing Top Personal Tax Rate,* National Bureau of Economics Working Paper 1761 (1985), shows that marginal tax rates above 43 percent were in the D range as they yielded less rather than more tax revenues in the early 1980s.

PERSPECTIVES
Soaking the Rich Through Tax Cuts
Richard Vedder and Lowell Gallaway, Ohio University

Almost a year ago [1984], the release of Internal Revenue Service data on 1982 income tax returns showed that higher-income Americans paid more in income taxes in 1982 than in 1981, whereas lower- and middle-income Americans paid less. The preliminary IRS data for 1983 tax returns are in, and repeat the pattern of the 1982 returns. Upper-income earners *are* paying a greater share of the tax burden after the Reagan tax-rate cuts.

A year ago, this interpretation was still open to question by critics and skeptics, while supply-siders proclaimed that since the top income-tax rate fell from 70% to 50% in 1982, the 1982 IRS data showed the tax cut was working just as they said it would. The incentives for higher-income Americans to engage in tax avoidance and even tax evasion were reduced and they responded accordingly. The fact that the number of returns from citizens with an adjusted gross income (AGI) of more than $1 million grew by nearly 60% amid the greatest recession in years was ample evidence that the tax cuts were working.

All of this, of course, was mildly embarrassing to Democratic presidential hopefuls who were spending most of last year trashing the Reagan administration for its tax policies that supposedly benefitted the rich and hurt the poor. However, a horde of commentators rose to their defense and attacked the supply-side view. They argued that the 1982 data were not typical. John Berry of the *Washington Post* suggested that the stock-market boom explained the rising affluence (and tax payments) of the rich, somehow assuming that the tax-rate reductions had no bearing on that boom. Joseph Minarik of the Urban Institute argued that because of inflationary "bracket creep," the payments from the rich typically rose and the 1982 results merely reflected a long-term trend.

Still others used different arguments. Donald Kiefer, a researcher for the Congressional Research Service, claimed that the wealthy, anticipating the tax-rate reductions, engaged in income-shifting tactics in late 1981 that swelled 1982 taxable income. Finally, some people maintained that because of rising nominal income, the definition of "rich" and "poor" was changing, meaning that a simple analysis of the data by constant-income classes led to distorted findings.

While supply-siders believe the bulk of these criticisms to be misdirected or exaggerated, the fact remains that conclusions were being drawn on the basis of a single year's observations. As Mr. Vedder said in a Joint Economic Committee study published last November ". . . the final word will be the 1983 data."

Well, the preliminary 1983 IRS data are in and

TABLE 15.2 Tax Payments by Income Groups, 1981 to 1983

Income Class[c]	Taxes Paid[a]			% of Total Taxes Paid[b]		
	1981	1982	1983	1981	1982	1983
$0–$15,000	$26,571	$23,949	$21,037	9.1%	8.4%	7.4%
$15,000–$30,000	80,475	74,196	67,000	27.6	26.0	23.6
$30,000–$50,000	88,322	86,363	84,736	30.3	30.2	29.8
$50,000–$100,000	52,156	51,732	55,179	17.9	18.1	19.4
Over $100,000	43,633	49,387	55,781	15.0	17.3	19.6
Over $1,000,000	4,901	6,955	10,231	1.7	2.4	3.6

a. In millions of dollars; refers to total tax liability.
b. These percentages do not add to 100 because of rounding.
c. Adjusted gross income.

TABLE 15.3   Changing Income of the Very Rich, 1981 to 1983[a]

Income Source	AGI Reported (in millions of dollars)		% of Total AGI	
	1981	1983	1981	1983
Rentier income[b]	$ 4,509	$ 7,147	40.5	28.2
Entrepreneurial income[c]				
Business[d]	329	4,012	3.0	15.8
Financial[e]	4,105	8,718	36.9	43.4
Human capital[f]	2,186	5,452	19.6	21.5
Total entrepreneurial income	6,620	18,182	59.5	71.8
Total income	11,129	25,329		

a. Very rich includes returns with an AGI of over $1,000,000.
b. Dividends, interest, rent, royalty income, and estate and trust income.
c. All income other than rentier income.
d. Small business corporations, farms, partnerships, and business and professional income.
e. Primarily capital gains.
f. Wages and salaries.

they further support the contention that as after-tax rates of return rise the supply of labor and capital also increases. As the first table [Table 15.2] indicates, affluent Americans (say, those with an AGI of more than $100,000) paid substantially more than in 1981. Poor and middle-income Americans (those making under $50,000 AGI) paid less in 1983 than in 1982, and far less than in 1981. While tax payments rose 28% from 1981 and 1983 for the affluent group, they decreased nearly 12% for the low- and middle-income groups.

The increase in payments from the super rich was particularly dramatic—those with an AGI of $1 million or more paid 108% more in 1983 than in 1981, and the number of "tax millionaires" more than doubled in the greatest explosion of millionaires in U.S. history.

These results are not surprising. In the afore-mentioned JEC study, an analysis of 29 years of tax data from 1954 to 1982 revealed that upper-income Americans have become highly sensitive to variations in marginal tax rates on both ordinary

and capital-gains type income. The study revealed that some Americans were in the backward-bending portion of the Laffer curve—where reductions in tax rates so stimulate growth in the tax base that total tax receipts from the group rise. Profs. James Gwartney of Florida State University, Richard Stroup of Montana State University and James Long of Auburn University have reached virtually identical conclusions using quite a different methodology and different data sources.

The rise in tax payments reflected mainly a boom in what might be termed "entrepreneurial" income—income from small businesses, partnerships, farms, etc., or from working. The second table [Table 15.3] indicates that passive or *rentier* income, in the form of dividends, interest, royalties and the like, grew far less rapidly. It would appear that a big surge in entrepreneurial activity has occurred in response to the increase in the part of income that individuals keep after taxation.

The one argument of the critics that has not been addressed is the notion that rising nominal

Soaking the Rich Through Tax Cuts
continued

income normally pushes more Americans into higher tax brackets, increasing the pool of persons with incomes in excess of a given amount. One way to deal with this argument is to look at the relative income of Americans, that is, to examine, say the top 10% of income recipients, regardless of what their income may be. Analysis using this procedure indicates that the shift in tax payments toward the rich is somewhat less dramatic than shown in the first table, but it is occurring nonetheless. The share of total income taxes paid by the top 1% of income recipients grew from 17.44% to 20.64% between 1981 and 1983, with the share of middle-income groups showing a noticeable decline.

A single index of progressivity is the "tax Gini coefficient." A value of 1 indicates perfect progressivity—one rich person pays all the taxes—while a value of 0 describes a situation in which everybody pays the same absolute tax, regardless of income. The tax Gini rose from .6488 to .6560 between

1981 and 1983, a move in the direction of greater progressivity. In other words, the 1981 tax cut seems to have been successful in promoting a key part of the liberal agenda of the past half-century, namely, "redistributive justice."

All of this, of course, speaks to the great tax debate beginning now in Washington. The Treasury, Kemp-Kasten and Bradley-Gephardt proposals all continue in the spirit of the 1981 legislation, further reducing marginal tax rates, raising the rate of return on investment in both human and physical capital, and stimulating growth, fairness and administrative simplicity in the tax system. The evidence from the period 1981 to 1983 indicates that these initiatives also hold the promise of making a welcome addition to the U.S.'s long-term economic vitality.

The Threat of Inflation

Finally, critics question the supply-side argument that, on balance, the nation is better off because of a tax rate cut. Cuts in marginal tax rates can increase deficit spending, which can eventually increase inflation.

Economists' response to this issue depends on whether they adhere to Keynesian or monetarist theory on matters of demand management. Keynesians tend to argue that in times of inflation, deficit spending will increase aggregate demand, thus adding to inflationary pressures. A cut in marginal tax rates may mean an immediate drop in tax collections and thus an increase in disposable income for consumers. Eventually it may stimulate an expansion of aggregate supply as well, but not until people have had a chance to respond to reduced tax rates by working, saving, and investing more. If spending increases rapidly but output increases slowly, the result will be a higher rate of inflation. (In terms of the equation of exchange, $MV = PQ$, deficit spending increases the velocity of money, V, necessitating an increase in P or Q on the other side of the equation. P will increase more rapidly than Q.)

Supply-side economists, on the other hand, tend to argue that the increase in the supply of goods and services stimulated by a tax cut will counteract any inflationary pressures from a deficit. Indeed they recommend that the Fed adopt an expansionary monetary policy when tax rates are reduced, to avoid deflation. Supply-side theorists criticized the Fed for adhering to monetarist theory from 1981 to 1986, the period of the Reagan tax cut. Growth of the money stock, they maintain, does not invariably lead to inflation. As long as monetary growth accommodates rapid growth in production, inflation should not be a problem. In 1984, they point out, the rate of inflation did not keep pace with the growth of the money stock, because output expanded unusually fast—at an annual rate of over 7 percent for much of that year. In fact, for the period 1980–1986 the M1 and M2 money stocks grew at about 9.5 percent per year, real GNP at 2.1 percent, and inflation at 6.1 percent. The unemployment rate also averaged 6.1 percent.

Supply-side theorists generally agree with monetarists that government expenditures will crowd out private expenditures. Government expenditures, in their view, are the ultimate tax on the economy, but they are not particularly distressed by the prospect of deficit spending crowding out private investment through higher interest rates. Lower tax rates should mean more resources available for investment. First, people will save more, supply-side theorists believe. Their greater saving (or nonconsumption) will free resources for use by investors, shifting purchases from consumption to investment. Second, the greater national income generated in response to reduced tax rates will also mean more resources available for investment—and reduced tax rates should draw back home those investment resources previously employed outside the country.

Supply-side theorists argue too that deficits created by tax rate cuts are likely to be short-lived (just how short-lived is a matter of dispute). With the increased national income generated by lower tax rates, government revenues will rise, wiping out or reducing the deficit. Over a period of years, then, government should run fewer deficits, borrow less, and crowd out less private investment than if tax rates were never reduced. (Keynesians made similar arguments in support of the 1964 Kennedy tax cut, but they believed that the increase in national income would result from an increase in aggregate demand.)

To ensure that government does not crowd out private investment, supply-side economists often recommend eliminating "fat," "waste," and "counterproductive programs" from the federal budget. (Exactly what constitutes fat and waste varies, as you can imagine, from one dispassionate economist or passionate policymaker to another.) Budgetary deficits can also be avoided by authorizing tax rate cuts to take effect in the future, thus encouraging businesses to invest now to take advantage of lower tax rates on future income. Future productivity, production, and national income will rise, and when tax rates are actually lowered, government revenues will be no lower than they otherwise would have been.

In general, supply-side economists have opposed efforts to eliminate government deficits by increasing tax rates. Smaller deficits may mean

Perestroika as Supply-Side Economics, Styled for the Soviet Union

General Secretary Mikhail Gorbachev of the Soviet Union and former President Ronald Reagan of the United States may disagree on many issues, but they have one common ground: They both believe that economic incentives matter. Oddly enough, they are both "supply siders," or so they profess in their own ways.

Accordingly, they both have recommended sweeping changes in their respective economies. They both contend that greater economic prosperity can be had only by reducing the onerous burden of government and by relying to a greater degree on decentralized decisionmaking.

President Reagan's supply-side criticisms of current government policies in the United States are well known. He does not like the way taxes and government subsidies dampen people's inclinations to work, save, and invest. He has a well-publicized disdain for welfare cheats.

What is not so well appreciated is that General Secretary Gorbachev has, in his book on *Perestroika,* marshalled criticisms against current policies in the Soviet Union that appear to be transatlantic echoes of Reagan's best critical efforts.[1]

Indeed, what is astounding about Gorbachev's review of Soviet economic and political problems is its frankness. He openly admits to economic stagnation and to personal and moral decay in the Soviet Union, due in large part to the Soviet system's excessive reliance on "officialdom, red tape, patronizing attitudes and careerism."[2] He tells his readers that "the political economy of socialism is stuck with outdated concepts and is no longer in tune with the dialectics of life."[3]

The general secretary explains that the blame

for their problems are directly attributable to a "specific feature of socialism"—namely, "the high degree of protection in our society."[4] Although such a feature may be a mark of achievement by some standards, it also has made "some people sponges." Because the state has virtually eliminated unemployment, "even a person dismissed for laziness or a breach of labor discipline must be given another job. Also, wage leveling has become a regular feature of everyday life: Even if a person is a bad worker, he gets enough to live fairly comfortably. The children of an outright parasite will not be left to the mercy of fate."[5] The country's problem is that

> dishonest people try to exploit these advantages of socialism; they know only their rights, but they do not want to know their duties: they work poorly, shirk and drink hard. There are quite a few people who have adapted the existing laws and practices to their own selfish interests. They give little to society, but nevertheless [have] managed to get from it all that is possible and what even seems more impossible; they have lived on unearned incomes.[6]

The reader is left to wonder if Reagan has ever been so passionate and articulate in or out of office. The reader, who may be steeped in western versions of recent Soviet history, cannot help wondering if a Soviet general secretary could have been so blunt (and eloquent) a decade ago and, if he had been, could have avoided being hog-tied and shipped out on the next Siberian express.

In no uncertain terms, Gorbachev rejects as unrealistic and destructive the communist adage,

1. Mikhail Gorbachev, *Perestroika: New Thinking for Our Country and the World* (New York: Harper & Row, 1987).
2. Ibid., pp. 54–55.
3. Ibid., p. 49.

4. Ibid., p. 30.
5. Ibid.
6. Ibid., p. 31.

"From each according to his ability, to each according to his needs." In the new, restructured Soviet economy policy will be guided by a much more practical party line of Lenin (and Reagan), "From each according to ability, to each according to his *work*."[7]

In blunt and subtle twists of Leninist philosophy, Gorbachev claims that renewed economic growth must be based to a substantially greater extent on market principles. He argues that no great nation can produce efficiently when orders are handed down from a central authority in Moscow. He also maintains that individuals and groups of individuals who are given the authority to make economic decisions, formerly made by the state, must be held responsible for their decisions. This means that they must be subjected to the risk of failure, even a loss of income and wealth, if not employment. Nonetheless, Gorbachev recognizes, in full concurrence with Reagan's most ardent market supporters, "Amazing things happen when people take responsibility for everything themselves. The results are quite different, and at times people are unrecognizable. Work changes and attitudes to it, too."[8]

Gorbachev's book is important for three principle reasons. First, he accepts criticisms of the Soviet economy that have long been made in the West. His candor is disarming.

Second, Gorbachev explains the logic of his proposed structural changes in the Soviet economy. The similarity between the economic logic underlying enacted and proposed changes in government policies in the Soviet and U.S. economies is remarkable. (Such similarities make one ques-

tion whether both political systems are being forced to respond to many of the same fundamental international economic forces that do not respect national boundaries—for example, the growing competitiveness in world markets.)

Gorbachev agrees with Reagan that decentralized decisionmaking is important. The main dispute between him and Reagan, or so Gorbachev suggests, is *how much* decentralization is politically and economically practical. Gorbachev wants to make sure that his country is left with a form of economic democracy (which Reagan finds objectionable) in which workers continue to have a say in how their firms operate, but he also wants them to be constrained by the dictates of profitmaking and financial survival (which Reagan finds agreeable).

Third, Gorbachev provides a written record of his internal and worldwide political intentions. He argues that, for example, the Soviet leadership is no longer interested in the persecution of its own people or the domination of others. In effect, he as much says his country must give up its missiles and its misadventure in Afghanistan in order to free up needed resources for the restructuring process. The country must become more open and more willing to encourage criticism of leaders, citizens, and institutions. *Glasnost*, the policy of expanding human rights and political freedoms, is crucial to economic revitalization, or so he says.

The Gorbachev book is intriguing reading because of how he reconciles greater reliance on markets with Marxist theory. It is important reading because it offers a great deal of hope—mainly hope that some of the resources now devoted to military posturing in international disputes may, in the not-too-distant future, be diverted to more productive uses.

7. Ibid.
8. Ibid., p. 97.

reduced demand for lendable funds. But if tax revenues increase, the result will be a reduced supply of lendable funds. People will earn less and have less to save after taxes. Some supply-side theorists contend that a tax rate increase can only compound the deficit problem.

As to monetary policy, supply-siders in general join the monetarists in advocating a steady, moderate, nondestabilizing growth in the money stock with some extremists even pushing for a return to a gold standard which they feel is less inflation prone. Although monetarists find a keen ally in supply-siders on some aspects of economic policymaking, their differences should not be minimized.

Economic Need Versus Political Reality

▲ 3. What variables determine the actual impact of supply-side policies?

According to many of its supporters, supply-side policy is not a quick fix, but a long-term economic plan based on improving incentives for investment by lowering tax rates. Its advocates do not believe that government can fine-tune the economy. Instead, they assert, time is needed to turn incentives into real plant and equipment and improved human skills. To make the needed investment, businesses and individuals must be convinced that tax rates will not only be cut but will be held down for some time to come.

Therein lies the Achilles' heel of Reaganomics, which initially was grounded in a three-year tax cut package. After the 1981 tax cut, taxpayers had little reason to believe the immediate future would be any different from the immediate past. Like the so-called tax cuts of the 1970s, the Reagan cuts seemed less likely to be permanent reductions than midcourse corrections in the generally upward movement of tax rates. Because long-term growth depends on expectations about future tax rates, many people remained cautious about investing, fearing that their earnings would go up in the smoke of higher taxes. The 1986 Tax Reform is still too recent to reach any definitive conclusions as to its long-run impact.

The needs of political leaders, however, who must keep their eyes on the near term and the next election, may be inconsistent with the needs of investors, who look to the long term and the after-tax return on their investments. Politicians seeking the funds to provide benefits to their constituents may take advantage of people's short-run inability to respond to tax increases. Much of taxpayers' current income may depend on past investments in physical and human capital, which are not readily changed in the short run. People will not destroy their plant and equipment or cast off their work-related skills just because tax rates rise. Thus politicians may decide to maximize short-run tax revenues, positioning the nation at the peak of the short-run Laffer curve. In the long run, of course, taxpayers will respond to higher tax rates by reducing their investments. Such a response would mean a long-run contraction in the nation's capital stock, income, and tax revenues.

If politicians do lower tax rates, however, the short-term result can be disastrous for them. Tax revenues will drop, at least in the short term, because people will not be able to expand their investments immediately in response to the tax cut. If government expenditures are not reduced, the result can be a larger budget deficit. Politicians may then be accused of fiscal imprudence. When the federal budget deficit reached $200 billion in the mid-1980s, after passage of the Reagan tax package, supporters of the tax cut were frequently chided for their irresponsibility. Critics reminded supply-side theorists that some of them had predicted that the tax cut would bring a smaller deficit, not a larger one. Moreover, politicians who vote for tax cuts can be accused of neglecting current social needs, since lower tax revenues restrict the government's ability to provide social services. Thus the political benefits of a tax cut may be available only to future political leaders.

Because of the conflict between the needs of the economy and the realities of the political system, some supply-side theorists have suggested the establishment of constitutional checks on the government's spending and taxing powers. The 1985 Gramm-Rudman-Hollings Bill that required the deficit to be decreased until balance was restored in 1991 was aimed in this direction. Although a replacement law overcame the unconstitutionality of the 1985 bill, the remaining loopholes make it questionable whether the budget will be balanced. At this point in time, it is not clear whether Congress really cares about a workable solution to the deficit problem. It appears—based largely on the open letters sent to Congress by 172 economists in 1982—that a majority of economists are against the balanced budget amendment on the grounds it would put a straitjacket on fiscal policy that has the potential to be an important countercyclical tool.

Chapter Review

Review of Key Questions

▲   *1. What are the basic propositions of supply-side economics?*

Supply-side economics is a macroeconomic theory that emphasizes long-run aggregate supply rather than short-run aggregate demand management. All the factors that influence aggregate supply—the resource base, level of technology, and social, political, and economic institutions such as incentives, taxes, and government regulation—are examined and emphasized. Supply-side advocates consider it "incentive economics" whereas critics consider it "voodoo economics." Supply-siders put a lot of time into investigating the size of the population and productive capital stock, the state of technology, tax rates, and expected rate of inflation. The motivation of people to work, save, invest, and increase long-run real output is crucial.

The theoretical roots of supply-side economics go back to classical economics. Supply-siders do not ignore demand management or consider it unimportant. They simply believe overemphasis in the past on demand now calls for an emphasis on supply, with keen attention paid to productivity, incentives, and capital formation. Supply-side is less interested in monetary policy than other long-run macroeconomic policies that determine long-run economic activity. One of the most important tenets of supply-side theory is that lowering tax rates gives people an incentive to work, save, and invest more than they would otherwise. Therefore a reduction in tax rates stimulates the economy through increased production rather than increased demand. Another important tenet of supply-side theory is that a cut in tax rates can alleviate unemployment by increasing people's incentives to work and employers' incentives to create jobs. A tax rate cut can also lower the inflation rate by encouraging investment, thus stimulating the economy through greater productivity and expanded production. Because tax collections depend on the national income level as well as on tax rates, the Laffer curve demonstrates that a reduction in tax rates can (but will not necessarily) increase tax collections. Therefore a reduction in tax rates need not force cutbacks in government programs; it might actually allow an expansion. Similarly, an increase in tax rates will not necessarily expand government revenues; it might reduce them instead.

In supply-side theory, a tax rate cut will shift the short-run aggregate supply curve outward, moderating the price effect of the outward shift in the aggregate demand curve. It will also shift the long-run aggregate supply curve outward. The net result is that potential output will increase, but the effect on prices is indeterminate.

▲   *2. What are the basic criticisms of supply-side economics?*

Supply-side theory has been criticized as to whether lower tax rates encourage people to work hard or longer and if so, how much. There is empirical evidence questioning the magnitude, the speed of adjustment, and even the direction of tax reductions on incentives. Economists are also in doubt as to where on the Laffer curve the American economy is. While tax cuts can in logic lead to an increase in tax revenues, empirically documented evidence that this is the situation now is unavailable. It is also possible that if aggregate demand is more powerful than aggregate supply, tax cuts can accelerate inflation and budget deficits. There is also the danger that tax cuts can be asymmetrical, redistributing income from the poor and to the rich, thus exacerbating income inequality.

▲   *3. What variables determine the actual impact of supply-side policies?*

The actual consequences of supply-side policy depend on three variables: (a) the responsiveness of workers, savers, and investors to a change in the tax rates; (b) the effect of a change in the tax rates on the total tax revenues collected; and (c) the relative impact of a change in the tax rates on aggregate supply and aggregate demand, and therefore on the rate of inflation. Whatever the practical impact of supply-side economics on actual economic activity in the past, now, or in the future, this philosophy has been useful in providing aggregate supply analysis and in bringing policymaking management more on a par with aggregate demand analysis and policymaking management.

Further Topics

The debate between supply-side theorists and other economists hinges largely on empirical questions. How much more will people work, save, and invest in response to a specific tax rate cut for a specific number of years? Will government tax revenues go up or down in response to a tax rate cut? Will a tax rate cut raise or lower inflation in the short run and the long run? Economists have only recently begun to address these questions from the perspective of supply-side theory. Unfortunately the answers are not yet clear.

As evidence of the validity of their theory, supply-side economists point to the effect of the 1964 Kennedy tax cut package and to the rise in national income after 1982 and the Reagan tax cuts. As we have seen, however, Keynesian theory attributes the rise in national income that followed those cuts to growth in aggregate demand, and monetarist theory attributes it to growth in the money stock. Because the forces of aggregate supply and demand interact, no one can be certain whether an increase in economic activity is a response to the pull of aggregate demand, as Keynesians and monetarists would contend, or to the push of aggregate supply.

Supply-side economists also point with pride to the very positive effects of state and local tax cuts in California and Puerto Rico during the 1970s. Both economies grew faster after property and income tax rates were reduced. Although many economists agree that a tax rate cut is likely to have some positive effect on growth, they differ as to how much of the growth in these economies was actually due to the tax cut. Other factors, such as changes in energy costs and in the comparative advantage of producing in those areas, may have been responsible for much of the economic growth in California and Puerto Rico.

We have focused in this chapter on the macroeconomic goals of supply-side economics, but their desires and accomplishments in the microeconomic area are also significant. In particular, they have pushed vigorously, and with an ample helping of success, to reduce what they perceive to be a significant overregulation in the U.S. economy that they believe has adversely affected productivity and costs. The late 1970s and early 1980s have seen a dramatic decline in government involvement or deregulation on both the economic (industrial)—e.g., transportation and financial—and social fronts (e.g., pollution, safety, health, and equal opportunities).

On the other hand, by 1987 some were predicting the harmony and commonality that may have existed among supply-siders may have diminished. For instance, a 1987 *Wall Street Journal* article carried the title "Supply-siders Suffer a Decline in the Demand for Their Policy Ideas."[5] The article discussed the bickering that now divides some of the supply-siders, with some even abandoning the supply-siders title to establish bonds with more mainstream economists. Although the article points out that the supply-side theories did not attract a large following in academia (e.g., the 18,000 members of the American Economic Association), the idea were enormously popular in Washington, D.C. In fact, the movement's "extraordinary success" of the late 1970s may have harmed the group's coalescence. It's a tough act to follow when you push for lower marginal tax rates and help drive the highest rate from 70 percent in 1981 to 28 (or 33 for some affluent taxpayers) percent in 1988. Jude Wanniski, however, one of the most influential ideologists who have helped shape the big 1981 tax cut, reminds people: "Don't bury us yet, 'cause we ain't dead."

---

5. Alan Murray, *Wall Street Journal,* August 18, 1987, pp. 1, 13.

One of the most heeded attacks on supply-side economics from the academic front came from Alan S. Blinder, who considers the movement intellectually negligible but politically potent. He put it this way:

> There is an old joke about the economist who, upon being asked "How's your wife?" responds: "Relative to what?" Compared to these three alternatives, Keynesian economics, for all its warts, looks pretty good. No wonder, then, that both President Reagan and Fed Chairman Volcker, after flirting with supply-side economics and monetarism respectively, scurried back to modern Keynesianism—though without using the name.[6]

Review of New Terms

Laffer curve   A diagram that shows the relationship between tax revenues collected and tax rates.

Supply-side economics   The macroeconomic theory that emphasizes aggregate supply management over aggregate demand management, and long-run growth over short-run cyclical swings.

Review Questions

1. Keynesians contend that a reduction in tax rates will stimulate production by increasing consumption demand. Supply-side economists say that it will stimulate production by increasing the supply of labor. Is there any real difference between the two theories? (◢ 2)

2. Why does the Laffer curve not slope continually upward toward the right, instead of eventually bending backward? (◢ 1)

3. What happens if tax rates are lowered when an economy is on the upper half of the Laffer curve? When it is on the bottom half? (◢ 1)

4. Suppose the nation is in a period of inflation, and you have been asked to formulate a remedy using the Keynesian model of the macroeconomy. Suppose further that the rich are taxed at very high rates, which place them on the upper portion of the Laffer curve, while the poor are taxed at very low rates, which place them on the bottom half of the Laffer curve. What would your solution be? Would your recommendations be politically acceptable? (◢ 2)

5. List all the empirical issues involved in the Keynesian/supply-side controversy. What are the difficulties in resolving them? (◢ 3)

6. List the current administration's tax and spending policies, and label them as monetarist, Keynesian, or supply-side. (◢ 1)

---

6. Alan S. Blinder, *Hard Heads, Soft Hearts* (Reading, Mass.: Addison-Wesley, 1987), p. 106.

Rational Expectations

You may fool all the people some of the time; you can even fool some of the people all the time; but you can't fool all of the people all the time.
  Abraham Lincoln

KEY QUESTIONS

▲ 1. How does Keynesian theory handle expectations?

▲ 2. What do the rational expectationists believe?

▲ 3. How does monetarism handle expectations?

▲ 4. What are criticisms of rational expectations theory?

NEW TERMS

Adaptive expectations theory
Efficient market hypothesis
Policy neutrality or policy
  ineffectiveness theorem

Rational expectations
Rational ignorance
Share economy

Keynesian theory suggests that unemployment can be alleviated by increasing government spending or expanding the money stock. Increased spending works directly on unemployment by increasing aggregate demand. Expansion of the money stock works indirectly by lowering interest rates, thus increasing investment demand.

Both government spending and the money stock virtually exploded during the late 1960s and early 1970s, but this did not reduce unemployment as Keynesian theory would have predicted. Instead, unemployment and inflation both rose during the 1970s (see Chapter 14). That experience frustrated many economists, who believe that the validity of any science, physical or social, resides in the correctness of its predictions.

The last twenty years have taught us that both demand and supply elements have significant impact on the macroeconomy. We also know that we cannot neglect our economic international interdependence on other countries. The U.S. role in the world economy is discussed in Part VI of this book. Chapter 15 described supply-side economists' attempts to reformulate and redirect macroeconomic theory and policy to recognize the neglected supply elements of the macroeconomy. The third lesson of the last twenty years—that expectations play an important causal role in the macroeconomy—has not yet been explored. This chapter examines rational expectations theory, another alternative to the traditional Keynesian model. To improve the predictive power of macroeconomic theory, this school emphasizes the role that expectations play in people's reactions to fiscal and monetary policy.

Expectations in Keynesian Theory

▲ 1. How does Keynesian theory handle expectations?

A cornerstone of rational expectations theory is the assumption that people will behave rationally—an idea that underlies microeconomic theory as well. That is, people are assumed to be capable of ranking their options from most preferred to least preferred and of acting on the basis of those priorities. They will develop expectations about the consequences of government fiscal and monetary policies and will act on those expectations in the future.

Rational expectations theorists contend that Keynesian predictions have been incorrect in the past because they did not recognize that government policies can change people's expectations and behavior. Rational expectationists also believe that output and input markets are perfectly competitive, and instantaneously assimilate information.

In a sense, rational expectations economic theory is an offshoot of a well-established relationship in finance theory called the **efficient market hypothesis.** Put simply, the efficient market hypothesis posits that new information traveling randomly is very rapidly assimilated by a large number of rational participants, no one group of which possesses market power. Because of this almost instantaneous adjustment to new information, no disequilibrium can last very long. For example, there is solid empirical evidence that daily stock market prices are efficient—they behave like a "random walk." Random walk has been likened to a drunk stumbling around, changing directions in a completely unpredictable fashion every few seconds.

In economics, if a variable follows a random walk a reasonable guess of the next period's value is this period's same value. However, such an estimate is just as likely to be wrong as right. This means that random walk events such as stock market prices cannot be predicted on the basis of the past history of price changes. Thus there are no sure ways to beat the market.

Similarly, **rational expectations theory** assumes that market participants formulate their expectations of the future, including future economic policy activities, on past, present, and projected future information. Their actions, driven by self-interest, over time make economic policies partially or completely ineffective, but also exploit all profitable opportunities. To do this, costly information needs to be used efficiently. This information efficiency is crucial to rational expectationists, but leads to this paradox: If the market is informationally efficient and gathering information costs money, then it doesn't pay to glean information, as the market already reflects it. If no traders gather information, though, the market won't reflect all the information, and so must pay to gather it. Remember, not all market participants need to be rational for the market to show rational expectations. As long as some marginal participants eliminate all unexploited opportunities, the whole market will be efficient.

The older, more naive **adaptive expectations theory** assumes that market participants formulate their expectations of the future, including their future economic policy activities, solely on past and current information. The most recent experience is accorded the greatest influence, with little attention paid to modeling market behavior. In contrast, rational expectationists believe that people use past, current, and future information, and pay considerable attention to modeling the structure of the economic sys-

Efficient market hypothesis: the theory that new information traveling randomly is very rapidly assimilated by a large number of rational participants, no one group of which possesses market power. Because of this almost instantaneous adjustment to new information, no disequilibrium can last very long.

Rational expectations theory: the macroeconomic theory that market participants formulate their expectations of the future, including future economic policy activities, on past, present, and projected future information.

Adaptive expectations theory: the macroeconomic theory that market participants formulate their expectations of the future, including their future economic policy activities, solely on past and current information.

tem. Rational expectationists believe that people do not make continual errors; they have a learning curve that eliminates systematic (but not random) forecasting errors. Although the validity of these two theories is the subject of considerable debate among economists, both adaptive and rational expectationists agree that the long-run Phillips curve is vertical at the natural rate of unemployment, with no unemployment-inflation tradeoff. However, adaptive expectationists believe that there is a short-run tradeoff of unemployment and inflation. Rational expectationists posit that there is no consistent tradeoff, even in the short run.

A central (and somewhat extreme) conclusion of many rational expectations models is **policy neutrality** or **policy ineffectiveness theorem** that fiscal and monetary policy will have no effect on national income and employment, in either the short run or the long run. That is, rational expectationists raise the disturbing possibility that government cannot systematically control the ups and downs of the business cycle by altering its budget or the size of the money stock. Clever people will inevitably learn to anticipate the consequences of such policies and will act to negate them. People on average correctly and completely anticipate the effects of government policies and therefore neutralize those policies. However, random surprises can occur, because only systematic forecasting errors can be obviated. At any rate, government should assume a passive role since rational people often take compensating actions to render macroeconomic policymaking counterproductive or at least unproductive.

Before we can appreciate the theoretical innovation of rational expectations, we must first understand the role of expectations, anticipated and

Policy neutrality or **policy ineffectiveness theorem:** the conclusion of many rational expectations models that fiscal and monetary policy will have no effect on national income and employment, in either the short run or the long run.

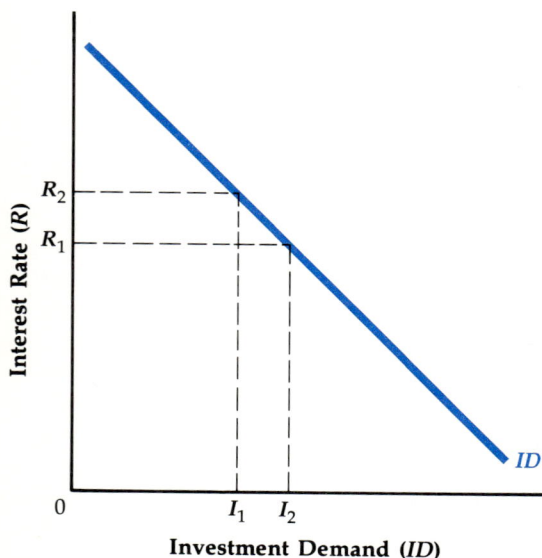

FIGURE 16.1 Investment Demand (*ID*) Curve
The level of investment spending varies inversely with the interest rate. When the interest rate falls from R_2 to R_1, investment spending rises from I_1 to I_2.

unanticipated, in traditional Keynesian thought. The Keynesian model does not ignore expectations. They play a part in determining the investment, consumption, and money demand functions.

Investment

Expectations about the future profitability of business are critically important in determining the position and slope of the planned investment curve. In Keynesian theory, investment expenditures are inversely related to the interest rate. When the interest rate falls—for example, from R_2 to R_1 in Figure 16.1—investment spending increases, from I_1 to I_2. The actual position of the investment demand curve, *ID*, depends on business people's assessment of the future profitability of their investment projects. The anticipated rate of return on an investment project determines whether a firm will borrow funds at prevailing interest rates.

An assumption implicit in Keynesian theory is that the investment demand curve does not change much in response to fiscal policy. Therefore when government demand rises, aggregate demand rises with it (see Figure 16.2). Keynesians do not normally consider the possibility that if government increases its deficit, business expectations may change, shifting the investment demand curve down, in the opposite direction from government demand. Investment may drop, but because of a rise in the interest rate, not a shift in investment demand. On balance, Keynesians believe, the

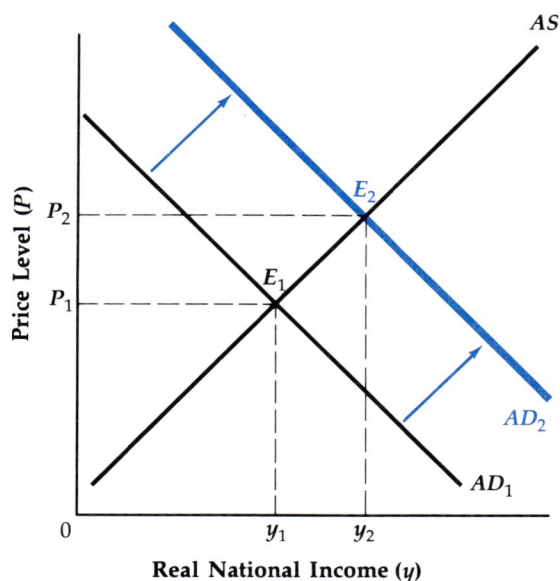

FIGURE 16.2 Fiscal Policy in the Keynesian Model
In Keynesian theory, an increase in government spending is not fully offset by a reduction in investment and consumption spending. As a result, an increase in government spending can cause the aggregate demand curve to shift out, from AD_1 to AD_2. The equilibrium shifts from E_1 to E_2 and the real national income level rises from y_1 to y_2, and the price level climbs from P_1 to P_2.

increase in government spending will outweigh any decrease in investment, shifting the aggregate demand curve up. The real national income and price levels will rise, from y_1 and P_1 to y_2 and P_2 in Figure 16.2.

Consumption

Expectations also play a role in determining consumption patterns. People's consumption decisions are based not only on current income, but on expected future income. The Keynesian analysis implicitly assumes that consumers' expectations, and therefore their consumption and saving patterns, remain more or less stable even if government fiscal and monetary policy change. In other words, when the government takes expansionary fiscal or monetary actions, the consumption function will not shift downward or upward, negating or reinforcing the effect of government policy. According to Keynesian theory, government expenditures affect consumption mainly through actual rather than anticipated changes in real income, prices, and interest rates.

Demand for Money

Finally, expectations play a role in the construction of the Keynesian demand for money curve. When interest rates fall, more and more people begin to expect them to rise again. They hold on to their money instead

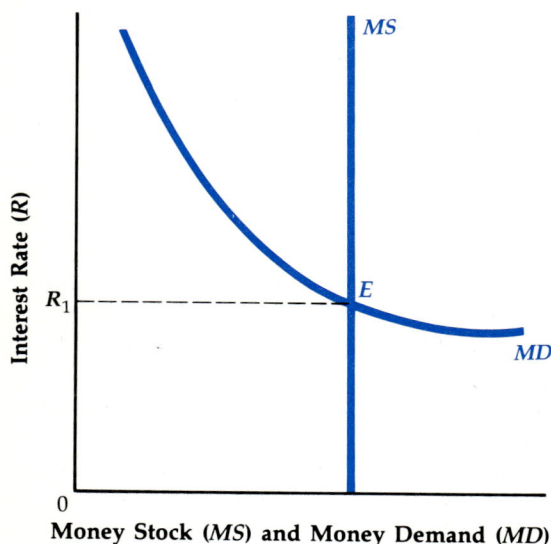

FIGURE 16.3 The Stock of and Demand for Money The nominal money stock, *MS*, is controlled by the Federal Reserve and is more or less fixed, or vertical. The quantity of money demanded, *MD*, is inversely related to the interest rate—the higher the cost of money, the lower the quantity demanded. The market interest rate, R_1, is established by the intersection of the two curves at the equilibrium point *E*.

of lending it, as the opportunity cost of holding money is lower. The quantity of money demanded is therefore inversely related to the interest rate. The lower the rate, the higher the quantity of money demanded. The demand for money can be represented by a downward sloping curve, as in Figure 16.3.

The actual market interest rate is established by the stock of, and demand for, money balances. (See Chapter 12 for a review of how interest rates are determined.) That is, the amount of money created by the Federal Reserve (which determines the stock of money) interacts with people's expectations about future interest rates (which influence their demand for money) to determine the interest rate. In Figure 16.3, the equilibrium interest rate is R_1, the rate at which the money stock and demand curves intersect.

A change in expectations about such things as "normal" bond prices and interest rates (and not merely a change in quantity demanded) can change the entire demand curve and therefore the interest rate—which in turn can influence investment. Thus, a change in expectations can be translated into a change in aggregate demand, national production, and employment. Keynesians have generally assumed, however, that the demand for money is relatively stable, at least in the short run. Hence they do not worry that government fiscal and monetary policy will be frustrated by changes in expectations that affect the demand for money.

Rational Expectations

◢ 2. What do the rational expectationists believe?

Rational expectations theorists argue that Keynesian thinking does not account fully for changes in people's expectations about the consequences of fiscal and monetary policy. They contend that in pursuit of their own self-interest, people—consumers, businesses, and workers—will gather and use effectively a rationally determined amount of information on the past consequences of government policy. Then they will act accordingly on a tolerably accurate assessment of the structural model of the economy. For instance, if expansionary fiscal policy has led to higher interest rates in the past (because of the government's increased demand for borrowed funds), people will come to expect higher interest rates as a result of increased government spending and will take steps to protect themselves. If bond speculators revise their expectations about "normal" interest rates and bond prices, the entire demand curve for money will shift as opposed to a movement along a given money demand curve. Those who have bonds will attempt to sell them, driving bond prices down and interest rates up in the process. Thus the expectation of higher interest rates leads almost immediately to higher interest rates. (A contractionary fiscal policy can have the opposite effect. People will anticipate lower interest rates, and in the process of reacting to their expectations, they will drive interest rates down.) In Keynesian terms, the demand for money curve shifts up with an increase in government spending.

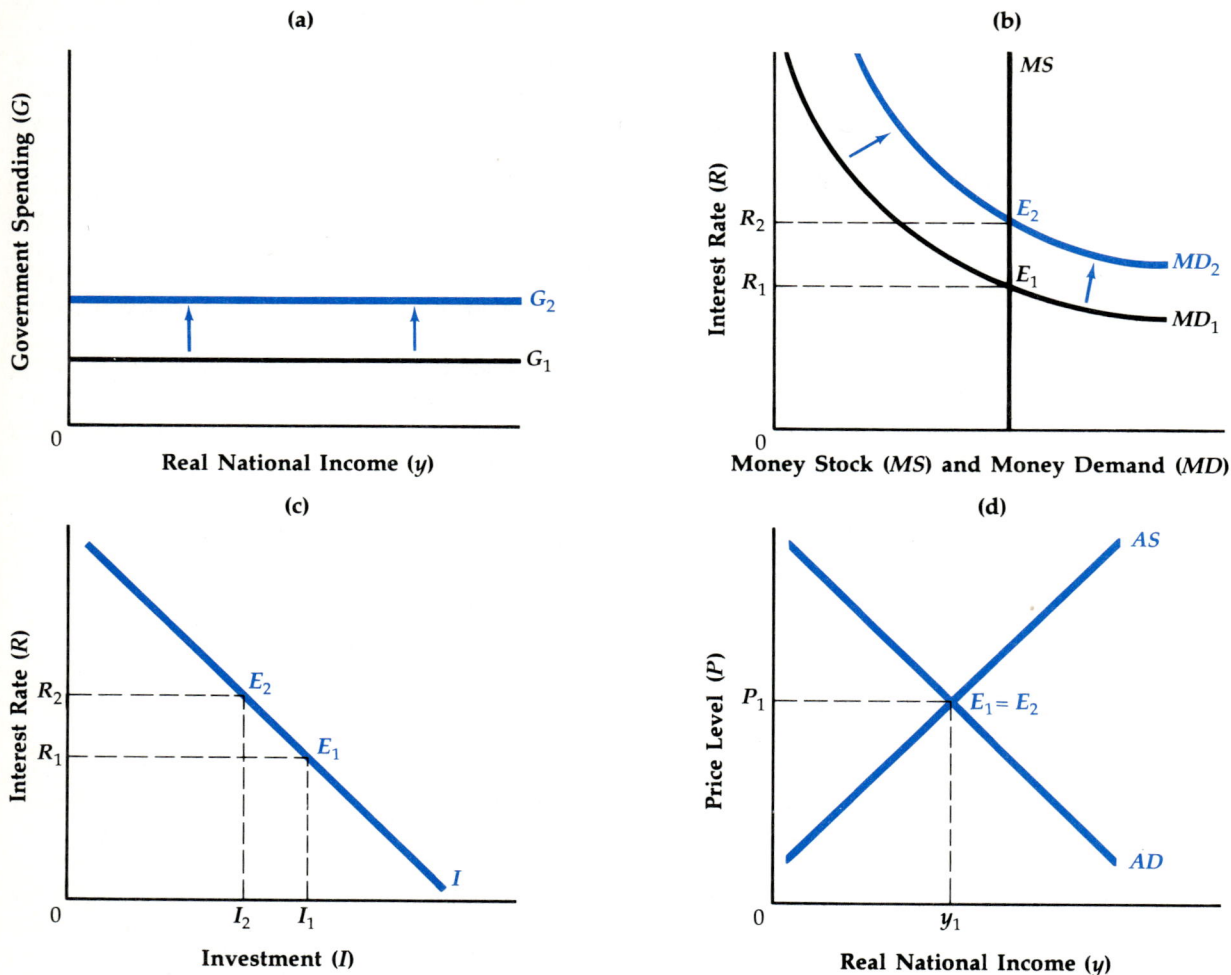

FIGURE 16.4   The Impact of Expectations on the Demand for Money (*MD*)
Suppose that government increases its expenditures from G_1 to G_2 (part (a)) and runs a larger deficit or a smaller surplus than people expect. According to rational expectations theory, the demand for money curve will shift up from MD_1 to MD_2, shifting the equilibrium from E_1 to E_2 and raising the market interest rate from R_1 to R_2 (part (b)). The higher interest rate will shift the investment equilibrium from E_1 to E_2 causing investment spending to fall from I_1 to I_2 (part (c)). The drop in investment offsets the impact of increased government spending, so that aggregate demand and supply do not change (part (d)). The nation's equilibrium price and real national income levels remain the same (P_1 and y_1) as the new equilibrium E_2 is the same as the old one E_1.

Suppose, for example, that the government increases its expenditures from G_1 to G_2 in Figure 16.4(a). Because experience has taught them that greater government spending is accompanied by greater budget deficits, people begin to expect interest rates to rise. This change in expectations will cause the demand for money curve to shift upward, as in Figure 16.4(b). People are now selling their bonds at high prices, so they can hold on to greater cash balances until bond prices drop and interest rates rise. Although the increase in government expenditures increases aggregate demand, the resulting upward shift in the demand for money curve boosts the interest rate from R_1 to R_2 (Figure 16.4(b) and (c)).

As the interest rate rises, the level of investment falls from I_2 to I_1 (see Figure 16.4(c)), counteracting the rise in government spending. In this instance the decrease in business investment, $I_2 - I_1$, just balances the expansion in government spending, $G_2 - G_1$. Aggregate demand remains constant (Figure 16.4(d)), and national income and employment are unaffected by the government's action.

Similarly, people may observe that prices rise faster when the Federal Reserve increases the rate of growth of the money stock. According to rational expectations theory, if there is such an acceleration in monetary growth, they will come to expect a higher rate of inflation. Business people will buy plant and equipment now, in anticipation of higher prices later. Wage earners will push for higher wages to protect their future purchasing power. Thus the very anticipation of price increases sets in motion forces that lead to higher prices. Any lag between the adoption of an expansionary monetary policy and the resulting increase in inflation is reduced (if not eliminated altogether) by the impact of people's expectations.

Various quite different models are used by theorists working in this relatively new area. In an effort to keep their models simple, many rational expectations theorists employ unrealistic assumptions about how expectations are formed. For example, some theorists base their models on these three extreme assumptions:

1. No cost is involved in gathering the necessary amount of information about the nature and structure of the economy and the consequences of fiscal and monetary policies.

2. Prices and wages are perfectly flexible, both upward and downward.

3. Transactions based on expectations of government policy changes and their consequences are costless.

Such assumptions make it relatively easy to conclude that people will fully and accurately anticipate the consequences of government policy, eliminating any time lag between the government action and its consequences.

Of course, in the real world, markets and people do not work with the perfection implied in these assumptions. Recognizing that discrepancy, rational expectations theorists may conclude that on average, people will fairly quickly formulate reasonably correct expectations about the consequences of government policy. Although some time may elapse between the government's action and its consequences, the lag will be much shorter than is usually assumed.

Clearly, clever people learn from experience. The Keynesian assumption that expectations are not changed by government policies may have been a useful working hypothesis during periods like the early 1960s, when people had had relatively little experience with such policies. When expansionary policy is pursued year after year, however, people will eventually begin to anticipate its consequences. When that happens, economic predictions based on constant expectations will begin to miss their mark. Before we can predict what will happen in response to fiscal and monetary policy actions, rational expectation theorists contend, we must understand one principle. People develop certain expectations based on past experience. When the rules of the game are changed, people's experience and expectations will change. When government changes its fiscal and monetary policies, it changes the rules of the game. People's expectations will change accordingly. Their behavior will be different, and so will the consequences of government policies. Indeed, once people come to understand what government is doing (or thinking of doing) to the economy, government will lose its ability to do anything to change the nation's real output and employment levels.

Rational Expectations Theory from Other Perspectives

3. How does monetarism handle expectations?

We have seen that rationally determined expectations can nullify the intended effect of government policy. To understand the principles of individual behavior that lie behind the phenomenon, we must return to monetarist theory.

In Chapter 14 we observed that the quantity of labor demanded and supplied is related to the real wage, W/P (see Figure 16.5). Assuming that the market originally clears at the intersection of the labor supply and demand curves at the equilibrium point E, the equilibrium real wage rate will be $(W/P)_2$ and the equilibrium employment level will be N_1. As we saw in Chapter 14, more rapid growth in the money stock will accelerate inflation. If prices rise faster than money wages, the real wage rate will fall, and employers will want to hire more workers. That is what happens in Figure 16.5. The real wage rate falls from $(W/P)_2$ to $(W/P)_1$, and employers increase employment from N_1 to N_2. As long as workers believe (incorrectly) that the increases in their money wages are increases in their real wages—that the real wage has gone *up*, to $(W/P)_3$—the quantity of labor supplied will expand from N_1 to N_2.

The resulting increase in employment will reduce the unemployment rate and increase real output. Once workers realize that their real wage has actually declined to $(W/P)_1$, however, they will demand higher money wages. The real wage will climb back up to $(W/P)_2$, negating the effects of

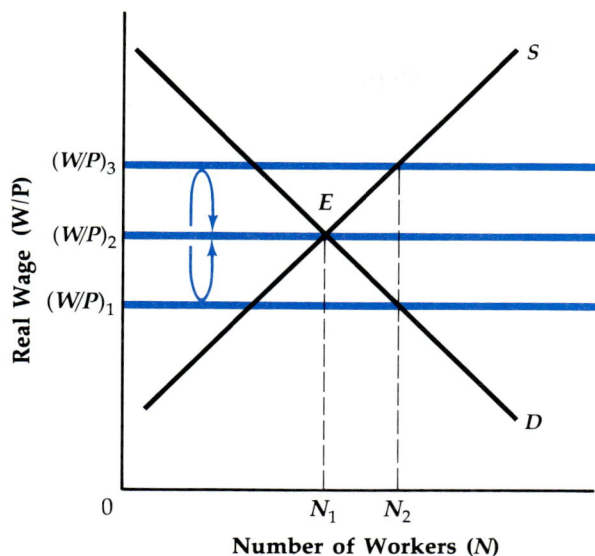

FIGURE 16.5 The Effect of Expansionary Monetary Policy on the Labor Market

Suppose the market originally clears at the equilibrium point E. Assume that an expansion in the money stock increases the price level. If employers interpret the increase as a reduction in the real wage from $(W/P)_2$ to $(W/P)_1$, they will expand the quantity of labor they demand, from N_1 to N_2. As long as workers interpret the resulting rise in their money wage as an increase in real wages, from $(W/P)_2$ to $(W/P)_3$, the quantity of labor supplied will also rise, from N_1 to N_2. The national output and income levels will rise. In rational expectations theory, workers and employers are not fooled by inflation. In other words, the inflation is anticipated and not unanticipated. Almost immediately wages will adjust to account for price increases, so that the real wage remain at $(W/P)_2$. Thus the quantity of labor employed will remain N_1, and national output and income will not expand.

the government-induced monetary expansion. Thus expansionary monetary policy can succeed only in the short run.

This process produces a long-run Phillips curve that is vertical rather than downward sloping (see Figure 16.6). When the inflation rate rises from IR_1 to IR_2, workers may at first be fooled into taking jobs at the lower real wage by not anticipating the change in government policy. Unemployment will drop from U_2 to U_1 as the equilibrium shifts from E_1 to E_2. When workers realize that the real wage has fallen, they will begin to turn down jobs offered at that rate. The unemployment rate will return to its previous level, U_2. Once workers have learned to anticipate the effects of monetary expansion, the Phillips curve will be vertical even in the short run.

Thus monetarists draw essentially the same conclusion as rational expectations theorists. The main difference between the two schools of thought lies in the speed of the adjustment process. According to rational expectations theory, people will learn to react very quickly, if not immediately, anticipating higher prices and interest rates as a result of expansionary fiscal and monetary policy. Instead of moving back along the short-run Phillips curve SPC_1 in Figure 16.6, the economy will move straight up the vertical long-run Phillips curve (LPC) almost immediately as the equilibrium shifts from E_1 to E_3. In other words, the short-run Phillips curve is also vertical, or practically so. And instead of the gradual rise in interest rates and fall in investment spending predicted by the monetarists, rational expectations theorists forecast that the change in expectations underlying the

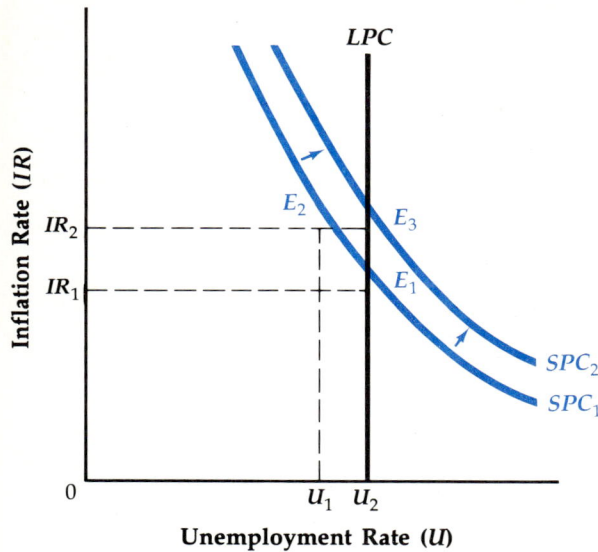

FIGURE 16.6 The Effect of Expansionary Monetary Policy on Unemployment

In Keynesian and monetarist theory, an increase in the inflation rate can move the economy up along the short-run Phillips curve SPC_1, as the equilibrium shifts from E_1 to E_2, reducing the unemployment rate from U_2 to U_1. In rational expectations theory, wages adjust immediately or almost immediately to the increase, shifting the Phillips curve from SPC_1 to SPC_2. The equilibrium shifts from E_1 to E_3 as the economy moves straight up along its vertical long-run Phillips curve, LPC, and the unemployment rate remains at U_2.

money and investment demands will bring an almost immediate, if not instantaneous, rise in interest rates and fall in investment.

Rational expectations theory can also be seen in terms of aggregate supply and aggregate demand. The economy is assumed initially to be in equilibrium at E_1 in Figure 16.7. As long as workers are deceived by an increase in the price level from P_1 to P_2—as a result of a policy change or action they did not expect—employment will increase, shifting the aggregate demand curve from AD_1 to AD_2. Real national income will rise from y_1 to y_2, moving from E_1 to E_2. As soon as workers demand higher wages, the aggregate supply curve will shift to the left, from SAS_1 to SAS_2. The equilibrium becomes E_3, at which point real national income will return to y_1 as producers cut back on production because of higher wages. Again, the monetarist and rational expectations views differ primarily as to the amount of time required for the adjustment. Monetarists tend to argue that people can be fooled for a short period of time. Rational expectations theorists argue that the downward adjustment of aggregate supply is immediate, or almost immediate. According to rational expectations theorists, the short-run aggregate supply curve is virtually vertical, just like the monetarists' long-run aggregate supply curve.

Thus the expansionary fiscal and monetary policy of the late 1960s and 1970s failed to reduce unemployment, because people anticipated and reacted to it, nullifying its effects. After only a few years of Keynesian fiscal policy, the government had played its hand too long. Some theorists argue that the same phenomenon explains the high real interest rates of the early

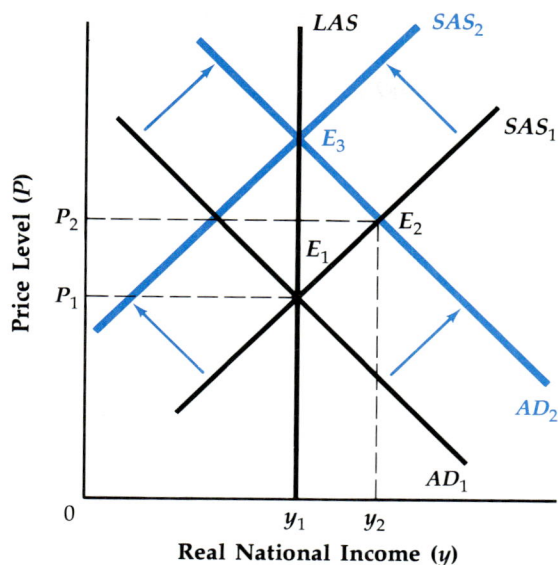

FIGURE 16.7 The Effect of Expansionary Monetary Policy on Aggregate Supply and Demand
The economy is originally in equilibrium at E_1. The increased consumption and investment spending caused by an expansionary monetary policy will shift aggregate demand from AD_1 to AD_2. The price level will rise from P_1 to P_2, and as long as workers are fooled (in the sense of an unanticipated or unexpected policy change) into believing their real wages have risen, the national output level will rise from y_1 to y_2 at E_2. Monetary policy will be ineffective, however, once people have learned that an expansionary monetary policy leads to a higher price level. Workers will demand higher wages, shifting the short-run aggregate supply curve in from SAS_1 to SAS_2 almost immediately. The result will be virtually no change in the real national income level as the equilibrium goes from E_1 to E_3 almost instantaneously. In rational expectations theory, the short-run (and long-run) aggregate supply curve is almost vertical, like the long-run aggregate supply curve (*LAS*) in monetarist theory.

and mid-1980s. People had learned to associate high federal deficits with high inflation and interest rates. Watching the deficit increase under President Reagan, they moved to protect themselves against another resurgence of inflation, in part by demanding high interest rates for their money. Like Lincoln, rational expectations theorists stress that you can't fool all of the people all the time.

Problems with Rational Expectations Theory

▲ **4. What are criticisms of rational expectations theory?**

Although supported by the monetarist, aggregate demand, and aggregate supply models, rational expectations theory and its implications are disputed by many economists. Several criticisms must be noted. The first two concern the extreme nature of the assumptions underlying rational expectations theory.

The Cost of Acquiring Information

Critics point out that rational expectations theory assumes too much of people. Adaptive expectationists feel that people make most actual decisions based on simple rules of thumb, rather than on complex, unrealistic economic models. Moreover, economists spend years studying and modeling the macroeconomy and still cannot accurately predict the timing and

Is the Federal Deficit a Burden?

Robert J. Barro, Harvard University

Everyone's talking about "large" recent budget deficits. In fact, the consensus is that the federal government's first priority should be to reduce the deficit. But be suspicious of this type of consensus: The last time I remember one this strong was in 1971 when every sensible person was supposed to believe that wage-price controls were a good idea. The current popular view on deficits falls into the same category—it is incorrect and is also likely to be discarded within a couple of years.

The appropriate first question is, how do today's deficits relate to history? Recent deficits—currently about 4%–5% of gross national product, or about $170 billion for fiscal 1984—are in line with what we would expect from experience, given the state of the economy. And they're in line with what we ought to be running. Under current conditions, I would be concerned if the deficit were either much larger or much smaller than it is.

Past U.S. deficits have had three main elements. The first is temporary federal expenditures, which arise primarily in wartime. In these cases a large budget deficit lessens the need to raise tax rates on a temporary basis. Since high tax rates blunt the incentives that help the economy deal with a war or other emergency, these kinds of deficits are a good idea. Wartime finance has, in fact, been the principal long-run source of the stock of public debt in the U.S. and other industrialized countries. But this factor has not been a consideration in recent years.

The second element is the business cycle. The federal deficit rises during recessions in order to avoid either large increases in tax rates or major cuts in government expenditures at these times. This process is well known and underlies the con-

struction of a full-employment deficit (which attempts to filter out the part of the deficit or surplus that derives from the business cycle). This element was the most important source of the budget deficits during the recessions of 1975–76 and 1980–83. Despite the strong recovery since early 1983, the continuing effect of the last recession still matters for the current deficit. I estimate that the remaining shortage of output below the full-employment level accounted for about $60 billion out of the total deficit of $170 billion for fiscal 1984.

The third item is net federal interest payments, which totaled $111 billion for fiscal 1984. This element, which was of minor significance until the rise of inflation in the late 1960s, has become the key force behind current budget deficits. The question is, how much of interest payments should be financed by a deficit rather than by higher taxes?

One part that is reasonable to finance by a deficit is that corresponding to expected inflation. If the government pays for this part with new debt, then—on this count—it just plans for a constant real debt over time. Using an estimate for expected inflation of 6% for 1984 (somewhat above the actual rate), the resulting contribution to the deficit was 6% times a stock of debt of about $1.2 trillion, or $70 billion–$75 billion.

A second element of interest payments appropriate to finance by a deficit is that corresponding to temporarily high real interest rates. These payments are analogous to other types of temporarily high government expenditures—such as wartime spending—that call for a deficit rather than an increase in taxes. In this way the government avoids unnecessary fluctuations in tax rates over time. I estimate that this component accounted for about 2½% (excess of current real interest rates above normal) times $1.2 trillion of debt, or roughly $30 billion of the fiscal 1984 deficit.

Overall, it was reasonable to finance about $100 billion–$105 billion of interest payments by a deficit. Adding in the $60 billion contribution from the residual effects of the recession leads to a total of $160 billion–$165 billion, or almost all of the actual figure of $170 billion.

The historical view of deficits and the accounting for the present situation also tell us what to expect for the future. Basically, deficits will fall greatly in fiscal years 1985 and 1986 only if there is rapid economic growth or if there are substantial declines in interest rates. Typical forecasts of these variables lead to projections of budget deficits for both years of about $170 billion, the same as in 1984. The potential for economic growth to reduce deficits below this figure is limited to about $60 billion, which is the contribution of prior recessions to the 1984 deficit. Thus, the main element that could reduce the deficit further is lower interest rates, whether because of reduced inflationary expectations or decreased real interest rates.

My forecast of a budget deficit of $170 billion for fiscal 1986 contrasts with the Congressional Budget Office's estimate last summer of $200 billion–$210 billion (the figure has been revised upward, but new accounting procedures and growth projections make the old number more appropriate for this comparative analysis). Basically, the CBO projection is for given spending and tax programs, whereas my forecast factors in the likely congressional responses. In other words, I see some combination of cuts in spending or increases in taxes that will total $30 billion–$40 billion for 1986.

It should be clear that there is a major interplay between recessions, interest rates and inflation on the one hand, and federal budget deficits on the other hand. But the channel that has been documented is from the economic variables to the deficit, and not the reverse. For example, recessions cause deficits (as is well known) but there is no evidence that shifts in the deficit have important effects on economic activity. Notably, the large deficits for 1983–84 did not prevent a strong investment-led economic recovery.

Similarly, an increase in interest rates (when it reflects either higher expected inflation or a temporary increase in real rates) can lead to a larger deficit. But, despite the efforts of many researchers to detect it, there is no evidence that shifts in deficits lead to higher interest rates, especially to the higher real rates that would deter investment.

The strongly held popular view is that large budget deficits—and the consequent rise in the real stock of public debt—tend to raise real interest rates and thereby crowd out private investment. Basically, this crowding-out view of deficits is a myth, which is reinforced mainly by repetition. It isn't supported by economic theory or empirical investigation.

In light of what has caused our recent deficits, and what they themselves are unlikely to cause, the national mania these days is rather hard to justify.

impact of government policy. How then can ordinary people be expected to make such predictions, virtually without cost or delay? Although this criticism may reflect the wounded professional dignity of economists, it is also consistent with common sense. In an imperfect world, adjustment to government policy may not be as costless, accurate, or reasonable as rational expectations theorists assume; on the other hand, uninformed people may elect to employ trend specialists or to heed their routinely available media predictions.

Because of the cost of obtaining information on economic conditions, people do not become perfectly informed. As a result they sometimes over- or underestimate the consequences of government policy actions. Thus an expansion in the money stock could have a perverse effect—an increase in labor's wage demands, a reduction in employment, and a contraction in national income—or the opposite could occur. That is, fiscal policy could have some temporary positive effect on employment and national income. Because of miscalculations and the time lags required to correct them, government fiscal and monetary policy can have at least some short-run effects on employment and national income. Policy need not be completely impotent, say critics of rational expectations theory.

Rational Ignorance

Rational expectations theory assumes that it is in people's self-interest to become aware of government policy. If government takes fiscal and monetary actions to influence citizens' welfare, people should have the necessary incentive to understand what government is doing. Critics stress that the macroeconomy is terribly complex, however, and that people have little incentive to keep abreast of government actions. One person can do little to influence the outcome of government policy. To varying degrees, people may be rationally ignorant about government policy—especially economic policy, a comparatively technical subject. While the effects of informed citizenry are stimulating for society as a whole, there may be little incentive for any individual to chart a course of truthseeking. Thus, **rational ignorance** occurs when the (marginal) costs of acquiring additional information exceed the (marginal) benefits at relatively low (perhaps zero) levels of information. The costs are relatively high because the macroeconomy is so complex, while the benefits are low because one person has little ability— and thus little incentive—to influence significantly the outcome of government policy.

Rational expectations theorists counter that it is not necessary to assume that everyone keeps abreast of government policy. Just a few people may adjust their expectations in response to government actions. Their response will produce a change in pricing signals, which will lead others to adjust their behavior. But the criticism is still relevant. If prices must be adjusted and then readjusted, for a short period at least, people are effectively fooled. Government fiscal and monetary actions can therefore have some short-run effect.

Rational ignorance: when the (marginal) costs of acquiring additional information exceed the (marginal) benefits at relatively low (perhaps zero) levels of information.

Changes in the Composition of National Output

Many rational expectations theorists conclude that fiscal and monetary policy has neither short-run nor long-run effects, but critics protest that if government actions change the composition of demand and the relative prices of goods and services, they necessarily affect the composition of the nation's output. For instance, expansionary fiscal policy can produce more government goods and services and fewer private goods and services, including private investment. Expansionary monetary policy can lower interest rates (at least in the short run), thus increasing investment. Such changes in the composition of output necessarily have a long-run effect on the national output level. For example, a reduction in private investment because of greater government spending can mean a reduction in the nation's future capital stock, productivity, and income level.

Many rational expectations theorists accept this criticism. Their point is that, contrary to Keynesian analysis, government cannot systematically influence the employment and production levels by managing aggregate demand.

Contract and Wage Rigidities

Many rational expectations models assume that prices and wages are perfectly flexible, but there are many institutional rigidities and viscosities in the real-world pricing system. Many producers, for instance, are bound by labor contracts that strictly prohibit wage and price adjustments for certain periods of time. As a result, wages cannot always be raised in response to a higher inflation rate. At least temporarily, real wages can fall while employment and national production expand.

To this criticism, rational expectations theorists may reply that experience will teach labor leaders to develop contracts that permit wage adjustments for inflation, including clauses for automatic cost-of-living increases. Perhaps the most widely discussed proposal to make wages more flexible is due to MIT Professor Martin L. Weitzman in his concept of a share economy.[1] Although Weitzman's proposal was offered to moderate the impact of a fall in aggregate demand in unemployment, it would, if successful, also make the rational expectations position more tenable. A **share economy** is a profit-sharing plan with a two-part wage scheme in which part of each worker's wages is independent of the firm's profitability and part is dependent. As a result, with a recession driven by a decline in aggregate demand, the attendant lower profits would automatically bring lower wages. This profit-sharing plan should both expand employment as employers respond to the fact that the risk is partially shifted to the workers and should reduce cylical unemployment and layoffs.

Share economy: a profit-sharing plan with a two-part wage scheme in which part of each worker's wages is independent of the firm's profitability and part is dependent.

1. Martin L. Weitzman, *The Share Economy* (Cambridge, Mass.: Harvard University Press, 1984).

PERSPECTIVES

Expectations and the Effects of Federal Deficits

William F. Shughart II, University of Mississippi

Almost two centuries ago the British economist David Ricardo (1772–1823) suggested that government expenditures will have the same effect on an economy whether the funds are raised through taxes or through deficit spending (borrowing). Ricardo's theorem is still debated among economists. It is especially controversial today, both because of the emergence of rational expectations theory and because the federal deficit is projected to run from $200 to $250 billion a year for the rest of the decade.

How do expectations influence the economy's response to a budget deficit? Deficit spending implies that the government will eventually have to raise taxes to pay off its creditors. Ricardo proposed that individuals will react to the expectation of higher future taxes just as they would to an increase in current taxes. Others have argued that individuals do not respond to deficits as they do to taxes. Instead, they see deficit spending as a way of shifting part of their tax liability to future generations. Whether or not one should be concerned about deficits depends, obviously, on which of these two views one subscribes to.

Suppose the government decides to increase spending this year by $1, but will return to its former level of spending next year, and each year thereafter. This year's extra spending could be financed by imposing a $1 tax surcharge this year. Taxpayers would then have $1 less to spend as they wished, but the government's budget would remain balanced.

Alternatively the government could pay for this year's extra spending by running a budget deficit. That is, the government would borrow $1 by issuing a bond on which the principal plus interest is due some time in the future. To keep the example simple, assume the loan would be repaid in one year. Although current taxes would not go up, next year's taxes would have to rise enough to cover the $1 of principal plus the interest on the bond, r. And the public would be aware of the impending increase.

Taxpayers could meet their increased future liability by buying a $1 bond that pays the same interest rate as the government's, r. By selling the bond next year, they would have just enough money—$1 + r$—to pay their taxes. As in the first case, they would be one dollar poorer this year. Therefore the extra dollar's worth of public spending would have the same effect whether it is financed by raising taxes or by running a deficit.

Weitzman believes that a share economy is more resistant to inflation because output will be higher, which naturally, given normal downsloping demand curves, holds down prices. On a theoretic level, critics contend that the share economy would provide just the opportunity employers have wanted to push wages down to peon levels. In addition, with the relative price of labor reduced, employers will shift to more labor-intensive technology that may be less socially desirable for long-term economic growth. On a practical level, there is serious doubt that labor unions will trade off the possibility of greater employment stability and more jobs for the certainty of reduced guaranteed wages. Also the measurement of profits could become a contentious labor and management issue. Although no one can be sure if the share system will work, the only major industrial country using something like it (Japan) has excelled at price stability, employment, and productivity for decades.

Of course, the government does not normally promise to repay the funds it borrows in one year. Government securities usually mature in four, ten, or even twenty years. In fact, the government can borrow money indefinitely, simply by issuing a new bond to pay off an old one when it comes due (a practice known as "rolling over" debt). In this way the government can delay repaying the principal, but it will still have to raise taxes enough to meet the interest payments on its debt.

Suppose, for instance, that a $1 increase in spending is financed by a bond that the government does not intend to retire when it matures. In that case, taxes in each future year must be higher by the amount of the interest, r. But again, taxpayers can meet their future tax liability by buying $1 worth of bonds this year. The r dollars in interest income they receive in each subsequent year will pay for their extra taxes. Ricardo's theorem still holds. The effect is the same whether the government raises taxes or borrows money to cover its extra spending.

But taxpayers do not live forever. Can they be expected to act as if they will? Some economists think that a concern for the welfare of their children would lead taxpayers to plan beyond their own lifetimes. They would make up for any tax burden the government imposed on their children by giving them larger inheritances. Otherwise part of their tax burden would be shifted to future generations.

Recent evidence suggests that the assumption that taxpayers would plan beyond their lifetimes may be wrong. An analysis of eighty-three federal budgets from 1900 through 1982 shows that holding other things constant (such as the size of government, interest payments on existing debt, and economic growth), increases in the average life-span are associated with declines in deficit spending. In other words, individuals may prefer deficits to taxes if they do not expect to be living when the government's bonds mature. If so, deficit spending may well be the equivalent of a tax on future generations. As such, it will reduce the amount of capital future generations will inherit, benefiting the living at the expense of those yet to be born.

See also W. F. Shughart II and R. D. Tollison, "The Vote Motive and the Debt: A Contingent Liability Approach," in J. M. Buchanan, C. K. Rowley, and R. D. Tollison, eds., *Deficits* (New York: Basil Blackwell, 1987), pp. 218–235.

Chapter Review

Review of Key Questions

1. *How does Keynesian theory handle expectations?*

    In Keynesian economics, expectations underlie the investment, consumption, and money demand curves. Keynesians tend to assume that changes in people's expectations do not entirely offset the impact of fiscal and monetary policy on aggregate demand. Thus, Keynesians do not believe that expectations can neutralize macroeconomic policymaking.

2. *What do the rational expectationists believe?*

    Rational expectations theory is an offshoot of the efficient market hypothesis that emphasizes that expectations and actual outcomes are in agreement for market participants. In both cases the market is informationally efficient. Naive adaptive expectations theory posits that people base their extrapolations of the future on actual historical outcomes in the past, with greater weight given to more recent events. This introduces systematic errors as recent rates of change are given less prominence than recent levels of economic variables. Rational expectations theory assumes that people understand how the economy works and will acquire information on the consequences of government fiscal and monetary policy, and will act on that information. The acquisition of information will change people's expectations for the future, altering the effectiveness of government policies. People weigh all available information, including the anticipated impact of current and future economic policymaking, as they formulate their expectations about the economic future. As in a chess match, strategy changes as opponents make their choices. In this way systematic (but not random) errors will tend to be eliminated. People will anticipate correctly and fully and take rational compensating actions to neutralize government policies. This means there will be policy neutrality, because macroeconomic policy is important in influencing real economic variables in both the short run and the long run. In its strictest and most extreme form, rational expectations theory assumes that prices and wages are completely flexible; that the acquisition of information on government policy costs nothing; and that adjustments based on changed expectations of the results of government policy also cost nothing. Given these assumptions, rational expectations theorists conclude that government fiscal and monetary policy should be passive; it will be completely ineffective, both in the short run and in the long run, because the aggregate supply curve is vertical. The fact that economic policy will have no real, but perhaps nominal, effects on GNP or employment is sometimes called the policy ineffectiveness theorem.

  ◢ *3. How does monetarism handle expectations?*

Monetarists, adaptive expectationists, and rational expectations theorists conclude that fiscal and monetary policy will have no long-run effect on the national income level. Monetarists believe, however, that fiscal and monetary policy may have a short-run effect on the national income level. Rational expectations theorists argue that even the short-run effect is practically nil. While economists are debating vigorously the merits of adaptive versus rational expectations theories, the two agree that the Phillips curve is vertical at the natural rate of unemployment in the long run. However, adaptive expectationists feel that there is an unemployment-inflation tradeoff in the short-run, whereas rational expectationists find no consistent tradeoff.

  ◢ *4. What are criticisms of rational expectations theory?*

Criticism of rational expectations theory focuses on the assumptions that underlie it. Critics contend that information is costly to acquire and that citizens have an incentive to remain ignorant of government policy. Some delay between the initiation of government fiscal or monetary policy and its impact on prices and interest rates must therefore be expected. Critics charge too that fiscal and monetary policies alter the composition of the nation's output—between public and private goods, between investment and consumption goods—and thus affect production and national income in the long run. Finally, critics point out that prices are not perfectly flexible. Labor contracts often fix wages, creating a time lag within which government policy can have some effect. For instance, the share economy proposal offers a way to make wages more flexible. Of course, the rational expectationists have a rational response to each of these matters, and so regard these criticisms as mere peccadilloes. The rational expectationists have created quite a stir in economics over the last decade. All in all, the debates among the various schools of thought—Keynesian, monetarist, supply-side, rational expectations—has been salutary as all sides open the windows to bring more and higher-quality information into their analyses and their policy recommendations.

Further Topics

Rational expectations theory is relatively new; only in the last several years has it received much attention. Because the theory is new, economists are still working to develop it and to test its usefulness in improving macroeconomic prediction. Many questions remain unsettled. For instance:

○ Why would a government devise a macroeconomic policy if they knew it would not (and the people also knew it would not) have any effect on the economy?

○ Do government policymakers overestimate their own power?

○ How is economic information transmitted in the macroeconomy?

Needless to say, these questions cannot be fully answered here. Refinements in theory can be expected with time, and tentative answers will be devised. For now, many see rational expectations as a rather sterile and unrealistic theory. It has made one important contribution to our understanding of government policy, however. That is the observation that the effectiveness of fiscal and monetary policy depend partly on the extent to which people correctly anticipate the impact of government policy and react accordingly. Insofar as government fiscal and monetary policy is effective, people have been fooled. The real value of rational expectations theory may lie in improved predictions and better understanding of the limits of government policy.

After admitting the valid theoretical points—although in his view fallacious empirical assertions—of rational expectations theory, a leading Keynesian, Alan S. Blinder, summed up his feelings this way:

Rational expectationists accused Keynesians of some pretty dubious activities—like harboring Phillips curves, bearing false witness of involuntary unemployment, and assault and battery with a dead econometric model. Keynesian econometric models are certainly no font of truth; they are homely and they have flaws. They also make mistakes, failing to predict both OPEC and bad harvests. Furthermore, they are guilty as charged of coping poorly with changes in expectations. But, ironically, the Phillips curve—once it is patched up to take account of supply shocks—is one of the strongest links in the Keynesian model. And the alternative models offered by new classical economics are not obvious improvements. Though elegant as theory, their empirical predictions are either nonexistent or comical. Finally, Keynesians do insist that they see involuntary unemployment in the land, no matter how many idealized theoretical models say that no such thing can exist. To a Keynesian, seeing is believing. New classicists insist on seeing what they believe.[2]

Review of New Terms

Adaptive expectations theory The theory that market participants formulate their expectations of the future, including their future economic policy activities, solely on past and current information.

Efficient market hypothesis The theory that new information traveling randomly is very rapidly assimilated by a large number of rational participants, no one group of which possesses market power. Because of this almost instantaneous adjustment to new information, no disequilibrium can last very long.

Policy neutrality or **policy ineffectiveness theorem** The conclusion of many rational expectations models that fiscal and monetary policy will have no effect on national income and employment, in either the short run or the long run.

Rational expectations theory The macroeconomic theory that market participants formulate their expectations of the future, including future economic policy activities, on past, present, and projected future information.

Rational ignorance When the (marginal) costs of acquiring additional information exceed the (marginal) benefits at relatively low (perhaps zero) levels of information.

Share economy A profit-sharing plan with a two-part wage scheme in which part of each worker's wages is independent of the firm's profitability and part is dependent.

Review Questions

1. This chapter focused on the effects of expansionary fiscal and monetary policies. What should be the effects of contractionary fiscal and monetary policies (a) when they are not expected and (b) when they are expected? (◢1, ◢2)

2. Suppose the marginal cost of acquiring information increases as more information is obtained. How would the increasing cost of information affect the theory of rational expectations? (◢4)

2. Alan S. Blinder, *Hard Head, Soft Hearts* (Reading, Mass.: Addison-Wesley, 1987), pp. 105–106.

3. Suppose money wages cannot be adjusted downward and the real
   wage is consequently held above equilibrium. With the aid of a
   graph, explain how an expansionary fiscal policy would affect employment (a) if its consequences were expected and (b) if its consequences were not fully expected. (◀ 1, ◀ 2)
4. We have discussed four commonly cited objections to rational expectations theory. Can you think of any others? (◀ 4)
5. How do expectations figure in Keynesian theory? (◀ 1)
6. How do monetarism and rational expectations theory differ? (◀ 3)

PART VI

The International Economy

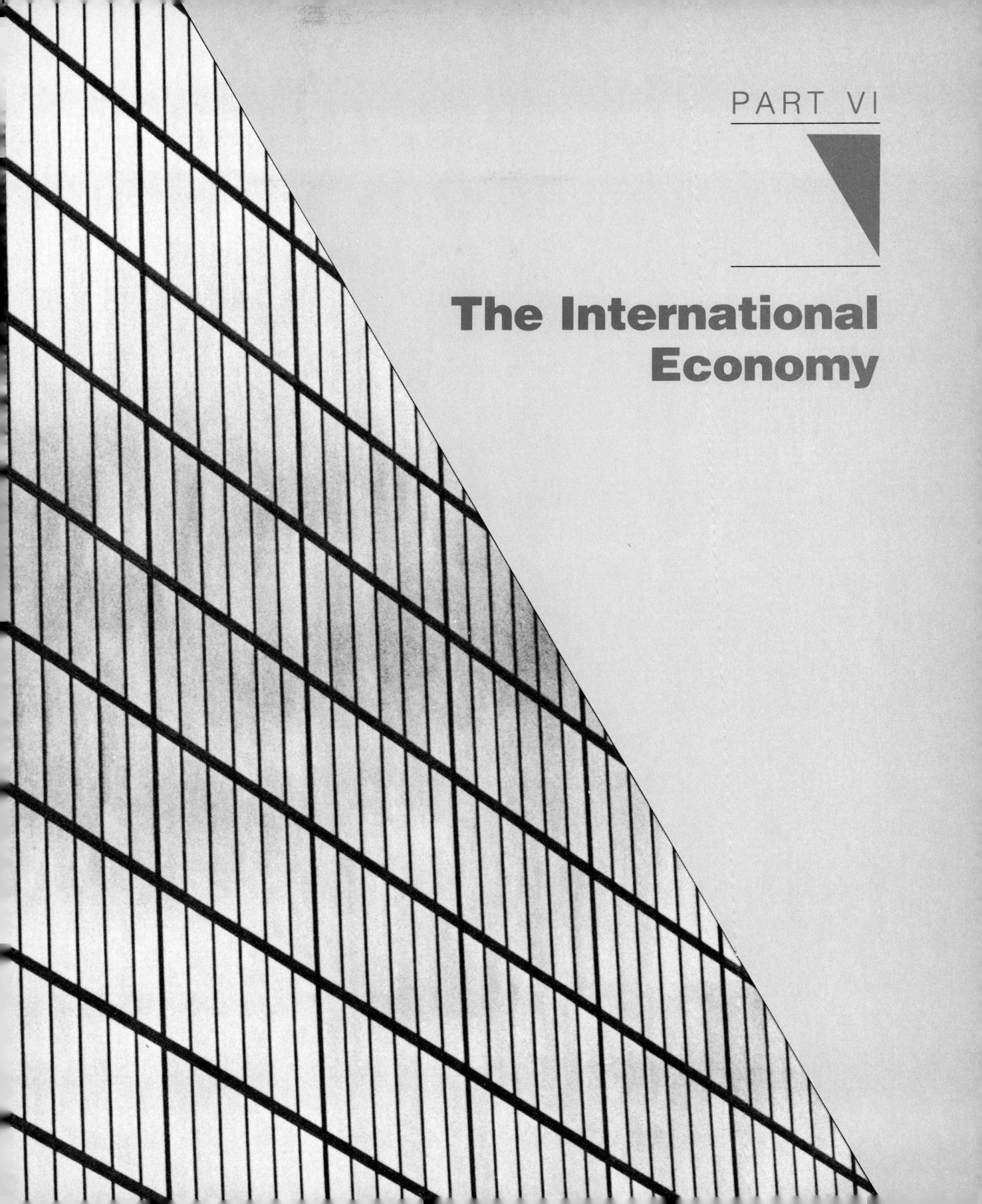

International Trade

It can be of no consequence to America, whether the commodities she obtains in return for her own, cost Europeans much, or little labor; all she is interested in, is that they shall cost her less labor by purchasing than by manufacturing them herself.
    David Ricardo

KEY QUESTIONS

▲ 1.   What does the balance of payments measure?

▲ 2.   How do nations gain from international trade?

▲ 3.   What are the distributional effects of international trade?

▲ 4.   What do trade restrictions such as tariffs and quotas do to international trade?

▲ 5.   What is good about free international trade?

▲ 6.   What arguments in favor of restricted international trade are valid?

NEW TERMS

Absolute advantage
Capital account
Capital account deficit
Capital account surplus
Comparative advantage
Current account
Current account deficit
Current account surplus

International balance of
  payments
Merchandise trade balance
Merchandise trade deficit
Merchandise trade surplus
Quota
Tariff
Terms of trade

Nations never really trade; people do. This simple point is important, for it allows us to approach international trade as an extension of models already developed, rather than a completely new topic. Earlier discussions focused on the local or national marketplace. In this and the following chapter, our marketplace will be the world.

Of course, there are differences between international and domestic trade—enough to make international economics an important subdiscipline of the profession. Some differences are obvious, like the many different national currencies, cultures, institutions, laws, languages, artificial barriers (tariffs, quotas, embargoes, health regulations), and countercyclical domestic policies, involved in international exchange. Others go largely unrecognized. An intangible but significant factor is the difference in people's attitudes toward domestic and international trade—call it nationalism. As Abraham Lincoln is supposed to have said, "Domestic trade is among us; international trade is between us and them." Yet people all over the world trade with each other for the same reason: They stand to gain from the transaction in spite of the politics. There is much greater immobility of resources than commodities between nations. International trade is a substitute for the international movement of human and property resources, especially people.

Understanding that trade is between people, not nations, is important for another reason. If we focus solely on gains from trade to nations, we may overlook the distributional effects of international commerce—the gains and losses to individuals. As we will see, while international trade increases a nation's total income, it reduces some individuals' incomes and increases others'. To evaluate objections to free trade among nations in proper perspective, we must recognize these hidden gains and losses.

Objections to free trade can be explained easily in terms of market theory. A major principle of economic theory is that each individual competitor has a vested interest in reducing competition. Competition forces product prices down and spurs product development and, in the long run, restricts business profits to only the risk-adjusted profit opportunities available elsewhere. Thus it is natural for domestic firms to seek protection from their foreign competitors—but protection only increases the prices consumers must pay. Carried to an extreme, protection based on the narrow interests of particular sectors of the economy can reduce everyone's income. On this basis rests the case for free international trade.

After examining the advantages of international trade from a purely national perspective, we will look at the distributional, or individual, effects. The chapter closes with a discussion of the pros and cons of protectionism.

The Balance of Payments

◢ 1. What does the balance of payments measure?

International balance of payments: a summary statement of the flow of all international economic and financial transactions between one nation—for example, the United States—and the rest of the world over some period of time, usually one year.

The benefits of international commerce to the United States are revealed in the international balance of payments statistics. The **international balance of payments** is a summary statement of the flow of all international economic and financial transactions between one nation—for example, the United States—and the rest of the world over some period of time, usually one year. These transactions involve individuals, businesses, and governments. The major elements of a flexible, floating, or free market exchange system with only private supply and demand forces operative, are the current account (involving merchandise goods, services, and gifts) and the capital account (involving financial assets). If there is a managed flexible or fixed exchange system that features official government intervention, there must also be an official reserve transaction account (including gold, foreign currencies, and special drawing rights at the International Monetary Fund, the world's Federal Reserve) that can be used if the combined current and capital accounts do not balance. Since the early 1970s, most countries have operated under a managed floating rate system that uses official reserve balances only moderately, leaving market forces the bulk of the responsibility for maintaining equilibrium. Therefore, we will discuss the official reserves transaction account in Chapter 18, *International Finance*.

International transactions include exports and imports of goods, services, and gifts, interest and dividend payments, and travel expenditures, as well as the flows of financial capital (purchases of financial assets, such as stocks and bonds, and real capital assets) across national boundaries. Transactions that create a demand for a country's currency on the foreign exchange market (e.g., exports) are a credit (+), inflow, or receipt item. Transactions that create a supply of a country's currency on the foreign exchange market (e.g., imports) are a debit (−), outflow, or payment item.

PERSPECTIVES
The Balance on Current Account
Edward L. Hudgins, Heritage Foundation

International economic transactions can be measured in several ways. The merchandise trade balance includes the dollar value of imports and exports. The balance on current account, a more complete measure, includes investment income receipts and payments and other minor transactions as well.

During the twenty-five years following World War II, the United States ran yearly surpluses in its merchandise trade. A **merchandise trade surplus** is the dollar amount by which exports of goods exceed imports of goods. Between 1946 and 1970, exports averaged $4 billion more than imports. Total exports increased from $11.8 billion to $42.5 billion, while imports went from $5 billion to $40 billion.

Except for two years since then, however, the United States has run a steadily increasing merchandise trade deficit. A **merchandise trade deficit** is the dollar amount by which imports of goods exceed exports of goods. Between 1977 and 1982, the deficit averaged $30 billion. In 1983 it climbed to $61 billion, and in 1984 doubled again to reach $123 billion.

During the same period, the balance on current account was more favorable. Ever since World War II, interest income from U.S. investments abroad has exceeded interest payments on foreign investments in the United States. In fact, the surplus interest income has usually been greater than the trade deficit. But from 1977 to 1979, the United States ran deficits on current account of $7.96 to $15.4 billion. That was nothing, however, compared with the staggering deficits of 1986 and 1987 (see Figure 17.1).

The major cause of these deficits in the balance on current account was an increase in imports. After a general decline during the 1970s, the U.S. dollar regained much of its historical strength abroad, allowing Americans to purchase more imports. The surplus of investment income receipts also decreased in these years, in part because of increased investment in the United States both by Americans, who began to invest less abroad, and by foreigners, who began to invest more in the United States.

Some economists see the deficit on current account as a problem. As long as the invest-

---

Merchandise trade balance: the difference between the dollar value of a nation's imported and exported goods—raw materials, agricultural and manufactured products, and capital and consumer products, but not services and financial assets.

Under double-entry bookkeeping, the balance of payments in the aggregate must balance, but separate accounts can be out of balance. For instance, a current account deficit might be made up by a capital account surplus. Balance, however, does not mean that disequilibrium situations won't occur.

The bulk of the United States' international receipts and payments transactions are exports and imports, which are summarized in the **merchandise trade balance.** The merchandise trade balance is the difference between the dollar value of a nation's imported and exported goods—raw materials, agricultural and manufactured products, and capital and consumer products, but not services and financial assets. The merchandise trade balance is only one element of the balance of payments; a problem here or elsewhere does not necessarily mean a problem for the entire balance of payments. Table 17.1 shows the Balance of Payments (International Trade and Transactions) for the United States in 1986. In 1986, the United

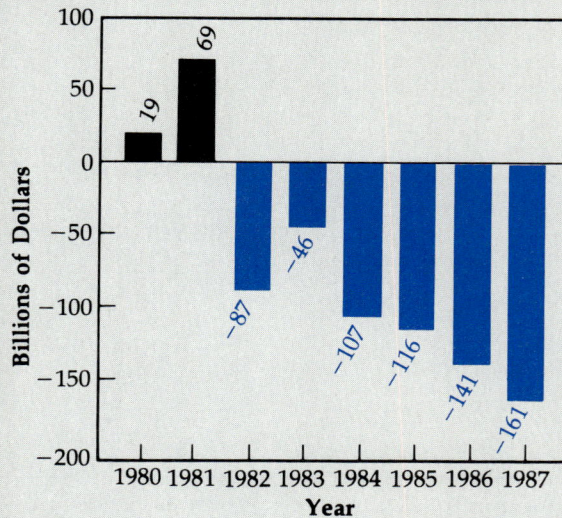

FIGURE 17.1 U.S. Balance on Current Account, 1980–1987

In 1980 and 1981 the United States recorded a small surplus on current account. By 1987, however, the nation was running a record deficit of $161 billion on current account—over three times its deficit in 1983.
Source: Economic Report of the President (Washington, D.C.: U.S. Government Printing Office, 1988) p. 366.

ment income surplus matches the trade deficit, they maintain, excess imports can be covered. But if the United States does not earn the equivalent of its excess imports in net investment income, it is in effect buying on credit. In the long run the United States will become a debtor nation, unable to import goods or to attract investment capital because of its high debt payments.

But other economists feel a deficit on current account reflects a passing situation, not an economic problem that demands government action. Excess imports, they argue, may be considered as paid for by the increased buying power of the dollar. That is, the strong dollar has benefited Americans by lowering the prices of imported goods. If too many dollars flow out of the United States, furthermore, the dollar will decrease in value. Over the long run, exports will increase and imports will decrease. Finally, excess dollars that flow out of the United States in payment for imports may well return in the form of foreign investment. Such an inflow of capital would help, not harm, American industry.

States exported goods and services valued at $224.3 billion, or approximately 5 percent of its GNP. It imported $368.7 billion worth of goods and services, or almost 9 percent of its total production. Imports exceeded exports by about $145 billion. This illustrates how exports and imports, in relative volume terms, are not as important in the United States as in some countries (such as the Netherlands, West Germany, Canada, Italy, and the United Kingdom), where exports range from 20 to almost 50 percent of GNP. Of course, U.S. absolute dollar volumes are the highest in the world because the United States is so big. Our three biggest imports are oil and gas, machinery, and automobiles, and our biggest exports are machinery, grain and cereal, and office equipment.

The difference between exports and imports was offset by other international transactions. In 1986, Americans received approximately $88 billion in interest and dividends from investments in foreign nations. Foreigners, on the other hand, received only about $63 billion in interest

---

TABLE 17.1   Balance of Payments (International Trade and Transactions) for the United States, 1986 (in billions of dollars)

Merchandise trade	
Exports	$ 224.3
Imports	−368.7
Investment income	
Receipts	88.3
Payments	−62.9
Net military transactions	−3.6
Net travel and transportation receipts	−9.9
Other services	11.4
Balance on goods and services	$ 125.7
Remittances, pensions, and other unilateral transfers (i.e., gifts)	−15.6
Balance on current account	$ 141.3
International capital flows	
U.S. assets abroad (capital outflows)	$−96.0
Foreign assets in the United States (capital inflows)	213.4
Balance on capital account	$ 117.4
Statistical discrepancy	23.9
Balance of current account, capital account, and statistical discrepancy	$ 0.0

Source: Economic Report of the President (Washington, D.C.: U.S. Government Printing Office, 1988), pp. 364–365.

Current account: the record of all the nation's international transactions other than capital flows and statistical discrepancies, including its merchandise trade, its investment income, its military transactions, its travel and transportation expenditures, its other services, and its remittances, pensions, and other unilateral transfers (i.e., gifts).

Current account deficit: the dollar amount by which a nation's imports of goods and services, interest and dividend payments to foreigners, gifts to foreigners, travel expenditures abroad, and other remittances to foreign nations exceed its exports of goods and services, interest and dividend receipts from foreign nations, gifts from abroad, foreign travel expenditures in this nation, and other remittances from abroad.

and dividends from investments in American businesses and securities. American tourists spent almost $10 billion more abroad than foreign tourists spent here, but "other services" sold to foreigners exceeded "other services" to Americans by about $11 billion. When remittances, pensions, and gifts were added, the United States had a large current account deficit of $141.3 billion.

Although a total balance of payments must always balance—in that the total credits must equal the total debits—any one part of the statement (e.g., current account or capital account) can be out of balance. This has the potential to cause disequilibrium. Disequilibrium calls for an adjustment or change in one or more factors, including exchange rates, domestic income, price levels or interest rates, or trade restrictions. A balance of payment deficit (surplus) generates a contractive (or expansive) impact on domestic aggregate demand, and thus employment, income, prices, and production as well.

The **current account** is the record of all the nation's international transactions other than capital flows and statistical discrepancies, including its merchandise trade, its investment income, its military transactions, its travel and transportation expenditures, its other services, and its private and governmental remittances, pensions, and other unilateral transfers (i.e., gifts). In simple terms, the current account records all international transactions involving goods, services, and gifts. A **current account deficit** is the dollar amount by which a nation's imports of goods and services, interest and dividend payments to foreigners, gifts to foreigners, travel expenditures abroad, and other remittances to foreign nations exceed its exports of goods and services, interest and dividend receipts from foreign nations, gifts from abroad, foreign travel expenditures in this nation, and other remittances from abroad. In contrast to the 1980s, during the 1960s and 1970s, the United States frequently ran a current account surplus. A current account surplus is the dollar amount by which a nation's exports of goods and services, interest and dividend receipts from foreigners, gifts from foreigners, foreign travel expenditures in this nation, and other receipts from abroad exceed the nation's imports of goods and services, interest and dividend payments to foreigners, gifts to foreigners, travel expenditures abroad, and other remittances to foreign nations.

Part of the income received from the sale of American goods abroad went into purchases of foreign stocks and bonds and overseas investment by U.S. firms. Such investments are not included in current account statistics, because they are not imports. Instead, they are included in the nation's capital account. The **capital account** is the record of a nation's assets or investments abroad and foreign investments in that nation. In 1986 Americans invested $96 billion abroad, while foreigners bought assets or invested $213.4 billion here. Thus the nation ran a capital account surplus of $117.4 billion. A **capital account surplus** is the dollar amount by which foreign investments in a nation—that is, capital inflows—exceed that nation's investments abroad—that is, capital outflows. In contrast to the 1980s, during the 1960s and 1970s, the United States frequently ran a capital account deficit: A **capital account deficit** is the dollar amount by which a nation's investments abroad—that is, capital outflows—exceed foreign investments in that nation—that is, capital inflows.

Many of the imports Americans bought were finished products like automobiles and television sets, their Japanese or German origins clearly identified. Other imports were raw materials, like crude oil and tin, or parts used in the production of other goods, like transistors and auto parts. Some of the imported raw materials were used to make products that were ultimately exported to other countries. More will be said about export-import balances in the following chapter. The point here is that all these international transactions were undertaken for mutual gain. Americans who bought foreign goods did so because they offered a better price-quality package than their U.S. counterparts. Americans who invested in foreign countries did so because they expected to earn a higher rate of return than would be possible on U.S. properties.

Collective Gains From Trade

Most of the gains from trade result from allocating resources in the most efficient manner and from the reduction in the social opportunity cost— each geographic area produces and exchanges those things for which it is best suited to produce. By nations producing where they are low opportunity cost producers and trading for commodities where they are high opportunity cost producers, joint output is maximized and consumption opportunities are enhanced. Adam Smith told us more than two hundred years ago about the nature of the gains from trade: "It is a maxim of every prudent master, never to attempt to make at home what it will cost him

---

Current account surplus: the dollar amount by which a nation's exports of goods and services, interest and dividend receipts from foreigners, gifts from foreigners, foreign travel expenditures in this nation, and other receipts from abroad exceed the nation's imports of goods and services, interest and dividend payments to foreigners, gifts to foreigners, travel expenditures abroad, and other remittances to foreign nations.

Capital account: the record of a nation's investments abroad and foreign investments in that nation.

Capital account surplus: the dollar amount by which foreign investments in a nation—that is, capital inflows—exceed that nation's investments abroad—that is, capital outflows.

Capital account deficit: the dollar amount by which a nation's investments abroad—that is, capital outflows—exceed foreign investments in that nation—that is, capital inflows.

◢ **2. How do nations gain from international trade?**

more to make than to buy."[1] Trade also allows a greater variety and wider choice of available products. The gains from international trade are clearest when there is no domestic substitute for an imported good. For example, the United States does not have any known reserves of chromium, manganese, or tin. For those basic resources, which are widely used in manufacturing, American firms must rely on foreign suppliers. The gains from trade are also clear for goods that are very costly or difficult to produce in the United States. For example, cocoa and coffee can be raised in the United States, but only in a greenhouse. Obviously it is less costly to import coffee in exchange for some other good, like wheat, for which the U.S. climate is better suited.

Foreign competition also offers benefits to the American consumer. By challenging the market power of domestic firms, foreign producers who market their goods in the United States reduce product prices and expand domestic consumption. Foreign competition also increases the variety of goods available. Without competition from the twenty or more foreign automobile producers who sell in the American market, the three U.S. automakers would each get a much larger percentage of the market. They would be less hesitant to raise their prices if consumers had fewer alternative sources of supply. Collusion among major manufacturers would also be much more likely without the presence of foreign competitors.

International trade also promotes specialization, whose benefits are fairly clear. By concentrating on producing a small number of goods and selling to the world market, a nation can reap the benefits of greater efficiency and economies of scale. Resource savings that are not initially obvious may be gained. Indeed, after considering the following example, some readers may doubt that international trade can be mutually beneficial.

Consider a world in which only two nations, the United States and Japan, produce only two goods, textiles and beef. Assume that the United States produces both textiles and beef more efficiently than Japan. That is, with the same resources, the United States can produce more beef and more textiles than Japan can. It has an absolute advantage in the production of both goods. An **absolute advantage** in production is the capacity to produce more units of output than a competitor can for any given level of resource use. A **comparative advantage** in production or cost is the relative advantage based on comparative ratios such that either the absolute advantage is greatest or the absolute disadvantage is smallest. Comparative advantage is more important for trade than absolute advantage. As long as the relative productivities or costs differ between individuals, regions, or nations, the participants can engage in mutually beneficial trade. Let's see how these differences work out for people.

Suppose that Lisa is worth $100 an hour in market work and only $10 an hour in home or household work. Her husband Gary is worth $8 an hour in the market and $4 in the home. Lisa has an absolute advantage in both tasks, but a comparative advantage in market work. She is ten times more productive in the market than at home; he is only twice as productive.

Absolute advantage: the capacity to produce more units of output than a competitor can for any given level of resource use.

Comparative advantage: the relative advantage in production or cost based on comparative ratios such that either the absolute advantage is greatest or the absolute disadvantage is smallest.

1. Adam Smith, *The Wealth of Nations* (New York: Random House, Modern Library edition, 1937), p. 422.

Her comparative advantage (largest advantage) is in the market; his comparative advantage (smallest disadvantage) is in the home. She should work in the market; and he should work at home. Their combined productivity would be $104 per hour (her $100 market rate plus his $4 home rate). If instead Gary worked in the market and Lisa worked at home, their combined productivity would be $18 (his $8 market rate plus her $10 home rate). They would be $86 (equal to $104 − $18) better off by utilizing their comparative advantage, with Lisa working in the market, where her comparative advantage lies (her greatest absolute advantage, $92 over his) and Gary working at home, where his comparative advantage lies (his absolute disadvantage is smallest, $6 less than hers).

Table 17.2 shows these absolute and comparative differences for nations. With the same labor, capital, and other resources, the United States can produce thirty units of textiles; Japan can produce twenty-five. If the same resources are applied to beef production, the United States still outproduces Japan, by ninety units to twenty-five. Under such conditions, one might think that trade with Japan could not possibly benefit the United States. The relevant question is not how efficient the United States is in absolute terms, however, but whether the people of the United States can make a better deal by trading with Japan than they can make by trading among themselves.

This is determined by examining the comparative advantage, or the ratios of advantage or differences in relative efficiencies. A nation has a comparative advantage where (1) its absolute advantage is greatest or (2) its absolute disadvantage is smallest. Generally, a nation will have a comparative advantage in those products that require in their production a large proportion of factors that are relatively abundant and inexpensive in that nation and a comparative disadvantage in those productions that are relatively scarce and expensive in that nation. It is a technological fact that different products generally require in their production different proportions of the factors.

TABLE 17.2 Comparative Cost Advantages, Beef and Textiles, United States and Japan

	Maximum Units of Textiles (Zero Beef Units)	Maximum Units of Beef (Zero Textile Units)	Domestic Cost Ratios in Each Nation	Mutually Beneficial Trade Ratio, Both Nations
United States	30	90	1 textile costs 3 beef	1 textile trades for 2 beef
Japan	25	25	1 textile costs 1 beef	

To determine which is the better deal, we must compare the costs of production. We know that there is an uneven distribution of economic resources among nations. This produces differences in productive capacities based on these differences in relative factor endowments. If each nation produces and trades the products in which it has a comparative cost advantage, trade can raise both their incomes. Remember that a comparative advantage is the capacity to produce a product at a lower cost than a competitor, in terms of the goods that must be given up. The United States may have an absolute advantage in the production of both beef and textiles, but it may have a comparative advantage only in the production of beef. In other words, the United States must forgo fewer units of textiles to obtain a unit of beef than Japan. Although a single nation could theoretically have an absolute advantage in all commodities, it could not have a comparative advantage in all commodities. With two nations and two commodities, *if a nation has a comparative advantage in one commodity it must have a comparative disadvantage in the other commodity*. Having a comparative advantage in beef necessarily means the United States cannot have a comparative advantage in textiles—a point that will become clear shortly.

In a sense, the United States trades with itself every time it produces either beef or textiles. If it produces beef, it incurs an opportunity cost: it gives up some of the textiles it could have produced. If it produces textiles, it gives up some beef. In Table 17.2, every time the United States produces one unit of textiles, it gives up three units of beef. (It can produce either thirty units of textiles or ninety of beef—a ratio of one to three.) Thus the United States can benefit by trading beef for textiles if it can give up fewer than three units of beef for each unit of textiles it gets from Japan.

Japan, on the other hand, gives up an advantage of one unit of beef for each unit of textiles it produces. If Japan can get more than one unit of beef for each unit of textiles it trades, it too can gain by trading. In short, if the trade ratio is greater than one unit of beef for one unit of textiles but less than three units of beef for one unit of textiles, trade will benefit both countries. The United States will gain because it has to give up fewer units of beef—two, perhaps, instead of three—than if it tried to produce the textiles itself. It can produce three units of beef, trade two of them for a textile unit, and have one extra beef unit left over—or it can trade all three units of beef for one and one-half units of textiles. Japan can produce one unit of textiles and trade it for two units of beef, gaining one textile unit in the process.

Both nations can gain from such a trade because each is specializing in the production of a good for which it has a comparative opportunity cost advantage.[2] Even though the United States has an absolute cost advantage in both products, Japan has a comparative advantage in textiles. One unit of textiles costs Japan one unit of beef; the same unit of textiles costs the United States three units of beef. Similarly, the United States has a compar-

_____

2. This specialization will be partial in the most likely case of increasing cost. With constant-cost (such as the linear production possibilities curves discussed later) or decreasing-cost, the specialization may be complete.

TABLE 17.3 Mutual Gains from Trade in Beef and Textiles, United States and Japan

	United States	Japan	Total, U.S. and Japan
Production and consumption levels before international trade	15 textiles 45 beef	3 textiles 22 beef	18 textiles 67 beef
Production levels in anticipation of international trade (complete specialization assumed)	0 textiles 90 beef	25 textiles 0 beef	25 textiles 90 beef

At an exchange ratio of 2 beef for 1 textile, United States and Japan agree to trade 40 beef for 20 textiles.

	United States	Japan	Total, U.S. and Japan
Consumption levels after international trade	20 textiles 50 beef	5 textiles 40 beef	25 textiles 90 beef
Increased consumption (before-trade consumption levels subtracted)	5 textiles 5 beef	2 textiles 18 beef	7 textiles 23 beef

ative cost advantage in the production of beef. One unit of beef costs the United States only one-third unit of textiles; it costs Japan a whole unit. If each country specializes in the commodities for which it has a comparative cost advantage, the two nations can save resources for use in further production.

Table 17.3 shows the gains in production each nation can realize under such an arrangement. Before trade, the United States produces 15 units of textiles and 45 of beef; Japan produces 3 units of textiles and 22 of beef. Total production is therefore 18 units of textiles and 67 units of beef. With trade, the United States produces 90 units of beef and Japan produces 25 units of textiles. At an international trade ratio of 1 unit of textiles to 2 units of beef, suppose the two nations agree to trade 40 units of beef for 20 units of textiles. The United States gets more beef—50 units as opposed to 45— and more textiles—20 units as opposed to 15. Japan also gets more of both commodities. Through specialization, total world production has risen from 18 to 25 units of textiles and from 67 to 90 units of beef. Both nations can now consume more of both commodities. In a very important sense, the world's aggregate real income has increased.

The same gain in aggregate welfare is shown graphically in Figure 17.2. On the left side of the figure, the U.S. production possibilities curve extends from 30 units of textiles on the horizontal axis to 90 units of beef on the vertical axis. Japan's production capability is shown on the right. Without trade, the United States chooses to produce at point *a*, 15 textile units and 45 beef units. At an exchange ratio of 2 beef units for 1 textile unit, the

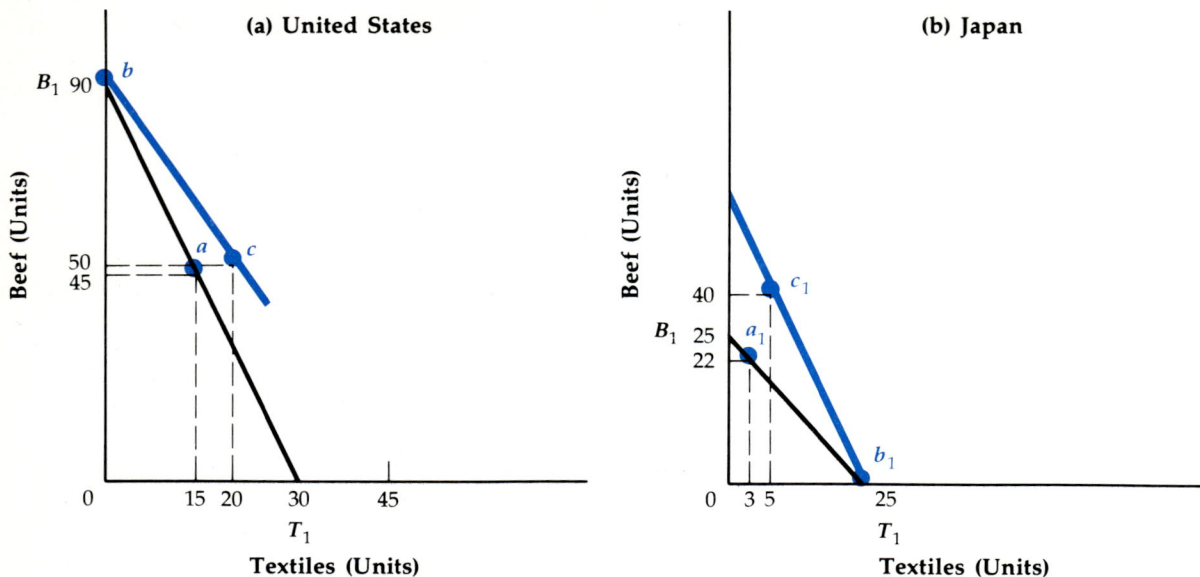

FIGURE 17.2 Production Gains from International Trade

The United States can produce any combination of beef and textiles along its production possibilities curve B_1T_1 (left panel). Without trade, it will choose to produce at point a, 45 units of beef and 15 units of textiles. If given the opportunity to trade two units of beef for one unit of textiles, however, the United States will specialize completely in beef (point b) and trade beef for textiles along the color line. Through trade, the United States moves from a to c, exporting 40 units of beef (90 units produced minus 50 consumed) and importing 20 units of textiles. In the process the nation increases its consumption of both beef and textiles, from 45 units of beef and 15 units of textiles to 50 units of beef and 20 units of textiles. (The color line does not intersect the horizontal axis because the United States cannot get more than 25 units of textiles from Japan.)

At the same time trade permits Japan (right panel) to shift its consumption from the black production possibilities curve to the color curve. By producing at b_1 and exporting 20 units of textiles in exchange for 40 units of beef, Japan too can expand its consumption, from a_1 to c_1.

United States can move up and to the left on its production possibilities curve. At the extreme, it will produce at point b, 90 units of beef and no textiles. It can then trade along the color outer line, exchanging 40 beef units for 20 textile units (point c). Through trade, the United States realizes a gain in aggregate welfare represented by the distance between points a and c. In other words, international trade permits the United States to consume at a point beyond its own limited production possibilities curve (the black line in the graph). In the same way, Japan realizes a gain in welfare equal to the difference between its consumption before trade, a_1, and its consumption after trade, c_1.

In the long run, a country's imports are paid for by its exports. Thus, by engaging in international trade, according to comparative advantage, a country gains by reducing its social opportunity cost. The social opportunity cost of imports is the exports required to pay for the imports. If the resources used to produce exports are less than those required to produce the goods domestically, there is a net social economic gain.

The Distributional Effects of Trade

▲ 3. What are the distributional effects of international trade?

As we have seen, even a nation that has an absolute advantage in every production process can benefit from trade. In reality, no such nation exists, but that just underscores the point that even in the unlikeliest of conditions, we can make the case for free trade. Furthermore, if voluntary trade takes place we must assume that both parties perceive that they will gain. Why else would they agree to the arrangement? How much each nation gains depends on the **terms of trade**—the ratio at which one commodity can be traded or exchanged for another commodity internationally; or on an aggregate basis, it is the ratio of the price of exports to the price of imports. The more favorable a nation's terms of trade, and therefore its exchange rate, the larger its share of gain in enhanced output.

Terms of trade: the ratio at which one commodity can be traded or exchanged for another commodity internationally; or on an aggregate basis, it is the ratio of the price of exports to the price of imports.

International trade remains a controversial subject, for although nations gain from trade, individuals within those nations may not. Individual gains tend to go to the firms that produce goods and services for export, losses tend to go to the firms that produce goods and services that are imported under free trade.

Gains to Exporters

Exporters of domestic goods gain from international trade because the market for their goods expands, increasing demand for their products. The increase in their revenue can be seen in Figure 17.3. When the demand curve shifts from D_1 to D_2, producers' revenues rise from P_1Q_2 (point a) to P_2Q_3 (point b). The more price-elastic or flatter the supply function (S), the larger the change in quantity and the smaller the change in price. The increase in revenues is equal to the shaded L-shaped area $P_2Q_3Q_2aP_1$. Producers benefit because they receive greater profits, equal to the shaded area above the supply curve, P_2baP_1. Workers and suppliers of raw materials benefit because their services are in greater demand, and therefore more costly. The cost of producing additional units for export is equal to the shaded area below the supply curve, Q_2abQ_3.

This graphic suggests why farmers supported the sales of wheat to the Soviet Union that began in the early 1970s. They complained loudly when the U.S. government suspended sales temporarily for political reasons. Many consumers and members of Congress objected to the wheat sales, however, on the ground that they would increase the domestic price of wheat and therefore of bread. In a narrow sense, consumers of exported products have an interest in restricting their exportation. Yet in the broad context of international trade, restrictions can work against the private interests of individuals, including even consumers of bread. Trade is ultimately a two-way street. To import goods and services that can be produced more cheaply abroad than at home, a nation must export something else. No nation will continually export part of what it produces without getting something in return. To the extent that exports are restricted to suit the special interests of some group, imports of other commodities also are restricted. Restrictions on the exportation of wheat may hold down the price of bread, but they can also increase the price of imported goods, like radios and television sets.

Losses to Firms Competing with Imports

While consumers gain from increased imports, domestic producers may lose from increased competition. Foreign producers can gain a foothold in the domestic market in three ways: (1) by providing a better product than domestic firms; (2) by selling essentially the same product as domestic firms, but at a lower price; and (3) by providing a product previously unavailable in the domestic market. Most people welcome the importation of a previously unavailable product, but producers who face competition from foreign suppliers have an incentive to object to importation. If imports are allowed, the domestic supply of a good increases. Domestic competitors will sell less, and they may have to sell at a lower price. In short, the employ-

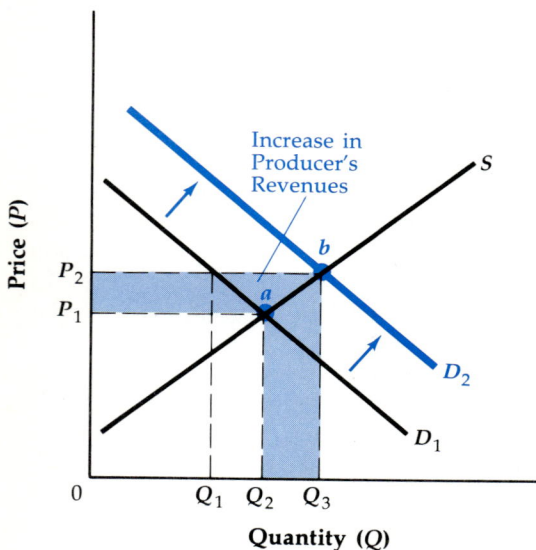

FIGURE 17.3 Gains from the Export Trade
The opening up of foreign markets to U.S. producers increases the demand for their products, from D_1 to D_2. As a result, domestic producers can raise their price from P_1 to P_2 and sell a larger quantity, Q_3 instead of Q_2. Revenues increase by the shaded area $P_2bQ_3Q_2aP_1$. The more price-elastic or flatter the supply function (S), the larger the change in quantity and the smaller the change in price.

ment opportunities and real income of domestic producers decline as a result of foreign competition.

Figure 17.4 shows the effects of importing foreign textiles. Without imports, demand is D and supply is S_1. In a competitive market, producers will sell Q_2 units at a price of P_2. Total receipts will be $P_2 \times Q_2$. The importation of foreign textiles increases the supply to S_2, dropping the price from P_2 to P_1. Because prices are lower, consumers increase their consumption from Q_2 to Q_3 and get more for their money. The more price-elastic or flatter the demand curve (D), the greater the change in quantity and the smaller the change in price.

Domestic firms, their employees, and their suppliers lose. Because the price is lower, domestic producers must move down their supply curve (S_1) to the lower quantity Q_1. Their revenues fall from P_2Q_2 to P_1Q_1. In other words, the revenues in the shaded L-shaped area $P_2aQ_2Q_1bP_1$ are lost. Of this total loss in revenues, owners of domestic firms lose the area above the supply curve, P_2abP_1. Workers and suppliers of raw materials lose the area below the supply curve, Q_2abQ_1. This is the cost domestic firms would incur in increasing production from Q_1 to Q_2, the payments that would be made to domestic workers and suppliers in the absence of foreign competition. If workers and other resources are employed in textiles because it is their best possible employment, the introduction of foreign products can be seen as a restriction on some workers' employment opportunities. In summary, while international trade lowers import prices and raises export prices in the domestic nation, the net impact is a reduced social opportunity cost curve that expands total output and consumption opportunities.

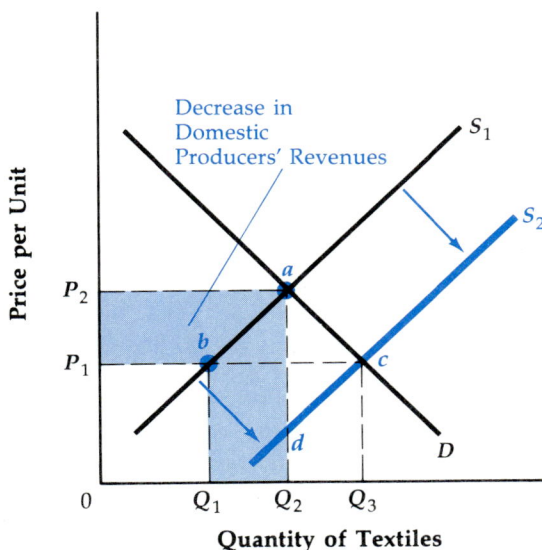

FIGURE 17.4 Losses from Competition with Imported Products
The opening up of the market to foreign trade increases the supply of textiles from S_1 to S_2. As a result, the price of textiles falls from P_2 to P_1, and domestic producers sell a lower quantity, Q_1 instead of Q_2. Consumers benefit from the lower price and the higher quantity of textiles they are able to buy, but domestic producers, workers, and suppliers lose. Producers' revenues drop by an amount equal to the shaded area P_2abP_1. Workers' and suppliers' payments drop by an amount equal to the shaded area Q_2abQ_1. Starting at point c, a tariff or tax equal to ad is levied, shifting the supply curve from S_2 to S_1. In an industry whose costs are increasing, the increase in price from P_1 to P_2 in the importing country is less than the increase in the tariff (ad), because a price fall in the exporting country absorbs some of the burden of the duty.

DIALOGUE
The Case for Textile Protection
James C. Self, Sr., Greenwood Mills, Inc.

When the question of international trade and the textile/apparel industry arises, those seeking to address the complex issues in print often ignore the facts of the real world. Example: The March 6th Associated Press story that appeared in numerous South Carolina newspapers, and was headlined "Double whammy, industry calls for protection, but imports machinery," is the one I read.

When textile manufacturers need new equipment, they are limited to buying machinery that is available. I know of only one American company that makes and sells a complement of yarn manufacturing machinery.

As for weaving machinery, in the late 1960s most American textile machinery manufacturers were acquired by nontextile conglomerates who greatly reduced funds for research and development. When our industry needed new weaving equipment, the more competitive machinery was available overseas. Today there is one domestic loom manufacturer; however, little is known about the sales volume of this equipment.

Dyeing and finishing machinery is available from both domestic and foreign sources; however, all roller printing machinery is produced overseas.

The U.S. textile/apparel industry has long been the whipping boy of our federal government. This was recognized in 1980 by then-presidential candidate Ronald Reagan, who in a letter to Sen. Strom Thurmond, wrote: "The Multifiber Arrangement (MFA) which is supposed to provide orderly international trade in fibers, textiles and apparels, was first negotiated under a Republican administration. The MFA expires at the end of 1981 and needs to be strengthened by relating import growth from all sources to domestic market growth. I shall work to achieve that goal."

Mr. Reagan's pledge proved to be nothing more than political rhetoric and, under his administration, imports flooded this country in record numbers. Proof of this can be seen in the textile and apparel deficit figures for 1980–1987:

1980—$4.7 billion
1981—$6.4 billion
1982—$7.9 billion
1983—$10.6 billion
1984—$16.2 billion
1985—$18.2 billion
1986—$21.3 billion
1987—$25.0 billion (estimated)

Interestingly, these quota increases are not limited to the underdeveloped nations of the world. The Canada-U.S. Free Trade Agreement is filled with serious implications for the U.S. textile industry. Moreover, a similar agreement with Mexico is expected to be announced soon.

The fact is our government has repeatedly failed to enforce the agreements already in force.

Now, Vice President George Bush has taken the position that we don't need to pass the Textile and Apparel Trade Act; we only need to enforce the laws already on the books. Where has Vice President Bush been for the last eight years? Is this more political rhetoric? Will we continue to sit by and watch the jobs of our friends and neighbors exported? I hope not!

Our industry employs nearly two million workers in all 50 states, and pays more than $25 billion a year in wages. It also:

○ Has more employees than the steel and automobile industries combined

○ Is the largest manufacturing employer of women and minorities

○ Employs two million additional workers in support and allied industries

○ Is composed of 5,000 textile companies; 20,000 apparel companies; 120,000 wool growing and shearing operations and 41,000 cotton farms and allied companies

○ Contributes $46 billion to the U.S. gross national product (includes fiber)

Part of the solution to our problems can be found in a recent article by Alan Wm. Wolff, former deputy U.S. special trade representative for the steel industry.

"Given the current international competitive environment, U.S. trade policy should not be based on ideological factors—free trade vs. protectionism—but on a realistic assessment of where the national interest lies.

"In a world in which trade in textiles and apparel is not governed primarily by market forces, but by extensive government intervention, the question remains what policy the United States should follow. World trade in textiles and apparel should be liberalized, but the initial burden of moving toward that liberalization lies on countries other than the United States.

"First and foremost, the major textile and apparel exporting nations should reduce their own protective barriers and eliminate their subsidies, export promotion schemes, cartels and other practices which currently distort international trade in textiles and apparel.

"Second, the major industrialized nations, most notably Japan and the European Economic Community, should open their markets to a degree commensurate with the United States, so that the burden of absorbing developing country exports is shared more equally.

"It is clear that the United States cannot—without incurring unacceptable costs—unilaterally open its market to imports while other markets remain heavily protected, nor can it commit its industry to a wholly unregulated competitive struggle with foreign firms which enjoy cost advantages such as subsidies and the absence of minimum wage, safety and environmental standards. Nor can the United States remain, in effect, the world's market of last resort, absorbing most of the developing countries' exports, simply because Japan and the EEC have implemented more restrictive import regimes."

A good example of other markets being heavily protected, as referred to by Mr. Wolff, is that a $10,000 automobile imported into Korea actually would sell for more than $47,000 with all duties and taxes added.

In summary, I believe in the U.S. textile/apparel industry and what it means to this nation of ours. All our industry asks is a chance to compete internationally on a level playing field. But to accomplish this, we must replace the myth of "free trade" with a "real world" policy of fair trade. And, of course, we can't do it without the support of our federal government, namely, speedy enactment of the Textile and Apparel Trade Act.

Reprinted with permission from the *Greenville (S.C.) News/Piedmont*, April 3, 1988, p. 3E.

The Case Against Textile Protection

Richard B. McKenzie, Clemson University

The textile industry, already one of our most protected industries, once again is looking to Washington for more restrictions on imports.

Under the auspices of the Fiber, Fabric and Apparel Coalition for Trade, the industry is fortifying its extensive lobbying efforts in Washington with an intensive television advertising campaign focused on the textile-producing states of Georgia, Alabama and North and South Carolina. What the PR campaign fails to mention, however, is that output in the industry and profits of many textile firms are at record highs and that the industry is

The Case Against Textile Protection

continued

operating at more than 90 percent capacity, a performance rate well above the national average for all industries.

The textile coalition also does not mention that, while still below their earlier peak, textile and apparel exports in 1987 (measured in constant dollars) were 36 percent above their low of 1985 (although still 25 percent below their peak of 1980), that unemployment rates in many textile states have been falling, or that employment in the textile industry actually increased in 1987.

The TV ads claim that between 1980 and 1986, 1,000 U.S. textile and apparel plants were closed and 350,000 textile and apparel jobs were lost to imports. These statistics do not bear up under scrutiny. This is because most of the lost textile jobs were eliminated not because of imports but because of the installation of more efficient and less labor-intensive equipment. Between 1973 and 1984 employment in the textile industry decreased by 270,000 to 710,000 from 980,000. Over the same period, worker productivity (measured in real dollar shipments per worker) rose by 49 percent. (Productivity advancements have been more dramatic over the past three years due to record investment levels.)

Productivity in various processes increased several hundred percent between 1970 and 1985 thanks to new, often computerized equipment. For example, productivity in fiber extrusion (the process of forming man-made fibers) increased by 300 percent. Air-jet looms—now the emerging norm for the production of long-run fabrics used for sheets and curtains—are more than 300 percent more productive than the looms they have replaced.

My research indicates that productivity increases alone could account for the loss of approximately 225,000 jobs, or 83 percent of the total decrease in employment in the textile industry between 1973 and 1984. In addition, other jobs were lost—and an untold number of textile and apparel plants were closed—because some firms couldn't keep up with the competition for labor and other resources from expanding non-textile firms in growing local economies.

Amid all the clamor for more protection from imports, it is refreshing to remember that employment and wages have risen in many states where the textile industry is heavily concentrated. Between the end of 1986 and 1987 employment in North and South Carolina, two very important textile states, rose by 2.6 percent (or by 127,000 workers) while total U.S. employment rose by 1.6 percent. Between 1980 and 1987, the average wage of textile production workers rose in real terms and increased from 78 to 82 percent of the average wage of all production workers in the country.

The protection the textile and apparel industry seeks would not, on balance, save American jobs, nor would it come cheap. Economist Laura Baughman, in a study for the International Business and Economic Research Corporation, a Washington-based consulting firm, estimates that the Textile and Apparel Trade Bill of 1987 would wipe out at least as many jobs in other American industries—most notably in the retail trade. It would also force consumers to spend an average of $8 billion more a year on imported and domestic textile products over the next decade. This means that each textile job saved (worth an average of $17,000 in annual wages to textile workers) might cost American consumers, on average, as much as $262,000 a year.

The industry tests the public's credulity when it suggests that every textile and apparel plant that closed in this decade did so solely because of imports. The public is asked to believe that none of the plants in question was mismanaged, had excessive costs, or was simply outmoded in an era of tremendous technological advancements in the textile industry.

The truth—as evidenced by recently expanding exports—is that there are U.S. textile firms that can compete with the best producers in the world, especially now that the dollar is weaker. American producers have been responsible for the closing of American plants—their own plants and ones that couldn't keep pace when they introduced new and more productive equipment. Contrary to what the industry suggests in its PR campaign, the count of lost textile jobs is a tribute to a revitalized and aggressive American industry. The elimination of jobs is one of the most difficult tasks of any economy, and the textile industry should be proud of its achievements in reducing employment.

By tying its economic future to government protection, the industry may well be worsening its competitive problems. Many young people may be understandably reluctant to go to work for an industry that is constantly bad-mouthing its ability to compete and whose future might turn from bright to bleak with changing political winds in Washington.

Indeed, the constant talk of gloom and doom appears to be discouraging university students from considering textiles as a career. Between 1983 and 1987, the number of university students majoring in technical fields (for example, textile engineering and chemistry) within the country's principal textile programs fell by 25 percent (from 1,409 to 1,050 majors).

Wilbur Newcomb, editor of the American Textile International, a trade magazine, took a courageous stand last year when he acknowledged in an editorial that additional textile protection may do nothing more than insulate from competition domestic producers who continue to operate with "50-year-old fly shuttle looms."

He added: "The screaming and yelling for a new textile bill can only fall on deaf ears right now, especially if the screamers really only want to 'protect' their totally outmoded plants. Now is the time to buy and build. Sales and profits are high. Stock values are higher. Consumers want to 'buy American.' Let's give them the best products at the best prices. But that can only be done with the latest technology. We can't keep crying 'imports' to cover large pockets of inefficiency remaining. Instead we need to make ours one of the most modern manufacturing industries in the nation—modern throughout."

Protecting the industry from competition is not likely to make it more competitive any more than forcing rival players to wear ankle weights would make a basketball team more competitive. On the contrary, protectionism can only lessen the market pressures that helped spur the industry to improve its productivity. It is ironic that the industry imports half its machinery from abroad, presumably because foreign machinery is cheaper and of better quality. Consumers should also have the right to purchase the best textile products, without being encumbered by trade restrictions.

The Effects of Trade Restrictions Such as Tariffs and Quotas

▲ **4. What do trade restrictions such as tariffs and quotas do to international trade?**

Tariff: a special tax or duty on imported or exported goods that can be a percentage of the price (*ad valorem* duty) or a specific amount per unit of the product (specific duty).

Quota: a physical or dollar value limit—mandatory or voluntary—on the amount of a good that can be imported or exported during some specified period of time.

Because foreign competition hurts some individuals, domestic producers, workers, and suppliers have an incentive to seek government restrictions on the imports of tradables. Of course, some industries such as communications, services, and utilities are largely nontradables and are therefore largely insulated from foreign competition without trade restrictions. Two forms of protection are commonly used, tariffs and quotas. A tariff is a special tax or duty on imported or exported goods that can be a percentage of the price (*ad valorem* duty) or a specific amount per unit of the product (specific duty). A tariff may be imposed to raise money for the levying country—typically, revenues are modest on commodities not produced in the levying country—or in the more likely case, to protect some industry against the cold winds of competition. A quota is a physical or dollar value limit—mandatory or voluntary—on the amount of a good that can be imported or exported during some specified period of time. There are other nontariff barriers such as controlling the flow of foreign exchange, licensing requirements, or health, quality, or safety restriction on products.

If tariffs are imposed on a foreign good such as textiles, the supply of textiles will decrease—say, from S_2 toward S_1 in Figure 17.4—and the price of imports will rise. Domestic producers will raise their prices too, and domestic production will go up. If the tariff is high and all foreign textiles are excluded, the supply will shift all the way back to S_1. A small tariff will have a more modest effect, shifting the supply curve only part of the way back toward S_1. The price of textiles will rise and domestic producers will expand their production, but imports will continue to come into the country. How much the price rises and the quantity falls after the imposition of the tariff depends on how price-elastic or flat the demand curve (D) is. The more elastic D is, the greater the fall in quantity and the greater the rise in price. The imposition of a duty can cause the taxed good in the importing country to increase by exactly the amount of the duty, less than the duty, or in the extreme case, not at all (depending on price elasticity). In the most likely case (of increasing cost conditions and a rising supply curve) a tariff will cause the price to increase in the importing country by less than the amount of the duty as the price falls in the foreign country. The tariff will cause the domestic and foreign price to differ by exactly the amount of the tariff, but the price increase in the importing country is equal to the tariff minus the fall in price in the exporting country. Thus, in Figure 17.4, starting from point c, the increase in the price in the importing country from P_1 to P_2 is less than the tariff equal to ad, shifting the supply curve from S_2 to S_1 as part of the duty is shifted to the exporting country where the price falls. For instance, a tariff of $3 per unit may cause the import price to rise by $2 and the export price to fall by $1 with both nations absorbing part of the burden of the tariff. Who bears the biggest burden is a matter of relative price elasticity, just as whether buyers or sellers bear the burden of a domestic excise tax. As always, the more inelastic the demand of the buyers and the more elastic the supply of the sellers, the bigger burden of any tax—domestic (e.g., excise) or foreign (e.g., an import duty)—that falls on the buyers.

A quota has the same general effect as a tariff, although its price-cost effect can be much more drastic. They both reduce the market supply, raise the market price, and encourage domestic production, thereby helping domestic producers and harming domestic consumers. A quota, however, can sever international price-cost links because the market mechanism for relating the prices of different nations is artificially stopped from functioning. Nonetheless, quotas are sometimes imposed by nations because they are a more certain and precise technique of control, and can be changed by administrative decree.

There are three main differences between quotas and tariffs. First, quotas firmly restrict the amount of a product that can be imported, regardless of market conditions. A quota may specify how much oil may be imported each day or how much sugar each year. Tariffs, on the other hand, permit any level of importation for which consumers are willing to pay. Thus, if demand for the product increases, imports may rise. (There is a hybrid called a "tariff quota" that sets the amount beyond which higher tariffs apply, but does not set a fixed limit on importation or exportation).

The first Reagan administration imposed quotas on steel, copper, textiles, and autos from Japan. In 1984 the so-called voluntary restraint program forced Japan to restrict auto sales in the United States to 1.84 million cars. Foreign cars now represent about 25 percent of U.S. sales. Because Japanese supply was not allowed to keep pace with the rapidly expanding U.S. demand, the price of Japanese cars rose, more expensive models were imported, and consumers faced longer waiting lists for Japanese cars. The prices of American cars also rose. These consequences led to the termination of the voluntary restraint program in 1985.

The second major difference between tariffs and quotas is that quotas are typically specified for each important foreign producer. Otherwise, all foreign producers would rush to sell their goods before the quota was reached. When quotas are rationed in this way, more detailed government enforcement is required. Tariffs place no such restriction on individual producers. Moreover, the tariff is collected by the government in custom duties while price enhancement with a quota goes as a windfall gain to the fortunate few with import licenses.

Finally, quotas enable foreign firms to raise their prices and extract more income from consumers. One economist estimated that the Reagan administration's voluntary restraint program permitted Japanese auto producers to raise their prices high enough to take an additional $2,500 per car, or $5 billion, out of the American market.[3] As a result of the protectionist shield, U.S. automakers raised domestic car prices $1,000 per car, or $8 billion per year, in 1984 and 1985. Tariffs, on the other hand, force foreign firms to lower their prices to offset the increase from the tariff. They also generate income for the federal government. Although tariffs

---

3. Robert Crandell, "Assessing the Impact of the Automobile Export Restraints upon U.S. Automobile Prices," mimeo, Brookings Institution, December 1985.

and quotas promote a less efficient allocation of the world's scarce resources, because of the private benefits to be gained from tariffs and quotas we should expect an industry to seek them as long as their market benefits exceed their political cost. Politicians are likely to expect votes and campaign contributions in return for tariff legislation that generates highly visible benefits to special interests. Producers (and labor) will usually make the necessary contributions, because the elimination of foreign competition promises increased revenues in the protected industries. The difference between the increase in profits due to import restrictions and the amount spent on political activity can be seen as a kind of profit in itself. Surprisingly, protectionism may sometimes also be supported by exporters, as a tariff or quota can stimulate net exports. Since protectionism also causes the exchange rate to appreciate, however, this discourages exports and offsets partially or wholly the tariff-driven increase in net exports.

Consumers, on the other hand, have reason to oppose tariffs or quotas on imported products. Such legislation inevitably causes prices to rise, as a tariff amounts to a subsidy to the domestic producer of the dutiable product, paid for largely by the consumers of that product in the form of higher prices. Consumers typically do not offer very much resistance, however, because the effects of tariffs and quotas are hard to perceive. Unlike a sales tax, the cost of a tariff is not rung up separately at the cash register, and many consumers do not reason through the complex effects of a tariff on consumer prices. In fact, many, if not most, consumers feel that tariffs on foreign automobile, steel, or copper producers are good for the nation and for themselves. "Buy American" slogans and advertisements emphasizing the need to preserve American jobs are generally effective in swaying public opinion. One comprehensive investigation showed that protection in thirty-one countries cost consumers $53 billion in 1984, while providing only $40 billion in benefits to the producers.[4]

As a group, consumers have less incentive to oppose tariffs than industry has to support them, as the costs to individual consumers and taxpayers are negligible and largely hidden. The benefits of a tariff accrue principally to a relatively small group of firms, whose lobby may already be well entrenched in Washington. These firms have a strong incentive to be fully informed on the issue and to make campaign contributions, but the harmful effects of a tariff are diffused over an extremely large group of consumers. The financial burden any one consumer bears may be very slight, particularly if the tariff in question is small, as most tariffs are. As a result, the individual consumer has little incentive to become informed on tariff legislation or to make political contributions to lobbies that support such legislation. Although consumers as a whole may share an interest in opposing tariffs, collective action must still be undertaken by individuals—and individuals will not incur the cost of organizing unless they expect to receive compensating private benefit.

At some level of increased cost, of course, consumers will find the necessary incentive to oppose tariff legislation. For this reason Congress

---

4. Gary C. Hufbauer, et al., *Trade Protection in the United States: 31 Case Studies* (Washington, D.C.: Institute for International Economics, 1986).

rarely passes tariffs high enough to make importation totally unprofitable. Even low tariffs reduce the nation's real income while redistributing it toward protected sectors. The size of the pie is reduced, but the protected few get a bigger slice. In spite of all the impediments to free trade imposed by the U.S. economy, there has been a substantial increase in our dollar volume of imports and exports over the last thirty years. Similarly, world trade has increased in the last three decades. Over 15 percent of the world's production is now consumed in a different nation than where it was produced. Put differently, the dollar value of imports to all countries has increased tenfold since 1960.

According to Alan S. Blinder,[5] the case against protectionism, described as a negative-sum game, where the losing consumers lose more than the winning protected producers win, involves even more problems. There are four other problems with trade restrictions. First, protectionism allows high-cost producers that would otherwise fail to survive. Second, trade restrictions have a habit of affecting other industries. For example, automobiles need protection because the ball bearings, steel, and textiles that provide inputs to automobiles are protected. Third, foreign nations often retaliate against protectionism. Tit-for-tat is the modus operandi in international trade: Country A raises barriers on product X because Country B did it to product Y. Fourth, trade restrictions aren't really job-saving or job-creating, but job-swapping. Protectionism raises the exchange rate, hurting exports in unprotected industries. Because in the long run the value of exports must be equal to the value of imports, we end up swapping jobs in efficient unprotected industries for those in inefficient protected industries.

The Case for Free Trade

▲ 5. What is good about free international trade?

We have seen how international trade can on balance increase the total incomes of the nations engaged in it, although export producers gain and import-substitute producers lose. By extension, we can conclude that anything that restricts the scope of trade between nations generally reduces their real incomes. To the extent that trade is a two-way street—that exports trade for imports, at least in the long run—a reduction in imports brings a reduction in exports. From our imports the Japanese get the dollars they need to buy American exports. If we reduce our imports, they will have fewer funds with which to buy from us. For this reason, U.S. farmers, who sell approximately one-third of their crops in foreign markets, actively opposed the protectionist movement led by textile, steel, and copper firms in the 1980s.

Yet what is true for one sector of the economy is not necessarily true for all. If all sectors are protected by tariffs, it is possible (but not inevitable) that all experience a drop in real income. Figure 17.5 illustrates the case of an economy with two industries, automobiles and textiles. Both industries must compete with imports. If neither seeks protection, both will operate in

5. Alan Blinder, *Hard Heads, Soft Hearts* (Reading, Mass.: Addison-Wesley, 1987), pp. 118–119, but the entire Chapter 4, pp. 109–135, is a delight to read.

cell I, at a combined real income of $50 ($20 for the textile industry and $30 for the automobile industry). If the textile industry seeks protection but the auto industry does not, they will move to cell II, where tariffs raise the textile industry's income from $20 to $23. The automotive sector's income falls to $25, so that the two industries' combined real income falls to $48. Consumers get fewer textiles at a higher price.

Similarly, if the auto industry seeks protection while the textile industry does not, the economy will move from cell I to cell III. Again, total real income falls from $50 to $49, but this time the auto industry is better off. Its income rises from $30 to $34, while the textile industry's income falls to

	Textile Industry Without Tariff Protection		Textile Industry With Tariff Protection	
Automobile Industry Without Tariff Protection	**Cell I**		**Cell II**	
	Real Income, Textile	Real Income, Auto	Real Income, Textile	Real Income, Auto
	$20	$30	$23	$25
Automobile Industry With Tariff Protection	**Cell III**		**Cell IV**	
	Real Income, Textile	Real Income, Auto	Real Income, Textile	Real Income, Auto
	$15	$34	$17	$26

FIGURE 17.5   Effects of Tariff Protection on Individual Industries: Case 1
If neither the textile nor the automobile industry obtains tariff protection, the economy will earn its highest possible collective income (cell I), but each industry has an incentive to obtain tariff protection for itself. If the textile industry alone seeks protection (cell II), its income will rise while the auto industry's income falls. If the auto industry alone seeks protection, its income will rise while textile income falls. If both obtain protection, the economy will end up in cell IV, its worst possible position. Income in both sectors will fall.

$15. Obviously, if one industry seeks protection, the other has an incentive to follow suit. If the textile industry counters with a tariff of its own, the economy will move from cell III to cell IV, and the industry's real income will rise from $15 to $17.

Without some constraint on both sectors, then, each has an interest in seeking protection regardless of what the other does. Yet if the economy winds up in cell IV, total real income will be lower than under any other conditions: only $43. Obviously the best course for the economy as a whole is to prohibit tariffs altogether, and in an economy with only two sectors, the cost of reaching an agreement is manageable. In the real world, however, there are many economic sectors, and the costs of reaching a decision are much greater.

In Figure 17.5, both industries end up with lower real incomes in cell IV, but in reality, the effects of multiple tariffs will be different in different sectors of the economy. Although total real income will fall, several sectors may realize individual gains. Consider Figure 17.6. Although total real income falls from cell I ($50) to cell IV ($48), the auto sector's income rises (from $30 to $31). In this case the textile sector bears the brunt of tariff protection, and the auto sector has a compelling interest in obtaining protective tariffs. The sectors of the economy that are most adept at manipulating the political process will be least willing to accept free trade.

Although it is true that for a nation some trade is better than no trade, it is not necessarily true that free trade is better than restricted trade. Even though protectionism promotes economic inefficiency in the aggregate, a nation may under certain conditions act like a monopolist and improve its share of the gains through trade restrictions. Similarly, the owners of relatively scarce factors of production may be better off with little or no trade.

Thus the case for free trade is a subtle one. As always, special-interest groups—entrepreneurs, labor organizations, consumer groups—will pursue their individual interests, competing for favors and benefits the same way they compete in the marketplace. Yet if all are to be treated equally by government, we must make the choice between free trade for all and protection for all.

Economists generally choose free trade for all, because of its obvious benefits to the nation as a whole. There are some legitimate exceptions to that rule, such as the required domestic production of public goods, which are discussed below. Yet even trade restrictions necessary for the public good are abused by those who would secure protection for private purposes.

The Case for Restricted Trade

6. What arguments in favor of restricted international trade are valid?

Proponents of tariffs rarely argue publicly that they will serve private interests, raise prices, and reduce the availability of goods. Instead, they typically advocate tariffs as the most efficient means of accomplishing some national objective. Any private benefits that would accrue to protected industries are generally portrayed as insignificant side effects.

	Textile Industry Without Tariff Protection		Textile Industry With Tariff Protection	
Automobile Industry Without Tariff Protection	Cell I		Cell II	
	Real Income, Textile	Real Income, Auto	Real Income, Textile	Real Income, Auto
	$20	$30	$23	$25
Automobile Industry With Tariff Protection	Cell III		Cell IV	
	Real Income, Textile	Real Income, Auto	Real Income, Textile	Real Income, Auto
	$15	$34	$17	$31

FIGURE 17.6   Effects of Tariff Protection on Individual Industries: Case 2
In this more realistic case, the auto industry gains from tariff protection, even if both sectors are protected (cell IV). The textile industry's income falls from $20 (cell I) to $17 (cell IV), but the auto industry's income rises from $30 (cell I) to $31 (cell IV). Thus the auto industry has no incentive to agree to the elimination of tariffs.

Although most arguments in favor of tariffs camouflage the underlying issues, one is partially valid. It has to do with the maintenance of national security.

The Need for National Security

Protariff arguments based on national or military security stress the need for a strong defense industry. If imports are completely unrestricted, certain industries needed in time of war or other national emergency could be undersold and run out of business by foreign competitors. In an emergency, the United States would then be dependent on possibly hostile foreign suppliers for essential defense equipment. (The nation could convert to production of war-related goods, but the conversion process might be prohibitively lengthy and complex.) Tariffs may create inefficiencies in the allocation of world resources, but that is one of the costs a nation must bear to maintain military self-sufficiency and hence a strong national defense.

Given the unsteady popularity of U.S. foreign policy and the uncertain support of allies, this argument has some merit. Other nations, like Israel, have found that they cannot count on the support of all their allies in time of war. Because France disagreed with Israeli policy in the Middle East, it held up shipment of spare parts for planes it had sold to Israel earlier. The United States could conceivably find itself in a similar position if it relies on foreign firms for planes, firearms, and oil.

Special-interest groups can easily abuse the national defense argument for tariffs. The textile industry, for example, promotes itself as a ready source of combat uniforms during wartime. Even candle manufacturers have petitioned Congress for increased tariff protection, on the grounds that candles are "a product required in the national defense."[6] In years past, U.S. oil producers, contending that a healthy domestic oil industry is vital to the national defense, have lobbied for protection from foreign oil imports. Although few would dispute the need for a reliable source of oil in wartime, the effects of a tariff are not entirely straightforward. By making foreign oil more expensive, a tariff increases consumption of domestic oil. Since oil is a finite resource, a tariff can ultimately make the United States more dependent on foreign energy sources in time of emergency.

Recent history illustrates the danger of dependence on foreign suppliers. In 1973, the OPEC oil cartel used U.S. dependence on its oil reserves as a bargaining tool in its efforts to reduce U.S. support for Israel. President Gerald Ford responded in 1974 by supporting a tariff on imported oil, to stimulate exploration for new domestic energy reserves. If the United States could become energy independent by the end of the 1980s, Ford argued, it would reduce the threat of political blackmail from the Middle East. In 1983, for the same reason, the Reagan administration granted tariff protection to specialty steel products, which are used extensively in high-technology defense systems.

Other Arguments

Most of the other arguments in support of tariffs are weak from a practical as well as a theoretical perspective. In fact, while protectionism is a growth industry in recent years, the costs to society exceed the benefits. It is sometimes argued that because workers are paid less in foreign countries, U.S. industries cannot hope to compete with foreign imports—but trade depends on the relative costs of production, not absolute wage rates in various nations. U.S. wages may be quite high in either absolute or relative terms. If

6. "Petition of the Candlemakers—1951," in *Readings in Economics,* ed. Paul Samuelson (New York: McGraw-Hill, 1973), 7th ed., p. 237.

U.S. workers are more productive than others, however, the costs of production can be lower in the United States than elsewhere.

The important point is what tariffs do to trade. In an earlier example of trade in textiles and beef, the United States was more efficient than Japan in the production of both products. That is, generally speaking, fewer resources were required to produce those goods in the United States than in Japan. Very possibly, the incomes of textile and beef workers would be higher in the United States than in Japan, but because Japanese firms had a comparative cost advantage in textiles (measured in terms of the number of units of beef forgone for each textile unit), they were able to undersell textile firms in the United States. If the U.S. imposed tariffs or quotas on imported textiles because Japan had a comparative advantage in that product, it would destroy the basis for trade between the two nations. Reducing imports will tend to reduce exports, at least in the long run.

A second questionable argument for tariffs is based on the faulty idea that the United States loses when money flows overseas in payment for imports. As Abraham Lincoln is reported to have said, "I don't know much about the tariff, but this I do know. When we trade with other countries, we get the goods and they get the money. When we trade with ourselves, we get the goods and the money."

Lincoln was clearly right when he said he did not know much about the tariff. He failed to recognize the real income benefits of international trade, which are reduced by tariffs. He seems to have confused the nation's welfare with its monetary holdings. It is true that if Americans buy goods from abroad, they get the goods and foreigners get the money.[7] What are foreigners going to do with the money they receive, however? If they never spend it, Americans will be better off, for they will have gotten some foreign goods in exchange for some paper bills, which are relatively cheap to print. At some point, however, foreign exporters will want to get something concrete in return for their labor and materials. They will use their dollars to buy goods from U.S. manufacturers. Again, trade is a give-and-take process, in which benefits flow to both sides.

A third argument often made is that foreign nations impose tariffs on U.S. goods; unless we respond in kind, foreign producers will have the advantage in both markets. This argument has a significant flaw. By restricting their imports, foreign nations reduce their ability to sell to the United States and other nations. To buy Japanese goods, for instance, Americans need yen. They get yen by selling to Japan. If Japan reduces its imports from the United States, Americans will have fewer yen to buy Japanese goods. So the Japanese are restricting their own exports with their tariffs. They harm themselves as well as Americans. If Americans respond to their actions by imposing tariffs of their own, they will reduce trade even further. The harm is compounded, not negated.

---

7. Actually, the transaction may not involve the transfer of paper money. It is more likely—as explained in the next chapter—that payment will be made by transferring funds from one bank account to another. The importer's bank balance will drop, and the exporter's bank balance will increase.

One sound reason for increasing tariffs is to strengthen our bargaining position in international trade conferences. By matching foreign restrictions, the United States may be able to force a multilateral reduction of tariffs. To the extent that all tariffs are reduced by such a strategy, world trade will be stimulated.

According to the fourth argument, tariffs increase workers' employment opportunities. If the government imposes tariffs on imported goods, the demand for American goods will rise. More workers will have jobs and can spend their income on goods and services produced by other Americans.

It is true that in the short run, more workers are likely to be hired because of tariffs, but in the long run reduced imports will result in reduced exports. The market for U.S. goods will shrink, increasing unemployment in the export industries.

Furthermore, if Americans reduce their demand for foreign goods to increase employment in the United States, their domestic recession will be transmitted to other nations. With fewer sales of foreign goods, fewer workers will be needed in foreign industries. Foreign governments may retaliate by imposing tariffs of their own. Tariffs will temporarily increase their employment levels and can be used as a bargaining tool in trade negotiations as well. The end result will be a reduction in total worldwide production and real income.

Finally, tariff advocates sometimes claim that new industries deserve protection because they are too small to compete with established foreign firms. If protected by tariffs, these new industries can expand their scale of production, lower their production costs, and eventually compete with foreign producers.

It is very difficult, however, for a government to determine which new industries may eventually be able to compete with foreign rivals. Over the long period of time that an industry needs to mature, conditions, including the technology of production, may change significantly. For a so-called infant industry to become truly competitive, furthermore, it must develop a comparative cost advantage, not just economies of scale.

Moreover, the mere likelihood that a firm will eventually be able to compete with its foreign rivals does not in itself warrant protection. Not until firms have become established will consumers receive the benefit of lower prices. In the interim, tariff protection hurts consumers by raising the prices they must pay. Proponents of protection must be able to show that the time-discounted future benefits to be gained by establishing an industry exceed the current costs of protecting it.

Finally, if a firm can expand, cover all its costs of production, and eventually compete with its foreign rivals, private entrepreneurs are not likely to miss the opportunity to invest in it. Through the stock and bond markets, firms with growth potential will be able to secure the funds they need for expansion. If a firm cannot raise capital from private sources, it may be because the return on the investment is too low in relation to the risk. Why should the government accept risks that the private market will not accept?

Chapter Review

Review of Key Questions

◢   *1. What does the balance of payments measure?*

A balance of payments is a summary statement of the flow of all economic and financial transactions between one country and the rest of the world over a given period of time (typically, one year). The major elements of a flexible exchange system, for which there is no official government intervention, are the current account (involving merchandise goods, services, and gifts) and capital account (involving financial assets). If there is a managed flexible or fixed exchange system where there is official government intervention, there is also an official reserve transaction account (including gold, foreign currencies, and special drawing rights at the International Monetary Fund, the world's Federal Reserve) that can be used if the combined current and capital accounts do not balance. Since the early 1970s most countries have operated under a managed floating rate system using official reserve balances only moderately, leaving market forces the bulk of the responsibility for maintaining equilibrium. Under double-entry bookkeeping, the balance of payments in the aggregate, but not each account, must balance. Items that increase the demand for a nation's currency are credits and items that increase the supply of a nation's currency are debits. For instance, a current account deficit might be made up by a capital account surplus. But balance does not preclude there being a disequilibrium situation. A balance of payments includes merchandise trade, investment income, net military transactions, travel, remittance, pensions, and gifts, and international capital flows. Although the trade balance only involves imports and exports, the goods and services balance considers imports and exports of all goods and services, and the current account balance involves not only goods and services, but also net investment income and transfers.

◢   *2. How do nations gain from international trade?*

When two nations trade with each other, both trading partners perceive that they will gain from the transaction: Each nation can achieve a larger real income given the volume of resources. Absolute advantage involves the ability of a nation to produce a good or service with lower costs or fewer resources because of its abundance of natural endowments or previous experience. Comparative or relative advantage occurs where a nation's absolute productive capacity or cost advantage is greatest or its absolute disadvantage is smallest. Even if one nation has an absolute advantage in the production of all goods and services, trade between nations can be mutually beneficial on the basis of relative or comparative advantage. All nations have a comparative advantage in some product. Generally, a nation will have its comparative advantage in those products that require the intensive use of the factors that the nation has a relative abundance of. The law of comparative advantage is that under competitive conditions each nation tends to (1) specialize (partly or completely) in and export those commodities in which it has a comparative advantage—those commodities that require in their production a large proportion of those resources that are relatively abundant and inexpensive in that nation—and (2) import those commodities in which it has a compar-

ative disadvantage—those commodities that require in their production a
large portion of those resources that are relatively scarce and expensive
in that nation. By specializing in those commodities for which they have
the greatest relative efficiency, nations can expand world productivity
and output. Nations gain from international trade although the greater
efficiency allows lower social opportunity costs, greater variety of available products, and enhanced competition. In the long run, the value of a
nation's imports and exports will equalize.

◢ *3. What are the distributional effects of international trade?*

While voluntary trade is mutually advantageous, the terms of trade
(or ratio of exchange) of the price of exports to the price of imports determine how much a nation gains from another nation. Although nations
as a whole always gain from international trade, not all individuals do.
Firms that produce for export can gain from foreign trade, along with
their employees, but free trade can hurt firms that must compete with
foreign producers. Consumers who buy products that are exported must
pay higher prices than they would in the absence of trade.

◢ *4. What do trade restrictions such as tariffs and quotas do to international trade?*

Tariffs are taxes placed on imports or exports based either on their
value (*ad valorem* duty) or per unit of output (specific duty). While the
major purpose of tariffs is protection of import-competing domestic
firms, (i.e., protective tariffs) in our early history the purpose was simply
to raise revenues for the nation (i.e., revenue tariffs). Quotas are mandatory (or voluntary physical) dollar value limits on the amount of a good
that can be imported or exported during a given time. Protectionism
promotes economic inefficiency. Tariffs and quotas reduce the supply of
goods on the market, raising domestic prices, and encouraging domestic
production. How much the import price rises depends on the price elasticity of demand and supply. Generally, the price in the import nation
rises and the price in the export nation falls, so that each trading partner
bears part of the actual burden of the tariff. Free trade promotes efficient resource allocation and economic growth.

◢ *5. What is good about free international trade?*

International trade tends to redistribute income in favor of the owners of abundant factors and against the owners of scarce factors, in that
it tends to make abundant factors scarce and more expensive and scarce
factors more abundant and cheaper. Producers who face foreign competition can benefit substantially from, and have a private interest in, tariff
or quota restrictions on imports. Consumers have little incentive to oppose tariff legislation, for the cost of opposition is generally greater than
the benefit to be gained from it (slightly lower prices). Yet the societal
costs—of the loss of efficiency resulting from protectionism—are greater
than its gains in home jobs saved, enhanced incomes of protected parties, and government tariff revenues. Tariffs and quotas on imports reduce international trade, and therefore the aggregate incomes of the
nations that engage in international commerce.

◢ *6. What arguments in favor of restricted international trade are valid?*

Restricted trade or protectionism in the tradeable goods sector includes tariffs, quotas, bans, and other devices. There are many argu-

ments in favor of protectionism: it improves terms of trade and bargaining power, reduces domestic unemployment and pauperization of labor, promotes national military security, encourages industrialization (in infant industries), enhances aggregate demand (by keeping money at home), and effects retaliation against previous protectionism by foreign nations. Tariffs and quotas sometimes serve the national interest, especially where national defense and security and infant industries are concerned. Most other arguments in favor of tariffs are seriously flawed, and even the two sometimes valid arguments are seriously abused.

Further Topics

The schedule of tariffs applied to goods coming into the United States is now larger than the Los Angeles telephone directory. Surely all those tariffs were not imposed in pursuit of the national interest, as in the maintenance of a strong defense industry. Most probably reflect the political influence of special-interest groups. Yet on balance, the overall tariffs are low, but they mask very high tariffs and even quotas on certain commodities—such as certain agricultural products, tobacco, motorcycles, and cooking utensils.

The case against such special-interest tariffs was wittily stated by the nineteenth-century French economist Frederic Bastiat. Pretending to represent the candle manufacturers of his day, he wrote to the French Chamber of Deputies in 1845:

> Gentlemen:
> . . . We are subjected to the intolerable competition of a foreign rival, who enjoys, it would seem, such superior facilities for the production of light, that he is enabled to *inundate* our *national market* at so exceedingly reduced price, that, the moment he makes his appearance, he draws off all customs for us; and thus an important branch of French industry . . . is suddenly reduced to a state of complete stagnation. This rival is no other than the sun.
>
> Our petition is, that it would please your honorable body to pass a law whereby shall be directed the shutting up of all windows, doors, skylights, shutters, curtains, in a word, all openings, holes, chinks, and fissures through which light of the sun . . . penetrates into our dwellings.[8]

Bastiat suggests that passage of his proposed law would be consistent with the Chamber's attempts to check the importation of "coal, iron, cheese, and goods of foreign manufacture, merely because and even in proportion as their price approaches zero."

Clearly, tariffs force consumers to pay more for domestic goods. To that extent they reduce aggregate real income. Unfortunately, because they benefit special-interest groups—and because the political process is easily exploited by special-interest groups—tariffs, like other taxes, are probably inevitable.

8. Frederic Bastiat, "A Petition," *Economic Sophisms* (Irvington-on-Hudson, N.Y.: Foundation for Economic Education, 1964; originally published 1845), pp. 56–60.

Review of New Terms

Absolute advantage The capacity to produce more units of output than a competitor can for any given level of resource use.

Capital account The record of a nation's investments abroad and foreign investments in that nation.

Capital account deficit The dollar amount by which a nation's investments abroad—that is, capital outflows—exceed foreign investments in that nation—that is, capital inflows.

Capital account surplus The dollar amount by which foreign investments in a nation—that is, capital inflows—exceed that nation's investments abroad—that is, capital outflows.

Comparative advantage The relative advantage in production or cost based on comparative ratios such that either the absolute advantage is greatest or the absolute disadvantage is smallest.

Current account The record of all the nation's international transactions other than capital flows and statistical discrepancies, including its merchandise trade, its investment income, its military transactions, its travel and transportation expenditures, its other services, and its remittances, pensions, and other unilateral transfers (i.e., gifts).

Current account deficit The dollar amount by which a nation's imports of goods and services, interest and dividend payments to foreigners, gifts to foreigners, travel expenditures abroad, and other remittances to foreign nations exceed its exports of goods and services, interest and dividend receipts from foreign nations, gifts from abroad, foreign travel expenditures in this nation, and other remittances from abroad.

Current account surplus The dollar amount by which a nation's exports of goods and services, interest and dividend receipts from foreigners, gifts from foreigners, foreign travel expenditures in this nation, and other receipts from abroad exceed the nation's imports of goods and services, interest and dividend payments to foreigners, gifts to foreigners, travel expenditures abroad, and other remittances to foreign nations.

International balance of payments A summary statement of the flow of all international economic and financial transactions between one nation—for example, the United States—and the rest of the world over some period of time, usually one year.

Merchandise trade balance The difference between the dollar value of a nation's imported and exported goods—raw materials, agricultural and manufactured products, and capital and consumer products—but not services and financial assets.

Merchandise trade deficit The dollar amount by which imports of goods exceed exports of goods.

Merchandise trade surplus The dollar amount by which exports of goods exceed imports of goods.

Quota A physical or dollar value limit—mandatory or voluntary—on the amount of a good that can be imported or exported during some specified period of time.

Tariff A special tax or duty on imported or exported goods that can be a percentage of the price (*ad valorem* duty) or a specific amount per unit of the product (specific duty).

Terms of trade The ratio at which one commodity can be traded or exchanged for another commodity internationally; or on an aggregate basis, it is the ratio of the price of exports to the price of imports.

Review Questions

1. Using supply and demand curves, show how a U.S. tariff on a foreign-made good will affect the price and quantity sold in the country of origin. (◢ 4)

2. How will an import quota on sugar affect the price of sugar produced and sold domestically? Sugar produced domestically and sold abroad? (◢ 4)

3. If a tariff is imposed on imported autos and the domestic demand for autos rises, what will happen to auto imports? If a quota is imposed on imported autos and the demand for autos increases, what will happen to auto imports? (◢ 4)

4. Given the following production capabilities for cheese and bread, which nation will export cheese to the other? What might be a mutually beneficial exchange rate for cheese and bread? (◢ 2)

	Cheese		Bread
France	40 units	or	60 units
Italy	10 units	or	5 units

5. "Tariffs on imported textiles increase the employment opportunities and incomes of domestic textile workers. They therefore increase aggregate employment and income." Evaluate this statement. (◢ 2, ◢ 3, ◢ 4, ◢ 5, ◢ 6)

6. Since the balance of payments must always balance, how can a disequilibrium situation occur? (◢ 1)

International Finance

The goal of every science is a conceptual model which shows how the pieces of its universe are related. Economists seek to become the Copernicuses of the international financial system, but their task is complicated since this system has changed substantially in the last one hundred years and continues to change.
    Robert Aliber

KEY QUESTIONS

▲ 1. What are international exchange rates?

▲ 2. How are international exchange rates determined?

▲ 3. How do floating, flexible, or freely fluctuating international exchange rates work?

▲ 4. What is a fixed or pegged international exchange rate system?

▲ 5. How does monetary adjustment operate under a fixed-rate system?

▲ 6. How does a persistent balance of payments problem get solved?

NEW TERMS

Appreciation
Depreciation
Devaluation
Dirty or managed floating exchange rate system
Fixed or pegged exchange rate system

Floating, flexible, or freely fluctuating exchange rate system
Foreign exchange
International exchange rate
J-curve phenomenon
Purchasing power parity theory
Revaluation

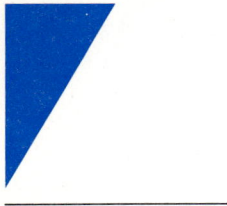

People rarely use barter in trade. Exchanging one toy for two pens or three pots for the rear end of a steer simply is not practical. Because the bartering seller must also be a buyer, buyers and sellers may have to incur very substantial costs to find one another, even in the domestic market. When people are hundreds or thousands of miles apart and separated by national boundaries and foreign cultures and languages, as they are in international trade, barter would be all the more complicated. We rarely see exporters acting as importers, exchanging specific exports for specific imports.

In the domestic economy, money reduces the cost of making exchanges. The seller of pots needs only to find a buyer willing to pay with bills, coins, or a check. He does not have to accept goods that may be difficult to store, use, and trade. In the international economy too, money facilitates trade, but well over a hundred different national currencies are in use. The French have the franc; the Japanese, the yen; the Americans, the dollar. To deal with this complication, a system of international exchanges emerged in which importers pay for the goods they buy in their currency. Before international trade can take place, it is usually necessary for the country buying to convert to the currency of the trading partner. Importers demand foreign currency and exporters supply it. How the international monetary system works, and the problems inherent in it, are the subjects of this chapter.

The Process of International Monetary Exchange

◢ 1. What are international exchange rates?

Imagine you own a small gourmet shop that carries special cheeses. You may buy your cheese either domestically—cheddar from New York, Monterey Jack from California—or abroad. If you buy from a domestic firm, it is easy to negotiate the deal and make payment. Because the price of cheese is quoted in dollars and the domestic firm expects payment in dollars, you can pay the same way you pay other bills—by writing a personal check. Only one national currency is involved.

Purchasing cheese from a French cheesemaker is a little more complicated, for two reasons. First, the price of the cheese will be quoted in francs. Second, you will want to pay in dollars, but the French cheesemaker must be paid in francs. Either you must exchange your dollars for francs, or the cheesemaker must convert them for you. At some point, currencies must be exchanged at some recognized exchange rate. **Foreign exchange** is the monetary means or instruments used to make monetary payments and transfers from one currency area to another. The funds available as foreign exchange include foreign coin and currency, deposits in foreign banks, and other short-term, liquid financial claims payable in foreign currencies.

International Exchange Rates

Before you buy, you will want to compare the prices of French and domestic cheeses. You must convert the franc price of cheese into its dollar equivalent. To do that, you need to know the international exchange rate between dollars and francs. The **international exchange rate** is the price of one national currency (like the franc) stated in terms of another national currency (like the dollar). In other words, the international exchange rate is the dollar price you must pay for each franc you buy. Table 18.1 gives you an example of the highly organized foreign exchange market where currencies of different nations are bought and sold; it shows the dollar prices of several foreign currencies as of the end of January 1988. This table appears in each issue of the *Wall Street Journal*. In February, 1988, the franc was then worth almost $0.18, the British pound cost a little more than $1.77, and the West German mark roughly $0.60.

Once you know the current exchange rate, conversion of currencies is not difficult. Assume that you want to buy F5,000 (read "5,000 francs") worth of cheese, and that the international exchange rate between dollars and francs is $0.10 (that is, $1 sells for F10). F5,000 at $0.10 apiece will cost you $500. For the rest of this chapter we will assume that the dollar price of the franc is $0.10 to make our arithmetic examples easier to follow.

The international exchange rate determines the dollar price of the foreign goods you want to buy. A different exchange rate would have changed the dollar price of cheese. For instance, suppose the exchange rate rose from $0.10 = F1 to $0.20 = F1. In the jargon of international finance, such a change represents a depreciation (a devaluation involves a depreciation relative to the monetary standard and not necessarily relative to other monies) of the dollar. A **depreciation** of the dollar (or any other national currency) is a reduction in the exchange value or purchasing power, brought about by market forces, in relation to other national currencies. The dollar is now cheaper in terms of francs: It takes fewer francs (F5) to buy a dollar than previously (F10).

The same change represents an appreciation of the franc. An **appreciation** of the dollar (or any other national currency) is an increase in the exchange value or purchasing power, brought about by market forces, in relation to other national currencies. Each franc will now buy a larger

Foreign exchange: the monetary means or instruments used to make monetary payments and transfers from one currency area to another. The funds available as foreign exchange include foreign coin and currency, deposits in foreign banks, and other short-term, liquid financial claims.

International exchange rate: the price of one national currency stated in terms of another national currency.

Depreciation: a reduction in the exchange value or purchasing power of one national currency, brought about by market forces, in relation to other national currencies.

Appreciation: an increase in the exchange value or purchasing power of one national currency, brought about by market forces, in relation to other national currencies.

fraction of a dollar—$0.20 as opposed to $0.10. From the perspective of the gourmet shop, the important point is that at the higher exchange rate, the dollar price of the cheese purchase is $1,000 ($0.20 times 5,000). If the exchange rate fell from $0.10 = F1 to $0.05 = F1, the price of the French cheese would decline to $250.

As you can see, your willingness to buy French cheese depends very much on the franc price of cheese and the exchange rate. If the franc price of cheese increases or decreases, your dollar price increases or decreases.

TABLE 18.1 International Exchange Rates (dollar prices of foreign currencies), January 29, 1988

Country	Dollar Price of Foreign Currency	Country	Dollar Price of Foreign Currency
Argentina (Austral)	.2500	Malta (Lira)	3.0798
Australia (Dollar)	.7105	Mexico (Peso)	
Austria (Schilling)	.08489	Floating rate	.0004529
Belgium (Franc)		Netherland (Guilder)	.5298
Commercial rate	.02856	New Zealand (Dollar)	.6600
Financial rate	.02849	Norway (Krone)	.1569
Brazil (Cruzado)	.01199	Pakistan (Rupee)	.0570
Britain (Pound)	1.7660	Peru (Inti)	.03030
Canada (Dollar)	.7843	Philippines (Peso)	.04796
Chile (Official rate)	.004095	Portugal (Escudo)	.007299
China (Yuan)	.2687	Saudi Arabia (Riyal)	.2666
Colombia (Peso)	.003742	Singapore (Dollar)	.4988
Denmark (Krone)	.1559	South Africa (Rand)	
Ecuador (Sucre)		Commercial rate	.5035
Official rate	.003774	Financial rate	.35
Floating rate	.004454	South Korea (Won)	.001276
Finland (Markka)	.2456	Spain (Peseta)	.008790
France (Franc)	.1765	Sweden (Krona)	.1661
Greece (Drachma)	.007477	Switzerland (Franc)	.7310
Hong Kong (Dollar)	.1288	Taiwan (Dollar)	.03501
India (Rupee)	.07651	Thailand (Baht)	.03963
Indonesia (Rupiah)	.0006024	Turkey (Lira)	.0009139
Ireland (Punt)	1.5868	United Arab (Dirham)	.2722
Israel (Shekel)	.6339	Uruguay (New Peso)	
Italy (Lira)	.0008078	Financial	.003448
Japan (Yen)	.007817	Venezuela (Bolivar)	
Jordan (Dinar)	2.9027	Official rate	.1333
Kuwait (Dinar)	3.6377	Floating rate	.0333
Lebanon (Pound)	.002237	W. Germany (Mark)	.5951
	.3929	SDR	1.36642

Special Drawing Rights (SDRs) are based on exchange rates for the U.S., West German, British, French and Japanese currencies. Source: International Monetary Fund.

The New York foreign exchange selling rates above apply to trading among banks in amounts of $1 million and more, as quoted at 3 p.m. Eastern time by Bankers Trust Co. Retail transactions provide fewer units of foreign currency per dollar.

Source: Wall Street Journal, February 1, 1988, p. 46.

TABLE 18.2 The Likely Long-Run Effects of Depreciation and Appreciation of the Dollar on U.S. Exports and Imports

	Depreciation of Dollar	Appreciation of Dollar
Price of exports	Decrease	Increase
Total dollar value of exports[a]	Increase	Decrease
Price of imports	Increase	Decrease
Total dollar value of imports[a]	Decrease	Increase

a. This assumes that the demand and supply functions for exports and imports are price elastic.

J-curve phenomenon: Although the initial impact of depreciation is often an increase in nominal spending on imports because higher prices cause a deterioration in the nominal trade balance, over time depreciation will tend to improve both nominal and real net exports.

Changes in the dollar price of francs have a similar effect. If the dollar depreciates (that is, if the price of francs in dollars rises), the dollar price of French cheese rises. Very likely you will be inclined to import less, since at the higher price your customers will buy less. If the dollar appreciates (that is, if the price of francs falls), the dollar price of French cheese falls. Very likely you will import more because you can lower your own price and sell more. In general, a depreciation of the dollar discourages imports; an appreciation of the dollar encourages imports. The likely long-run results of changes in the international rate of exchange are summarized in Table 18.2. In contrast, in the short run a depreciation can worsen a country's balance of trade according to the J-curve phenomenon because elasticities are smaller. Although the initial impact of depreciation is often an increase in nominal spending on imports because higher prices cause a deterioration in the nominal trade balance, the **J-curve phenomenon** of currency depreciation states that over time depreciation will tend to improve both nominal and real net exports.[1] Thus, although a depreciation in the exchange rate will eventually achieve a balance-of-trade equilibrium as shown in Table 18.2, it may take some time. In general, long-run price elasticities are greater—often considerably greater—than short-run price elasticities. As a rule, economic agents respond reasonably quickly and significantly to changes in economic stimuli.

During the first half of this decade, the U.S. dollar appreciated in relation to most major currencies.[2] The dollar price of the French franc, for

1. Rudiger Dornbush and Paul Krugman, "Flexible Exchange Rates in the Short Run," *Brookings Papers on Economic Activity* (March 1976), pp. 537–575.

2. William Branson and James Love, *The Real Exchange Rate and Employment in U.S. Manufacturing: State and Regional Results* (NBER Working Paper No. 2435, 1988) estimated that the dramatic appreciation of the U.S. dollar between the early 1980s until the first quarter of 1985, which made U.S. products relatively more expensive in other nations, led to the loss of about 1.1 million jobs—about 6 percent of 1985 employment—in American manufacturing. Five largely rural states lost the most jobs as a percentage of their 1985 manufacturing work force: North Dakota 25%; Nevada 19%; Wyoming, Kansas, and West Virginia 17%. Several industrial Northeast states, such as New Jersey, Massachusetts, and New York, were hardly affected.

International Economics Talks: A Who's Who

Peter Kilborn, New York Times

In recent weeks, several groups of international financial leaders have met to discuss or take action on freeing world trade, lowering the value of the dollar and easing the international debt crisis, in which many developing countries are struggling to repay hundreds of billions of dollars of loans.

The heavy debt of these developing countries has made it difficult for them to buy goods in the world marketplace. That, coupled with the strength of the dollar, which makes American goods more expensive abroad and imports cheaper, has hurt American exports. In turn, this has prompted calls for trade legislation to protect American industry, a response that the Reagan Administration opposes. The Administration has begun to offer alternative strategies at the international meetings—proposals for dealing with the trade and debt problems. The following is a brief description of the groups involved in the talks.

General Agreement on Tariffs and Trade

Function: Established in Geneva in 1947 as a vehicle for promoting world trade. The organization, also known as GATT, has held seven rounds of trade liberalization talks since its founding.

Members: 90 industrialized and developing countries, representing about four-fifths of international trade. The Soviet Union is not a member.

Issues: At a meeting in Geneva last week, the group unanimously agreed to open a new round of formal talks on freeing trade, setting in motion meetings that will last for several years. The Reagan Administration sought the new round to help defuse pressures in Congress for measures that would restrict imports. Such measures, the Administration argued, could lead to a worldwide recession. The United States and other industrial countries want the new talks to remove barriers to trading in services, including establishing telecommunications, insurance and banking operations in

many third world countries. This is opposed by some developing nations, who argue it would prevent them from developing their own technology and service industries.

International Monetary Fund

Function: Established by an agreement at the United Nations Monetary and Financial Conference at Bretton Woods, N.H., in 1944 to encourage international cooperation on monetary matters, including maintaining stable exchange rates and overseeing the payment of international debts. Makes short-term loans to nations, both rich and poor, with balance-of-payments deficits, in concert with individual governments and private banks. The loan pool comes from contributions from member nations. In return for such help, the fund imposes tight controls on a borrower's economy. Such controls include restrictions on government spending and wage rates that are designed to keep inflation down.

Members: 149 industrial and developing countries. The I.M.F.'s managing director is Jacques de Larosiere.

Issues: Latin American debtor nations have recently stepped up resistance to I.M.F. austerity requirements, arguing that policies that stimulate their economies would allow the region to grow out of its crushing debt problems. The group is now holding its joint annual meeting with the World Bank in Seoul, South Korea, where Treasury Secretary James A. Baker 3d is expected to announce tomorrow that the United States now supports the growth-oriented approach. He is also expected to urge support for a wider role for the World Bank in solving the debt crisis. Secretary Baker met with leading commercial bankers last week, reportedly urging them to provide fresh loans to debtor nations, a move that many banks— whose portfolios are already filled with shaky loans to developing nations—have said they would resist.

The World Bank

Function: Also established by the Bretton Woods agreement. Formally called the International Bank for Reconstruction and Development, it makes direct loans for specific projects such as highways and power plants in developing countries. It currently lends about $12 billion a year, and unlike the I.M.F., it does not provide tight controls on a borrower's economy.

Members: Same as I.M.F. The United States is its largest contributor. Its president is A. W. Clausen, former chairman of the Bank of America.

Issues: At the meetings in Seoul this week, the United States is expected to urge a greater role for the bank. This would include higher maximum lending levels to developing and debtor countries, partly through collaboration with the I.M.F. and commercial banks. The new loans would not be limited to specific projects but could be used to bolster the borrower's general economy. In exchange for the support of the commercial banks, the Administration is expected to ask the World Bank to provide loan guarantees to safeguard the private lenders. Developing countries have expressed reservations about increased cooperation between the World Bank and the I.M.F., fearing that would lead to tougher loan conditions.

Group of Five

Function: Meets informally to discuss sensitive international monetary problems.

Members: Finance ministers of United States, Britain, France, West Germany and Japan, the major non-Communist industrialized countries. Sets agenda for the larger Group of 10.

Issues: At a meeting at the Plaza Hotel in New York on Sept. 22, the ministers agreed to intervene in world currency markets to drive down the value of the dollar against other currencies, making American goods more competitive abroad. The move to lower the dollar was, in part, an effort by the Reagan Administration to defuse pressure in Congress for protectionist legislation, and ramifications for their trade. The move marked a shift by the Administration, which has generally resisted intervention to change the dollar's value.

Group of 10

Function: Established in 1962. Meets formally to discuss monetary issues.

Members: Finance ministers and central bank governors of the United States, Canada, Japan, Britain, West Germany, France, Belgium, Italy, the Netherlands and Sweden. It actually has 11 members, because Switzerland joined several years ago.

Issues: The same as for the Group of Five.

Group of 24

Function: Represents developing countries in international monetary and trade matters.

Members: Representatives of eight developing countries each from Asia, Africa and Latin America. The Group of 24 is the steering committee for a much larger group that includes about 125 developing nations. Its chairman is Juan V. Sourrouille, Economy Minister of Argentina.

Issues: Group seeks easier credit and fewer restrictions on I.M.F. loans, and is said to want World Bank lending to rise to $20 billion a year by 1990.

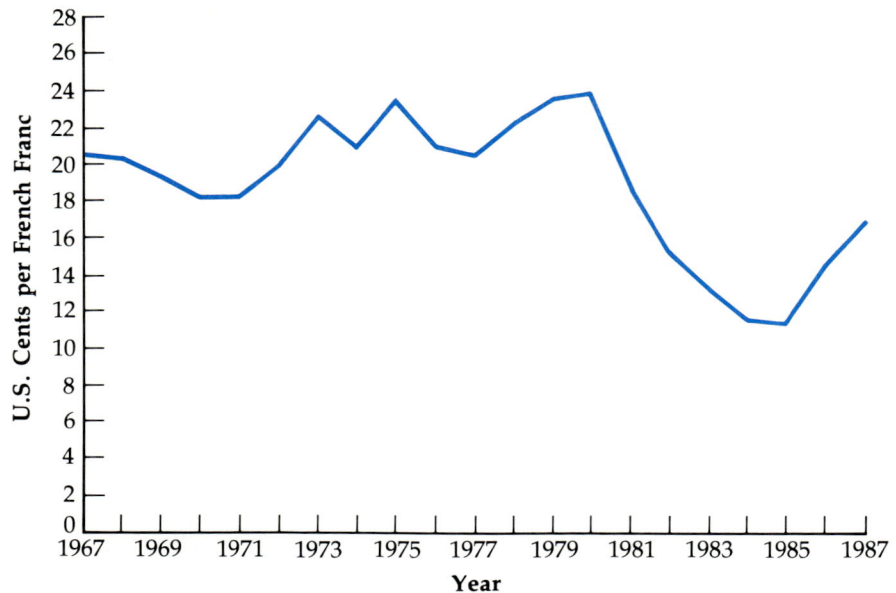

FIGURE 18.1 The Changing Dollar Price of the Franc, 1967–1987
The dollar price of the French franc has fluctuated considerably in recent years. For instance, it fell from 1967 to 1970, rose from 1971 to 1973, fell in 1974, rose in 1975, fell from 1976 to 1977, rose from 1978 to 1980, declined from 1981 to 1985, and started to rise again after 1985. From a high of about $0.24 in 1980, it fell to just above $0.11 in 1984.
Source: Economic Report of the President (Washington, D.C.: U.S. Government Printing Office, 1988), p. 371, reciprocals of figures in Table B-108 that has currency unit per U.S. dollar.

instance, began to tumble in the early 1980s, falling from just below $0.24 in 1980 to just above $0.11 in late 1984 and then back to almost $0.17 in 1987 (see Figure 18.1). As the dollar value of the franc fell, French goods and travel in France became less expensive for Americans. U.S. goods and foreign travel in the United States became more expensive for the French. Beginning in 1985, the U.S. dollar began depreciating in relation to most major currencies. For instance, the real exchange rate—the U.S. exchange adjusted for changes in the purchasing power between the U.S. and the rest of the world or the ratio of the foreign price of U.S. goods to the foreign price of the rest of the world's goods—fell about 15 percent between early 1985 and late 1986.

Because long-run price elasticities are large, a depreciation in the exchange rate will (according to the J-curve phenomenon) eventually attain a balance-of-trade equilibrium. But in the short-run, where price elasticities are small, a depreciation can worsen a country's balance of trade. Thus, the depreciation in the U.S. dollar that began in late 1985 will take some time to work itself out. For one thing, because the United States is a large economy, importers tend not to adjust their U.S. prices immediately in response to changes in the exchange rates. Many exporters to the United States try to keep the dollar price of foreign products unchanged in the United States, even when the exchange rate has increased or decreased sharply. Thus, when the dollar is weak as in 1986 and 1987, prices are relatively constant and profit margins, such as on Japanese automobiles, fell abruptly. When the dollar is strong, as in the early 1980s, the U.S. prices didn't fall as much as exchange rates rose and importation was quite profitable. A gray market developed when people began buying cars in Europe and sending them to the United States for resale. The United States' international trade deficit significantly increased in the early 1980s for several reasons: (1) the U.S. dollar had been strong and appreciating for some years before that; (2) the United States recovered from the 1980–1982 world recession more rapidly than did the major countries it trades with; and (3) third-world countries, shackled by excessive indebtedness, reduced export purchases.

The Exchange of National Currencies

Assume you have figured the dollar price of cheese using the exchange rate and find it satisfactory. Since your American customers pay for their groceries in dollars, that is the only currency you have to make the payment. Yet cheesemakers in France need francs to pay for their groceries. Therefore the French cheese exporter must ultimately be paid in francs.

How can you make payment in dollars while the French exporter is paid in francs? A bank will exchange your dollars for you. Banks deal in national currencies for the same reason that business people trade in commodities: to make money. An automobile dealer buys cars at a low price with the hope of selling them at a higher price. Banks do the same thing, except that their commodities are national currencies. They buy dollars and pay for them in francs or yen, with the idea of selling them at a profit.

If you pay for your French cheese in dollars, you write a check against your checking account and send it to the French firm.[3] The French cheesemaker will accept the check knowing that your dollars can be traded for francs (that is, sold to a French bank) at the current rate of exchange. If the exchange rate is $0.10 = F1, and you have sent the cheesemaker a check for $500, the exporter will receive F5,000 for your check from the French bank. Remember that banks, even foreign ones, have accounts with other banks, just as individuals do. The French bank will deposit your check with its U.S. banker. Your bank balance will fall, and the French bank's balance at the U.S. institution will rise. Then the French bank will sell (or trade) the dollars it has on account for francs.

---

3. Instruments of exchange other than checks are often used in international transactions. The process, however, is the same.

In the process of buying and selling dollars, the French bank may make a profit. Suppose, for example, that the French bank buys dollars from the French cheesemaker at a rate of $0.10 = F1 (or $1 = F10), paying F5,000 for $500. It can then sell its dollars to a French importer for a higher franc price—say $0.09 = F1 (or $1 = F11.11). It will receive F5,555 for its $500— a net gain of F555.

This hypothetical purchase of French cheese leads to an important observation. Any U.S. import, be it cheese or watches, will increase the dollar holdings of foreign banks. So will American expenditures abroad, whether for tours or for foreign stocks and bonds. Americans must have francs for such transactions; therefore they must offer American dollars in exchange. In most instances, foreign banks end up holding the dollars that Americans have sold.

In the same way, U.S. exports reduce the dollar holdings of foreign banks. Exports are typically paid for out of the dollar accounts of foreign banks. Foreign expenditures on trips to the United States or on the stocks and bonds of U.S. corporations have the same effect. They reduce the dollar holdings of foreign banks and increase the foreign currency holdings of U.S. banks. If American expenditures abroad exceed foreign expenditures here, the dollar holdings of foreign banks will rise—and vice versa.

If American expenditures abroad exceed foreign expenditures here for a long time, foreign banks will eventually accumulate all the dollars they can reasonably expect to use—that is, to sell back to their citizens for the purchase of American goods. Foreign banks then have several options. First, they may sell their dollar holdings to other foreign commercial banks in exchange for francs, marks, or krona. Second, they may sell their dollars to their government—or, more properly, to their government's central bank (for example, the Bank of France).

The market may already be saturated with dollars, however. No one, including the central bank, may want to buy dollars at the going price, $0.10 = F1 in our illustration. In that case, foreign banks can induce people to buy dollars by lowering their price. For instance, they can alter the exchange rate from $0.10 = F1 to $0.15 = F1. In so doing they increase the price of francs and decrease (depreciate) the price of dollars.

A depreciation in the U.S. dollar in the exchange rate will have several effects, all tending to reduce the number of dollars coming onto the international money market. As explained earlier, the exchange will make French goods more expensive for Americans to buy. Thus it will tend to reduce U.S. imports, and accordingly the number of dollars that must be exchanged for foreign currencies. Depreciation will also tend to reduce the price of American goods to foreigners. For instance, at an exchange rate of $0.10 = F1, the franc price of a $1 million American computer is F10 million. At an exchange rate of $0.15 = F1, the franc price of the same computer is F6.66 million—a substantial reduction in price. To buy American goods at the new lower franc price, the French will increase their demand for dollars. Again, the quantity of dollars being offered on the money market will fall, and the growth in foreign dollar holdings will be checked.

Determination of the Exchange Rate

2. How are international exchange rates determined?

Like the price of anything else, exchange rates are determined by the forces of demand and supply, although government may interfere to alter the rate from what market forces alone would have produced. When there is no official or government interference, the rates are free or floating.

When government intervenes, by buying or selling currency in the foreign exchange rates by a central bank or other some official government agency, the exchange rates are fixed or pegged. From 1945 to 1971 exchange rates were basically fixed. Since 1971, however, rates have been set flexibly with some government intervention in a **dirty or managed floating exchange rate system,** in which the prices of currencies are partly determined by competitive market forces and partly determined by official government intervention.

Dirty or managed floating exchange rate system: an international monetary exchange system in which the prices of currencies are partly determined by competitive market forces and partly determined by official government intervention.

National currencies have a market value—that is, a price—because individuals, firms, and governments use them to buy foreign goods, services, and securities. There is a market demand for a national currency like the franc. Furthermore, the demand for the franc (or any other currency) slopes downward, like curve D in Figure 18.2. To see why, look at the market for francs from the point of view of a U.S. resident As the dollar price of the franc falls, the price of French goods to Americans also falls. As a result Americans will want to buy more French goods. They will require a larger quantity of francs to complete their transactions.

The supply of francs coming onto the market reflects the French people's demand for American goods, services, and securities. To get American goods, the French need dollars. They must pay for those dollars with

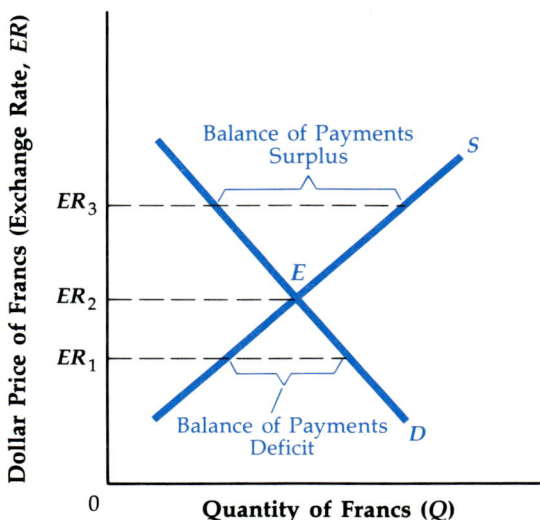

FIGURE 18.2 Supply and Demand for Francs on the International Currency Market
The international exchange rate between the dollar and the franc is determined by the forces of supply and demand with the equilibrium at E. If the exchange rate is below equilibrium, say at ER_1, the quantity of francs demanded, shown by the demand curve, will exceed the quantity supplied, shown by the supply curve. Competitive pressure will push the exchange rate up. If the exchange rate is above equilibrium, say at ER_3, the quantity supplied will exceed the quantity demanded, and competitive pressure will push the exchange rate down. Thus the price of a foreign currency is determined in much the same way as the price of any other commodity.

francs, and in doing so they supply francs to the international money market. As the dollar price of the franc rises, the price of American goods to the French falls. To buy a larger quantity of American goods at the lower franc price, the French need more dollars; they must offer more francs to get them. Therefore the quantity of francs supplied on the market rises. Thus the supply curve for francs slopes upward to the right, like curve S in Figure 18.2.

The buyers and sellers of francs make up what is loosely called the international money market in francs. Banks are very much involved in such markets. They buy francs from the sellers (suppliers) and sell to the buyers (demanders). As in other markets, the interaction of suppliers and demanders determines the market price. That is, given the supply and demand curves in Figure 18.2, in a competitive market the dollar price of the franc will move toward the equilibrium point at E involving the intersection of the supply and demand curves. The equilibrium price, or exchange rate, will be ER_2, the price at which the quantity of francs supplied exactly equals the quantity of francs demanded.

At the market equilibrium point there is no build-up of dollars or francs in the accounts of foreign banks. French and U.S. banks have no reason to modify the exchange rate to encourage or discourage the purchase or sale of either currency. To use a financial expression, the net balance of payments coming into and going out of each nation is zero.

If the exchange rate is below equilibrium level—say ER_1—the quantity of francs demanded will exceed the quantity supplied (see Figure 18.2). An imbalance in the balance of payments will develop. In the jargon of international finance, the United States will develop a balance of payments deficit—a shortfall in the quantity of a foreign currency supplied. (This is a conceptual definition. When it comes to defining the balance of payments deficit in a way that can be measured by the Department of Commerce, economists are in considerable disagreement.)

As in other markets, this imbalance will eventually right itself. Because of the excess demand for francs, French banks will accumulate excess dollar balances. French banks will have more dollars than they can sell and fewer francs than they need. Competitive pressure will then push the exchange rate back up to ER_2. People who cannot buy francs at ER_1 will offer a higher price. As the price of francs rises, French goods will become less attractive to Americans, and the quantity of francs demanded will fall. Conversely American goods will become more attractive to the French, and the quantity of francs supplied will rise.

Similarly, at an exchange rate higher than ER_2—say ER_3—the quantity of francs supplied will exceed the quantity demanded (see Figure 18.2). A balance of payments surplus—an excess quantity of a foreign currency supplied—will develop. The surplus will not last forever, however. Eventually the exchange rate will fall back toward ER_2, causing an increase in the quantity of francs demanded and a decrease in the quantity supplied. In short, in a free foreign currency market, the price of a currency is determined in the same way the prices of other commodities are determined.

Market Adjustment to Changes in Money Market Conditions

◢ 3. How do floating, flexible, or freely fluctuating international exchange rates work?

By modifying exchange rates to correct for imbalances in payments, the money market can accommodate vast changes in the economic conditions of nations engaged in trade. A good example is the way the market handles a change in consumption patterns. These changes in consumption, and hence in foreign exchange rates, can be caused by changes in a nation's tastes and preferences, real income, level of prices (including interest rates), costs, and expectations as to future exchange rates. If all countries' exchange rates move with the relative rates of inflation, only real (terms of trade) changes would affect the relative prices of home-country to foreign-country goods. However, while floating exchange rates tend to eliminate automatically any balance-of-payment problems, they may diminish the volume of trade because of the uncertainty and instability of the terms of trade. In fact, since flexible exchange rates were reintroduced in 1971 the volume of world trade has actually grown despite considerable volatility and turbulence.

The two major advantages of a floating system are that exchange rates are automatically determined exclusively by free market forces, without government intervention, controls, or regulations. Moreover, external adjustment, under favorable conditions, is attained without requiring major domestic or internal price, income, or employment changes. Its two major disadvantages are: (1) uncertainty and instability in the form of frequent and large fluctuations discourages international trade, transactions, and investment; and (2) there is the possibility of exchange rate fluctuations leading to cumulative disequilibrium rather than stable equilibrium.

Suppose American preferences for French goods—say, wines and perfumes—increase for some reason. The demand for francs will rise, because Americans will need more francs to buy the additional French goods they desire. If, as in Figure 18.3, the U.S. demand for francs shifts from D_1 to D_2, the quantity of francs demanded at the old equilibrium exchange rate of ER_1 will exceed the quantity supplied. Those who cannot buy more francs at ER_1 will offer to pay a higher price. The exchange rate will rise toward the new equilibrium level of ER_2 as the equilibrium point shifts from E_1 to E_2. As the dollar depreciates in value, the imbalance in payments is eliminated.

Now suppose Americans' real incomes rise. Assuming that the consumption of goods and services goes up with real income—we call these normal goods and services—Americans will be likely to demand more foreign imports, both directly and in the form of domestic goods that incorporate foreign parts or materials. Either way, an increase in real incomes leads to an increase in the demand for foreign currencies. Again the demand for francs will rise, as in Figure 18.3. The exchange rate will rise with it to bring the quantity supplied into line with the quantity demanded.

A change in the rate of inflation can have a similar effect on the exchange rate. If the inflation rates are about the same in two nations that

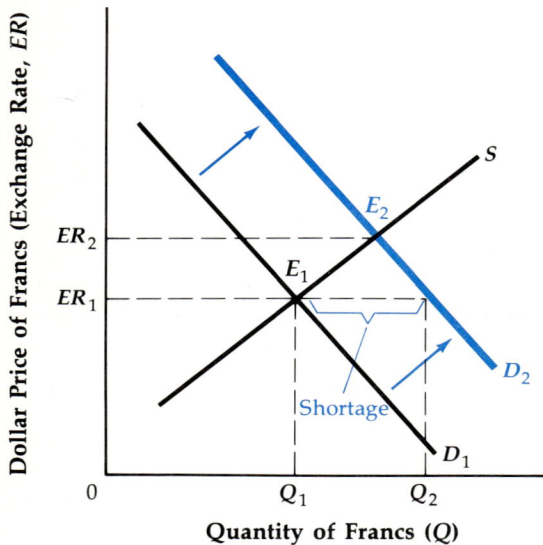

FIGURE 18.3 Effect of an Increase in Demand for Francs
An increase in the demand for francs will shift the demand curve from D_1 to D_2, pushing the equilibrium from E_1 to E_2. At the initial equilibrium exchange rate, ER_1, a shortage will develop. Competition among buyers will push the exchange rate up to the new equilibrium level, ER_2.

Purchasing power parity theory: the theory that if the inflation rates are about the same in two nations that trade with each other, the exchange rate between their currencies will remain stable, *ceteris paribus*.

trade with each other, the exchange rate between their currencies will remain stable, *ceteris paribus*, according to the **purchasing power parity theory**. Because the relative prices of goods in the two nations stay the same, people will have no incentive to switch from domestic to imported goods, or vice versa. If one nation's inflation rate exceeds another's, however, the relative prices of foreign and domestic goods change. If prices increase faster in the United States, for example, Americans will want to buy more foreign goods and fewer domestic goods. Foreigners, on the other hand, will have an incentive to buy more goods from their own countries, where prices are not rising as fast as in the United States. In sum, a higher U.S. inflation rate spells a rise in the demand for foreign currencies, a fall in their supply, and a depreciation of the dollar. Similar flows occur when there are interest rate differentials between nations.

Figure 18.4 illustrates the process for prices in general. As U.S. demand for foreign goods rises, the demand curve for francs shifts outward, from D_1 to D_2, shifting the equilibrium from E_1 to E_2. As foreign demand for U.S. products falls, the supply curve for francs shifts to the left, from S_1 to S_2. At the initial equilibrium exchange rate of ER_1, a shortage of francs will develop. The exchange rate will rise to ER_2, eliminating the shortage and reestablishing balance in the money market. At the higher rate, Americans must pay a higher dollar price for foreign goods. The rise in the exchange rate has evened out the difference in the two nations' inflation rates.

In the short run, supply and demand are most influenced by anticipations as to the direction in which an exchange rate is likely to move. For example, if the franc is expected to increase in value, people who have

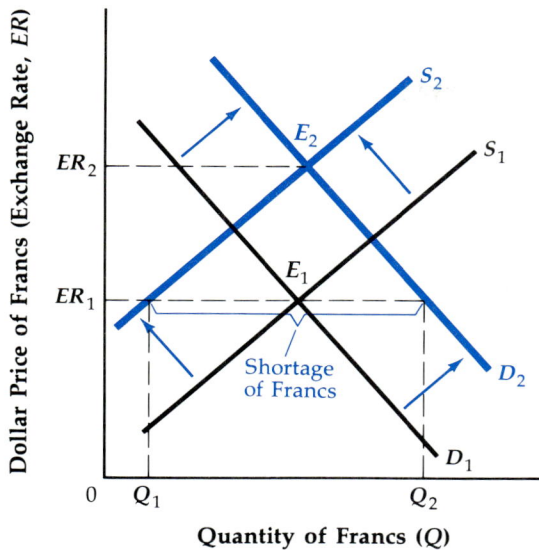

FIGURE 18.4 Effect of an Increase in Inflation on the Supply and Demand for Francs
If the rate of inflation is higher in the United States than in France, the demand for francs will rise from D_1 to D_2, while the supply of francs will contract from S_1 to S_2. The dollar price of francs will rise from ER_1 to ER_2, as the equilibrium shifts from E_1 to E_2.

payments to make in that currency will tend to buy the currency and make payments sooner. Economic and political news—such as an unanticipated change in monetary policy—has an almost immediate impact.

Control of the Exchange Rate: The Fixed or Pegged Rate System

◢ 4. What is a fixed or pegged international exchange rate system?

Floating, flexible, or freely fluctuating exchange rate system: an international monetary exchange system in which the prices of currencies are determined by competitive market forces.

Fixed or pegged exchange rate system: an international monetary exchange system in which the prices of currencies are established and maintained by government intervention.

So far our analysis of the international money market has assumed a floating, or flexible, system of exchange in which exchange rates are determined by private demand and supply forces in the market. A **floating, flexible, or freely fluctuating exchange rate system** is one in which the prices of currencies are determined by competitive market forces. Until 1971, however, international exchange rates were controlled by governments. Rates were not permitted to move in response to changes in supply and demand. Because rates were fixed for long periods of time by government decree, this system is generally referred to as a fixed exchange rate system. A **fixed or pegged exchange rate system** is one in which the prices of currencies are established and maintained by government intervention. Although the fixed-rate system is no longer in use among major nations, it merits some discussion because of its historical importance and because of periodic high-level discussions—especially in the late 1980s—about returning to it.

To understand that a properly working fixed exchange rate system can be better than a floating-rate system, consider the problems that would arise if *each state* in the United States had its own currency. The exchange rate

PERSPECTIVES

American Competitiveness and the Overlooked Capital Account Surplus

Policy commentators often discuss U.S. international-trade flows in goods as if they are the only meaningful transactions in the nation's balance of international payments, which, of course, is hardly the case but which does permit policy discussions to proceed in terms of a deficit. As noted in the text, a *deficit* cannot exist in the context of the entire balance of payments. Because of double-entry bookkeeping methods employed in recording international transactions, *the (full) balance of payments must balance*! An import entry in the trade account of the balance of payments, for example, must be exactly offset by another entry somewhere else in the balance-of-payments accounts. If this entry is not made with an export, then it may be made with a capital flow, a part of the capital account (a subsection of the full balance of payments).

Double-entry bookkeeping is used to accommodate the unbreakable principle that trade is a two-way exchange. What is bought from abroad by Americans or from the domestic market by foreigners must be paid for in some way—either in terms of dollars, other goods or services, securities, or trade credit (or some combination of all these payment methods). Recognizing the double-entry nature of the nation's international books makes two points evident. First, a trade deficit must be offset by a surplus in some other balance of payments account. As a matter of fact, as shown in Figure 18.5, the United States had a sharply rising capital account surplus beginning in 1983, the same year that the balance of merchandise trade deficit surfaced (see Figure 18.6). Furthermore, as obvious in Figure 18.6 (and as expected), the merchandise trade and capital ac-

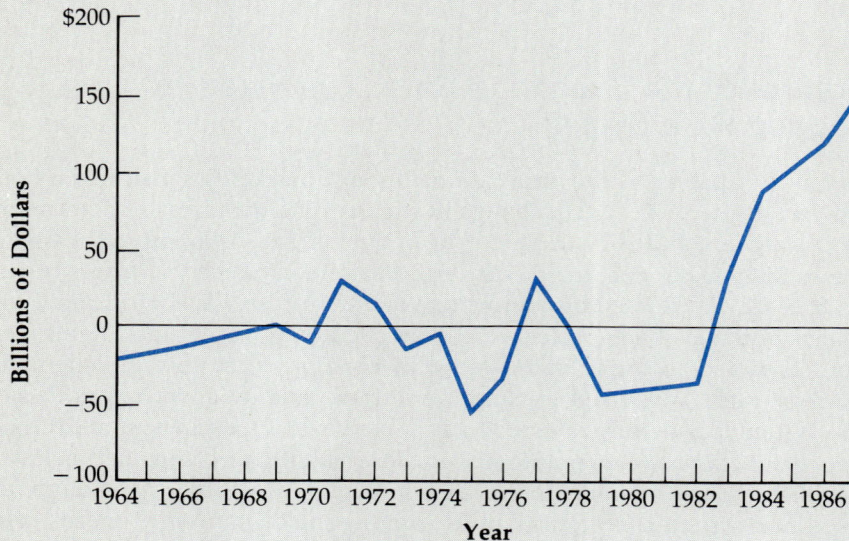

FIGURE 18.5   Balance on U.S. Capital Outflows and Inflows, 1964–1987 (1987 dollars)

count balances moved between deficits and surpluses in almost identical countercycles (to each other) throughout the 1964–1987 period.[1]

Second, the data on trade and capital balances say nothing about causal effects—what caused what. Policymakers who worry about the *trade* deficit seem to believe that trade deficits are directly caused by increases in imports or reductions in exports. This convinces some observers that the deficits are due to the growing (relative) aggressiveness of foreign producers who are able to outcompete American producers both in foreign and domestic markets.

1. The reason that the two account balances do not *exactly* offset each other is that several transaction categories, mainly services and remittances, are left out of the trade balances.

From this perspective, the trade deficit is seen as a major (if not the only) cause of the capital-account surplus, not the other way around. Americans buy more from foreigners than foreigners buy from Americans, inadvertently leaving foreigners with more dollars than they can use on American goods. Foreigners stored the dollars (practically by default) in American bank accounts or in securities (all forms of capital inflows).

The causal connection between the trade-and-capital-account balances is hardly so neat and self-revealing. Clearly, foreigners do sell goods to Americans and do hold on to some of the dollars they receive in exchange, but the dollars must also be valued and demanded (for a variety of reasons) by foreigners, otherwise they would not give up their valuable goods for the dollars. Both parties must value the things received in exchange, or

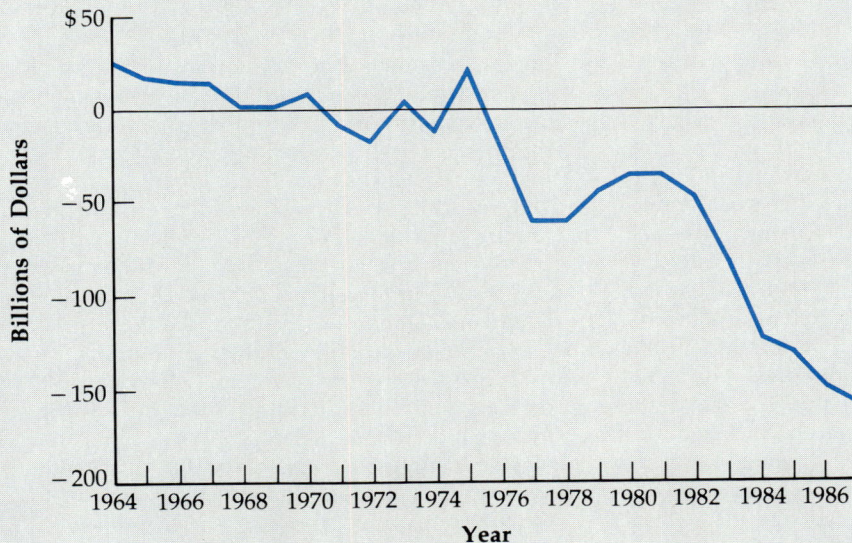

FIGURE 18.6   Balance on U.S. Merchandise Trade, 1964–1987 (1987 dollars)

American Competitiveness and the Overlooked Capital Account Surplus

continued

else the exchange across national boundaries would not happen (at least, not on a continuing basis).

Having acknowledged that obvious point, it is not necessarily the case that the trade of foreign goods for U.S. dollars is motivated exclusively by the Americans' demand for the goods. It could be just as forcefully argued that the exchange is motivated by the foreigners' demand for the dollars—which can reflect their demand for U.S. cash balances, securities, or future goods and services.

This line of argument is elementary but crucial to an appreciation of just what trade deficits do—or more accurately, do not—tell us about the competitiveness of the U.S. economy. Indeed, the argument casts considerable doubt on any proposition that a U.S. merchandise trade deficit necessarily mirrors a lack of competitiveness among Americans. Clearly, the trade deficit indicates that Americans find foreign goods attractive and competitive, but it indicates that in the United States foreigners find something—cash, securities, physical assets, or future goods and services—attractive and competitive.

Whether the foreign goods are *more* attractive to Americans than American cash and securities are to foreigners absolutely cannot be determined because the relative (subjective) values to the different people involved in the exchange cannot be measured. In addition, the question of relative attractiveness may be largely irrelevant. What may be more important is that the exchange made across national boundaries is mutually beneficial to the people (not countries) involved.

The problem of assessing the relative competitiveness of Americans with reference solely to the balance of merchandise trade is made more difficult when it is understood that all Americans—goods producers and security brokers—actually compete with one another for the dollar claims held and obtained by foreigners through the sale of their goods and services in the United States. In

other words, domestic goods producers are often perceived to be competing directly with their counterparts in other countries for domestic and foreign sales. When U.S. imports rise and exports fall and trade deficits result, this perception of international competition makes it appear that U.S. goods producers have been outcompeted, on net, by their foreign counterparts. However, U.S. goods producers are also in direct competition with U.S. security (and physical asset) brokers in the domestic markets. Both U.S. goods producers and security brokers seek to outcompete each other by offering better deals to foreigners for their dollars.

A trade deficit may emerge simply because American security brokers have offered foreigners a better deal on the securities they have to sell than American goods producers have to offer. The foreigners therefore use the dollars earned on the sale (of what constitute U.S. merchandise imports) to buy U.S.-created stocks and bonds (or physical assets), not U.S.-produced consumer or investment goods that can be transported abroad.

Alternately, because of the relatively greater attractiveness of the U.S. security deals, foreigners may be encouraged to sell more goods in U.S. markets so that they can buy a greater number of U.S. securities. However the capital inflow is ignited, the more competitive U.S. security brokers, offering improved deals on U.S. investments, can cause a rise in foreigners' demand for U.S. dollars. This leads to an appreciation of the dollar on international exchange markets and, in turn, to more attractive prices of foreign goods in U.S. markets and to less attractive prices of U.S. goods in foreign markets. In the process, economic life may be made more troublesome for U.S. export and import-competing industries, but trouble for the noncompetitive wherever it is found is endemic to market competition. This is true in the international and domestic economies.

would vary among all the states. The resulting risks and inconveniences would severely hamper interstate trade. For instance, a worker in New York City who commutes from New Canaan, Connecticut, would have to face fluctuating exchange rates on a daily basis when riding subways, buying gas, eating lunch, whatever.

The fixed exchange rate has one advantage over the floating rate: it is stable. Because even a small change in the exchange rate can cause significant losses to people who have already concluded business deals, a flexible exchange rate can increase the risks involved in international trade. For example, suppose you agree to purchase cheese at an exchange rate of $0.10 = F1. You promise to pay the exporter $500, and the French cheese-maker expects to receive F5,000. By the time you send the check, however, the rate has moved to $0.11 = F1. The exporter will now receive only F4,545 ($500 ÷ 0.11). She loses F455.

If the exchange rate moves in the opposite direction, of course, the exporter will gain. In addition, the French cheesemaker can hedge against short-term losses by agreeing, at the time she closes the deal, to sell the proceeds at a given exchange rate, perhaps a fraction of a cent less than the current rate of $.10 = F1. In long-term deals, however, traders inevitably risk losing money because of changes in exchange rates. They incur a risk cost that is translated into higher prices. Under a fixed-rate system, exchange rates move only periodically. The risk cost is reduced, and the prices of foreign goods can be lower.

Like any other form of price control, however, control of foreign exchange rates creates its own problems. If the exchange rate is fixed—at ER_1 in Figure 18.3, for example—and the supply and demand curves remain stable, there is no problem. There is no need for government to fix the rate either, however. It will remain at ER_1 as long as the supply and demand curves for currency stay put.

Problems can develop when market conditions change but the exchange rate is fixed. If the demand for francs increases from D_1 to D_2 in Figure 18.3, a shortage of francs will develop on the international money market. Those who want francs at the fixed price will be unable to get all they want. The government may have to ration the available francs and police the market against black marketeering. If black markets are not controlled, the price of currency will rise—illegally perhaps, but it will rise nonetheless. In the end, the exchange rate will not really be controlled.

Perhaps the chief disadvantage of a fixed rate system is that the level of internal prices and costs in each nation is affected by external economic and monetary developments over which a nation has little or no control. Nations must play according to the rules of the game and submit their internal economy to the dictates of external equilibrium.

Monetary Adjustment Under the Fixed-Rate System

5. How does monetary adjustment operate under a fixed-rate system?

Under the conditions just described, the United States government can keep the exchange rate fixed if it finds some way to fill the gap between the quantity of francs supplied and demanded. Under the fixed exchange system, governments hold currency reserves for just this purpose. Accordingly, the U.S. government sells some of its francs at the officially established price (ER_1 in Figure 18.3), eliminating the upward pressure on the exchange rate. To do so, however, the government must have collected reserves at times when the quantity of francs supplied exceeded the quantity demanded. During such periods, the government generally buys the excess francs with dollars specially created for the purchase.

If a shortage of francs persists, however—if the imbalance in the balance of payments is fundamental rather than temporary—it can only be corrected by a shift in market conditions. An increase in the demand for U.S. goods, for instance, might correct a persistent imbalance. Until market conditions change, maintaining sufficient currency reserves can become a real problem. A persistent shortage of currencies, often referred to as a liquidity problem, can be remedied temporarily in several ways.

Gold Reserves

For centuries governments have used gold as an international monetary reserve, defining their national currencies in terms of it. The U.S. government might establish the price of gold at $500 an ounce, for example; the French government, at F5000 an ounce. In case of a currency shortage, these gold reserves can be used to fill the gap between quantity supplied and demanded. If a shortage of francs develops on the money market, for instance, the U.S. government can sell some of its gold to France and receive F5000 for each ounce. The government can then sell the francs on the money market, filling the gap at the official exchange rate.

In practice, the process may not work exactly that way. Given the shortage of francs, foreign banks may continue to exchange francs for dollars and then sell their dollars to the Bank of France, which will exchange them for gold. The final outcome is the same, however. Gold is traded for francs, and the shortage of francs is eliminated.

Conversely, if there is a shortage of dollars, the French government can keep the price of the dollar from rising above the official level by selling some of its gold to the United States. It then exchanges (sells) its dollars for francs.

Currency Reserves

From the 1930s until 1971, when exchange rates were allowed to float, most nations kept a combination of gold and currency as monetary reserves. Many kept the U.S. dollar, which has come to be accepted throughout the world as a form of *key* or *reference* exchange. A Brazilian exporter, for example, might accept dollars from a German importer because he is confident that they can be converted into Brazilian currency.

Foreign banks too have been willing to hold large amounts of dollars, partly because of the dollar's acceptability in business transactions and partly because banks know foreigners will always demand a large variety of U.S. goods. Before 1971, banks could trade their dollars in for gold at any time. Since gold was more expensive to store, however, they chose to hold dollars. Note that these foreign banks got their dollars from the sale of goods and services to Americans. To the extent that they still hold them for the purpose of carrying out other transactions, people in the United States have struck a tremendous deal. They have traded money—a paper product relatively cheap to produce—for foreign textiles, automobiles, and appliances, which are much more expensive to produce.

The International Monetary Fund (IMF)

The International Monetary Fund (IMF) was created at the close of the Second World War to expand international reserves further. By depositing part of its gold reserves and a specified amount of its currency in the IMF, a nation receives the right to borrow other foreign currencies at a modest interest rate. It can then use those currencies to fill a gap between outgoing and incoming foreign payments. Borrowing rights are restricted to 125 percent of a nation's deposit with the IMF.

Suppose the United States' deposit is $1 billion. At the established exchange rates, the United States can borrow as much as $1.25 billion worth of francs, pounds, yen, or any other currency. When its need for extra reserves has slackened, the United States can pay back the currencies it has borrowed. The method works well. Over the years member nations have raised their deposits at the IMF, increasing the quantity of foreign currencies they can borrow.

Currency Swaps

At times nations have increased one another's currency reserves simply by trading their currencies. For instance, the United States might agree to swap some of its dollars for West German marks. Each nation then has more of the other's currency available to cover a balance of payments deficit, should one occur. In addition, during periods of international monetary crisis, when buyers and sellers of a particular currency no longer accept the official exchange rate, nations can lend money to each other. The borrowed funds can be used to fill a balance of payments gap and prevent the exchange rate from rising.

Reserves acquired through currency swaps are meant to be used only to correct temporary imbalances in a nation's international accounts, or to get it through financial difficulties. During periods when incoming payments exceed outgoing payments, nations are expected to rebuild their depleted reserves. In the 1960s, however, the system failed to work as expected. Some nations, particularly the United States and Great Britain, failed to correct their persistent balance of payment deficits. Once they got additional reserves, they used them up. In effect, the United States and

Britain were using currency swaps to trade their paper currency for the goods and services of other nations.

To correct a fundamental imbalance of payments, a nation might adopt anti-inflationary policies or impose tariffs on imports. It might also take measures to improve the competitiveness of its industry. (More will be said on this subject later.)

Special Drawing Rights (SDRs)

Gold has been used for centuries as an international reserve. It is, however, expensive to mine and store. To use gold as a currency reserve, a nation must not only get it out of the ground, but go to the trouble and expense of storing it. It must maintain expensive security systems to prevent the gold from being stolen. Although gold has an important role in international finance, its benefits come at considerable expense to all who use it.

Gold reserves have another disadvantage: they increase only as new gold is mined and distributed. Yet growth in world trade can quickly widen the gap between a nation's outgoing and incoming payments. If the exchange rate is to be held constant, the growing gap must be filled with a larger quantity of reserves. Unfortunately, growth in world trade can easily outstrip not only growth in gold reserves, but growth in reserves from other sources.

Fearing that currency imbalances might impede world trade, and recognizing the expense of increasing world gold reserves, members of the IMF developed plans for a new monetary reserve system, called Special Drawing Rights (SDRs) in the 1960s. Unlike other reserves, SDRs are merely bookkeeping entries in the IMF accounts. Once a nation has an SDR account, it can use SDRs to settle imbalances in any currency. It can sell some of its SDRs to France for francs (or to Germany for marks), and use the francs (or marks) to fill the balance of payments gap. Because SDRs can be used much as gold is used, they are sometimes called paper gold.

Even though SDRs are only bookkeeping entries, they are a form of international money. The members of the IMF have agreed to accept SDRs in settlement of their accounts, just as they accepted gold in the past. Just as the general acceptability of the U.S. dollar gives the bills in your wallet value in domestic transactions, the general acceptability of SDRs gives them value. Money is what people will generally accept in trade. The difference between these IMF liabilities called SDRs and the demand deposit liabilities of a commercial bank is that the volume of SDRs outstanding does not fluctuate with the extension and repayment of loans. The amount issued is decided by the IMF with allocations made at specific intervals on the basis of the nation's IMF quota, which in turn depends on its world trade volume. In summary, SDRs are preferred to gold in that SDRs earn interest, cost almost nothing to produce and store, represent an equitable manner of distributing reserve assets, and provide a method for controlling the growth of world liquidity. Table 18.3 shows how important SDRs have become in recent years, representing about 22 percent of the U.S. total reserve assets

---

TABLE 18.3   U.S. Reserve Assets (millions of dollars)

Type	1979[a]	1987[a]
Gold stock, including Exchange Stabilization Fund[b]	$11,172	$11,078
Special Drawing Rights (SDRs)[c,d]	2,724	10,283
Reserve position in International Monetary Fund[c]	1,253	11,349
Foreign currencies[e]	3,807	13,088
Total	$18,956	$45,798

a. End of period.
b. Gold held under earmark at Federal Reserve Banks for foreign and international accounts is not included in the gold stock of the United States. Gold stock is valued at $42.22 per fine troy ounce.
c. Beginning July 1974, the IMF adopted a technique for valuing the SDR based on a weighted average of exchange rates for the currencies of member countries. From July 1974 through December 1980, sixteen currencies were used; from January 1981, five currencies have been used: British, French, Japanese, U.S., and West German. The U.S. SDR holdings and reserve position in the IMF also are valued on this basis beginning July 1974.
d. Includes allocations by the International Monetary Fund of SDRs as follows: $867 million on January 1, 1970; $717 million on January 1, 1971; $710 million on January 1, 1972; $1,139 million on January 1, 1979; $1,152 million on January 1, 1980; and $1,093 million on January 1, 1981; plus transactions in SDRs.
e. Valued at current market exchange rates.
Source: Federal Reserve Bulletin (January 1980, March 1988), p. A54.

at the end of 1987 compared with 14 percent at the end of 1979. Also note that while U.S. foreign currencies and IMF reserves increased sharply along with SDRs, the gold stock component stayed roughly constant in absolute terms and declined sharply in relative terms, falling from about 59 percent of the total in 1979 to 24 percent in 1987.

Correcting a Persistent Balance of Payments Deficit

▲ **6. How does a persistent balance of payments problem get solved?**

International reserves of gold, foreign currencies, and SDRs are useful in solving temporary balance of payment problems. If outgoing payments exceed incoming payments for long, a nation's reserves will eventually run out. It will not be able to prop up the value of its currency without resorting to elaborate corrective measures, most of which are either economically inefficient or politically unacceptable.

Tax increases, expenditure decreases, and a reduction in the growth of the money stock may help to reduce inflation temporarily, but at the cost of a drop in total real income. The lower inflation rate will make domestically produced goods more attractive, both at home and abroad—and a lower aggregate real income will mean people will have less to spend, both on domestic goods and on imports. This reduced demand for foreign goods will be translated into a reduced demand for foreign currencies. As a result, the gap between the supply of and demand for any particular foreign currency will narrow, reducing the short-run balance of payments deficit.

Many economists believe this was precisely the policy President Dwight Eisenhower followed during his term of office (1953–1961). Politically it is a controversial approach. By lowering total real income and production, this method of correcting a balance of payments deficit can add to the nation's unemployment. Although a reduction in the inflation rate may seem attractive, increased short-term unemployment is a high price to pay for an improved balance of payments.

Tariffs on imported goods and/or restrictions on the flow of funds into foreign investments are another way of correcting a persistent balance of payments deficit. Both approaches tend to reduce the immediate demand for foreign currencies. Although these policies have been used by almost all governments at one time or another, they expose citizens to all the negative effects of restrictions on international trade described in the preceding chapter.

After all else has been tried, a nation may be forced to depreciate or devaluate its currency. Given a fixed exchange rate of $0.10 = F1, for instance, the United States could correct a balance of payments deficit by depreciating the dollar (or revising the exchange rate upward) to $0.20 = F1. The rules of the IMF provide for such a change, which would make U.S. exports more attractive to foreigners and foreign imports less attractive to Americans. Thus it would reduce the quantity of francs demanded and increase the quantity of francs supplied on the international money market. In Figure 18.7, with the exchange rate at ER_1, the balance of payments deficit is the difference between the quantity of francs demanded, Q_2, and the quantity supplied, Q_1. At ER_1, the exchange rate is below equilibrium. Depreciation of the dollar moves the exchange rate up

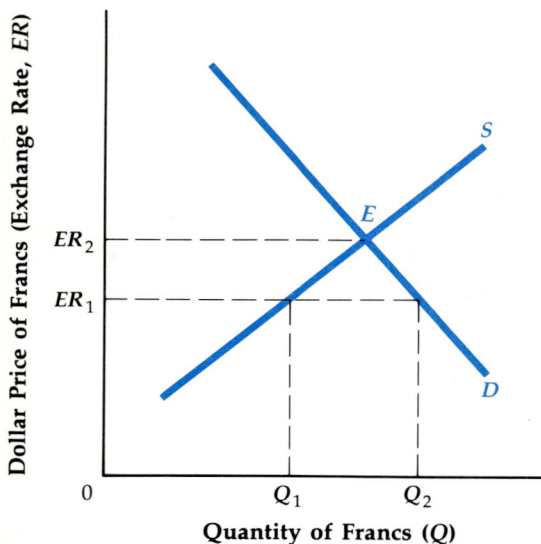

FIGURE 18.7   Balance of Payments Deficit
Given a supply of francs equal to S and a demand for francs equal to D, an exchange rate of ER_1 will cause a balance of payments deficit equal to the difference between Q_2 and Q_1. At ER_1, the exchange rate is below equilibrium; more francs are demanded than supplied. Depreciation of the dollar through a rise in the exchange rate, from ER_1 to ER_2, will eliminate the deficit as the equilibrium is reached at E.

toward the equilibrium rate of ER_2, reducing the gap between supply and demand.

Devaluation: under a fixed standard, the reduction of a domestic currency brought about by government intervention in its official price in relation to a foreign currency.

Revaluation: under a fixed standard, the rise of domestic currency brought about by government intervention in its official price in relation to a foreign currency.

Devaluation of a domestic currency under a fixed standard is a reduction brought about by government intervention in its official price in relation to a foreign currency. **Revaluation** of a domestic currency under a fixed standard is a rise brought about by government intervention in its official price in relation to a foreign currency. If all nations simultaneously devalued by raising the price of gold by the same percentage under a gold standard, there would be devaluation but not depreciation. In other words, devaluation involves a depreciation relative to the monetary standard and not necessarily relative to foreign currencies.

The Demise of the Fixed-Rate System

In August 1971, President Richard Nixon withdrew the United States' commitment to maintain fixed exchange rates between the dollar and other national currencies. In so doing, he allowed the overvalued U.S. dollar to seek a new equilibrium level and to move, or float, with changes in money market conditions. The demise of the fixed exchange rate system—sometimes called the adjustable peg system, since nations could adjust the rates periodically—was inevitable. The United States had run a balance of payments deficit almost every year since 1950. Its gold reserves, valued at $35 an ounce, had dwindled from a high of $23 billion in 1950 to $12 billion in 1971—they have since stabilized at about $11 billion. At the same time, about $80 billion had accumulated in foreign bank accounts. Although many of those dollars were necessary to the transaction of world trade, it was becoming clear that the market was saturated with overvalued dollars.

In the mid-1960s, moreover, people had begun to expect depreciation of the dollar and the British pound. Every year or so there would be a run on the dollar or the pound. Panicky investors would try to exchange their dollars or pounds for some other currency, like German marks. Such crises became progressively more frequent in the late 1960s and early 1970s. By August 1971, they had so destabilized the fixed exchange rate system that it was certain to be abandoned. The only question was the timing of the change to a floating exchange rate system.

Fear of depreciation can disrupt the international money market for two reasons. First, depreciation of a currency reduces the value of foreign holdings of that currency in terms of other world currencies. For example, at an exchange rate of $0.10 = F1, a $100 bank account is worth F1,000. At $0.20 = F1, however, that same $100 is worth only F500. To avoid a loss from an expected depreciation, people will try to sell the currency in question and buy others. In other words, at times of international monetary crisis, the demand for undervalued foreign currencies like francs will increase. The greater demand for francs will widen the gap between the quantity demanded and the quantity supplied, thus increasing the amount of reserves needed to bring the quantity supplied into line with the quantity demanded.

American Competitiveness and the Balance of Trade

No matter how it is measured, America's balance of international trade has deteriorated dramatically during the 1980s. Few international analysts think that deficits will go away in the near future; some predict that large (if not progressively larger) trade deficits will linger into the 1990s. Most Washington policy pundits worry that the country's worsening trade balance signals a degeneration of the country's "competitiveness," the new Washington buzzword made so prominent by the Reagan administration that it is sometimes called the "C-word" in Washington policy circles.

The presumed trade problems of the United States are measured in several ways, but the most easily understood measure is the balance on *merchandise trade*, which covers only U.S. exports and imports of goods.[1] Figure 18.8 vividly portrays the striking growth of the U.S. merchandise trade deficit in the period from 1976 to 1987. In 1975, the United States had a modest trade surplus of nearly $19 billion, measured in 1987 dollars. By the following year, the trade balance on exports and imports had switched to a deficit of under $58 billion in constant (1987) dollars. By 1987, however, the merchandise trade balance had grown in real terms by more than 200 percent, to a whopping deficit of nearly $160 billion.[2]

During the 1982–1987 period, relative to real gross national product (GNP), the trade deficit also grew substantially. In 1982, the deficit was just above .2 percent of GNP. In 1987 the deficit represented slightly less than 3.5 percent of GNP. Other measures of the deficit on goods and services and current account grew both absolutely

and relatively in concert with the merchandise trade deficit.[3]

Does the United States face a competitive crisis? There is much disagreement over the answer. Many commentators considering the raw trade figures certainly think so. The country has had persistent trade deficits in its history, for example, in the early 1970s, but never as large as the ones reported in 1984 through 1987. Nevertheless, an answer to the competitiveness question is not as clear as might be imagined on first appraisal of the deficit record. The answer depends on how the export and import data—which encompass economic opportunities as well as problems—are viewed.

Taken by itself, the trade deficit can be misleading because it is the *net* of exports and imports. The total rise in the deficit in the 1980s could therefore have been due only to a fall in exports. A $160 billion drop in exports between 1982 and 1987 might have, indeed, been a major policy concern, since it would have meant a virtual collapse (more than a 60 percent reduction) in exports during a five-year period. (U.S. exports in 1982 were only $249 billion, measured in 1987 dollars.)

However, the rapid rise in the trade deficit between 1982 and 1987 was actually due to a combination of export and import forces. Real imports grew by 27 percent between 1981 and 1987, while real exports fell by nearly 12 percent.

Obviously, some exporters were being outcompeted in foreign markets, but focusing on exports and imports, instead of on the *net* of the inflows and outflows of goods, is important for two reasons. First, the shift in imports relative to exports could be largely explained, as it has been, to a relatively more rapid rate of economic growth in

---

1. Two other commonly cited measures of U.S. "trade" problems include the balance on goods and services (which adds net military transactions, investment income, travel, transportation, and other services to merchandise trade) and balance on current account (which adds remittances, pensions, and other unilateral payments to the balance on goods and services).

2. All trade and deficit figures for 1987 are preliminary, based on annualized figures for the first three quarters.

3. The deficit on goods and services and on current account tended to be lower in all years than the deficit on merchandise trade. This was generally because of the net inflow of investment income and the surplus in trade of services.

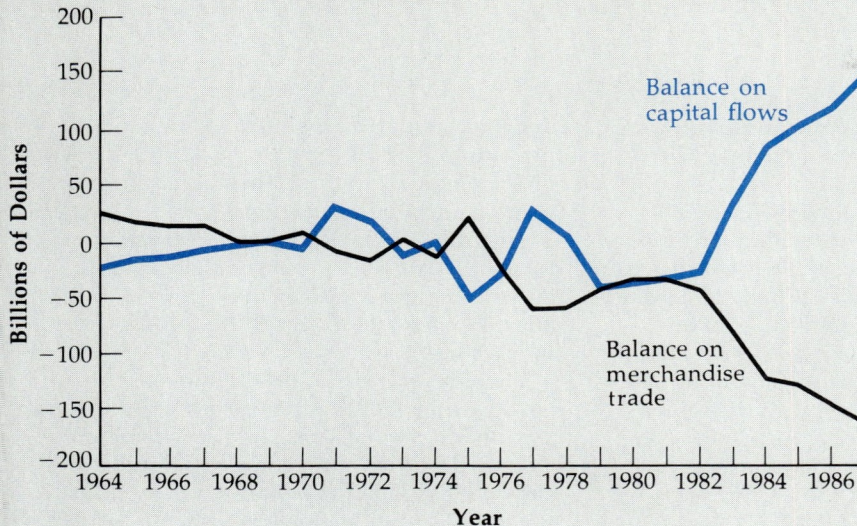

FIGURE 18.8 Balance on Merchandise Trade and Capital Flows, 1964–1987 (1987 dollars)

▬ Balance
▬ Net

the United States.[4] The growth in U.S. demand has, as recognized, led to an expansion of imports because more foreign resources need to be bought in order to produce more domestic output. More foreign goods will be bought with the rise in domestic income, but the growth in domestic demand has also led to a contraction of the ability of the U.S. economy to export. The growth in domestic demand has pulled resources away from export production.

Seen from this perspective, the balance of trade deficits could have been moderated. Barring an expansion of foreign demand, however, correction in the balance of trade would have called for a reduction in domestic demand. This, in turn, would imply a lower rate of growth in domestic production and income and higher unemployment at a time when unemployment rates were already

high by historical standards—hardly a means of improving domestic competitiveness.

Second, between the late 1970s and 1985, the U.S. dollar appreciated in value more than 30 percent against an index (called the "trade-weighted index") of fifteen other currencies; this means that U.S. exporters were, during the period, facing stiffer price competition in foreign markets. Given the rise in U.S. export prices in foreign markets and the relative rise in U.S. domestic demand, it may be deemed somewhat remarkable that U.S. exports did not drop by more than 12 percent in the period and that they were actually moving gradually upward after 1983.[5] One reason that exports did not fall by a greater percentage must be that, during the period, many (but, of course, not all) U.S. exporters were becoming more aggressive—more competitive, not

4. Ralph C. Bryant and Gerald Holtham, "The External Deficit: Why? Where Next? What Remedy?" *Brookings Review* (Spring 1987): 29.

5. Bryant and Holtham conclude "paradoxically that the deficit is 'too' easy to explain." Ibid.

American Competitiveness and the Balance of Trade

continued

less so. Improvement in the competitiveness of American industries has been reflected in their reductions of production costs.

On the import side, the rapid appreciation of the dollar meant a rapid decrease in import prices, which, of course, caused competitive problems for several domestic industries. U.S. firms were having to defend their market positions against lower priced foreign goods, but at the same time, most U.S. industries were not being pushed out of their markets. The sales and employment levels in most U.S. industries continued to rise, while only a few levels contracted.[6] On balance, once the recovery from the last recession of the early 1980s was

6. Norman Fieleke notes in a study of the impact of rising trade deficits on industry, "A common view is that rising import competition signifies unemployment and plant closings. In fact, no such simple correlation prevails." Norman S. Fieleke, "The Foreign Trade Deficit and American Industry," Federal Reserve Bank of Boston *New England Economic Review* (July/August 1985): 52. Fieleke explains that import penetration can be misleading when aggregate demand is rising. While American industries may have done better, if the dollar had not appreciated, "it is clearly premature to lament the downfall of American industry." Ibid.

underway, industrial production and manufacturing output generally rose. Also during the period, most domestic import-competing industries were, in effect, demonstrating that they were capable of holding their own against competition made tougher by an adverse shift in the exchange rate—an outcome that is hardly descriptive of a systematic crippling of the competitiveness of American industries.

There is really no unresolved mystery about why the trade deficit after 1984 continued to expand when the dollar began a precipitous depreciation, a drop that was generally still underway in early 1988. When the dollar depreciates rapidly, the prices of U.S. imports rise while the prices of U.S. exports fall. Because trading channels could not be adjusted as rapidly as prices, the dollar value of imports rose at the same time the dollar value of exports fell, widening the export/import gap. However, once producers in the domestic and foreign markets have sufficient time to adapt to new exchange rates, the trade gap can be expected to narrow (as it was narrowing in 1987 and early 1988). Whether the gap will be eliminated is an uncertain issue.

Second, speculators will try to make a profit on any expected depreciation of a currency. If a person holding dollars can buy francs at $0.10 apiece and sell them back at $0.20, he will make a profit of $0.10 on each franc. This speculative activity increases the demand for francs, again widening the gap between the quantity demanded and the quantity supplied. During the 1950s and 1960s, when the British experienced substantial balance of payments deficits, speculation in the pound was active.

The 1980s were a period of substantial unrest in the international sphere. The United States and third-world countries experienced weak currencies and high-level deficits. There were also more severe fluctuations in exchange rates and more persistent balance-of-trade payment imbalances than hoped for. There were high-level discussions among nations regarding the need for revision in the international monetary system, perhaps even bringing back some form of a pegged or fixed-rate system—such as the gold standard.

Chapter Review

Review of Key Questions

◢   *1. What are international exchange rates?*

Foreign exchange involves the monetary means used to make monetary payments transfers from one nation to another. Sellers want to be paid in their currency; thus their trading partner needs to acquire units of that currency. Any nation's imports create a demand for foreign currency. Any nation's exports create a demand for its domestic currency. In the long run, the monetary value of a nation's imports and exports must be equal. The international exchange rate affects the relative prices of domestic and foreign products. Under a free or flexible exchange rate system under which there is no government intervention with the forces of supply and demand, if a national currency is overvalued it will tend to depreciate or decline in exchange value or purchasing power relative to other national currency; if it is undervalued, a national currency will tend to increase in exchange value. In the short run when elasticities are small, the balance-of-trade equilibrium, according to the J-curve phenomenon, may worsen. But in the long run when elasticities are greater, depreciation generally should improve the balance of trade. Whereas the U.S. trade deficit worsened in the early 1980s, a depreciating dollar should eventually help matters. The highly organized foreign exchange market brings together buyers and sellers of different currency.

◢   *2. How are international exchange rates determined?*

Like any price, the exchange rate, or price paid for foreign currency on the foreign exchange market, is determined by supply and demand. Changes in the real exchange rate (i.e., terms of trade) will change the relative prices of foreign and domestic products, eventually altering import and export levels. Specifically, depreciation of the dollar will lower imports to the United States and increase exports from the United States. Appreciation of the dollar will have the opposite effect. According to the J-curve phenomenon, although a depreciation will eventually achieve a balance-of-trade equilibrium, there may be a short-run worsening of trade. Changes in inflation rates that are captured in every country's nominal exchange rate affect the real exchange rate. From the end of World War II to 1971, most of the world was on a fixed exchange rate system. Since 1971 most countries have operated under a dirty or managed float exchange rate system, where there is official government intervention with private demand and supply to moderate exchange rate swings.

◢   *3. How do floating, flexible, or freely fluctuating international exchange rates work?*

Under a floating, flexible, or freely fluctuating exchange rate system, international exchange rates are determined by the interaction of supply and demand of domestic and foreign currencies. Changes in consumer tastes, total real income, and speculation can alter the real exchange rate (or terms of trade). If the purchasing power parity theory works, anticipated changes in the rate of inflation in prices and interest rates and in the future levels of exchange rates will only shift the nominal exchange rate. A nation's currency tends to depreciate when the rate of inflation and economic growth are high and real interest rates are low at home, tastes and preferences favor foreign over home goods, and people's expectations are poor regarding a nation's prospects. The reverse situation leads to an appreciation of a currency. Although flexible exchange rates automatically tend eventually to eliminate balance of payments problems, some people think they harm trade because of the uncertainty and instability over the terms of trade.

4. What is a fixed or pegged international exchange rate system?

Under a fixed rate system there is official government intervention in the private market. This system places the burden of the equilibrium process on the domestic economy rather than on the balance of payments. While the system is automatic, internal economic policymaking must be sacrificed to achieve external equilibrium. While the pure gold standard pegged exchange rates within a narrow range, other systems allow wider but still prescribed limits. When those bounds are reached, official government intervention occurs.

5. How does monetary adjustment operate under a fixed-rate system?

Under a fixed exchange rate system, nations use gold and currency reserves, loans from the International Monetary Fund, currency swaps, and special drawing rights to fill periodic—but not long-run structural—gaps between the quantity of a currency supplied and the quantity demanded. SDRs and other non-gold assets have become increasingly important in recent years. Insufficient reserves call for direct (exchange) controls, protectionism, or undesirable macroeconomic adjustments at home (such as higher interest and unemployment rates and lower inflation rates).

6. How does a persistent balance of payments problem get solved?

A fixed exchange rate system lessens the risk, uncertainty, and instability involved in trade, but tends to create balance of payment problems. The United States dropped fixed exchange rates in 1971; most other industrial nations followed by 1973. There have been persistent discussions of returning to "the way we were." In the short run, international reserves of gold, foreign currencies, and SDRs are used in solving temporary balance of payments problems. Changes in domestic income, interest rates, and price levels through domestic monetary policy is another solution. Devaluation or depreciation are more drastic measures. After all of these have been tried, wholesale structural changes in an economy may be necessary.

Further Topics

A stable set of international exchange rates is needed for the smooth operation of international trade. Continual and significant variations in exchange rates introduce an unwanted element of risk into international commerce, reducing the volume of trade. Control of exchange rates through a fixed-rate system, however, has serious practical defects.

Under a floating exchange rate system, exchange rates vary in response to changes in consumer taste and the technology of production. Such fluctuations are not only useful but necessary. Exchange rates also vary with changes in domestic and foreign inflation and interest rates, national income levels, and expectations as to the future exchange rates. In short, the international monetary system mirrors the stability or instability, actual and anticipated, of the world's national economies. If the nations of the world are pursuing inappropriate domestic policies, they cannot expect the international monetary system to remain stable.

Review of New Terms

Appreciation An increase in exchange value or purchasing power of one national currency, brought about by market forces, in relation to other national currencies.

Depreciation A reduction in the exchange value or purchasing power of one national currency, brought about by market forces, in relation to other national currencies.

Devaluation Under a fixed standard, the reduction of a domestic currency brought about by government intervention in its official price in relation to a foreign currency.

Dirty or managed floating exchange rate system An international monetary exchange system in which the prices of currencies are partly determined by competitive market forces and partly determined by official government intervention.

Fixed or pegged exchange rate system An international monetary exchange system in which the prices of currencies are established and maintained by government intervention.

Floating, flexible, or freely fluctuating exchange rate system An international monetary exchange system in which the prices of currencies are determined by competitive market forces.

Foreign exchange The monetary means or instruments used to make monetary payments and transfers from one currency area to another. The funds available as foreign exchange include foreign coin and currency, deposits in foreign banks, and other short-term, liquid financial claims.

International exchange rate The price of one national currency stated in terms of another national currency.

J-curve phenomenon Although the initial impact of depreciation is often an increase in nominal spending on imports because higher prices cause a deterioration in the nominal trade balance, over time depreciation will tend to improve both nominal and real net exports.

Purchasing power parity theory The theory that if the inflation rates are about the same in two nations that trade with each other, the exchange rate between their currencies will remain stable, *ceteris paribus*.

Revaluation Under a fixed standard, the rise of a domestic currency brought about by government intervention in its official price in relation to a foreign currency.

Review Questions

1. If a nation appreciates its currency in relation to other national currencies, what will be the effect on other nations' exports and imports? On the willingness of that nation's citizens to invest abroad? (◢ 1, ◢ 2, ◢ 3)

2. Will a tax on imports and a subsidy on exports have the same effect on trade as depreciation of a nation's currency? (◢ 2)

3. Suppose the exchange rate between the pound and the dollar is fixed. If both the United States and Great Britain double the price of gold in terms of their own national currencies, what will be the effect on trade between the two nations? Assuming that other nations hold the price of gold in their own currencies constant, how will the change in the dollar and pound prices of gold affect trade between the United States and Britain and the rest of the world? (◢ 4, ◢ 5)

4. Develop cases for and against the fixed exchange rate system. (◢ 4, ◢ 5)

5. Do you agree that if a nation runs a persistent balance of payments surplus—that is, if its outgoing international payments fall consistently short of its incoming payments—it is trading goods and services for foreign currencies? Why might a nation be unwilling to incur an extended balance of payments surplus? (◢ 6)

International Trade and the Macroeconomy

I am raising the question why any of us should worry about this particular statistic [the trade deficit], and why the U.S. government should take any responsibility for it. The people who have the trade deficit—who are buying more abroad than they are selling—are doing so voluntarily. If they were worried much they would stop. I had a trade deficit in 1986 because I took a vacation in France. I didn't worry about it; I enjoyed it.
    Herbert Stein

KEY QUESTIONS

◢ 1. How do international transactions fit into the Keynesian model of the macroeconomy?

◢ 2. How do international transactions fit into the monetarist model of the macroeconomy?

◢ 3. How do international transactions fit into the supply-side model of the macroeconomy?

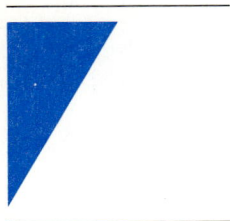

The last two chapters explained how trade across national boundaries can increase the incomes of the parties involved in the trades and how those trades are made possible through the exchange of national currencies. This chapter extends our analysis of the income and employment effects of international trade by reintroducing the macroeconomic theories studied earlier in Chapters 5 through 16.

As we learned in our earlier discussions of macroeconomics, much controversy surrounds the usefulness of various theories of how the macroeconomy works. Nevertheless, by exploring several schools of macroeconomic thought, we gained insights regarding how the different schools interpret the impact of changes in broad sectors of the economy, summarized in aggregate demand and aggregate supply. We were also able to explore the policy recommendations of adherents to the different schools of thought.

In this chapter we continue our discussion of the macroeconomy by introducing exports and imports as sources of changes in aggregate demand and aggregate supply—and, therefore, as sources of changes in national income and production, unemployment and employment, and prices. Specifically, we are concerned in this chapter with how Keynesian, monetarist, and supply-side macroeconomic theorists appraise the interactive effects of the domestic macroeconomy and exports and imports.

The Keynesian Perspective

▲ 1. How do international transactions fit into the Keynesian model of the macroeconomy?

In the Keynesian model, the macroeconomy moves principally in response to changes in aggregate demand. When aggregate demand rises, the national income and employment levels rise by some multiple (generally assumed to be greater than 1) of the change in aggregate demand. The price level can also be expected to change in the same direction as aggregate demand. That is to say, an increase in aggregate demand can be expected to lead to an increase in national income and production, an increase in employment (and a reduction in unemployment), and an increase in the price level. A decrease in aggregate demand has the exact opposite effects.

Aggregate demand can change in response to changes in consumption, investment, and government expenditures. As we studied, consumption expenditures can change due to changes in current and forward-looking national income, prices, wealth, and taxes. Investment can change in response to changes in the (real) interest rates and profit expectations and also to changes in taxes on business income. Government expenditures may also change because of specific legislative actions or because government expenditures (for example, unemployment compensation) are directly linked to the level of national income and employment.

In the Keynesian model, international trades are also sources of increases and decreases in aggregate demand. The existence of the potential for trade across national boundaries can, as studied earlier, increase a country's production possibilities curve. The greater efficiency in production can cause both aggregate supply and demand to expand, with a resulting improvement in national income.

The Circular Flow of Income

These points are no different from what we have already argued in Chapter 17. The most theoretically interesting points relate to the way exports and imports are treated in Keynesian theory.

Exports represent expenditures on American goods, a source of demand on American productive capacity. An exogenous increase in exports amounts to an increase in demand for American goods and services. Similarly, a decrease in exports amounts to a decrease in aggregate demand.

Imports, on the other hand, represent expenditures on foreign goods. An exogenous increase in imports therefore represents a decrease in aggregate demand on the productive capacity of the domestic economy, and vice versa. This is true to the extent that greater imports represent a shift in purchases by Americans from domestic to foreign goods and services.

Taken by themselves, exports represent an injection (similar to investment and government expenditures studied earlier) into the macroeconomy. Exports are described by the appropriately labeled arrow in Figure 19.1 pointing toward the circular flow of income diagram, first introduced in Chapter 2 and reconsidered in greater detail in Chapter 10. Imports, being a withdrawal from the circular flow (on par with saving and taxes), are described in Figure 19.1 by the appropriately labeled arrow pointing outward from the circular flow.

As long as all outward arrows (saving, taxes, and imports) equal all inward arrows (investment, government expenditures, and exports) the macroeconomy is in Keynesian equilibrium. Aggregate demand from all sectors is then matched by aggregate production, and producers do not have any reason to either expand or contract their production levels. Hence, the production and employment levels will remain stable. In mathematical notation, Keynesian equilibrium occurs where:

$$I + G + Ex = S + T + Im$$

where I = private investment
         G = government expenditures
      Ex = exports
         S = saving
        T = taxes
     Im = imports

Alternately, equilibrium occurs where national income and production equal aggregate demand, or where:

$$Y = C + I + G + (Ex - Im)$$

where Y = national income
         C = consumption expenditures

This statement means, very simply, that when total expenditures from all foreign and domestic sources equal the value of total production, there is no reason for production (and national income and employment) to expand or contract.

    Notice that equilibrium in national income, production, and employment does not require that the government budget be balanced or that exports and imports be balanced. All that is required is that in order to achieve equilibrium, the aggregate of the injections must equal the aggregate of the withdrawals, which means that any deficit or surplus in the federal budget must be offset by a surplus or deficit in the international trade account (or by an appropriate difference in saving and investment).

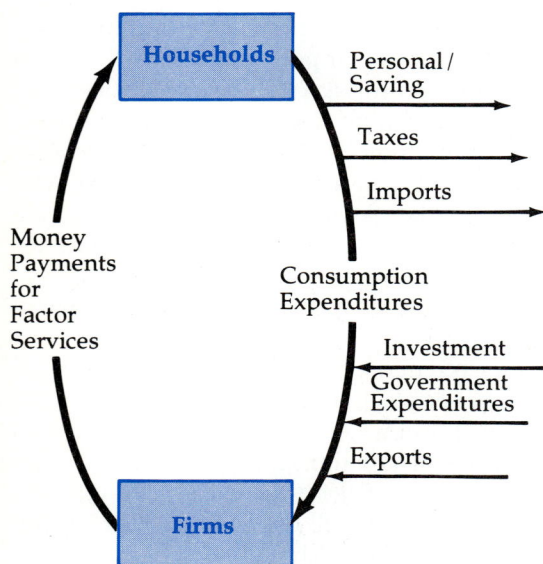

FIGURE 19.1   The Circular Flow of Income and International Trade
In the Keynesian model of the macroeconomy, exports are an injection (and add to aggregate domestic demand), while imports are a withdrawal (and reduce aggregate domestic demand). An increase in imports will lower national income and employment. An increase in exports, on the other hand, will raise national income and employment. When national income rises or falls (due to a change in investment, consumption, or government expenditures), imports will move in the same direction.

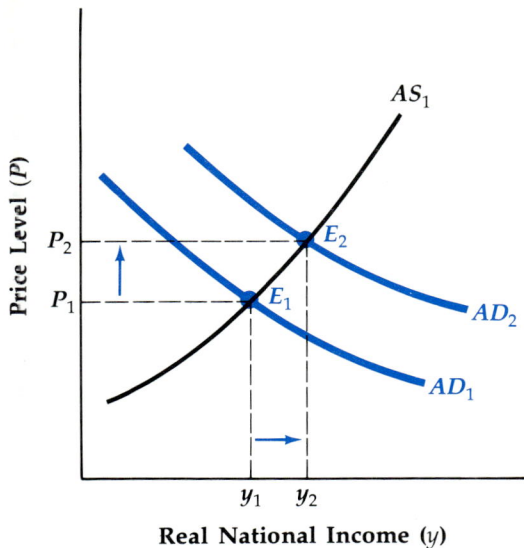

FIGURE 19.2 The Keynesian Aggregate Demand and Supply Model
A reduction taxes will cause the aggregate demand curve to shift rightward. Real national income will rise from y_1 to y_2, and the price level will rise from P_1 to P_2. Because of the increase in national income, imports will rise.

Changes in Aggregate Demand and Supply

From the Keynesian macroeconomic perspective, it follows that national income will rise with an increase in exports unmatched by an increase in imports, *ceteris paribus*. In addition, there will be a multiplier effect: the increase in the national income level will be some multiple, presumably greater than 1, of the increase in exports. If, for example, exports increase by $1 billion and the multiplier is 1.5, national income will increase by $1.5 billion. Employment will also rise (and unemployment will also fall).

Consider Figure 19.2, which replicates our aggregate demand and aggregate supply model of the macroeconomy first studied in Chapter 13. Early in our discussion of Keynesian macroeconomics (see Chapter 11) we said that the multiplier was directly related to the marginal propensity to consume (*MPC*): the higher the marginal propensity to consume, the larger the multiplier (and the greater the increase in national income, given any exogenous change in aggregate demand).[1] This is because the multiplier (*m*) was defined in that simple model as:

$$m = 1/(1 - MPC) = 1/MPS$$

where the *MPC* = marginal propensity to consume
    MPS = marginal propensity to save (which equals $1 - MPC$)

1. Robert E. Hall and John B. Taylor, *Macroeconomics: Theory, Performance and Policy,* 2nd ed. (New York: W. W. Norton, 1988), p. 195, estimate that over the period 1953–1986 the short-run (long-run) MPC was .76 (.91).

The direct relationship between the *MPC* and the multiplier still holds with the inclusion of exports and imports in the Keynesian model. However, with international trade in the model, the multiplier effect of any given change in aggregate demand is never quite as large as indicated earlier. This is because imports have the same effect on the resulting change of the economy as do taxes: imports drain away purchases that would otherwise be realized by domestic producers.

When the national income begins to expand in response to an increase in aggregate demand (whether from greater investment, government expenditures, or exports), imports begin to rise (along with saving and taxes) for two reasons.

> First, producers seeking to satisfy the greater domestic demand will want to import more raw materials (example: oil), parts (example: automobile transmissions), and machinery (example: textile looms) from abroad.

> Second, with rising income, consumers will want to supplement their domestic purchases with goods (examples: wines and clothes) and services (example: travel) from foreign countries.

As a consequence, given the increase in aggregate demand and with exports and imports in the model, Keynesian macro-equilibrium is reestablished with a smaller increase in income and a smaller multiplier effect—regardless of the cause of the increase in aggregate demand, whether from an increase in consumption, investment, government, or export expenditures. Imports, in other words, dampen the expansion—and reduce the size of the multiplier. Imports also dampen any contraction in the economy. The decrease in the national income is moderated by a reduction in purchases from abroad—that is, fewer imports. As a result, the domestic economy does not feel the full effect of any changes in aggregate demand.[2]

The Exchange Rate System

Obviously, exports and imports complicate Keynesian macroeconomic analysis. However, as complicated as the foregoing discussion may sound, several important technical details have been left out. The impact of exogenous changes in exports and imports—or any other injection or withdrawal—on the national economy depends critically on the international exchange rate system in place—that is, with whether the dollar value of foreign currencies on international money markets is fixed by government fiat or whether it is allowed to move in value with changes in market forces.

Our foregoing analysis has implicitly assumed that the exchange rate is fixed. Therefore, when exports increase, there is no necessary offsetting

---

2. Because income does not rise as much with imports in the model, saving and taxes, two other leakages from the circular flow, do not rise as much as they otherwise would. The decreases in these leakages partially, but not totally, offset the moderating influence on the rise in national income.

change in imports. The increase in exports does not change the international price of the dollar (it is held stable by government) and therefore does not directly affect the American prices of imported goods and services. Therefore, an increase in exports can in fact lead to an increase in national income with some subsidiary increase in imports due to the expansion in employment and income. Fiscal policy can have all of the effects discussed earlier. An increase in government spending or a reduction in taxes can cause national income to rise (with some subsidiary increase in imports due to the expansion of employment and income).

However, under a fixed exchange rate system, monetary policy may be largely ineffective. This is because an increase in the money stock can cause interest rates to fall and capital to flow to foreign countries (because U.S. investors will then want to place their money at higher interest rates abroad). At the same time, any increase in national income due to lower interest rates and greater investment spending in this country can be expected to raise imports. The result is that the demand for foreign currencies will rise, and in order to hold the exchange rate stable at its official rate, the government will have to buy dollars. The government will then be forced to buy back the dollars it initially sought to add to the money stock.

Under a flexible exchange rate system, our conclusions about the impact of exogenous changes in domestic demand and fiscal and monetary policies are substantially different. In the main, the effectiveness of fiscal and monetary policies are reversed.

Under a flexible exchange rate system, an exogenous increase in exports will be accompanied by an increase in the demand for dollars on the foreign exchange market (foreigners will need more dollars to buy the greater quantity of American goods). The increase in the demand for dollars will lead to an appreciation of the international value of the dollar. The increase in the dollar's value will make American exports more expensive, dampening the original increase in aggregate demand due to exports. The increase in the dollar's value will also make foreign goods cheaper, shifting domestic demand from American to foreign goods and again reducing the demand in the American economy. The net effect of the exchange rate change should be that the national income level is undisturbed (except to the extent that the shifts in demand cause temporary and minor adjustments in the allocation of resources).

In a similar manner, other changes in domestic demand—whether from changes in consumption, investment, or government expenditures—can be expected to have neutralizing effects on imports and exports. For example, suppose that investment expenditures increase for some reason (businesses become more profitable or the corporate income tax is reduced on new plant and equipment). Normally, the increase in investment spending would necessarily mean an increase in aggregate demand and therefore in national employment and income. However, the increase in demand for loanable funds by Americans can drive interest rates up (which will temper somewhat American investment spending). The higher interest rates can attract capital from foreigners who want a higher return on their funds, and the capital inflow will translate into an increase in demand for dollars on international markets. The dollar will appreciate, causing the price of foreign imports to Americans to fall (with more actual goods imported) and the prices of American goods to foreigners to rise (with fewer actual goods exported). The exogenous increase in investment spending is therefore offset by a reduction in one injection (exports) and an expansion in another withdrawal (imports).

Because of capital flows, fiscal policies will be largely neutralized under a flexible exchange rate system. An increase in the government's budget deficit (due to an increase in government expenditures and/or a reduction in taxes) can be expected to put upward pressure on interest rates. The higher interest rates can be expected to attract foreign capital and appreciate the dollar, which will increase imports and reduce exports.[3]

Monetary policy, however, can be quite effective under a flexible exchange rate system. This is because in the Keynesian model, an increase in the money stock will lower interest rates in the United States, causing a capital outflow (because U.S. investors will then want to invest abroad at relatively higher interest rates) and a depreciation of the dollar. The depreciation will then spur exports and retard imports, resulting in an increase in aggregate demand—and, therefore, more national employment and more income.

The Monetarist Perspective

▲ **2. How do international transactions fit into the monetarist model of the macroeconomy?**

Keynesian economics is mainly concerned with explaining short-run changes in national income and employment, primarily through changes in aggregate demand. Monetarism, by contrast, is basically concerned with explaining the price level and inflation. Monetarism is called by that name because of its adherents' focus on the influence of the stock of money and its growth rate on the price level and rate of inflation. Monetarists contend that fiscal and monetary policies have few long-run effects on real national income and employment (except to the extent that government taxes and expenditures affect people's incentives to produce). Hence, when they study the international economy (and international macroeconomics) monetarists are primarily concerned with the influence that the money stock and monetary policy have on price levels in different countries and on the determination of international exchange rates.

The monetary approach to international macroeconomics was originally developed to explain the movements of gold and silver in a world where the precious metals constituted the international currency. The

---

3. Whether fiscal policies are *totally* neutralized by capital flows actually depends on the size of the U.S. economy relative to the rest of the world. If the United States is a "small" country vis-à-vis the rest of the world, fiscal policies will be totally ineffective. This is because the rush of capital from around the world to the U.S. economy will have such a large impact on the international price of the dollar that the increase in imports and reduction in exports will completely offset the increase in the budget deficit.

quantity theory of money can be thought of as holding for the world economy as a whole. The equation of exchange, or

$$MV = Py$$

can also be interpreted as applying to the entire world economy. If the equation of exchange applies to the world economy, then M is the world stock of gold and silver, V is the velocity of circulation of gold and silver, P is the average world price level, and y is real world output.

According to quantity theory, when the quantity of international currency increases, the world price level will rise. A major gold discovery, then, will be expected to lead to inflation throughout the world in the long run. Inflation and deflation in the world economy therefore depends on changes in the stocks of gold and silver. (Note the implicit assumption that the world economy is at full employment in the long run.)

The simple extension of the quantity theory to the world economy explains the world price level. Another question involves the distribution of gold and silver throughout the different nations. That distribution is simply a matter of demand and supply. If the quantity of money demanded exceeds the quantity supplied in some nation, gold flows in. If the quantity supplied exceeds the quantity demanded, gold flows out. In equilibrium, the quantity of international money demanded will equal the quantity supplied in each nation and in the world economy as a whole.

The simple quantity theory model can explain worldwide inflation or deflation in a gold standard world. The model must be altered slightly, however, when we apply it to a world where each nation has its own currency and no single international currency exists. In a world of floating (or flexible) exchange rates—the exchange rate between two currencies is determined in the international currency market—the quantity theory holds for each nation with respect to its own currency. In other words, the rate of inflation in Japan is determined by the rate of growth of the Japanese money stock, while the rate of inflation in France is determined by the French money stock.

Domestic money, then, determines domestic price levels. The only international prices are the exchange rates between different currencies. The monetary approach to the determination of the exchange rate between currencies adopts the view that exchange rates are determined by purchasing power parity.

Absolute purchasing power parity holds that the exchange rate between two currencies will be equal to the ratio of the domestic price levels in the two countries. If the two countries are the United States and Japan, the exchange rate of dollars per yen, E, will be equal to

$$E = P/P_j$$

where P is the price level in the United States and P_j is the price level in Japan. If the American price level rises relative to the Japanese price level, the exchange rate will rise, as the dollar depreciates relative to the yen. In other words, it will now take more dollars to buy yen (see Chapter 18).

DIALOGUE
Twin Deficits: The Dangers
Russell Shannon, Clemson University

During the 1970s when the rate of inflation rose above 10 percent—first in 1974 and again in 1979—news reporters began using the awesome term "double digits."

In the 1980s, however, although inflation subsided, the federal budget deficit jumped from $78.9 billion in 1981 to $127.9 billion in 1982—more than twice the previous peak achieved during World War II. Then the nation's merchandise trade balance—which in recent times had been persistently positive until the early 1970s—suddenly leaped from a deficit of $67 billion in 1983 to $112.5 billion in 1984.[1] Apparently we had entered an even more troubling era of "double deficits."

Paul A. Volcker, then chairman of the Federal Reserve Board, sounded the alarm. Testifying before a congressional committee in February 1984, he warned that unless immediate action was taken to curb the deficits, "finally they will undercut all that has been achieved with so much effort and so much pain."[2]

But Volcker's warning went unheeded. Both deficits deepened. The federal budget deficit soared above the $200 billion level in 1983, 1985, and 1986, and the trade deficit rose steadily until it reached a peak of $159.2 billion in 1987.[3]

In October 1987, when the stock markets suddenly plunged on "Black Monday," many people believed that their worst fears were being realized. It was widely argued that the first order of business was to bring down the government's budget deficit. Presumably, a sharp decline in the trade deficit would follow.

The logical link between the two deficits, though indirect, is clear. First of all, when the federal government's expenditures exceed its tax revenues, it must finance the deficit by borrowing, which is as certain to raise interest rates as an increased demand for pizza would raise its price.[4] Sure enough, interest rates on U. S. government securities reached unprecedented levels in the early 1980s.

Second, when interest rates rise here relative to those in foreign countries, they attract the eyes of investors worldwide. In order to acquire our financial assets, however, foreign investors must convert their yen, pounds, marks, and other currencies to dollars. This increased demand will tend to raise our exchange rate—the price of the dollar. Just as predicted, as the federal government's budget deficit rose and our interest rates increased, the value of the dollar climbed from a multilateral trade-weighted value of 87.4 in 1980 to 143.2 in 1985.

Of course, the greater value of the dollar was good news to American consumers because foreign products became cheaper to buy. Merchandise imports rose from $250 billion in 1980 to $338 billion in 1985, an increase of 35 percent. Because American products became more costly to foreign consumers, however, our exports actually *fell*, from $224 billion in 1980 to $216 billion in 1985. (See Figure 19.3.)

The federal government's budget deficit and the merchandise trade deficit go hand-in-hand. Perhaps the most important question is, however, "Why should we worry about them?" In fact, there are several reasons for concern.

---

1. Unless otherwise noted, all data are from the *Economic Report of the President, 1988.*

2. Paul A. Volcker, "Facing Up to the Twin Deficits," *Challenge* (1987): 33.

3. David Wessel, "U.S. Trade Deficit Narrowed Slightly in Fourth Quarter," *Wall Street Journal,* February 25, 1988, p. 56.

4. The Ricardian equivalence theorem contests this view, arguing instead that taxpayers, intelligent enough to realize that greater government borrowing will require higher taxes to pay off the interest and the debt, increase their saving, thereby helping make more funds available and thus keeping interest rates down. See Robert J. Barro, *Macroeconomics* (New York: John Wiley, 1984), Ch. 15. However, several statistical studies support the more conventional view. In one such case, Khan H. Zahid concluded that there was "a significant positive impact of deficits on real interest rates in the U.S. during the period 1971–80." "Government Budget Deficits and Interest Rates: The Evidence since 1971, Using Alternative Deficit Measures," *Southern Economic Journal* 54 (January 1988): 730. Similarly, Paul Wachtel and John Young discovered that "an increase in the projected deficit leads to an increase in interest rates." "Deficit Announcements and Interest Rates," *American Economic Review* 77 (December 1987): 1011.

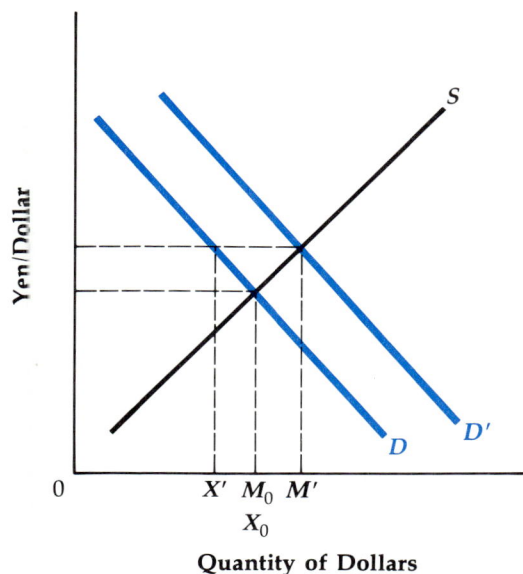

Quantity of Dollars

FIGURE 19.3
The diagram at left shows the market for dollars in terms of Japanese yen. The demand curve D shows that Japanese will want more dollars to buy American goods if they can pay fewer yen for them: the inverse relationship between quantity and price is typical. But Americans will be apt to supply more dollars to buy Japanese products if they can get *more* yen for their dollars; thus the supply curve S slopes upward. In a situation of floating exchange rates (and ignoring all other countries), the value of the dollar would tend to settle at the point where the two curves intersect, making our imports (M_0) just equal to the value of our exports (X_0). But now add additional demand for dollars by Japanese investors who find American interest rates relatively more attractive, so we get the demand curve D'. Clearly, the value of the dollar goes up, causing Americans to import more (M'). But American producers are put at a disadvantage, and our exports drop to X'. Now we have a deficit in our balance of trade, measured by the distance between X' and M'.

First of all, partly because of increased competition from foreign producers, literally millions of jobs have been destroyed in America's manufacturing industries. From a peak of just over 21 million workers in 1979, manufacturing employment plummeted to fewer than 18.5 million in 1984, a decline of almost 12 percent. Although almost a million jobs had been restored in manufacturing by the end of 1987, the implications for the future of the United States as an industrial power seem sobering.

Second, along with financial investments here, foreigners now own all or part of many American-based firms, from advertising companies to producers of television sets. This development provides opportunities for foreigners to influence not only our economy but our social and political arenas as well.

Third, this foreign investment in the United States requires that interest payments be made to foreign borrowers. The United States was a net *lender* of funds to the rest of the world for most of the twentieth century. We earned substantial interest income, which served to offset or at least diminish the burden of our trade deficit. In the third quarter of 1987, however, we began making net interest payments abroad: The United States had become a net debtor. To pay this interest, we must do more than just bring our trade relations in balance: We must run a surplus of exports over imports to have an overall balance on the current account.

Finally, the interest payments required to finance the budget deficit have become an increasing burden on the American taxpayer. From $53.3 billion in 1980, about 8.7 percent of total federal outlays, they jumped to over $142.6 billion in 1987, soaking up 13.3 percent of federal expenditures. That represents a sizeable transfer from taxpayers in general to those people wealthy enough to hold part of the national debt.

This is ample evidence that the two deficits are not only related but have resulted in many present and potential problems, both financial and real. It is certainly easy to understand why some people actually believe that the double deficits spell double trouble.

Dialogue continued

Mouse Wisdom: Foreign Trade and Economic Health

William R. Allen, University of California, Los Angeles

"Nonsense!" remarked nonsensical mouse Karl. "President Reagan says our trade deficit is a sign of a healthy economy."

"Why is that nonsensical?" asked sensible mouse Adam.

"We are on an import binge," answered Karl. "As we buy more merchandise abroad than we sell, we transfer billions of dollars to foreigners. Since they aren't using the dollars to buy our goods, they buy our real estate, stocks, Treasury

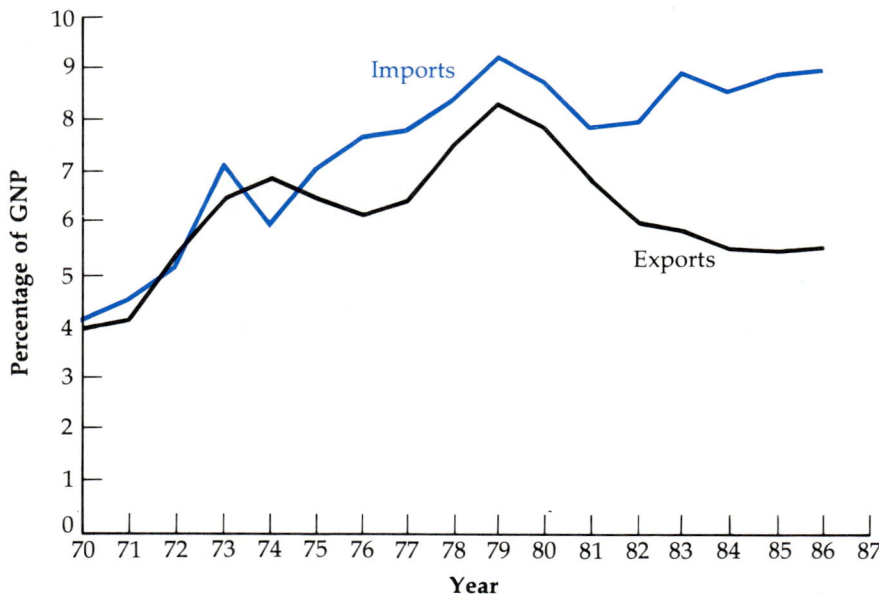

FIGURE 19.4 Merchandise Imports and Exports as a Percentage of National Production, 1970–87

Sources: Economic Report of the President, 1987; Economic Indicators (November 1987) The Wall Street Journal.

Relative purchasing power parity does not try to explain the level of exchange rates. Rather, it tries to explain the changes in the exchange rate. According to the theory of relative purchasing power parity, the rate of change of the exchange rate will be equal to the difference in the rates of inflation in the two economies. The basic formula for relative purchasing power parity is

$$\%\Delta E = \%\Delta P - \%\Delta P_j$$

where $\%\Delta E$ is the rate of change of the exchange rate, $\%\Delta P$ is the rate of inflation in the United States, and $\%\Delta P_j$ is the rate of inflation in Japan. The securities and other assets. It's baloney to argue that these purchases occur because foreigners have confidence in our economy. The problem is our orgy of imports."

"But imports are what we *gain* from foreign trade, and exports are what we *pay*," admonished Adam.

"Yes," conceded Karl, "but by enabling foreigners to send financial indebtedness. Think of all the future goods we'll have to export to pay that debt."

"But if we use the financial capital from abroad to obtain directly or indirectly more equipment and other useful assets," added Adam, "we will produce more output and income in the future. After paying our foreign debt, we can still come out ahead. Borrowing can be sensible."

"Not," cried Karl, "if we irresponsibly consume, instead of invest, all these imports."

"Since 1980," said Adam, "a third of the increase in our trade deficit has been due to increased imports of tools and equipment. In any case, there has been no import binge. The large trade deficits after 1981 occurred because exports collapsed, not because imports surged. As a percentage of national output, imports averaged about the same from 1976 to 1981 as from 1982 to 1987. But exports tumbled from an average of 7 percent of national output in the earlier period to 5.8 percent in the later."

"Exports fell as a percentage of national output," continued Adam, "because our economy grew faster than those of our trading partners. Between 1982 and 1986, our industrial production grew nearly twice as fast as the average for Canada, Japan, France, West Germany, Italy, and Great Britain. Because of the slower growth of foreign economies, their purchases of our goods did not keep pace with our purchases of their goods. And debt-troubled nations—such as Mexico, our third largest trading partner—cut their buying of our goods in order to divert foreign exchange to meet their foreign debts."

"I see," Karl finally agreed. "The superior performance of our economy has caused exports to fall as a fraction of national output. And the relative strength and soundness of our economy has encouraged foreigners to invest here. Perhaps our trade deficit has been a sign of a robust economy. But," he smirked, "this is an election year, and it is more fun—and easier—to bash the president than to understand foreign trade."

Reprinted with permission from the *Midnight Economist* (San Francisco, Calif.: Institute for Contemporary Studies, February 1988), pp. 3–4.

theory thus predicts that if the rate of inflation is higher in the United States than in Japan, the exchange rate will rise. To take a simple numerical example, if the rate of inflation in the United States is 5 percent and the rate of inflation in Japan is 3 percent, the exchange rate should rise (and the dollar depreciate) by 2 percent.

In recent years much evidence has been collected on the validity of purchasing power parity, both relative and absolute. The evidence, for the most part, shows that the hypothesis explains most exchange rates and changes in exchange rates in the long run—especially between Western industrial countries. Purchasing power parity does not, however, hold exactly. The reason may simply be the problem of comparing price levels calculated in different ways and based on different baskets of goods. Also, central banks often intervene to prevent exchange rates from moving to the level set by international markets.

The monetary approach to exchange rates, then, assumes that long-run changes in exchange rates are determined by differences in foreign and domestic rates of inflation. The monetary approach starts with the idea that movements in exchange rates are determined by the demand and supply of money. If the quantity of money supplied exceeds the quantity demanded in some economy, its exchange rate will depreciate. If the quantity of money demanded exceeds the quantity supplied, its exchange will appreciate.

The monetary approach can be illustrated with the case of the exchange rate between the currencies of the United States and Japan. If the quantity of dollars supplied exceeds the quantity demanded, the price of yen in terms of dollars will rise while the price of dollars in terms of yen will fall. As the simple supply and demand model predicts, the excess supply of dollars drives down the price of dollars. The monetary approach, then, is simply a matter of supply and demand. The demand side can be illustrated with the Cambridge cash balances version of the equation of exchange, or

$$M = kPy$$

Inflation occurs if the money stock grows more rapidly than the demand for money. If M is the stock of money and k is the fraction of income people wish to hold as money, then the rate of inflation is determined by

$$\%\Delta P = \%\Delta M - \%\Delta k - \%\Delta y$$

where $\%\Delta P$ is the rate of inflation, $\%\Delta M$ is the rate of growth of the money stock, $\%\Delta k$ is the rate of growth of the demand for money coefficient, and $\%\Delta y$ is the rate of growth of real income.

The formula can then be expanded to explain the change in the exchange rate. From relative purchasing power parity, we can write

$$\%\Delta E = \%\Delta P - \%\Delta P_j$$

If we substitute the inflation equation into the exchange rate equation, we get

$$\%\Delta E = \%\Delta M - \%\Delta k - \%\Delta y - \%\Delta P_j$$

This equation tells us that the rate of change of the exchange rate will be equal to the rate of growth of the domestic money supply *minus* the rate of growth of k, the rate of growth of real GNP, and the rate of inflation in Japan.

The equation can be used to explain recent changes in the exchange rate. For example, a rise in the exchange rate or a fall in the value of the dollar could be caused by the relatively slow rate of inflation in Japan or by a decline in the k. The rapid appreciation of the dollar in the early 1980s may have been the result of a decline in the rate of growth of the money stock, the rising rate of economic growth, and the rising willingness to hold dollars.

The monetary approach, then, views the international economy much as it views the domestic economy. In the long run, exchange rates, like inflation, are a monetary phenomenon. Attempts to affect real economic activity by manipulating exchange rates will possibly have short-run effects, but cannot have any long-run effects. Another hallmark of the monetary approach is that most real factors, such as the balance of trade, are not thought to matter much in the long run.

One question that the monetary approach cannot answer is: Is the floating exchange rate system a good thing? Critics argue that instability in the form of the rapid movements in exchange rates can create uncertainty and thereby discourage investment. Those who support floating rates, however, argue that they allow a nation to pursue an independent domestic monetary policy. Furthermore, many observers believe that a fixed exchange rate system is no longer possible. In a rapidly changing world—and change is particularly rapid in international markets—prices must be allowed to change. Fixed exchange rates may therefore be incompatible with the current world economy. On the other hand, there are those who feel that many of our current economic problems could be helped by a return to the fixed gold standard. For instance, New York Congressman Jack Kemp is an ardent advocate of a return to a gold standard that he perceives will decrease inflation, stabilize production and employment, and promote economic growth and international trade.

The Supply-Side Perspective

▲ 3. How do international transactions fit into the supply-side model of the macroeconomy?

A central tenet of supply-side economics is that people alter their behavior as incentives change. If a given economic activity is made more attractive, people will engage in more of it; if less attractive, they will do it less. For instance, supply siders contend that a permanent marginal (not average) tax rate cut alters the relative price of work and leisure, making work more attractive, and alters the relative price of saving versus consumption, making saving more attractive.

According to supply-siders, people do not work to pay taxes but to obtain goods and services (including savings) they can buy after taxes. People do not save to reduce their wealth but to increase their wealth (and to purchase more goods and services in the future). Therefore, the higher the after-tax return on savings, the more will be saved, *ceteris paribus*. In general, lower marginal tax rates enhance the after-tax return from more work, investment, saving, and other activities that become less heavily taxed and decrease the return from leisure-intensive activities, tax shelters, and the consumption of tax-deductible goods and services, and other methods of tax avoidance and evasion.

In terms of our aggregate demand and aggregate supply model in Figure 19.5, lower marginal tax rates cause the aggregate supply curve to shift outward to the right from AS_1 to AS_2. This shift in the graph causes the country's real output and national income level to increase from y_1 to y_2 and the price level to fall from P_2 to P_1. The aggregate supply curve may

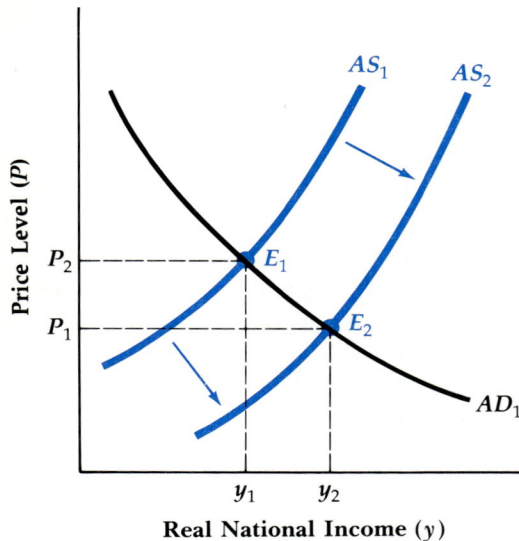

FIGURE 19.5 The Supply-Side Aggregate Demand and Aggregate Supply Model
A reduction in tax rates will cause the aggregate supply curve to shift rightward from AS_1 to AS_2. Real national income will rise from y_1 to y_2 at the same time the price level falls from P_2 to P_1. Because of the increase in national income, imports will rise.

also be moved to the right by a reduction in inefficient government regulations of people and businesses and by a reduction in subsidies that discourage people from producing efficiently or encourage people to abstain from working altogether. These are basic supply-side points covered in Chapter 15, that focused exclusively on the effects within the domestic economy.

International Complications

There is a close link between successful supply-side macroeconomic policy and international trade. Both supply-side theory and international trade theory focus on production, cost, and supply. Indeed, as we saw in Chapter 17, the basis for international trade is the theory of comparative advantage that emphasizes differences in relative production capabilities and costs in different countries. Mutual gains from exchanges cause trades, domestic or international, to exist in the first place.

A successful supply-side policy that heightens efficiency and productivity and lowers costs (such as tax reform and deregulation) shifts outward the nation's aggregate supply curve, as above, regardless of the amount of international trade. However, the inclusion of international trade and capital flows into the analysis complicates the supply-side analysis, but the effects are easily understood. The increase in national income caused by the above outward shift in the aggregate supply curve can be expected (1) to increase the country's trade deficit (because more foreign imports will be needed to satisfy higher output levels and the greater consumer demand for more domestic *and* foreign products) and (2) to increase the country's capital surplus through greater capital inflows and lower capital outflows (because a greater number of foreign investors will want to take advantage of the higher after-tax returns in the domestic economy and more domestic investors will want to switch their investment from foreign economies to the domestic economy).

For example, according to supply-side economists, the enactment of President Ronald Reagan's 1981 cut in tax rates and 1986 tax reform packages caused a rise in expected after-tax return on U.S. capital relative to capital abroad. This caused an increase in capital inflows and a reduction in capital outflows—and a capital account surplus in the U.S. balance of payments. The resulting increase in demand for U.S. dollars and the resulting reduction in the supply of dollars on international money markets caused the dollar to appreciate. The appreciation of the dollar through 1985 made U.S. goods more expensive abroad and foreign goods less expensive in the United States, giving a rising balance of trade deficit in the 1982–1985 period. The U.S. trade deficit was further aggravated by an increase in demand for imported resources to feed the U.S. industrial expansion and to satisfy the increase in demand for imported consumer products caused by an expansion in U.S. wages and salaries.

Supply-siders argue that by the mid-1980s the greater investment spawned by lower marginal tax rates and improved tax incentives for investment in the 1981 tax act began to pay off for U.S. industry through improved productivity growth and lower relative production costs or of manufactured goods. After languishing in the 1970s, U.S. manufacturing productivity was rising at an annual rate of 3.7 percent in 1986, beating Japan's 2.8 percent and most other industrial nations. The resulting decline in U.S. manufacturing costs taken together with a 25 percent depreciation of the dollar in 1986 gave U.S. producers an edge in export prices and raised U.S. import prices. With a further decline in the value of the dollar, the balance of trade deficit began, albeit gradually, to improve in 1987 and early 1988.

Exchange Rates

Some, but certainly not all, supply-siders believe that economic growth is critically dependent on some level of stability in international exchange rates. They reason that people interested in improving their income over a long stretch of time need to make their plans based on an expected and stable value of the dollar in international markets. If the exchange rate fluctuates wildly, international trades are made riskier and thus more costly. Accordingly, stability in the exchange rates is needed to foster trades, or so they contend. These supply-siders reason that we need to return to the gold standard or some other system of fixed exchange rates. Fixed exchange rates can cause a further increase in all nations' aggregate supply curves as well as more real income. By not having fixed exchange rates in the 1980s, the U.S. economy did not grow as rapidly as it could have grown, and future growth will be retarded because of past instability in international exchange rates.

Supply-siders, as might be expected, do not speak with one voice on exchange rate policies. Some supply-siders maintain that government cannot do an effective job of controlling the prices of any domestic good and is unlikely to be able to control very effectively international exchange rates. This is because too many forces are at work in the international economy for government to be able to hold the line for very long on any established "fixed" set of exchange rates. As a consequence, these supply-siders fear that a fixed exchange rate system may be subject to sudden and dramatic changes and such changes may cause a reduction in transactions across national boundaries primarily because the changes in the prevailing fixed rates may be unpredictable.

Chapter Review

Review of Key Questions

1. *How do international transactions fit into the Keynesian model of the macroeconomy?*

   Keynesian macroeconomics focuses on the relationship between aggregate demand and national income. In this model, *ceteris paribus*, exports increase aggregate demand; imports reduce aggregate demand. This means that greater exports can lead to an increase in national income and employment, while greater imports can have the opposite effects. An increase in aggregate demand caused by, say, a reduction in taxes can give rise to an expansion in real income and employment, an increase in the price level, and a rise in imports (due to the higher income and price level).

2. *How do international transactions fit into the monetarist model of the macroeconomy?*

   Monetarists focus their analytical attention on the role of money in the national economy. The equation of exchange, $MV = Py$, holds in the international economy, just as it does in the domestic economy. An increase in the money stock worldwide can be expected to result in a higher world price level. Changes in the stock of money in any particular country can be expected to affect that country's price level and, through domestic prices, the international exchange rate. If the money stock in the domestic economy is raised, its price level will also rise. Foreigners will be discouraged from buying its exports, and domestic residents will be encouraged to buy more imports. The country's currency will depreciate to prevent the emergence of a balance of trade deficit.

3. *How do international transactions fit into the supply-side model of the macroeconomy?*

   Supply-siders are concerned with how policy changes influence aggregate supply. A reduction in tax rates can encourage people to work harder and longer and to save and invest more. The result is an increase in aggregate supply, a reduction in the price level, and an increase in real income and employment. In the short run, such a tax-rate change may be expected to increase the balance of trade deficit for several reasons. First, a greater after-tax return in the domestic economy can cause a greater capital inflow and a lower capital outflow. Second, the greater real income and production can be expected to lead to greater imports. Third, the change in capital flows can cause the dollar to appreciate (at least until efficiency improvements in the domestic economy reduce the relative cost of domestic goods).

Further Topics

International trade will likely be a growing topic of concern for policy-makers. This is because trade across national boundaries continues to grow in real terms and relative to total domestic production of all countries. As never before, domestic economies are becoming more and more integrated, meaning more and more dependent on foreign sources of supply of resources and on foreign markets for production outlets. Few countries can ignore the international consequences of domestic policies. Unfortunately, economists differ over how domestic policies affect international trade and capital flows. They therefore differ over policy solutions. Nevertheless, policies adopted in different countries are likely to have a growing effect on the domestic economy.

Review Questions

1. Suppose that government boosts its tax rates and at the same time keeps its expenditures constant. Suppose also that the world is on a flexible exchange rate system. According to a Keynesian macroeconomist, what would be the impact of the tax-rate increase on exports, imports, capital inflows, and capital outflows? (◢ 1)
2. Answer question 1 from the perspective of a monetarist. (◢ 2)
3. Answer question 1 from the perspective of a supply-sider. (◢ 3)
4. Would your answers for any of the above questions be materially different if all exchange rates were fixed? (◢ 1, ◢ 2, ◢ 3)

Comparative Economic Systems

[I]nappropriate, wasteful, and sometimes harmful commodities have been produced and sold as the logical embodiment of the accepted principle which in a capitalist economy governs what is produced—the maximization of profit.
    Barry Commoner

KEY QUESTIONS

▲ 1. What are the principal economic systems?

▲ 2. What is the basis of the Marxian critique of capitalism?

▲ 3. How does Soviet communism work?

▲ 4. What elements of democratic socialism can be found in mixed capitalist economies?

NEW TERMS

Capitalism

Communism

Democratic socialism

Economic system

National economic planning

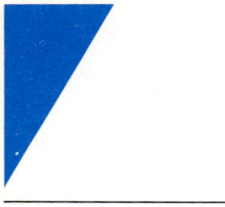

In his *Wealth of Nations* in 1776, Adam Smith explained how the invisible hand of self-interest, tempered by competition, could effectively satisfy society's economic needs. The American economic system rests largely on Smith's theory. Our supermarkets, shopping centers, fast-food chains, and computer companies are bastions of free enterprise. Yet the federal government frequently thrusts a visible foot into the operations of the market, setting standards, propping up prices, interfering with imports, or encouraging employment.

In the Soviet Union, on the other hand, the economy is carefully controlled. Still, financial incentives must be employed to stimulate production, and many goods are sold on the open market. Not long ago, in fact, many economists believed that over time the United States and the Soviet Union, like a married couple, would come to resemble each other more and more.[1] Despite reforms, however, recent years have given little evidence that the Soviet hierarchy is abandoning its control of the economy. And the United States seems to be moving away from government intervention, particularly in transportation, communication, and banking.

At the same time, the economies of Western Europe are showing signs of economic ambivalence. Under Margeret Thatcher's Conservative government in Great Britain, government interference has sometimes taken precedence over the free market. In France, the Socialist regime of Francois Mitterrand has retreated from some traditional socialist objectives. History is similarly ambiguous. In ancient times, trade stretched far across the Mediterranean. Yet the Code of Hammurabi and the construction of the pyramids in Egypt attest to persistent government efforts to manipulate and control economic activity.

---

1. Neil H. Jacoby and James E. Howell, *European Economics—East and West: Convergence of Five European Countries and the United States* (Cleveland: World Publishing, 1967).

This chapter explores some of the various "isms" under which government control and free enterprise blend in the modern world. Despite some important differences, there are many startling similarities in the way various economies operate.

Economic Systems

1. What are the principal economic systems?

In this book we have studied the production and distribution of goods and services in a mixed private market economy. In such an economy resource allocation is determined by the interaction of market supply and demand, as modified by government. Most productive resources are privately owned, and their use is privately determined, subject to government regulations.

Economic system: a set of institutions involved in making and implementing economic decisions.

The way a mixed private market, or capitalist, economy deals with the economic problem is not, however, the only possible way. Many different economic systems exist both in theory and actuality. An **economic system** according to one definition, is a set of institutions involved in making and implementing economic decisions. Mixed capitalism as practiced in the United States is one economic system. Different countries make economic decisions in different ways, so economic systems differ from country to country—even within the capitalist or socialist worlds. In addition to actual economic systems, many different theoretical systems exist. In making sense of the vast array of actual and possible economic systems, it is helpful to classify them into four basic categories:

1. *Market capitalism.* Resources are privately owned. Markets determine the allocation of resources. Examples include nineteenth-century England and America and (possibly) twentieth-century Hong Kong.

2. *Mixed capitalism.* Private ownership and market allocation are modified by substantial government regulation and government ownership. Examples include the United States, Japan, Canada, and most of Western Europe.

3. *Planned socialism.* Resources are owned by the state. Government plans determine resource allocation. Examples include the Soviet Union and East Germany.

4. *Market socialism.* Resources are owned by the state or by some smaller collective. Markets determine resource allocation. Examples include Yugoslavia and (possibly) Hungary.

The categorization of the economic systems of particular nations is extremely difficult because no pure systems exist. Socialist nations contain elements of capitalism, and capitalist nations contain elements of socialism.

Also, many nations change their economic systems. China, for example, appears to be undergoing great changes in its economic system (see the *Perspectives* on China in this chapter).

Although many variations of the principal economic systems operate in the world today, the great issue in comparative systems remains the choice between capitalism, with its reliance on private decision making, and socialism, with its reliance on collective decision making. Socialism, moreover, has made great progress in the twentieth century. Two principal types of socialism challenge capitalism throughout the world: (1) revolutionary socialism as represented in the writings of Karl Marx and the practice of Soviet Communism, and (2) democratic socialism as represented by the increasingly socialistic policies of ostensibly capitalist European nations. Both types represent important alternatives to capitalism.

Capitalism and Its Critics

▲ **2. What is the basis of the Marxian critique of capitalism?**

Capitalism: an economic system based on private property and free enterprise.

Capitalism, defined as an economic system based on private property and free enterprise, is the philosophical basis for the free market system that exists today in the United States and many other nations. In its pure form, it has never enjoyed unqualified support anywhere. English writers like William Blake deplored the "dark, satanic mills" that fouled the air over the English countryside. "Supply-and-demand,—Alas!" wrote Thomas Carlyle in 1843,[2] and in 1862 John Ruskin complained, "To this . . . professed and organized pursuit of Money . . . is owing *All* the evil of modern days."[3] Today, the writings of environmentalist Barry Commoner and economist John Kenneth Galbraith, among others, reflect a wariness toward the free market and the quest for profit. Of all the critics of capitalism, however, none is more notable than the man who made *capitalism* a household word: the German philosopher and economist Karl Marx.

Marxian Communism

Karl Marx (1818–1883) did not favor a return to a traditional agricultural economy. Indeed, he commended capitalists for rescuing "a considerable part of the population from the idiocy of rural life."[4] Although he accepted the writings of the classical economists Adam Smith and David Ricardo, he

---

2. Quoted in Neil H. Jacoby and James H. Howell, *European Economics—East and West: Convergence of Five European Countries and the United States* (Cleveland: World Publishing, 1967), p. 2.

3. Quoted in Bernard Murchland, *Humanism and Capitalism: A Survey of Thought on Morality* (Washington: American Enterprise Institute for Public Policy Research, 1984), p. 7.

4. Karl Marx and Friedrich Engels, *The Communist Manifesto* (New York: Appleton-Century-Crofts, 1955), p. 14.

PERSPECTIVES
The Competitive Japanese Economy

Katsuro Sakoh, Johns Hopkins University

Japan has experienced remarkable economic success since the end of World War II. In 1981 Japan's GNP surpassed that of the Soviet Union, making it the second-largest economy in the world. By 1986 its current dollar GNP had climbed to $1,658 billion, compared with $4,235 billion in the United States—a nation with twice its population. In terms of GNP per capita, Japan ranked fourth in the world.

The driving forces of Japan's phenomenal success have been private entrepreneurs and a well-educated labor force. Unlike European governments, the Japanese government has tried to avoid owning and operating major industries. Instead, it has concentrated on keeping taxes low by holding down expenditures on social welfare, quality of life, and national defense. (Japan's tax-revenue-to-GNP ratio is the lowest of the developed nations.) This relatively low tax burden has allowed the Japanese to achieve a high rate of saving—20 percent, or almost three times that of Americans. In turn, high savings have produced a high rate of capital investment and rapid technological improvements in the private sector.

This free market environment enabled Japan to shift quickly from an agricultural orientation in the 1950s to an industrial orientation in the 1960s and a service orientation in recent years. Today, 57 percent of Japanese workers are employed in service industries—only 12 percentage points less than in the United States. Contrary to popular perception, these changes in economic structure have been carried out mostly by small private companies rather than by government direction. In the private sector as a whole, nearly 70 percent of the labor force works for companies with fewer than 200 employees. Almost all the workers in agriculture; more than three-quarters of the work-

ers in construction, wholesale, retail, and personal service industries; and more than half of the workers in manufacturing are employed by small companies. The majority—perhaps two-thirds—of these workers are not guaranteed permanent employment.

Japan has achieved its economic success despite some formidable obstacles. The nation is small, the size of Montana, with no fossil fuels and few natural resources. To survive and grow, it must import most of its raw materials. During the oil crises of 1973 and 1978, Japan suffered high inflation, severe economic recession and negative growth rates, and large balance of trade deficits. As a result of that recession, the government is carrying a huge budget deficit. In 1983 Japan's debt-to-GNP ratio was 51 percent, compared with 43 percent in the United States.

Though Japan is heavily dependent on foreign trade for its well-being, trade is not the main source of its phenomenal economic growth. Japan's export-to-GNP ratio was only 13 percent in 1984—much lower than the ratio in any major industrial nation except the United States.[1] During the two oil crises of the 1970s, the buying power of Japan's exports deteriorated more than 30 percent. But the nation overcame that handicap by investing heavily in energy-saving measures and more productive technology. Once more, Japan became competitive in the world market. Like its rapid recovery from the devastation of World War II, Japan's strength today is due to its imaginative, hard-working, consumer-oriented private sector.

1. The figures are 48 percent for the Netherlands; 27 percent for West Germany; 25 percent for Canada; 20 percent for the United Kingdom; and 7 percent for the United States.

viewed capitalist activities as at best a temporary necessity. To Marx, capitalism was merely a brief period of transition between a grim past and the more prosperous future. For Marx had observed a more fully developed capitalism than had Adam Smith, one in which the blessings of the division of labor were obscured by such problems as unemployment, urban squalor, and worker alienation.

Marx's ideas are often summed up in the phrase "dialectical materialism." The word *dialectic* is derived from the Greek word for the process of developing philosophical ideas. Ancient Greek philosophers originated the technique of posing an idea, or hypothesis, against a contrasting idea, or antithesis. Through discussion thinkers would eventually merge the two ideas to create a new idea, or synthesis. The process, however, did not end there. The synthesis became the new hypothesis, and a new antithesis spawned a new synthesis.

In the early nineteenth century, the German philosopher Friedrich Hegel applied the concept of dialectics to historical development. He suggested that human evolution could be seen as a continuous process of hypothesis, antithesis, and synthesis. Marx extended the idea by specifying social classes as the opposing forces in the dialectical process. Medieval lords and serfs, pitted against each other, had been replaced by the bourgeois capitalists and the paid laborers ("proletariat") of modern times. Marx noted that each historical era had its own peculiar mode of production— the windmill of earlier times had given way to the steam engine. The Marxian dialectical process had a distinctly economic, or material, base.

Like Hegel, Marx saw human history as a broad upward sweep through time. In London, where (from 1849) he took refuge from political persecution at home, Marx developed his theory. He started with the classical labor theory of value. For Adam Smith, that theory had meant emancipation from the mercantilist belief that the value of the world's output was rigidly fixed and could not increase. Trade was not a zero-sum game, Smith saw; what France gained, England would not necessarily lose. But the opening words of *The Wealth of Nations*, "Labour . . . supplies . . . all the necessities and conveniences of life," meant something quite different to Marx. He took the idea one step further and argued that only labor created value. The capitalist was an unnecessary parasite who had freed workers from bondage to the land, but was unnecessary to their future advancement.

The capitalist was, of course, the owner of the means of production: the machinery and tools that workers used. Forces of competition compelled capitalists to acquire more and more capital. To purchase it, Marx charged, capitalists paid workers less than the value of their output—a tendency David Ricardo had already described. In effect, capitalists expropriated part of the value produced by workers. Capitalists did not live on the surplus value produced by workers; instead, they used it to purchase more capital.

Meanwhile, instead of benefiting from the improved productivity created by new equipment, workers lost their jobs. As more and more of them were fired, they joined the "reserve army of the unemployed," a ready source of eager labor that depressed wages. Because workers were unable to buy the output of the new factories, capitalists would suffer wrenching business failures. Eventually, Marx believed, the reserve army of the unemployed would become so large and so desperate that it would rise up and overthrow the remaining capitalists in a bloody revolution. Such a violent transition had marked the advent of capitalism in France, and Marx expected history to repeat itself. The coming revolution would usher in the new and final era of communism. **Communism**, as conceived by Marx, was a classless society that would emerge from the downfall of capitalism and the establishment of socialism. In practical terms, communism is an economic system in which virtually all the means of production are owned and controlled by the state.

In the period after the revolution, which Marx called the dictatorship of the proletariat, property rights would be abolished and a new society would emerge. Because workers would no longer be the slaves of capitalists, they would spontaneously become more productive. The state, which had merely been a device to suppress the workers, would eventually wither away. Although Marx dwelt only briefly on the nature of the new society, he apparently believed that it would be both productive and satisfying. According to the famous slogan, production and distribution would be based on the principle "from each according to his ability, to each according to his need."

Marx may have been wrong about the threat that capital posed to labor, and naive to believe that a totally classless society was possible. For many oppressed peoples, however, his writings have served as a beacon of hope and inspiration, and for many communist leaders, from Lenin to Mao to Castro, his writings have provided the foundation for new revolutionary goals. Still, what is called communism today, especially in the Soviet Union, is very unlike the ideal state Marx envisioned. The economist Joseph Schumpeter once remarked that "There is, between the true meaning of Marx's message and . . . [Soviet] practice and ideology, at least as great a gulf as there was between the religion of humble Galileans and the practice and ideology of the princes of the church or the warlords of the Middle Ages."[5]

Soviet Communism

In the late nineteenth century, Russia was governed by a repressive monarchy whose abuses encouraged revolutionary activity. There were some spurts of economic development in the 1890s and the early twentieth century, but industry was largely directed and controlled by government, and the economy remained overwhelmingly agricultural. On the eve of the Communist Revolution, then, czarist Russia had not nearly reached the

Communism: as conceived by Marx, a classless society that would emerge from the downfall of capitalism and the establishment of socialism. In practical terms, an economic system in which virtually all the means of production are owned and controlled by the state.

◢ 3. How does Soviet communism work?

5. Joseph A. Schumpeter, *Capitalism, Socialism, and Democracy*, 3d ed. (New York: Harper & Row, 1950), p. 3.

stage of capitalist development that Marx had predicted would precede a workers' revolution.

Nevertheless revolutionary uprisings occurred in early 1917. They were largely a spontaneous reaction to Russia's devastating losses in the First World War. A provisional regime set up under Alexander Kerensky seemed to offer the possibility of a more democratic government. Then a man named Lenin appeared on the scene.

Leninism

Lenin, whose real name was Vladimir Ilyich Ulyanov, was a native Russian whose father had taught mathematics and physics. As a young man Lenin had been exiled to Siberia because of his efforts to promote more power for the working class. In contrast to Marx, who thought that capitalism would be overthrown by a spontaneous working-class mass uprising, Lenin believed that revolution should be brought about by the concerted effort of a small group of professionals. In 1903, at a meeting in London, his determination on that point had split the Russian revolutionary party in two. Lenin's smaller group had adroitly termed itself the Bolsheviks, which means "majority." The other group became known as the Mensheviks, or the minority.

In 1917 Lenin was in exile again, this time in Switzerland. There he aided the Germans in a devious plan to neutralize their enemy on the eastern front. By helping Lenin return to Russia, Winston Churchill observed, the Germans deployed "the most grisly of all weapons" in a war already distinguished by the use of poison gas and flame throwers. "They transplanted Lenin in a sealed truck like a plague bacillus from Switzerland into Russia."[6]

In October 1917 Lenin led the Bolsheviks in overthrowing Kerensky's provisional government. As the Germans had hoped, he withdrew Russia from the war, thus eliminating one of their enemies. Several years of struggle, however, were required before Lenin could consolidate his control of the country. During this period of "war communism," industry was nationalized, wages were equalized, and crops were confiscated to feed the army and urban workers. By 1921, when Lenin finally claimed political success, the economy was faltering so badly that he was forced to retreat temporarily from his ideological objectives. His New Economic Policy (NEP) provided more freedom to farmers and small businesspeople in an effort to restore production to previous levels.

This new, more open society did not last. Lenin died in January 1924 without designating his successor. After a struggle for power, Joseph Stalin emerged as the new supreme leader. In 1928, after consolidating his power, Stalin began dismantling the NEP.

---

6. Quoted in Alan Moorehead, *The Russian Revolution* (New York: Perennial Library, Harper & Row, 1965), p. 171.

Stalinism

National economic planning: the process of deciding collectively on national economic objectives, and of developing policies and programs for accomplishing those objectives.

Stalin's overriding goal was the rapid industrialization of the Russian economy through national economic planning. **National economic planning** is the process of deciding collectively on national economic objectives, and of developing policies and programs for accomplishing those objectives. To achieve his end Stalin set up Gosplan, the Soviet central planning agency. In the first of a series of five-year plans, bureaucrats in Gosplan established mandatory economic goals for various sectors of the economy. The last vestiges of the NEP program were swept away, and the secret police regained the pervasive control they had held during the period of war communism.

Whereas Lenin had come to believe that greater freedom was the key to enhancing agricultural output, Stalin rejected that view. He abolished private farms and combined them into huge collectives, running some like factories in which workers earned wages. Farmers did not gain the benefit of improvements in productivity. Instead, most of the food was earmarked for workers in urban areas, to support their construction and factory work. In essence, farmers were forced to accept subsistence wages to support the rapid accumulation of capital in industry—an ironic reincarnation of the capitalist system Marx had condemned.

At least initially, Stalin's plans for raising farm productivity through collectivization backfired. The peasants so resented the new system that they retaliated by destroying their crops and slaughtering their livestock. Such discord was inconsistent with Marx's prediction of a placid and productive postrevolutionary society. Conflict was supposed to be the result of class distinctions, and classes had presumably been wiped out. So Stalin resolved the dilemma by blaming the difficulties of forced collectivization on the *kulaks* (prosperous peasant farmers who had done well for themselves under the NEP). Eventually he announced that the kulaks would be "liquidated," and several thousand of them were shot.[7]

Stalin's repressive policies did not last, but neither did Soviet agriculture flourish. Eventually Soviet planners had to establish incentives to stimulate production. Instead of paying equal wages to all, they rewarded more productive workers. In recent years peasants have been allowed to farm small plots of land near their homes and to sell the produce in local markets. Peasants naturally tend to use these plots to produce agricultural items whose market value is high—milk and eggs, for instance. Still, the productivity of the privately farmed land testifies to the value of incentives. The collectively farmed lands, which produce less valuable foodstuffs like wheat, are not nearly as productive. In recent years, the Soviets have had to import grain regularly from capitalist nations.

The lack of a profit motive also presented problems in Soviet industry. Managers of Soviet plants were expected to meet quotas, not to satisfy the

---

7. Calvin Hoover, *Memoirs of Capitalism, Communism, and Nazism* (Durham, N.C.: Duke University Press, 1965), pp. 111–114.

PERSPECTIVES

A Traveler's View of Emerging Capitalism in China

Laurence S. Moss, Babson College

Ten years ago no one imagined China would reach out to embrace capitalist economic methods. During Mao Zedong's Cultural Revolution, bands of teenagers had roamed China's countryside, burning books, destroying historical monuments, and dragging reluctant counterrevolutionaries through the streets. Thousands of citizens were forced to renounce their bourgeois-capitalist ways and close their flourishing commercial institutions.

Today the news media are filled with reports of China's return to capitalism. It is not yet clear how far the dismantling of China's centrally planned economy will proceed. But Premier Deng Xiaoping, China's pragmatic new leader, has obviously set out to accomplish what Mao would never have allowed: the liberalization of trade and the toleration of Western lifestyles.

The change in government policy has been most dramatic in the agricultural sector. In 1958, Mao's Great Leap Forward literally abolished most private landholding, consolidating farm management in huge regional collectives. The merging of small peasant farms and village lands was supposed not only to help in the mechanization of farming and the improvement of productivity, but to foster the spiritual rebirth of the Communist people. Unfortunately, the move did not produce the promised results. The stifling of personal incentives disrupted the whole economy for most of a decade.

Starting in 1980, however, the Chinese government declared a series of agricultural reforms that amounted to wholesale abandonment of collective land management. Most provincial landholdings were abolished, and small village and family farms were restored to their former owners. Farmers are now required to turn over only part of their output to the government. Any surplus is theirs to consume or to trade for cash in the cities. Government officials also encouraged the development of an agricultural futures market by allowing farmers to contract ahead of time for delivery of their crops. The idea was to give farmers an incentive to vary the composition of their output as market conditions warranted.

Trade works best when buyers and sellers can communicate easily with one another. In most Chinese cities the government has now granted sidewalk space to traders, and even blocked off traffic on selected streets. Traders still need licenses, but they are said to be relatively easy to acquire. In hopes of making a profit, a person may set up a trading booth and offer beans, clothing, ginseng roots, or dried beetles to passing shoppers. In one outdoor market in the city of Guangzhou, Western travelers recently saw a vendor offer several packages of Wrigley's chewing gum at premium prices. Another vendor, equipped with a dentist's chair, white apron, and surgical pliers, offered to pull aching teeth for

demands of customers. A factory manager who had been told to produce a million pairs of shoes could satisfy his quota most easily by making all of them the same size—and many managers did just that. Knitting factories made caps but not sweaters, because caps were easier to make. Lampshade factories made all their products one color—orange. And in the lighting fixtures industry, where quotas were established in terms of weight, a small number of extremely heavy products was produced.

Such tales may be exaggerated, but they demonstrate the problem of establishing an effective system of incentives. While the Soviet government can take pride in its military and space technology, it has not been able to passers-by who found the wait at the state hospital painfully long.

The free market principles operating in the open air markets can also be observed in Chinese factories. Managers are encouraged to negotiate Western-style contracts promising bonuses if a job is completed under budget and penalties if deadlines are not met. In Guangzhou the manager of a jade factory is now allowed to negotiate contracts with business people from Hong Kong without the approval of the Central Communist Party in Beijing (Peking). Only the small bureaucracy of Guangzhou province watches over his dealings. Contracts with foreigners are more likely to be approved if they provide employment for Chinese laborers or help to augment the state-owned Bank of China's foreign exchange holdings. Among other companies R. J. Reynolds (tobacco), Gillette (razor blades), Foxboro (automatic controls), and IBM (computers) have entered into joint ventures in China. To foreign travelers, the most obvious joint ventures are the smart high-rise hotels, some with indoor pools and revolving restaurants, that cater to the thousands of tourists who visit China each day.

In addition to the opportunities now available to entrepreneurs, a private labor market provides extra disposable income to many Chinese citizens. Tourists who read Chinese report seeing hand-painted signs along the roadways offering wages for after-hours labor on construction projects. Taxicab drivers in Beijing say that after they have paid a fixed sum to the government, they are free to work for themselves. Workers use their extra earnings to purchase television sets and refrigerators, or to establish small businesses in the open air market.

The Chinese citizens' ability to reorganize production methods or reallocate capital in response to changing market conditions is more limited. The days of total police control of citizens' movements seem to be over. Individuals can now travel freely within each of China's provinces, without signing in and out of police stations. As a result, some middleman activity is possible. Goods can be moved from countryside to city to even out maladjustments in supply and demand. But can individuals start a labor union and strike? Can entrepreneurs issue stocks or engage in other sophisticated venture capital arrangements? In 1985 the government allowed a company in Shanghai to offer stock, but it is not yet clear whether that action was the harbinger of a new China or only a tentative experiment. Only time will tell whether Chinese capitalism will last.

See also Laurence S. Moss, "Capitalism in China" (Babson Park, Mass.: Economics Department, Babson College, 1985).

match Western economies and Japan in the production of consumer goods and services. Competition with the United States spurs Soviet military and space achievements. The lack of competition holds back the Soviet consumer products sector.

Marx's classless society has not yet emerged in the Soviet Union. The ruling class has privileges that workers do not. A reporter who lived in the Soviet Union observed that special stores reserved for the elite "insulate the Soviet aristocracy from chronic shortages, endless waiting in line, rude service, and other daily harassments that plague ordinary citizens. Here the politically anointed can obtain rare Russian delicacies like caviar, smoked salmon, the best canned sturgeon, export brands of vodka or unusual vintages of Georgian and Moldavian wines, choice meat, fresh fruits and vegetables in winter that are rarely available elsewhere."[8]

Soviet industry may have become even more inefficient in recent years. During his brief tenure as premier (1982–1984) Yuri Andropov tried earnestly to improve productivity, but there are few signs that he was successful. Mikhail Gorbachev, who became Soviet leader in 1985, has instituted further reforms to try to halt the decline in productivity. Suggestions that the Soviet economy is tottering on the brink of collapse are probably exaggerated, however. Like their czarist predecessors, party members enjoy power and privileges they will not readily forgo, and there are no strong signs of unrest among the Soviet people. In fact, the similarities between czardom and communism in Russia are so great that one is reminded of the old French proverb: the more things change, the more they stay the same.

Democratic Socialism

▲ **4. What elements of democratic socialism can be found in mixed capitalist economies?**

Democratic socialism: an economic system that combines government ownership of productive resources with full political democracy.

Many advocates of socialism, either market or planned, believe that the authoritarian political system of the Soviet Union does not have to accompany a socialist economy. They believe that political democracy is perfectly compatible with socialist economic institutions. **Democratic socialism**—an economic system in which the government owns major plants in industries such as coal, transportation, steel, and banking, and operates them in the public interest—combines government ownership of productive resources with full political democracy. According to its supporters, democratic socialism is characterized by both political and economic democracy.

Although many socialists reject parts of Marxian economics, most accept the belief that capitalist profits are unearned. Socialism allows the unearned profits to be turned over to the workers. Another advantage of socialism would be an end to the exploitation of labor by capitalists. If the government owns industry, the earning of enterprises can be used to improve working conditions and raise wages. Moreover, under democratic socialism the use of the surplus earnings of government enterprises can be determined through the democratic process. The result, according to democratic socialists, will be a distribution of wealth and power more just and equal than under either democratic capitalism or authoritarian socialism.

Marx said that socialism would be established by a violent revolution. Democratic socialists, by contrast, believe that socialism can be established gradually through the democratic political process. Indeed, it only requires an extension of existing policies and institutions. Government ownership of industry is already common in capitalist nations, especially those of Europe.

In the United States, the postal service has always been owned by government. Today public elementary and secondary schools and land-grant colleges are all run by state, county, or local governments. (The

---

8. Hedrick Smith, *The Russians* (New York: Quadrangle, New York Times Book Co., 1976), p. 26.

historian Arnold Toynbee once called the American public schools the most socialistic system of education in the world.) In the 1930s, the federal government entered the electricity business by establishing the Tennessee Valley Authority. More recently it has taken control of ailing railroads to establish Amtrak and Conrail, although Conrail reverted to private ownership in 1985. Still, outright government ownership of plant and equipment is relatively limited.

In Europe, industry has been far more extensively socialized. At the end of the Second World War, Britain's new Labour government nationalized several major industries. In Austria at about the same time, a substantial segment of industry that had been confiscated by the Nazis during the war was placed under government control. More recently, governments in Norway, Sweden, and France have assumed ownership of many industries.

One study of nationalization estimated the percentages of basic industry owned by the public in several Western European nations as follows:[9]

Austria	65%
France	55
Italy	45
Norway	40
Sweden	30
Great Britain	25
West Germany	20

The Effects of Nationalization

Originally, industries were nationalized in order to prevent the exploitation of workers and to distribute unearned profits. Over the years, however, motivations have changed. Government officials began taking over industries simply because they were failing. In Britain, Rolls Royce was nationalized not by a Labour administration with socialist leanings, but by a Conservative government. Similar moves have become common in Norway and Sweden.

In a free-market economy, persistent losses are usually taken as a signal that a firm should reorganize or go out of business. Of course, during recessions and sometimes for other reasons, producers may endure temporary losses, expecting better times, but continued losses suggest that the firm is producing the wrong product or managing resources inefficiently. Like a thermostat that turns on the furnace when the temperature in a building falls too low, losses reveal a need for change.

Sometimes unprofitable companies can be rescued by astute managers. For instance, Lee Iacocca turned Chrysler from a failing enterprise into a profitable company. His efforts were assisted by government loan guarantees (which critics maintain was a wasteful use of funds). If nothing else, the example shows there are other ways for government to restore a company's

9. R. Joseph Monsen and Kenneth D. Walters, *Nationalized Companies: A Threat to American Business* (New York: McGraw-Hill, 1983), p. 17.

PERSPECTIVES
Yugoslavia: A Modified Communist Economy
Russell Shannon, Clemson University

Perhaps no nation has a paper currency more appropriate to its economy than Yugoslavia. Instead of a monarch or a president, the face of the 10 dinar note shows a smiling factory worker outfitted with cap, gloves, and shovel. On the back of the note, a sprawling industrial complex belches smoke into the air. For a nation whose industries are publicly owned and guided by workers' committees, the bill seems fitting.

A nation only a bit larger than Wyoming, Yugoslavia has a population density similar to that of industrial states like Ohio and Pennsylvania. Though it is a communist nation, its economy resembles a free market system more than the centrally planned system of the Soviet Union.

In the state-owned factories, self-management by workers is the rule. Workers are elected to a council, which may then select a management committee. The council or committee makes basic decisions about production, pricing, and pay. Profits are divided among workers or reinvested in the operation. Firms tend to be market oriented, because the workers suffer if their products do not satisfy consumers. And workers are paid according

to the value of their output. Although parts of this arrangement seem to resemble the free market system, Yugoslavs insist that their approach is true to the Marxist ideal of a dictatorship of the proletariat.

Worker management has produced moderately successful results for the Yugoslavs. From 1952 to 1965, Yugoslavia's per capita growth in GNP was second only to Japan's. In 1980 its output, $73.2 billion worth, almost equaled that of Iran, a nation with half as many more people. Compared with other nations, however, Yugoslavia's per capita GNP, $3,000 in 1980, was small. In the same year, the communist nations of East Germany, Czechoslovakia, and Hungary produced per capita GNPs of $5,000 to $8,000. And the free market nations of Japan, France, and West Germany enjoyed GNPs of $9,000 to $12,500 per capita. Yugoslavia has also been plagued by persistently high inflation—50 percent or more a year—and high unemployment.

Worker-run industries have certain problems. A group of basically untrained, inexperienced managers often cannot run an enterprise efficiently on

profitability besides outright ownership. John Kenneth Galbraith, an economist who favors the nationalization of failing industries, insists that once a company has been nationalized, it should be run according to strict principles of profit and loss. The manager appointed by the state "must have extensive autonomy in decision-making. . . . [Public management] must be held accountable for results by the orthodox standards of cost and return. This is not a capitalist test of efficiency; it is the universal and only test."[10]

What sounds good in theory does not necessarily work in practice, however. Scholars have found that "the government as owner is interested in whether the company contributed to the nation's export drive, whether it

10. John Kenneth Galbraith, quoted in R. Joseph Monsen and Kenneth D. Walters, *Nationalized Companies: A Threat to American Business* (New York: McGraw-Hill, 1983), p. 71.

a day-to-day basis. In practice, factories must be run by a general director selected by the worker management committee. Directors are supposed to serve limited terms, but frequently retain control for many years. Workers' personal interests may also bias their business decisions. Workers commonly prefer to distribute profits among themselves rather than to reinvest them in the business. As a result, funds for new equipment or for research and development are usually scarce. At the same time, workers may be so anxious to preserve their jobs that they keep an operation going when it is no longer useful to society. And discipline is so lax in worker-run factories that the nation's output is seriously reduced.

Yugoslavia's economic problems probably originate as much in its historical circumstances as in its Marxist ideology, however. Split for centuries between the Austro-Hungarian Empire in the north and the Ottoman Empire in the south, the nation was not united until near the end of World War I. Yugoslavia is a nation of two alphabets, three religions, four languages, five ethnic groups, and six republics. Substantial economic disparities

between the northern and southern regions intensify the natural rivalries and conflicts among these groups. For these reasons the central planning approach used in most communist economies simply will not work in Yugoslavia. It was tried in the 1940s under Marshal Tito's government, but failed miserably. The decentralized organization of local workers' groups fits the fragmented nature of Yugoslav society much better.

In 1980 the death of President Tito, one of the few unifying influences in the nation, left Yugoslavia in a precarious situation. As one observer worried, "So extensive is the autarky of the republics that there is now less economic cooperation and exchange among the various Yugoslav republics than among the members of the Common Market."[1] Even under the best economic systems, the many barriers to Yugoslavia's prosperity, symbolized by the four languages printed on its currency, might still thwart the nation's prospects.

1. Milovan Djilas, "Yugoslav Unity Fragments Without Tito," *Wall Street Journal*, March 13, 1985, p. 35.

managed to avoid laying off employees, and whether it kept domestic prices under control. One rarely hears about the state-owned company's return on investment, its return on capital, or the profitability of its assets."[11] Macroeconomic goals—the desire to promote exports, the Keynesian urge to achieve high employment, and the monetarist aim to suppress inflation—tend to replace the profit motive in state-run companies.

Political considerations also influence the management of publicly owned firms. When the chairman of British Steel announced plans to reduce employment because of lagging demand in 1975, the secretary of industry objected, and the chairman was replaced. More recently, Conservative Prime Minister Margaret Thatcher refused to fund a new factory for a state-owned microelectronics firm unless it were located in Wales, where unemployment is high. Such political intervention raises costs, which either

11. Ibid., p. xi.

consumers or taxpayers must ultimately pay for. It also "creates chaos for the managers of nationalized firms."[12] Too often, the short-term interests of politicians conflict radically with the long-run goals of industry.

Nowhere is the conflict between political and economic goals more obvious than in government attempts to deal with inflation. It has been charged that "state companies tend to nearly freeze their prices in the year before national elections and then raise them rapidly in the following year."[13] Even in nonsocialist nations like the United States, politicians sometimes resort to this practice. President Richard Nixon imposed comprehensive wage and price controls just before the presidential campaign of 1972. As a result, the American economy was plagued by shortages. In his memoirs, Nixon admitted that "the . . . decision to impose [controls] was politically necessary and immensely popular in the short run. But in the long run I believe that it was wrong. The piper must always be paid, and there was an unquestionably high price for tampering with the orthodox economic mechanism."[14]

Small wonder that the income statements of nationalized firms are often awash in a sea of red ink. As one book put it, "In the state firm, there is a bottom line, but it is political, not financial."[15] The same conclusion also applies to economic planning in a socialist economy.

The Effects of Economic Planning

Early socialists argued that capitalists took a narrow personal view in their production decisions, preferring individual gain to the general good of society. Government planning, they suggested, would improve economic performance. As the eminent Polish economist Oskar Lange put it, under socialism, "the Central Planning Board has a much wider knowledge of what is going on in the whole economic system than any private entrepreneur can ever have."[16]

It is probably true that a group of planners can have broader knowledge than a single capitalist. In a competitive economy of many producers, both actual and potential, the collective knowledge of producers far exceeds that of any planning board. Even with the best of intentions, then, government planning may be more prone to error than the market process.

Consider the case of Japan, which was at roughly the same stage of development as Russia at the turn of the century. Japan's economic growth has now far outstripped the Soviet Union's. Many believe that Japan's cen-

12. Ibid., p. 42.

13. Ibid., p. 44.

14. Richard M. Nixon, *Memoirs of Richard Nixon* (New York: Grosset and Dunlap, 1978), p. 521.

15. R. Joseph Monsen and Kenneth D. Walters, *Nationalized Companies: A Threat to American Business* (New York: McGraw-Hill, 1983), p. 128.

16. Oskar Lange, *On the Economic Theory of Socialism* (New York: McGraw-Hill, 1964), p. 89.

tral planning agency, the Ministry for International Trade and Industry (MITI), is largely responsible for the nation's success. Yet MITI actively discouraged two Japanese firms, Honda and Toyo Kogyo, from entering the automobile industry. Both have nevertheless achieved great success. As one scholar has noted, in Japanese manufacturing, "cement, paper, glass, bicycles, and motorcycles are huge success stories, even though MITI did little to help or hinder them."[17]

Those who envy Japan's industrial prowess, then, should not necessarily credit it to economic planning. MITI and other Japanese planning agencies have made many mistakes (and achieved many successes as well). Skeptics doubt that state planning and central control of the economy will produce more efficient results than the free market system. Instead, it might well produce improvements in job security, redistribution of income, and personal gain for politicians.

Chapter Review

Review of Key Questions

◢ *1. What are the principal economic systems?*

The four principal economic systems are market capitalism, mixed capitalism, planned socialism, and market socialism. The principal division in the world, however, is between capitalism and socialism.

◢ *2. What is the basis of the Marxian critique of capitalism?*

Capitalists paid workers less than the value of their output and used the surplus value to purchase more capital. The accumulation of capital, however, inevitably brought about the destruction of capitalism itself. As capital increased, unemployment and misery increased, leading eventually to a bloody revolution that would overthrow capitalism and establish socialism.

◢ *3. How does Soviet communism work?*

Central planning, rather than the market, determines the allocation of resources and the distribution of output. Planners establish economic goals that managers of enterprises are expected to meet. The lack of profits often leads to incentive problems among Soviet workers and managers.

◢ *4. What elements of democratic socialism can be found in mixed capitalist economies?*

Governments own and operate many enterprises in capitalist nations. In the United States, the federal government owns the postal service, the Tennessee Valley Authority, and several transportation

---

17. Arthur T. Denzau, *Will an "Industrial Policy" Work for the United States?* (St. Louis: Center for the Study of American Business, Washington University, 1983), p. 10.

enterprises. State and local governments operate transportation enterprises. State and local governments also operate utilities, schools, and other enterprises. In Europe, government ownership of basic industries is common.

Further Topics

In recent years, the governments of Western Europe have been nationalizing ailing industries at an unprecedented rate. The election of a Conservative government in Britain did little to reverse the trend. In the United States the Reagan administration, supposedly committed to the free market, has restricted imports of steel, textiles, sugar, cars, and motorcycles, and has slowed the process of deregulation in the trucking industry.

Perhaps Marx was correct, then. Capitalism may be only a temporary phase in the world's economic development. Yet instead of moving toward a new Socialist order, the world seems to be reverting back to older policies.

Marx saw the capitalist economy as the servant of producers' self-interest. The free market economy, however, has proved far more responsive to consumers—and has limited their freedom less—than the planned economy of the communist state.[18] Although capitalism is based on producers' self-interest, in the long run the producers' interest is to satisfy their customers. As Adam Smith wrote, "Consumption is the sole end and purpose of all production."[19] Both authoritarian and democratic socialism shift the focus away from consumers, replacing the invisible hand of self-interest with the visible and often clumsy foot of government.

Review of New Terms

Capitalism An economic system based on private property and free enterprise.

Communism As conceived by Marx, a classless society that would emerge from the downfall of capitalism. In practical terms, an economic system in which virtually all the means of production are owned and controlled by the state.

Democratic socialism An economic system that combines government ownership of productive resources with full political democracy.

Economic system A set of institutions involved in making and implementing economic decisions.

National economic planning The process of deciding collectively on national economic objectives, and of developing policies and programs for accomplishing those objectives.

18. Calvin B. Hoover, *The Economy, Liberty, and the State* (New York: Twentieth Century Fund, 1959), p. 18.

19. Adam Smith, *An Inquiry into the Nature and Causes of the Wealth of Nations* (New York: Random House Modern Library Edition, 1937), p. 625.

Review Questions

1. Can a nation's economic system ever be independent of its political system? Why or why not? (◢ 1)

2. Why do you think that Marx's prediction of a working-class revolution in advanced capitalist nations has not come true? (◢ 2)

3. What is the difference between socialism and communism? (◢ 2)

4. How might a capitalist economy be converted to democratic socialism? (◢ 1, ◢ 2, ◢ 4)

5. What changes did Stalin make in the economic system Lenin created in the Soviet Union? (◢ 3)

6. Do you think that it is possible to introduce fundamental reforms into the Soviet economy? (◢ 3)

7. Planning is usually associated with socialism. Yet many capitalist nations have planning agencies. How do you think planning works in capitalist economies? (◢ 1, ◢ 4)

Economic Growth and Development

The bourgeoisie, during its rule of scarce one hundred years, has created more massive and more colossal productive forces than have all preceding generations together. Subjection of Nature's forces to man, machinery, application of chemistry to industry and agriculture, steam navigation, railways, electric telegraph, clearing of whole continents for cultivation, canalization of rivers, whole populations conjured out of the ground—what earlier century had even a presentiment that such productive forces slumbered in the lap of social labor?
  Karl Marx

KEY QUESTIONS

▲ 1. What is the difference between economic growth and economic development?

▲ 2. What are some important differences between developing countries and developed countries?

▲ 3. How might a developing country become a developed country?

▲ 4. What are the economic problems faced by developing countries?

▲ 5. How can developing countries solve their economic problems?

NEW TERMS

Economic development
Economic growth

Most of the nations of the world can be classified as rich or poor, have or have-not. Among the have-nots—a category that includes most of the world's countries—are China and India, which together represent more than a third of the world's population. Mass poverty exists in these societies. People often lack basic food, clothing, or shelter, and have little opportunity to obtain the education taken for granted in developed countries. The enormous gap between poor nations and rich increases the potential for world conflict.

This chapter examines the reasons why some countries are far more developed economically—and therefore richer—than others. Developing countries share certain characteristics, such as low income, high population growth, and technological underdevelopment, that are linked to their economic difficulties. We will also explore some theories of what conditions are required for economic development to occur and look at the obstacles to economic growth, such as inadequate rates of saving. Finally we will consider some of the proposed remedies for economic underdevelopment.

Prerequisites for Growth and Development

1. What is the difference between economic growth and economic development?

Economic growth: the expansion of a nation's capacity to produce the goods and services its people want.

Economic development: the structural and other changes that accompany economic growth.

The terms economic growth and economic development are often used interchangeably, but they have slightly different meanings. **Economic growth** is the expansion of a nation's capacity to produce the goods and services its people want. Because the productive capacity of an economy depends fundamentally on the quantity and quality of its resources, as well as on its level of technology, economic growth must involve the expansion and improvement of those factors of production. Especially important are the accumulation of capital through saving and investment; improvements in human skills; and technological advances.

Economic development is the structural and other changes that accompany economic growth. It includes but goes beyond the improvements in technology and skills that promote economic expansion.

An economy can have economic growth without economic development, but not vice versa. A nation that relies on oil exports for much of its income can increase its growth rate by pumping more oil, but its economic development may be minimal unless new industries and outputs are created. Development of those new industries requires investment, which must be funded by increases in oil exports. The distinction is similar to the difference between growth and development in human beings. Growth generally means increases in height or weight. Development means changes in learning capacity, physical coordination, or the ability to adapt to new circumstances. The second depends, at least in a person's early years, on the first.

There are a number of prerequisites for economic growth and development. Most of the developed countries have at least several of the following.

1. Sufficient quantity and quality of labor. The existence of a large labor force in itself does not guarantee growth and development—India is an excellent case in point. A labor force must have the education and job skills to deal with new products and methods of production.

2. Sufficient quantity and quality of capital in the form of raw material, machines, and equipment. The supply of capital depends on the level of saving, which is the difference between income and consumption. In countries where people exist at a subsistence level, there is little difference between income and consumption. Capital is generally in short supply in the less developed countries.

3. Sufficient quantity and quality of natural resources. This factor is helpful but not crucial. The United States' vast natural resources obviously contributed to its economic development. By contrast, Japan, which has few natural resources, has attained a high level of growth and development because of high savings and the quality of its labor force.

4. A sufficiently high level of technology (the knowledge of how to convert resources into goods and services). Technology is generally more important to the efficiency of production than to the introduction of new goods or the improvement of existing goods. Different combinations of land, labor, and capital simply require different levels and types of technology.

5. Favorable sociocultural factors. It has been said that the Protestant work ethic, which applauds hard work, diligence, and thrift, was partly responsible for the economic development of the United States.[1]

---

1. Max Weber, *The Protestant Ethic and the Spirit of Capitalism* (New York: Scribner, 1930).

TABLE 21.1 GNP per Capita for Selected Countries in 1985, by Level of Development (U.S. Dollars)					
Low-Income Countries		**Lower Middle-Income Countries**		**Middle-Income Countries**	
Country	Per Capita Income	Country	Per Capita Income	Country	Per Capita Income
Ethiopia	$110	Indonesia	$ 530	Chile	$1,430
Bangladesh	150	Philippines	580	Brazil	1,640
Zaire	170	Egypt	610	Portugal	1,970
India	270	Ivory Coast	660	Malaysia	2,000
Kenya	290	Nicaragua	770	Mexico	2,080
Sudan	300	Thailand	800	Argentina	2,130
China	310	Nigeria	800	South Korea	2,150
Pakistan	380	Guatemala	1,250	Algeria	2,550

Characteristics of Developing Countries

▲ **2. What are some important differences between developing countries and developed countries?**

Three-fourths of the world's population lives in less developed countries, which include most of the nations of Latin America, Africa, and Asia. Some of these countries are in more advanced stages of economic development than others. Although Mexico is far less developed than the United States, the average Mexican citizen enjoys much better living conditions than the average farmer in Bangladesh. Mexico's per capita income is only one-sixth that of the United States, but it is fifteen times greater than that of Bangladesh. Nevertheless, some characteristics are common to developing countries. These include low per capita income and a more inequitable distribution of income than that of developed countries.[2]

Income

Countries are sometimes classified as developed or developing on the basis of their GNP per capita—a rough measure of the value of goods and services produced and available to the average person.[3] Among the poorest countries of the world by this measure are China, India, Bangladesh, and

---

2. See also Harvey Leibenstein, *Economic Backwardness and Economic Growth* (New York: Macmillan, 1957), pp. 40–41.

3. The United Nations classifies countries as either more developed or less developed. More developed regions comprise all of Europe, the United States, Canada, Australia, Japan, New Zealand, and the Soviet Union. All other regions are classified as less developed. There is not much difference, however, between the per capita income of Portugal, which is considered more developed, and the per capita income of Mexico, which is considered less developed.

TABLE 21.1   (continued)

Upper Middle-Income Countries		High-Income Countries	
Country	Per Capita Income	Country	Per Capita Income
South Africa	$2,010	Soviet Union	$ 6,751 (1983)
Yugoslavia	2,070	United Kingdom	8,460
Venezuela	3,080	France	9,540
Greece	3,550	West Germany	10,940
Spain	4,290	Japan	11,300
Israel	4,990	Sweden	11,890
Hong Kong	6,230	Canada	13,680
Singapore	7,420	United States	16,690

Note: The average per capita income of all developed countries is $9,190; the average per capita income of all less developed countries is $750.

Source: The World Bank, *World Development Report 1987*, Table 1, pp. 202–203.

Pakistan. Together they include almost 40 percent of the world's population but produce less than 2 percent of the world's gross national product. The annual GNP per capita for those countries is less than 3 percent of the U.S. level, which was $16,690 in 1985. Ethiopia had a GNP per capita of only $110 in 1985, or about 1 percent of Sweden's. The poverty represented by that abstract figure shows up tangibly in nutritionally inadequate diets, primitive and crowded housing, the absence of medical services, and the general unavailability of schooling.

Table 21.1 shows per capita GNP in countries at various stages of development. The first category, the poorest countries—those with per capita incomes of $400 or less—includes both China and India, the two largest countries in the world. In the second category, Indonesia and Nigeria, with per capita GNPs between $400 and $1300, are still not much better off than China and India. Sixty percent of the world's population lives in countries that would fall in one of these two categories. In the third category, which includes Mexico and Brazil, countries have higher incomes and at least some industrial base. These countries are in the early stages of economic development. The fourth category includes areas in an advanced stage of development, like Hong Kong and Spain. The highest category includes the Soviet Union and the developed market economies of the United States, Japan, and Western Europe.

Some countries with high per capita GNPs defy classification. The United Arab Emirates' per capita GNP is $19,270, higher than that of the United States or Switzerland. The United Arab Emirates, however, relies on oil exports for its income. Its high per capita income does not reflect advanced economic development. Nor does per capita GNP tell us anything about income distribution. In fact, income is distributed less equally in the

TABLE 21.2 Income Distribution in Selected Countries, Developing and Developed (percentage share of household income, by quintile)

Country	Year	First Fifth	Second Fifth	Third Fifth	Fourth Fifth	Last Fifth	Top 10 Percent
Developing							
India	1976	7.0%	9.2%	13.9%	20.5%	49.4%	33.6%
Kenya	1976	2.3	6.6	11.5	19.2	60.4	45.8
Peru	1972	1.9	5.1	11.0	21.0	61.0	42.9
Malaysia	1973	3.5	7.7	12.4	20.3	56.1	39.8
Panama	1973	2.0	5.2	11.0	20.0	61.8	44.2
Brazil	1972	2.0	5.0	9.4	17.0	66.6	50.6
Mexico	1977	2.9	7.0	12.0	20.4	57.7	40.6
Argentina	1970	4.4	9.7	14.1	21.5	50.3	35.2
Developed							
United Kingdom	1979	7.0	11.5	17.0	24.8	39.7	23.4
Japan	1979	8.7	13.2	17.5	23.1	36.8	21.2
Finland	1981	6.3	12.1	18.4	25.5	37.6	21.7
West Germany	1978	7.9	12.5	17.0	23.1	39.5	24.0
Sweden	1981	7.4	13.1	16.8	21.0	41.7	28.1
Norway	1982	6.0	12.9	18.3	24.6	38.2	22.8

Source: The World Bank, *World Development Report 1987*, Table 26, pp. 252–253.

less developed countries than in developed countries, as Table 21.2 shows. In Mexico, for example, the top 10 percent of households received about 40 percent of the national income. The bottom 60 percent of households received only about half that amount, 22 percent. In Japan, the top 10 percent of families received about the same amount of income as the bottom 40 percent. In the poorest of the less developed countries, there is no middle class. An enormous (and growing) gulf separates rich and poor.

Over time, economic growth and technological development can lead to greater equality in income distribution. Time, however, is not on the side of most developing countries. In these countries, rapid population growth tends to cancel out increases in national income per capita.

Economic Growth Versus Population Growth

Economic growth is important to a nation's development for several reasons. It increases the amount of goods and services available to consumers for personal use. It expands the supply of resources available for capital formation, and it gives government the resources it needs to discharge its social responsibilities. Table 21.3 shows the average annual growth rates for selected countries, developed and developing, from 1965 to 1985. With few exceptions, growth rates were higher in the developed countries.

In the low-income countries, especially those of Africa, slow growth accentuates and perpetuates poverty. In the poorest country in the world,

TABLE 21.3 Average Annual Growth Rate of GNP Per Capita (U.S. Dollars), Selected Countries, 1965–1985 (percent)

	Per Capita Income	Growth Rate		Per Capita Income	Growth Rate
Chad	$ 80	−2.3	Italy	$ 6,520	2.6
Bangladesh	150	0.4	Belgium	8,280	2.8
Ethiopia	110	0.2	United Kingdom	8,460	1.6
Zaire	170	−2.1	Austria	9,120	3.5
India	270	1.7	Netherlands	9,290	2.0
Haiti	310	0.7	France	9,540	2.8
China	310	4.8	Australia	10,830	2.0
Pakistan	380	2.6	Finland	10,890	3.3
Sudan	300	−0.4	West Germany	10,940	2.7
Indonesia	530	4.8	Denmark	11,200	1.8
Zambia	390	−1.6	Japan	11,300	4.7
Nigeria	800	2.2	Sweden	11,890	1.8
Peru	1,010	0.2	Canada	13,680	2.4
Chile	1,430	−0.2	Norway	14,370	3.3
Brazil	1,640	4.3	Switzerland	16,370	1.4
Mexico	2,080	2.7	United States	16,690	1.7

Source: The World Bank, *World Development Report 1987,* Table 1, pp. 202–203.

Chad, income per capita declined significantly from 1965 to 1985. Three other poor countries, Zaire, Chile, and Zambia, had static economies. India, with one of the largest populations in the world, grew at a rate of only 1.7 percent annually. To make matters worse, in countries like India, population gains often offset economic growth. Because their resources are consumed at home, poor countries have little to export to earn the income necessary for economic development.

Although the overall rate of population growth has been declining worldwide since the late 1970s, the population is still growing year by year. In 1986 world population increased by 79 million people, bringing the total to 4.94 billion—twice as many as forty years ago.[4] Current projections suggest the world's population will be about 6.2 billion by the end of this century. Almost all the increase will come in Latin America, Africa, and Asia, where birth rates are high and mortality rates are declining. These are the countries that can least afford population increases. The population of China and India is projected to increase by 450 million persons by the year 2000. The population of Bangladesh and Pakistan is likely to increase by 90 million.

Table 21.4 shows past population growth rates and projected future rates for selected countries, along with per capita GNP, which reflect a

---

4. U.S. Bureau of the Census, *Statistical Abstract of the United States* (Washington, D.C.: U.S. Government Printing Office, 1987), p. 814.

country's capacity to support an increase in population. The countries with very low per capita GNP tend to be those with the highest population growth rates. Income and population growth are inversely related. Sweden, which had a per capita GNP of $11,890 in 1985, has one of the lowest population growth rates in the world. It is projected to have about the same population in the year 2000 as it did in 1985. Bangladesh, which had a per capita GNP of $150 in 1985, is projected to have 40 million more people by the year 2000.

Social Services

There are two kinds of capital, social overhead capital and physical capital. Social overhead capital includes the structure and equipment required to support and develop human resources—housing, hospitals, and schools. Physical capital consists of directly productive capital: the plant and equipment used in industry and agriculture. Neither kind of capital can be created without a supply of savings. Yet as we have seen, incomes are too low to permit much saving in poor countries. Inevitably, the low rate of saving translates into a low rate of capital formation. The result is that poor countries cannot afford the medical services and educational facilities needed to improve the quality of their labor forces.

Table 21.5 shows the difference among countries in medical and educational services. In Bangladesh, there is one physician to 9,700 persons; in

TABLE 21.4   Population Growth, Past and Projected, Selected Countries, 1980–2000

Country	Per Capita GNP, 1985 (U.S. Dollars)	Annual Average Population Growth		Population (millions)	
		1980–1985	1985–2000	1985	2000
Bangladesh	$ 150	2.6%	2.3%	101	141
India	270	2.2	1.8	765	996
China	310	1.2	1.3	1040	1274
Pakistan	380	3.1	2.7	96	146
Indonesia	530	2.1	1.8	162	212
Egypt	610	2.8	2.2	49	67
Nigeria	800	3.3	3.4	100	163
Brazil	1,640	2.3	1.8	136	178
Malaysia	2,000	2.5	1.9	16	21
Mexico	2,080	2.6	2.2	79	110
Algeria	2,550	3.3	2.9	22	34
Italy	6,520	0.3	0.1	57	58
United Kingdom	8,460	0.1	0.1	57	57
West Germany	10,940	−0.2	−0.2	61	59
Sweden	11,890	0.1	0.0	8	8
United States	16,690	1.0	0.6	239	262

Source: The World Bank, *World Development Report 1987*, Table 1, pp. 202–203; Table 27, pp. 254–255.

the United States, one to every 500. In Uganda, only 8 percent of high-school-age people are in school, and only 1 percent of college-age people are in college. In Japan, the figures are 95 percent and 30 percent.

Agriculture and Technology

One of the most fundamental characteristics of the developing countries is that a high percentage of the population is employed in agriculture. In most of these countries it would be possible to reduce the number of workers employed in agriculture without changing technology and still obtain the same output. Farming techniques are primitive, tools and equipment limited. Modern equipment is neither easy to import nor highly demanded, and agricultural output consists mostly of high-calorie cereals and raw materials. Relatively little protein food is produced, since it requires more acres per calorie than cereals do.

Table 21.6 shows the percentage of the labor force employed in agriculture, industry, and services in various countries. In a poor country like Bangladesh, 75 percent of the working-age population is employed in agriculture, compared with 3 percent in the United States. In the highly developed countries, employment in the service industries actually exceeds employment in manufacturing. The United States is one such postindustrial economy: employment in services far exceeds employment in industry and agriculture combined.

TABLE 21.5   Health and Education in Selected Countries, Developed and Developing

Country	Population per Physician	Percentage of Age Group in Secondary Schools	Percentage of Age Group in Higher Institutions
Bangladesh	9,700	19%	5%
Ethiopia	88,120	12	1
Uganda	24,500	8	1
India	3,700	34	9
China	1,730	37	1
Pakistan	2,910	15	2
Kenya	10,140	19	1
Indonesia	12,300	39	7
Nigeria	12,000	29	3
Mexico	1,200	55	15
Italy	750	74	26
Japan	740	95	30
United States	500	95	57
Sweden	410	83	38
Soviet Union	270	100	21
Canada	550	93	37

Source: The World Bank, *World Development Report 1987*, Table 30, pp. 260–261; Table 31, pp. 262–263.

TABLE 21.6 Labor Force Participation Rates in Agriculture, Industry, and Services, Selected Countries

Country	Agriculture	Industry	Services
	Percentage of 1980 Labor Force Employed in		
Bangladesh	75%	6%	19%
Ethiopia	80	7	13
India	70	13	17
China	74	14	12
Niger	91	2	7
Pakistan	55	16	30
Sudan	71	8	21
Indonesia	57	13	30
Thailand	71	10	19
Syria	32	32	36
Brazil	31	27	42
Mexico	37	29	35
Greece	31	29	40
Italy	12	41	48
West Germany	6	44	50
United States	3	31	66

Source: The World Bank, *World Development Report 1987,* Table 32, pp. 264–265.

Technologically, many developing countries are divided between two coexisting modes of production. One is modern, capital intensive, export oriented, and often foreign owned and managed. The other is traditional, labor intensive, dedicated to supplying the home market or the family, and domestically owned.[5] The first is technologically advanced and highly productive. The second is technologically dated and underproductive. In small cottage industries, each worker may perform every step in the production process.

This technological dualism can create social divisions, for new products and production methods often require people to change their beliefs and ways of living. Workers accustomed to different modes of production will have different values and different economic goals.

Theories of Economic Development

▲ 3. How might a developing country become a developed country?

Over time economists have developed a considerable body of thought on the conditions necessary for economic development. We will summarize some of the more important theories here.

5. Bruce Herrick and Charles P. Kindleberger, *Economic Development,* 4th ed. (New York: McGraw-Hill, 1983), p. 520.

Classical Theory

The classical economists of the late eighteenth and early nineteenth centuries—Adam Smith, David Ricardo, Thomas Malthus, and John Stuart Mill—saw technological progress as the key to development. Increasing mechanization permitted the efficient division of labor, improving productivity. Such technological progress depended in turn on the accumulation of capital, which itself depended on the level of profits.

Classical economists worried that profits were linked to population growth. As profits increased, employment and total wages paid would rise with them, encouraging workers to have more children. (It was assumed that an unlimited amount of labor, including child labor, was available at a subsistence wage.) Population growth would tend to absorb profits, creating a drag on economic development. To feed the growing population, farmers would have to put marginal land into use or till the best land more intensively. Diminishing marginal returns would cause prices to rise, pushing up labor costs. Profits would go down, and the accumulation of capital would decline. To stay ahead of the population growth, therefore, technology would have to improve continually.

Marxist Theory

Karl Marx contended that economic conditions were the basic forces that shaped society. Marx saw technological change as the prime mover in the development of medieval feudalism into industrial capitalism. Capitalism was merely another stage in the evolution of society toward its final form: the communist state.

Like the classical economists, Marx believed that economic development depended on technological progress, which depended on the accumulation of capital and ultimately on profits. He saw low wages as the key to the accumulation of capital (see Chapter 20). Marx argued that labor was the sole source of value in the productive process. Capitalists would try to pay labor a subsistence wage and claim the surplus value for themselves. Eventually consumption would decline, causing recurrent economic crises. Ultimately economic instability would wreck the capitalist system. Workers would revolt against the capitalists and establish socialism. Economic growth and development would accelerate, preparing the way for the new communist society.

Rostow's Takeoff Theory

Probably the most prominent of recent theories of economic development is Walt Rostow's takeoff theory.[6] According to Rostow, nations pass through five stages in the process of economic development.

6. Walt Whitman Rostow, *The Stages of Economic Growth: A Non-Communist Manifesto* (New York: Cambridge University Press, 1971).

1. *The traditional society.* In this first stage, most resources are concentrated in agriculture. There is no cumulative, self-reinforcing process of material improvement, such as exists in industrial societies. As a result there is little social mobility. All societies before the Renaissance were traditional societies.

2. *Prerequisites for takeoff.* In the second stage, the prerequisites for sustained, systematic social change are created. At least part of the population in traditional societies must abandon its fatalistic outlook on life. There must be entrepreneurs willing to take risks in finance and manufacturing. Social respect must come to depend on economic achievement rather than inherited status. Finally, a leading sector—mining, petroleum, or some other industry—must propel the takeoff.

3. *Takeoff.* In this stage, which lasts twenty to thirty years, the pace of social and economic change suddenly accelerates. The process is fueled by an increase in the percentage of the gross national product that is saved and invested, and by the establishment of manufacturing. Social customs, governmental forms and practices, and economic institutions continue to evolve.

4. *The drive to maturity.* This is a period of self-sustaining increases in gross national product, both overall and per capita. During this stage, which lasts about sixty years, industry acquires the most advanced technology available. Manufacturers become capable of producing whatever they wish, subject only to the constraints of the market and the availability of resources.

5. *Mass consumption.* The last stage of economic development is one of mass consumption of durable goods and services. The production of such goods and services enables most of the population to attain a high living standard.

Rostow's theory has been criticized on several counts. It does not fit historical fact very closely. Some countries' economies do not take off suddenly, but develop steadily over a long period of time. The theory is also vague on what causes growth in each stage, and what distinguishes one stage from the next. Nevertheless Rostow's theory offers valuable insight into the changes that must occur before a nation in the traditional stage of development can develop economically.

Other Theories

Two other theories of economic development deserve brief mention. The *big push theory* offers a potential solution to the vicious circle of low income, low saving, low investment, low productivity, and low income. The idea is that a large infusion of investment, primarily from foreign sources, into different industries will enlarge markets, creating support industries. As industries buy from each other, the economy will grow, income and saving will rise, and the circle will be broken.

PERSPECTIVES
The Value of Children in Developing Countries
Martin Schnitzer, Virginia Tech

If population growth is an obstacle to economic development, why are birth control programs difficult to implement in less developed countries? For one thing, traditional cultural barriers must be overcome. To the male head of the household, a large family may be a symbol of social prestige. And religion may prohibit the use of contraceptives.

But economic factors also play a part. A large family can mean economic security for parents, for each additional child represents an earning asset. The economic motive is especially strong in agricultural areas, where farmers need extra labor to work the land. Parents also depend on children to care for them in their old age. Thus the mone-

tary benefits of having many children far outweigh the costs.

In the developed countries, it is usually the other way around. As living standards increase, it costs more to provide the goods and services needed to raise children. In addition there is the opportunity cost of raising children—the amount of time parents put into caring for children, compared with other uses they could have made of that time. A woman who leaves the labor force to have children may lose considerable income. No wonder people with high incomes want fewer children than people with low incomes. The alternative uses for their time—making money, enjoying leisure pursuits—are quite attractive.

The *dependency theory* relates the problems of the developing countries to their former colonial status. Most developing countries were once possessions of mercantilist nations like Spain, England, France, the Netherlands, and Portugal. Their natural resources were exploited by the mother countries, and they were prevented from developing technologically. These colonies eventually achieved independence, but they remained economically and psychologically dependent on Europe. Many of the new African countries still rely on foreign military and financial advisers, for example.

Obstacles to Economic Development

4. What are the economic problems faced by developing countries?

Economic development has been proceeding slowly or not at all in many of the developing countries. Per capita GNP is not only low, but stagnant. In some countries, during some periods, it has actually fallen. The fact is, economic development is an extremely elusive objective. Among the most significant obstacles to its achievement is overpopulation.

Overpopulation

Perhaps the chief obstacle to economic development in developing countries is people. Because people provide the most important factor of production, labor, one might conclude that more people would obviously mean more GNP. That belief, however, assumes access to large amounts of natural resources and capital. More people means not only more labor and output, but more mouths to feed. The more people, the less capital and natural resources per capita. Unfortunately, many less developed countries are experiencing runaway population growth.

Population Doubling

In 1798 the English economist Thomas Malthus published *An Essay on the Principle of Population*. Malthus took a pessimistic view. He suggested that the world's population was growing faster than its food supply. On the basis of scattered empirical evidence, including data from the North American colonies, Malthus calculated that populations tended to double every twenty-five years, in geometric progression, whereas the food supply tends to increase arithmetically. For example:

Year	0	25	50	75	100	125	150	175	200
Population	1	2	4	8	16	32	64	128	256
Food	1	2	3	4	5	6	7	8	9

Malthus based his proposition on two assumptions that have subsequently been disproved: first, that technological change could not increase the food supply faster than the population was increasing; second, that population growth could be limited only by an increase in the death rate. Nevertheless, there was some truth in Malthus's predictions. It took over four thousand years of recorded history for China to reach a population of 500 million, but then only a little more than three decades to increase to one billion. It is true that whatever a nation's size, natural resources, and level of development, a large population and a high birth rate will bring increasing problems in the future.

Table 21.7 shows the birth and death rates and the time required for a doubling of population for selected countries. The United States, with a birth rate of 16 per 1,000 and a death rate of 9 per 1,000, will double its population in 99 years.[7] Mexico, with a birth rate of 30 per 1,000 and a death rate of 6 per 1,000, will double its population in just 29 years. West Germany and East Germany, with negative and zero rates of growth respectively, will never double their population unless their growth increases. Worldwide, the population doubling-time for developed countries is 120 years; for developing countries, it is 33 years. The gap is even wider if we compare Western Europe (398 years), with Africa (24 years). Again we see the link between economic growth and population growth. In 1986, the GNP per capita for Africa was $620; it was $11,380 for Western Europe.

Urbanization

Urbanization compounds population problems through congestion. Overcrowding in cities promotes pollution, unemployment, and a greater demand for human services. The increased stress can cause disease—not only communicable diseases like tuberculosis but heart disease, cancer, and

---

7. Mary M. Kent and Carl Haub, "1988 World Population Data Sheet" (Washington, D.C.: Population Reference Bureau, April 1988).

TABLE 21.7 Birth and Death Rates and Population Doubling-Time for Selected Countries, Developed and Less Developed, 1988

Developed Countries	Birth Rate (thousands)	Death Rate (thousands)	Doubling-Time (years)	Developing Countries	Birth Rate (thousands)	Death Rate (thousands)	Doubling-Time (years)
All countries	15	9	120	All countries	31	10	33
Soviet Union	20	10	68	China	21	7	49
United States	16	9	99	India	33	13	35
Japan	11	6	133	Indonesia	27	10	40
West Germany	10	11	—	Brazil	28	8	34
East Germany	13	13	—	Bangladesh	43	17	26
Italy	10	10	3465	Pakistan	43	15	24
United Kingdom	13	12	408	Nigeria	46	17	24
France	14	10	166	Mexico	30	6	29
Canada	15	7	94	Philippines	35	7	25
Sweden	12	11	673	Vietnam	34	8	27

Source: Mary M. Kent and Carl Haub, "1988 World Population Data Sheet" (Washington, D.C.: Population Reference Bureau, April 1988).

other ailments attributable to a breakdown in the body's immunity. The problems of urbanization are particularly acute in less developed countries, which lack the financial resources to provide remedial services.

By the end of this century, at least twenty-two of the world's cities will have populations of more than 10 million. Sixty will have more than 5 million.[8] Most of these, like Mexico City, now the second largest city in the world, are located in developing countries.

Food Shortages

The larger a nation's population, the greater its demand for food. In most overpopulated countries, the strong demand for food has left little saving and has hampered industrial development. The rural population competes with a rising tide of urban consumers for the limited agricultural output.

Here again we see the vicious circle of poverty in operation. The inability to industrialize reduces the potential of developing countries to earn money from exports, which could be used to import additional food. Food shortages produce nutritional deficiencies and ultimately ill health. And poor health reduces productivity, output, and income.

Lack of an Infrastructure

Infrastructure is a broad concept that includes the highways, railways, airports, sewage facilities, housing, and social amenities provided in developed areas. Once in place, the infrastructure encourages both economic and social development. Because developing countries generally do not have

8. United Nations, Department of International and Social Affairs, *Population Bulletin of the United Nations,* No. 14 (1983), p. 24.

infrastructures, industrial firms will not normally locate plants there. Products manufactured for mass consumption simply cannot be distributed and used without transportation and communication facilities, skilled labor, and waste disposal plants.

Schools

Educational facilities are a key component of an area's infrastructure. Because education is directly related to the quality of life, it constitutes a form of social capital. A low literacy rate can retard economic development. A high literacy rate can assist it. No nation with a highly educated population is poor.

Literacy is directly related to a country's stage of economic development. There is a positive correlation between a low standard of living and a high rate of illiteracy. It has been estimated that one-third of the world's people are illiterate,[9] and that most of them live in countries with high birth rates, large populations, and little money to spend on education. This general lack of educational opportunities reinforces the distribution between the haves and the have-nots, perpetuating class differences as well as slowing economic development.

Roads

A system of roads is vital to economic and social development. Without roads, transportation becomes much more expensive. The cost of air transport is prohibitively high for most products, and railroad networks serve only a limited number of major access points.

Poor countries usually do not have the resources to develop and maintain an adequate road system. Their limited capital is simply insufficient to surmount natural barriers to transportation. For example, the lack of highways across the Sierra Madre and Andes mountains has long inhibited the east-west development of Mexico and South America. Transportation is especially hard to develop in countries dominated by mountain ranges, like Bolivia and Peru.

Other Facilities

Dams, bridges, and waste disposal and communication facilities are vitally important assets that less developed countries usually lack. Dams provide the water supply and electric power necessary for economic and social development. Bridges create more efficient transportation by directly linking areas separated by water bodies. Waste disposal facilities control communicable diseases like cholera and typhoid fever, which can be spread by rats and other animals that feed on garbage dumped in city streets. Finally, communication facilities must be reliable enough to allow the transaction of business on a regular basis. In the less developed countries, government-owned telephone and telegraph services are notoriously inefficient.

---

9. United Nations, Department of International and Social Affairs, *Population Bulletin of the United Nations,* No. 14 (1983), p. 25.

Other Obstacles

Low Savings Rate

Savings are an important prerequisite for capital formation, for they free resources for use in the production of plant and equipment. An inability to raise capital is therefore a serious obstacle to economic development. Here again developing countries are caught in a vicious circle. Small savings mean a small capital stock and a small gross national product. If GNP is small, almost all of it will be consumed in subsistence goods like food, leaving little to be saved. Capital formation will remain low, along with the standard of living and the rate of economic development.[10]

The unequal distribution of income in developing countries exacerbates the saving problem. The vast majority of workers in these countries do not earn enough income to accumulate any savings. Instead, a minority of households receives most of the income. In Mexico, as we have seen, the top 10 percent of income earners receives about 40 percent of the national income. In Brazil, the top 10 percent receives about 50 percent of the nation's earnings. Members of this privileged group could provide the saving necessary for capital formation, but they usually invest their money in real estate, which offers them a quick, high return on investment, or in foreign assets. Swiss bonds, which cannot be expropriated by a new government, may be extremely attractive to investors living in politically unstable countries.

Limited Range of Exports

The developing countries tend to export agricultural products, raw fuels, and metals. Many depend on a single product for most of their export income. About 80 percent of Nigeria's total export earnings is from oil, for instance. Needless to say, such dependence on only one primary product can make a country extremely vulnerable to the ups and downs of the marketplace.

When oil prices were high in the early 1970s, for example, Nigeria's income increased. It ran a surplus in its balance of payments and used foreign earnings to improve its living standards. Increased public spending improved Nigeria's infrastructure, bettering its opportunities for development. During the early 1980s, however, world demand for oil began to decline. Oil prices fell by about $6 per barrel from a peak of $35 in 1980. As revenues from oil exports declined, Nigeria developed a deficit in its balance of payments. It must now pay off a large foreign debt incurred when oil prices were high, with earnings received when prices are low.

Countries that depend on the export of agricultural products and minerals are usually at a disadvantage in trade with developed countries. The terms of trade—that is, the quantity of exports required to pay for a given amount of imports—tend to favor the developed countries. Brazilian coffee

10. Ragnar Nurkse, *Problems of Capital Formation in Underdeveloped Countries* (New York: Oxford University Press, 1953).

and Mexican oil, for example, are much more subject to shifts in price than American computers or Japanese cars. The demand for agricultural products and minerals tends to be price inelastic, so that when prices fall, they are not offset by a large increase in quantity demanded. When coffee prices decline, then, Brazil will have to give up more income to import the same number of computers or cars. At the same time, America and Japan will give up less income to acquire Brazil's coffee.

Sociocultural Factors

Sociocultural factors can also impede economic development.[11] In countless ways, culture influences individual and group behavior, determining how and when things will be done. Status distinctions based on education, caste, politics, religion, or sex can hold back employment of productive labor. Language differences can make communication and job training difficult, but culture can also contribute to development. If the use of machinery and equipment creates an industrial culture that is alien to the old agrarian ways, the new culture will speed the transition to a developed economy. Cultural conformity keeps groups of people working together, either for or against new ideas and ways of living.

Cultural attitudes and values underlie population problems as well as productivity rates. The norm in most developing countries is to have large families. Religious prohibitions on birth control contribute to this pattern, but so do the limited social roles of women. Women in these countries occupy a secondary position that allows them little education or opportunity for work outside the home.

Status distinctions and religious values are also important determinants of economic advancement. Business has a lower status than other professions in some developing societies. Furthermore, economic development often conflicts with religious tradition. The overthrow of the Shah of Iran in 1979 was led largely by a fundamentalist Moslem clergy in revolt against Western materialism. Finally, traditional tribal conflicts can hamper development.

Remedies for Economic Underdevelopment

◢ **5. How can developing countries solve their economic problems?**

There is no easy way for poor countries to become rich. Many problems must be overcome, notably population growth. The mismatch between population growth and income growth in many developing countries works against economic development.

Changes in the developed countries' economic and financial policies could relieve some of the difficulties of the developing countries. Foreign

---

11. For a discussion of sociocultural factors and their impact on development, see Edmund Leach, *Social Anthropology* (New York: Oxford University Press, 1982); and W. Arthur Lewis, *The Theory of Economic Development* (Homewood, Ill.: Irwin, 1955).

trade can be an instrument of growth. If governments of the developed countries would drop some of their import restrictions, developing countries would be able to earn more income. Through foreign aid programs, developed countries could also lend funds for investment to developing countries.

Foreign Aid

Foreign aid is the transfer of income from rich nations to poor nations for the purpose of promoting their economic development. The transfer may be made as outright grants or as loans carrying lower interest rates and longer repayment periods than usual. (In 1985, the average interest rate for public borrowing in Bangladesh was 1.0 percent, and the average length of repayment was forty-one years.) Foreign aid may also take a variety of physical forms, from technical assistance to food supplies. Military assistance may be considered a form of foreign aid, although its impact on economic development is debatable.

Since the end of the Second World War, a battery of international financial institutions has sprung up to assist developing countries. Among these are the International Bank of Reconstruction and Development (IBRD), the International Development Association (IDA), and the International Finance Corporation (IFC). All these organizations attempt to promote economic and social progress through the creation of modern economic and social infrastructures. All three make loans to countries or firms for such purposes as roads, irrigation projects, and electric generating plants. The IFC, for example, makes loans to firms, on the condition that the project benefit the economy of the less developed country and have a reasonable prospect of making a profit. Finally, the World Health Organization (WHO), an agency of the United Nations, assists less developed countries in improving their health services.

Besides these international institutions, the United States and other developed nations have their own programs of assistance for developing countries. The Overseas Private Investment Corporation (OPIC), an American agency, provides direct loans for development projects at low interest rates. The Export-Import Bank (Eximbank), although originally created for other purposes, has recently allocated most of its funds for the use of developing countries. In addition, most Western European countries provide technical or financial assistance to the developing countries.[12] In the Third World, or politically nonaligned, countries of Africa, Asia, and the Middle East, the Soviet Union is increasingly providing technical and capital assistance. Economic aid to those countries is now a major factor in the contest for power between the United States and the Soviet Union.

---

12. Foreign aid as a percentage of gross national product varies considerably by country. In 1983, for example, 0.24 percent of the U.S. GNP went to foreign aid, compared with 1.10 percent for Norway. Japan contributed 0.33 percent of its GNP to foreign aid, West Germany 0.48 percent.

PERSPECTIVES
Harry Gordon Johnson (1923–1977)

Harry Gordon Johnson, one of the most versatile and prolific economists of the twentieth century, was born in Toronto and educated at the University of Toronto, Cambridge University, and Harvard University. During his career he taught at Cambridge University, Manchester University, the London School of Economics, the University of Chicago, and the Graduate School of International Studies in Geneva. In addition, he served as a visiting professor and occasional lecturer at universities throughout the world.

In a profession where few scholars publish more than a handful of articles during their careers, Johnson wrote twenty-seven books and fourteen pamphlets, edited another twenty-five books, and published hundreds of articles and reviews.[1] His books and articles displayed his amazingly wide interests, ranging from the economics of John Maynard Keynes to the geometry of two-by-two general equilibrium models to the literary style of Mickey Spillane (and much in-between).

One of Johnson's continuing concerns was development economics (or the economics of growth). He criticized much of the development economics of the 1960s and 1970s, particularly the notion that the developed countries of the world were responsible for the lack of development of the developing countries. He could not understand the willingness of intellectuals in Europe and America to accept the blame for the poverty of Asia and Africa. To Johnson, the ancestors of the Europeans had engaged in activities that created wealth for their descendents; the ancestors of the people in the developing countries had not. It was as simple as that.

Johnson believed that there was no such thing as an economics of development that was somehow separate from ordinary micro- and macroeconomics. The same principles that held for a developed country held for the developing countries. For example, he argued against attempts to cartelize international markets in the products produced by developing countries on the same grounds that most economists oppose cartels in a domestic economy: Monopoly is inefficient and cartels are likely to be unstable.

What should developing countries do to achieve economic growth and development? According to Johnson,

> Economic development is primarily a process of domestic economic and social transformation of a society or nation into one that seeks economic improvement and is organized to allow and encourage its citizens to undertake the investment in material, human, and intellectual capital required for steady accumulation.[2]

The internal transformation of the society, then, caused economic development.

Johnson was particularly interested in the role of trade and trade policy in promoting development. He believed that an open economy was the best policy to promote development—especially for small nations. Protection was almost always a mistake and could be disastrous for countries too small to generate domestic markets for their products. It was unlikely that such nations would be able to develop without foreign trade. If protectionist measures were adopted, then the country was cutting off its main hope of development. The correct policy for a small economy was to reduce protectionist barriers and to encourage those industries in which it was likely to have a comparative advantage in international markets.

Although foreign trade could contribute to development, internal factors played a far more important role. Political stability and predictable economic policies could create a favorable environment for the transformation of a developing nation. Investment in education and training could increase the efficiency of the domestic labor market. Finally, Johnson repeatedly emphasized that tax policies should not discourage the accumulation and innovation that are essential to economic growth and development.

1. A recent bibliography of Johnson's works was fifty-three pages long. See Vicki M. Longawa, editor and compiler, "Harry G. Johnson: A Bibliography," *Journal of Political Economy* 92 (August 1984): 659–711.

2. Harry G. Johnson, "The New International Economic Order," Selected Papers No. 49, Graduate School of Business, University of Chicago (1977), p. 9.

Foreign aid is not a miracle cure for economic underdevelopment. Military aid can do little to promote economic development, unless it permits a country to divert defense funds to more productive uses. The benefits of aid may end up in the hands of a few, instead of reaching a broad segment of the population. If aid is used for consumption instead of investment, it will generate few lasting economic benefits. Moreover, many foreign aid projects take time to develop. Many projects do not produce directly marketable output until several years after commencement.

Other Solutions

In the last three decades many developing countries have made substantial economic and social progress. In general, this development has come about in one of three ways.

1. Exportation of a major resource, with no real progress toward industrialization. The Arab oil-producing countries have achieved very high per capita incomes through their oil exports, for example.

2. Industrialization and protective tariffs and quotas. The Mexican government, for example, has encouraged manufacturing both directly, through controls on investment and trade, and indirectly, through taxes, subsidies, and other measures influencing resource and product prices. At the same time it has restricted imports to limit the competition faced by new industries.

3. Industrialization and the export of manufactured goods. Taiwan and South Korea have pursued this approach successfully. Both nations have relied mainly on the incentives of the market system, with some direction and control from the state. A high rate of investment has been a major contributor to economic growth in these nations.

These methods may not be relevant to the poorest countries in the world, which have little of value to export and little potential for industrialization. Investment in India and other poor countries is limited by their inability to absorb capital; by low levels of saving; and by adverse foreign exchange rates. Developing countries cannot control many of the factors that influence their development prospects—such as the economic well-being of the developed countries, their source of trade and foreign aid.

In the end the key to development may lie in the right combination of government policy and private initiative. Some East Asian countries have succeeded this way. Government policies have expanded exports by keeping exchange rates competitive, while restricting imports on the basis of price. They have maintained high real interest rates, which have encouraged saving and ensured that investment is directed to the areas of highest return. Yet in these countries resources are allocated by the market, to ensure their most productive use. In China, the government recently introduced a series of measures to restructure the economy and increase the rate of development. Business enterprises are to have greater autonomy; there will be greater reliance on the market to determine output; and government monopolies will be broken up through competition.

Chapter Review

Review of Key Questions

◢   *1. What is the difference between economic growth and economic development?*

Economic growth is the expansion of a nation's output; it is usually measured as the increase in real gross national product per capita. Economic development refers to the structural and other changes that accompany economic growth. An economy can grow without developing, but it cannot develop without growth.

◢   *2. What are some important differences between developing countries and developed countries?*

Real GNP per capita is far lower in the developing countries than in the developed countries. Population growth tends to be more rapid in the developing countries, while levels of health, education, and social services are far lower. The proportion of the labor force employed in agriculture is much higher in the developing countries, while industry is technologically far behind the economies of the developed countries.

◢   *3. How might a developing country become a developed country?*

Many theories purport to explain why and how economic growth and development take place. Three theories are particularly influential. (a) Classical theory stresses the role of capital accumulation and technological progress. (b) Marxist theory also focuses on technology and accumulation, but includes the class struggle between capitalists and workers as an important force in development. (c) Rostow's theory assumes that all economies pass through five stages, starting as traditional societies and eventually becoming mass consumption societies. The crucial stage is the takeoff, when growth and development accelerate.

◢   *4. What are the economic problems faced by developing countries?*

The major problems facing less developed countries are (a) overpopulation and relatively high rates of population growth, (b) an inadequate infrastructure, (c) heavy reliance on the export of a small number of primary products, and (d) a low rate of savings and investment. Other problems include religious and cultural biases against modernization.

◢   *5. How can developing countries solve their economic problems?*

The most commonly proposed remedies are (a) control of population growth, (b) foreign aid, and (c) greater reliance on markets and the profit incentive in the allocation of resources.

Further Topics

Almost half the world's population lives in countries with a GNP per capita of $400 a year or less. Another 500 million people live in countries with a per capita income of between $400 and $1,300 a year. These countries are in the beginning stages of economic development. Yet many countries with higher per capita incomes, like Mexico and Brazil, are by no means modern industrial economies. Similarly, in the oil-exporting countries, per capita incomes are high, but the level of development is low.

Developing countries face many challenges in their efforts to advance. The first is to attract enough investment, either through saving or aid, to provide a satisfactory rate of economic growth. They must also build an infrastructure that provides the services necessary for industrial development. Negative sociocultural attitudes must also be overcome. Probably the most important obstacle to conquer is high population growth. If population grows rapidly, most of a nation's investment must be devoted to maintaining per capita income at current levels rather than to increasing it.

Review of New Terms

Economic development The structural and other changes that accompany economic growth.

Economic growth The expansion of a nation's capacity to produce the goods and services its people want.

Review Questions

1. On what basis is a country classified as developing? (◢ 1, ◢ 2)
2. What are the typical features of a developing economy? (◢ 2)
3. What role does trade play in economic development? (◢ 4, ◢ 5)
4. Describe Rostow's theory of the stages of economic development. (◢ 3)
5. What is the typical attitude toward family size in traditional societies? Why? (◢ 4)
6. What do you consider the most important obstacle to economic development in the developing countries? Why? (◢ 4)
7. Give some examples of sociocultural factors that block economic development. (◢ 2, ◢ 3, ◢ 4)
8. Why are developing countries at a disadvantage in their trade with developed countries? (◢ 4)
9. When and how are people a liability rather than an asset in achieving economic development? (◢ 2, ◢ 4)
10. What trade policies should developing countries adopt? Why? (◢ 5)

PART VII

The Political Economy

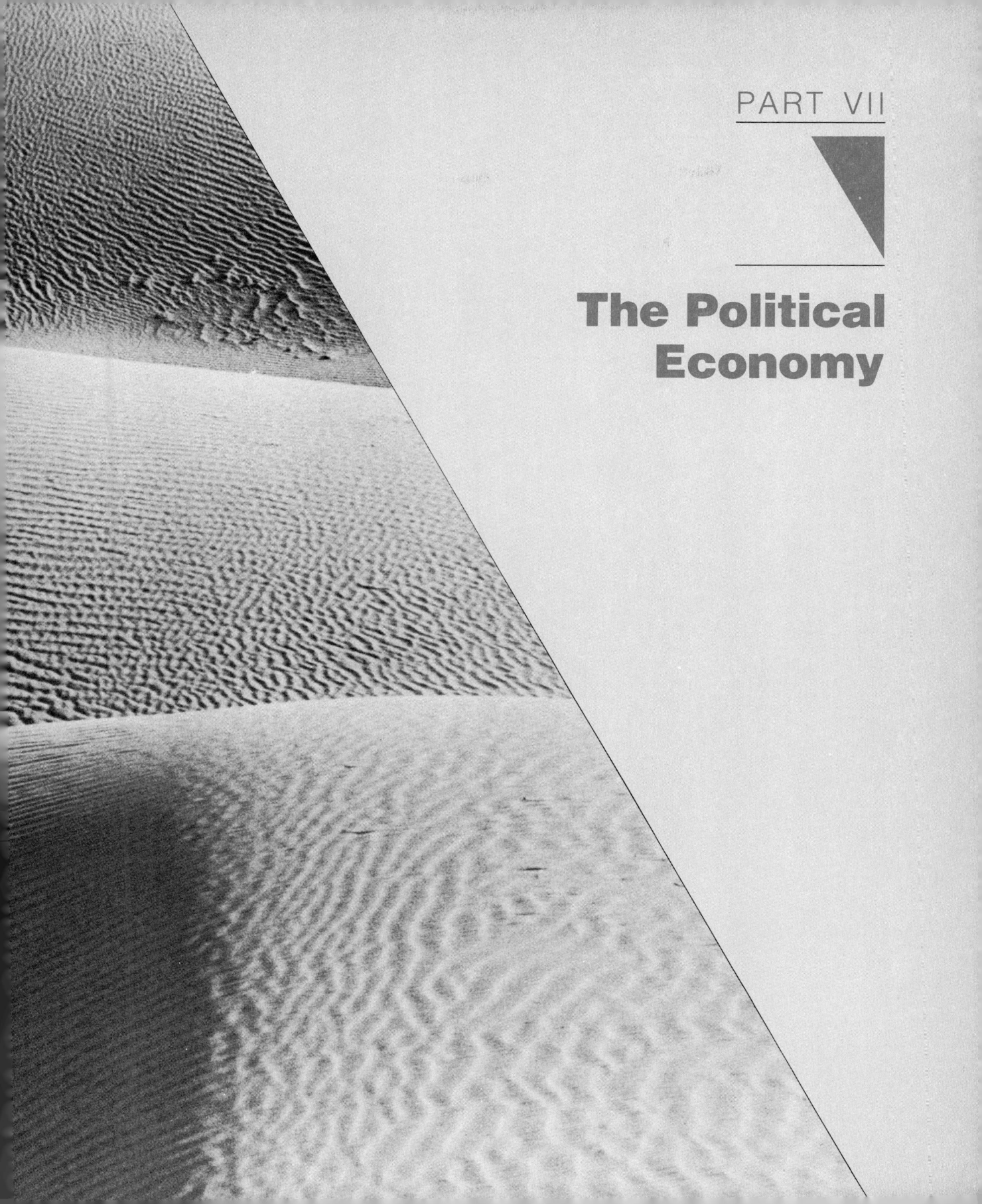

Public Choice: The Economics of Government

I have no fear, but that the result of our experiment will be, that men may be trusted to govern themselves without a master. Could the contrary be proved, I should conclude, either that there is no God, or that he is a malevolent being.
    Thomas Jefferson

KEY QUESTIONS

1. Why do candidates in two-party political systems tend to move toward the "middle of the road"?

2. How does the rule for determining winners in elections affect the decisions that are made in a political system?

3. What are the sources of inefficiency in democratic political systems?

4. How can competition among governments improve the effectiveness of government programs?

5. How do government bureaucracies determine their levels of production?

6. How can bureaucracies be made more competitive and efficient?

NEW TERMS

Median voter
Unanimity rule

Previous chapters have discussed the effects of various government policies on the market system. We looked at government efforts to control the external costs of pollution. We considered the economic impact of price controls and consumer protection laws on the market for final goods and services. We examined the effects of government agricultural policy. Throughout the analysis we have focused on assessing the economic efficiency of government policy. We said little about how government policy is determined or why government prefers one policy to another.

In this chapter, we will shift our focus to the functioning of government itself. Using economic principles, we will examine the process through which government decisions are made and carried out in a two-party democratic system, and consider its consequences. Today, when government production accounts for a substantial portion of the nation's goods and services, no student of economics can afford to ignore these issues.

The Central Tendency of a Two-Party System

◢ 1. Why do candidates in two-party political systems tend to move toward the "middle of the road"?

In a two-party democratic system, elected officials typically take middle-of-the road positions. Winning candidates tend to represent the moderate views of the many voters who are neither liberals nor conservatives. For this reason there is generally little difference between Republican and Democratic candidates. Even when the major parties' candidates differ strongly, as Ronald Reagan and Walter Mondale did at the start of their 1984 presidential campaign, they tend to move closer together as the campaign progresses.

Figure 22.1 illustrates politicians' incentives to move toward the center. The bell-shaped curve shows the approximate distribution of voters along the political spectrum. A few voters have views that place them in the wings of the distribution, but most cluster near the center. Assuming that citizens will vote for the candidate who most closely approximates their own political position, a politician who wants to win the election will not choose a position in the wings of the distribution.

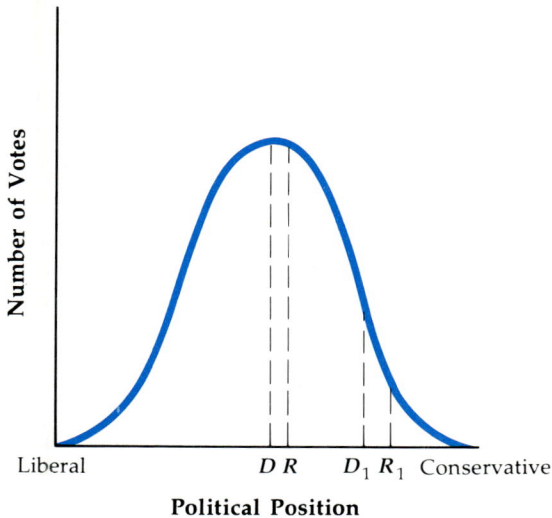

FIGURE 22.1 The Political Spectrum
A political candidate who takes a position in the wings of a voter distribution, such as D_1 or R_1, will win fewer votes than a candidate who moves toward the middle of the distribution. In a two-party election, therefore, both candidates will take middle-of-the-road positions, such as D and R.

Suppose, for instance, that the Republican candidate chooses a position at R_1. The Democratic candidate can easily win the election by taking a position slightly to the left, at D_1. Although the Republican will take all the votes to the right of R_1 and roughly half the votes between R_1 and D_1, the Democrat will take all the votes to the left. Clearly the Democrat will win an overwhelming majority.

The smart politician, therefore, will choose a position near the middle. Then the opposing candidate must also move to the middle, or accept certain defeat. Suppose, for instance, that the Republican candidate chooses position R, but the Democrat remains at D_1. The Republican will take all the votes to the left of R and roughly half the votes between R and D_1. She will have more than the simple majority needed to beat her Democratic opponent. In short, both candidates will choose political positions in the middle of the distribution.

Politicians can misinterpret the political climate, of course. Even with polls, no one can be certain of the distribution of votes before an election. Just as producers find the optimum production level though trial and error, politicians may suffer several defeats before finding the true center of public opinion. Inevitably, however, political competition will drive them toward the middle of the distribution, where the median voter group resides. The **median voter** is the voter in the middle of the political distribution.

Median voter: the voter in the middle of the political distribution.

The recent history of presidential elections illustrates how politicians play to the views of the median voter. After an election in which the successful candidate won by a wide margin, the losing party has moved toward the position of the winning party. After Barry Goldwater lost by a wide margin to Lyndon Johnson in 1964, the Republican party made a deliberate effort

PERSPECTIVES
The Mathematics of Voting and Political Ignorance
Gordon Tullock, University of Arizona

Public problems are normally more important than private problems, but the decision by any individual on a private problem is likely to be more important than his decision on a public problem, simply because most people are not so situated that their decision on public matters makes very much difference. It is rational, therefore, for the average family to put a great deal more thought and investigation into a decision such as what car to buy than into a decision on voting for president. As far as we can tell, families, in fact, act quite rationally in this matter, and the average family devotes almost no time to becoming informed on political matters but will carefully consider the alternative when buying a car. Why is that the case?

In order to address the question we need first to ask a more basic question: What is the payoff to the individual from voting? Assume that you are in possession of some information and have decided that you favor the Democratic party or, if it is a primary, some particular candidate. The payoff could be computed from the following expression:

$$BDA - C_v = P$$

B = benefit expected to be derived from success of your party or candidate

D = likelihood that your vote will make a difference

A = your estimate of the accuracy of your judgment ($-1 < A < +1$)

C_v = cost of voting

P = payoff

Certain aspects of this expression deserve a little further discussion. The B refers, of course, not to the absolute advantage of having one party or candidate in office, but the difference between the candidate and his or her opponent. The factor labeled A, the estimate of the accuracy of the voter's judgment, is included here because we are

preparing to consider variations on the amount of information held by the individual, and the principal effect of being better informed is that your judgment is more likely to be correct. The factor labeled A can take any value from minus 1, which represents a certainty that the judgments will be wrong, to plus 1, which indicates that the voter is sure he or she is right. The choice of this rather unusual way of presenting what is really a probability figure is due solely to its use in the particular equation, not to any desire to change the probability notational scheme. For the equation to give the right answer, it is necessary that A have a value of zero when the individual thinks that he has a fifty-fifty chance of being right.

The factor labeled D is the likelihood that an individual's vote will make a difference in the election; that is, the probability that the result if he were to vote would be different than it would be if he were not to vote. For an American presidential election, this is less than one in 10 million. C_v is the cost, in money and convenience, of voting. For some people, of course, it may be negative. They may get pleasure, or at least the negative benefit of relief of social pressure, from voting. If we view voting as an instrumental act, however—something we do not because it gives us pleasure directly but because we expect it to lead to some desirable goal—then our decision to vote or not will depend on weighing the costs and benefits.

Let us put a few figures into our expression. Suppose I feel that the election of the "right" candidate as president is worth $10,000 to me. I think I am apt to be right three times out of four, so the value of A will be .5, D will be figured as .000,000,1. Assuming that my cost of voting is $1.00, the expression gives ($10,000 × .5 × .000,000,1) − $1.00 = −$.9995. It follows from this that I should not bother voting.

It will, however, be worthwhile to consider a few variations on the expression. In the first place, it is frequently argued that this line of reasoning would lead to no one voting. This is not true. If people began making these computations and then refraining from voting, this would raise the value of D, since the fewer the voters, the more likely that any given vote will affect the outcome. As more and more people stopped voting, D would continue to rise until the left side of the expression equaled the right. At this equilibrium there would be no reason for nonvoters to begin to vote or for voters to stop. Presumably the people voting would be those among the population who were most interested in politics, since D would have the same value for everyone but $(B \times A)$ would approximate a positive function of political interest.

The equation, if it is thought to be in any way descriptive of the real world, would imply that people would be more likely to vote in close elections. This hypothesis has been tested and found to be correct.

Let us now complicate our model. An additional factor, C_i, the cost of obtaining information, has been included in the first equation.

$$BDA - C_v - C_i = P$$

This is, of course, the cost of obtaining additional information, since the voter will have at least some information on the issues as a result of his contact with the mass media. Of course, A is a function of information ($A = f(I)$), and hence each increase in information held will increase A and thus raise both the benefits and the costs. The problem for the rational individual contemplating whether or not he or she should vote would be whether there are any values of C_i that would lead to a positive value payoff.

Suppose, for example, that the investment of $100.00 (mostly in the form of leisure forgone) in obtaining more information would raise the value of A from .5 to .8. Using the same amounts for the other values as we used previously, $P =$ −$100.9992. Clearly, this is even worse than the original outcome. Furthermore, these figures are

realistic. The cost of obtaining enough information to significantly improve your vote is apt to very much outweigh the effect of the improvement. This is particularly true for the average voter, who does not have much experience or skill in research and who would put a particularly high negative evaluation on the time spent in this way.

A further implication of our reasoning must be pointed out. There may be social pressures that make it wise for the individual to make the rather small investment necessary for voting. In terms of our equation, C_v may be negative. In these cases, voting would always be rational. Becoming adequately informed, however, is much more expensive. Further, it is not as easy for your neighbors (or your conscience) to see whether you have or have not put enough thought into your choice. Thus, it would almost never be rational to engage in much study in order to cast a "well-informed" vote. For certain people (and presumably most readers of this book will fall within this category) A may already be quite high. For intellectuals interested in politics, the amount of information acquired about the different issues for reasons having nothing to do with voting may be quite great. Further, for this group of people, the value put on the well-being of others may be higher than in the rest of the population. It may be, then, that these people would get a positive payoff from voting even though the average citizen would get negative returns from taking the same action. Thus, for many of the readers of this book, voting may be rational. I have my doubts, however. The value put on the well-being of others must be extremely great. Further, my own observation of intellectuals interested in politics would not confirm that A is high for them. They may have a great deal of information, but this seems to have been collected to confirm their basic position, not to change it.

Excerpted with revisions and permission from Gordon Tullock, *Toward a Mathematics of Politics* (Ann Arbor, Mich.: University of Michigan Press, 1972), pp. 111–114.

to pick a more moderate candidate. As a result, the contest between Richard Nixon and Hubert Humphrey in 1968 was practically a dead heat. After George McGovern was defeated by Richard Nixon in 1972, Democrats realized they too needed a less extreme candidate. Their choices in 1976 and 1984, Jimmy Carter and Walter Mondale, were more moderate.

The Economics of the Voting Rule

▲ 2. How does the rule for determining winners in elections affect the decisions that are made in a political system?

So far we have been assuming that a winning candidate must receive more than 50 percent of the vote. Although most issues that confront civic bodies are determined by simple-majority rule, not all collective decisions are made on that basis, nor should they be. Some decisions are too trivial for group consideration. The cost of a bad decision is so small that it is uneconomical to put the question up for debate. Other decisions are too important to be decided by a simple majority. Richard Nixon was elected president with only 43 percent of the popular vote in 1968 (when a third-party candidate, George Wallace, took almost 14 percent), but Nixon's impeachment would have required more than a majority of the Senate and the House of Representatives. In murder cases, juries are required to reach unanimous agreement. In such instances, the cost of a misguided decision is high enough to justify the extra time and trouble required to achieve more than a simple majority.

The voting rule that government follows helps determine the size and scope of government activities. If only a few people need to agree on budgetary proposals, for example, the effect can be to foster big government. Under such an arrangement, small groups can easily pass their proposals, expanding the scope of government activity each time they do so. However, under a voting rule that requires unanimous agreement among voters—a **unanimity rule**—very few proposals will be agreed to or implemented by government. There are very few issues on which everyone can agree, particularly when many people are involved.

Unanimity rule: a voting rule that requires unanimous agreement among voters.

A unanimity rule can be exploited by small groups of voters. If everyone's vote is critically important, as it is with a unanimous voting rule, then everyone is in a strategic bargaining position. Anyone can threaten to veto the proposed legislation unless he is given special treatment. Such tactics increase the cost of decision making.

Government represents people's collective interest, but the type of voting rule used determines the particular interests it represents and the extent to which it represents them.

The Inefficiencies of Democracy

▲ 3. What are the sources of inefficiency in democratic political systems?

As a form of government, democracy has some important advantages. It disperses the power of decision making among a large number of people, reducing the influence of individual whim and personal interest. Thus it provides some protection for individual liberties. Democracy also gives political candidates an incentive to seek out and represent voters' interests.

Competition for votes forces candidates to reveal what they are willing to do for various interest groups. Like the market system, however, the democratic system has some drawbacks as well. In particular, democracy is less than efficient as a producer of some goods and services.

The fact that the democratic form of government is inefficient in some respects does not mean that we should replace it with another decision-making process, any more than we should replace the market system, which is also plagued by inefficiencies. Instead, we must measure the costs of one type of production against the other, and choose the more efficient means of production in each particular case. We must weigh the cost of externalities in the private market against the cost of inefficiencies in the public sector. Neither system is perfect, so we must choose carefully between them.

Median Voter Preferences

When you buy a good like ice cream in the marketplace, you can decide how much you want. You can adjust the quantity you consume to your individual preferences and your ability to pay. If you join with your neighbors to purchase some public service, however, you must accept whatever quantity of service the collective decision-making process yields. How much of a public good government buys depends not only on citizens' preferences, but on the voting rule that is used.

Consider police protection, for instance. Perhaps you would prefer to pay higher taxes in return for a larger police force and a lower crime rate. Your neighbors might prefer a lower tax rate, a smaller police force, and a higher crime rate, but public goods must be purchased collectively, no matter how the government is organized. If preferences differ, you cannot each have your own way. Under a democracy, the preferences of the median voter group will tend to determine the types and quantities of public goods produced. If you are not a member of that group, the compromise that is necessary to a democracy inflicts a cost on you. You probably will not receive the amount of police protection you want.

The Simple-Majority Voting Rule

Any decision that is made less than unanimously can benefit some people at the expense of others. Because government expenses are shared by all taxpayers, the majority that votes for a project imposes an external cost on the minority that votes against it. Consider a democratic community composed of only five people, each of whom would benefit to some degree from a proposed public park. If the cost of the park, $500, is divided evenly among the five, each will pay a tax of $100. The costs and benefits to each taxpayer are shown in Table 22.1. Because the total benefits of the project ($550) exceed its total costs ($500), the measure will pass by a vote of three to two, but the majority of three imposes net costs of $50 and $75 on taxpayers D and E.

When total benefits exceed total costs, as in this example, decision by majority rule is fairly easy to live with, but sometimes a project passes even though its cost exceeds its benefits. Table 22.2 illustrates such a situation. Again, the $500 cost of a proposed park is shared equally by five people. Total benefits are only $430, but again they are unevenly distributed. Taxpayers A, B, and C each receive benefits that outweigh a $100 tax cost. Thus, A, B, and C will pass the project, even though it cannot be justified on economic grounds.

It is conceivable that many different measures, each of whose costs exceeded its benefits, could be passed by separate votes under such a system. If all the measures were considered together, however, the package could be defeated. Consider the costs and benefits of three proposed projects—a park, a road, and a school—shown in Table 22.3. If the park is put to a vote by itself, it will receive majority support from A, B, and C. Similarly, the road will pass with the support of A, C, and E, and the school will pass with the support of C, D, and E. If all three projects are considered together, however, they will be defeated. Voters A, B, and D will reject the package (see column 4).

TABLE 22.1   Costs and Benefits of a Public Park for a Five-Person Community

Individuals (1)	Dollar Value of Benefits to Each Person (2)	Tax Levied on Each Person (3)	Net Benefit (+) or Net Cost (−) [(2) − (3)] (4)	Vote For or Against (5)
A	$200	$100	+$100	For
B	150	100	+ 50	For
C	125	100	+ 25	For
D	50	100	− 50	Against
E	25	100	− 75	Against
Total	$550	$500		

TABLE 22.2   Costs and Benefits of a Public Park for a Five-Person Community, Alternative Schedule

Individuals (1)	Dollar Value of Benefits to Each Person (2)	Tax Levied on Each Person (3)	Net Benefit (+) or Net Cost (−) [(2) − (3)] (4)	Vote For or Against (5)
A	$140	$100	+$ 40	For
B	130	100	+ 30	For
C	110	100	+ 10	For
D	50	100	− 50	Against
E	0	100	− 100	Against
Total	$430	$500		

TABLE 22.3 Costs and Benefits of a Park, a Road, and a School for a Five-Person Community

Individuals	Park (1) Benefit	Cost	Vote	Road (2) Benefit	Cost	Vote	School (3) Benefit	Cost	Vote	Total, 3 Projects (4) Benefit	Cost	Vote
A	$120	$100	For	$250	$ 200	For	$ 50	$ 400	Against	$ 420	$ 700	Against
B	120	100	For	50	200	Against	50	400	Against	220	700	Against
C	120	100	For	250	200	For	500	400	For	870	700	For
D	50	100	Against	50	200	Against	500	400	For	600	700	Against
E	50	100	Against	250	200	For	500	400	For	800	700	For
Total	$460	$500		$850	$1,000		$1,600	$2,000		$2,910	$3,500	

Many if not most measures that come up for a vote in a democratic government benefit society more than they burden it. Moreover, voters in the minority camp can use "logrolling" (vote trading) to defeat some projects that might otherwise pass. For instance, voter A can agree to vote against the park if voter D will vote against the school. Our purpose is simply to demonstrate that, in some instances, the democratic process can be less than cost efficient.

Political Ignorance

In some ways, the lack of an informed citizenry is the most severe problem in a democratic system. The typical voter is not well informed about political issues and candidates. In fact, the average individual's welfare is not perceptibly improved by knowledge of public issues.

A simple experiment will illustrate this point. Ask everyone in your class to write down the name of his or her congressional representative. Then ask them for the name of the opposing candidate in the last election. You may be surprised by the results. In one survey, college juniors and seniors, most of whom had taken several courses in economics, political science, and sociology, were asked how their U.S. senators had voted on some major bills. The students scored no better than they would have done by guessing.[1] In the United States as a whole, most voters do not even know which party controls Congress,[2] and public opinion polls indicate that most voters greatly underestimate the cost of programs like Social Security.[3]

1. Richard B. McKenzie, "Political Ignorance: An Empirical Assessment of Educational Remedies," *Frontiers of Economics* (Blacksburg, Va.: University Publications, 1977).

2. Donald E. Stokes and Warren E. Miller, "Party Government and the Saliency of Congress," *Public Opinion Quarterly* 26 (Winter 1962): 531–546.

3. Edgar Browning, "Why the Social Insurance Budget Is Too Large in a Democracy," *Economic Inquiry* 13 (September 1974): 373–388.

PERSPECTIVES
Prisoner's Dilemma: Why People Cooperate

James Gleick, New York Times

You and your accomplice have been caught red-handed. Together your best hope is to cooperate by remaining silent: You will each get off with a 30-day sentence. But either of you can do better for yourself: Double-cross your partner and you will go free while he serves 10 years. The problem is, if you each betray the other, you will both go to prison—and not just for 30 days, but for eight years.

When you think about it, you realize that no matter what your partner chooses, you are better off choosing betrayal. Unfortunately, he is aware of it too—so the inexorable tide of self-interest is bound to carry both up the river for eight years. If only you could have cooperated . . .

That, in a bitter nutshell, is the "prisoner's dilemma."

Half a game-theory paradox, half a behavioral metaphor, the prisoner's dilemma has become a central model for psychologists, political scientists, biologists and economists trying to understand the dynamics of competition and—more important—cooperation.

Much of game theory devotes itself to a logic pursued for its own sake. The prisoner's dilemma has proved a robust exception, finding unexpected applications far from its abstract origins. One reason is the simplicity of its basic message: that cooperation arises from a combination of restraint and retaliation. It is a game-theory modernization of the eye-for-eye rule.

"There's been a renewal of interest in the last few years in using game theory in a wide variety of subjects," said Robert Axelrod, a political scientist at the University of Michigan who has become a one-man clearing-house for research using the model. "The prisoner's dilemma is so simple and suggestive that it provides a way of thinking about some very fundamental problems."

The model was one of the main themes of a symposium on behavioral economics this month at Harvard University, where psychologists and economists discussed ways to quantify decision-making. And the prisoner's dilemma is stimulating theoretical work by biologists studying animals from monkeys to fish to tree swallows, as well as by management scientists studying corporate executives.

The real power of the prisoner's dilemma model comes when the subjects play not once but many times—what is known as the iterated prisoner's dilemma. In a standard version, subjects play for points, paired under the supervision of a psychologist who will pay a dollar for each point.

Over the long run, both subjects will do best to cooperate every time. Yet in any one round, not knowing what the opponent will do, each subject has an overpowering temptation to betray the other, or defect.

The iterated prisoner's dilemma asks whether continual betrayal is inevitable or whether you can devise a strategy that will change your opponent's behavior, eliciting cooperation. Should you start off by cooperating? How should you respond if your opponent betrays you?

The basic prisoner's dilemma model is more than three decades old, invented by two scientists at the Rand Corporation. The modern era of prisoner's dilemma research, however, began in 1978, when Dr. Axelrod decided to test different strategies experimentally, by pitting them against each other in a series of computer tournaments. Contestants submitted tiny programs that competed with one another in a computerized round-robin prisoner's dilemma universe.

The most fertile legacy of Dr. Axelrod's original tournaments was the discovery of what is, in almost all circumstances, the best strategy for playing the prisoner's dilemma. It is called "Tit for Tat," and it can be summed up this way: Do unto your opponent as he has just done unto you.

Tit for Tat is a paradox unto itself. As long as your opponent cooperates, you cooperate. If he betrays you, then the next time you betray him back. If he cooperates again, then next time you cooperate. In the crowded field of the first computer tournament, Tit for Tat did better than strategies that always betrayed, or betrayed at random, or used sophisticated statistical strategies that required many lines of computer code.

Those strategies never lost when playing Tit for

Tat—they couldn't. But when they were playing each other, they tended to do badly, because they defected too much. Tit for Tat actually encouraged a wide variety of its competitors to cooperate, and when the overall scores were added up, it always came out on top.

The mathematicians, psychologists, economists and sociologists who participated in the tournaments came up with other appealing strategies. For example, Tit for Two Tats—wait until your opponent betrays you twice before punishing him with a betrayal of your own. In the language of prisoner's dilemma theorists, Tit for Tat is "nice," since it never betrays first. It is "responsive," since it reacts to its opponent. A typical not-nice strategy was Tranquilizer, which lulled its opponent for a few moves and then tried to exploit it by betraying him. Tit for Two Tats was not just "nice," it was "forgiving."

But none proved better. The magic of Tit for Tat is its simplicity. An opposing strategy can easily recognize it and respond. It is "retaliatory" enough not to be easily exploited, yet forgiving enough to allow a pattern of mutual cooperation to develop.

As a metaphor, the success of Tit for Tat suggests why it may be advantageous to cooperate in circumstances that might seem to favor nasty behavior. Dr. Axelrod himself, in his book "The Evolution of Cooperation," describes spontaneous out-breaks of nonhostility across the trenches in World War I—outbreaks that senior commanders tried in vain to quell. Dr. Axelrod and other political scientists also suggest the applicability of the prisoner's dilemma to the nuclear arms race, in which short-term advantages can lead to long-term disadvantages for both sides.

"It's become incredibly useful in business and economics," said John R. Hauser, a professor of management science at the Massachusetts Institute of Technology's Sloan School of Management. Research is still only embryonic, but every rock we look under there are more and more exciting things to help us understand major phenomena."

For example, the Sloan School is conducting a similar computer tournament using the prisoner's dilemma as a way of comparing marketing strategies. Marketing scientists there believe that they have already gained some new insights into how competing businesses manage to "cooperate" without actually resorting to collusion—an antitrust official's nightmare.

They are adding complications to the basic model—three or more options, for example, instead of just cooperation and defection. They hope to determine how companies such as airlines and automobile manufacturers get into promotion wars, and especially how they get out of them.

In economics as in other realms of the prisoner's dilemma, success requires a willingness not to measure oneself against any one opponent. "You don't tend to compare yourself to other people," Dr. Hauser said. "However, it turns out that if I do that I'm hurting myself very badly."

Examining less corporate forms of behavior, scientists have used the model in studying the evolution of territorial cooperation among, for example, howler monkeys and stickleback fish. Traditionally, explanations of cooperative behavior have tended to focus on genetic kinship, assuming that animals sacrifice their self-interest to promote the survival of their genes in offspring of siblings.

"This is a new way to look at interactions between animals," said Michael P. Lombardo of Rutgers University. "It's useful for modeling interactions between parties with a conflict of interest." Dr. Lombardo studied three swallows on Long Island, where breeders and nonbreeders compete for limited nest sites.

During nesting season, when Dr. Lombardo sneaked around leaving evidence of cooperation and betrayal, Tit for Tat proved to be the best model of behavior.

As natural situations get more complex, though, direct biological applications of the model seem more limited. Some of the more enduring lessons of the prisoner's dilemma may be in the less scientific regions of human existence.

If voters were better informed on legislative proposals and their implications, government might make better decisions. In that sense, political information is a public good that benefits everyone. Nevertheless, as we have seen before, in large groups people have little incentive to contribute anything toward the production of a public good. Their individual contributions simply have little effect on the outcome.

To remain politically free, people must exercise their right to determine who will represent them. The result is that they often cast their votes on the basis of impressions received from newspaper headlines or television commercials—impressions carefully created by advertisers and press secretaries.

Special Interests

The problem of political ignorance is especially acute when the benefits of government programs are spread more or less evenly, so that the benefits to each person are relatively small. Benefits are not always spread evenly; subgroups of voters—farmers, labor unions, or civil servants—often receive more than their proportional share. Members of such groups thus have a special incentive to acquire information on legislative proposals. Farmers can be expected to know more about farm programs than the average voter. Civil servants will keep abreast of proposed pay increases and fringe benefits for government workers, and defense contractors will take a private interest in the military budget.

Congressional representatives, knowing they are being watched by special-interest groups, will tend to cater to their wishes. As a result, government programs will be designed to serve the interests of groups with political clout, not the public as a whole.

Cyclical Majorities

In their personal lives, most people tend to act consistently on the basis of rational goals. If an individual prefers good A to good B, and good B to good C, the rational individual will choose A over C repeatedly. Collective decisions made by majority rule are not always consistent. Consider a community of three people, whose preferences for goods A, B, and C are as follows.

Individual	Order of Preference
I	A, B, C
II	B, C, A
III	C, A, B

Suppose these three voters are presented with a choice between successive pairs of goods, A, B, and C. If the choice is between good A and good B, which will be preferred collectively? The answer is A, because individuals I and III both prefer it to B. If A is pitted against C, which will be preferred? The answer is C, because individuals II and III both prefer it to A. Since the group prefers A to B and C to A, one might think it would prefer C to B, but note that if C and B are put up to a vote, B will win. A cyclical, or revolving, majority has developed in this group situation. This phenomenon can lead to continual changes in policy in a government based on collective decision making.

Although there is no stable majority, the individuals involved are not acting irrationally. People with perfectly consistent personal preferences can make inconsistent collective choices when acting as a group. Fortunately, the larger the number of voters and issues at stake, the less likely a cyclical majority is to develop. Still, citizens of a democratic state should recognize that the political process may generate a series of inconsistent or even contradictory policies.

The Efficiencies of Competition Among Governments

▲ **4. How can competition among governments improve the effectiveness of government programs?**

In the private sector, competition among producers keeps prices down and productivity up. A producer who is just one of many knows that any independent attempt to raise prices or lower quality will fail. Customers will switch to other products or buy from other producers, and sales will fall sharply. To avoid being undersold, therefore, the individual producer must minimize its production costs. Only a producer who has no competition— that is, a monopolist—can afford to raise the price of a product without fear of losing profits.

These points apply to the public as well as the private sector. The framers of the Constitution, in fact, bore them in mind when they set up the federal government. Recognizing the benefits of competition, they established a system of competing state governments loosely joined in federation. As James Madison described it in *The Federalist* papers, "In a single republic, all the power surrendered by the people is submitted to the administration of a single government; and the usurpations are guarded against by a division of the government into distinct and separate departments."[4]

Under the federal system, the power of local governments is checked not just by citizens' ability to vote, but by their ability to move somewhere else. If a city government raises its taxes or lowers the quality of its services, residents can go elsewhere, taking with them part of the city's tax base. Of course, many people are reluctant to move, and so government has a measure of monopoly power, but competition among governments affords at least some protection against the abuses of power.

Local competition in government has its drawbacks. Just as in private industry, large governments realize economies of scale in the production of

---

4. Alexander Hamilton, John Jay, and James Madison, *The Federalist: A Commentary on the Constitution of the United States,* no. 51 (New York: Random House, Modern Library edition, 1964), pp. 338–339.

services. Garbage, road, and sewage service can be provided at lower cost on a larger scale. For this reason, it is frequently argued that local governments, especially in metropolitan areas, should consolidate. Moreover, many of the benefits offered by local governments spill over into surrounding areas. For example, people who live just outside San Francisco may benefit from its services, without helping to pay for them. One large metropolitan government, including both city and suburbs, could spread the tax burden over all those who benefit from city services.

Consolidation can be a mixed blessing, however, if it reduces competition among governments. A large government restricts the number and variety of alternatives open to citizens and increases the cost of moving to another locale by increasing the geographical size of its jurisdiction. Consolidation, in other words, can increase government's monopoly power. As long as politicians and government employees pursue only the public interest, no harm may be done. In fact, the people who run government have interests of their own. So the potential for achieving greater efficiency through consolidation could easily be lost in bureaucratic red tape. Studies of consolidation in government are inconclusive, but it seems clear that consolidation proposals should be examined carefully.

The Economics of Government Bureaucracy

▲ 5. How do government bureaucracies determine their levels of production?

Bureaucracy is not limited to government. Large corporations like General Motors and AT&T employ more people than the governments of some nations. They are bigger than the major departments of the federal government—although no company, of course, is as large as the federal government as a whole. Yet corporate bureaucracy tends to work more efficiently than government bureaucracy. The reason may be found in the fact that it pursues one simple objective—profit—that can be easily measured in dollars and cents.

Certainly the reason cannot be that stockholders are better informed than voters. Most stockholders are rationally ignorant of their companies' doings, for the cost of becoming informed outweighs the benefits. Even in very large corporations, however, some individuals hold enough stock to make the acquisition of information a rational act. Often such stockholders sit on the company's board of directors, where their interest in increasing the value of their own shares makes them good representatives of the rest of the stockholders. The crucial point is that this informed stockholder has one relatively simple objective—profit—and can find out relatively easily whether the corporation is meeting it. The voter, on the other hand, has a complicated set of objectives and must do considerable digging to find out whether they are being met.

Because most corporations function in competitive markets, furthermore, the stockholder's drive toward profit is reinforced. General Motors knows that its customers may switch to Toyota if it offers them a better deal. In fact, stockholders can sell their General Motors stock and buy stock in Toyota. Thus corporate executives make decisions on the basis of the consumer's well-being—not because they wish to serve the public good but because they want to make money.

Government bureaucracies, on the other hand, tend to produce public goods and services for which there is no competition. No built-in efficiencies guard the taxpayer's interests in a government bureaucracy. Both government bureaucrats and corporate executives base their decisions on their own interests, not those of society, but competition ensures that the interests of corporate decision makers coincide with those of consumers. No such safeguards govern the operations of government bureaucracies. Bureaucracies are constrained by political, as opposed to market, forces.

From the economist's point of view, one of the advantages of the profit-maximizing goal of competitive business is that it enables predictions. Although some business people pursue other goals—personal income, power, respect in the business—their behavior can generally be well explained in terms of the single objective, profit. There is no single goal like profit that drives the government bureaucracy. Different bureaucracies pursue different objectives. We do not have time or space to consider all the possible objectives of bureaucracy, but we will touch on three: monopolistic profit maximization, size maximization, and waste maximization.

Profit Maximization

Assume that police protection can be produced at a constant marginal cost, as shown by the horizontal marginal cost curve in Figure 22.2. The demand for police protection is shown by the downward-sloping demand curve D. If individuals could purchase police service competitively at a constant price of P_1, the optimum amount of police service would be Q_2, the amount at which the marginal cost of the last unit of police service equals its marginal benefit. The total cost would be $P_1 \times Q_2$ (or the area $0P_1aQ_2$), leaving a consumer surplus equal to the triangular area P_1P_3a.

Police protection is usually delivered by regional monopolies, however. That is, all police services in an area are supplied by one organization. These regional monopolies have their own goals and their own decision-making process, which do not necessarily match the individual taxpayers'. If police service must be purchased from such a profit-maximizing monopoly, service will be produced to the point where the marginal cost of the last unit produced equals its marginal revenue: Q_1. The monopolist will sell that quantity above cost at price P_2, making a profit equal to the rectangular area P_1P_2ed.

At the monopolized production level, there is still some surplus—the triangular area P_2P_3e—left for consumers, but they are worse off than under competitive market conditions. They get less police protection (Q_1 instead of Q_2) for a higher price (P_2 instead of P_1).

This analysis presumes that the police are capable of concealing their costs. If taxpayers know that P_2 is an unnecessarily high price, the outcome will be the same as under competition. They will force the police to produce Q_2 protection for a price of P_1.

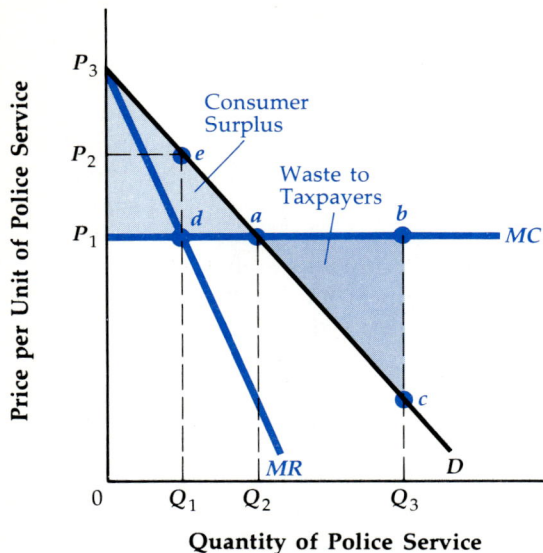

FIGURE 22.2 Bureaucratic Profit Maximization
Given the demand for police service, D, and the marginal cost of providing it, MC, the optimum quantity of police service is Q_2. A monopolistic police department interested in maximizing its profits will supply only Q_1 service at a price of P_2, however. (A monopolistic bureaucracy interested in maximizing its size would expand police service to Q_3.)

Size Maximization

In fact, a government bureaucracy is unlikely to take profit as its overriding objective, if only because bureaucrats do not get to pocket the profit. Instead, government monopolies may try to maximize the size of their operations. For if a bureaucracy expands, those who work for it will have more chance of promotion. Their power, influence, and public standing will improve, along with their offices and equipment.

What level of protection will a police department produce under such conditions? Instead of providing Q_1 service and misrepresenting its cost at P_2, it will probably provide Q_3 service—more than taxpayers desire—at the true price of P_1. The bill will be $P_1 \times Q_3$, or the area $0P_1bQ_3$ in Figure 22.2 Note that the net waste to taxpayers, shown by the shaded area abc, exactly equals the consumer surplus, P_1P_3a. By extending service to Q_3, the police have squeezed out the entire consumer surplus and spent it on themselves.

Waste Maximization

Instead of maximizing the amount of service they offer, bureaucrats may choose to maximize waste. They can increase their salaries, improve their working conditions, or reduce their workloads. All such changes increase the cost of providing a given amount of service.

Figure 22.3 shows how far a bureau can go in increasing the cost of, or budget for, its services. The marginal cost curve MC_1 is the minimum cost of providing additional police protection. The optimum quantity of police

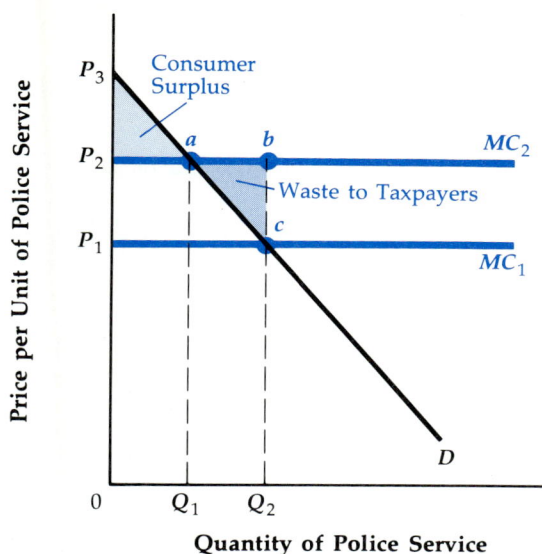

FIGURE 22.3 Bureaucratic Waste Maximization
Given a demand for police service D and a marginal cost of providing it MC_1, the optimum quantity of police service will be Q_2. A monopolistic bureaucracy, however, may seek to maximize waste by inflating its costs to MC_2. It will supply Q_2 units of police protection at a tax price of P_2 instead of P_1. The shaded area abc shows the waste created, which exactly equals the consumer surplus P_2P_3a.

protection is therefore Q_2, the same as in Figure 22.2, but if the police pad their costs, the marginal cost curve will shift up to MC_2. The bureau's budget climbs from $P_1 \times Q_2$ to $P_2 \times Q_2$. Note that beyond Q_1, the marginal cost of additional police service is now greater than its marginal benefit, indicated by the demand curve. Again, the police are wasting taxpayers' money, as shown by the shaded triangular area abc. By moving their cost curve to MC_2, they have managed to extract all the consumer surplus (shown by the triangular area P_2P_3a) and to spend it on unnecessary frills.

In real life, most bureaucratic monopolies may pursue both size maximization and waste maximization. For each unit of service they provide, they will try to expand both the size of their operation and the funds spent on it—but they do have to make tradeoffs between the two objectives. Whenever they expand their size, they must forgo a certain amount of expansion in their cost per unit of service. There is, after all, only so much consumer surplus that can be extracted from the system.

Figure 22.4 shows one possible combination of size and budget maximization. In this case the department chooses to expand its service from Q_1 to Q_2. Having done so, it can expand its cost per unit only to MC_2. Again, the shaded triangular area that indicates waste, abc, just equals the consumer surplus P_2P_3a.

Fortunately government bureaucracies do not usually achieve perfect maximization of size or waste. For one thing, most legislatures have at least some information about the production costs of various services, and bureaucrats may not be willing to do the hard work necessary to exploit their position fully. If bureaucracy does not manage to capture the entire consumer surplus, citizens will realize some net benefit from their investment.

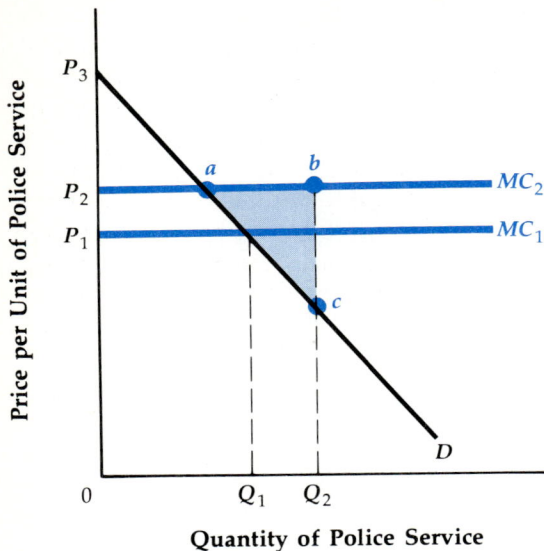

FIGURE 22.4 Size and Waste Maximization Combined
The monopolistic bureaucracy may choose to increase both its size and the cost of its service. Any increase in one must come at the cost of the other, however, for together the two increases must not exceed the consumer surplus. Here net waste, shown by the shaded triangular area abc, is divided between size and cost increases. The area between the two marginal cost curves MC_1 and MC_2 represents waste maximization. The area below the marginal cost curve MC_1 represents size maximization. The whole area abc exactly equals the consumer surplus, P_2P_3a.

Making Bureaucracy More Competitive

6. How can bureaucracies be made more competitive and efficient?

What can be done to make government bureaucracy more efficient? Perhaps the development of managerial expertise at the congressional level would encourage more accurate measurement of the costs and benefits of government programs. Cost-benefit analysis alone, however, will not necessarily help. As long as special-interest groups, including those of government employees, exist, the potential for waste can be substantial.

A better solution to bureaucratic inefficiency may be to increase competition in the public sector. In the private marketplace, buyers do not attempt to discover the production costs of the companies they buy from. They simply compare the various products offered, in terms of price and quality, and choose the best value for their money. A monopoly of any kind, of course, makes that task difficult if not impossible, but the existence of even one competitor for a government bureaucracy's services would allow some comparison of costs. The more different sources of a service, the flatter the demand curve faced by each source, and the more efficient it must be to stay in business.

How exactly can competition be introduced into bureaucracy? First, proposals to consolidate departments should be carefully scrutinized. What appears to be wasteful duplication may actually be a source of competition in the provision of service. In the private sector, we would not expect the consolidation of General Motors, Ford, and Chrysler to improve the efficiency of the auto industry. If anything, we would favor the breakup of the large firms into separate, competing companies. Why then should we merge the sanitation departments of three separate cities?

A second way to increase the competitiveness of government services is to contract for them with private producers. Many government activities that must be publicly financed need not necessarily be publicly produced. In the United States, highways are usually built by private companies but repaired and maintained by government. Competitive provision of maintenance as well as construction might reduce costs. Other services that might be "privatized" are fire protection, garbage collection, and education.

Finally, competition can be increased simply by dividing a bureaucracy into several smaller departments with separate budgets, thus increasing competition. Such a change would reduce the costs citizens must bear to move to an area that offers better or cheaper government services. The loss (or threat of loss) of constituents can put pressure on government to improve its performance.

Chapter Review

Review of Key Questions

1. *Why do candidates in two-party political systems tend to move toward the "middle of the road"?*

    In a two-party democracy, political candidates will tend to represent the interests of the median voter group. If a candidate takes a political position in the wing of the distribution of voters, then the opposing candidate will establish a position slightly closer to the middle of the distribution and win the election. To win, each candidate will be swayed by the forces of political competition to move close to the middle. If either of the candidates moves away from the middle or from the other candidate, then votes, and possibly the election, will be lost.

2. *How does the rule for determining winners in elections affect the decisions that are made in a political system?*

    The simple-majority rule can minimize the cost of reaching collective agreement. It is not the only possible voting rule, however, nor does it minimize the cost of all collective agreements. Some issues are too important to be decided by simple-majority; others are too trivial to require voter attention.

3. *What are the sources of inefficiency in democratic political systems?*

    Inefficiencies occur in democracies for five overriding reasons. First, political decisions in two-party systems reflect the wishes of the median voter. This means that many voters will have to adjust their consumption, or use, of public goods and services to the level chosen by the median voter. Second, simple-majority rule can result in the passage of measures for which the total costs exceed the total benefits to all voters. Third, voters are often politically ignorant, meaning they are not well informed on the true consequences of their votes. Fourth, because many voters have few private incentives to become well informed and active in political decisions, special-interest groups frequently have influence on political decisions that is disproportionate to their numbers. Finally, the democratic process can also result in inconsistent choices (through what is called "cyclical majorities").

▲ *4. How can competition among governments improve the effectiveness of government programs?*

Decentralized forms of government, like the federal-state arrangements in the United States, foster efficiency in the public sector by providing citizens with alternatives to their local government. Their local government must produce and tax efficiently to keep people and other resources (important components of the tax base of any government) in its districts.

▲ *5. How do government bureaucracies determine their levels of production?*

Public bureaucracies can operate in much the same ways as private monopolies do; that is, they can produce at an inefficient output level and impose excessive costs in the form of taxes and the prices that are charged on the users of their services. Public bureaucracies can become too large, both because legislators do not know the true cost of government services and because bureaucrats benefit personally from government expansion. Instead of maximizing profits, bureaucratic governments will tend to maximize government size and waste. The result is that without alternative sources of the services, users of the services may receive few, or no, net benefits from the existence of many government bureaucracies.

▲ *6. How can bureaucracies be made more competitive and efficient?*

Government efficiency can be increased by the introduction of competition into the provision of public services. That goal can be accomplished either by increasing the number of departments that provide a service or by requiring government to compete with private firms.

Further Topics

This chapter has used cost-benefit analysis to develop an economic model of government. In government as well as private industry, producers in a monopolistic market position will tend to exploit the lack of competition for their service. A government bureau that has no competitors is in an enviable bargaining position vis-à-vis legislators and taxpayers. As the sole producer of a service, it can charge higher prices and deliver poorer service than competitive producers would.

In many cases, then, the performance of government bureaucracies can be improved by the introduction of competition for their services. Where possible, alternative sources of a government-provided good or service should be encouraged. If government bureaus have to compete with other producers by lowering their prices or increasing the quality of their service, they will be forced, like private producers, to reveal not just what they want to do, but the limit of what they will do for the consumer's business.

The democratic system provides checks and balances to control the exploitation of power in government. Voters can vote not to re-elect officeholders who abuse the public trust. They may not do so reliably, however, because of imperfect information. The fact that democracy is not a completely efficient system does not mean that a nondemocratic form of government is preferable.

Review of New Terms

Median voter The voter in the middle of the political distribution.

Unanimity rule A voting rule that requires unanimous agreement among voters.

Review Questions

1. Is it desirable, in your opinion, that government generally adopts policies intended to please the median voter group? Why or why not? (◢ 1, ◢ 2)

2. It is sometimes said that a rational decision must be based on perfect information. Would it be rational for a voter to acquire perfect information about politics? Would it be possible? (◢ 3)

3. What effect does increased competition have on the slope of an individual firm's demand curve? Why? How does a change in the slope of a firm's demand curve affect its efficiency? How do these effects apply to government bureaucracy? (◢ 4, ◢ 5)

4. "Competition forces producers to reveal what they are willing to do at the limit, not just what they want to do." How does this statement apply to government bureaucracy, and to legislators' ability to control it? (◢ 5)

5. Write down all the government-provided services you can think of. Which of them *must* be provided by government bureaucracy? Which could be provided through competitive contract? (◢ 6)

The Nobel Laureates in Economics

Nobel prizes in physics, chemistry, medicine or physiology, literature, and peace were first awarded in 1901. Alfred Nobel requested that the prizes be given to those who had made the most important discovery or contribution in their respective fields, and that the prizes be given without respect to the candidates' nationality. The Nobel Prize in Economics was not a part of Alfred Nobel's bequest. Indeed, it was set up and endowed in 1968 by the Central Bank of Sweden, and is officially called "The Central Bank of Sweden Prize in Economics in Memory of Alfred Nobel."

In general, the Nobel Prize in Economics has been given annually according to the same rules and principles as the original Nobel prizes. However, the original Nobel awards tend to be granted for specific achievements; the Nobel Prize in Economics has, to date, been granted to economists in recognition of a whole career of path-breaking contributions, normally work that redirected much research within the economic profession.

The first Nobel Prize in Economics was awarded in 1969. Because the selection committee has given joint prizes in several years, there were a total of 25 Nobel Laureates in Economics as of 1987. Fifteen (or 60 percent) of the Nobel Laureates in Economics were teaching at American universities at the time of their awards.

Ragnar Frisch (1895–1973)
Jan Tinbergen (b. 1903)

In 1969, Frisch and Tinbergen were awarded the first Nobel Prize in Economics for their pioneering work in the field of econometrics, the application of mathematical and statistical methods to economics. The rise of econometrics may well be the most important development in economics in this century. When Frisch and Tinbergen began their work, few economists knew what econometrics was. Now, virtually all economists study econometrics as a matter of course.

R. Frisch

J. Tinbergen

Paul Samuelson (b. 1915)

In 1970, the Nobel Prize was bestowed on Samuelson for his broad influence over economic thought and policies in the years since World War II, an era in which his influence and example increased the use of mathematical analysis in the study of economics. His contribution to the theories of international trade, public finance, money, and market dynamics have all permanently altered the way economists think about the world.

P. Samuelson

S. Kuznets

Simon Kuznets (1901–1985)

In 1971, Kuznets received the Nobel Prize for his development and use of the measure Gross National Product. Kuznets used his measure (and others as well) to describe and interpret economic growth in the long run.

K. J. Arrow

J. R. Hicks

Kenneth J. Arrow (b. 1921)
John R. Hicks (b. 1904)

In 1972, their trailblazing work in the fields of general economic equilibrium theory earned the Nobel Prize for Hicks and Arrow. General equilibrium theory provides a picture of the economy as a whole. Arrow and Hicks showed how to model the complex interrelationships among the prices and outputs of goods and the prices and outputs of factors of production.

W. Leontief

Wassily Leontief (b. 1906)

In 1973, the Nobel Prize was awarded to Leontief for his original creation and development of the input-output method and its uses in various economic applications. The input-output model remains one of the most important applications of general equilibrium analysis. It has also become an essential part of economic planning in nonmarket economies.

G. Myrdal

F. A. Hayek

Gunnar Myrdal (1878–1987)
Friedrich August von Hayek (b. 1899)

In 1974, Myrdal and Hayek won the Nobel Prize for monetary theory and analysis of the interdependence of economic and social factors; the two men themselves disagreed on the role of government in the economy. Hayek believed that government represented the greatest threat to human liberty; Myrdal, in contrast, enthusiastically supported the growth of the Swedish welfare state.

T. C. Koopmans

L. Kantorovich

Tjalling C. Koopmans (1910–1985)
Leonid Kantorovich (1912–1986)

In 1975, the Nobel Prize was awarded to Koopmans and Kantorovich for their important work on the efficient allocation and use of economic resources. The joint award to an American citizen and a Soviet citizen highlighted the fact that the problems of resource allocation are similar in the two economic systems.

M. Friedman

Milton Friedman (b. 1912)

In 1976, Friedman received the Nobel Prize for his contributions to the fields of consumption theory, macroeconomic stabilization, and monetary history. His restatement of the quantity theory of money and his empirical studies of the role of money in the economy led to a rebirth of monetary economics. Friedman also vigorously defended free markets.

J. Meade

James Meade (b. 1907)
Bertil Ohlin (1899–1979)

In 1977, Meade and Ohlin were awarded the Nobel Prize for their seminal contributions to international trade theory. Their work on world economics, done in the 1930s and 1950s, is relevant to this day. The costs and benefits of trade (and of interference with trade) are once again major political issues in both developed and developing nations.

B. Ohlin

Herbert A. Simon (b. 1916)

In 1978, Simon won the Nobel Prize for his ground-breaking research in the late 1940s and 1950s on the way economic decisions are made. A social scientist himself, he challenged accepted theory, arguing for new ways of viewing business behavior. He believed that the standard assumption that firms maximize profits could not explain most behavior. According to Simon, firms are content to achieve "satisfactory" profits.

H. A. Simon

A. Lewis

Arthur Lewis (b. 1915)
Theodore W. Schultz (b. 1902)

In 1979, Lewis, an outspoken critic of industrialized nations' neglect of their underdeveloped neighbors; and Schultz, an expert in agricultural and human capital economics, were awarded the Nobel Prize for their important contributions to the study of the problems of economic development and poverty. Lewis argued that excess supplies of labor in peasant agriculture could be reallocated to industry in developing nations. Schultz emphasized the importance of human capital to economic development.

T. W. Schultz

L. R. Klein

Lawrence R. Klein (b. 1920)

In 1980, Klein was given the Nobel Prize in Economics for his creation of econometric models to be used in forecasting and analyzing the fluctuating economy. Forecasting has become a major field in economics, with both private firms and universities involved in predicting the economic future. Forecasters rely heavily on the models first developed by Klein.

J. Tobin

James Tobin (b. 1918)

In 1981, Tobin earned the Nobel Prize for his creation of a new investment theory, the portfolio selection theory, which argued that business and household investors counterbalance risks when investing. He also originated the q-ratio, a concept that helped explain the investment decisions firms make. His other contributions include developing new measures of economic welfare, showing the role of money in economic growth, and exploring various aspects of the demand for money.

G. J. Stigler

George J. Stigler (b. 1911)

In 1982, Stigler received the Nobel Prize in Economics. A leader of the "Chicago School" of economics, Stigler received the prize in recognition of his important studies of the way markets work, their organization and structure, and the causes and effects of public regulation. Stigler questioned the then-prevailing belief that consumer protection was the sole aim of government regulation. He argued that producer protection often motivated regulators.

Gerard Debreu (b. 1912)

In 1983, Debreu received the Nobel Prize for devising a mathematical model that scientifically substantiated the theory of general equilibrium that had been introduced in 1776 by Adam Smith as "the invisible hand." Debreu showed mathematically how prices operated to balance supply and demand.

G. Debreu

Sir Richard Stone (b. 1913)

In 1984, the Nobel Prize was awarded to Stone for his creation of the national income account, a tool for measuring a country's total income and expenditures. The method he created is useful in comparing economies of capitalist countries, and was adopted by the United Nations, the International Monetary Fund, and the World Bank.

R. Stone

Franco Modigliani (b. 1918)

In 1985, Modigliani received the Nobel Prize for his theories of savings and corporate finance. Specifically, he proposed that people save mostly for their own retirement and not for their descendants, and that the market value of a company's shares is based on the company's prospects, not its debt. His theories of finance remain part of the foundation for that branch of economics.

F. Modigliani

James McGill Buchanan (b. 1919)

In 1986, the academy honored Buchanan for his work in integrating an understanding of political decision making (public choice) into the study of economics. He argued that politicians acted not out of a sense of public duty but out of self-interest, thus yielding a "regime of permanent budget deficits." Buchanan believed that the remedy for the problem was not to change politicians but rather to impose constitutional constraints on the behavior of elected officials.

J. M. Buchanan

Robert M. Solow (b. 1924)

In 1987, Solow was given the Nobel Prize for his influential theory of economic growth. He had argued since the mid-1950s that it was technology, not capital, that was most important to a country's economic development. Unlike earlier models of economic growth, Solow's model could be used to study the actual experience of nations over time.

R. M. Solow

Glossary

A

Absolute advantage The capacity to produce more units of output than a competitor can for any given level of resource use.

Action (administrative) lag The time elapsed between the general recognition of a problem and the implementation of a policy to correct it.

Adaptive expectations theory The theory that market participants formulate their expectations of the future, including their future economic policy activities, solely on past and current information.

Aggregate demand The presumed negative relationship between the general price level and the total quantity of goods and services consumers, businesses, and government want to buy in the economy during a given period of time.

Aggregate supply The presumed positive relationship between the general price level and the total quantity of goods and services produced in the economy during a given period of time.

Appreciation An increase in the exchange value or purchasing power of one national currency, brought about by market forces, in relation to other national currencies.

Asset demand for money The combined precautionary and speculative reasons for holding money.

Automatic fiscal stabilizer A built-in tax or expenditure that increases total planned spending in times of recession and lowers it in times of economic expansion, without special explicit action on the part of the administration and Congress.

Average tax rate The percentage of total income that is paid in taxes, obtained by dividing total taxes paid by total taxable income.

B

Balanced-budget multiplier Equal and same sign changes in government spending and taxes result in a net change in aggregate demand and national income of that same magnitude.

Bracket creep (or taxflation) The loss of purchasing power that occurs if progressive tax brackets are not indexed: people are pushed into higher tax brackets by inflation as money incomes (but not real incomes) rise, and pay a higher percentage of their incomes to the government.

Budget deficit The amount by which outlays exceed receipts during any given accounting period.

Budget surplus The amount by which receipts exceed outlays during any given accounting period.

Business cycle A recurring but irregular swing in general economic activity, or a smaller pattern of ups and downs within a major long-term trend.

C

Cambridge equation $MD = kPy$, where k represents the fraction of income people wish to hold in the form of money.

Capital account The record of a nation's investments abroad and foreign investments in that nation.

Capital account deficit The dollar amount by which a nation's investments abroad—that is, capital outflows—exceed foreign investments in that nation—that is, capital inflows.

Capital account surplus The dollar amount by which foreign investment in a nation—that is, capital inflows—exceed that nation's investments abroad—that is, capital outflows.

Capital (investment goods) Any output of a production process that is designed to be used later in other production processes. Includes plant and equipment.

Capitalism An economic system based on private property and free enterprise.

Checkable deposits Any deposits against which checks or their equivalent can be written.

Circular flow of income The integrated flow of resources, goods, and services between or among broad sectors of the economy, like producers, consumers, and governments.

Classicism A macroeconomic theory that emphasizes that the economy in the long run will, if unimpeded, achieve equilibrium at full employment and neutrality of money.

Coincident indicator An index of business conditions that tends to move up or down roughly in line with general economic activity, like real GNP.

COLA A cost-of-living adjustment clause found in some wage contracts to compensate workers in part or in full for erosion of their real purchasing power by inflation (as measured by the CPI).

Common access resources Resources owned in common instead of privately by individuals. Thus individuals may not be excluded from their use.

Communism As conceived by Marx, a classless society that would emerge from the downfall of capitalism and the establishment of socialism. In practical terms, an economic system in which virtually all the means of production are owned and controlled by the state.

Comparative advantage The relative advantage in production or cost based on comparative ratios such that either the absolute advantage is greatest or the absolute disadvantage is smallest.

Competition The process by which market participants, in pursuing their own interests, attempt to outdo, outprice, outproduce, and outmaneuver each other.

Composite index of leading indicators A combined index of twelve leading economic indicators of business activity that tends to move up or down several months before measures of general economic activity, like real GNP, move.

Consumer price index (CPI) The ratio of the cost of specific consumer items included in a representative consumer market basket in any one survey year to the cost of those items in the base year (currently 1967).

Consumer unit A household of people who pool their money.

Consumption function The assumed direct relationship between the national income level and the planned or desired consumption expenditures of households.

Consumption goods Goods that are produced to be used and enjoyed more or less immediately by their purchasers.

Contractionary gap When actual GNP is less than potential (i.e., full employment) GNP.

Corporate income taxes Government revenues collected on a corporation's computed profits, as reported on its profit and loss statements. A corporation's taxable profits are computed by sub-tracting its business expenses from its sales revenues.

Cost (opportunity cost) The value of the most highly preferred alternative not taken.

Cost-push or sellers' or suppliers' inflation A general rise in prices that occurs when restrictions are placed on the supply of one or more resources, or when the price of one or more resources is increased.

Crowding out The theory that an increase in government spending tends to cause—working through an increase in the real interest rate—a partial or total offset in total planned expenditures of decreased private spending, thereby making fiscal policy less effective or totally ineffective.

Current account The record of all the nation's international transactions other than capital flows and statistical discrepancies, including its merchandise trade, its investment income, its military transactions, its travel and transportation expenditures, its other services, and its remittances, pensions, and other unilateral transfers (i.e., gifts).

Current account deficit The dollar amount by which a nation's imports of goods and services, interest and dividend payments to foreigners, gifts to foreigners, travel expenditures abroad, and other remittances to foreign nations exceed its exports of goods and services, interest and dividend receipts from foreign nations, gifts from abroad, foreign travel expenditures in this nation, and other remittances from abroad.

Current account surplus The dollar amount by which a nation's exports of goods and services, interest and dividend receipts from foreigners, gifts from foreigners, foreign travel expenditures in this nation, and other receipts from abroad exceed the nation's imports of goods and services, interest and dividend payments to foreigners, gifts to foreigners, travel expenditures abroad, and other remittances to foreign nations.

Cyclical unemployment Unemployment that is caused by downswings of the business cycle—that is, by a broad-based reduction in the overall level of spending in the economy.

D

Decrease in demand A decrease in the quantity demanded at each and every price, represented graphically by a leftward, or inward, shift of the supply curve.

Decrease in supply A decrease in the quantity producers are willing and able to offer at each and every price, represented graphically by a leftward, or inward, shift of the supply curve.

Demand   The assumed inverse relationship between the price of a good or service and the quantity consumers are willing and able to buy during a given period, all other things held constant.

Demand for money   The willingness of people to hold money.

Demand-pull or buyers' inflation   A general rise in prices that occurs when total planned expenditures increase faster than total production.

Democratic socialism   An economic system that combines government ownership of productive resources with full political democracy.

Depository institutions   Private, profit-seeking financial institutions, including commercial banks and thrift institutions such as credit unions, mutual savings banks, savings banks, and savings and loan institutions (S&Ls) that handle transaction accounts and checkable deposits.

Depreciation   A reduction in the exchange value or purchasing power of one national currency, brought about by market forces, in relation to other national currencies.

Devaluation   Under a fixed standard, the reduction of a domestic currency brought about by government intervention in its official price in relation to a foreign currency.

Dirty or managed floating exchange rate system   An international monetary exchange system in which the prices of currencies are partly determined by competitive market forces and partly determined by official government intervention.

Discount rate   The interest rate the Federal Reserve charges on loans to depository institutions such as commercial banks.

Diseconomies of scale   Increases in per-unit cost due to an increase in the rate of production when the use of all resources is expanded.

Disposable personal income   Personal income minus tax payments (as well as some minor non-tax payments).

Dissaving   Any net withdrawal from accumulated past savings, or any net increase in borrowing.

E

Econometric model   A statistical equation or set of equations that describes economic data.

Econometrics   The science of the statistical testing of economic theory and prediction.

Economic development   The structural and other changes that accompany economic growth.

Economic growth   The expansion of a nation's capacity to produce the goods and services its people want.

Economic system   A set of institutions involved in making and implementing economic decisions.

Economics   The study of how people cope with scarcity—with the pressing problem of how to allocate their limited resources among their competing wants to satisfy as many of those wants as possible.

Economies of scale   Decreases in per-unit cost due to an increase in the rate of production when the use of all resources is expanded.

Efficiency   The maximization of output through careful allocation of resources, given the constraints of supply (producer's costs) and demand (consumer's preferences).

Efficient market hypothesis   The theory that new information traveling randomly is very rapidly assimilated by a large number of rational participants, no one group of which possesses market power. Because of this almost instantaneous adjustment to new information, no disequilibrium can last very long.

Entrepreneur   An enterprising person who discovers potentially profitable opportunities and organizes, directs, and manages productive ventures.

Equation of exchange ($MV = PQ$)   A statement of mathematical equality between the product of the money stock (M) and the velocity of money (V) and the product of the price level (P) and the national output level (Q).

Equilibrium income level   The income level (not necessarily at full employment) at which producers have no reason to change their output level because leakages equal injections.

Equilibrium price   The price toward which a competitive market will move, and at which it will remain once there, everything else held constant. The price at which the market "clears"—that is, at which the quantity demanded by consumers is matched exactly by the quantity offered by producers.

Equilibrium quantity   The output (or sales) level toward which the market will move, and at which it will remain once there, everything else held constant. Reached when the quantity demanded equals the quantity supplied (at the equilibrium price).

Excess reserves   The amount of a depository institutions (such as a bank's) total reserves minus the required reserves.

Excise taxes   Taxes levied on specific products or services, for specific purposes. Excise taxes are normally a percentage of the purchase price.

Expansionary gap   The gap that occurs when actual GNP is greater than potential (i.e., full employment) GNP.

Expenditure approach   The approach to calculating GNP which sums the dollar value of all final products.

External benefits   Benefits of production and consumption that are received by people not directly involved in the production, consumption, or exchange of a good. Positive effects on some third party.

External costs Costs of production and consumption that are imposed on people not directly involved in the production, consumption, or exchange of a good. Negative effects on some third party.

Externalities The positive (beneficial) or negative (harmful) effects that market exchanges have on people who do not participate directly in those exchanges. Third party or "spillover" effects.

F

Federal funds rate The interest charged by one depository institution to another for a temporary loan based on the use of unneeded balances at Federal Reserve banks.

Fiat money A medium of exchange or store of value that cannot be redeemed for anything other than a replica of itself.

Final goods and services Those goods and services that are purchased by their ultimate users rather than for further processing or resale.

Financial intermediary A financial institution that assembles the funds of savers or lenders to lend to borrowers at interest rates that generally cover at least the cost of operation (including normal profit).

Fiscal drag Possibly restrictive effect on the economy of the automatic increase in tax revenues arising from an increase in national income, where such tax revenue is not matched by corresponding increases in expenditures or decreases in taxes.

Fisher effect An economic principle which states that the nominal (market) rate of interest is equal to the real rate of interest (based on the real productivity of capital) plus the rate of anticipated inflation.

Fixed or pegged exchange rate system An international monetary exchange system in which the prices of currencies are established and maintained by government intervention.

Floating, flexible, or freely fluctuating exchange rate system An international monetary exchange rate system in which the prices of currencies are determined by competitive market forces.

Foreign exchange The monetary means or instruments used to make monetary payments and transfers from one currency area to another. The funds available as foreign exchange include foreign coin and currency, deposits in foreign banks, and other short-term, liquid financial claims.

Frills multiplier (f) The value of f is greater than the simplest multiplier (m), as it adds an additional source of income at each round. Stated as an equation, $f = 1/(1 - MPC - MPI)$, where MPC is the marginal propensity to consume and MPI is the marginal propensity to invest.

Full-bodied commodity money A medium of exchange or store of value that has some intrinsic value as a consumer good or factor of production. It has some economic use apart from its monetary role.

Full employment The employment level that occurs when the quantity of labor demanded equals the quantity of labor supplied at a competitive market-determined real wage rate.

G

GNP gap The difference between potential GNP (i.e., full employment) and actual GNP.

Gross national product (GNP) The current market value in dollars of all final goods and services produced in the economy in a given period.

H

Hidden unemployed Underemployed and discouraged workers who quit looking for work after long periods of rejection and are thus not considered unemployed, as they are not actively seeking work.

Hidden unemployment Unemployment that involves people not counted in statistics as unemployed because they are either underemployed involuntarily at part-time jobs, or they are working at jobs for which they are overqualified, or they are discouraged and have quit looking for work.

Hyperinflation An abrupt and substantial rise in prices (e.g., 50 percent or more per month) that causes the value of currency to deteriorate so quickly that people become reluctant to accept and hold money.

I

Impact (operational) lag The time elapsed between the implementation of a corrective policy and when the economic impact of that policy is felt.

Implicit GNP price deflator index A price index that shows the cost of buying the final goods and services included in the GNP during some year relative to the cost of buying these same items during a base year (currently, 1982).

Increase in demand An increase in the quantity demanded at each and every price, represented graphically by a rightward, or outward, shift in the demand curve.

Increase in supply An increase in the quantity producers are willing and able to offer at each and every price, represented graphically by a rightward, or outward, shift in the supply curve.

Inflation A sustained rise in the general level of quality-adjusted prices over a period of time; it causes both costs and benefits.

Inflation premium The additional interest required by, and thus included in, the nominal market interest rate as compensation and protection against erosion of purchasing power due to inflation.

Injection (inflow) An introduction of income into the circular flow.

Intermediate goods and services Goods and services that are purchased for further processing in producing another good or service for resale.

International balance of payments A summary statement of the flow of all international economic and financial transactions between one nation—for example, the United States—and the rest of the world over some period of time, usually one year.

International exchange rate The price of one national currency stated in terms of another national currency.

Investment The purchase of capital goods—plant and equipment, residential structures, and changes in inventory—that can be used in the production of other goods and services.

Investment function The assumed relationship between national income and total planned expenditures on new equipment, construction, and inventory.

J

J-curve phenomenon Although the initial impact of depreciation is often an increase in nominal spending because higher prices cause a deterioration in the nominal trade balance, over time depreciation will tend to improve both nominal and real net exports.

K

Keynesianism A macroeconomic theory that emphasizes that the economy is inherently unstable and requires an activist discretionary government policy to stop unemployment and inflation.

Keynes's law The macroeconomic principle stating that "demand creates its own supply"—that is, that the demand for goods and services creates an equal production of those goods and services.

L

L M3 plus other liquid assets not included in other aggregates such as bankers' acceptances, commercial paper, and Treasury bills.

Labor Any way in which human energy, physical or mental, can be usefully expended.

Labor force All persons sixteen years of age or older (i.e., adults) who are willing and able to work and who are counted as either employed or unemployed.

Labor force participation rate The number of adult civilian people in the labor force divided by the adult civilian noninstitutionalized population.

Laffer curve A diagram that shows the relationship between tax revenues collected and tax rates.

Lagging indicator An index of business activity that tends to move up or down several months after measures of general economic activity, like real GNP, move.

Land The surface area of the world and everything in nature—minerals, chemicals, plants—that is useful in the production process.

Leading indicator An index of business activity that tends to move up or down several months before measures of general economic activity, like real GNP, move.

Leakage (outflow) A withdrawal of income from the circular flow.

Linear regression A statistical technique used to find the equation describing the straight line that comes closest to the plotted points of a curve.

Liquidity The ease with which any asset can be converted on short notice into spendable form with little or no loss of value.

Liquidity trap When people under certain unlikely conditions hoard all increases in the money stock so that the demand for money curve is horizontal (i.e., infinitely interest-elastic).

Long-run aggregate supply A function or curve that shows the assumed fixed relationship between the total production of goods and services and the price level over an extended period of time.

Long-run equilibrium The price-quantity combination that will exist after firms have had time to change their production facilities (or some other resource that is fixed in the short run).

Lump-sum tax A constant tax that produces the same amount of tax revenue at each level of national income.

M

M1 The total of the public's (as opposed to the financial institutions') holdings of currency (paper bills and coins), demand deposits at commercial banks, traveler's checks, and other bank accounts against which checks can be written, such as NOW (negotiable order of withdrawal) and ATS (automatic transfer service) accounts.

M2 M1 plus savings accounts and small-denomination (less than $100,000) time deposits and certificates of deposit, plus money market accounts and other highly liquid assets.

M3 M2 plus large-denomination time deposits and other relatively minor components.

Macroeconomic policy The manipulation of taxes, federal expenditures, and the money supply to promote a high and stable level of employment and production, price level stability, and economic growth.

Macroeconomics The study of the national economy as a whole or its major components. Deals with the "big picture," not the details, of the nation's economic activity.

Marginal efficiency of investment (MEI) The expected yield or expected rate of net profit on additions to the capital stock or investment.

Marginal propensity to consume The percentage of any change in income (ΔY) that consumers are inclined to spend (ΔC). Stated as a ratio, $MPC = \Delta C/\Delta Y$.

Marginal propensity to save The percentage of any change in national income (ΔY) that consumers are inclined to save (ΔS). Stated as a ratio, $MPS = \Delta S/\Delta Y$.

Market The process by which buyers and sellers determine what they are willing to buy and sell and on what terms. That is, the process by which buyers and sellers decide the prices and quantities of goods to be bought and sold.

Market shortage The amount by which the quantity demanded exceeds the quantity supplied at a given price. Graphically, the shortfall in supply that occurs at any price below the intersection of the supply and demand curves.

Market surplus The amount by which the quantity supplied exceeds the quantity demanded at a given price. Graphically, the excess supply that occurs at any price above the intersection of the supply and demand curves.

Measure of (or net) economic welfare A measure that adjusts GNP for non-market bads and goods to obtain a better measure of quality of life or social welfare.

Median voter The voter in the middle of the political distribution.

Merchandise trade balance The difference between the dollar value of a nation's imported and exported goods—raw material, agricultural and manufactured products, and capital and consumer products—but not services and financial assets.

Merchandise trade deficit The dollar amount by which imports of goods exceed exports of goods.

Merchandise trade surplus The dollar amount by which exports of goods exceed imports of goods.

Microeconomics The study of the individual markets—for corn, records, books, and so forth—that operate within the broad national economy.

Misery (or discomfort) index The equally weighted sum of the CPI inflation rate and the civilian unemployment rate.

Monetarism A macroeconomic theory that emphasizes a nonactivist economic policy; monetarists believe that the economy is inherently stable and will usually return to its natural state after any temporary disequilibrium.

Money Any generally accepted medium of exchange or trade that also serves as a store of purchasing power.

Money illusion The mistaken belief that an increase in market price, stated in dollars, represents an increase in real market price.

Money stock The sum of all identified forms of money held by the public (as opposed to financial institutions) at a given point in time.

Multiplier The ratio of a final change in national income (ΔY) to the initial change in total planned expenditures (ΔTPE) that stimulated it: m = final change in Y/initial change in $TPE = \Delta Y/\Delta TPE$.

N

National economic planning The process of deciding collectively on national economic objectives, and of developing policies and programs for accomplishing those objectives.

National income The total income payment made to owners of human and physical productive resources for the use of those resources during a given period.

National or public debt The total amount owed by the Federal government in the form of outstanding U.S. Treasury securities as a result of past net budget deficits.

Natural rate of unemployment The maximum sustainable rate of output consistent with equilibrium in the structure of real wages at any point in time. The minimum percentage of the labor force that is unemployed because of structural problems in the economy and transitional movement among jobs.

Net national product (NNP) Gross national product minus an allowance for replacement of worn-out plant and equipment (called the capital consumption allowance).

Neutrality of money The classical economist's belief that changes in the money supply will affect the general price level, but not relative prices.

Nominal, money, or current dollar gross national product The gross national product with no adjustments made for price changes.

Normative economics That branch of economic inquiry which deals with value judgments—with what prices, production levels, incomes, and government policies ought to be.

O

Okun's law For every 1 percent increase in actual unemployment greater than the natural rate there is produced a 2½ percent increase in the GNP gap.

Open market operations The purchase and sale by the Federal Reserve of U.S. government securities, which can be bills, notes, or bonds.

P

Paradox of thrift The theory that if people attempt to save more at every level of income, they will end up earning less in the aggregate and saving no more (and possibly less) than before.

Peak The phase of the business cycle that occurs when general economic activity is no longer rising.

Perfect competition A market composed of numerous independent sellers and buyers of an identical product, such that no one individual buyer has the ability to affect the market price by changing the production level. Entry into and exit from a perfectly competitive market is unrestricted.

Personal income The part of national income that is paid to individuals as opposed to businesses.

Phillips curve A graphical representation of the presumed short-run inverse relationship between unemployment and inflation, assuming a certain expected rate of inflation.

Planned investment Anticipated, scheduled purchases of plant and equipment, residential homes, and inventory.

Policy neutrality or policy ineffectiveness theorem The conclusion of many rational expectations models that fiscal and monetary policy will have no effect on national income and employment, in either the short run or the long run.

Political business cycle When politicians destabilize the economy to gain short-run voter support by manipulating macroeconomic policy to stimulate the economy before elections and contract it after elections.

Positive economics That branch of economic inquiry that is concerned with the world as it is rather than as it should be. Deals only with the consequences of changes in economic conditions or policies.

Potential GNP The total amount of output that could be produced under full employment.

Potential output (or GNP) The maximum sustainable rate of output (i.e., real GNP) that involves no tendency for inflation to accelerate or decelerate, associated with the natural rate of unemployment.

Precautionary demand for money The desire to hold money balances in order to finance unexpected or emergency purchases of goods and services.

Price ceiling The government-determined price above which a specified good cannot be sold.

Price floor The government-determined price below which a specified good cannot be sold.

Private goods Goods that are bought or produced and used by people as individuals or as members of small voluntary groups.

Producer price index (PPI) The ratio of nonretail prices in any year to nonretail prices in the base year (currently, 1967).

Production possibilities curve (production possibilities frontier) A graphical representation of the various combinations of goods that can be produced when all resources are fully and efficiently employed.

Public goods Goods that are bought or produced and used by large groups of people or by governments.

Purchasing power parity theory The theory that if the inflation rates are the same in two nations that trade with each other, the exchange rate between their currencies will remain the same, *ceteris paribus*.

Q

Quantity theory The theory that a change in the stock of money will, in the long run and other things being the same, lead to a proportional change in the price level.

Quota A physical or dollar value limit—mandatory or voluntary—on the amount of a good that can be imported or exported during some specified period of time.

R

Rational expectations theory The macroeconomic theory that market participants formulate their expectations of the future, including their future economic policy activities, on past, present, and projected future information.

Rational ignorance When the (marginal) costs of acquiring additional information exceed the (marginal) benefits of relatively low (perhaps zero) levels of information.

Real balances or wealth effect The change in real

wealth resulting from a change in the purchasing power of nominal wealth.

Real balances or real wealth effect The manner in which deflation tends to increase the real value of financial assets with fixed money values held by private economic agents, and thus increases the consumption function and increases aggregate spending and national income in the economy.

Real or constant dollar gross national product The gross national product adjusted for price changes using the implicit GNP price deflator.

Real wage rate The nominal or money wage rate (the number of dollars a person earns per hour or day) adjusted for inflation or deflation. The real wage rate measures a worker's actual purchasing power.

Recession A downward movement in general economic activity, especially in national production and unemployment.

Recognition lag The time elapsed between the initial occurrence of a problem and the recognition of that problem.

Recovery An upward movement in general economic activity, especially in national production and employment.

Representative commodity money Certificates or notes that can be converted into given quantities of a specific commodity, like gold or silver.

Reserve deposits The accounts that depository institutions hold in Federal Reserve Banks. (A depository institution's reserve deposit balance plus its vault cash equals its total reserves.)

Reserve requirement ratio The portion of a depository institution's (such as a bank's) reserves that by law cannot be used to create money.

Reserve requirements The amount of reserves, expressed as a percentage of deposits, held by depository institutions in the form of cash holdings in their own vaults or on deposit at the Federal Reserve Bank (or at another depository institution for nonmember banks) that cannot be used to create money through loans.

Reserves The cash a depository institution has in its vault plus its deposits at the Federal Reserve Bank.

Resource cost-income approach The approach to calculating GNP which sums the dollar income payments to all resources.

Resources Things used in the production of goods and services.

Revaluation Under a fixed standard, the rise of a domestic currency brought about by government intervention in its official price in relation to a foreign currency.

S

Saving That portion of income not spent. Represents forgone expenditures on real goods and services.

Saving function The assumed direct relationship between nominal national income and the amount of income saved (not spent on goods and services).

Say's law The macroeconomic principle that supply creates its own demand—that is, that the production of a supply of goods and services creates an equal demand for goods and services.

Scarcity The fact that we cannot all have everything we want all the time.

Share economy A profit-sharing plan with a two-part wage scheme in which part of each worker's wages is independent of the firm's profitability and part is dependent.

Short-run aggregate supply A curve or function that shows the assumed positive relationship between the total production of goods and services and the price level over a given period of time.

Short-run equilibrium The price-quantity combination that will exist as long as producers do not have time to change their production facilities (or some other resource that is fixed in the short run).

Simplest multiplier The reciprocal of the marginal propensity to save. Stated as an equation, $m = 1/MPS = 1/(1 - MPC)$.

Specialization of labor The process of dividing and assigning different production tasks to individuals with differing skills and talents.

Speculative demand for money The desire to hold money in anticipation of a decrease in the price of other assets and in anticipation of future profits.

Stagflation The combination of persistently high rates of unemployment and inflation.

Structural inflation A general rise in prices that occurs when producers cannot readily shift production in response to changes in the structure of the economy.

Structural unemployment Unemployment that is caused by major changes in the skills needed by workers.

Supply The assumed relationship between the quantity of a good producers are willing and able to offer during a given period and the price, everything else held constant.

Supply-side economics A macroeconomic theory that emphasizes supply management and increased incentives to work, save, and invest over demand management when formulating macroeconomic policy to attain maximum employment, production, economic growth, and price stability.

T

Target Any economic variable—usually some monetary aggregate—that the Fed manages in the attempt to attain certain macroeconomic goals.

Tariff A special tax or duty on imported or exported goods that can be a percentage of the price (*ad valorem* duty) or a specific amount per unit of the profit (specific duty).

Technology The knowledge of how resources can be combined in productive ways.

Terms of trade The ratio at which one commodity can be traded or exchanged for another commodity internationally; or on an aggregate basis, it is the ratio of the price of exports to the price of imports.

Theory A set of abstractions about the real world. An economic theory is a simplified explanation of how the economy or part of the economy functions or would function under specific conditions.

Total expenditure function The relationship of total planned expenditures to national income, normally assumed to be a direct relationship.

Transactions demand for money The desire to hold money balances in order to carry out anticipated purchases of goods and services.

Transitional (frictional or search) unemployment Unemployment that occurs when people move from one job to another requiring similar skills.

Trend A long-run directional change, up or down, in some economic variable—for example, real GNP.

Trough The bottom of the business cycle, the point at which general economic activity ceases to fall.

U

Unanimity rule A voting rule that requires unanimous agreement among voters.

Underemployed workers Those people either working at part-time jobs although they would prefer full-time jobs or working for jobs for which they are overqualified in terms of training, education, or experience.

Underground economy Unreported legal and illegal activities excluded from traditional GNP estimates.

Unemployment rate The ratio of the number of people estimated to be unemployed to the number of people estimated to be in the labor force, stated as a percentage.

Unplanned investment Unanticipated, unscheduled purchases of plant and equipment, residential construction, and inventory.

V

Value added The amount of additional market value or income created at any stage of production.

Variable-rate or adjustable-rate mortgage (ARM) A mortgage whose interest rate is adjusted periodically to agree with some market interest rate—for example, the rate on a specific type of government or corporate bond.

Velocity (V) The rate of turnover or circulation of the money stock (M) relative to GNP; thus, $V = GNP/M$.

Velocity of money (V) The average number of times a dollar is used during a given period. It is the circulation or turnover ratio for money (M) relative to GNP (PQ) or $V = PQ/M$.

Index

Boldfaced page numbers indicate the first occurrence of key terms; page numbers followed by (table) indicate information from tables; page numbers followed by (fig.) indicate information from figures; entries followed by NL appear in the Appendix, *Nobel Laureates in Economics*.

Smith, Adam: (*cont.*)
  labor theory of value, 536
  on market system, 8–9
  Work: *Wealth of Nations,* 6, 8, 9,
    30, 532, 536
Smoot-Hawley Tariff (1931), 296
Social class, dialectics of, 536
Social contract, protection of
    property rights by, 86
Social cycles, law of, 161
Socialism, *see* Communism; Demo-
    cratic socialism; Market
    socialism; Planned socialism
Social Security
  cost-of-living adjustments, 232
  financial crisis of, 90–91
Solow, Robert M., NL
Sourrouille, Juan V., 485
South Africa
  currency of, 482 (table)
  developmental level of, 555
    (table)
South Carolina, 85, 460, 461, 462
South Korea, 461
  currency of, 482 (table)
  developmental level of, 554
    (table)
  developmental strategy, 571
Soviet Union, 457, 532, 533, 535,
    544, 546, 569
  application of supply-side theory
    in, 412–413
  Communist system of, 537–542
  developmental level of, 554n.2,
    555 & table, 559 (table),
    565 (table)
  GNP growth rates, 151 (table)
Spain, 563
  currency of, 482 (table)
  developmental level of, 555 &
    table
  marginal tax rates vs. govern-
    ment revenues, 396 & table
Spanish Conquest, 212–213, 377
Special Drawing Rights (SDRs),
    balancing of currency sup-
    ply and demand with, 500–
    501, 501 (fig.)
Special interests
  influence in democracies, 588
  and international trade restric-
    tions, 458, 466, 469, 471
Specialization of labor
  defined, **28**
  production-cost advantages to,
    31–32
  and production opportunities,
    28–29

Specialization of labor: (*cont.*)
  in world economy, 451–457,
    453 (table), 455 (table), 456
    (fig.)
Speculation, in money, 263
Speculative demand for money,
    177, 330–332, 331 (fig.)
Spillane, Mickey, 571
Stagflation, **150,** 394
Stalin, Joseph, 538–539
State, the, *see* Government
Stein, Herbert, 511
Stigler, George J., NL
Stocks, control of corporations
    through, 590
Stone, Courtenay C., 386–388
Stone, Richard, NL
Stroup, Richard, 409
Structural inflation, **142**
Structural unemployment, **146,**
    147
Substitution effect, 50, 71
  demand shift as function of, 52,
    53
  nondeductible to tax-deductible
    goods, 399
Substitution of resources, and
    production opportunities,
    28
Sudan, 554 (table), 557 (table),
    560 (table)
Sunspot theory, 251
Supply
  creation by demand, 255
  creation of demand by, 251–252
  decrease in, **55,** 56 & fig.
  defined, **53**
  equilibrium price/quantity
    movements as function of,
    59 & fig.
  increase in, **55**–56, 56 (fig.)
  of labor, 247, 248–250, 249
    (fig.), 250 (fig.)
  of national currency, 489 (fig.),
    489–490
    correcting imbalance with
      demand, 501–503, 502
      (fig.)
    and fixed exchange rate, 497–
      501, 501 (table)
    impact of marginal tax rates,
      527
    and international gold flows,
      519
    movement of exchange rate
      with, 524
    positive relationship with
      world price level, 519

Supply: (*cont.*)
  response to anticipated ex-
    change rate, 492–493, 503,
    506
  response to changes in market
    for goods, 492, 493 (fig.)
  positive relationship with price,
    53–55, 54 (fig.), 55 (table)
  production costs as determinant
    of, 54–56
  shifts in, in long-run market, 66
    (fig.), 67, 68 (fig.)
  See also Aggregate supply; Pro-
    duction
Supply shocks, 352–353, 353 (fig.)
Supply-side theory
  advocacy of flat-rate taxation,
    406–407
  basic tenets of, **159,** 162, **395,**
    398–400, 401 (fig.), 525–
    526, 526 (fig.)
  criticism of, 401–407, 410–411,
    414
  perspective on international
    trade, 526–528
  and short-run political impera-
    tives, 414–415
  Soviet application of, 412–413
Surplus, *see* Market surplus
Surplus value, 536, 561
Survey of Current Business, 109
Sweden
  currency of, 482 (table)
  developmental level of, 555 &
    table, 556 (table), 557 (ta-
    ble), 558 (table), 559 (table),
    565 (table)
  marginal tax rates vs. govern-
    ment revenues, 396 & table
  membership in international
    financial organizations, 485
  nationalized industry of, 543
Switzerland
  currency of, 482 (table)
  developmental level of, 455, 457
    (table)
  inflation rate in, 140, 141 (table)
  marginal tax rates vs. govern-
    ment revenues, 396 (table)
  membership in international
    financial organizations, 485
Syria, 560 (table)

Taiwan
  currency of, 482 (table)
  developmental strategy, 571